W9-BRP-727

Dear NFT User,

Thanks for picking up the 2009 edition of the Not For Tourists Guide to Chicago! If this is the first time you've picked up the guide, welcome to the family. Whether you're a new resident to Chicago, moving to a different neighborhood, or if you live in the suburbs but commute regularly to Chicago for work or culture, we are sure you will find this friendly little guidebook invaluable for navigating the CTA, planning urban adventures, and orienting yourself with every 'hood in the city from Beverly to Rogers Park. And since we're written by locals, you are getting a true insider's perspective on dining options, nightlife, and daily essentials for nearly every square inch of the Chicago city limits. Need a cuppa joe in Edison Park? Look no further. Need to grab a bite to eat after the Sox game? We've got it here. Need an ATM by Garfield Park? A liquor store in Logan Square? A plumber at 3 am? Interested in exploring Chicago's gallery or theater scene, but don't know where to start? Want to know a good hotel to shack up your in-laws or the location of the closest FedEx office? Don't worry, we've got you covered.

If you're already a loyal NFT user, then you'll be happy to know that this new edition has been thoroughly updated, with scores of new nightlife, dining, and shopping listings—all told, we make over 1,000 changes to the guide each year, meaning the 2009 guide will be as indispensable this year as the 2008 guide was last year, as in, don't leave home without it.

Of course, all things are subject to change—and that is where NFT online comes in! Visit us at www.notfortourists.com, and you'll be privy to all the latest updates, not to mention web-only features (free PDF files of all of our maps, the ability to review listings, location-based searching, and so much more). There is also a place on our site for your feedback, so if your favorite local spot deserves a mention in the guide, or if you have anything else to contribute, fill out the form and help us continue to make the NFT Guide to Chicago the most accurate, comprehensive, and downright handy guide to life in the Windy City.

Cordially Yours,

Kathie, Jane, Rob, & Craig

Table of Contents

Map 1 • River North / Fulton Market District

Crisscrossed by rail tracks, I-90/94, and the Chicago River, this area is transitioning from industrial to residential as the loft-conversion craze in River North, Greek Town, and West Loop Gate expands. The Blommer Chocolate Company pumps sweet, chocolate-coated air into the streets all day. Diabetics, beware.

Banks

- **Chase** • 500 N Kingsbury St
- **LaSalle** • 600 W Chicago Ave
- **LaSalle** • 770 N Halsted St
- **New Century** • 363 W Ontario St
- **MB Financial** • 306 N Halsted St
- **Washington Mutual** • 501 N Milwaukee Ave

Car Washes

- **River West Hand Car Wash** •
  478 N Milwaukee Ave
- **We Wash III** • 452 N Halsted St

○Landmarks

- **The Blommer Chocolate Co** • 600 W Kinzie St

ⓟParking

Map 1 • River North / Fulton Market District

Dance-loving clubbers flock to Funky Buddha for its eclectic sounds and organic cocktails. Those looking for a simple, nostalgic night order up a round of Manhattans while popping quarters in the jukebox at The Motel Bar. Impress your date with an alfresco meal at French-Japanese fusion restaurant Japonais.

Coffee

- **Caribou Coffee** • 600 N Kingsbury St

Copy Shops

- **Cushing & Color Chicago** • 420 W Huron St

Gyms

- **David Barton Gym** • 600 W Chicago Ave
- **East Bank Club** • 500 N Kingsbury St
- **Sharper Fitness** • 401 W Ontario St, 4th Fl

Nightlife

- **Emmit's Irish Pub & Eatery** •
  495 N Milwaukee Ave
- **Funky Buddha Lounge** • 728 W Grand Ave
- **The Motel Bar** • 600 W Chicago Ave
- **Rednofive & Fifth Floor** • 440 N Halsted St
- **Richard's Bar** • 491 • N Milwaukee Ave

Restaurants

- **Brasserie Ruhlmann** • 500 W Superior St
- **Carnivale** • 702 W Fulton St
- **Iguana Café** • 517 N Halsted St
- **Japonais** • 600 W Chicago Ave
- **La Scarola** • 721 W Grand Ave
- **Powerhouse** • 215 • N Clinton St
- **Reza's** • 432 W Ontario St
- **Scoozi!** • 410 W Huron St
- **Timo** • 464 N Halsted St
- **Tony Rocco's River North** • 416 W Ontario St
- **Zealous** • 419 W Superior St
- **Zocalo** • 358 W Ontario St

Shopping

- **Doolin's** • 511 N Halsted St

Monolithic Merchandise Mart casts its shadow over River North, helping the area maintain its industrial edge even if all of the former warehouse spaces are now upscale lofts or designer showrooms. A former art gallery haven, only the most successful (and staid) have persevered—edgier artistes have migrated to lower rents on the near west side.

$ Banks

- **Bank of America** • 49 E Chicago Ave
- **Bank of America** • 601 N Dearborn St
- **Bank of America (ATM)** • 320 N Wells St
- **Bank of America (ATM)** • 521 N State St
- **Bank of America (ATM)** •
  59 E Chicago Ave
- **Bank of America (ATM)** • 640 N Wells St
- **Charter One** • 33 W Grand Ave
- **Charter One (ATM)** • 35 E Wacker Dr
- **Charter One (ATM)** • 451 N State St
- **Chase** • 230 W Grand Ave
- **Chase** • 340 N State St
- **Chase** • 35 W Wacker Dr
- **Chase** • 71 W Chicago Ave
- **Chase** • 600 • N Dearborn St
- **Chase (ATM)** • 101 E Erie St
- **Chase (ATM)** • 222 Merchandise Mart Plz
- **Chase (ATM)** • 321 N Clark St
- **Chase (ATM)** • Walgreens •
  641 N Clark St
- **Citibank** • 400 N Clark St
- **Citibank (ATM)** • 343 N LaSalle St
- **Citibank (ATM)** • 7-Eleven •
  418 N State St
- **Citibank (ATM)** • 7-Eleven •
  714 N Clark St
- **Fifth Third** • 222 Merchandise Mart Plz
- **Fifth Third** • 42 E Ontario St
- **Fifth Third (ATM)** • 350 Orleans St
- **Fifth Third (ATM)** • 401 N Wells St
- **Fifth Third (ATM)** • 431 N Wells St
- **First American (ATM)** • 310 W Chicago
  Ave
- **First American (ATM)** •
  Renaissance Hotel • 1 W Wacker Dr
- **First American (ATM)** • Hilton Garden
  Inn Downtown • 10 E Grand Ave
- **First American (ATM)** • 200 W Ohio St
- **First American (ATM)** • 213 W Grand Ave
- **First American (ATM)** • 225 W Wacker Dr
- **First American (ATM)** •
  Courtyard Marriott • 30 E Hubbard St
- **First American (ATM)** • 30 W Huron St
- **First American (ATM)** • 325 N Wells St
- **First American (ATM)** • House of Blues
  Hotel Chicago • 333 N Dearborn St
- **First American (ATM)** • 401 N Wells St
- **First American (ATM)** • 50 E Ohio St
- **First American (ATM)** • 640 N La Salle St
- **First American (ATM)** • 70 W Erie St
- **First American (ATM)** •
  Howard Johnson Inn • 720 N La Salle St
- **First American (ATM)** •
  Howard Johnson Inn • 721 N Wells St
- **First American (ATM)** • 734 N Clark St
- **First American (ATM)** • 750 N Clark St
- **First American (ATM)** • 750 N Rush St
- **Harris Trust & Savings** • 33 W Ohio St
- **Lakeside** • 55 W Wacker Dr

- **LaSalle** • 515 N La Salle St
- **LaSalle (ATM)** • CVS • 121 W Kinzie St
- **LaSalle (ATM)** • CVS • 344 W Hubbard St
- **LaSalle (ATM)** • 77 W Wacker Dr
- **MB Financial (ATM)** • 100 W Grand Ave
- **MB Financial (ATM)** • 615 N Wells St
- **MB Financial** • 1 E Wacker Dr
- **MB Financial** • 33 W Huron St
- **New Century (ATM)** • 441 N Wabash Ave
- **North** • 501 N Clark St
- **North Community** • 448 N Wells St
- **North Community** • 800 N State St
- **TCF** • 635 N Dearborn St
- **TCF (ATM)** • DePaul University •
  333 N State St
- **TCF (ATM)** • 7-Eleven • 343 N La Salle St
- **TCF (ATM)** • 7-Eleven • 418 N State St
- **TCF (ATM)** • 550 N State St
- **TCF (ATM)** • 7-Eleven • 714 N Clark St
- **Washington Mutual** • 431 N Orleans St
- **Washington Mutual** • 710 N Wabash Ave

Car Washes

- **River North Hand Car Wash** •
  356 W Superior St

Car Rental

- **Enterprise** • 10 E Grand Ave •
  312-670-7270
- **Enterprise** • 160 W Kinzie St •
  312-494-3434
- **Hertz** • 401 N State St • 312-372-7600

Gas Stations

- **BP Connect** • 631 N La Salle Dr
- **Citgo** • 750 N Wells St
- **Shell** • 350 W Chicago Ave

o Landmarks

- **Courthouse Place** • 54 W Hubbard St
- **House of Blues** • 329 N Dearborn St
- **Marina Towers** • 300 N State St
- **Merchandise Mart** •
  222 Merchandise Mart Plz
- **Rock 'N Roll McDonald's** •
  600 N Clark St
- **Sotheby's** • 215 W Ohio St
- **Trump International Hotel and Tower** •
  330 N Wabash Ave

P Parking

Rx Pharmacies

- **CVS** • 121 W Kinzie St
- **CVS Pharmacy** • 344 W Hubbard St
- **Jewel-Osco** • 550 N State St
- **Walgreens** • 641 N Clark St ⊕

Pizza

- **Alibi Restaurant** • 23 W Hubbard St
- **Bacino's On Wacker** • 75 E Wacker Dr
- **Bella Bacino's** • 75 E Wacker Dr
- **Buca Di Beppo** • 521 N Rush St
- **California Pizza Kitchen** • 52 E Ohio St
- **Delicious** • 308 W Erie St
- **Gino's East** • 633 N Wells St
- **Giordano's** • 730 N Rush St
- **Lou Malnati's Pizzeria** • 439 N Wells St
- **Pizza Ria** • 405 N Wabash Ave
- **Pizzeria Due** • 619 N Wabash Ave
- **Pizzeria Ora** • 545 N La Salle St
- **Pizzeria Uno** • 29 E Ohio St
- **Rizzata's Pizzeria** • 300 W Grand Ave
- **Rosati's Pizza and California Style Deli** •
  126 W Grand Ave

Post Offices

- **US Post Office** •
  222 Merchandise Mart Plz
- **US Post Office** • 540 N Dearborn St

Schools

- **Adler School of Professional
  Psychology** • 65 E Wacker Pl
- **Argosy University** • 350 N Orleans St
- **Associated Colleges of the Midwest** •
  205 W Wacker Dr
- **Chicago School of Professional
  Psychology** • 325 N Wells St
- **Feltre** • 22 W Erie St
- **Frances Xavier Ward Middle** •
  751 N State St
- **Illinois Institute of Art** • 350 N Orleans St

Supermarkets

- **Jewel-Osco** • 550 N State St
- **Trader Joe's** • 44 E Ontario St
- **Whole Foods Market** • 30 W Huron St

Tourista-style eateries dominate the landscape around these parts, but if you remain vigilant you will be rewarded. For example, Fulton's on the River serves up tasty (and pricey) prime steaks and scrumptious oysters. As for nightlife, Lincoln Park and Wicker Park cross paths at Martini Ranch. Andy's jazz bar is a destination for aging beatniks, and Rossi's on State Street is a dive in the best sense of the word.

☕ Coffee

- **Cosi** • 55 E Grand Ave
- **Dunkin' Donuts** • 20 E Chicago Ave
- **Dunkin' Donuts** • 404 N Wabash Ave
- **Dunkin' Donuts** • Merchandise Mart Plz
- **Ohio House Coffee Shop** • 600 N La Salle Dr
- **Starbucks** • Marriott Courtyard • 30 E Hubbard St
- **Starbucks** • 35 E Wacker Dr
- **Starbucks** • 38 E Ontario St
- **Starbucks** • 414 N Orleans St
- **Starbucks** • 42 E Chicago Ave
- **Starbucks** • 430 N Clark St
- **Starbucks** • 470 Merchandise Mart Plz
- **Starbucks** • Embassy Suites • 600 N State St
- **Starbucks** • 750 N Franklin St
- **Starbucks** • 30 E Erie St

🖨 Copy Shops

- **FedEx Kinko's** • 350 N Clark St
- **FedEx Kinko's** • 444 N Wells St ♿
- **Icon Printing** • 18 W Hubbard St
- **Office Depot** • 352 W Grand Ave
- **Printwell** • 20 W Hubbard St
- **Quantity Photo & Print** • 119 W Hubbard St
- **The UPS Store** • 40 E Chicago Ave
- **The UPS Store** • 446 N Wells St

🏋 Gyms

- **Crunch Fitness** • 350 N State St
- **Crunch Fitness** • 38 E Grand Ave
- **Executive Sports & Fitness Center** • 77 W Wacker Dr
- **Lakeshore Athletic Club** • 441 N Wabash Ave
- **Lawson YMCA** • 30 W Chicago Ave
- **Lifestart** • 10 E Ontario St

🔧 Hardware Stores

- **Clark & Barlow Hardware** • 353 W Grand Ave
- **Gordon's Ace Hardware & Paint** • 440 N Orleans St
- **Katonah Architectural Hardware** • 222 Merchandise Mart Plz

🍾 Liquor Stores

- **Artisan Cellar** • 222 Merchandise Mart Plz
- **Ben'z Liquors** • 15 E Ohio St
- **Binny's Beverage Depot** • 213 W Grand Ave
- **Copperfield's** • 70 W Huron St
- **Dalal Food & Liquor** • 414 N State St
- **Galleria Market** • 340 W Superior St
- **Hart Davis Hart Wine** • 363 W Erie St
- **Holiday Wines & Spirits** • 6 W Chicago Ave
- **Marina Food & Liquor** • 300 N State St
- **Plaza Market** • 405 N Wabash Ave
- **Rossi's Liquors** • 412 N State St
- **Superior Liquor** • 750 N Clark St
- **White Hen Pantry** • 645 N State St

🍸 Nightlife

- **Andy's** • 11 E Hubbard St
- **Bin 36** • 339 N Dearborn St
- **Blue Chicago** • 736 N Clark St
- **Blue Frog Bar & Grill** • 676 N La Salle Dr
- **Brehon Pub** • 731 N Wells St
- **Buzz Club** • 308 W Erie St
- **Gentry** • 440 N State St
- **Green Door Tavern** • 678 N Orleans St
- **Howl at the Moon** • 26 W Hubbard St
- **Martini Park** • 151 W Erie St
- **Martini Ranch** • 311 W Chicago Ave
- **Ontourage** • 157 W Ontario St
- **Pippin's Tavern** • 806 N Rush St
- **Pops for Champagne** • 601 N State St
- **Redhead Piano Bar** • 16 W Ontario St
- **Rockwell Lounge** • 710 N Clark St
- **Rossi's** • 412 N State St
- **Spy Bar** • 646 N Franklin St
- **Sound Bar** • 226 W Ontario St
- **Streeter's Tavern** • 50 E Chicago Ave
- **Swirl Wine Bar** • 111 W Hubbard St
- **Vision** • 640 N Dearborn St

🐾 Pet Shops

- **Pet Stuff** • 509 N La Salle St
- **Petco** • 440 N Orleans St

🍽 Restaurants

- **1492 Tapas Bar** • 42 E Superior St
- **A Mano** • 335 N Dearborn St
- **Aigre Doux** • 230 W Kinzie St
- **Avenues** • Peninsula Hotel • 108 E Superior St
- **Ballo** • 445 N Dearborn St
- **Ben Pao** • 52 W Illinois St
- **Blue Water Grill** • 520 N Dearborn St
- **Brasserie Jo** • 59 W Hubbard St
- **Brett's Kitchen** • 233 W Superior St
- **Café Iberico** • 739 N La Salle Blvd
- **Chicago Chop House** • 60 W Ontario St
- **Club Lago** • 331 W Superior St
- **Crofton on Wells** • 535 N Wells St
- **Cyrano's Bistrot & Wine Bar** • 546 N Wells St
- **David Burke's Primehouse** • 616 N Rush St
- **Frontera Grill** • 445 N Clark St
- **Fulton's on the River** • 315 N La Salle St
- **Gaylord Fine India Cuisine** • 678 N Clark St
- **Gene & Georgetti** • 500 N Franklin St
- **Gino's East** • 633 N Wells St
- **Graze** • 35 W Ontario St
- **Keefer's** • 20 W Kinzie St
- **Kevin** • 9 W Hubbard St
- **Kinzie Chophouse** • 400 N Wells St
- **Klay Oven** • 414 N Orleans St
- **Lawry's The Prime Rib** • 100 E Ontario St
- **Le Lan** • 749 N Clark St
- **Lou Malnati's Pizzeria** • 439 N Wells St
- **Maggiano's Little Italy** • 516 N Clark St
- **Mr Beef** • 666 N Orleans St
- **Nacional 27** • 325 W Huron St
- **Naha** • 500 N Clark St
- **Osteria Via Stato** • 620 N State St
- **Pizzeria Uno** • 29 E Ohio St
- **Quartino** • 626 N State St
- **Redfish** • 400 N State St
- **Rosebud on Rush** • 720 N Rush St
- **Roy's** • 720 N State St
- **Ruth's Chris Steak House** • 431 N Dearborn St
- **Shanghai Terrace** • Peninsula Hotel • 108 E Superior St
- **Shaw's Crab House & Blue Crab Lounge** • 21 E Hubbard St
- **Smith & Wollensky** • 318 N State St
- **Sullivan's Steakhouse** • 415 N Dearborn St
- **Sushi Naniwa** • 607 N Wells St
- **Tizi Melloul** • 531 N Wells St
- **Topolobampo** • 445 N Clark St
- **Vermillion** • 10 W Hubbard St
- **Vong's Thai Kitchen** • 6 W Hubbard St
- **Wildfire** • 159 W Erie St

🛍 Shopping

- **American Girl Place** • 111 E Chicago Ave
- **Jazz Record Mart** • 27 E Illinois St
- **Jonathan Adler** • 676 N Wabash Ave
- **Mig and Tig Furniture** • 540 N Wells St
- **Montauk** • 401 N Wells St
- **Paper Source** • 232 W Chicago Ave

📼 Video Rental

- **Blockbuster** • 700 N State St
- **Hubbard's Street Books** • 109 W Hubbard St

The tiny, densely populated blocks of Streeterville are home to big stores, big restaurants, and big hotels, as well as the maze that is the Northwestern University Medical campus. The hoity-toity residents of the premier high-rises sip on their champagne and laugh at the shopping bag-toting provincials who look like ants so, so far below.

$ Banks

- **Banco Popular** • 717 N Michigan Ave
- **Bank of America** • 500 N Michigan Ave
- **Bank of America (ATM)** • 600 N Michigan Ave
- **Bank of America (ATM)** • 600 E Grand Ave
- **Chase** • 605 N Michigan Ave
- **Chase (ATM)** • Northwestern Hospital • 251 E Huron St
- **Chase (ATM)** • Northwestern Hospital • 250 E Superior St
- **Chase (ATM)** • 255 E Grand Ave
- **Chase (ATM)** • Walgreens • 342 E Illinois St
- **Chase (ATM)** • Rehabilitation Institute of Chicago • 345 E Superior St
- **Chase (ATM)** • Walgreens • 430 N Michigan Ave
- **Chase (ATM)** • Walgreens • 757 N Michigan Ave
- **Chase** • 355 E Illinois St
- **Citibank** • 539 N Michigan Ave
- **First American** • Prentice Women's Hospital • 250 E Superior St
- **First American** • 643 N Fairbanks Ct
- **First American (ATM)** • 400 N Michigan Ave
- **First American (ATM)** • 165 E Ontario St
- **First American (ATM)** • 226 E Ontario St
- **First American (ATM)** • 233 E Erie St
- **First American (ATM)** • 247 E Ohio St
- **First American (ATM)** • 393 E Illinois St
- **First American (ATM)** • 401 N Michigan Ave
- **First American (ATM)** • Wrigley Building • 410 N Michigan Ave
- **First American (ATM)** • 541 N Fairbanks Ct
- **First American (ATM)** • 633 N St Clair St
- **First American (ATM)** • 676 N St Clair St
- **Harris Trust & Savings** • 352 E Illinois St
- **Harris Trust & Savings (ATM)** • 455 N Cityfront Plz Dr
- **LaSalle (ATM)** • 474 N Lake Shore Dr
- **LaSalle (ATM)** • 520 N Michigan Ave
- **LaSalle (ATM)** • 800 N Michigan Ave
- **North** • 360 E Ohio St
- **Northern Trust** • 201 E Huron St
- **Northern Trust (ATM)** • Northwestern Hospital • 251 E Huron St
- **Shore Bank (ATM)** • 700 N Michigan Ave
- **US (ATM)** • 200 E Huron St
- **US (ATM)** • 320 E Superior St
- **US (ATM)** • Northwestern University • 357 E Chicago Ave
- **US (ATM)** • 710 N Lake Shore Dr

Car Washes

- **River North Experts** • 161 E Chicago Ave

Emergency Rooms

- **Northwestern Memorial** • 251 E Huron St

Landmarks

- **Billy Goat Tavern** • 430 N Michigan Ave
- **Chicago Spire** • 400 N Lake Shore Dr
- **Museum of Contemporary Art** • 220 E Chicago Ave
- **Tribune Tower** • 435 N Michigan Ave
- **Wrigley Building** • 400 N Michigan Ave

Parking

Pharmacies

- **Dominick's** • 255 E Grand Ave
- **Walgreens** • 342 E Illinois St
- **Walgreens** • 430 N Michigan Ave
- **Walgreens** • 757 N Michigan Ave ◎
- **Walgreens** • 201 E Huron St

Pizza

- **Gino's East Pizza** • 162 E Superior St
- **Pompei Bakery** • 212E Ohio St

Post Offices

- **US Post Office** • 227 E Ontario St

Schools

- **Near the Pier Development Center** • 540 N Lake Shore Dr
- **Northwestern University** • 211 E Superior St

Supermarkets

- **Dominick's** • 255 E Grand Ave
- **Fox & Obel Food Store** • 401 E Illinois St
- **Treasure Island** • 680 N Lake Shore Dr

Map 3 · **Streeterville / Mag Mile**

1

2

Lake Michigan

E Walton St

E Delaware Pl

E Chestnut St

N Mies Van Der Rohe Way

N Dewitt Pl

E Pearson St

A

Loyola University (Water Tower Campus)

Seneca Park

Lake Shore Park

32

E Chicago Ave

GOLD COAST

E Superior St

Northwestern University (Chicago Campus)

N McClurg

Lake Shore Dr

N Lake Shore Dr

Outer Harbor

E Huron St

VA Lakeside Med Center

E Huron St

N Fairbanks Ct

E Erie St

N Michigan Ave

N St Clair St

Ohio Street Beach

E Ontario St

B

2

E Ohio St

Navy Pier

PAGE 234

N Peshtigo Ct

E Grand Ave

100E

200E

N Seneca St

400E

N McClurg Ct

N New St

N Park Dr

N Columbus Dr

E Illinois St

N Fairbanks Ct

E Hubbard St

University of Chicago Gleacher Center

E Kinzie St

STREETERVILLE

N Old Ford Plaza Dr

E North Water St

River Rd

Chicago River

6

C

E Wacker Dr

100E

N Stetson Ave

300E

N Columbus Dr

N Field Blvd

Du Sable Harbor

South Water St

N Garland Ct

N Beaubien Ct

1/4 mile

.25 km

Young singles pose artfully at the Museum of Contemporary Art's First Friday series, featuring a deejay, free finger food, and a cash bar. And speaking of cash, drop a wad of it dining at the posh French food emporium Les Nomades, or Rick Tramanto and Gale Gand's trendsetting Tru. For slumming it, hit the Billy Goat Tavern.

Coffee

- **Argo Tea** • 250 E Superior St
- **Dunkin' Donuts** • 200 E Ohio St
- **Dunkin' Donuts** • 401 E Ontario St
- **Einstein Bros Bagels** • 300 E Ohio St
- **Starbucks** • 165 E Ontario St
- **Starbucks** • Chicago Downtown Courtyard • 155 E Ontario St
- **Starbucks** • Northwestern Memorial Hospital • 251 E Huron St
- **Starbucks** • Dominick's • 255 E Grand Ave
- **Starbucks** • 401 E Ontario St
- **Starbucks** • 444 N Michigan Ave

Copy Shops

- **AlphaGraphics** • 645 N Michigan Ave
- **FedEx Kinko's** • 540 N Michigan Ave
- **Kwik Kopy** • 500 N Michigan Ave
- **Press Type and Copy** • 541 N Fairbanks Ct
- **The UPS Store** • 207 E Ohio St

Farmers Markets

- **Museum of Contemporary Art/Streeterville (Jun–Oct; Tues, 10am–6pm)** • E Chicago Ave & Mies Van der Rohe Wy

Gyms

- **Holmes Place** • 355 E Grand Ave
- **Lakeshore Athletic Club** • 333 E Ontario St
- **Onterie Fitness Center** • 446 E Ontario St
- **Woman's Athletic Club** • 626 N Michigan Ave

Hardware Stores

- **Streeterville Ace Hardware** • 680 N Lake Shore Dr

Liquor Stores

- **Market Place FoodUncork It** • 393 E Illinois St

Movie Theaters

- **AMC Loews 600** • 600 N Michigan Ave
- **AMC River East** • 322 E Illinois St
- **Museum of Contemporary Art Movie Theater** • 220 E Chicago Ave

Nightlife

- **Billy Goat Tavern** • 430 N Michigan Ave
- **Dick's Last Resort** • 435 E Illinois St
- **Reagle Beagle** • 160 E Grand Ave
- **Timothy O'Toole's Pub** • 622 N Fairbanks Ct

Pet Shops

- **Streeterville Pet Spa and Boutique** • 401 E Ontario St

Restaurants

- **Bandera** • 535 N Michigan Ave
- **Billy Goat Tavern** • 430 N Michigan Ave
- **Capital Grille** • 633 N St Clair St
- **Copperblue** • 580 E Illinois St
- **D4 Irish Pub & Café** • 345 E Ohio St
- **De La Costa** • 465 E Illinois St
- **Emilio's Tapas Sol y Nieve** • 215 E Ohio St
- **Fox & Obel Café** • 401 E Illinois St
- **Grand Lux Café** • 600 N Michigan Ave
- **Heaven on Seven** • 600 N Michigan Ave
- **Hot Diggity Dogs** • 251 E Ohio St
- **Indian Garden** • 247 E Ontario St
- **Kamehachi** • 240 E Ontario St
- **Les Nomades** • 222 E Ontario St
- **Nomi** • Park Hyatt • 800 N Michigan Ave
- **Sayat Nova** • 157 E Ohio St
- **Tru** • 676 N St Clair St
- **Volare** • 201 E Grand Ave
- **Wave** • 644 N Lake Shore Dr

Shopping

- **Apple Store** • 679 N Michigan Ave
- **Chicago Place** • 700 N Michigan Ave
- **Disney Store** • 717 N Michigan Ave
- **Garrett Popcorn Shop** • 670 N Michigan Ave
- **Neiman-Marcus** • 737 N Michigan Ave
- **Niketown** • 669 N Michigan Ave
- **Ralph Lauren** • 750 N Michigan Ave
- **Tiffany & Co** • 730 N Michigan Ave

Trains, buses, gyros, and loft spaces define this transitioning 'hood. Proximity to the Loop, the Expressway, Union Station, Ogilvie Transportation Center, and the Greyhound Bus Depot may seem just right for hip, urban commuters. Nonetheless, many pockets maintain a gritty vibe (particularly around said Greyhound station—isn't that always the case?).

$ Banks

- **Bank of America** • 105 N Halsted St
- **Bank of America** • 2 N Riverside Plz
- **Bank of America (ATM)** • Amtrack-Union Station • 225 S Canal St
- **Bank of America (ATM)** • 400 W Madison St
- **Charter One** • 555 W Jackson Blvd
- **Charter One (ATM)** • 101 S Clinton St
- **Charter One (ATM)** • 627 W Jackson Blvd
- **Charter One (ATM)** • 833 W Van Buren St
- **Chase** • 1 N Halsted St
- **Chase** • 300 S Riverside Plz
- **Chase** • 550 W Adams St
- **Chase (ATM)** • Chicago Union Station • 225 S Canal St
- **Chase (ATM)** • 525 W Monroe St
- **Chase (ATM)** • Chicago-Kent College of Law • 565 W Adams St
- **Chase (ATM)** • 567 W Lake St
- **Citibank** • 500 W Madison St
- **Citibank (ATM)** • 7-Eleven • 567 W Lake St
- **Corus** • 10 S Riverside Plz
- **Fifth Third** • 222 S Riverside Plz
- **Fifth Third** • 100 S Halsted St
- **Fifth Third (ATM)** • Union Station • 225 S Canal St
- **First American (ATM)** • 117 S Clinton St
- **First American (ATM)** • 500 W Monroe St
- **First American (ATM)** • 517 W Jackson Blvd
- **First American (ATM)** • 550 W Washington St
- **First American (ATM)** • Crowne Plaza • 733 W Madison St
- **Harris Trust & Savings (ATM)** • 555 W Madison St
- **Harris Trust & Savings (ATM)** • 626 W Jackson Blvd
- **LaSalle** • 540 W Madison St
- **LaSalle (ATM)** • 130 S Canal St
- **LaSalle (ATM)** • 550 W Van Buren St
- **MB Financial** • 800 W Madison St
- **MB Financial (ATM)** •811 W Lake St
- **New Century (ATM)** • 225 S Canal St
- **New Century (ATM)** • Union Station • 225 S Canal St
- **TCF** • 120 S Riverside Plz
- **TCF (ATM)** • 400 W Madison St
- **US (ATM)** • 111 N Canal St
- **Washington Mutual** • 555 W Monroe St

Car Rental

- **Enterprise** • 555 W Madison St • 312-906-8300
- **Hertz** • 225 S Canal St • 312-928-0538

Gas Stations

- **Fulton & Des Plaines** • 225 N Des Plaines St

Landmarks

- **Dugan's Drinking Emporium** • 128 S Halsted St
- **Union Station** • 200 S Canal St

P Parking

Pharmacies

- **CVS** • 400 W Madison St
- **CVS** • 130 S Canal St
- **Dominick's** • 1 N Halsted St ⊘
- **Walgreens** • 111 S Halsted St ⊘
- **Walgreens** • 250 S Wacker Dr

Pizza

- **Bacino's** • 118 S Clinton St
- **Giordano's** • 815 W Van Buren St
- **Leona's** • 848 W Madison St
- **Sbarro** • 500 W Madison St

Post Offices

- **US Post Office** • 168 N Clinton St

Schools

- **Chicago-Kent College of Law** • 565 W Adams St
- **Frances Xavier Warde** • 120 S Desplaines St

Supermarkets

- **Dominick's** • 1 N Halsted St ⊘

Randolph Street's funky, contemporary restaurant row kicks off here and continues westward. Meanwhile, back in the old country, shouts of "Opa!" ring out on Halsted Street in Greek Town. The stretch steams in the summer, when many of the restaurants offer patio dining. Stop in at the Athenian Candle Co to stock up on "Law Be Gone" room spray and "Lover Come Back" floor wash.

Coffee

- **Bean Addiction** • 555 W Madison St
- **Caribou Coffee** • 222 S Riverside Plz
- **Caribou Coffee** • 500 W Madison St
- **Dunkin' Donuts** • 2 N Riverside Plz
- **Dunkin' Donuts** • 500 W Madison St
- **Dunkin' Donuts** • 555 W Lake St
- **Krispy Kreme Doughnuts** • 210 S Canal St
- **Saxpys Coffee** • 605 W Lake St
- **Starbucks** • Dominick's • 1 N Halsted St
- **Starbucks** • 10 S Riverside Plz
- **Starbucks** • 139 S Clinton St
- **Starbucks** • 40 N Clinton St
- **Starbucks** • 400 W Madison St
- **Starbucks** • 550 W Van Buren St
- **Starbucks** • 600 W Lake St

Copy Shops

- **American Color Laboratory** • 611 W Adams St
- **Comet Press** • 812 W Van Buren St
- **FedEx Kinko's** • 127 S Clinton St ◎

Farmers Markets

- **Riverside Plaza (Jun–Oct; every other Thurs)** • 2 N Riverside Plz

Gyms

- **Fitness Formula** • 444 W Jackson Blvd
- **Lifestart** • 555 W Monroe St

Hardware Stores

- **Chicago Wholesale Hardware** • 171 N Halsted St

Liquor Stores

- **Bennett Special Wines** • 802 W Washington Blvd
- **Just Grapes (wine only)** • 560 W Washington Blvd
- **Monemvassia Wines** • 801 W Adams St
- **Presidential Market** • 555 W Madison St

Nightlife

- **Dylan's** • 118 S Clinton St
- **Snuggery Saloon & Dining Room** • Union Station • 225 S Canal St

Restaurants

- **Athena** • 212 S Halsted St
- **Avec** • 615 W Randolph St
- **Blackbird** • 619 W Randolph St
- **Butter** • 130 S Green St
- **Costa's** • 340 S Halsted St
- **Dine** • Crowne Plaza Chicago Metro Hotel • 733 W Madison St
- **Extra Virgin** • 741 W Randolph St
- **Gold Coast Dogs** • Union Station • 225 S Canal St
- **Greek Islands** • 200 S Halsted St
- **J&C Inn** • 558 W Van Buren St
- **Lou Mitchell's** • 565 W Jackson Blvd
- **Meli** • 301 S Halsted St
- **Nine** • 440 W Randolph St
- **Nine Muses** • 315 S Halsted St
- **Parthenon** • 314 S Halsted St
- **Pegasus Restaurant and Taverna** • 130 S Halsted St
- **Red Light** • 820 W Randolph St
- **Robinson's No 1 Ribs** • Union Station • 225 S Canal St
- **Rodity's** • 222 S Halsted St
- **Santorini** • 800 W Adams St
- **Sepia** • 123 N Jefferson St
- **Starfish** • 804 W Randolph St
- **Sushi Wabi** • 842 W Randolph St
- **Wild** • 3130 N Broadway St

Shopping

- **Athenian Candle Co** • 300 S Halsted St
- **Greek Town Music** • 330 S Halsted St

Map 5 • The Loop

N

1 · 2

W Carroll Ave

Merchandise Mart Plz

Chicago River

E Wacker Pl

Eisenhower Expy Access Rd

2

E Haddock Pl

W Haddock St

N Wells St

N Garvey Ct

N Dearborn St

E Wacker Pl

A W Lake St · W Lake St · State · E Benton Pl · Randolph · PAGE 212

Clark · Lake

N La Salle St

James R Thompson Center · Monument with Standing Beast · W Randolph St

Chicago Cultural Center

City Hall Green Roof · W Couch Pl · Macy's

N Clark St

Daley Civic Plaza · Washington

W Court Pl · Randolph

N State St

Washington · W Washington St · Washington · E Washington St

N Hadden Ct

N Wabash Ave

N Garland Ct

Joan Miro Sculpture

W Calhoun Pl · The Four Seasons

N Franklin St

N Wacker Dr

Court Pl

100W

W Madison St · Madison

Chicago Mercantile Exchange · W Arcade Pl

B ◄4 · THE LOOP · 6► · S Michigan Ave · N Michigan Ave

200W

W Monroe St · Monroe · Monroe · Adams

S Wacker Dr

S Franklin St

W Marble Pl

W Adams St · Rookery Building · Flamingo · Adams

Quincy L Station · Sears Tower · W Quincy St

300S

Quincy · Chicago Board of Trade · Monadnock Building · Jackson

S Clark St

S Dearborn St

S State St

Monadnock Building

La Salle · Library · DePaul University (Loop Campus) · PAGE 245

C · E Van Buren St · Roosevelt University

Chicago Board Options Exchange/ Chicago Stock Exchange

7 · 8 · La Salle

S Wells St

S Federal St

Harold Washington Library Center · PAGE 213

La Salle · E Congress Pkwy

290 · Eisenhower Expy

La Salle Street Station

S La Salle St

S Plymouth Ct

E Congress Pkwy

1/4 mile · .25 km

W Harrison St · E Harrison St · Harrison

The Loop derives its moniker from the L tracks that lasso the city's heart. This here is the bustling financial and business district, where banks are plentiful and parking is pricey. The intersection of State and Madison is literally ground zero (0 east, 0 west, 0 north, 0 south) for Chicago's easy-to-follow street numbering grid. Watching over it all is the Sears Tower, North America's tallest building...for the moment, at least...

$ Banks

- **Amalgamated** • 1 W Monroe St
- **Associated** • 200 N La Salle St
- **Banco Popular** • 415 N La Salle St
- **Bank of America** • 105 W Madison St
- **Bank of America** • 205 W Monroe St
- **Bank of America** • 231 S La Salle St
- **Bank of America** • 33 N Dearborn St
- **Bank of America (ATM)** • 100 W Lake St
- **Bank of America (ATM)** • 20 S State St
- **Bank of America (ATM)** • 233 S Wacker Dr
- **Bank of America (ATM)** • 300 S Wacker Dr
- **Bank of America (ATM)** • 302 W Adams St
- **Bank of America (ATM)** • 64 E Madison St
- **Charter One** • 150 S Wacker Dr
- **Charter One** • 2 S State St
- **Charter One** • 400 S La Salle St
- **Charter One** • 71 S Wacker Dr
- **Charter One (ATM)** • 200 N Dearborn St
- **Chase** • 10 S Dearborn St
- **Chase** • 120 S La Salle St
- **Chase** • 200 W Jackson Blvd
- **Chase** • 30 S Wacker Dr
- **Chase (ATM)** • 400 S La Salle St
- **Chase (ATM)** • 333 W Wacker Dr
- **Chase (ATM)** • 200 S Wacker Dr
- **Chase (ATM)** • 161 N Clark St
- **Chase (ATM)** • 131 S Dearborn St
- **Chase (ATM)** • Walgreens • 15 W Washington St
- **Chase (ATM)** • 16 W Adams St
- **Chase (ATM)** • 191 N Clark St
- **Chase (ATM)** • Walgreens • 200 W Adams St
- **Chase (ATM)** • Walgreens • 201 W Madison St
- **Chase (ATM)** • Walgreens • 240 W Randolph St
- **Chase (ATM)** • 30 S Dearborn St
- **Chase (ATM)** • Walgreens • 300 S State St
- **Chase (ATM)** • 425 S State St
- **Chase (ATM)** • 55 W Monroe St
- **Chase (ATM)** • 66 W Washington St
- **Chase (ATM)** • 70 W Madison St
- **Chicago Community** • 51 W Jackson Blvd
- **Citibank** • 11 S La Salle St
- **Citibank** • 222 W Adams St
- **Citibank** • 69 W Washington St
- **Citibank (ATM)** • 216 W Jackson Blvd
- **Citibank (ATM)** • 209 S La Salle St
- **Citibank (ATM)** • 1 W Monroe St
- **Citibank (ATM)** • 125 S Clark St
- **Citibank (ATM)** • 7-Eleven • 180 N Franklin St
- **Citibank (ATM)** • 25 E Washington St
- **Citibank (ATM)** • 7-Eleven • 29 E Madison St
- **Citibank (ATM)** • 7-Eleven • 318 W Adams St
- **Citibank (ATM)** • 7-Eleven • 33 E Adams St
- **Citibank (ATM)** • 7-Eleven • 343 S Dearborn St
- **Citibank (ATM)** • 7-Eleven • 48 N Wells St
- **Citibank (ATM)** • 7-Eleven • 58 E Lake St
- **Citibank (ATM)** • 69 W Washington St
- **Cole Taylor** • 111 W Washington St
- **Fifth Third** • 1 N Wacker Dr
- **Fifth Third** • 1 S Dearborn St
- **Fifth Third** • 161 N Clark St
- **Fifth Third** • 175 W Jackson Blvd
- **Fifth Third** • Sears Tower • 233 S Wacker Dr
- **Fifth Third** • 57 E Randolph St
- **Fifth Third (ATM)** • 101 N Wacker Dr
- **First** • 161 N Clark St
- **First** • 20 N Wacker Dr
- **First American** • 33 W Monroe St
- **First American** • 50 E Adams St
- **First American (ATM)** • 55 E Adams St
- **First American (ATM)** • 111 W Jackson Blvd
- **First American (ATM)** • 123 N Wacker Dr
- **First American (ATM)** • 145 S Wells St
- **First American (ATM)** • 171 W Randolph St
- **First American (ATM)** • 172 W Adams St
- **First American (ATM)** • 190 S La Salle St
- **First American (ATM)** • 200 W Madison St
- **First American (ATM)** • 208 S Wabash Ave
- **First American (ATM)** • 222 N La Salle St
- **First American (ATM)** • 234 S Wabash Ave
- **First American (ATM)** • 25 E Washington St
- **First American (ATM)** • 303 W Madison St
- **First American (ATM)** • 311 S Wacker Dr
- **First American (ATM)** • 326 S Wells St
- **First American (ATM)** • 60 E Randolph St
- **Harris** • 111 W Monroe St
- **Harris** • 141 W Jackson Blvd
- **Harris** • 99 W Washington St
- **Harris (ATM)** • 115 S La Salle St
- **Harris (ATM)** • 311 W Monroe St
- **Lakeside** • 141 W Jackson Blvd
- **LaSalle** • 100 S Wacker Dr
- **LaSalle** • 120 N La Salle St
- **LaSalle** • 135 S La Salle St
- **LaSalle** • 201 S State St
- **LaSalle** • 203 N La Salle St
- **LaSalle** • 77 S Dearborn St
- **LaSalle (ATM)** • 200 N State St
- **LaSalle (ATM)** • 175 N State St
- **LaSalle (ATM)** • 79 W Monroe St
- **LaSalle (ATM)** • 55 E Monroe St
- **LaSalle (ATM)** • 30 E Lake St
- **LaSalle (ATM)** • 24 W Madison St
- **LaSalle (ATM)** • 18 W Monroe St
- **LaSalle (ATM)** • 5 S Wabash Ave
- **LaSalle (ATM)** • 151 W Randolph St
- **LaSalle (ATM)** • 175 W Jackson Blvd
- **LaSalle (ATM)** • 180 N LaSalle St
- **LaSalle (ATM)** • 201 W Madison St
- **LaSalle (ATM)** • CVS • 208 W Washington St
- **LaSalle (ATM)** • 226 W Jackson Blvd
- **LaSalle (ATM)** • 230 W Washington St
- **LaSalle (ATM)** • 55 W Lake St
- **LaSalle (ATM)** • Hyatt Center • 71 S Wacker Dr
- **MB Financial** • 1 S Wacker Dr
- **MB Financial** • 2 S La Salle St
- **MB Financial (ATM)** • 223 W Jackson Blvd
- **MB Financial (ATM)** • 216 N Wabash Ave
- **MB Financial (ATM)** • 223 W Jackson Blvd
- **Northern Trust** • 50 S La Salle St
- **Northern Trust (ATM)** • 10 S La Salle St
- **Northern Trust (ATM)** • 111 S Wacker Dr
- **Northern Trust (ATM)** • 181 W Madison St
- **Shore** • 333 S State St
- **TCF** • 29 E Madison St
- **TCF (ATM)** • DePaul University • 1 E Jackson Blvd
- **TCF (ATM)** • 7-Eleven • 125 S Clark St
- **TCF (ATM)** • Osco • 37 S State St
- **TCF (ATM)** • 7-Eleven • 180 N Franklin St
- **TCF (ATM)** • 7-Eleven • 29 E Madison St
- **TCF (ATM)** • 7-Eleven • 33 E Adams St
- **TCF (ATM)** • 7-Eleven • 343 S Dearborn St
- **TCF (ATM)** • 7-Eleven • 48 N Wells St
- **US** • 209 S La Salle St
- **US** • 25 E Washington St
- **US (ATM)** • 333 S Wabash Ave
- **Washington Mutual** • 100 W Randolph St
- **Washington Mutual** • 230 W Monroe St
- **Washington Mutual** • 247 S State St
- **Washington Mutual** • 311 S Wacker Dr
- **Washington Mutual** • 41 N Wabash Ave
- **Washington Mutual** • 70 W Madison St

🚗 Car Rental

- **Avis** • 214 N Clark St • 312-782-6825
- **Enterprise** • 65 E Lake St • 312-251-0200
- **Enterprise** • 201 W Madison St • 312-553-5230
- **Enterprise** • 303 W Lake St • 312-332-7783
- **Enterprise** • 425 S Wells St • 312-939-6001
- **Hertz** • 181 W Washington Blvd • 312-726-1476
- **National/Alamo** • 203 N La Salle St • 312-236-2581

○ Landmarks

- **Chicago Board of Trade** • 141 W Jackson Blvd
- **Chicago Board Options Exchange** • 400 S La Salle St
- **Chicago Cultural Center** • 78 E Washington St
- **Chicago Mercantile Exchange** • 20 S Wacker Dr
- **Chicago Stock Exchange** • 440 S La Salle St
- **City Hall Green Roof** • 121 N LaSalle St
- **Daley Civic Plaza** • 50 W Washington St
- **Flamingo** • 219 S Dearborn St
- **The Four Seasons** • 70 W Madison St
- **Harold Washington Library Center** • 400 S State St
- **James R Thompson Center** • 100 W Randolph St
- **Joan Miro Sculpture** • 69 W Washington St
- **Macy's** • 111 N State St
- **Monadnock Building** • 53 W Jackson Blvd
- **Monument with Standing Beast** • 100 W Randolph St
- **Quincy L Station** • 220 S Wells St
- **Rookery Building** • 209 S La Salle St
- **Sears Tower** • 233 S Wacker Dr

📖 Libraries

- **Harold Washington Public Library** • 400 S State St
- **The Swedenborg Library** • 77 W Washington St, Rm 1700

P Parking

℞ Pharmacies

- **CVS** • 137 S State St
- **CVS** • 105 S Wabash Ave
- **CVS** • 175 W Jackson Blvd
- **CVS** • 208 W Washington Blvd
- **Walgreens** • 15 W Washington St
- **Walgreens** • 16 W Adams St
- **Walgreens** • 191 N Clark St
- **Walgreens** • 200 W Adams St
- **Walgreens** • 201 W Madison St
- **Walgreens** • 240 W Randolph St
- **Walgreens** • 300 S State St
- **Walgreens** • 79 W Monroe St

🍕 Pizza

- **Bacci Pizzeria** • 120 N Wells St
- **Bacci Pizzeria** • 105 W Madison St
- **Bonivino Restaurant** • 111 W Van Buren St
- **California Pizza Kitchen** • 30 N La Salle St
- **Exchequer Pub** • 226 S Wabash Ave
- **Giordano's** • 223 W Jackson Blvd
- **Giordano's** • 310 W Randolph St
- **Jimmy John's** • 216 W Washington St
- **Little Pompeii** • 131 S Dearborn St
- **Little Pompeii** • 181 W Madison St
- **Pizano's Pizza & Pasta** • 61 E Madison St
- **Pizza Broker** • 400 S Financial Pl
- **Reggie's Pizza Express** • 411 S Wells St
- **Ricobenes Pizzeria** • 222 N Wells St

✉ Post Offices

- **US Post Office** • 100 W Randolph St
- **US Post Office** • 211 S Clark St
- **US Post Office** • Sears Tower • 233 S Wacker Dr
- **US Post Office** • 5 S Wabash Ave

🏫 Schools

- **Alternative Safe Schools** • 125 S Clark St
- **Chicago City Colleges** • 226 W Jackson Blvd
- **Chicago School of Massage Therapy** • 18 N Wabash Ave
- **DePaul University** • 1 E Jackson Blvd
- **Harold Washington College** • 30 E Lake St
- **Harrington College of Design** • 200 W Madison St
- **International Academy of Design and Technology** • 1 N State St
- **John Marshall Law** • 315 S Plymouth Ct
- **Keller Graduate School of Management** • 225 W Washington St
- **LINC Alternative High** • 125 S Clark St
- **MacCormac College** • 29 E Madison St
- **Robert Morris College** • 401 S State St
- **School of the Art Institute** • 37 S Wabash Ave

Map 5 · **The Loop**

Ⓝ

W Carroll Ave

Merchandise Mart Plz

Chicago River

W Haddock Pl

E Haddock Pl

E Wacker Pl

N Garland Ct

Eisenhower Expy
Access Rd

1

2

▲ **2**

N Garvey Ct

N Dearborn Ct

A

W Lake St

W Lake St

State

Lake

E Benton Pl

Clark

W Couch Pl

W Couch Pl

Randolph

**PAGE
212**

N Wells St

N La Salle St

N Clark St

W Randolph St

N State St

Chicago
Cultural
Center

N Wacker Dr

N Court Pl

W Court Pl

W Court Pl

E Washington St

N Franklin St

Washington

W Washington St

Washington

N Michigan Ave

Chicago River

N Wabash Ave

N Garland Ct

W Calhoun Pl

W Calhoun Pl

N Holden Ct

300W

100W

Madison

B

◄ **4**

2

S Franklin St

W Arcade Pl

W Arcade Pl

2

2

THE LOOP

6 ►

S Michigan Ave

W Monroe St

Monroe

Monroe

100S

W Marble Pl

Adams

S Wacker Dr

Sears Tower

2

W Adams St

200S

S Clark St

S Dearborn St

S State St

Quincy

W Quincy St

W Quincy St

Jackson

3

E Jackson Blvd

S Wells St

300S

DePaul University
(Loop Campus)

**PAGE
245**

C

La Salle

Library

E Van Buren St

S Franklin St

400S

S Federal St

Roosevelt
University

7 ▼

290

8 ▼

Eisenhower Expy

La Salle

E Congress Pkwy

La Salle
Street
Station

S La Salle St

S Plymouth Ct

E Harrison St

W Harrison St

Harrison

| 1/4 mile | .25 km |

State Street provides the retail draw (just don't mention Marshall Fields…). For a spot of culture, check out the aptly named Chicago Cultural Center, the Harold Washington Center, or Daley Plaza for imaginative seasonal events. For original dining, try the historic Atwood Café and the bustling three-restaurant Italian Village.

Coffee

- Argo Tea • 1 N Dearborn St
- Argo Tea • 140 S Dearborn St
- Argo Tea • 16 W Randolph St
- Capra's Café • 46 S Clark St
- Caribou Coffee • 10 S La Salle St
- Caribou Coffee • 200 N La Salle St
- Caribou Coffee • 311 W Monroe St
- Caribou Coffee • 55 W Monroe St
- Cosi • 203 N La Salle St
- Cosi • 230 W Monroe St
- Cosi • 230 W Washington St
- Cosi • 28 E Jackson Blvd
- Cosi • 33 N Dearborn St
- Dunkin' Donuts • 400 S Financial Pl
- Dunkin' Donuts • 166 W Washington St
- Dunkin' Donuts • 105 W Madison St
- Dunkin' Donuts • 39 W Jackson Blvd
- Dunkin' Donuts • 27 E Lake St
- Dunkin' Donuts • 100 W Randolph St
- Dunkin' Donuts • 125 S Clark St
- Dunkin' Donuts • 201 N Clark St
- Dunkin' Donuts • 201 W Madison St
- Dunkin' Donuts • 205 W Randolph St
- Dunkin' Donuts • 215 W Lake St
- Dunkin' Donuts • 220 W Washington St
- Dunkin' Donuts • 229 W Jackson Blvd
- Dunkin' Donuts • 230 S State St
- Dunkin' Donuts • 27 W Lake St
- Dunkin' Donuts • 31 E Adams St
- Dunkin' Donuts • 333 S State St
- Dunkin' Donuts • 439 S Dearborn St
- Dunkin' Donuts • 6 N Wabash Ave
- Dunkin' Donuts • 62 E Jackson Blvd
- Dunkin' Donuts • 75 E Washington St
- Intelligentsia Coffee • 53 E Randolph St
- Intelligentsia Coffee • 53 W Jackson Blvd
- Lavazza • 111 W Jackson Blvd
- Lavazza • 134 N La Salle St
- Lavazza • 27 W Washington St
- Liberty Coffee and Tea • 401 S La Salle St
- Starbucks • 200 W Madison St
- Starbucks • 100 S Wacker Dr
- Starbucks • 105 W Adams St
- Starbucks • Marshall Fields • 111 N State St
- Starbucks • 111 W Washington St
- Starbucks • 131 S Dearborn St
- Starbucks • 150 N Wacker Dr
- Starbucks • CT&T Bldg • 161 N Clark St
- Starbucks • 175 W Jackson Blvd
- Starbucks • 180 N La Salle St
- Starbucks • 200 W Adams St
- Starbucks • 209 W Jackson Blvd
- Starbucks • 21 S Clark St
- Starbucks • AT&T Bldg • 227 W Monroe St
- Starbucks • Bank of America Bldg • 231 S La Salle St
- Starbucks • Sears Tower • 233 S Wacker Dr
- Starbucks • 25 E Washington Blvd
- Starbucks • 30 N La Salle St
- Starbucks • 303 W Madison St
- Starbucks • 311 S Wacker Dr
- Starbucks • 39 S La Salle St
- Starbucks • 40 W Lake St
- Starbucks • 55 E Jackson Blvd
- Starbucks • 66 W Washington St
- Starbucks • 68 E Madison St
- Starbucks • 70 W Madison St

Copy Shops

- 24 Seven Copies • 222 N La Salle St ⊕
- Acme Copy • 218 S Wabash Ave
- Advance Instant Printing • 5 S Wabash Ave
- AlphaGraphics • 208 S La Salle St
- Best Imaging • 20 E Randolph St
- Copy Corps • 20 N Clark St
- Document Technologies • 105 W Adams St
- Fastrac Printing • 220 S State St
- FedEx Kinko's • 101 N Wacker Dr
- FedEx Kinko's • 111 W Washington St
- FedEx Kinko's • 2 N La Salle St
- FedEx Kinko's • 200 W Jackson Blvd
- FedEx Kinko's • 227 W Monroe St
- FedEx Kinko's • 29 S La Salle St ⊕
- FedEx Kinko's • 400 S La Salle St
- FedEx Kinko's • 55 E Monroe St
- FedEx Kinko's • 6 W Lake St
- Instant Printing • 180 N La Salle St
- Instant Printing • 200 S Clark St
- Kwik Kopy • 11 S La Salle St
- Landmark Document Services • 200 W Adams St
- Loop Legal Copies • 318 W Adams St
- Record Copy Services • 30 N La Salle St
- Reproduction Consultants • 218 S Wabash Ave
- Sir Speedy • 311 S Wacker Dr
- Staples Copy & Print Centers • 111 N Wabash Ave
- The UPS Store • 27 N Wacker Dr
- Viking Printing & Copying • 53 W Jackson Blvd
- Williams Lea • 300 W Adams St

Farmers Markets

- Daley Plaza (May–Sep; Thurs 7 am–3 pm) • W Washington St & S Dearborn St, N of W Washington St
- Federal Plaza (May–Oct; Tues, 7 am–3 pm) • Adams St & Dearborn St
- The Park at Jackson & Wacker (June–Oct; Thurs, 7 am–3 pm) • 311 S Wacker Dr at Sears Tower

Gyms

- Bally Total Fitness • 25 E Washington St
- Buckingham Athletic Club • 440 S La Salle St
- Curves (women only) • 39 S La Salle St
- Equinox • 200 W Monroe St
- Executive Fitness Center • Palmer House Hilton • 17 E Monroe St
- Fitness Image Incorporated • 9 N Wabash Ave, 4th Fl
- Lifestart • 1 N Franklin St
- Lifestart • 161 N Clark St
- Lifestart • 20 N Wacker Dr
- Lifestart • 200 S Wacker Dr
- Metropolitan Fitness Club • Sears Tower • 233 S Wacker Dr, 67th Fl
- Women's Workout World (women only) • 208 S La Salle St
- World Gym • 150 S Wacker Dr

Hardware Stores

- Ace Hardware • 312 W Adams St
- Lens Ace Hardware • 272 W Lake St
- Sears • 2 N State St

Liquor Stores

- Cal's • 400 S Wells St
- G&J Gifts & Liquor • 167 N Wells St
- Lake-Wells Food And Liquors • 201 West Lake St
- Rothschild Liquor Mart • 55 W Van Buren St, Ste 350
- Wabash Food & Liquor • 234 S Wabash Ave

Movie Theaters

- Chicago Cultural Center • 78 E Washington St
- Gene Siskel Film Center • 164 N State St

Nightlife

- Cal's • 400 S Wells St
- Exchequer Pub • 226 S Wabash Ave
- Manhattans • 415 S Dearborn St
- Miller's Pub • 134 S Wabash Ave
- Petterino's • 150 N Dearborn St

Restaurants

- Atwood Café • 1 W Washington St
- Billy Goat Tavern • 330 S Wells St
- Everest • 440 S La Salle St
- Gold Coast Dogs • 159 N Wabash Ave
- Gold Coast Dogs • 17 S Wabash Ave
- Hannah's Bretzel • 180 W Washington St
- Heaven on Seven • 111 N Wabash Ave
- La Cantina Enoteca • Italian Village Restaurant Complex • 71 W Monroe St
- La Rosetta • 70 W Madison St
- Lockwood • 17 E Monroe St
- Miller's Pub • 134 S Wabash Ave
- Nick's Fishmarket & Grill • 51 S Clark St
- Oasis Café • 21 N Wabash Ave
- Plymouth Restaurant • 327 S Plymouth Ct ⊕
- Russian Tea Time • 77 E Adams St
- Trattoria No 10 • 10 N Dearborn St
- The Village • Italian Village Restaurant Complex • 71 W Monroe St
- Vivere • 71 W Monroe St

Shopping

- American Music World • 111 N State St
- Carson Pirie Scott • 1 S State St
- Gallery 37 Store • 66 E Randolph St
- Kramer's Health Food Center • 230 S Wabash Ave
- Rock Records • 175 W Washington St
- Sears • 2 N State St

Map 6 • **The Loop / Grant Park**

A giant silver bean and 50-foot-tall animated faces...yes, really! Millennium Park is definitely the Chicago show-stopper, with its unique blend of artwork and landscaping. Further down Michigan Avenue, the more traditional Grant Park brings highbrow and lowbrow culture side by side. Tasteful music or Taste of Chicago, there's something for everyone.

$ Banks

- **Associated** • 130 E Randolph St
- **Associated** • 200 E Randolph St
- **Associated** • 225 N Michigan Ave
- **Bank of America (ATM)** • 404 S Michigan Ave
- **Chase** • 150 N Michigan Ave
- **Chase (ATM)** • 151 N Michigan Ave
- **Chase (ATM)** • 11 N Michigan Ave
- **Chase (ATM)** • 30 N Michigan Ave
- **Chase (ATM)** • Walgreens • 300 N Michigan Ave
- **Citibank** • 100 S Michigan Ave
- **Citibank** • 233 N Michigan Ave
- **Citibank (ATM)** • 7-Eleven • 174 N Michigan Ave
- **Citibank (ATM)** • 360 N Michigan Ave
- **Fifth Third** • 400 E South Water St
- **First American (ATM)** • Hard Rock Hotel •
  230 N Michigan Ave
- **LaSalle (ATM)** • 122 S Michigan Ave
- **LaSalle (ATM)** • 205 N Michigan Ave
- **MB Financial** • 303 E Wacker Dr
- **Midwest Bank & Trust Company** •
  300 S Michigan Ave
- **Midwest Bank & Trust Company (ATM)** •
  332 S Michigan Ave
- **New Century (ATM)** • 211 N Stetson Ave
- **North Community** • 180 N Michigan Ave
- **TCF (ATM)** • 7-Eleven • 174 N Michigan Ave
- **TCF (ATM)** • 500 S Columbus Dr
- **US** • 360 N Michigan Ave
- **US (ATM)** • 111 E Wacker Dr
- **Washington Mutual** • 206 N Michigan Ave

Car Rental

- **Hertz** • 151 E Wacker Dr

Landmarks

- **American Windows** • Art Institute •
  111 S Michigan Ave
- **Art Institute of Chicago** • 111 S Michigan Ave
- **Auditorium Building** • 430 S Michigan Ave
- **Cloud Gate** • Millennium Park
- **The Crown Fountain** • N Michigan Ave b/w
  E Madison St & E Monroe Dr
- **Fine Arts Building** • 410 S Michigan Ave

- **Jay Pritzker Pavilion** • Millennium Park
- **Prudential Building** • 1 Prudential Plz
- **Santa Fe Building** • 224 S Michigan Ave
- **Symphony Center** • 220 S Michigan Ave

P Parking

Rx Pharmacies

- **Walgreens** • 30 N Michigan Ave
- **Walgreens** • 300 N Michigan Ave

Pizza

- **Giordano's** • 135 E Lake St
- **Sbarro** • 233 N Michigan Ave

Post Offices

- **US Post Office** • 200 E Randolph St

Schools

- **American Academy of Art** • 332 S Michigan Ave
- **Career Works Alternative** • 200 N Michigan Ave
- **Institute for Clinical Social Work** •
  200 N Michigan Ave
- **National-Louis University** • 122 S Michigan Ave
- **Roosevelt University** • 430 S Michigan Ave

Map 6

Park Grill's front yard morphs from an ice skating rink in winter to an outdoor café in summer. Take in a free concert at the spectacular Pritzker Pavilion, or paddle in the crowd-pleasing Crown Fountain. For those long winter months the Art Institute's free Thursday nights are ideal, whilst the Symphony Center offers Afterwork Masterworks for commuters.

Coffee

- **Caribou Coffee** • 20 N Michigan Ave
- **The Coffee Beanery** • 150 N Michigan Ave
- **Cosi** • 116 S Michigan Ave
- **Cosi** • 233 N Michigan Ave
- **Dunkin' Donuts** • 406 S Michigan Ave
- **Dunkin' Donuts** • 233 N Michigan Ave
- **Dunkin' Donuts** • 300 E Randolph St
- **Dunkin' Donuts** • 303 E Wacker Dr
- **Starbucks** • 151 N Michigan Ave
- **Starbucks** • Millenium Station • 130 E Randolph St
- **Starbucks** • Amoco Bldg • 200 E Randolph St
- **Starbucks** • 202 N Michigan Ave
- **Starbucks** • Illinois Ctr • 225 N Michigan Ave

Copy Shops

- **AlphaGraphics** • 180 N Stetson Ave
- **FedEx Kinko's** • 111 E Wacker Dr
- **FedEx Kinko's** • 130 E Randolph St
- **FedEx Kinko's** • 225 N Michigan Ave
- **FedEx Kinko's** • 34 S Michigan Ave
- **Sir Speedy** • 130 E Randolph St
- **Swift Impressions** • 333 N Michigan Ave

Farmers Markets

- **Prudential Plaza (Jun–Oct; Thurs, 7 am–3 pm)** • E Lake St & N Beaubien Ct

Gyms

- **Curves (women only)** • 180 N Stetson Ave
- **Lakeshore Athletic Club** • 211 N Stetson Ave

Liquor Stores

- **Gourmet Pantry** • 155 N Michigan Ave

Nightlife

- **Houlihan's** • 111 E Wacker Dr

Restaurants

- **Aria** • Fairmont Chicago Hotel • 200 N Columbus Dr
- **Artist's Café** • 412 S Michigan Ave
- **Bennigan's** • 150 S Michigan Ave
- **China Grill** • Hard Rock Hotel • 230 N Michigan Ave
- **The Gage** • 24 S Michigan Ave
- **The Green at Grant Park** • 352 E Monroe St
- **Park Grill** • 11 N Michigan Ave

Shopping

- **ArchiCenter** • 224 S Michigan Ave
- **Art & Artisans** • 108 S Michigan Ave
- **Museum Shop of the Art Institute** • 111 S Michigan Ave
- **Poster Plus** • 200 S Michigan Ave
- **Precious Possessions** • 28 N Michigan Ave

Map 7 · **South Loop / River City**

N

1   2

W Jackson Blvd

300S

W Gladys Ave
W Gladys Ave

W Gladys Ave

W Van Buren St

300W   200W

S Franklin St

S Wells St

S Sherman St

4

5

UIC-Halsted

A   Clinton

W Tilden St

Eisenhower Expy

290

P

US Postal
Distribution Center

Old Post
Office

W Harrison St

600S

S Clinton St

Chicago River

W Vernon Park Pl

W Vernon Park Pl

River City

W Lexington St

P

26

S Des Plaines St

600W   500W

W Polk St   W Polk St

B

SOUTH
LOOP

W Cabrini St

8

W Arthington St

800S

W Taylor St   W Taylor St

1000S

W De Koven St

S Union Ave

90
94

W Grenshaw St

$

200W

$

$

Maxwell Street Market
W Roosevelt Rd

$ $

Dan Ryan Expy

1200S

10

2 $

Rx

C   W 12th Pl

W 12th Pl

W 12th Pl

S Jefferson St

S Clinton St

Canal St

W O'Brien St

W 13th St

S Ruble St

W Maxwell St   W Maxwell St

| 1/4 mile | .25 km |

Bertrand Goldberg's brilliant River City, the sprawling condo development compound hugging the Chicago River's eastern shore, has not exactly stimulated a commercially-developed utopia. Despite the residents, it's still mostly warehouses, semi-trucks, and the US Postal Distribution Center. The only remnant of the former US Customs office— relocated in 2006—is the concentration of immigration attorneys.

$ Banks

- **Bank of America** • 430 W Roosevelt Rd
- **Chase** • 1130 S Canal St
- **Chase (ATM)** • Walgreens • 501 W Roosevelt Rd
- **First American** • 1101 S Canal St
- **Harris Trust & Savings** • 522 W Roosevelt Rd
- **South Central** • 525 W Roosevelt Rd

Gas Stations

- **Citgo** • 1004 S Desplaines St
- **Marathon** • 1121 S Jefferson St

Landmarks

- **Maxwell Street Market (Sun, 7 am–3 pm)** • Canal St b/w Taylor St & Roosevelt Rd
- **Old Post Office** • 404 W Harrison St
- **River City** • 800 S Wells St
- **US Postal Distribution Center** • 433 W Harrison St

P Parking

℞ Pharmacies

- **Walgreens** • 501 W Roosevelt Rd ⓓ

Pizza

- **Atinos Pizza** • 570 W Roosevelt Rd
- **Aurelio's Pizza** • 506 W Harrison St

✉ Post Offices

- **US Post Office** • 358 W Harrison St
- **US Post Office** • 433 W Harrison St

Manny's is essential for folks who enjoy sarcasm with their pastrami; pack a wire—you never know what you'll overhear. The 24-hour White Palace Grill has sopped up late night booze since 1939. Although a shadow of its former self, the Maxwell Sunday Market remains a haven for tube socks, churros, and trashy treasures.

Map

Coffee

- **Dunkin' Donuts** • 1121 S Jefferson St
- **Dunkin' Donuts** • 500 W Roosevelt Rd
- **Starbucks** • 1101 S Canal St

Copy Shops

- **Staples** • 1130 S Canal St

Farmers Markets

- **Maxwell Street Market (Sun, 7 am–3 pm)** • Canal St b/w Taylor St & Roosevelt Rd

Pet Shops

- **Petsmart** • 1101 S Canal St

Restaurants

- **Bake for Me** • 608 W Roosevelt Rd
- **Manny's Coffee Shop** • 1141 S Jefferson St
- **White Palace Grill** • 1159 S Canal St ⊕

Shopping

- **Adam Joseph's Hats** • 544 W Roosevelt Rd
- **Fishman's Fabrics** • 1101 S Des Plaines St
- **Lee's Foreign Car Service** • 727 S Jefferson St
- **Morris & Sons** • 557 W Polk St

Map 8 • **South Loop / Printers Row / Dearborn Park**

The University Center, which houses students from nearby Columbia, Roosevelt, and DePaul, has injected a much needed youthful flavor into this empty-nester 'hood. The Dearborn Street corridor known as Printer's Row, once a publishing enclave, now sports student-friendly bars and restaurants. Look both ways before crossing Congress, as cars zip on and off the expressway like they're training for NASCAR.

$ Banks

- **Bank of America (ATM)** • 1104 S Wabash Ave
- **Bank of America (ATM)** • 623 S Wabash Ave
- **Charter One (ATM)** • 600 S Dearborn St
- **Chase** • 550 S Dearborn St
- **Chase** • 850 S Wabash Ave
- **Chase (ATM)** • 717 S Dearborn St
- **Chase (ATM)** • 1167 S State St
- **Chase (ATM)** • Walgreens • 2 E Roosevelt Rd
- **Chase (ATM)** • 800 S Wells St
- **Chicago Community** • 47 W Polk St
- **Citibank (ATM)** • 7-Eleven • 525 S State St
- **First American (ATM)** • 711 S State St
- **First American (ATM)** • 24 E Congress Pkwy
- **First American (ATM)** • 524 S Wabash Ave
- **First American (ATM)** • 600 S Clark St
- **LaSalle (ATM)** • 50 E Congress Pkwy
- **MB Financial** • 557 S State St
- **MB Financial (ATM)** • 525 S State St
- **TCF** • Jewel • 1224 S Wabash Ave
- **TCF (ATM)** • 7-Eleven • 525 S State St
- **Washington Mutual** • 620 S Dearborn St

⬤ Car Washes

- **Kendo's Hand Car Wash** • 700 S Clark St
- **River City Car Wash** • 800 S Wells St

Car Rental

- **Budget** • 714 S Wabash Ave • 312-935-3440

🅿 Gas Stations

- **BP** • 50 W Congress Pkwy

o Landmarks

- **Columbia College Center for Book & Paper Arts** • 1104 S Wabash Ave
- **Former Elliot Ness Building** • 618 S Dearborn St
- **Old Dearborn Train Station** • 47 W Polk St
- **Pacific Garden Mission** • 646 S State St

🅿 Parking

℞ Pharmacies

- **Jewel-Osco** • 1224 S Wabash Ave ⊚
- **Target** • 1154 S Clark St
- **Walgreens** • 2 E Roosevelt Rd

Pizza

- **Edwardo's Natural Pizza** • 521 S Dearborn St
- **Got Pizza** • 719 S State St
- **KFC & Pizza Hut Express** • 612 S Wabash Ave
- **Pat's Pizzeria** • 638 S Clark St
- **Trattoria Caterina** • 616 S Dearborn St

Schools

- **Daystar Education Association** • 800 S Wells St
- **Jones College Prep** • 606 S State St
- **Renaissance Prep** • 719 S State St

Map 8 • **South Loop / Printers Row / Dearborn Park**

Sundries / Entertainment

Blackie's is the real deal, the oldest and most racially-mixed bar in the neighborhood. Hackney's bar food is way underrated. Same goes for South Loop Club—sit by a window here to take in the always-interesting street scene at this funky intersection. Meanwhile, restaurateur Shawn McClain (Spring, Green Zebra) gets carnivorous at his latest venture, Custom House, on Congress and Dearborn.

Coffee

- **Caribou Coffee** • 800 S Wabash Ave
- **Caribou Coffee** • 41 E 8th St
- **Dunkin' Donuts** • 600 S Wabash Ave
- **Mezicera** • 728 S Dearborn St
- **Starbucks** • Target • 1154 S Clark St
- **Starbucks** • 31 E Roosevelt Rd
- **Starbucks** • 555 S Dearborn St

Copy Shops

- **FedEx Kinko's** • 700 S Wabash Ave
- **The UPS Store** • 47 W Polk St

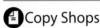Farmers Markets

- **Printer's Row (Jun–Oct; Sat, 7 am–2 pm)** • S Dearborn St & W Polk St

Gyms

- **Bally Total Fitness** • 800 S Wells St
- **Fitness Formula** • 1151 S State Ave
- **XSport Fitness** • 819 S State St

Hardware Stores

- **South Loop Ace Hardware** • 725 S State St

Liquor Stores

- **George's Cocktail Lounge** • 646 S Wabash Ave
- **Printers Row Wine Shop** • 719 S Dearborn St
- **Warehouse Liquors** • 634 S Wabash Ave

Nightlife

- **Buddy Guy's Legends** • 754 S Wabash Ave
- **George's Cocktail Lounge** • 646 S Wabash Ave
- **Kasey's Tavern** • 701 S Dearborn St
- **South Loop Club** • 701 S State St
- **Tantrum** • 1023 S State St

Restaurants

- **Amarit** • 600 S Dearborn St
- **Blackie's** • 755 S Clark St
- **Cafe Mediterra** • 728 S Dearborn St
- **Custom House** • 500 S Dearborn St
- **Eleven City Diner** • 1112 S Wabash Ave
- **Hackney's** • 733 S Dearborn St
- **Orange** • 75 W Harrison St
- **South Loop Club** • 701 S State St
- **SRO** • 610 S Dearborn St
- **Tamarind** • 614 S Wabash Ave
- **Trattoria Caterina** • 616 S Dearborn St

Shopping

- **Printers Row Fine & Rare Books** • 715 S Dearborn St
- **Sandmeyer's Book Store** • 714 S Dearborn St

Video Rental

Map 8

Map 9 • **South Loop / South Michigan Ave**

N

East Jackson Dr

1

2

Rose Garden

E Van Buren St

Roosevelt University

400S

E Congress Plaza Dr

PAGE 282

Van Buren Street Station

6

Monroe Street Harbor

E Congress Pkwy

$

Buckingham Fountain

E Congress Plaza Dr

E Harrison St

Spirit of Music Garden

2 2

Rose Garden

PAGE 220

Grant Park

Lake Michigan

Columbia College

PAGE 242

E Balbo Ave

100E

Chicago Hilton and Towers

$

P

S Columbus Dr

S Lake Shore Dr

E 8th St

$

8

Johnson Publishing Headquarters

S Michigan Ave

Hutchinson Field

E 9th St

$

E 11th St

P

11th Pl

Roosevelt Road Station

P

41

S Holden Ct

S Wabash Ave

Agora

1200S

E Roosevelt Rd

Museum Campus

John G Shedd Aquarium

Roosevelt

$

P

PAGE 232

E Solidarity Dr

E 13 St

11

E Solidarity Dr

Field Museum of Natural History

McFetridge Dr

1/4 mile

.25 km

Built atop the rubble of the Great Chicago Fire of 1871, Grant Park is now affectionately known as Chicago's front yard. Spin around and you are guaranteed a view—Lake Michigan, Museum Campus, the city skyline, or the gardens of the park itself. While rather desolate in the winter, warm weather brings out Frisbee players, inline skaters, joggers, boaters, and sun-worshippers galore.

$ Banks

- **Citibank (ATM)** • 800 S Michigan Ave
- **First American (ATM)** • 1200 S Lake Shore Dr
- **First American (ATM)** • Congress Plaza Hotel • 520 S Michigan Ave
- **First American (ATM)** • Chicago Hilton and Towers • 727 S Michigan Ave
- **New City** • 900 S Michigan Ave

o Landmarks

- **Agora** • S Michigan Ave & E Roosevelt Rd
- **Buckingham Fountain** • Columbus Dr & E Congress Pkwy
- **Chicago Hilton and Towers** • 720 S Michigan Ave
- **John G Shedd Aquarium** • 1200 S Lake Shore Dr
- **Johnson Publishing Headquarters** • 820 S Michigan Ave
- **Spirit of Music Garden** • 601 S Michigan Ave

Libraries

- **Asher Library-Spertus Institute** • 610 S Michigan Ave
- **Library of Columbia College** • 624 S Michigan Ave

P Parking

Schools

- **Columbia College** • 600 S Michigan Ave
- **East-West University** • 816 S Michigan Ave
- **Spertus College** • 610 S Michigan Ave

Chicago's front yard boasts gardens, recreation courts and fields, and the Shedd Aquarium. Dancers gather at the Spirit of Music Garden for the outdoor SummerDance series, and the skyrocketing water display known as Buckingham Fountain, accompanied by lights and music, occurs daily and hourly for twenty minutes from dusk until 10 pm, April through October.

Nightlife

- **Kitty O'Shea's** • 720 S Michigan Ave
- **Savoy Bar and Grill** • 800 S Michigan Ave
- **Spertus Cafe** • 610 S Michigan Ave

Restaurants

- **Kitty O'Shea's** • 720 S Michigan Ave
- **Oysy** • 888 S Michigan Ave
- **Yolk** • 1120 S Michigan Ave

Shopping

- **Spertus Shop** • 610 S Michigan Ave

Map 10 • East P

SOUTH LOOP

EAST PILSEN

CHINATOWN

University of Illinois at Chicago

Roosevelt

Jefferson Park

Ping Tom Memorial Park

Chinatown Square

Cermak-Chinatown

Chinatown Gate

On Leong Merchants Association Building

Raymond Hilliard Apartments

Halsted

Connector

1/4 mile .25 km

The developer John Podmajersky has a monopoly on the once-affordable loft rentals in East Pilsen that house so many of Chicago's working artists. Across the river in Chinatown, development continues to clip along with the same breakneck speed as the dim sum carts at the bustling expanse of Three Happiness during their popular Sunday brunch.

Map

$ Banks
- **American Metro** • 2144 S Archer Ave
- **Cathay Bank** • 222 W Cermak Rd
- **Cathay Bank** • 250 W Cermak Rd
- **Charter One** • 2131 S China Pl
- **Charter One** • 2263 S Wentworth Ave
- **Chase** • 1340 S Canal St
- **Chase (ATM)** • Walgreens • 316 W Cermak Rd
- **Citibank** • 2022 S Archer Ave
- **International Bank of Chicago** • 208 W Cermak Rd
- **Lakeside** • 2200 S Archer Ave
- **South Central** • 2335 S Wentworth Ave
- **Washington Mutual** • 1226 S Canal St

Gas Stations
- **Shell** • 1741 S Ruble St

Landmarks
- **Chinatown Gate** • S Wentworth Ave & W Cermak Rd
- **Chinatown Square** • S Archer Ave
- **On Leong Merchants Association Building** • 2216 S Wentworth Ave
- **Ping Tom Memorial Park** • 300 W 19th St
- **Raymond Hilliard Apartments** • 2111 S Clark St

Libraries
- **Chinatown Public Library** • 2353 S Wentworth Ave

P Parking

Rx Pharmacies
- **Dominick's** • 1340 S Canal St
- **Walgreens** • 316 W Cermak Rd

Pizza
- **Connie's Pizza** • 2373 S Archer Ave
- **Domino's** • 1234 S Canal St

Post Offices
- **US Post Office** • 2345 S Wentworth Ave

Schools
- **John C Haines Elementary** • 247 W 23rd Pl
- **National Teacher's Academy** • 55 W Cermak Rd
- **Pui Tak Christian** • 2301 S Wentworth Ave
- **South Loop Elementary** • 1212 S Plymouth Ct
- **St Therese** • 247 W 23rd St

Supermarkets
- **Dominick's** • 1340 S Canal St
- **Richwell Market** • 1835 S Canal St
- **Tai Wah Grocery** • 2226 S Wentworth Ave

Map 10 · **East F**

N

University of Illinois at Chicago

PAGE 254

1

2

W Taylor St   W Taylor St   W Taylor St

W De Koven St

W Grenshaw St

7 W Roosevelt Rd   **8**   Roosevelt   Roosevelt

W 12th Pl

W O'Brien St

W 12th Pl

SOUTH LOOP

W 13th St

A

W Maxwell St

W 13th St

W Liberty St

E 14th St

W 14th St

E 14th St

W Barber St

W 14th Pl

W 14th St

90

94   W 15th St   W 15th St

W 15th St   W 15th St

◄26

W 16th St   W 16th St   E 16th St

Jefferson Park

W 17th St   **EAST**   W 17th St

W 17th St   **PILSEN**

E 18th St

W 18th Pl   W 18th St   W 18th St

B

W 19th St

W 19th Pl

W 19th St

W Cullerton St

E Cullerton St

W 20th Pl

W 21st St

◄11►

W 21st St

600W   500W   **Cermak-Chinatown**   E 21st St

100E

◄52   W Cermak Rd

W 22nd Pl   **2**

W 22nd Pl

W 23rd St   W 22nd Pl   **2**

W Alexander St   **2**

W 23rd St   **3**

CHINATOWN   **90**   W 23rd St

W 23rd Pl   **Connector**

C

W 24th Pl   W 24th St

Halsted   W 24th Pl

W 24th St

55

Stevenson Expy   **55**

E 24th Pl

W 25th Pl   **90**   **13**

W 26th St   **94**   W 26th St   W 26th Pl   E 26th St

W 27th St   W 27th St   W 27th St

| 1/4 mile | .25 km |

Would-be collectors make their rounds sipping wine and looking for the next Ed Paschke at the annual gallery crawl in East Pilsen; second Fridays of the month are a staple. Find cookware, finger traps, rice candy, and bamboo back-scratchers galore while shopping Chinatown, and stop in at Joy Yee's Noodles for a tapioca freeze.

Coffee

- **Starbucks** • Dominick's • 1340 S Canal St
- **Tasty Place** • 2339 S Wentworth Ave

Copy Shops

- **Athena** • 1882 S Normal Ave
- **FedEx Kinko's** • 1242 S Canal St ⊕

Hardware Stores

- **Home Depot** • 1300 S Clinton St
- **Turek & Sons True Value** • 1333 S Jefferson St
- **Zweifel True Value Hardware** • 345 W 25th Pl

Liquor Stores

- **Vetoux Fine Wine** • 1601 S Canal St

Restaurants

- **Chi Café** • 2160 S Wentworth Ave
- **Double Li** • 228 W Cermak Rd
- **Emperor's Choice** • 2238 S Wentworth Ave
- **Evergreen** • 2411 S Wentworth Ave
- **Happy Chef Dim Sum House** • 2164 S Archer Ave
- **Joy Yee's Noodle Shop** • 2159 S China Pl
- **Lao Sze Chuan Spicy City** • 2172 S Archer Ave
- **Penang** • 2201 S Wentworth Ave
- **Phoenix** • 2131 S Archer Ave
- **Three Happiness** • 209 W Cermak Rd
- **Won Kow** • 2237 S Wentworth Ave

Shopping

- **Chinatown Bazaar** • 2221 S Wentworth Ave
- **Pacific Imports** • 2200 S Wentworth Ave
- **Sun Sun Tong** • 2260 S Wentworth Ave
- **Ten Ren Tea & Ginseng Co** • 2247 S Wentworth Ave
- **Woks 'n' Things** • 2234 S Wentworth Ave

McCormick Place, once known as McCormick's Folly because it obstructed the Burnham Plan's lakefront view, is now the inspiration for a South Loop renaissance. A postmodern cubic crowning for Soldier Field and the creation of the Museum Campus remodel its reputation closer to the economic dynamo it was originally envisioned to be.

Banks

- **Chase** • 1934 S State St
- **Chase (ATM)** • 2525 S Michigan Ave • Mercy Hospital
- **Chase (ATM)** • Soldier Field • 1600 S Lake Shore Dr
- **Fifth Third (ATM)** • 1300 S Lake Shore Dr
- **First American** • 1241 S Wabash Ave
- **Harris Trust & Savings** • 1300 S Wabash Ave
- **Lakeside** • 2141 S Indiana Ave
- **Lakeside (ATM)** • Stevenson Expy & Martin Luther King Dr
- **LaSalle** • 1400 S Lake Shore Dr
- **LaSalle** • 2301 S Dr Martin L King Jr Dr
- **MB Financial (ATM)** • 1250 S Michigan Ave
- **TCF (ATM)** • 425 E McFetridge Dr
- **Washington Mutual** • 1556 S Michigan Ave

Car Washes

- **State Street Hand Car Wash** • 1701 S State St
- **Strictly By Hand** • 2009 S Wabash Ave
- **Z-Wash** • 1522 S Wabash Ave

Car Rental

- **Hertz** • 2300 S Dr Martin L King Jr Dr • 312-567-0380

Gas Stations

- **BP** • 1221 S Wabash Ave

Emergency Rooms

- **Mercy** • 2525 S Michigan Ave

Landmarks

- **Adler Planetarium & Astronomy Museum** • 1300 S Lake Shore Dr
- **America's Courtyard** • Lakefront, south of Adler Planetarium
- **The Chicago Daily Defender** • 2400 S Michigan Ave
- **The Chicago Legend** • 2109 S Wabash Ave
- **Clarke House** • 1827 S Indiana Ave
- **The Field Museum** • 1400 S Lake Shore Dr

- **Hillary Rodham Clinton Women's Park and Gardens of Chicago** • S Prairie Ave, b/w 18th St & 19th St
- **Hyatt Regency McCormick Place** • 2233 S Dr Martin L King Jr Dr
- **McCormick Place** • 2301 S Lake Shore Dr
- **National Vietnam Veterans Art Museum** • 1801 S Indiana Ave
- **Northerly Island Park** • Lakefront, south of Adler Planetarium
- **Quinn Chapel, African Methodist Episcopal Church** • 2401 S Wabash Ave
- **Second Presbyterian Church** • 1936 S Michigan Ave
- **Soldier Field** • 425 E McFetridge Dr
- **The Wheeler Mansion** • 2020 S Calumet Ave
- **Willie Dixon's Blues Heaven Foundation** • 2120 S Michigan Ave

Pharmacies

- **CVS** • 2545 S Dr Martin L King Jr Dr

Pizza

- **Big Daddy's Pizzeria** • 2137 S State St
- **Pal Joey's Restaurant & Lounge** • 440 E Roosevelt Rd

Police

- **1st District (Central)** • 1718 S State St

Post Offices

- **US Post Office** • 2035 S State St

Schools

- **Detour 2 Discovery Day** • 2001 S Wabash Ave
- **Loop Learning Center** • 2001 S Michigan Ave
- **Ray Graham Training Center** • 2347 S Wabash Ave

Though many Capone-related landmarks became casualties of '90s gentrification, the South Loop still boasts attractions like a burgeoning restaurant scene. Trendies dine at theatrical spots like Opera while old-schoolers flock to live jazz at Velvet Lounge or toss back suds at Wabash Tap. Prestigious addresses of the Prairie Avenue Historic District attract history buffs.

25 26
10 11

Coffee

- **Café Au Lait** • 1900 S State St
- **Dunkin' Donuts** • 1575 S Michigan Ave
- **Dunkin' Donuts** • 1231 S Wabash Ave
- **Starbucks** • McCormick Con Ctr—Mezzanine • 2301 S Dr Martin L King Jr Dr
- **Starbucks** • McCormick Con Center—North Food Ct • 2301 S Lake Shore Dr

Farmers Markets

- **South Loop Farmers Market (Jun–Oct; Sat, 7 am–2 pm)** • 18th St & Wabash Ave

Gyms

- **Curves (women only)** • 77 E 16th St
- **Phenomenal Fitness** • 1450 S Michigan Ave

Nightlife

- **Chicago Legends** • 2109 S Wabash Ave
- **Reggie's** • 2105 S State St
- **Velvet Lounge** • 67 E Cermak Rd
- **Wabash Tap** • 1233 S Wabash Ave

Pet Shops

- **Dogone Fun** • 1717 S State St
- **Downtown Pets (Fish only)** • 1619 S Michigan Ave
- **Soggy Paws** • 1912 S State St

Restaurants

- **Carolina Caramel Room for Dessert** • 1511 S State St
- **Chef Luciano** • 49 E Cermak Rd
- **Chicago Firehouse Restaurant** • 1401 S Michigan Ave
- **Cuatro** • 2030 S Wabash Ave
- **Gioco** • 1312 S Wabash Ave
- **Kroll's** • 1736 S Michigan Ave
- **La Cantina Grill** • 1911 S Michigan Ave
- **NetWorks** • Hyatt Regency • 2231 S Dr Martin L King Jr Dr
- **Opera** • 1301 S Wabash Ave
- **Room 21** • 2110 S Wabash Ave• Triad • 1933 S Indiana Ave
- **Zapatista** • 1307 S Wabash Ave

Shopping

- **Blue Star Auto Stores** • 2001 S State St
- **Cycle Bicycle Shop** • 1465 S Michigan Ave
- **Waterware** • 1829 S State St

Nestled just north of the old stockyards, this area's jumbo land parcels and warehouses ripe for conversion have spurred pockets of development. Most notable is tony Bridgeport Village, set smack–dab on a stretch of the Chicago River known as Bubbly Creek. The waterway got its name because animal carcasses dumped by the former stockyards turned it into a gaseous stew and, despite the pricey homes along its banks, the bubbles still linger.

$ Banks

- **Chase** • 3145 S Ashland Ave
- **Chicago Community** • 1110 W 35th St
- **Washington Federal** • 2869 S Archer Ave

Car Washes

- **Pershing Road Car Wash** • 940 W Pershing Rd

Gas Stations

- **Citgo** • 970 W Pershing Rd

Landmarks

- **Library Fountain** • W 34th St & Halsted St
- **McGuane Park** • 2901 S Poplar Ave
- **Monastery of the Holy Cross** • 3111 S Aberdeen St
- **St Mary of Perpetual Help** • 1039 W 32nd St
- **Wilson Park** • S May St & W 34th Pl

Pharmacies

- **Dominick's** • 3145 S Ashland Ave ☺

Pizza

- **Lina's Pizza** • 3132 S Morgan St
- **Little Caesar's Pizza** • 3010 S Halsted St

Schools

- **Armour Branch** • 911 W 32nd St
- **Charles N Holden Elementary** • 1104 W 31st St
- **Philip D Armour Elementary** • 950 W 33rd Pl
- **St Barbara Elementary** • 2867 S Throop St

Supermarkets

- **Dominick's** • 3145 S Ashland Ave ☺

51

Map
| 15 | 16 | 17 |
| 54 | 57 | 18 | 19 | 20 |

Never a destination spot, this area nonetheless has some offbeat institutions with old-school flavor. Bustling lunch stop Best's Kosher Outlet Store is a working-class favorite for made to order sandwiches and all-beef dogs.

Coffee

- **Bridgeport Coffeehouse** • 3101 S Morgan St
- **Dunkin' Donuts** • 970 W Pershing Rd
- **Zhou B Café** • 1029 W 35th St

Hardware Stores

- **Cremieux Supply** • 3015 S Archer Ave
- **Elston Ace Hardware** • 1514 W 33rd St

Liquor Stores

- **All Star Food & Liquors** • 2911 S Archer Ave
- **Ashland S** • 3162 S Ashland Ave

Shopping

- **Best's Kosher Outlet Store** • 1000 W Pershing Rd
- **Bridgeport Antiques** • 2963 S Archer Ave

Video Rental

- **Blockbuster** • 3145 S Ashland Ave

Bridgeport exemplifies how the "City That Works" actually works. The stomping grounds of the Daley family and de facto political center of the city, Bridgeport is also the quintessential Chicago neighborhood with its close–knit residents, legions of patronage workers, and distinctive "dese, dem, and dose" vernacular.

$ Banks

- **Charter One** • 600 W 37th St
- **Chase** • 757 W 35th St
- **Chase (ATM)** • 142 W 35th St
- **Chase (ATM)** • Walgreens • 3000 S Halsted St
- **Chase (ATM)** • 3241 S Federal St
- **Citibank** • 3430 S Halsted St
- **First American (ATM)** • 659 W 31st St
- **LaSalle (ATM)** • 333 W 35th St
- **Marquette** • 615 W 31st St
- **Marquette (ATM)** • 501 W 31st St
- **South Central** • 3032 S Halsted St
- **TCF (ATM)** • Jewel • 3033 S Halsted St
- **TCF (ATM)** • Osco • 741 W 31st St

Car Washes

- **J&J Full Service Car Wash** • 349 W 31st St
- **Looking Good Hand Car Wash** • 3540 S Halsted St

Gas Stations

- **Citgo** • 501 W 31st St
- **Clark Oil** • 444 W 26th St
- **Marathon** • 659 W 31st St
- **Mobil** • 243 W Pershing Rd
- **Shell** • 215 W 31st St

ₒLandmarks

- **Illinois Institute of Technology** • 31st to 35th St, b/w Dan Ryan Expy & Michigan Ave
- **Old Neighborhood Italian American Club** • 3031 S Shields Ave
- **Richard J Daley House** • 3536 S Lowe Ave

Libraries

- **Daley Public Library** • 3400 S Halsted St

℞ Pharmacies

- **CVS** • 741 W 31st St
- **Walgreens** • 3000 S Halsted St

Pizza

- **Fratellini Pizza** • 3258 S Wells St
- **Freddie's Pizza & Pasta Parlor** • 701 W 31st St
- **Little Caesar's Pizza** • 3010 S Halsted St
- **Phil's Pizza** • 3551 S Halsted St
- **Punky's Pizza & Pasta** • 2600 S Wallace St
- **Ricobene's Pizzeria** • 252 W 26th St

Police

- **9th District (Deering)** • 3501 S Lowe Ave

Schools

- **Big Picture Company High** • 2710 S Dearborn St
- **Bridgeport Catholic Academy** • 3700 S Lowe Ave
- **Bridgeport Catholic Academy North** • 512 W 28th Pl
- **Crispus Attucks Elementary** • 3813 S Dearborn St
- **George B McClellan Elementary** • 3527 S Wallace St
- **Illinois Institute of Technology** • 3300 S Federal St
- **James Ward Elementary** • 2701 S Shields Ave
- **KIPP Chicago Youth Village Academy** • 2710 S Dearborn St
- **Mark Sheridan Math & Science Academy** • 533 W 27th St
- **Robert Healy Annex** • 3040 S Parnell Ave
- **Robert Healy Elementary** • 3010 S Parnell Ave
- **Robert S Abbott Elementary** • 3630 S Wells St
- **Santa Lucia** • 3017 S Wells St
- **St Jerome** • 2805 S Princeton Ave
- **Vandercook College of Music** • 3140 S Federal St
- **Williams Elementary** • 2710 S Dearborn St
- **Williams Middle** • 2710 S Dearborn St

The 2005 World Champion White Sox proved the southside mantra: you don't have to be glitzy to get the job done. Ditto for much-maligned US Cellular Field, where pure baseball and terrific sightlines trump drunken revelry at cross-town Wrigley. Aside from ballpark fare, Schaller's Pump serves the best steak sandwich and hash browns in town.

Coffee

- **Dunkin' Donuts** • 749 W 31st St
- **Starbucks** • 3506 S State St

Gyms

- **Curves (women only)** • 3252 S Wallace St

Hardware Stores

- **Joe Harris Paint & True Value Hardware** • 3301 S Wallace St
- **Windy City Hardware** • 3364 S Halsted St

Liquor Stores

- **Bridgeport Liquors** • 3411 S Halsted St
- **Express Food & Liquor** • 3904 S Wentworth Ave
- **JJ Peppers** • 659 W 31st St

Nightlife

- **Cobblestone's Bar and Grill** • 514 W Pershing Rd
- **Jimbo's Lounge** • 3258 S Princeton Ave
- **Schaller's Pump** • 3714 S Halsted St

Restaurants

- **Carbón** • 300 W 26th St
- **Franco's Ristorante** • 300 W 31st St
- **Freddie's Pizza & Pasta Parlor** • 701 W 31st St
- **Gio's** • 2724 S Lowe Ave
- **Kevin's Hamburger Heaven** • 554 W 39th St ⊚
- **Pancho Pistola's** • 700 W 31st St
- **Phil's Pizza** • 3551 S Halsted St
- **Schaller's Pump** • 3714 S Halsted St
- **Stages** • 657 W 31st St
- **Ramova Grill** • 3510 S Halsted St
- **Wing Yip Chop Suey** • 537 W 26th St

Shopping

- **Ace Bakery** • 3241 S Halsted St
- **Augustine's Spiritual Goods** • 3327 S Halsted St
- **Bridgeport News Travel & Tours** • 3252 S Halsted St
- **Health King Enterprises Chinese Medicinals** • 238 W 31st St
- **Henry's Sports & Bait Shop** • 3130 S Canal St
- **Let's Boogie Records & Tapes** • 3321 S Halsted St

Map 14 • **Prairie Shores / Lake Meadows**

Ⓝ

W 25th St
W 24th St

55
1
E 25th St
2

11
Monument to the
Great Northern
Migration

**PRAIRIE
SHORES**

E 26th St

*Lake
Michigan*

**SOUTH
COMMONS**

E 27th St

27th St

E 28th St

E 28th St

E 28th Pl

E 29th St

St. James
Catholic Church

E 29th Pl

E 30th St

E 30th St

Dunbar
Park

100E   200E
400E

E 31st St

Olivet
Baptist
Church

E 31st St

Lake
Meadows
Park

THE GAP

E 32nd St

Griffin
Funeral
Home

E 32nd St

E 32nd St

E 32nd Pl

McCormick
Tribune Campus

Illinois College
Of Optometry

**LAKE
MEADOWS**

IIT Student
Housing

E 33rd St

E 33rd Blvd

E 33rd St

E 33rd St

Groveland Park

Burnham
Park

**Illinois
Institute
of Tech**

E 34th St

E 34th St

Early Chicago
Defender Building

Interesting
Benches

E 34th St

E Groveland Park

41

E Woodland Park Ave

Woodland Park

246

35th-
Bronzville-IIT

Sunset
Café

E 35th St

2

Victory Monument

Black Metropolis
Convention &
Tourism

Supreme
Life
Insurance
Company

E 35th St

Douglas
Tomb

Overton
Hygenic
Building

Chicago Bee
Building

E 36th St

Eighth
Regiment
Armory

Ida B Wells/
Barnett Home

E Browning Ave

E 36th St

Stateway
Gardens
Park

Chicago Bee
Branch Public Library

E 36th St

E 36th Pl

Ellis Park

E Carver Plz

E 37th Pl

E 37th St

Anderson
Park

Wabash
Avenue
YMCA

3

E 37th Pl

E 38th St

Madden
Park

E 38th St

E 38th St

2

16

Bronzville
Bed & Breakfast

E 38th Pl

E Pershing Rd

17

E Oakwood Blvd

E Oakwood St

| 1/4 mile | | .25 km | |

Named after two rather imposing urban apartment complexes, this area also includes the spiritual heart of Chicago's African-American community, Bronzeville. Spots of sparkling new townhouses are interspersed with the occasional dowdy walk-up building. Given the recent reinvestment in Burnham Park, a jaunt to consider the thriving skate park and other amenities is a fine idea.

15	16	17	
54	57	18	19	20

Banks

- **Chase** • 3500 S King Dr
- **Chase (ATM)** • Walgreens • 3405 S King Dr
- **Citibank (ATM)** • 7-Eleven • 3201 S State St
- **Harris Trust & Savings (ATM)** • 3201 S State St
- **Lakeside (ATM)** • 2900 S Ellis Ave
- **Lakeside (ATM)** • 2929 S Ellis Ave
- **LaSalle (ATM)** • 3901 S State St
- **Shore** • 3401 S Dr Martin L King Jr Dr
- **TCF (ATM)** • 7-Eleven • 3201 S State St
- **TCF (ATM)** • Jewel • 443 E 34th St
- **Washington Mutual** • 3501 S King Dr

Car Rental

- **Enterprise** • 2640 S Michigan Ave • 312-808-1228

Gas Stations

- **BP** • 343 E 35th St
- **BP/Amoco** • 3101 S Michigan Ave
- **Citgo** • 437 E Pershing Rd

Emergency Rooms

- **Michael Reese** • 2929 S Ellis Ave

Landmarks

- **Black Metropolis Convention & Tourism Council** • 3501 S King Dr, Ste 1E
- **Bronzeville Bed & Breakfast** • 3911 S Dr Martin L King Jr Dr
- **Chicago Bee Building** • 3647 S State St
- **Chicago Bee Branch Public Library** • 3647 S State St
- **Douglas Tomb** • E 35th St & Lake Park Ave
- **Dunbar Park** • S Indiana Ave & E 31st St
- **Early Chicago Defender Building** • 3435 S Indiana Ave
- **Eighth Regiment Armory** • 3533 S Giles Ave
- **Griffin Funeral Home** • 3232 S King Dr
- **Ida B Wells / Barnett Home** • 3624 S King Dr
- **IIT Student Housing** • 3303 S State St
- **Interesting Benches** • S Dr Martin L King Jr Dr b/w E 33rd St & E 35th St
- **McCormick Tribune Campus Center** • 3201 S State St
- **Monument to the Great Northern Migration** • S Dr Martin L King Jr Dr & E 26th St
- **Olivet Baptist Church** • 3101 S King Dr
- **Overton Hygenic Building** • 3619 S State St
- **St James Catholic Church** • 2929 S Wabash Ave
- **Sunset Café** • 315 E 35th St

- **Supreme Life Insurance Company Head Office** • 3501 S King Dr
- **Victory Monument** • 35th St & King Dr
- **Wabash Avenue YMCA** • 3763 S Wabash Ave

Libraries

- **Chicago Bee Public Library** • 3647 S State St
- **King Public Library** • 3436 S Dr Martin L King Jr Dr

Pharmacies

- **Walgreens** • 3405 S Dr Martin L King Jr Dr

Police

- **21st District (Prairie)** • 300 E 29th St

Schools

- **Albert Einstein Parent/Com Train Academy** • 3663 S Wabash Ave
- **Chicago Military Academy** • 3519 S Giles Ave
- **Christ the King Lutheran** • 3701 S Lake Park Ave
- **Dawson Technical Institute** • 3901 S State St
- **De la Salle Institute** • 3455 S Wabash Ave
- **Donoghue Elementary** • 707 E 37th St
- **Doolittle East Primary** • 535 E 35th St
- **Doolittle Middle** • 535 E 35th St
- **Douglas Community Academy** • 3200 S Calumet Ave
- **Drake Elementary** • 2722 S Dr Martin L King Jr Dr
- **Dunbar Vocational Career Academy** • 3000 S Dr Martin L King Jr Dr
- **Illinois College of Optometry** • 3241 S Michigan Ave
- **JJ Pershing School for Humanities** • 3113 S Rhodes Ave
- **Lindblom College Preparatory High** • 707 E 37th St
- **McKinley Lakeside High** • 2929 S Wabash Ave
- **Milburn High** • 545 E Oakwood Blvd
- **Phillips Academy** • 244 E Pershing Rd
- **University of Chicago-Donoghue** • 707 E 37 St
- **Wells Elementary** • 244 E Pershing Rd
- **William J & Charles H Mayo Elementary** • 249 E 37th St
- **Young Women's Leadership High** • 2641 S Calumet Ave
- **Your School of Beauty Culture** • 116 E Pershing Rd
- **Youth Connection Charter-YCCS** • 3424 S State St
- **Youth Connection High** • 10 W 35th St

Supermarkets

- **Jewel-Osco** • 443 E 34th St

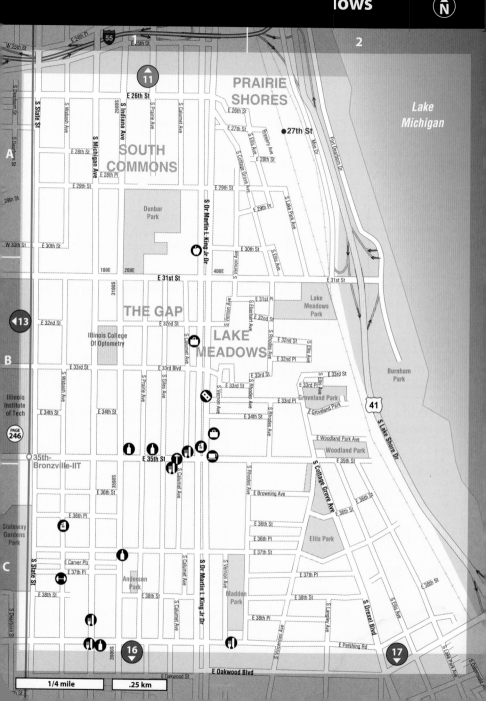

This area of the city is fairly abuzz with neat–o buildings that reflect the city's influential African–American community, including the Ida B. Wells/Barnett House and former head-quarters of the Chicago Bee. As curious suburbanites and newcomers return to rehab forlorn structures throughout the neighborhood, the area has begun to experience a 21st–century "urban renewal."

Coffee

- **Dunkin' Donuts** • 3481 S Dr Martin L King Jr Dr

Copy Shops

- **Bronzeville Postnet** • 122 E 35th St
- **The UPS Store** • 3473 S Dr Martin L King Jr Dr

Farmers Markets

- **Bronzeville (Jun-Oct; Sat, 7 am-2 pm)** •
  3000 S Dr Martin L King Jr Dr

Gyms

- **Wabash YMCA** • 3763 S Wabash Ave

Hardware Stores

- **Meyers Ace Hardware** • 315 E 35th St

Liquor Stores

- **Abu-Elreish** • 252 E 35th St
- **Abu-Elreish** • 3700 S Indiana Ave
- **Poorwood Food & Liquors** • 200 E 35th St
- **Rothchild Liquor Marts** • 124 E Pershing Rd

Restaurants

- **Blue Sea Restaurant** • 427 E Pershing Rd
- **Chicago Rib House** • 3851 S Michigan Ave
- **Hong Kong Delight** • 327 E 35th St
- **Pearl's Place** • 3901 S Michigan Ave
- **Wings Around the World** • 321 E 35th St

Shopping

- **Ashley Stewart** • 3455 S Dr Martin L King Jr Dr
- **Avenue** • 3429 S Dr Martin L King Jr Dr

Video Rental

- **Blockbuster** • 3349 S Dr Martin L King Jr Dr

Map

| 15 | 16 | 17 |
| 54 | 57 | 18 | 19 | 20 |

Christmas 1865 was a bad day for livestock, as the sprawling Union Stock Yards opened, all beasts on the lookout. All that's left now is the imposing limestone gate (moment of silence). While cattle around the country breathed a collective sigh when the Yards closed, this area headed south afterward and is still in recovery.

 Banks

- **Chase (ATM)** • Walgreens • 4701 S Halsted St
- **First American (ATM)** • 4640 S Halsted St

 Gas Stations

- **Citgo** • 4300 S Wentworth Ave
- **Econo-Gas** • 4248 S Wentworth Ave

 Libraries

- **Canaryville Public Library** • 642 W 43rd St

 Pharmacies

- **Walgreens** • 4700 S Halsted St

Pizza

- **Pizza Nova** • 558 W 43rd St
- **TNT Pizza & Beef** • 601 W Root St

Police

- **2nd District (Wentworth)** • 5101 S Wentworth Ave

 Post Offices

- **US Post Office** • 4101 S Halsted St

Schools

- **Alexander Graham Elementary** •
  4436 S Union Ave
- **Bronzeville Academic Center** • 220 W 45th Pl
- **Francis Parkman Elementary** • 245 W 51st St
- **Garfield Alternative High** • 220 W 45th Pl
- **John H Sengstacke Achievement Academy** •
  4747 S Union Ave
- **Sengstacke Academic Preparation** •
  4747 S Union Ave
- **St Gabriel Elementary** • 4500 S Wallace St
- **Thomas A Hendricks Community Academy** •
  4316 S Princeton Ave
- **Tilden Career Communty Academy High** •
  4747 S Union Ave
- **Tilden High** • 4747 S Union Ave

Supermarkets

- **Fairplay Finer Foods** • 4640 S Halsted St

Canaryville and Fuller Park have retained scrappy and salt–of–the–earth sensibilities for years. The Union Stock Yards' closing in 1971 hit the community hard, and until recently it was a stone's throw away from the largest public housing complex in Chicago. Even urbanologists may be hard pressed to find much to do on a casual visit.

| 15 | 16 | 17 |
| 54 | 57 | 18 | 19 | 20 |

Map

Nightlife

• **Kelley's Tavern** • 4403 S Wallace St

Hardware Stores

• **Discount Hardware** • 601 W 47th St

Liquor Stores

• **Bravo Liquors** • 619 W 43rd St
• **Root Inn** • 234 W Root St
• **Shamsan Food & Liquor** • 737 W 51st St

Far from its glorious roots, Bronzeville is trying to make a comeback from years of poverty, crime, empty lots, and dilapidated project housing. Today, there are many buppy implants, restored greystones, and overpriced condos. If you can wait out this slow rebirth and the recent changing of the aldermanic guard (the hat went splat after 23 years), once again, Bronzeville should become a great place to visit and an even better place to live.

 Banks
- **Chase (ATM)** • Walgreens • 5036 S Cottage Grove Ave
- **Harris Trust & Savings (ATM)** • 4859 S Wabash Ave
- **Illinois Service Federal Savings** • 4619 S King Dr
- **Northern Trust (ATM)** • McDonald's • 740 E 47th St
- **Shore** • 4659 S Cottage Grove Ave

 Gas Stations
- **Amoco** • 4300 S State St
- **Citgo** • 123 E 51st St
- **Marathon** • 4700 S Michigan Ave

 Emergency Rooms
- **Provident** • 500 E 51st St

Landmarks
- **Corpus Christi Church** • 4920 S King Dr
- **Drexel Fountain** • S Drexel Blvd & E Oakwood Blvd
- **Harold Washington Cultural Center** • 4701 S King Dr
- **Jamaican Consulate/Jamaican Market Place** • 4655 S King Dr, Ste 104
- **Liberty Baptist Church** • 4849 S King Dr
- **Provident Hospital** • 500 E 51st St
- **Robert S Abbott Home** • 4742 S King Dr
- **Steele Life Gallery** • 4655 S King Dr

 **Libraries**
- **Hall Public Library** • 4801 S Michigan Ave

 Pharmacies
- **Walgreens** • 5036 S Cottage Grove Ave

 Pizza
- **Pizza Ria** • 4300 S Michigan Ave

 Post Offices
- **US Post Office** • 4601 S Cottage Grove Ave

 Schools
- **Anthony Overton, CPC** • 4935 S Indiana Ave
- **Anthony Overton Elementary** • 221 E 49th St
- **Bronzeville Scholastic Institute** • 4934 S Wabash Ave
- **Cain's Barber College** • 365 E 51st St
- **Carruthers Center for Inner City Studies, Northeastern Illinois University** • 700 E Oakwood Blvd
- **Colman Elementary** • 4655 S Dearborn St
- **DuSable Leadership Academy of B Shabazz** • 4934 S Wabash Ave
- **Dyett Academy Center** • 555 E 51st St
- **Hales Franciscan High** • 4930 S Cottage Grove Ave
- **Helen J McCorkle Elementary** • 4421 S State St
- **Holy Angels Elementary** • 545 E Oakwood Blvd
- **Irvin C Mollison Elementary** • 4415 S Dr Martin L King Jr Dr
- **Jean Baptiste Du Sable High** • 4934 S Wabash Ave
- **John Farren Elementary** • 5055 S State St
- **Ludwig Von Beethoven Elementary** • 25 W 47th St
- **Melville W Fuller Elementary** • 4214 S St Lawrence Ave
- **St Elizabeth Elementary** • 4052 S Wabash Ave
- **William Reavis Elementary** • 834 E 50th St
- **Williams Preparatory School of Medicine** • 4934 S Wabash Ave
- **Woodson North Middle** • 4414 S Evans Ave
- **Woodson South CPC** • 4511 S Evans Ave
- **Woodson South Elementary** • 4444 S Evans Ave

 Supermarkets
- **Save A Lot** • 4701 S Cottage Grove Ave

Map 16 · **Bronzeville**

Jokes & Notes and the Harold Washington Cultural Center are main attractions, as are Afrocentric Bookstore, headquarters of the black literati, and the Steele Life Gallery, showcasing contemporary multicultural art. Sensual Steps offers sleek footwear during the day and frequent evening events. Blu 47 and the The Negro League Café offer upscale soul food.

Coffee
• **Bronzeville Coffee House** • 528 E 43rd St

Hardware Stores
• **Brooks Hardware** • 103 E 47th St

Liquor Stores
• **Calumet Food & Liquor** • 315 E 43rd St

Nightlife
• **Jokes & Notes** • 4641 S King Dr

Restaurants
• **Ain't She Sweet Café** • 4532 S Cottage Grove
• **Barbara's** • 353 E 51st St
• **Blu 47** • 4655 S King Dr
• **Harold's Chicken Shack** • 307 E 51st St
• **Negro League Café** • 301 E 43rd St
• **Sweet Potatoes Café** • 501 E 47th St

Shopping
• **Afrocentric Bookstore** • 4655 S King Dr
• **Ibiza** • 233 E 47th St
• **Issues Barber & Beauty Salon** •
  3958 S Cottage Grove Ave
• **Jordan's Closet** • 106 E 51st St
• **Leaders 1354** • 4351 S Cottage Grove Ave
• **New Apparel Health Foods** • 641 E 47th St
• **Parker House Sausage Co** • 4605 S State St
• **Sensual Steps** • 4518 S Cottage Grove Ave
• **Stnx Galleria** • 4200 S Prairie Ave

Many a 19th-century suburb prided itself on wide lawns and tranquil settings, and Kenwood was no exception. Though it was annexed to Chicago over one hundred years ago, the suburban feeling lingers. These days, the architecturally enriched neighborhood contains everything from the residence of Louis Farrakhan to the oldest Jewish congregation in the city, KAM Isaiah Israel.

$ Banks

- **Chase (ATM)** • Walgreens • 1320 E 47th St
- **Citibank** • 1310 E 47th St
- **Harris Trust & Savings** • 901 E 47th St
- **Hyde Park (ATM)** • 4301 S Lake Park Ave

Gas Stations

- **Amoco** • 5048 S Cornell Ave
- **BP** • 5130 S Lake Park Ave

o Landmarks

- **Drexel Square Park** • Drexel Blvd, from 51st St to 39th St
- **Louis Farrakhan Home** • 4855 S Woodlawn Ave
- **Little Black Pearl Art & Design Center** • 930 E 50th St
- **Rainbow/PUSH Coalition Headquarters** • 1060 E 47th St
- **South Kenwood Mansions** • b/w S Dorchester Ave, S Ellis Ave, E Hyde Park Blvd, & E 47th St

Libraries

- **Blackstone Public Library** • 4904 S Lake Park Ave

P Parking

Rx Pharmacies

- **Walgreens** • 1320 E 47th St

Pizza

- **Domino's** • 1453 E Hyde Park Blvd
- **Italian Fiesta Pizzeria** • 1400 E 47th St

Schools

- **Ancona Montessori** • 4770 S Dorchester Ave
- **Ariel Community** • 1119 E 46th St
- **Ariel Community Academy** • 1119 E 46th St
- **Creative Mansion Childrens Academy** • 4745 S Ellis Ave
- **Dr Martin Luther King Jr High** • 4445 S Drexel Blvd
- **Florence B Price Elementary** • 4351 S Drexel Ave
- **Kenwood High** • 5015 S Blackstone Ave
- **Miriam Canter Middle** • 4959 S Blackstone Ave
- **North Kenwood Oakland Charter** • 1014 E 47th St
- **North Kenwood/Oakland Elementary** • 1119 E 46th St
- **Robinson Elementary** • 4225 S Lake Park Ave
- **Shoesmith Elementary** • 1330 E 50th St

Supermarkets

- **Village Foods** • 1521 E Hyde Park Blvd

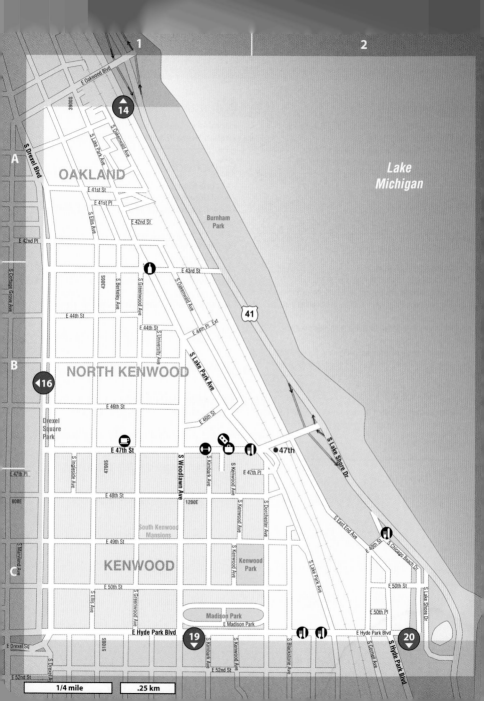

Inquisitive urbanistas will want to come down here to take a look at the Little Black Pearl Art & Design Center, which offers visual arts classes, a swanky art café and gallery. The old homes of retail capitalists like Julius Rosenwald and famed meat–packer, Gustavus Swift add historical value to this community. With few eateries in the area, visitors may want to dine in neighboring Hyde Park and wander over to Lake Michigan.

Coffee

• **Hidden Pearl Café** • 1060 E 47th St

Gyms

• **Bally Total Fitness** • 1301 E 47th St

Liquor Stores

• **One Stop Food & Liquors** • 4301 S Lake Park Ave

Restaurants

• **Fung's Chop Suey** • 1400 E 47th St
• **Kenny's Ribs & Chicken** • 1461 E Hyde Park Blvd
• **Lake Shore Café** • 4900 S Lake Shore Dr
• **Original Pancake House** • 1517 E Hyde Park Blvd

Shopping

• **South Shore Decor** • 1328 E 47th St

For decades, the western border of Washington Park was defined by the Robert Taylor homes. Recently, the housing projects have disappeared and the community has seen a mini–revival. The eastern half of the park is dominated by the massive park itself and its DuSable Museum of African–American History, pond, track, and swimming pool.

Banks
• **Charter One (ATM)** • 6319 S Vernon Ave

Car Washes
• **Adam's Car Wash** • 48 E Garfield Blvd
• **Dylan's Hand Car Wash & Detail** • 5437 S Wabash Ave

Gas Stations
• **Adam's Car Wash** • 48 E Garfield Blvd
• **Citgo** • 368 E Garfield Blvd

Landmarks
• **Aquatic Center & Refectory** • 5531 S Martin Luther King Jr Dr
• **DuSable Museum of African-American History** • 740 E 56th Pl
• **Former Home of Jesse Binga** • 5922 S Dr Martin L King Jr Dr
• **Washington Park** • 5531 S Martin Luther King Dr

Libraries
• **Bessie Coleman Public Library** • 731 E 63rd St

Pizza
• **B&B Pizza King** • 4 W Garfield Blvd

Post Offices
• **US Post Office** • 700 E 61st St

Schools
• **ACE Technical High** • 5410 S State St
• **Austin O Sexton Elementary** • 6020 S Langley Ave
• **Beasley Academic Elementary** • 5255 S State St
• **Betsy Ross Elementary** • 6059 S Wabash Ave
• **Chicago International Elementary - Washington Park Campus** • 6105 S Michigan Ave
• **Edmund Burke Elementary** • 5356 S King Dr
• **John Foster Dulles High** • 6311 S Calumet Ave
• **Oneida Cockrell, CPC** • 30 E 61 St
• **William W Carter Elementary** • 5740 S Michigan Ave

Supermarkets
• **Family Food Market** • 723 E 63rd St

Map 18 · **Washington Park**

Map 18

While family reunions, baseball games, and pan–African festivals are the dominant leisure activities in Washington Park today, the park used to feature carriage rides, horse--racing, and other pursuits that loomed large in the social lives of Gilded Age dandies. Walking through the park, you'll build up a big appetite. The home cookin' of Ms. Lee or Rose will help fill you up.

Copy Shops
• **JJC Creative Services** • 130 E Garfield Blvd

Hardware Stores
• **Boulevard Ace Hardware** • 227 E Garfield Blvd

Liquor Stores
• **Home Liquors Food Mart** • 301 E 61st St
• **Jordan Food & Liquor** • 315 E Garfield Blvd
• **Rothschild Liquor Marts** • 425 E 63rd St

Restaurants
• **Ms Lee's Good Food** • 205 E Garfield Blvd
• **Rose's BBQ Chicken** • 5426 S State St

Map 19 · **Hyde Park**

Neo–Gothic buildings and large–scale urban renewal come together in Hyde Park, one of the South Side's most diverse and eclectic communities. The University of Chicago draws an impressive band of intellectuals together, while others remain oblivious to their presence. Visitors should wander by the Robie House, Rockefeller Chapel, and the retail chaos along 53rd Street.

 ## $ Banks

- **Bank of America** • 1439 E 53rd St
- **BankFinancial** • 1354 E 55th St
- **BankFinancial** • E 55th St & S Lake Park Ave
- **Chase** • 1204 E 53rd St
- **Chase (ATM)** • Istria Café • 1520 E 57th St
- **Chase (ATM)** • 1554 E 55th St
- **Chase (ATM)** • Bernard Mitchell Hospital • 5815 S Maryland Ave
- **Citibank** • 5812 S Ellis Ave
- **Citibank (ATM)** • University of Chicago Business School • 5807 S Woodlawn Ave
- **Cole Taylor** • 824 E 63rd St
- **First American (ATM)** • 1226 E 53rd St
- **First American (ATM)** • 1424 E 53rd St
- **First American (ATM)** • 1467 E 53rd St
- **Hyde Park** • 1311 E 57th St
- **Hyde Park** • 1525 E 53rd St
- **Hyde Park (ATM)** • 1518 E 53rd St
- **Hyde Park (ATM)** • 1526 E 55th St
- **LaSalle (ATM)** • 1228 E 53rd St
- **Northern Trust (ATM)** • McDonald's • 5220 S Lake Park Ave
- **Washington Mutual** • 1364 E 53rd St

Car Washes

- **Hyde Park Mobile Car Wash** • 1330 E 53rd St

Car Rental

- **Enterprise** • 5508 S Lake Park Ave • 773-288-0500

Gas Stations

- **Mobil** • 1330 E 53rd St

 ## Emergency Rooms

- **University of Chicago** • 5841 S Maryland Ave
- **University of Chicago Children's** • 5721 S Maryland Ave

 ## oLandmarks

- **Frederick C Robie House** • 5757 S Woodlawn Ave
- **Midway Plaisance Park & Skating Rink** • S Ellis Ave & S University Ave, from E 59th St to E 60th St
- **Nichols Park** • 1300 E 55th St
- **Nuclear Energy Sculpture** • 5600 S Ellis Ave
- **Oriental Institute Museum** • 1155 E 58th St
- **Rockefeller Memorial Chapel** • 5850 S Woodlawn Ave
- **University of Chicago** • S University Ave & E 57th St

 ## Libraries

- **University of Chicago Harper Memorial Library** • 1116 E 59th St

P Parking

R Pharmacies

- **CVS** • 1228 E 53rd St
- **Walgreens** • 1554 E 55th St ⊕

 ## Pizza

- **Caffe Florian** • 1450 E 57th St
- **Edwardo's Natural Pizza** • 1321 E 57th St
- **Giordano's** • 5309 S Blackstone Ave
- **Homemade Pizza** • 1546 E 55th St
- **Leona's** • 1236 E 53rd st
- **Medici on 57th** • 1327 E 57th St
- **Pizza Capri** • 1501 E 53rd St

 ## Post Offices

- **US Post Office** • 1510 E 55th St
- **US Post Office** • 956 E 58th St

 ## Schools

- **Andrew Carnegie Elementary** • 1414 E 61st Pl
- **Bret Harte Elementary** • 1556 E 56th St
- **Charles Kozminski Elementary** • 936 E 54th St
- **Chicago Theological Seminary** • 5757 S University Ave
- **Donoghue Charter** • 1313 E 60 St
- **Hyde Park Day** • 1375 E 60th St
- **John Fiske Elementary** • 6145 S Ingleside Ave
- **Lutheran School of Theology at Chicago** • 1100 E 55th St
- **McCormick Seminary** • 5460 S University Ave
- **Meadville Lombard Theological** • 5701 S Woodlawn Ave
- **Phillip Murray Language Academy** • 5335 S Kenwood Ave
- **Sonia Sahnkman Orthogenic** • 1365 E 60th St
- **St Thomas the Apostle Elementary** • 5467 S Woodlawn Ave
- **Toyota Technological Institute at Chicago** • 1427 E 60th St
- **University of Chicago** • 5801 S Ellis Ave
- **University of Chicago Laboratory** • 1362 E 59th St
- **William H Ray Elementary** • 5631 S Kimbark Ave

 ## Supermarkets

- **Bonne Sante Health Food** • 1512 E 53rd St
- **Treasure Island Supermarket** • 1526 E 55th St

Map 19 · **Hyde Park**

Woodlawn Tap is a regular haunt for the college crowd and townies despite the lacking nightlife. Bookstore Row on 57th Street provides a literary surge, while restaurants include the delivery-and–counter-seating-only Ribs 'n' Bibs, the four way chili of Mellow Yellow, and the only cafeteria that has been the subject of a sociological treatise, the Valois.

15	16	17	
54	57	18	19	20

Coffee

- **Argo Tea** • 5758 S Maryland Ave
- **Dunkin' Donuts** • 1411 E 53rd St
- **Einstein Bros Bagels** • University of Chicago • 5706 S University Ave
- **Istria Café** • 1520 E 57th St
- **Starbucks** • 1174 E 55th St
- **Starbucks** • 1500 E 53rd St
- **Third World Café** • 1301 E 53rd St

Copy Shops

- **FedEx Kinko's** • 1315 E 57th St
- **The UPS Store** • 1507 E 53rd St

Farmers Markets

- **Hyde Park (Jun-Oct; Thurs, 7 am-2 pm)** • E 52nd Pl & Harper Ave

Gyms

- **Curves (women only)** • 1424 E 53rd St
- **Curves (women only)** • 1514 E 63rd St

Hardware Stores

- **Elston Ace Hardware** • 5420 S Lake Park Ave

Liquor Stores

- **Binny's Beverage Depot** • 1531 E 53rd St
- **Fair Discount** • 801 E 63rd St
- **Kimbark Liquors & Wine Shop** • 1214 E 53rd St
- **Magic Mart** • 1467 E 53rd St
- **Woodlawn Tap & Liquor Store** • 1172 E 55th St

Movie Theaters

- **University of Chicago Doc Films** • 1212 E 59th St

Nightlife

- **Seven Ten Lanes** • 1055 E 55th St
- **Woodlawn Tap** • 1172 E 55th St

Pet Shops

- **Hyde Park Pet** • 5210 S Harper Ave

Restaurants

- **Bonjour Café Bakery** • 1550 E 55th St
- **C'Est Si Bon** • 5225 S Harper Ave
- **Calypso Café** • Harper Ctr • 5211 S Harper Ave
- **Cedars Mediterranean Kitchen** • 1206 E 53rd St
- **Chant** • 1509 E 53rd St
- **Daley's Restaurant** • 809 E 63rd St
- **Dixie Kitchen and Bait Shop** • 5225 S Harper Ave
- **Hyde Park Gyros** • 1368 E 53rd St
- **Kikuya Japanese Restaurant** • 1601 E 55th St
- **La Petite Folie** • Hyde Park Shopping Ctr • 1504 E 55th St
- **Maravilla's Mexican Restaurant** • 5211 S Harper Ave
- **Medici on 57th** • 1327 E 57th St
- **Mellow Yellow** • 1508 E 53rd St
- **Nathan's** • 1372 E 53rd St
- **Noodles Etc** • 1460 E 53rd St
- **Ribs 'n' Bibs** • 5300 S Dorchester Ave
- **Salonica** • 1440 E 57th St
- **Thai 55 Restaurant** • 1607 E 55th St
- **Valois** • 1518 E 53rd St

Shopping

- **57th Street Books** • 1301 E 57th St
- **The Baby PhD Store** • 5225 S Harper Ave
- **Borders** • 1539 E 53rd St
- **Dr Wax Records and Tapes** • 5225 S Harper Ave
- **Futons N More** • 1370 E 53rd St
- **House of Africa** • 1510 E 63rd St
- **Hyde Park Records** • 1377 E 53rd St
- **O'Gara & Wilson** • 1448 E 57th St
- **Powell's** • 1501 E 57th St
- **Toys Et Cetera** • 1502 E 55th St
- **Wesley's Shoe Corral** • 1506 E 55th St
- **Wheels and Things** • 5210 S Harper Ave

Video Rental

- **Hollywood Video** • 1530 E 53rd St

Here, Hyde Park is known for its luxury apartment buildings, part of Burnham Park known as "The Point," and the Museum of Science and Industry. After exploring 57th Street beach, visitors can stumble into the Museum to find a demonstration coal mine, preserved cross–sections of humans, and a fairy castle all in one place.

$ Banks

- **Harris Trust & Savings** • 5493 S Cornell Ave
- **LaSalle** •5700 S Lake Shore Dr

oLandmarks

- **Osaka Garden/Wooded Island** •
  Just south of the Museum of Science and Industry,
  b/w the West and East Lagoons
- **Promontory Point Park** • 5491 S Shore Dr

 Pizza

- **Cholie's Pizza** • 1601 E 53rd St

 Schools

- **Akiba-Schechter Jewish Day** • 5235 S Cornell Ave
- **Catholic Theological Union** • 5416 S Cornell Ave
- **Hyde Park Academy** • 6220 S Stony Island Ave

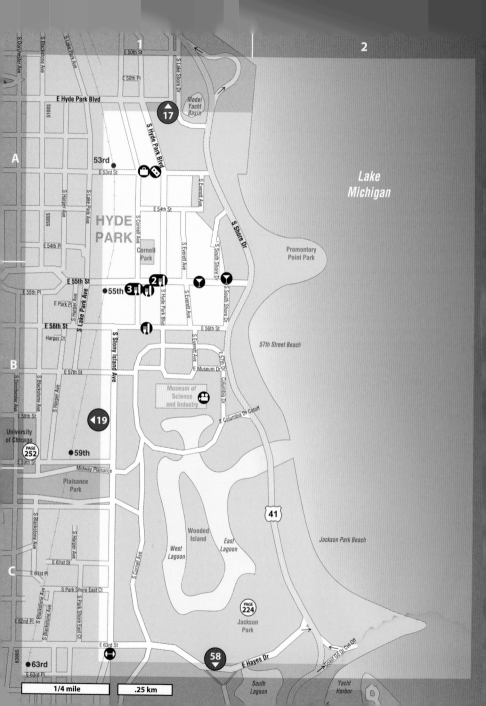

Eschewing the buzz of Hyde Park, East Hyde Park is a bit more tranquil, though don't count out the thousands who flock to the Museum of Science and Industry and the rather popular beaches in the area. Walking over to Promontory Point is a good idea for those who like to people–watch, and the canopy of trees along South Hyde Park Boulevard during the spring and summer are a most welcome pause from the less–than–polite Chicago humidity.

Copy Shops

• **Post Link** • 1634 E 53rd St

Gyms

• **Southside YMCA** • 6330 S Stony Island Ave

Movie Theaters

• **Henry Crown MSI Omnimax** • Museum of Science & Industry • 5700 S Lake Shore Dr

Nightlife

• **Bar Louie** • 5500 S South Shore Dr
• **The Cove** • 1750 E 55th St

Restaurants

• **Café Corea** • 1603 E 55th St
• **Morry's Deli** • 5500 S Cornell Ave
• **Nile Restaurant** • 1611 E 55th St
• **Orly's Café** • 1660 E 55th St
• **Piccolo Mondo** • 1642 E 56th St
• **Siam Thai Cuisine** • 1639 E 55th St
• **Snail's Thai Cuisine** • 1649 E 55th St

Shopping

• **Art's Cycle Sales & Service** • 1652 E 53rd St

Video Rental

• **Blockbuster** • 1644 E 53rd St

While yuppies rehab Victorians and developers strike gold, the young, arty community that paved the way is finding it harder and harder to stomach rising rents in this former ethnic enclave. Proximity to downtown and the expressway, as well as the hotbed of commercial growth—from dive bars to edgy boutiques and nightclubs—still make this a desirable place to live, even if traffic and parking now rival Lincoln Park.

$ Banks

- **Bank of America** • 1525 N Milwaukee Ave
- **Chase** • 1849 W North Ave
- **Chase** • 1959 W Division St
- **Chase (ATM)** • Walgreens • 1372 N Milwaukee Ave
- **Chase (ATM)** • Walgreens • 2440 W North Ave
- **Citibank** • 1445 N Milwaukee Ave
- **Citibank (ATM)** • 7-Eleven • 1400 N Milwaukee Ave
- **First American (ATM)** • 1515 N Milwaukee Ave
- **First American (ATM)** • 1550 N Milwaukee Ave
- **First American (ATM)** • 1601 N Paulina St
- **LaSalle** • 2222 W Division St
- **LaSalle (ATM)** • 1145 N Western Ave
- **LaSalle (ATM)** • 1431 N Claremont Ave
- **LaSalle (ATM)** • 2233 W Division St
- **MB Financial** • 936 N Western Ave
- **Midwest Bank & Trust Company** • 1601 Milwaukee Ave
- **North Community** • 1555 N Damen Ave
- **North Community** • 2000 W Division St
- **TCF** • Jewel • 1341 N Paulina St
- **TCF (ATM)** • 7-Eleven • 1400 N Milwaukee Ave
- **Washington Mutual** • 1811 W North Ave

Car Washes

- **Elite Car Wash** • 823 N Western Ave

Gas Stations

- **BP** • 2405 W Augusta Blvd
- **Citgo** • 1720 W North Ave
- **Citgo** • 823 N Western Ave
- **Clark Oil** • 1949 W Augusta Blvd
- **Shell** • 1600 N Western Ave
- **Shell** • 1950 W Division St

Emergency Rooms

- **St Elizabeth's** • 1431 N Claremont Ave
- **St Mary of Nazareth** • 2233 W Division St

Landmarks

- **Coyote Building** • 1600 N Milwaukee Ave
- **Crumbling Bucktown** • 1579 N Milwaukee Ave

- **Division Street Russian Bath** • 1916 W Division St
- **Flat Iron Building** • 1579 N Milwaukee Ave
- **Holy Trinity Orthodox Cathedral and Rectory** • 1121 N Leavitt St
- **Wicker Park** • Pierce St & Hoyne St

Pharmacies

- **CVS** • 2418 W Division St
- **Jewel-Osco** • 1341 N Paulina St
- **Walgreens** • 1372 N Milwaukee Ave
- **Walgreens** • 2440 W North Ave

Pizza

- **Leona's** • 1936 W Augusta Blvd
- **Lou Malnati's Pizzeria** • 1520 N Damen Ave
- **Piece** • 1927 W North Ave
- **Pizza Hut** • 1601 N Western Ave
- **Pizza Metro** • 1707 W Division St

Police

- **13th District (Wood)** • 937 N Wood St

Schools

- **A N Pritzker Elementary** • 2009 W Schiller St
- **Albert R Sabin** • 2216 W Hirsch St
- **Christopher Columbus Elementary** • 1003 N Leavitt St
- **De Diego Elementary** • 1313 N Claremont Ave
- **Frederic Chopin Elementary** • 2450 W Rice St
- **Hans Christian Andersen Elementary** • 1148 N Honore St
- **Josephinum High** • 1501 N Oakley Blvd
- **Roberto Clemente Community High** • 1147 N Western Ave
- **St Helen Elementary** • 2347 W Augusta Blvd
- **St Nicholas** • 2200 W Rice St

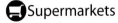 Supermarkets

- **Jewel-Osco** • 1341 N Paulina St

Lincoln Park West, as it's known by some, remains one of the hippest parts of town for young artist-types, densely packed with faux-hawks, scooters, and wearable art. Fashion-forward boutiques, veggie-friendly eats, and cool cafés abound. Indie bands and avant-garde jazz wail through the night from Empty Bottle while brainy hipsters frequent Quimby's and Myopic books.

Map

Coffee

- **Alliance Bakery** • 1736 W Division St
- **Barista Café** • 852 N Damen Ave
- **Café Ballou** • 939 N Western Ave
- **Caffe Gelato** • 2034 W Division St
- **Letizia's Natural Bakery** • 2144 W Division St
- **Starbucks** • 1588 N Milwaukee Ave
- **Starbucks** • 1701 W Division St
- **Sweet Thang** • 1921 W North Ave
- **Windy City Cyber Café** • 2246 W North Ave

Copy Shops

- **Copymax** • 1573 N Milwaukee Ave
- **FedEx Kinko's** • 1800 W North Ave ⊕

Farmers Markets

- **Wicker Park/Bucktown (Jun–Oct; Sun, 7 am–2 pm)** • W Schiller St & N Damen Ave

Gyms

- **Bucktown Fitness Club** • 2100 W North Ave
- **Cheetah Gym** • 1934 W North Ave

Liquor Stores

- **Carlos Food & Liquor** • 1401 N Western Ave
- **Ola's Liquor** • 947 N Damen Ave
- **Sahar Food & Liquor** • 1761 W Division St
- **Universal Food & Liquor** • 1803 W North Ave
- **Wicker Park Liquor** • 2006 W Division St

Nightlife

- **Beachwood Inn** • 1415 N Wood St
- **Between Boutique Cafe & Lounge** • 1324 N Milwaukee Ave
- **Borderline** • 1954 W North Ave
- **Cleo's** • 1935 W Chicago Ave
- **Club Foot** • 1824 W Augusta Blvd
- **Davenport's** • 1383 N Milwaukee Ave
- **Debonair Social Club** • 1575 N Milwaukee Ave
- **Double Door** • 1572 N Milwaukee Ave
- **Empty Bottle** • 1035 N Western Ave
- **Empire Liquors** • 1566 N Milwaukee Ave

- **Estelle's Café & Lounge** • 2013 W North Ave
- **Gold Star Bar** • 1755 W Division St
- **Happy Village** • 1059 N Wolcott Ave
- **Inner Town Pub** • 1935 W Thomas St
- **Innjoy** • 2051 W Division St
- **Jun Bar** • 2050 W Division
- **Lava Lounge** • 1270 N Milwaukee Ave
- **Phyllis' Musical Inn** • 1800 W Division St
- **Pontiac Café** • 1531 N Damen Ave
- **Rainbo Club** • 1150 N Damen Ave
- **Rodan** • 1530 N Milwaukee Ave
- **Small Bar** • 2049 W Division St
- **Subterranean Cabaret & Lounge** • 2011 W North Ave
- **Vintage Wine Bar** • 1942 W Division St
- **The Violet Hour** • 1520 N Damen Ave

Pet Shops

- **Doggy Style Pet Shop** • 2023 W Division St
- **Wicker Pet** • 2029 W North Ave

Restaurants

- **Bin Wine Café** • 1559 N Milwaukee Ave
- **Bite** • 1039 N Western Ave
- **Blue Line Club Car** • 1548 N Damen Ave
- **Bluefin** • 1952 W North Ave
- **Bob San** • 1805 W Division St
- **The Bongo Room** • 1470 N Milwaukee Ave
- **Cleo's** • 1935 W Chicago Ave
- **Cold Comfort Café & Deli** • 2211 N North Ave
- **Earwax** • 1561 N Milwaukee Ave
- **Feast** • 1616 N Damen Ave
- **Flash Taco** • 1570 N Damen Ave
- **Handlebar** • 2311 W North Ave
- **Jerry's** • 1938 W Division St
- **Las Palmas** • 1835 W Division St
- **Letiza's Natural Bakery** • 2144 W Division St
- **Mas** • 1670 W Division St
- **Milk & Honey** • 1920 W Division St
- **Mirai Sushi** • 2020 W Division St
- **People Lounge** • 1560 N Milwaukee Ave
- **Picante** • 2016 W Division St
- **Piece** • 1927 W North Ave
- **Smoke Daddy** • 1804 W Division St
- **Spring** • 2039 W North Ave
- **Su-Ra** • 2257 W North Ave
- **Sultan's Market** • 2057 W North Ave
- **Thai Lagoon** • 2322 W North Ave
- **Thai Village** • 2053 W Division St
- **Tre Via** • 1575 N Milwaukee Ave

Shopping

- **American Apparel** • 1563 N Milwaukee Ave
- **An Je Nu** • 1747 W Division St
- **Akira** • 1814 W North Ave
- **Asrai Garden** • 1935 W North Ave
- **Black Walut Gallery** • 2135 W Division St
- **The Brown Elephant** • 1459 N Milwaukee Ave
- **Casa de Soul** • 1919 W Division St
- **Cattails** • 1935 W Division St
- **City Soles** • 2001 W North Ave
- **DeciBel Audio** • 1429 N Milwaukee Ave
- **G-Star** • 1525 N Milwaukee Ave
- **Grow** • 1943 W Division St
- **Habit** • 1951 W Division St
- **hejfina** • 1529 N Milwaukee Ave
- **Jade** • 1557 N Milwaukee Ave
- **Language** • 1537 N Milwaukee Ave
- **Lille** • 1923 W North Ave
- **Myopic Books** • 1564 N Milwaukee Ave
- **Nina** • 1655 W Division St
- **Paper Doll** • 2048 W Division St
- **Penelope's** • 1913 W Division St
- **Plein Aire** • 2036 W Division St
- **Porte Rouge** • 1911 W Division St
- **Quimby's Bookstore** • 1854 W North Ave
- **Ragstock** • 1433 N Milwaukee Ave
- **Reckless Records** • 1532 N Milwaukee Ave
- **Ruby Room** • 1743 W Division St
- **Silver Moon** • 1755 W North Ave
- **The Silver Room** • 1442 N Milwaukee Ave
- **Symmetry** • 1925 W Division St
- **Tatine** • 1742 W Division St
- **Una Mae's Freak Boutique** • 1422 N Milwaukee Ave
- **Untitled** • 1941 W North Ave

Video Rental

- **Blockbuster** • 1303 N Milwaukee Ave
- **Brainstorm** • 1648 W North Ave
- **Earwax** • 1561 N Milwaukee Ave
- **Mass Video** • 2014 W Division St

89

Gritty Goose Island industry crosses paths with arty fringes of East Ukrainian Village. Lovely historical churches exist, often buried under scaffolding. Expressway access abounds, and there's a cab stand by the Nelson Algren fountain on Milwaukee. Elston is a popular route to crisscross the city. Wave to the Morton Salt Girl as you pass by.

Banks

- **Bank of America** • 1590 N Clybourn Ave
- **Bank of America (ATM)** • 1000 W North Ave
- **Chase** • 1230 N Milwaukee Ave
- **Community Bank of Ravenswood** •
  1414 N Ashland Ave
- **Fifth Third** • 1209 N Milwaukee Ave
- **First American (ATM)** • 1000 W North Ave
- **First American (ATM)** • 1132 W Blackhawk St
- **First American (ATM)** • 939 W North Ave
- **Harris Trust & Savings** • 1242 N Ashland Blvd
- **MB Financial** • 1200 N Ashland Ave
- **New Century** • 1554 W North Ave
- **Washington Mutual** • 1555 W Division St

Car Washes

- **Hertz** • 939 W North Ave
- **Turtle Wax Car Wash** • 1550 N Fremont St

Gas Stations

- **Amoco** • 1600 N Elston Ave
- **BP** • 1334 W Division St
- **Gas Depot** • 1551 W North Ave
- **Shell** • 1400 W Division St

Landmarks

- **House of Crosses** • 1544 W Chestnut St
- **Morton Salt Elston Facility** •
  Elston Ave & Blackhawk St
- **Nelson Algren Fountain** •
  Division St & Ashland Blvd
- **North Avenue Bridge** • W North Ave
- **Polish Museum of America** •
  984 N Milwaukee Ave
- **Pulaski Park/Pulaski Fieldhouse** •
  Blackhawk St & Cleaver St
- **St Stanislaus Kostka Church** •
  1351 W Evergreen Ave
- **Weed Street District** •
  b/w Chicago River & Halsted St

Parking

Pizza

- **California Pizza Kitchen** • 939 W North Ave
- **Little Caesar's Pizza** • Kmart • 1360 N Ashland Ave
- **Pizza Hut** • 1601 W Division St
- **Pizza Metro II** • 925 N Ashland Ave

Post Offices

- **US Post Office** • 1635 W Division St

Schools

- **College of Office Technology** • 1520 W Division St
- **Elizabeth Peabody Elementary** •
  1444 W Augusta Blvd
- **Holy Trinity High** • 1443 W Division St
- **Montessori-Near North** • 1434 W Division St
- **Noble Street High** • 1010 N Nobel St
- **Rudy Lozano Elementary** • 1424 N Cleaver St
- **William H Wells High** • 936 N Ashland Ave

Supermarkets

- **Laura's Grocery** • 1051 N Ashland Ave
- **Stanley's Fresh Fruit & Vegetables** •
  1558 N Elston Ave
- **Whole Foods Market** • 1000 W North Ave

Map 22 · **Noble Square / Goose Island**

N

GOOSE ISLAND

NOBLE SQUARE

Turning Basin

Weed Street District

Pulaski Park

Eckhart Park

Stanton Park

North Branch Chicago River

Chicago River

Dan Ryan Expy

North/Clybourn

Division

Chicago

Connector

Grand

29

21

31

24

90

94

90

1600W

800W

1200N

800N

800W

1200W

1600W

Streets (labels):
W Cortland St
N Elston Ave
W Bloomingdale Ave
N Hermitage Ave
N Paulina St
N Marshfield Ave
N Ashland Ave
W Wabansia Ave
W Willow St
N Throop St
N Ada St
W Wabansia Ave
W Concord Pl
N Magnolia Ave
N Clifton Ave
N Mendell St
N Sheffield Ave
N Bissell St
W Wisconsin St
N Dayton St
W Willow St
N Clybourn Ave
W Willow St
W Concord Pl
W North Ave
N Racine Ave
W Pierce Ave
N Bosworth Ave
W Le Moyne St
W Julian St
W Beach Ave
N Dean St
W Le Moyne St
W Le Moyne St
N Cherry Ave
W Blackhawk St
N Fremont St
W Blackhawk St
N Kingsbury St
W Eastman St
N Burling St
W Schiller St
W Fair Pl
W Goethe St
W Scott St
W Evergreen Ave
N Greenview Ave
N Cleaver St
N Ada St
W Blackhawk St
W Blackhawk St
W Blackhawk St
W Potomac Ave
W Potomac Ave
W Crystal St
W Crystal St
N Eastman Ave
W Evergreen Ave
W Division St
N Hooker St
N Hickory Ave
N North Branch St
N Cherry Ave
N Mozart St
W Evergreen Ave
N Paulina St
N Marshfield Ct
N Maud Ave
Division
W Haddon Ave
W Haddon Ave
W Thomas St
Milwaukee Ave
W Cortez St
W Cortez St
N Bliss St
W Haines St
N Halsted St
W Cortez St
W Cortez St
N Willard Ct
N Elston Ave
Chicago River
W Augusta Blvd
W Walton St
N Noble St
W Chestnut St
W Pearson St
N Bishop St
N Elizabeth St
W Chestnut St
N May St
W Fry St
N Peoria St
W Fry St
W Chicago Ave
Chicago
N Aberdeen St
N Carpenter St
N Morgan St
N Sangamon St
W Superior St
W Huron St
800W
W Superior St
W Huron St
1600W
W Ontario St
W Ancona St
N Ada St
N Elizabeth St
N Willard Ct
W Ancona St
N Green St
W Erie St
W Ontario St
W Ohio St
N Racine Ave
W Ohio St
W Race Ave
W Grand Ave
N Paulina St
N Armour St
N Throop St

1/4 mile   .25 km

Funky shops and studios cluster around Milwaukee, Division, and Ashland. Savor ceviche with humorously-monikered margaritas at El Barco, or share pub grub in Corosh's courtyard patio. Clubby Weed Street district is a breeding laboratory, while at Exit, the pierced and leather–clad pretend there still is a punk scene in Chicago.

Map

Coffee

- **Dunkin' Donuts** • 1200 N Milwaukee Ave
- **Dunkin' Donuts** • 1244 N Ashland Ave
- **Peet's Coffee and Tea** • 1000 W North Ave
- **Ritz Tango Café** • 933 N Ashland Ave
- **Starbucks** • 1001 W North Ave

Copy Shops

- **Carnegie Printers** • 868 N Milwaukee Ave

Gyms

- **Crunch Fitness** • 939 W North Ave

Hardware Stores

- **Ace Hardware** • 1013 N Ashland Ave
- **Home Depot** • 1232 W North Ave

Liquor Stores

- **Crater Food & Liquor** • 1144 N Milwaukee Ave

Nightlife

- **Crobar** • 1543 N Kingsbury St
- **Exit** • 1315 W North Ave
- **Hot Shots** • 1440 N Dayton St
- **Joe's** • 940 W Weed St
- **Republic** • 1520 N Fremont St
- **Zentra** • 923 W Weed St

Restaurants

- **Buenos Aires Forever** • 939 N Ashland Ave
- **Corosh** • 1072 N Milwaukee Ave
- **El Barco Mariscos Seafood** • 1035 N Ashland Blvd
- **La Pasadita** • 1132 N Ashland Ave
- **Luc Thang** • 1524 N Ashland Blvd
- **NYC Bagel** • 1001 W North Ave
- **Podhalanka** • 1549 W Division St
- **Sangria Restaurant and Tapas Bar** • 901 W Weed St
- **Schwa** • 1466 N Ashland Ave
- **Usagi Ya** • 1178 N Milwaukee Ave

Shopping

- **Cost Plus World Market** • 1623 N Sheffield Ave
- **Dusty Groove Records** • 1120 N Ashland Ave
- **Irv's Luggage Warehouse** • 820 W North Ave
- **Restoration Hardware** • 938 W North Ave
- **Transitions Bookplace** • 1000 W North Ave
- **Vintage Pine** • 904 W Blackhawk St

Map 23 • **West** ... le

This neighborhood was once the heart of the city's produce and meat markets. United Center, a.k.a. The House That Mike Built, infused energy into the area. A few food supplier warehouses still exist, mixing in with new loft conversions. And, by the way, after some patchy years, the new Bulls seem to be on the verge of giving loyal hoops fans something to be excited about again.

Banks

- **Chase (ATM)** • Rush University Medical Center • 1700 W Van Buren St
- **Chase (ATM)** • 1650 W Chicago Ave
- **Chase (ATM)** • Walgreens • 2316 W Madison St
- **Citibank (ATM)** • McDonald's • 2005 W Chicago Ave
- **Fifth Third (ATM)** • 1901 W Madison St
- **LaSalle (ATM)** • 1900 W Van Buren St
- **MB Financial** • 820 N Western Ave
- **MidAmerica** • 2100 W Chicago Ave
- **MidAmerica** • 2154 W Madison St
- **Self Reliance Ukrainian American Federal Credit Union** • 2332 W Chicago Ave
- **US** • 2021 W Chicago Ave
- **TCF (ATM)** • Osco • 2427 W Chicago Ave

Car Washes

- **Quiroga's Detail & Hand Car Wash** • 2036 W Grand Ave

Gas Stations

- **Marathon** • 101 N Western Ave
- **Shell** • 45 N Western Ave

Landmarks

- **First Baptist Congregational Church** • 1613 W Washington Blvd
- **Metropolitan Missionary Baptist Church** • 2151 W Washington Blvd
- **Ukrainian Cultural Center** • 2247 W Chicago Ave
- **Ukrainian National Museum** • 2249 W Superior St
- **United Center** • 1901 W Madison St

Libraries

- **Mabel Manning Public Library** • 6 S Hoyne Ave
- **Malcolm X College Library** • 1900 W Van Buren St
- **Midwest Public Library** • 2335 W Chicago Ave

Pharmacies

- **CVS** • 2427 W Chicago Ave ♿
- **Walgreens** • 2340 W Madison St

Pizza

- **Bacci Pizzeria** • 2343 W Chicago Ave
- **Naty's Pizza 2** • 1757 W Chicago Ave
- **Pizza Ria** • 1744 W Grand Ave
- **Village Pizza** • 2356 W Chicago Ave

Post Offices

- **US Post Office** • 116 S Western Ave

Schools

- **Best Practice High** • 2040 W Adams St
- **Crane Achievement Academy** • 2245 W Jackson Blvd
- **Cregier Tech Prep** • 2040 W Adams St
- **Dett R Nathaniel Elementary** • 2306 W Maypole Ave
- **Ellen Mitchell Branch** • 2315 W Erie St
- **Ellen Mitchell Elementary** • 2233 W Ohio St
- **Foundations Elementary** • 2040 W Adams St
- **Healy High** • 100 N Western Ave
- **Henry Suder Elementary** • 2022 W Washington Blvd
- **Irene C Hernandez Achievement Center** • 2245 W Jackson Blvd
- **Malcolm X College** • 1900 W Van Buren St
- **Mancel Talcott Elementary** • 1840 W Ohio St
- **Nia Middle** • 2040 W Adams St
- **Phoenix Military Academy** • 145 S Campbell Ave
- **St Malachy Elementary** • 2252 W Washington Blvd
- **Victor Herbert Elementary** • 2131 W Monroe St
- **West Town High** • 2021 W Fulton St
- **William H Brown Elementary** • 54 N Hermitage Ave
- **Wilma Rudolph Learning Center** • 110 N Paulina St

Supermarkets

- **Dominick's** • 2021 W Chicago Ave
- **Ukrainian Village Grocery** • 2204 W Chicago Ave

Map 23 • **West**

W Watton St
W Iowa St
W Rice St
W Chicago Ave
N 600

21

W Walton St
W Pearson St
W Fry St
W Rice St
W Lee Pl
W Superior St
W Huron St
Superior Park
W Superior St
N Western Ave
N Oakley Blvd
N Leavitt St
N Hoyne Ave
N Damen Ave
N Wolcott Ave
N Wood St
N Hermitage Ave
N Marshfield Ave
N Paulina St
N Ashland Ave
N Armour St
N Greenview Ave

A

Smith Park

WEST TOWN

W Ohio St
W Race Ave
W Grand Ave
W Ontario St
W Race Ave
N Artesian Ave

Western Ave

◀50

W Ferdinand St
W Hubbard St
W Anson Pl
W Carroll Ave
W Fulton St
W Walnut St
N Claremont Ave
N Bell Ave
N Jessie Ave
N Seeley Ave
N Winchester Ave
N Hart St
N Hermitage Ave
N Oswego St
N Marshfield Ave

W Kinzie St.

W Arbor P
W Carroll
W Fultor

N Justine S
N Latin St

B

2400W
2000W
1600W

Ashland

W Lake St
W Maypole Ave

24▶

Union Park

W Washington Blvd
W Warren Blvd

NEAR WEST SIDE

W Madison St

United Center
PAGE 268

W Arcade Pl
W Monroe St
S Western Ave
S Oakley Blvd
S Bell Ave
S Hamilton Ave
S Hoyne Ave
S Seeley Ave
S Winchester Ave
S Wolcott Ave
S Honore St
S Wood St
N Paulina St
W Ogden Ave
S Ashland Ave
S Latin Av

W Monroe St
Rockwell Park
Touhy Park

W Adams St
W Quincy St

C

W Gladys Ave
W Gladys Ave
W Van Buren St
S Claremont Ave
S Laflin St
N Damen Ave

W Jackson Blvd

Medical Center

S Hermitage Ave
S Marshfield Ave

Western

Eisenhower Expy
290
25

Medical Center

W Van Buri

W Congress Pkwy
W Congress Pkwy
W Harrison St
S Bell Ave
S Hoyne Ave
W Congress Pkwy
W Harrison St
W Flournoy St
S Marshfield Ave
W Flourno

Claremont

St Lukes Medical Center

1/4 mile
.25 km

W Campbell Park Dr
W Flournoy St
W Flournoy

Between the architectural haven Salvage One, cowboy costumer Alcala's, designer toy store Rotofugi, and gardening boutique Sprout Home, the shopping is anything but ordinary in this neck of the woods. Get your coffee with a side of hipster at Atomix. Speaking of hipsters, watch them try to dance at the DJ-friendly, photography-themed club, Darkroom.

Coffee

- **Atomix** • 1957 W Chicago Ave
- **Bleeding Heart Bakery** • 2018 W Chicago Ave
- **Intelligentsia Roasting Works Tours** • 1850 W Fulton St
- **Village Café** • 2304 W Chicago Ave

Liquor Stores

- **DiCarlo's Armanetti Liquors** • 515 N Western Ave
- **Main St Liquors** • 2000 W Madison St
- **Westlake** • 2349 W Lake St

Nightlife

- **Cleo's** • 1935 W Chicago Ave
- **Darkroom** • 2210 W Chicago Ave
- **Guess Hookah** • 1829 W Chicago Ave
- **High Dive** • 1938 W Chicago Ave
- **Sak's Ukrainian Village Restaurant** • 2301 W Chicago Ave
- **Tuman's** • 2159 W Chicago Ave

Pet Shops

- **Windy City Parrot** • 2007 W Fulton St

Restaurants

- **A Tavola** • 2148 W Chicago Ave
- **Painted Lady Organic Eatery** • 2018 W Chicago Ave
- **China Dragon Restaurant** • 2008 W Madison St
- **Old Lviv** • 2228 W Chicago Ave
- **Sunrise Café** • 2012 W Chicago Ave
- **Takie Outit** • 2132 W Chicago Ave
- **Tecalitlan Restaurant** • 1814 W Chicago Ave

Shopping

- **Alcala's** • 1733 W Chicago Ave
- **Painted Lady Organic Eatery** • 2018 W Chicago Ave
- **Donofrio's Double Corona Cigars** • 2058 W Chicago Ave
- **Guess Hookah** • 1829 W Chicago Ave
- **H&R Sports** • 1739 W Chicago Ave
- **Modern Times** • 2100 W Grand Ave
- **Pistol Bazaar** • 1717 W Chicago Ave
- **Rotofugi** • 1953 W Chicago Ave
- **Salvage One Architectural Elements** • 1840 W Hubbard St
- **SoKo Fashion** • 1925 W Chicago Ave
- **Sprout Home** • 745 N Damen Ave
- **Tomato Tattoo** • 1855 W Chicago Ave

Food distribution centers and wholesalers, warehouses, and loading docks rub shoulders with an alternative gallery scene, trendy restaurants, and hot clubs in this transitional 'hood where condo-and loft-development is king and Oprah Winfrey is queen. Young Cusack–wannabes take classes at the Chicago Academy for the Arts. Break a leg.

Banks

- **American Chartered** • 932 W Randolph St
- **Banco Popular** • 1445 W Chicago Ave
- **Bank of America** • 140 S Ashland Ave
- **Bank of America (ATM)** • 1601 W Chicago Ave
- **Broadway** • 900 W Van Buren St
- **Charter One (ATM)** • 7-Eleven • 954 W Monroe St
- **Charter One (ATM)** • White Hen • 200 S Racine
- **Chase** • 923 W Washington Blvd
- **Citibank (ATM)** • 745 N Milwaukee Ave
- **First American (ATM)** • 1001 W Madison St
- **First American (ATM)** • 324 S Racine Ave
- **First Eagle National** • 1201 W Madison St
- **LaSalle** • 850 W Jackson Blvd
- **MB Financial** • 1420 W Madison St
- **North Community** • 1244 W Grand Ave
- **North Community** • 1600 W Chicago Ave
- **South Central** • 160 N Morgan St
- **TCF (ATM)** • Osco • 771 N Ogden Ave
- **US** • 745 N Milwaukee Ave
- **Washington Mutual** • 1301 W Madison St
- **Washington Mutual** • 1656 W Chicago Ave

Car Washes

- **Bert's Car Wash** • 1231 W Grand Ave
- **Randolph St Auto Spa** • 1308 W Randolph St
- **Shell** • 1001 W Jackson Blvd
- **Strictly by Hand II** • 1125 W Van Buren St

Car Rental

- **Enterprise** • 318 S Morgan St • 312-432-9780

Gas Stations

- **BP** • 1600 W Van Buren St
- **Citgo** • 1535 W Grand Ave
- **Marathon** • 1100 W Grand Ave
- **Marathon** • 335 N Ogden Ave
- **Marathon** • 649 N Ashland Ave
- **Shell** • 1001 W Jackson Blvd
- **Shell** • 1160 W Van Buren St
- **Shell** • 505 N Ashland Ave

Landmarks

- **Eckhart Park/Ida Crown Natatorium** • 1330 W Chicago Ave
- **Harpo Studios** • 1058 W Washington Blvd
- **Jackson Boulevard Historic District** • W Jackson Blvd & W Adams St b/w S Ashland Ave & S Laflin St

Libraries

- **Eckhart Park Branch** • 1330 W Chicago Ave

Parking

Pharmacies

- **CVS** • 771 N Ogden Ave
- **Walgreens** • 1650 W Chicago Ave

Pizza

- **D'Agostino's Pizzeria** • 752 N Ogden Ave
- **Moretti's** • 1645 W Jackson Blvd
- **Penny's Pizza** • 230 S Ashland Ave
- **Pie-Eyed Pizza** • 1111 W Chicago Ave
- **Romero's Fast Food** • 1521 W Grand Ave
- **Salerno's Restaurant** • 1201 W Grand Ave
- **Tomato Head Pizza Kitchen** • 945 W Randolph St

Police

- **12th District (Monroe)** • 100 S Racine Ave

Schools

- **American Quality** • 850 W Jackson Blvd
- **Calphalon Culinary Center** • 1000 W Washington Blvd
- **Chicago Academy for the Arts** • 1010 W Chicago Ave
- **Esperanza Community Services** • 520 N Marshfield Ave
- **James Otis Elementary** • 525 N Armour St
- **Mark Skinner Classical** • 1443 N Ogden Ave
- **Midwest Apostolic Bible College** • 14 S Ashland Ave
- **Near North Special Ed Center** • 739 N Ada St
- **Philo Carpenter Elementary** • 1250 W Erie St
- **Santa Maria Addolorata** • 1337 W Ohio St
- **UNO Charter School Network Elementary** • 954 W Washington Blvd
- **Whitney Young High** • 211 S Laflin St

Supermarkets

- **Bari Foods** • 1120 W Grand Ave

Dining options in River West are plentiful to say the least. Of all the choices, we like DeCero for their contemporary pan–Latin spin and Green Zebra for innovative vegetarian choices. La Sardine packs 'em in like, well, sardines, for their Tuesday evening three–course fixed price special. Later on, go sip at Tasting Room on Randolph Street. On Tuesdays all of their wines by the glass are half price.

25	26			
		10	11	
52	12	13	14	

Coffee

- **Bialy's Café** • 1421 W Chicago Ave
- **Dunkin' Donuts** • 1535 W Grand Ave
- **Dunkin' Donuts** •
  901 W Washington Blvd
- **Mercury Café** • 1505 W Chicago Ave
- **Muse Café** • 817 N Milwaukee Ave
- **Sip Coffee House** • 1223 W Grand Ave
- **Starbucks** • 1001A W Madison St
- **Starbucks** • 520 N Ogden Ave
- **Starbucks** • 946 W Randolph St
- **Swim Café** • 1357 W Chicago Ave

Copy Shops

- **AlphaGraphics** •
  1017 W Washington Blvd
- **The UPS Store** • 516 N Ogden Ave
- **The UPS Store** • 910 W Van Buren St

Gyms

- **Cardinal Fitness of Madison Ave** •
  1301 W Madison St
- **Curves (women only)** •
  1151 W Madison St
- **West Loop Gym** • 1024 W Kinzie St
- **Westloop Athletic Club** •
  1380 W Randolph St

Hardware Stores

- **Imperial Hardware** •
  1208 W Grand Ave

Liquor Stores

- **Casey's Liquors** • 1444 W Chicago Ave
- **Randolph Wine Cellars** •
  1415 W Randolph St
- **Rothchild Liquor Marts** •
  1532 W Chicago Ave
- **Tasting Room** • 1415 W Randolph St

Nightlife

- **Betty's Blue Star Lounge** •
  1600 W Grand Ave
- **Cobra Lounge** • 235 N Ashland Ave
- **Fulton Lounge** • 955 W Fulton Market
- **J Patricks** • 1367 W Erie St
- **Juicy Wine Company** •
  694 N Milwaukee Ave

- **Mahoney's Bar & Grill** •
  551 W Ogden Ave
- **Matchbox** • 770 N Milwaukee Ave
- **Players Bar & Grill** • 551 N Odgen Ave
- **Relax Lounge** • 1450 W Chicago Ave
- **Sonotheque** • 1444 W Chicago Ave
- **Stanley's Kitchen & Tap on Racine** •
  324 S Racine Ave
- **Tasting Room** • 1415 W Randolph St
- **Twisted Spoke** • 501 N Ogden Ave
- **Victor Hotel** • 311 N Sangamon

Pet Shops

- **Pet Care Plus** • 1328 W Lake St

Restaurants

- **Amelia's Mexican Grille** •
  1235 W Grand Ave
- **Aroma** • 941 W Randolph St
- **Avenue M** • 695 N Milwaukee Ave
- **Bella Notte** • 1374 W Grand Ave
- **Bombon Café** • 38 S Ashland Ave
- **Breakfast Club** • 1381 W Hubbard St
- **Burger Baron** • 1381 W Grand Ave
- **Butterfly Sushi Bar and Thai Cuisine** •
  1156 W Grand Ave
- **Café Central** • 1437 W Chicago Ave
- **Cannella's on Grand** •
  1132 W Grand Ave
- **Carmichael's Chicago Steak House** •
  1052 W Monroe St
- **Chicago Chocolate Café** •
  847 W Randolph St
- **Coalfire** • 1321 W Grand Ave
- **DeCero** • 814 W Randolph St
- **Fan Si Pan** • 1618 W Chicago Ave
- **Flo** • 1434 W Chicago Ave
- **Follia** • 953 W Fulton St
- **Green Zebra** • 1460 W Chicago Ave
- **Habana Libre** • 1440 W Chicago Ave
- **Hacienda Tecalitlan** •
  820 N Ashland Blvd
- **Ina's** • 1235 W Randolph St
- **Jak's Tap** • 901 W Jackson Blvd
- **Jerry's Sandwiches** •
  1045 W Madison St
- **La Sardine** • 111 N Carpenter St
- **Marche** • 833 W Randolph St
- **May Street Market** •
  1132 W Grand Ave
- **Misto** • 1118 W Grand Ave
- **Moto** • 945 W Fulton Market
- **Otom** • 951 W Fulton Market

- **Salerno's Pizza and Pasta** •
  1201 W Grand Ave
- **Silver Palm** • 768 N Milwaukee Ave
- **Sushi X** • 1136 W Chicago Ave
- **Swim Café** • 1357 W Chicago Ave
- **Twisted Spoke** • 501 N Ogden Ave
- **Vinnie's Sandwich Shop** •
  1204 W Grand Ave
- **Vivo** • 838 W Randolph St
- **West Town Tavern** •
  1329 W Chicago Ave
- **Windy City Café** •
  1062 W Chicago Ave
- **Wishbone** • 1001 W Washington Blvd

Shopping

- **Aesthetic Eye** • 1520 W Chicago Ave
- **Casati** • 949 W Fulton Market
- **Chicago Avenue Discount** •
  1637 W Chicago Ave
- **Design Inc** • 1359 W Grand Ave
- **Douglas Dawson Gallery** •
  400 N Morgan St
- **duchess** • 1043 W Grand Ave
- **Jan's Antiques** • 225 N Racine Ave
- **MK Brody** • 1101 W Randolph St
- **Ouest** • 1063 W Madison St
- **Pet Care Plus** • 1328 W Lake St
- **Phaiz** • 673 N Milwaukee Ave
- **The Realm** • 1430 W Chicago Ave
- **Roots** • 1140 W Grand Ave
- **RR#1 Chicago Apothecary** •
  814 N Ashland Blvd
- **Snap** • 470 N Ogden Ave
- **Terry's Toffee** • 1117 W Grand Ave
- **Upgrade Cycle Works** •
  1130 W Chicago Ave
- **Xyloform** • 1423 W Chicago Ave

Video Rental

- **Blockbuster** • 1015 W Madison St
- **Grand Slam Video** •
  1369 W Grand Ave

The conglomerated facilities making up the Illinois Medical District comprise the second–largest such quarter in the nation. Cook County (Stroger) Hospital broke ground in 1874. Its trauma center is among America's finest, if unfaithful to its "ER" rendering. Go elsewhere for non-emergency care to avoid waiting. New buildings in the Tri–Taylor area house green MDs.

$ Banks

- **Bank of America** • 1705 W 18th St
- **Bank of America** • 2332 W Cermak Rd
- **Bank of America (ATM)** • 1717 W Polk St
- **Bank of America (ATM)** • 1801 W Taylor St
- **Bank of America (ATM)** • 818 S Wolcott Ave
- **Chase** • 2000 W Cermak Rd
- **Chase (ATM)** • Rush Presbyterian Hospital • 1750 W Harrison St
- **Chase (ATM)** • 1850 W Roosevelt Rd
- **Chase (ATM)** • Walgreens • 1931 W Cermak Rd
- **Chase (ATM)** • 2111 W Roosevelt Rd
- **Chase (ATM)** • Rush University Medical Center • 600 S Paulina St
- **Chase (ATM)** • Veterans Affairs Hospital • 820 S Damen Ave
- **First American (ATM)** • 2200 S Western Ave
- **LaSalle (ATM)** • 1701 W Taylor St
- **LaSalle (ATM)** • 818 S Wolcott Ave
- **Metropolitan** • 2201 W Cermak Rd
- **Metropolitan** • 2235 W Cermak Rd
- **TCF** • 818 S Wolcott Ave
- **TCF (ATM)** • UIC Sport/Fitness West • 828 S Wolcott Ave

Car Washes

- **G Express Hand Car Wash** • 2323 W 18th St

Gas Stations

- **Citgo** • 2107 S Western Ave
- **Independent** • 1721 S Paulina St
- **Mobil** • 2401 W Ogden Ave
- **Shell** • 2401 W Roosevelt Rd

Emergency Rooms

- **John H Stroger** • 1900 W Polk St
- **Rush-Presbyterian St Luke's** • 1650 W Harrison St
- **St Anthony's** • 2875 W 19th St
- **University of Illinois at Chicago** • 1740 W Taylor St
- **VA Medical Center** • 820 S Damen Ave

Landmarks

- **18th St L station** • W 18th St & S Paulina St
- **Bowler Row Houses** • 2148 W Bowler St
- **Oakley Row Houses** • 801 S Oakley Ave
- **Vietnam Survivors Memorial** • 815 S Oakley Ave

P Parking

Pharmacies

- **Walgreens** • 1931 W Cermak Rd

Pizza

- **Aurelio's Pizza** • 1545 S Western Ave
- **Bacci Pizzeria** • 2301 W Taylor St
- **Damenzo's** • 2324 W Taylor St
- **Pisa Pizza** • 2050 W Cermak Rd
- **Pizza Hut** • 2337 W Cermak Rd
- **Pizza Nova** • 1842 W 18th St

Schools

- **Chicago Hope Academy** • 2189 W Bowler St
- **Chicago Lighthouse Development** • 1850 W Roosevelt Rd
- **Children of Peace Elementary** • 1900 W Taylor St
- **Josiah L Pickard Elementary** • 2301 W 21st Pl
- **Nancy Jefferson** • 1100 S Hamilton Ave
- **Octavio Paz Middle** • 2401 W Congress Pkwy
- **Orozco Elementary** • 1940 W 18th St
- **Rush Day** • 1720 W Polk St
- **Rush University** • 600 S Paulina St
- **St Ann Grade** • 2211 W 18th Pl
- **University of Illinois at Chicago** • 840 S Wood St
- **University of Illinois College of Medicine** • 808 S Wood St
- **Washington Irving Elementary** • 749 S Oakley Blvd
- **William E Gladstone Elementary** • 1231 S Damen Ave

Supermarkets

- **Aldi** • 1739 W Cermak Rd
- **Fairplay Finer Foods** • 2200 S Western Ave

Map 25

Residents of the Tri–Taylor building boom go a few blocks east to Little Italy or north to River West for nightlife and fine dining. Local options include Lu–Lu's (for a quick lunch) and the Ferrara bakery, with assorted treats for carry-out and a limited dine-in menu. Further south, Pilsen bleeds into the Heart of Chicago, and there's no shortage of low–priced, dependable Mexican grub.

Coffee

- **Dunkin' Donuts** • 1710 W 18th St
- **Dunkin' Donuts** • 1713 W Polk St
- **Dunkin' Donuts** • 2356 W Cermak Rd
- **Dunkin' Donuts** • 2401 W Ogden Ave

Copy Shops

- **PrintWorks Plus!** • 1720 W 18th St

Hardware Stores

- **Mitchell Hardware & Paints** • 2141 W Cermak Rd

Liquor Stores

- **Helen's Grocery & Liquors** • 2300 W 21st St
- **Three Star Liquor** • 2015 S Damen Ave

Restaurants

- **Carnitas Uruapan Restaurant** • 1725 W 18th St
- **Damenzo's** • 2324 W Taylor St
- **El Charco Verde** • 2255 W Taylor St
- **Ferrara Bakery** • 2210 W Taylor St
- **Lu-Lu's Hot Dogs** • 1000 S Leavitt St
- **TJ's Family Restaurant** • 1928 W Cermak Rd

Shopping

- **Accents Flowers and Gifts** • 2246 W Taylor St
- **Salvation Army Thrift Store** • 2024 S Western Ave

Video Rental

- **Blockbuster** • 2425 W Cermak Rd
- **Pedraza Video** • 1758 W 19th St

Map 26 • **University Village/Little Italy/Pilsen**

N

1

2

W Marshfield Ave
W Gladys Blvd
W Gladys Ave

W Van Buren St

24

Racine

S Tilden St

S Carpenter St

UIC-Halsted

290

W Congress Pkwy

4

S Ashland Ave

W Flournoy St

W Harrison St

$

W Harrison St

W Vernon Park Pl

A

Polk

S Paulina St

S Marshfield Ave

W Flournoy St

S Loomis

W Westgate Ter

W Flournoy St

S Ada St

S Lytle St

S Racine Ave

S May St

S Aberdeen St

S Carpenter St

S Miller St

4 $

W Polk St

7

W Cabrini St

W Lexington St

W Lexington St

Arrigo Park

W Polk St

S Morgan St

University of
Illinois at Chicago
East Campus

W Cabrini

W Polk St

S Bishop St

S Laflin Pl

National Italian-
American Sports
Hall of Fame

W Arthington St

W Cabrini St

W Arthington St

Sheridan
Park

PAGE
254

Garibaldi Pl

S Throop St

S Lytle St

W Taylor St

W Taylor St

W Fillmore St

$

W Grenshaw St

S Lytle St

S Blue Island Ave

W Roosevelt Rd

$

W Washburne Ave

S Morgan St

800W

Halsted St

W 12th Pl

S Ruble St

W 12th St

1600W

R

1200W

W Washburne Ave

W 13th St

W O'Brien St

W 13th St

S Laflin St

S Laflin Cir

UNIVERSITY VILLAGE / LITTLE ITALY

S Aberdeen St

W Maxwell St

S Sangamon St

S Peoria St

S Newberry Ave

$

B

25

S Laflin St

Plgd
Park

Throop St

W 13th St

W Hastings St

W Liberty St

W Liberty St

S Miller St

Dan Ryan Expy

W 14th St

W 14th St

W 14th Pl

Addams
Park

W 14th Pl

W 14th Pl

W 14th St

W Barber St

W 15th St

S Laflin St

W 15th St

W South Water Market

W 15th St

90

94

18th

R

W 16th St

W 17th St

S Miller St

Carpenter St

S Sangamon St

S Peoria St

10

W 16th St

$

W 17th St

W 17th St

W 17th St

$

S Throop St

S Ada St

S May St

S Carpenter St

Halsted

W 18th St

W 18th St

$

W 18th Pl

PILSEN

S Blue Island Ave

W 18th Pl

S Shelby Ct

S Sangamon St

S Peoria St

W 18th St

W 19th St

W 19th Pl

$

W 19th St

W Marshfield Ave

C

W 19th St

S Throop St

W 19th Pl

W 19th St

S Cullerton St

S Ashland Ave

S Miller St

W 20th Pl

S Morgan St

S Sangamon St

W 20th St

Dvorak
Park

S Blue Island Ave

S Laflin St

S Loomis St

W 21st St

S Throop St

S Albert St

W 20th Pl

S Canalport Ave

W 21st St

W 21st Pl

S Racine Ave

S Carpenter St

W 21st St

S Morgan St

S Peoria St

12

S Canalport Ave

W Cermak Rd

W 22nd Pl

| 1/4 mile | | .25 km |

Map

25	26
	10 11
52	12 13 14

Banks

- **Bank of America (ATM)** • 700 S Halsted St
- **Bank of America (ATM)** • 750 S Halsted St
- **Charter One (ATM)** • 1524 W Taylor St
- **Chase** • 1130 W Taylor St
- **Chicago Community** • 1800 S Halsted St
- **Citibank** • 1200 W Taylor St
- **Citibank (ATM)** • 7-Eleven • 1350 S Halsted St
- **First American (ATM)** • 1218 S Halsted St
- **First American (ATM)** • 1438 W Taylor St
- **Lakeside** • 1055 W Roosevelt Rd
- **LaSalle** • 1212 S Ashland Ave
- **LaSalle (ATM)** • 1200 W Harrison St
- **LaSalle (ATM)** • 750 S Halsted St
- **MB Financial** • 1618 W 18th St
- **MidAmerica** • 1314 S Halsted St
- **Midwest Bank & Trust Company (ATM)** • 1810 S Blue Island Ave
- **South Central** • 1400 W 18th St
- **TCF** • 750 S Halsted
- **TCF** • Jewel • 1220 S Ashland Ave
- **TCF (ATM)** • 7-Eleven • 1350 S Halsted St
- **Washington Federal** • 1410 W Taylor St

Car Washes

- **Speed Hand Car Wash** • 1700 S Ashland Ave
- **We Wash** • 2042 S Halsted St

Gas Stations

- **BP Amoco** • 1602 W Cermak Rd
- **Citgo** • 1491 W Roosevelt Rd
- **Marathon** • 1549 W Roosevelt Rd

Landmarks

- **National Italian American Sports Hall of Fame** • 1431 W Taylor St

Libraries

- **Lozano Public Library** • 1805 S Loomis St
- **Roosevelt Public Library** • 1101 W Taylor St
- **University of Illinois at Chicago Library** • 801 S Morgan St

Parking

Pharmacies

- **CVS** • 1713 S Ashland Ave
- **Jewel-Osco** • 1220 S Ashland Ave

Pizza

- **Aldo's Pizza** • 1901 S Racine Ave
- **Benny's Pizza II** • 1244 W 18th St
- **Caire's Pizza** • 1165 W 18th St
- **Chubby's Pizza** • 1429 W 18th St
- **Leona's** • 1419 W Taylor St
- **Pizza Tango** • 1013 W 18th St
- **Pompeii Bakery** • 1531 W Taylor St
- **Reggio's Pizza** • 1339 S Halsted St

Post Offices

- **US Post Office** • 1859 S Ashland Ave

Schools

- **Andrew Jackson Language Academy** • 1340 W Harrison St
- **Benito Juarez High** • 2150 S Laflin St
- **Bernice F Joyner CPC** • 1315 S Blue Island Ave
- **City as Classroom High** • 1814 S Union Ave
- **Galileo Scholastic Academy** • 820 S Carpenter St
- **Jane Addams High** • 1814 S Union St
- **John A Walsh Elementary** • 2015 S Peoria St
- **John M Smyth Elementary** • 1059 W 13th St
- **Joseph Jungman Elementary** • 1746 S Miller St
- **Joseph Medill Elementary** • 1301 W 14th St
- **Laurance Armour Day School RPS** • 630 S Ashland Ave
- **Manuel Perez Elementary** • 1241 W 19th St
- **McKinley Evgc** • 1326 W 14 Pl
- **Montefiore High** • 1310 S Ashland Ave
- **Moses Montefiore Middle** • 1310 S Ashland Ave
- **Perez Annex** • 2001 S Throop St
- **Peter Cooper Dual Language Academy** • 1624 W 19th St
- **Pilsen Academy** • 1420 W 17th St
- **Simpson Academy for Young Women** • 1321 S Paulina St
- **St Ignatius College Prep** • 1076 W Roosevelt Rd
- **St Pius V Elementary** • 1919 S Ashland Ave
- **St Procopius** • 1625 S Allport St
- **Thomas Jefferson Elementary** • 1522 W Fillmore St
- **Walsh Elementary** • 2015 S Peoria St

Supermarkets

- **Conte Di Savoia** • 1438 W Taylor St
- **Jewel-Osco** • 1220 S Ashland Ave

Sprawling over the city's Near West Side is the University of Illinois at Chicago. Little Italy is close at hand, and if you look closely you will note the presence of a number of thriving Italian neighborhood clubs here. Make sure and stop by Conte Di Savoia for some picnic supplies and a spare bottle of limoncello.

Coffee

- **Café Jumping Bean** • 1439 W 18th St
- **Café Mestizo** • 1646 W 18th St
- **Caribou Coffee** • 1328 S Halsted St
- **Caribou Coffee** • 811 W Maxwell St
- **Dunkin' Donuts** • 1651 W Roosevelt Rd
- **Efebos Internet Café** • 1640 S Blue Island Ave
- **Jamoch's Caffe** • 1066 W Taylor St
- **Kristoffer's Café & Bakery** • 1733 S Halsted St
- **Mi Cafetal** • 1519 W 18th St
- **Starbucks** • 1430 W Taylor St
- **Stivers Coffee** • 2215 S Union Ave

Copy Shops

- **Postnet** • 1258 S Halsted St
- **The UPS Store** • 1137 W Taylor St

Gyms

- **Energym** • 2201 S Halsted St
- **Go Time** • 1601 S Morgan St
- **World Gym** • 1822 S Bishop St

Hardware Stores

- **Alvarez Hardware** • 1323 W 18th St
- **La Brocha Gorda** • 974 W 18th St
- **Seigle's Lumber (lumber only)** • 977 W Cermak Rd
- **Torres Hardware** • 1836 S Ashland Ave

Liquor Stores

- **Amador Liquors** • 1167 W 18th St
- **Conte Di Savoia (wine only)** • 1438 W Taylor St
- **El Trebol Liquors** • 1135 W 18th St
- **F&R Liquor** • 2129 S Halsted St
- **Guadalajara Food & Liquors** • 1527 W 18th St
- **Harbee Liquor** • 1345 W 18th St
- **Lush Wine and Spirits** • 1306 S Halsted St
- **Taylor St Food & Liquor** • 1152 W Taylor St
- **Tito Hacienda** • 1854 S Blue Island Ave

Nightlife

- **Bar Louie** • 1321 W Taylor St
- **Bevi Amo Wine Bar** • 1358 W Taylor St
- **Hawkeye's Bar & Grill** • 1458 W Taylor St
- **The Illinois Bar & Grill** • 1421 W Taylor St
- **Junior's Sports Lounge** • 724 W Maxwell St
- **Skylark** • 2149 S Halsted St

Restaurants

- **Al's Number 1 Italian Beef** • 1079 W Taylor St
- **Carm's Beef and Snack Shop** • 1057 W Polk St
- **Chez Joel** • 1119 W Taylor St
- **Couscous** • 1445 W Taylor St
- **De Pasada** • 1519 W Taylor St
- **Demitasse** • 1066 W Taylor St
- **Francesca's** • 1400 W Taylor St
- **Franconello's Italian Restaurant** • 1301 S Halsted St
- **Golden Thai** • 1509 W Taylor St
- **Japonica** • 1422 W Taylor St
- **Kohan Japanese Restaurant** • 730 W Maxwell St
- **La Cebollita** • 1723 S Ashland Ave
- **La Vita** • 1359 W Taylor St
- **May Street Café** • 1136 W Cermak Rd
- **Mundial-Cocina Mestiza** • 1640 W 18th St
- **New Rosebud Café** • 1500 W Taylor St
- **Nuevo Leon** • 1515 W 18th St
- **Pizza Tango** • 1013 W 18th St
- **Playa Azul** • 1514 W 18th St
- **Steak 'n Egger** • 1174 W Cermak Rd
- **Sweet Maple Café** • 1339 W Taylor St
- **Taj Mahal** • 1512 W Taylor St
- **Taqueria Los Comales** • 1544 W 18th St
- **Taylor Street Taco Grill** • 1412 W Taylor St
- **Tuscany** • 1014 W Taylor St
- **WOW Café & Wingery** • 717 W Maxwell St

Shopping

- **Conte Di Savoia** • 1438 W Taylor St
- **Lush Wine and Spirits** • 1306 S Halsted St
- **Scafuri Bakery** • 1337 W Taylor St

Essentials

Map 27

Seems like all the young artists in Wicker Park and Bucktown have picked up and moved a few blocks northwest to budget-friendlier Logan Square. Between the wide open boulevard, tasty taquerias, a handful of dive bars, and a sea of vintage Schwinns, this area has everything you could want...except a central grocery store.

Banks

- **Banco Popular** • 2525 N Kedzie Blvd
- **Charter One** • 2500 W North Ave
- **Chase** • 2235 N Milwaukee Ave
- **Chase** • 2639 N Milwaukee Ave
- **Chase (ATM)** • 3110 W Armitage Ave
- **Citibank (ATM)** • 7-Eleven • 2020 N California Ave
- **Citibank (ATM)** • 2295 N Milwaukee Ave
- **Citibank (ATM)** • 7-Eleven • 2401 N Milwaukee Ave
- **First American (ATM)** • 2701 W North Ave
- **Northern Trust** • 2814 W Fullerton Ave
- **TCF (ATM)** • Osco • 2053 N Milwaukee Ave
- **Washington Mutual** • 2741 N Milwaukee Ave

Car Washes

- **California Car Wash** • 2340 N California Ave
- **Dreamwash** • 2524 W North Ave
- **Logan Square Car Wash** • 2436 N Milwaukee Ave

Gas Stations

- **Amoco** • 2800 W Fullerton Ave
- **BP/Amoco** • 2801 W Armitage Ave
- **Citgo** • 2338 N Sacramento Ave
- **Citgo** • 3142 W North Ave
- **Shell** • 2801 W Fullerton Ave

oLandmarks

- **Illinois Centennial Monument** •
  3100 W Logan Blvd
- **Logan House** • 2656 W Logan Blvd

Libraries

- **Humboldt Park Public Library** • 1605 N Troy St
- **Logan Square Public Library** •
  3030 W Fullerton Ave

Pharmacies

- **CVS** • 2053 N Milwaukee Ave
- **Walgreens** • 3110 W Armitage Ave
- **Walgreens** • 3320 W Fullerton Ave

Pizza

- **Big Tony's Pizza** • 3276 W Fullerton Ave
- **Congress Pizzeria** • 2033 N Milwaukee Ave
- **Domino's** • 2455 W Fullerton Ave
- **Marcello's Father & Son Restaurant** • 2475 N Milwaukee Ave
- **Lucky Vito's Pizzeria** • 2171 N Milwaukee Ave

Police

- **14th District (Shakespeare)** • 2150 N California Ave

Post Offices

- **US Post Office** • 2339 N California Ave
- **US Post Office** • 2901 W Armitage Ave

Schools

- **Bernhard Moos Elementary** •
  1711 N California Ave
- **Charles R Darwin Elementary** •
  3116 W Belden Ave
- **Harriet Beecher Stowe Elementary** •
  3444 W Wabansia Ave
- **Humboldt Community Christian** •
  1847 N Humboldt Blvd
- **J W Von Goethe Elementary** • 2236 N Rockwell St
- **Lorenz Brentano Math & Science Academy** •
  2723 N Fairfield Ave
- **The Lutheran Day Nursery** • 1802 N Fairfield Ave
- **Richard Yates Elementary** • 1839 N Richmond St
- **Salem Christian** • 2845 W McLean Ave
- **Salomon P Chase Elementary** • 2021 N Point St
- **St Augustine College West** •
  3255 W Armitage Ave
- **St John Berchman's** • 2511 W Logan Blvd
- **St Sylvester's** • 3027 W Palmer Blvd

Supermarkets

- **Provenance Food and Wine** •
  2528 N California Ave

Quit your whining. Just because Starbucks moved in, that doesn't mean the 'hood's lost its indie status. The heart of Logan, the actual square, hosts a few of the pioneering favorites: Lula Café, which keeps the crowds coming for its innovative, seasonally-focused cuisine, and Wolfbait & B-Girls, a mecca for made-in-Chicago clothing designers.

Coffee

- **Dunkin' Donuts** • 2247 N Milwaukee Ave
- **Dunkin' Donuts** • 2565 W Fullerton Ave
- **No Friction Café** • 2023 N California Ave
- **Starbucks** • 2543 N California Ave

Copy Shops

- **Klein Printing Co** • 3035 W Fullerton Ave

Farmers Markets

- **Logan Square**
  (Jun–Oct; every other Tues, 11 am–4 pm) •
  W Logan Blvd & N Kedzie Blvd

Gyms

- **Curves (women only)** • 3143 W Fullerton Ave

Hardware Stores

- **Gillman's Hardware** • 2118 N Milwaukee Ave
- **Monroy's Hardware Store** • 2511 W North Ave

Liquor Stores

- **Foremost Liquor Store** • 2300 N Milwaukee Ave
- **Foremost Liquor Store** • 3301 W North Ave
- **International Liquor Store** • 2001 N California Ave
- **Logan Liquors** • 2639 N Kedzie Ave
- **Provenance Food and Wine** • 2528 N California Ave
- **Red Star Liquors** • 2715 N Milwaukee Ave
- **Yafai Liquors** • 2700 W North Ave

Movie Theaters

- **Logan Theater** • 2646 N Milwaukee Ave

Nightlife

- **Fireside Bowl** • 2648 W Fullerton Ave
- **Ronny's** • 2101 N California Ave
- **Streetside Café** • 3201 W Armitage Ave
- **Tini Martini** • 2169 N Milwaukee Ave
- **Two Way Lounge** • 2928 W Fullerton Ave

- **Whirlaway** • 3224 W Fullerton Ave
- **The Winds Café** • 2657 N Kedzie Blvd

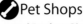Pet Shops

- **... and Feathers Bird Studio (Birds only)** •
  2406 W Fullerton Ave
- **The Barking Lot** • 1616 N Washtenaw Ave
- **Jules Pet Shop** • 2062 N Milwaukee Ave

Restaurants

- **Azucar** • 2647 Kedzie Ave
- **Bonsoiree Café and Delicacies** •
  2728 W Armitage Ave
- **Borinquen Restaurant** • 1720 N California Ave
- **Buona Terra Ristorante** • 2535 N California Ave
- **Café Bolero** • 2252 N Western Ave
- **Caliente** • 2556 W Fullerton Ave
- **Calvin's BBQ** • 2540 W Armitage Ave
- **Choi's Chinese Restaurant** • 2638 N Milwaukee Ave
- **Dunlay's on the Square** • 3137 W Logan Blvd
- **El Cid** • 2115 N Milwaukee Ave
- **El Nandu** • 2731 N Fullerton Ave
- **El Pollo Loco** • 2715 N Milwaukee Ave
- **Fat Willy's Rib Shack** • 2416 W Schubert Ave
- **Hachi's Kitchen** • 2521 N California Ave
- **Johnny's Grill** • 2545 N Kedzie Blvd
- **Lula Café** • 2537 N Kedzie Blvd
- **Mama's Apple** • 2139 N Milwaukee Ave
- **Sai Mai** • 2532 N California Ave
- **Taqueria Moran** • 2226 N California Ave

Shopping

- **Boulevard Bikes** • 2535 N Kedzie Blvd
- **Disco City** • 2630 N Milwaukee Ave
- **Fleur** • 3149 W Logan Blvd
- **Provenance Food and Wine** • 2528 N California Ave
- **Threads, Etc** • 2327 N Milwaukee Ave
- **Wolfbait & B-Girls** • 3131 W Logan Blvd

Video Rental

- **Blockbuster** • 2251 N Milwaukee Ave
- **Hi-Fi Video** • 3129 W Armitage Ave
- **Morelia Video** • 2381 N Milwaukee Ave

Separated from Lincoln Park by the freeway, Bucktown is not quite as well situated, but its (slightly) more affordable real estate has brought in the young professionals in droves. Still patchy, gentrification is gaining pace, with an ongoing influx of polished boutiques and hip baby stores. Meanwhile, the thriving art scene that once characterized Bucktown is but a memory.

Banks

- **Charter One** • Dominick's • 2550 N Clybourn Ave
- **Chase** • 1757 W Fullerton Ave
- **Chase (ATM)** • Walgreens • 2001 N Milwaukee Ave
- **Citibank (ATM)** • McDonalds • 1951 N Western
- **Citibank (ATM)** • 7-Eleven • 2010 N Damen Ave
- **Cole Taylor** • 1965 N Milwaukee Ave
- **Fifth Third** • 2785 N Clybourn Ave
- **Harris Trust & Savings** • 2196 N Elston Ave
- **MidAmerica** • 1830 W Fullerton Ave
- **MidAmerica** • 1955 N Damen Ave
- **MidAmerica** • 2300 N Western Ave
- **Northern Trust (ATM)** • 2346 N Western Ave
- **TCF (ATM)** • 7-Eleven • 2010 N Damen Ave
- **Washington Mutual** • 2790 N Clybourn Ave

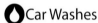Car Washes

- **Bucktown Hand Car Wash** • 2036 W Armitage Ave
- **Clybourn Express & Car Wash** •
  2452 N Clybourn Ave
- **Express Car Wash** • 2111 W Fullerton Ave
- **Fast Eddie's Hand Car Wash** • 1828 W Webster Ave
- **Prestige Hand Wash** • 1843 N Milwaukee Ave
- **Wash Express** • 1657 N Milwaukee Ave

Car Rental

- **Enterprise** • 1842 N Milwaukee Ave • 773-862-4700

Gas Stations

- **BP** • 2357 W Fullerton Ave
- **Citgo** • 1768 W Armitage Ave
- **Citgo** • 2501 N Western Ave
- **Marathon** • 2346 N Western Ave
- **Mobil** • 1750 N Western Ave
- **Shell** • 2357 W Fullerton Ave

○Landmarks

- **Margie's Candies** • 1960 N Western Ave

Libraries

- **Bucktown/Wicker Park Public Library** •
  1701 N Milwaukee Ave

Pharmacies

- **Dominick's** • 2550 N Clybourn Ave ⊕
- **Target** • 2656 N Elston Ave
- **Walgreens** • 2001 N Milwaukee Ave ⊕

Pizza

- **Chuck E Cheese's** • 1830 W Fullerton Ave
- **Homemade Pizza Co** • 1953 W Wabansia Ave
- **John's Restaurant & Lounge** •
  2104 N Western Ave
- **My Pie Pizza** • 2010 N Damen Ave
- **Plazzio's Pizza** • 1901 N Western Ave
- **Sonny's Pizza** • 2431 N Western Ave

Schools

- **Antonia Pantoja High** • 2435 N Western Ave
- **Casimir Pulaski Fine Arts Academy** •
  2230 W McLean Ave
- **Chicago International Elementary - Bucktown Campus** • 2235 N Hamilton Ave
- **St Mary of the Angels** • 1810 N Hermitage Ave
- **Thomas Drummond Elementary** •
  1845 W Cortland St
- **William H Prescott Elementary** •
  1632 W Wrightwood Ave

Supermarkets

- **Aldi** • 1767 N Milwaukee Ave
- **Aldi** • 2600 N Clybourn Ave
- **Always Open** • 1704 N Milwaukee Ave
- **Costco** • 2746 N Clybourn Ave
- **Dominick's** • 2550 N Clybourn Ave ⊕
- **Goddess and the Grocer** • 1646 N Damen Ave
- **Olivia's Market** • 2014 W Wabansia Ave

Map

Map 28 • **Bucktown**

You need never be hungry, thirsty, or poorly clothed in Bucktown—or have to walk more than a block or two. Budget and upscale still co-exist, for now; Margie's Candies and Meritage Cafe, and Goddess and the Grocer. Caffé De Luca is the spot for coffee, while Hot Chocolate is stroller-heaven by day, chic eatery by night. Find your niche, or better yet, do it all.

Coffee

- **Caffé De Luca** • 1721 N Damen Ave
- **Coffee Beanery** • 2158 N Damen Ave
- **Dunkin' Donuts** • 1746 N Western Ave
- **Dunkin' Donuts** • 1909 N Western Ave
- **Dunkin' Donuts** • 1927 W Fullerton Ave
- **Red Hen Bread** • 1623 N Milwaukee Ave
- **Starbucks** • Dominick's • 2550 N Clybourn Ave
- **Starbucks** • 2577 N Elston Ave
- **Starbucks** • Target • 2656 N Elston Ave

Copy Shops

- **Office Max** • 1829 W Fullerton Ave
- **Staples Copy & Print Centers** • 2484 N Elston Ave
- **The UPS Store** • 1658 Milwaukee Ave

Farmers Markets

- **Bucktown (Jun-Oct; every other Sun, 7 am-2 pm)** •
  W Belden Ave & N Western Ave

Gyms

- **Ladies Workout Express (women only)** •
  1722 N Western Ave
- **Mid-Town Athletic Club** • 2020 W Fullerton Ave

Hardware Stores

- **Home Depot** • 2570 N Elston Ave
- **Menard's** • 2601 N Clybourn Ave

Liquor Stores

- **Bon Song Liquors** • 2000 N Leavitt St
- **Bucktown Food & Liquor** • 2422 W Fullerton Ave
- **Danny's** • 2222 N Western Ave
- **MW Food & Liquor** • 1950 N Milwaukee Ave
- **Wine and Ciders** • 2211 N Elston Ave

Movie Theaters

- **Kerasotes Chicago City North 14** • 2600 N Western Ave

Nightlife

- **Cans** • 1640 N Damen Ave
- **Charleston Tavern** • 2076 N Hoyne Ave
- **Cleo's** • 2048 W Armitage Ave
- **Cortland's Garage** • 1645 W Cortland St
- **Danny's Tavern** • 1951 W Dickens Ave
- **Darwin's** • 1935 N Damen Ave
- **Gallery Cabaret** • 2020 N Oakley Ave
- **Green Eye Lounge** • 2403 W Homer St
- **Lemmings** • 1850 N Damen Ave
- **The Liar's Club** • 1665 W Fullerton Ave
- **The Map Room** • 1949 N Hoyne Ave

- **The Mutiny** • 2428 N Western Ave
- **Northside Bar & Grill** • 1635 N Damen Ave
- **Quenchers Saloon** • 2401 N Western Ave

Pet Shops

- **Petsmart** • 2665 N Elston Ave

Restaurants

- **Arturo's Tacos** • 2001 N Western Ave
- **Bluebird** • 1749 N Damen Ave
- **Café Laguardia** • 2111 W Armitage Ave
- **Café Matou** • 1846 N Milwaukee Ave
- **Club Lucky** • 1824 W Wabansia Ave
- **Coast Sushi Bar** • 2045 N Damen Ave
- **Hollywood Grill** • 1601 W North Ave ⊕
- **Honey 1 BBQ** • 2241 N Western Ave
- **Hot Chocolate** • 1747 N Damen Ave
- **Il Covo** • 2152 N Damen Ave
- **Irazu** • 1865 N Milwaukee Ave
- **Jane's** • 1655 W Cortland St
- **La Bonita** • 2165 N Western Ave
- **Le Bouchon** • 1958 N Damen Ave
- **Margie's Candies** • 1960 N Western Ave
- **Meritage Café & Wine Bar** • 2118 N Damen Ave
- **Rinconcito Sudamericano** • 1954 W Armitage Ave
- **Rio's D'Sudamerica** • 2010 W Armitage Ave
- **Riverside Deli & Café** • 1656 W Cortland St
- **Silver Cloud Club & Grill** • 1700 N Damen Ave
- **Takashi** • 1952 Damen Ave
- **Think Café** • 2235 N Western Ave
- **Vella Cafe** • 1912 N WEstern Ave

Shopping

- **Beta Boutique** • 2016 W Concord Pl
- **Bleeker Street Antiques** • 1946 N Leavitt St
- **G Boutique** • 2131 N Damen Ave
- **Goddess and the Grocer** • 1646 N Damen Ave
- **Jean Alan** • 2134 N Damen Ave
- **Mark Shale Outlet** • 2593 N Elston Ave
- **p.45** • 1643 N Damen Ave
- **Pagoda Red** • 1714 N Damen Ave
- **Pavilion Antiques** • 2055 N Damen Ave
- **Red Balloon Company** • 2060 N Damen Ave
- **Robin Richman** • 2108 N Damen Ave
- **Scoop NYC** • 1702 N Milwaukee Ave
- **T-Shirt Deli** • 1739 N Damen Ave
- **Tangerine** • 1719 N Damen Ave
- **Veruca Salt** • 1937 N Damen Ave
- **Vienna Beef Factory Store** • 2501 N Damen Ave
- **Village Discount Outlet** • 2032 N Milwaukee Ave
- **Vive La Femme** • 2115 N Damen Ave

Video Rental

- **Blockbuster** • 1704 N Milwaukee Ave

Map 29 • DePaul / Wrightwood / Sheffield

N

W George St
W Wolfram St
W Wolfram St
Diversey
W Diversey Ave
W Diversey School Ct
N Paulina St
N Marshfield Ave
N Ashland Ave
N Greenview Ave
N Bosworth Ave
N Janssen Ave
N Lakewood Ave
N Racine Ave
N Magnolia Ave
N Wilton Ave
N Mildred Ave
N Dayton Ave
N Burling St
N Orchard St

43

W Schubert Ave
W Schubert Ave

A

WEST
DEPAUL
W Drummond Pl
W Drummond Pl
W Wrightwood Ave

Pumpkin
House   **2 $**

Wrightwood
Park
W Lill Ave
W Draper St
W Lill Ave
W Altgeld St

WRIGHTWOOD
NEIGHBORS
W Montana St
W Montana St
Biograph
Theater
N Sheffield Ave
N Halsted St

W Montana St
N Surrey Ct

Rx $**   **$ **$**
W Fullerton Pkwy
W Fullerton Pkwy

$ **P**   **✉**   **$**   Fullerton
DePaul University
(Lincoln Park Campus)   **Rx**
McCormick Row
House District

Children's
Memorial
Hospital
N Children's Plz

W Medill Ave
W Medill Ave
N Clifton Ave

PAGE 244   **2 $**

B
1600W

N Clybourn Ave
N Bosworth Ave
N Wayne Ave
N Southport Ave
N Lakewood Ave
N Magnolia Ave
1200W
Trebes
Park
W Webster Ave
W Belden Ave
2 $

30 ▶
800W
N Fremont St
N Edward Ct
Oz Pa

P   **3 $**
W Shakespeare Ave
W Dickens Ave
N Nursey St
N Kenmore Ave
W Dickens Ave

SHEFFIELD
NEIGHBORS

N Dominick St
W McLean Ave
W Armitage Ave
Armitage   **2 $**
N Burling St

$
W Homer St
W Armitage Ave
N Mendell St
N Holly Ave
N Maud Ave
W Cortland St
N Seminary Ave
N Kenmore Ave
N Bissell St
N Dayton St

C

94
90
Clybourn
Cortland Street
Drawbridge
N Elston Ave
N Besly Ct
$
$
W Wisconsin St
RANCH
TRIANGLE

N Clifton Ave
N Magnolia Ave
N Racine Ave
N Marcey St
N Poe St
$
P
W Willow St

W Bloomingdale Ave
N Throop St
N Willow St
N Wabansia Ave
N Ada St
N Concord Pl
North Branch Chicago River
$
Rx
W Concord Pl
W Concord Pl

W Wabansia Ave
N Ashland Ave
N Marshfield Ave
Dan Ryan Expy
22
W North Ave
North/Clybourn

N Hermitage Ave
N Paulina St
W Pierce Ave
N Bosworth Ave
W Le Moyne St
W Weed St
W Blackhawk St

1/4 mile   .25 km

28 ◀
N Wood St
N Clybourn Ave
W Medill Ave

There's the good—neighborhood parks and quiet, tree-lined streets with elegant homes—the bad—an overabundance of frat boys and traffic jams—and the ugly—the occasional weekend puke puddle (DePaul University is right in the middle, you know). But it's this variety, we think, that gives this neighborhood its charm

Banks

- **Associated (ATM)** • 1224 W Webster Ave
- **Bank of America** • 2163 N Clybourn Ave
- **Charter One (ATM)** • 7-Eleven • 2710 W Lincoln Ave
- **Chase** • 2170 N Clybourn Ave
- **Chase** • 935 W Armitage Ave
- **Chase (ATM)** • Lakeshore Athletic Club • 1340 W Fullerton Ave
- **Chase (ATM)** • Walgreens • 1520 W Fullerton Ave
- **Chase (ATM)** • Dominick's • 959 W Fullerton Ave
- **Citibank** • 1251 W Fullerton Ave
- **Citibank (ATM)** • 7-Eleven • 1942 N Elston Ave
- **Citibank (ATM)** • 1953 N Clybourn Ave
- **Citibank (ATM)** • 7-Eleven • 2181 N Clybourn Ave
- **Citibank (ATM)** • 7-Eleven • 2600 N Lincoln Ave
- **Citibank (ATM)** • 7-Eleven • 957 W Armitage Ave
- **Fifth Third** • 900 W Armitage Ave
- **First American (ATM)** • De Paul University Schmidt Academic Center • 2320 N Kenmore Ave
- **LaSalle (ATM)** • 1714 N Sheffield Ave
- **TCF** • 1400 W Fullerton Ave
- **TCF** • 2250 N Sheffield Ave
- **TCF (ATM)** • 7-Eleven • 2181 N Clybourn Ave
- **TCF (ATM)** • DePaul University • 2235 N Sheffield Ave
- **TCF (ATM)** • DePaul University • 2320 N Kenmore Ave
- **TCF (ATM)** • 7-Eleven • 2600 N Lincoln Ave
- **TCF (ATM)** • 7-Eleven • 957 W Armitage Ave
- **US** • 1953 N Clybourn Ave
- **Washington Mutual** • 2053 N Clybourn Ave
- **Washington Mutual** • 2662 N Lincoln Ave

Car Washes

- **Simon's** • 1439 W Shakespeare Ave
- **We'll Clean** • 2261 N Clybourn Ave
- **White Glove Car Wash** • 1415 W Shakespeare Ave

Gas Stations

- **BP** • 1607 W Fullerton Ave
- **Mobil** • 1106 W Fullerton Ave
- **Mobil** • 1901 N Elston Ave
- **Mobil** • 2670 N Lincoln Ave

Landmarks

- **Biograph Theater** • 2433 N Lincoln Ave
- **Cortland Street Drawbridge** • 1440 W Cortland St
- **McCormick Row House District** • W Chalmers Pl, W Belden Ave, & W Fullerton Pkwy
- **Pumpkin House** • 1052 W Wrightwood Ave

Libraries

- **Lincoln Park Public Library** • 1150 W Fullerton Ave

Parking

Pharmacies

- **CVS** • 1714 N Sheffield Ave ⊛
- **Dominick's** • 959 W Fullerton Ave ⊛
- **Walgreens** • 1520 W Fullerton Ave ⊛

Pizza

- **Amato's Pizza** • 953 W Willow St
- **Homemade Pizza** • 850 W Armitage Ave
- **Lou Malnati's Pizzeria** • 958 W Wrightwood Ave
- **Pat's Pizzeria** • 2679 N Lincoln Ave
- **Pequod's Pizzeria** • 2207 N Clybourn Ave
- **Tomato Head Pizza Kitchen** • 1001 W Webster Ave
- **Via-Carducci's Italian Eatery** • 1419 W Fullerton Ave

Post Offices

- **US Post Office** • 2405 N Sheffield Ave

Schools

- **DePaul University (Lincoln Park Campus)** • 2250 N Sheffield Ave
- **Jefferson Center/Factory Branch** • 2032 N Clybourn Ave
- **Jonathan Burr Elementary** • 1621 W Wabansia Ave
- **Oscar F Mayer Elementary** • 2250 N Clifton Ave
- **St James Lutheran** • 2101 N Fremont St
- **St Josephat** • 2245 N Southport Ave

Supermarkets

- **Dominick's** • 959 W Fullerton Ave ⊛
- **Trader Joe's** • 1840 N Clybourn Ave
- **Treasure Island** • 2121 N Clybourn Ave

119

Map 29 · DePaul / Wrightwood / Sheffield

Facets Multimedia runs a regular schedule of obscure arthouse cinema, and you can rent the videos, too. For music, Hideout is a second home for Bloodshot Records fans. Aging punk rockers pay their rent in whiskey at Delilah's, while frat boys hang at Gin Mill to pick up chicks. Post-class drinks at Red Lion are a time-honored tradition for graduate students; sometimes lectures are even held upstairs.

Coffee

- **Ambrosia Café** • 1963 N Sheffield Ave
- **Argo Tea** • 958 W Armitage Ave
- **Bean Café** • DePaul University • 2235 N Sheffield Ave
- **Dunkin' Donuts** • 1982 N Clybourn Ave
- **Einstein Bros Bagels** • 2212 N Clybourn Ave
- **Savor the Flavor** • 2545 N Sheffield Ave
- **Starbucks** • 1001 W Armitage Ave
- **Starbucks** • 1157 W Wrightwood Ave
- **Starbucks** • 1245 W Fullerton Ave
- **Starbucks** • 2200 N Clybourn Ave
- **Starbucks** • 2454 N Ashland Ave
- **Starbucks** • 2475 N Lincoln Ave
- **Starbucks** • Dominick's • 959 W Fullerton Ave

Copy Shops

- **FedEx Kinko's** • 2300 N Clybourn Ave ⊚
- **Sir Speedy** • 1711 N Clybourn Ave
- **The UPS Store** • 1341 W Fullerton Ave
- **The UPS Store** • 858 W Armitage Ave

Gyms

- **Bally Total Fitness** • 1455 W Webster Ave
- **Crunch Fitness** • 2727 N Lincoln Ave
- **Lakeshore Athletic Club** • 1320 W Fullerton Ave
- **Webster Fitness Club** • 957 W Webster Ave

Hardware Stores

- **Armitage Hardware & Building Supply** • 925 W Armitage Ave

Liquor Stores

- **J&R Liquor & Foods** • 2401 N Ashland Ave
- **Park West Liquor & Smoke Shop** • 2581 N Lincoln Ave
- **Sam's Wine and Liquor Warehouse** • 1720 N Marcey St
- **Wine Discount Center** • 1826 N Elston Ave
- **Wine Shippers** • 1425 W Fullerton Ave

Movie Theaters

- **Facets Multimedia** • 1517 W Fullerton Ave
- **Kerasotes Chicago Webster** • 1471 W Webster Ave

Nightlife

- **Deja Vu** • 2624 N Lincoln Ave
- **Delilah's** • 2771 N Lincoln Ave
- **Gin Mill** • 2462 N Lincoln Ave
- **The Grand Central** • 950 W Wrightwood Ave
- **Green Dolphin Street** • 2200 N Ashland Ave
- **Hideout** • 1354 W Wabansia Ave
- **Hog Head McDunna's** • 1505 W Fullerton Ave
- **Irish Eyes** • 2519 N Lincoln Ave
- **Kincade's** • 950 W Armitage Ave
- **Local Option** • 1102 W Webster Ave
- **Nic and Dino's Tripoli Tavern** • 1147 W Armitage Ave
- **The (Prop) House** • 1675 N Elston Ave
- **Red Lion Pub** • 2446 N Lincoln Ave
- **Rose's Lounge** • 2656 N Lincoln Ave
- **Webster Wine Bar** • 1480 Webster Ave
- **Wrightwood Tap** • 1059 W Wrightwood Ave

Pet Shops

- **Barker & Meowsky** • 1003 W Armitage Ave
- **Chicago Pet Care** • 1341 W Fullerton Ave
- **Galloping Gourmutts** • 2736 N Lincoln Ave
- **Kriser's Feeding Pets For Life** • 2037 N Clybourn Ave
- **Petco** • 2000 N Clybourn Ave

Restaurants

- **Ambrosia Café** • 1963 N Sheffield Ave
- **Goose Island Brewing Company** • 1800 N Clybourn Ave
- **Green Dolphin Street** • 2200 N Ashland Ave
- **Ja'Grill** • 1008 W Armitage Ave
- **John's Place** • 1200 W Webster Ave
- **Metropolis** • 2009 N Bissel St
- **Minnies** • 1969 N Halsted St
- **Red Lion Pub** • 2446 N Lincoln Ave
- **Sai Café** • 2010 N Sheffield Ave

- **Salt & Pepper Diner** • 2575 N Lincoln Ave
- **Shine & Morida** • 901 W Armitage Ave
- **State** • 935 W Webster Ave
- **Sweet Mandy B's** • 1208 W Webster Ave
- **Taco & Burrito House** • 1548 W Fullerton Ave
- **Tsuki** • 1441 W Fullerton Ave
- **Twisted Lizard** • 1964 N Sheffield Ave
- **Vosges Haut Chocolat** • 951 W Armitage Ave

Shopping

- **Active Endeavors** • 853 W Armitage Ave
- **Dirk's Fish** • 2070 N Clybourn Ave
- **Isabella Fine Lingerie** • 1101 W Webster Ave
- **Jayson Home & Garden** • 1885 N Clybourn Ave
- **Kaveri** • 1211 W Webster Ave
- **Left Bank** • 1155 W Webster Ave
- **Lush Cosmetics** • 859 W Armitage Ave
- **Mint** • 2150 N Seminary Ave
- **Sam's Wine and Liquor Warehouse** • 1720 N Marcey St
- **Tabula Tua** • 1015 W Armitage Ave
- **Uncle Dan's** • 2440 N Lincoln Ave
- **Vosges Haut Chocolat** • 951 W Armitage Ave
- **Wine Discount Center** • 1826 N Elston Ave

Video Rental

- **Facets Multimedia** • 1517 W Fullerton Ave

Good luck finding anyone that considers Lincoln Park anything other than cushy, with its Graystone mansions and tree-lined streets. It's heaven or hell, depending on your tolerance for Trixies and Chads (the 'hood's vapid, label-conscious denizens) and traffic congestion. Parking spots are fleeting fantasies; hop on that Schwinn (or the L) to get anywhere.

💲 Banks

- **Bank of America** • 2041 N Clark St
- **Bank of America** • 2401 N Clark St
- **Bank of America (ATM)** •
  2240 N Lincoln Ave
- **Bank of America (ATM)** •
  2621 N Clark St
- **BankFinancial** • 2424 N Clark St
- **Bridgeview** • 1970 N Halsted St
- **Charter One (ATM)** • White Hen •
  2004 N Halsted St
- **Chase** • 1700 N Wells St
- **Chase** • 2501 N Clark St
- **Chase** • 2603 N Halsted St
- **Chase (ATM)** • Children's Memorial
  Hospital • 2300 N Childrens Plz
- **Chase (ATM)** • 2317 N Clark St
- **Citibank** • 2001 N Halsted St
- **Citibank** • 2555 N Clark St
- **Citibank (ATM)** • 7-Eleven •
  2264 N Clark St
- **Citibank (ATM)** • McDonald's •
  2400 N Lincoln Ave
- **Citibank (ATM)** • 7-Eleven •
  2619 N Clark St
- **Citibank (ATM)** • McDonald's •
  2635 N Clark St
- **Corus** • 2401 N Halsted St
- **Fifth Third (ATM)** • 2060 N Clark St
- **First American** • 356 W Armitage Ave
- **First American (ATM)** •
  1925 N Lincoln Ave
- **First American (ATM)** •
  1935 N Sedgwick St
- **First American (ATM)** •
  1970 N Lincoln Ave
- **First American (ATM)** • Starbucks •
  2521 N Clark St
- **First American (ATM)** •
  2246 N Clark St
- **First American (ATM)** •
  2306 N Clark St
- **First American (ATM)** •
  2717 N Clark St
- **First American (ATM)** •
  Lincoln Park Hospital •
  551 W Webster Ave
- **LaSalle (ATM)** • 401 W Armitage Ave
- **MidAmerica** • 2021 N Clark St
- **North Community** • 2000 N Halsted St
- **North Community** • 2201 N Halsted St
- **North Community** • 2335 N Clark St
- **North Community** • 2500 N Clark St
- **TCF (ATM)** • 7-Eleven • 2264 N Clark St
- **TCF (ATM)** • Osco • 2414 Lincoln Ave
- **TCF (ATM)** • 7-Eleven • 2619 N Clark St
- **Washington Mutual** • 2744 N Clark St

⛽ Gas Stations

- **BP** • 1647 N La Salle Dr
- **Shell** • 2600 N Halsted St

➕ Emergency Rooms

- **Children's Memorial** •
  2300 Children's Plz
- **Lincoln Park** •
  550 W Webster Ave

◯ Landmarks

- **Dewes Mansion** •
  503 N Wrightwood Ave
- **Kauffman Store and Flats** •
  2312 N Lincoln Ave
- **Lincoln Park Boat Club** •
  N Cannon Dr & Fullerton Pkwy
- **Lincoln Park Conservatory** •
  2391 N Stockton Dr
- **Lincoln Park Cultural Center** •
  2045 N Lincoln Park W
- **Lincoln Park Zoo** • N Cannon Dr,
  south of W Fullerton Pkwy
- **Midwest Buddhist Temple** •
  435 W Menomonee St
- **Oz Park** • 2021 N Burling St
- **Peggy Notebaert Nature Museum** •
  2430 N Cannon Dr
- **The Point at Diversey** •
  Lakefront at Diversey Harbor
- **Theurer-Wrigley House** •
  2466 N Lakeview Ave
- **Waterlily Pond** • Fullerton, just west
  of the zoo entrance

🅿 Parking

℞ Pharmacies

- **CVS** • 2414 N Lincoln Ave
- **CVS** • 401 W Armitage Ave
- **Walgreens** • 2317 N Clark St

✳ Pizza

- **Bacino's** • 2204 N Lincoln Ave
- **Brick's Chicago** • 1909 N Lincoln Ave
- **Café Luigi** • 2548 N Clark St
- **Chicago Pizza & Oven Grinder** •
  2121 N Clark St
- **Domino's** • 2231 N Lincoln Ave
- **Edwardo's Natural Pizza** •
  2622 N Halsted St
- **Lincoln Park Pizza** •
  2245 N Lincoln Ave
- **My Pie Pizza** • 2417 N Clark St
- **O' Fame** • 750 W Webster Ave
- **Pizza Capri** • 1733 N Halsted St
- **Ranalli's** • 2301 N Clark St

✉ Post Offices

- **US Post Office** • 2368 N Clark St
- **US Post Office** • 2500 N Clark St
- **US Post Office** • 2643 N Clark St

🚌 Schools

- **Abraham Lincoln Elementary** •
  615 W Kemper Pl
- **Francis W Parker High** •
  330 W Webster Ave
- **La Salle Language Academy** •
  1734 N Orleans St
- **Lincoln Park High** •
  2001 N Orchard St
- **Louisa May Alcott Elementary** •
  2625 N Orchard St
- **St Clement** • 2524 N Orchard St
- **Walter L Newberry Math & Science
  Academy** • 700 W Willow St

🛒 Supermarkets

- **Big Apple Finer Foods** •
  2345 N Clark St
- **Lincoln Park Market** • 2500 N Clark St
- **Treasure Island** • 1639 N Wells St

Map 30 · Lincoln Park

Frat types and DePaul students frequent Lion Head Pub/The Apartment, so check out a cooler venue like Kingston Mines if you're sick of the college crowd. Beyond the bevy of frat bars and Irish pubs, there's awesome, cheap Indian fare at Hema's Kitchen II and a laid-back vibe for bookish folks at the Bourgeois Pig coffee shop. Posh stores like Cynthia Rowley and Lululemon await you and your wallet on every corner.

Coffee

- **Argo Tea** • 2485 N Clark St
- **Bourgeois Pig Café** • 738 W Fullerton Ave
- **Caribou Coffee** • 2453 N Clark St
- **Cosi** • 2200 N Clark St
- **Einstein Bros Bagels** • 2530 N Clark St
- **Icosium Kafe** • 2433 N Clark St
- **Savories** • 1651 N Wells St
- **Screenz** • 2717 N Clark St
- **Siena Coffee** • 2308 N Clark St
- **Starbucks** • 2063 N Clark St
- **Starbucks** • 2200 N Halsted St
- **Starbucks** • 2275 N Lincoln Ave
- **Starbucks** • 2525 1/2 N Clark St

Copy Shops

- **Screenz** • 2717 N Clark St
- **The UPS Store** • 2038 N Clark St
- **The UPS Store** • 2506 N Clark St

Farmers Markets

- **Chicago's Green City Market (May–Oct, Wed & Sat, 7 am–1:30 pm)** • 1750 N Clark St
- **Lincoln Park (Jun–Oct; Sat, 7 am–2 pm)** • W Armitage Ave & N Orchard St
- **Lincoln Park Zoo (Jun–Sept; 4th Sun of month, 9 am–4 pm)** • 2001 N Stockton Dr

Gyms

- **Equinox** • 1750 N Clark St
- **Lincoln Park Fitness Center** • 444 W Fullerton Pkwy

Hardware Stores

- **Home Depot** • 2665 N Halsted St
- **Wahler Brothers True Value** • 2551 N Halsted St

Liquor Stores

- **Chalet Wine & Cheese Shop** • 2000 N Clark St
- **Country Fresh Finer Foods** • 2583 N Clark St

- **Diamond Importers** • 528 W Wrightwood Ave
- **Dynamic Liquors** • 2132 N Halsted St
- **Miska's Liquor** • 2353 N Clark St
- **S&S Food & Liquor** • 2427 N Clark St
- **Savings Unlimited** • 2353 N Clark St

Nightlife

- **B.L.U.E.S.** • 2519 N Halsted St
- **Bacchus** • 2242 N Lincoln Ave
- **Gamekeepers** • 345 W Armitage Ave
- **Glascott's** • 2158 N Halsted St
- **GoodBar** • 2512 N Halsted St
- **Hidden Shamrock** • 2723 N Halsted St
- **Kingston Mines** • 2548 N Halsted St
- **Lion Head Pub & The Apartment** • 2251 N Lincoln Ave
- **Neo** • 2350 N Clark St
- **Park West** • 322 W Armitage Ave
- **The Second City** • 1616 N Wells St
- **Victory Liquors** • 2610 N Halsted St
- **Wise Fools Pub** • 2270 N Lincoln Ave

Restaurants

- **Alinea** • 1723 N Halsted St
- **Austrian Bakery & Deli** • 2523 N Clark St
- **Boka** • 1729 N Halsted St
- **Brick's Chicago** • 1909 N Lincoln Ave
- **Café Ba-Ba-Reeba!** • 2024 N Halsted St
- **Café Bernard** • 2100 N Halsted St
- **Charlie Trotter's** • 816 W Armitage Ave
- **Dunlay's** • 2600 N Clark St
- **Emilio's Tapas** • 444 Fullerton Pkwy
- **Ethel's Chocolate Lounge** • 819 W Armitage Ave
- **Fattoush** • 2652 N Halsted St
- **Frances' Deli** • 2552 N Clark St
- **Geja's Café** • 340 W Armitage Ave
- **Hai Yen** • 2723 N Clark St
- **Hema's Kitchen II** • 2411 N Clark St
- **Hey Sushi** • 2630 N Clark St
- **Karyn's** • 1901 N Halsted Ave
- **Landmark** • 1633 N Halsted St
- **Lito's Empanadas** • 2566 N Clark St
- **Mon Ami Gabi** • 2300 N Lincoln Park W
- **Molly's Cupcakes** • 2536 N Clark St
- **Nookies** • 1746 N Wells St
- **Nookies, Too** • 2114 N Halsted St
- **North Pond** • 2610 N Cannon Dr
- **O' Fame** • 750 W Webster Ave

- **Original Pancake House** • 2020 N Lincoln Park W
- **Piattini** • 934 W Webster Ave
- **PS Bangkok** • 2521 N Halsted St
- **Red Rooster** • 2100 N Halsted St
- **Robinson's No 1 Ribs** • 655 W Armitage Ave
- **Salvatore's Ristorante** • 525 W Arlington Pl
- **Sedgwick's Bar & Grill** • 1935 N Sedgwick St
- **Sushi O Sushi** • 346 W Armitage Ave
- **Sushi Para II** • 2256 N Clark St
- **Swirlz Cupcakes** • 705 W Belden Ave
- **Taco Burrito Palace #2** • 2441 N Halsted St
- **Tilli's** • 1952 N Halsted St
- **Toro** • 2546 N Clark St
- **Twin Anchors** • 1655 N Sedgwick St
- **Vinci** • 1732 N Halsted St
- **Wiener's Circle** • 2622 N Clark St

Shopping

- **A New Leaf** • 1818 N Wells St
- **Art & Science** • 1971 N Halsted St
- **Barneys New York Co-Op** • 2209 N Halsted St
- **Buy Popular Demand** • 2629 N Halsted St
- **Cynthia Rowley** • 808 W Armitage Ave
- **Dave's Records** • 2604 N Clark St
- **Ethan Allen** • 1700 N Halsted St
- **GNC** • 2740 N Clark St
- **Lori's Designer Shoes** • 824 W Armitage Ave
- **Lululemon** • 2104 N Halsted St
- **Nau** • 2118 N Halsted St
- **Old Town Triangle** • 1763 N North Park Ave
- **Sally Beauty Supply** • 2727 N Clark St
- **White Elephant** • 2300 Children's Plz

With its narrow, cobble-stoned streets lined with Queen Anne-style homes and rehabbed cottages, Old Town's appropriate moniker perfectly encapsulates its nineteenth century charms. Once the infamous epicenter of '60s bohemian counterculture, the historic area is now home to upscale independent shops, restaurants, and the crumbling Cabrini Green housing projects.

Banks

- **Bank of America** • 1419 N Wells St
- **Chase** • 1350 N Wells St
- **Chase** • 424 W Division St
- **Chase (ATM)** • 1200 N Sandburg Terrace
- **Chase (ATM)** • 1599 N Clybourn Ave
- **Chase (ATM)** • Walgreens • 1601 N Wells St
- **Chase (ATM)** • 820 N La Salle Dr
- **Citibank** • 1525 N Wells St
- **Fifth Third** • 837 W North Ave
- **First American (ATM)** • 1317 N Wells St
- **First American (ATM)** • 1500 N Wells St
- **First American (ATM)** • 1543 N Sedgwick St
- **First American (ATM)** • Amoco/BP • 1560 N Halsted St
- **First American (ATM)** • 160 W Division St
- **LaSalle** • 1565 N Clybourn Ave
- **LaSalle (ATM)** • 900 N North Branch St
- **North Community** • 1561 N Wells St
- **Washington Mutual** • 1565 N La Salle Blvd
- **Washington Mutual** • 609 W North Ave

Car Washes

- **Gold Coast Car Wash** • 875 N Orleans St
- **We'll Clean** • 1520 N Halsted St

Car Rental

- **Enterprise** • 523 W North Ave • 312-482-8322

Gas Stations

- **Mobil** • 1234 N Halsted Ave

oLandmarks

- **Steppenwolf Theatre** • 1650 N Halsted St

Libraries

- **Near North Public Library** • 310 W Division St

Parking

Pharmacies

- **Dominick's** • 424 W Division St ⊚
- **Walgreens** • 1601 N Wells St ⊚

Pizza

- **Corlioni Pizzeria** • 349 W Oak St
- **Domino's** • 143 W Division St
- **Marcello's Father & Son Restaurant** • 645 W North Ave
- **Mangia Roma** • 1623 N Halsted St
- **Old Towne Pizza Pub** • 1339 N Wells St
- **Pizza Ria** • 1599 N Clybourn Ave

Police

- **18th District (Near North)** • 1160 N Larrabee St

Schools

- **Catherine Cook Elementary** • 226 W Schiller St
- **Catherine Ferguson CPC** • 1420 N Hudson Ave
- **Chicago Grammar** • 900 N Franklin St
- **Cornerstone Academy** • 1111 N Wells St, 4th Fl
- **Edward Jenner Academy of the Arts** • 1119 N Cleveland Ave
- **Franklin Fine Arts Center** • 225 W Evergreen Ave
- **Friedrick Von Schiller Middle** • 640 W Scott St
- **George Manierre Elementary** • 1420 N Hudson Ave
- **Immaculate Conception** • 1431 N North Park Ave
- **Lake Shore Preparatory** • 300 W Hill St
- **Moody Bible Institute** • 820 N La Salle Blvd
- **Ruben Salazar Bilingual Education Center** • 160 W Wendell St
- **Walter Payton Preparatory** • 1034 N Wells St

Supermarkets

- **Dominick's** • 424 W Division St ⊚

Old Jerusalem, the venerable shawarma and falafel stop, is an inexpensive Middle Eastern alternative to neighborhood's often pricey eateries. Fudge Pot freshly bakes up its chewy namesake and molds chocolate into any shape imaginable. Drink to life or drown your sorrows until 4 am with an eclectic mix of barflies and colorful locals at Old Town Ale House.

Coffee
- **Dunkin' Donuts** • 1234 N Halsted St
- **Dunkin' Donuts** • 333 W North Ave
- **Einstein Bros Bagels** • 1549 N Wells St
- **Starbucks** • 1229 N Clybourn Ave
- **Starbucks** • 200 W North Ave
- **Starbucks** • 424 W Division St

Copy Shops
- **The UPS Store** • 1235 N Clybourn Ave
- **The UPS Store** • 333 W North Ave

Farmers Markets
- **City Farm (Jun–Oct; 3 pm–7 pm)** •
  1204 N Clybourn Ave

Gyms
- **A Women's Gym (women only)** • 1248 N Wells St
- **Crunch Fitness** • 820 N Orleans St
- **Energy Training Center** • 900 N North Branch St
- **Fitness Formula** • 1235 N La Salle Dr
- **Wells St Athletic Club** • 1513 N Wells St
- **XSport Fitness** • 230 W North Ave ⊕

Hardware Stores
- **Tipre Hardware** • 229 W North Ave

Liquor Stores
- **Galleria Liquor** • 1559 N Wells St
- **Green Oak Food & Liquor** • 956 N Larrabee St
- **House of Glunz** • 1206 N Wells St
- **Old Town Liquors** • 1200 N Wells St
- **Ollie's Food** • 1012 N Larrabee St

Movie Theaters
- **AMC Loews Pipers Alley 4** • 1608 N Wells St

Nightlife
- **boutique** • 809 W Evergreen Ave
- **Burton Place** • 1447 N Wells St
- **McGinney's Tap** • 313 W North Ave
- **Old Town Ale House** • 219 W North Ave
- **Spoon** • 1240 N Wells St
- **Weeds** • 1555 N Dayton St
- **Zanies Comedy Club** • 1548 N Wells St

Pet Shops
- **Collar & Leash** • 1435 N Wells St
- **Furry Beastro** • 1500 N Wells St
- **Old Town Aquarium (Fish only)** • 1538 N Wells St
- **Shure Pets** • 1556 N La Salle Dr

Restaurants
- **Bistrot Margot** • 1437 N Wells St
- **Chic Café** • Cooking and Hospitality Institute • 361 W Chestnut St
- **Dinotto Ristorante** • 215 W North Ave
- **Fireplace Inn** • 1448 N Wells St
- **Fresh Choice** • 1534 N Wells St
- **Garlic and Chili** • 1232 N La Salle Dr
- **Kamehachi** • 1400 N Wells St
- **Kiki's Bistro** • 900 N Franklin St
- **Las Pinatas** • 1552 N Wells St
- **Mangia Roma** • 1623 N Halsted St
- **Michael's** • 101 W North Ave
- **Mizu** • 315 W North Ave
- **MK** • 868 N Franklin St
- **O'Brien's** • 1528 N Wells St
- **Old Jerusalem** • 1411 N Wells St
- **Old Town Brasserie** • 1209 N Wells St
- **Salpicon** • 1252 N Wells St
- **Topo Gigio Ristorante** • 1516 N Wells St
- **Wells on Wells** • 1617 N Wells St

Shopping
- **Crate & Barrel Outlet Store** • 1864 N Clybourn Ave
- **Etre** • 1361 N Wells St
- **Fleet Feet Sports** • 210 W North Ave
- **Fudge Pot** • 1532 N Wells St
- **Jumbalia** • 1429 N Wells St
- **Nicole Miller** • 1419 N Wells St
- **Old Town Gardens** • 1555 N Wells St
- **The Spice House** • 1512 N Wells St
- **Up Down Tobacco** • 1550 N Wells St
- **Village Cycle** • 1337 N Wells St

Video Rental
- **Blockbuster** • 400 W Division St
- **Video Shmideo** • 345 W North Ave

Map 32 • **Gold Coast / Mag Mile**

1

2

PAGE 226

Lincoln Park

N Sedgwick St
N Orleans St
N Lincoln Park W
N Cleveland Ave
W Menomonee St
W Willow St
W Saint Paul Ave
N Wells St
W Eugenie St
W Concord St
W Concord Ln
W Concord Pl

Sedgwick

N North Park Ave

30

W North Blvd

N Stockton Dr

N La Salle St

W Germania Pl

N Dearborn Pkwy

W Burton Pl

N State St

W Burton Pl

E Burton Pl

N Astor St

N Lake Shore Dr

W Schiller St

E Schiller St

Lake
Michigan

Charnley-Persky
House

41

N Orleans St

N North Park Ave

N Wieland St

Evergreen Ave

31

N Clark St

Old Playboy
Mansion

E Banks St

N Stone St

E Scott St

N Ritchie Ct

W Goethe St

W Scott St

N Sutton Pl

Clark/Division

E Division St

GOLD
COAST

N State St

E Elm St

E Cedar St

W Elm St

W Hill St

W Wendell St

E Bellevue
Pl

N Lake Shore Dr

W Maple St

Dr Scholl
College
of Podiatry

W Oak St
200W

Newberry
Library

N Dearborn St

100E

W Walton St

N Ernst Ct

3P

E Walton St

W Locust St

W Delaware Pl

John Hancock
Building

N Mies Van Der
Rohe Way

2P

W Delaware Pl

E Delaware Pl

2P

2P

E Chestnut St

41

W Chestnut St

Moody
Bible
Institute

800N

Water Tower
Place and Park

Lake Shore Drive
Apartments

W Institute Pl

Chicago

2

Loyola University
(Water Tower Campus)

Seneca
Park

Lake
Shore
Park

3

W Chicago Ave

Chicago

E Chicago Ave

N Orleans St

N Franklin St

C

W Superior St

E Superior St

N La Salle Dr

W Huron St

N Clark St

W Erie St

N Dearborn St

W Ontario St

N Wabash Ave

W Ontario St

N State St

W Ohio St

N Rush St

E Erie St

N Michigan Ave

N Saint Clair St

E Ontario St

N Fairbanks Ct

N McClurg Ct

E Huron St

E Ohio St

Milton Lee
Olive Park

N Peshtigo Ct

Grand

E Ohio St

E Grand Ave

E Illinois St

1/4 mile

.25 km

Between the tourist traps like Navy Pier, sticky bars on Division Street, and pick-up joints on Rush (that's the Viagra Triangle to you and me), it's easy for locals to make fun. But the Gold Coast/Mag Mile (actually only three-quarters of a mile, but who's counting?) is also home to some of Chicago's most impressive architecture, libraries (including the Newberry), and beautiful beaches.

$ Banks

- **Bank of America** • 1167 N State St
- **Bank of America (ATM)** • 45 W Division St
- **Charter One** • 1201 N Clark St
- **Chase** • 1122 N Clark St
- **Chase** • John Hancock Ctr • 875 N Michigan Ave
- **Chase (ATM)** • Walgreens • 1200 N Dearborn St
- **Chase (ATM)** • Loyola University Water Tower • 25 E Pearson St
- **Chase (ATM)** • Walgreens • 933 N State St
- **Citibank** • 68 E Oak St
- **Delaware Place** • 190 E Delaware Pl
- **Diamond** • 100 W North Ave
- **Fifth Third** • 29 W Division St
- **First American (ATM)** • 163 E Walton Pl
- **First American (ATM)** • 8 W Division St
- **Harris Trust & Savings** • 1000 N Lakeshore Dr
- **LaSalle** • 940 N Michigan Ave
- **LaSalle (ATM)** • 1201 N State St
- **North Community** • 2 W Elm St
- **Northern Trust** • 120 E Oak St
- **Oak** • 1000 N Rush St
- **Park National** • 801 N Clark St
- **TCF** • Jewel • 1210 N Clark St
- **TCF (ATM)** • Osco • 1165 N Clark St
- **TCF (ATM)** • 7-Eleven • 921 N State St
- **Washington Mutual** • 1200 N State Pkwy

Car Rental

- **Enterprise** • 850 N State St • 312-951-6262
- **Hertz** • Westin • 909 N Michigan Ave • 312-481-5193

Gas Stations

- **Shell** • 130 W North Ave

Landmarks

- **Charnley-Persky House** • 1365 N Astor St
- **John Hancock Building** • 875 N Michigan Ave
- **Lake Shore Drive Apartments** • 860 Lake Shore Dr
- **The Newberry Library** • 60 W Walton St
- **Old Playboy Mansion** • 1340 N State St
- **Water Tower Place and Park** • 845 N Michigan Ave

Libraries

- **The Newberry Library** • 60 W Walton St

P Parking

Pharmacies

- **CVS** • 1165 N Clark St
- **CVS** • 1201 N State Pkwy ⊙
- **Walgreens** • 1200 N Dearborn St ⊙
- **Walgreens** • 933 N State St

Pizza

- **California Pizza Kitchen** • 835 N Michigan Ave
- **Chi-Town Pizza** • 11 W Division St
- **Edwardo's Natural Pizza** • 1212 N Dearborn St
- **Papa Milano** • 951 N State St
- **Pizano's Pizza & Pasta** • 864 N State St

Post Offices

- **US Post Office** • 875 N Michigan Ave

Schools

- **Archbishop Quigley Prep Seminary** • 103 E Chestnut St
- **Latin School of Chicago** • 59 W North Blvd
- **Loyola University (Downtown Campus)** • 820 N Michigan Ave
- **William B Ogden Elementary** • 24 W Walton St

Supermarkets

- **The Goddess and the Grocer** • 25 E Delaware Pl
- **Jewel-Osco** • 1210 N Clark St
- **Potash Brothers** • 1525 N Clark St
- **Potash Brothers** • 875 N State St
- **Treasure Island** • 75 W Elm St

Map 32 · **Gold Coast / Mag Mile**

N

1

2

Stockton Dr

PAGE
226
Lincoln
Park

W Menomonee St

W Willow St

W Saint Paul Ave

W Eugenie St

N Lincoln Park W

N Orleans St

N Wells St

W Concord Pl

W Concord Ln

N Sedgwick St

A

30

W North Blvd

Sedgwick

W Germania Pl

W Burton Pl

W Burton Pl

N Sandburg Ter

N State St

N Dearborn Pkwy

E Burton Pl

N Lake Shore Dr

W Schiller St

E Schiller St

N Astor St

N La Salle St

41

31

N Clark St

W Evergreen Ave

N Sutton Pl

E Banks St

N Ritchie Ct

N Stone St

*Lake
Michigan*

W Goethe St

W Scott St

N 120W

N Felton Ct

E Scott St

Clark/Division

5

E Division St

B

W Elm St

E Elm St

3

**GOLD
COAST**

2

E Cedar St

W Maple St

Dr Scho
College
of Podiatry

6

E Bellevue
Pl

N Lake Shore Dr

W Wendell St

4

W Oak St
200W

4

8

100E

W Walton St

100W

5

2

W Walton St

E Walton St

N Michigan Ave

N Lake Shore Dr

W Locust St

W Delaware Pl

2

W Delaware Pl

4

41

W Delaware Pl

N Ernst Ct

N Mies Van Der Rohe Way

W Chestnut St

2

W Chestnut St

**Moody
Bible
Institute**

E Chestnut St

W Institute Pl

2

E Pearson St

3

Chicago

2

**Loyola University
(Water Tower Campus)**

**Seneca
Park**

Lake Shore
Park

3

W Chicago Ave

Chicago

E Chicago Ave

C

W Superior St

E Superior St

N La Salle Dr

N Orleans St

N Franklin St

W Huron St

E Huron St

N Dearborn St

N Wabash Ave

N Rush St

N Michigan Ave

N St Clair St

N Fairbanks Ct

N McClurg Ct

W Erie St

E Erie St

W Ontario St

E Ontario St

N Mies Van Der
Rohe Way

N Peshtigo Ct

W Ohio St

N Clark St

N 109

N State St

E Ohio St

E Ohio St
**Milton Lee
Olive Park**

N Lake Shore Dr

Fair Ct

Grand

E Illinois St

E Grand Ave

| 1/4 mile | | .25 km | |

Gucci, The Ritz-Carlton, Chanel, Barney's, Prada; they don't call it the Gold Coast for nothing. But with Urban Outfitters and H&M, there's plenty for us regular folk as well. Splurge on creative Italian at Spiaggia or dress up and go old school as the Pump Room. And admit it: You've marveled at the view from atop the Hancock's Signature Lounge where Pina Coladas cost $12. Now that's classy.

Coffee

- **Argo Tea** • 819 N Rush St
- **Cyber Café** • 25 E Pearson St
- **Dunkin' Donuts** • 101 W Division St
- **Einstein Bros Bagels** • 44 E Walton St
- **Gloria Jean's Gourmet Coffee** • 1031 N State St
- **Maui's Kaanapali Estate Coffee** • 900 N Michigan Ave
- **Sarah's Pastries & Candies** • 11 E Oak St
- **Starbucks** • 1 E Delaware Pl
- **Starbucks** • 106 W Germania Pl
- **Starbucks** • 111 E Chestnut St
- **Starbucks** • 39 W Division St
- **Starbucks** • 828 N State St
- **Starbucks** • 932 N Rush St

Copy Shops

- **FedEx Kinko's** • 1201 N Dearborn St
- **Office Supply Store** • 875 N Michigan Ave
- **The UPS Store** • 47 W Division St

Farmers Markets

- **Near North (Jun–Oct; Sat, 7 am–2 pm)** • 15 W Division St

Gyms

- **Equinox** • 900 N Michigan Ave
- **Fitness Formula** • 1030 N Clark St

Hardware Stores

- **Gordon's Ace Hardware** • 24 W Maple St
- **Potash Bros Ace Hardware** • 110 W Germania Pl

Movie Theaters

- **The Alliance Francaise** • 810 N Dearborn St

Nightlife

- **Backroom** • 1007 N Rush St
- **Butch McGuire's** • 20 W Division St
- **Coq d'Or** • 140 E Walton St
- **Cru Wine Bar** • 25 E Delaware Pl
- **Dublin's** • 1050 N State St
- **Finn McCool's** • 15 W Division St
- **The Hunt Club** • 1100 N State St
- **Jilly's Retro Club** • 1007 N Rush St
- **Le Passage** • 937 N Rush St
- **Leg Room** • 7 W Division St
- **loft** • 15 W Division St
- **Mothers** • 26 W Division St
- **She-nanigans** • 16 W Division St
- **Signature Lounge** • John Hancock Ctr • 875 N Michigan Ave, 96th Fl
- **Underground Wonder Bar** • 10 E Walton St
- **The Whisky** • 1015 N Rush St
- **Zebra Lounge** • 1220 N State St

Pet Shops

- **Pet Stuff** • 1201 N Clark St
- **Tails in the City** • 1 E Delaware Pl

Restaurants

- **Ashkenaz** • 12 E Cedar St
- **Bistro 110** • 110 E Pearson St
- **Bistrot Zinc** • 1131 N State St
- **Café des Architectes** • Sofitel Chicago Water Tower • 20 E Chestnut St
- **Cape Cod Room** • Drake Hotel • 140 E Walton St
- **Carmine's** • 1043 N Rush St
- **Fornetto Mei** • 107 E Delaware Pl
- **Gibson's Steakhouse** • 1028 N Rush St
- **Hugo's Frog Bar & Fish House** • 1024 N Rush St
- **Il Mulino New York** • 1150 N Dearborn St
- **Le Colonial** • 937 N Rush St
- **Le Petit Paris** • 260 E Chestnut St
- **McCormick & Schmick's** • 41 E Chestnut St
- **Morton's of Chicago** • 1050 N State St
- **Original Pancake House** • 22 E Bellevue Pl
- **Pane Caldo** • 72 E Walton St
- **Pump Room** • Omni Ambassador East Hotel • 1301 N State Pkwy
- **Spiaggia** • 980 N Michigan Ave
- **Table Fifty-Two** • 52 W Elm St
- **Tavern on Rush** • 1031 N Rush St
- **Tempo** • 6 E Chestnut St ⊛
- **Tsunami** • 1160 N Dearborn St

Shopping

- **Anthropologie** • 1120 N State St
- **Barney's New York** • 25 E Oak St
- **BCBG** • 55 E Oak St
- **Bloomingdale's** • 900 N Michigan Ave
- **Bravco Beauty Center** • 43 E Oak St
- **Chanel at the Drake Hotel** • 935 N Michigan Ave
- **Club Monaco** • 900 N Michigan Ave
- **Diesel** • 923 N Rush St
- **Elements** • 102 E Oak St
- **Europa Books** • 832 N State St
- **Flight 001** • 1133 N State St
- **Frette** • 41 E Oak St
- **G'bani** • 949 N State St
- **Gucci** • 900 N Michigan Ave
- **H&M** • 840 N Michigan Ave
- **Hermes** • 110 E Oak St
- **Hershey's Chicago** • 822 N Michigan Ave
- **Intermix** • 40 E Delaware Pl
- **Jake** • 939 N Rush St
- **Lush Cosmetics** • 835 N Michigan Ave
- **MAC** • 40 E Oak St
- **Paul Stuart X/S** • John Hancock Ctr • 875 N Michigan Ave
- **Prada** • 30 E Oak St
- **Pratesi** • 67 E Oak St
- **Tod's** • 121 E Oak St
- **Ultimate Bride** • 106 E Oak St
- **Ultimo** • 114 E Oak St
- **Urban Outfitters** • 935 N Rush St
- **Water Tower** • 835 N Michigan Ave

Map 33 · **West Rogers Park**

N

1

2

Dobson St

W Howard St

W Jerome St

W Birchwood Ave

W Fargo Ave

W Jarvis Ave

W Sherwin Ave

W Chase Ave

N Kedzie Ave

N Albany Ave

N Sacramento Ave

N Francisco Ave

N California Ave

N Fairfield Ave

N Talman Ave

N Maplewood Ave

N Artesian Ave

N Campbell Ave

N Oakley Ave

N Bell Ave

N Ridge Blvd

N Hoyne Ave

W Birchwood

A

W Fargo Ave

W Jarvis Ave

W Chase Ave

Rogers Park/
West Ridge
Historical Society

Rogers Park

W Jarlath St

N Claremont Ave

N Bell Ave

N Hamilton Ave

W Touhy Ave

High Ridge
YMCA

Bernard
Horwich JCC

W Fitch Ave

W Touhy Ave

WEST ROGERS PARK

W Estes Ave

W Greenleaf Ave

W Greenleaf Ave

◄ **46**

W Estes Ave

W Lunt Ave

2800W

2400W

34 ►

W Coyle Ave

W Morse Ave

Indian Boundary
Park

N Wolcott Ave

N Rockwell St

N Washtenaw Ave

N Francisco St

N Mozart St

Lerner
Park

N Morse Ave

N Oakley Ave

N Bell Ave

N Hamilton Ave

B

W Farwell Ave

W Pratt Ave

N 6300

W Pratt Ave

Chippewa
Park

Warren Park

W North Shore Ave

N Western Ave

W Albion Ave

N Richmond St

N California Ave

N Fairfield Ave

N Washtenaw Ave

N Maplewood Ave

N Claremont Ave

N Oakley Ave

N Bell Ave

N Leavitt St

N Hamilton Ave

N Hoyne Ave

C

W Arthur Ave

N Troy Ave

N Albany Ave

N Whipple St

N Sacramento Ave

Thillen's
Stadium

W Devon Ave

Croatian
Cultural Center

India
Town

N Talman Ave

N Rockwell St

N Maplewood Ave

N Campbell Ave

N Artesian Ave

W Devon Ave

35

36

W Highland Ave

W Rosemont Ave

1/4 mile

.25 km

West Rogers Park has an intimate, residential feel that draws many families and retirees. Cultures mix fluidly in this community. Between the Hebrew schools, the Russian shops, and the Indian markets are residential streets and five different parks with batting cages, sledding hills, baseball diamonds, tennis courts, and jogging paths. Nice.

Banks

- **Chase** • 7015 N Western Ave
- **Chase (ATM)** • Walgreens • 7510 N Western Ave
- **Citibank** • 2801 W Devon Ave
- **Devon** • 6445 N Western Ave
- **First Commercial** • 2201 W Howard St
- **First Commercial** • 7050 N Western Ave
- **LaSalle** • 2545 W Devon Ave
- **LaSalle** • 2855 W Touhy Ave
- **Shore Bank** • 7555 N California Ave
- **TCF (ATM)** • 7-Eleven • 2200 W Devon Ave
- **TCF (ATM)** • 7-Eleven • 2741 W Touhy Ave
- **TCF (ATM)** • Osco • 2825 W Devon Ave

Car Washes

- **Fast Carwash** • 7139 N Western Ave

Gas Stations

- **Marathon** • 7130 N Western Ave

Landmarks

- **Bernard Horwich JCC** • 3003 W Touhy Ave
- **Croatian Cultural Center** • 2845 W Devon Ave
- **High Ridge YMCA** • 2424 W Touhy Ave
- **India Town** • W Devon Ave, near Washtenaw Ave
- **Indian Boundary Park** • 2500 W Lunt Ave
- **Rogers Park/West Ridge Historical Society** • 7344 N Western Ave
- **Thillen's Stadium** • Devon & Kedzie Ave
- **Warren Park** • 6601 N Western Ave

Libraries

- **Northtown Public Library** • 6435 N California Ave

Pharmacies

- **CVS** • 2825 W Devon Ave
- **Walgreens** • 7510 N Western Ave ⊙

Pizza

- **Domino's** • 3144 W Devon Ave
- **Eastern Style Pizza** • 2911 W Touhy Ave
- **Gulliver's Pizzeria & Restaurant** • 2727 W Howard St
- **Pizza Hut** • 951 Howard St
- **Villa Palermo Pizza** • 2154 W Devon Ave

Schools

- **ABC Academy Inc** • 2714 W Pratt Bl
- **Bethesda Lutheran Elementary** • 6803 N Campbell Ave
- **Brisk Academy - Yeshivas Brisk** • 3000 W Devon Ave
- **Consolidated Hebrew High** • 2828 W Pratt Blvd
- **Daniel Boone Elementary** • 6710 N Washtenaw Ave
- **Decatur Classical** • 7030 N Sacramento Ave
- **George Armstrong Elementary** • 2110 W Greenleaf Ave
- **Hanna Sacks Girls' High** • 3021 W Devon Ave
- **Ida Crown Jewish Academy** • 2828 W Pratt Blvd
- **Jewish Children Bureau** • 3145 W Pratt Blvd
- **Lubavitch Boy's High** • 2756 W Morse Ave
- **Rogers Elementary** • 7345 N Washtenaw Ave
- **St Margaret Mary Elementary** • 7318 N Oakley Ave
- **St Scholastica High** • 7416 N Ridge Blvd
- **Virginia Frank Child Dev Center** • 3033 W Touhy Ave
- **Yeshiva Shearis Yisroel** • 2620 W Touhy Ave

Supermarkets

- **Jewel-Osco** • 2485 W Howard St
- **New York Kosher** • 2900 W Devon Ave
- **North Water Market** • 2626 W Devon Ave

Coffee

- **Dunkin' Donuts** • 3132 W Devon Ave
- **Dunkin' Donuts** • 7578 N Western Ave

Copy Shops

- **Progress Press** • 7315 N Western Ave
- **UNIK Business Center** • 2337 W Devon Ave

Gyms

- **Curves (women only)** • 7300 N Western Ave
- **High Ridge YMCA** • 2424 W Touhy Ave

Hardware Stores

- **Basco Plumbing & True Value** • 2953 W Devon Ave
- **Chicago Coast True Value** • 6942 N Western Ave

Liquor Stores

- **Adelphi Liquors** • 2351 W Devon Ave
- **M&Y Liquor & Grocery Store** • 2252 W Devon Ave
- **Old City Liquor Limited** • 2222 W Devon Ave

Nightlife

- **Cary's Lounge** • 2251 W Devon Ave
- **McKellin's** • 2800 W Touhy Ave
- **Mullen's Sports Bar and Grill** • 7301 N Western Ave

Restaurants

- **Afghan Restaurant** • 2818 W Devon Ave
- **Annapurna** • 2608 W Devon Ave
- **Arya Bhavan** • 2508 W Devon Ave
- **Ben Tre** • 3146 W Touhy Ave
- **Café Montenegro** • 6954 N Western Ave
- **Candlelite** • 7452 N Western Ave
- **Chopal** • 2240 W Devon Ave
- **Ghandi India Restaurant** • 2601 W Devon Ave
- **Good Morgan Kosher Fish Market** • 2948 W Devon Ave
- **Hashalom** • 2905 W Devon Ave

- **Hema's Kitchen** • 6406 N Oakley Ave
- **Indian Garden** • 2546 W Devon Ave
- **Mysore Woodland's** • 2548 W Devon Ave
- **Siam Pasta** • 7416 N Western Ave
- **Sukhadia's** • 2559 W Devon Ave
- **Tiffin** • 2536 W Devon Ave
- **U Lucky Dawg** • 6821 N Western Ave
- **Udupi Palace** • 2543 W Devon Ave
- **Uru-Swati** • 2629 W Devon Ave
- **Viceroy of India** • 2520 W Devon Ave

Shopping

- **Argo Georgian Bakery** • 2812 W Devon Ave
- **Al Mansoor** • 2600 W Devon Ave
- **AutoZone** • 2555 W Touhy Ave
- **Cheesecakes by JR** • 2841 W Howard St
- **Chicago Harley Davidson** • 6868 N Western Ave
- **Levinson's Bakery** • 2856 W Devon Ave
- **Office Mart** • 2801 W Touhy Ave
- **Raj Jewels** • 2652 W Devon Ave
- **Resham's** • 2540 W Devon Ave
- **Taj Sari Palace** • 2553 W Devon Ave
- **Tel-Aviv Kosher Bakery** • 2944 W Devon Ave
- **Three Sisters Deli** • 2854 W Devon Ave

Video Rental

- **Atlantic Video Rentals (Indian)** • 2541 W Devon Ave
- **Blockbuster Videos** • 7300 N Western Ave
- **Elita Video (Russian)** • 2753 W Devon Ave
- **Golden Video** • 2761 W Devon Ave
- **New Devon Video** • 2304 W Devon Ave
- **Super Star Video (Indian and Pakistani)** • 2538 W Devon Ave
- **Sur Sangeet Video (Indian)** • 2521 W Devon Ave
- **Western Video** • 7424 N Western Ave

Loyola students, civic-minded young professionals, new immigrants, and old hippies populate this dense and lively 'hood. It's becoming increasingly more unaffordable to inhabit, but the middle-class residents keep fighting to keep the area mixed income. The lakefront, easy access to public transportation, cultural diversity, and Loyola Campus make it pleasant, although crime and gang activity continue to be a problem.

$ Banks

- **Bank of America (ATM)** • 6359 N Broadway St
- **Chase** • 1763 W Howard St
- **Chase** • 6415 N Sheridan Rd
- **Chase (ATM)** • 1523 W Jarvis Ave
- **Chase (ATM)** • 6525 N Sheridan Rd
- **Chase (ATM)** • Walgreens • 7410 N Clark St
- **Citibank (ATM)** • 6401 N Sheridan Rd
- **First American (ATM)** • 6604 N Sheridan Rd
- **First American (ATM)** • 6740 N Ridge Blvd
- **First Commercial** • 6930 N Clark St
- **First Commercial** • 6945 N Clark St
- **Harris Trust & Savings** • 6538 N Sheridan Rd
- **LaSalle** • 7516 N Clark St
- **LaSalle (ATM)** • 7507 N Clark St
- **MB Financial** • 6443 N Sheridan Rd
- **TCF (ATM)** • 7-Eleven • 1404 W Pratt Blvd
- **Washington Mutual** • 1425 W Morse Ave

Car Washes

- **Rogers Park Auto Body Shop** • 6828 N Clark St

Gas Stations

- **Citgo** • 1500 W Devon Ave
- **Citgo** • 7138 N Sheridan Rd
- **Marathon** • 7550 N Sheridan Rd
- **Mobil** • 7201 N Clark St
- **Shell** • 6346 N Clark St
- **Shell** • 6401 N Ridge Blvd

Landmarks

- **Angel Guardian Croatian Catholic Church** • 6346 N Ridge Ave
- **Robert A Black Golf Course** • 2045 W Pratt Blvd

Libraries

- **Rogers Park Public Library** • 6907 N Clark St

Parking

Pizza

- **Carmen's of Loyola Pizzeria** • 6568 N Sheridan Rd
- **Giordano's** • 6836 N Sheridan Rd
- **Hamilton's Pub** • 6341 N Broadway St
- **JB Alberto's** • 1324 W Morse Ave
- **Leona's** • 6935 N Sheridan Rd
- **Vince's Pizzeria** • 1527 W Devon Ave

Police

- **24th District (Rogers Park)** • 6464 N Clark St

Post Offices

- **US Post Office** • 1723 W Devon Ave
- **US Post Office** • 7056 N Clark St
- **US Post Office** • 7617 N Paulina St

Schools

- **Chicago Math & Science Academy** • 1709 W Lunt Ave
- **Chicago Waldorf** • 1300 W Loyola Ave
- **Eugene Field Elementary** • 7019 N Ashland Blvd
- **Jordan Elementary** • 7414 N Wolcott Ave
- **Joyce Kilmer Elementary** • 6700 N Greenview Ave
- **Loyola University of Chicago** • 6525 N Sheridan Rd
- **New Field Primary** • 1707 W Morse Ave
- **North Shore Academy for Children** • 6711 N Sheridan Rd
- **Pactt Learning Center** • 7101 N Greenview Ave
- **Paideia Academy** • 6631 N Bosworth Ave
- **Peace Academy** • 6631 N Bosworth Ave
- **Roger C Sullivan High** • 6631 N Bosworth Ave

Supermarkets

- **Dominick's** • 1763 W Howard St
- **Morse Fruit & Meat Market** • 1430 W Morse Ave
- **New Leaf Natural Grocery** • 1261 W Loyola Ave
- **Rogers Park Fruit Market** • 7401 N Clark St

Heartland Café, featuring health-nut fare, a lefty gift shop, and live music, is the grand-papi stop. Mexican eateries offering authentic food at low prices dot Clark Street, while Howard Street's Caribbean American Bakery and Tickie's give you a sweet taste of Afro-Caribbean culture. The gay bar Jackhammer features an all-welcoming queer talent showcase.

Coffee

- **Charmers** • 1500 W Jarvis Ave
- **Dunkin' Donuts** • 1200 W Loyola Ave
- **Dunkin' Donuts** • 6970 N Clark St
- **Ennui Café** • 6981 N Sheridan Rd
- **Starbucks** • Dominick's • 1763 W Howard St
- **Starbucks** • 6738 N Sheridan Rd

Copy Shops

- **SOS Copies** • 6604 N Sheridan Rd
- **The UPS Store** • 1400 W Devon Ave

Farmers Markets

- **Loyola/Rogers Park**
  (Jul–Oct, some sundays, 7 am–2 pm) •
  W Devon Ave & N Broadway St

Gyms

- **Bally Total Fitness** • 7529 N Clark St

Hardware Stores

- **Clark-Devon Hardware** • 6401 N Clark St

Liquor Stores

- **Dino's Liquors** • 6400 N Clark St
- **Golden Valley Liquors** • 1339 W Morse Ave
- **Hahn Liquors** • 1410 W Devon Ave
- **Lian's Liquor & Grocery** • 6507 N Clark St
- **Morse Liquors** • 1400 W Morse Ave
- **Sandy's Food & Meat Market** •
  1534 W Howard St
- **Summit Grocery** • 7300 N Rogers Ave

Movie Theaters

- **Village North Theaters** • 6746 N Sheridan Rd

Nightlife

- **Duke's Bar** • 6920 N Glenwood Ave
- **Hamilton's Pub** • 6341 N Broadway St
- **Jackhammer** • 6406 N Clark St
- **Lamp Post** • 7126 N Ridge Blvd
- **No Exit** • 6970 N Glenwood Ave
- **Poitin Stil** • 1502 W Jarvis Ave
- **Red Line Tap** • 7006 N Glenwood Ave
- **Touche** • 6412 N Clark St

Pet Shops

- **Aquarium Gem** • 6623 N Clark St

Restaurants

- **A&T Grill** • 7026 N Clark St
- **Buffalo Joe's** • 1841 W Howard St
- **Café Suron** • 1146 W Pratt Blvd
- **Capt'n Nemos** • 7367 N Clark St
- **Caribbean American Bakery** • 1539 W Howard St
- **Dagel & Beli Shop** • 7406 N Greenview Ave
- **Deluxe Diner** • 6349 N Clark St ⊙
- **El Famous Burrito** • 7047 N Clark St
- **Ennui Café** • 6981 N Sheridan Rd
- **Ghareeb Nawaz** • 2032 W Devon Ave
- **Grande Noodles and Sushi Bar** • 6632 N Clark St
- **Heartland Café** • 7000 N Glenwood Ave
- **La Cazuela Mariscos** • 6922 N Clark St
- **Lake Side Café** • 1418 W Howard St
- **Morseland** • 1218 W Morse Ave
- **Panini Panini** • 6764 N Sheridan Rd
- **Quesadillas y Mariscos Dona Lolis** • 6924 N Clark St
- **Taste of Peru** • 6545 N Clark St
- **Thai Spice** • 1320 W Devon Ave
- **Tickie's Belizean Cuisine** • 7605 N Paulina St

Shopping

- **Mar-Jen Discount Furniture** • 1536 W Devon Ave
- **New Leaf Natural Grocery** • 1261 W Loyola Ave

Video Rental

- **Hollywood Video** • 1751 W Howard St
- **Pratt Video** • 6810 N Sheridan Rd
- **Syed Video** • 6808 N Clark St

This quiet enclave snuggled between the Chicago River and Rosehill Cemetery is home to many Koreans, Middle Easterners, and Eastern Europeans. Seedy hotels on Lincoln Avenue, once reputable, are being torn down due to their less-than-stellar reputations, making the area desirable for young families priced out of Ravenswood and Andersonville.

Banks

- **Charter One** • 5650 N Lincoln Ave
- **Chase** • 5224 N Lincoln Ave
- **Chase (ATM)** • 5233 N Lincoln Ave
- **Chase (ATM)** • Walgreens • 3019 W Peterson Ave
- **Chase (ATM)** • Walgreens • 5627 N Lincoln Ave
- **Citibank (ATM)** • 5562 N Lincoln Ave
- **First Commercial** • 2935 W Peterson Ave
- **TCF (ATM)** • 7-Eleven • 5562 N Lincoln Ave
- **Washington Mutual** • 5341 N Lincoln Ave

Gas Stations

- **BP** • 2751 W Peterson Ave
- **Citgo** • 5447 N Kedzie Ave
- **Citgo** • 5547 N Kedzie Ave
- **Marathon** • 2500 W Peterson Ave
- **Mobil** • 2758 W Peterson Ave

Landmarks

- **Lincoln Avenue Motels** • N Lincoln Ave b/w W Foster Ave & W Devon Ave

Libraries

- **Budlong Woods Public Library** • 5630 N Lincoln Ave

Pharmacies

- **Walgreens** • 3019 W Peterson Ave ⊚
- **Walgreens** • 5627 N Lincoln Ave

Pizza

- **T's Grand Slam Pizza** • 5701 N California Ave
- **Tel Aviv Kosher Pizza** • 6349 N California Ave

Police

- **20th District (Foster)** • 5400 N Lincoln Ave

Schools

- **Budlong Elementary** • 2701 W Foster Ave
- **DeWitt Clinton Elementary** • 6110 N Fairfield Ave
- **Joan Dachs Bais Yaakov Elementary** • 3200 W Peterson Ave
- **Joan Dachs Bais Yaakov Elementary** • 6110 N California Ave
- **Kiddie Kollege** • 6025 N California Ave
- **Little Harvard Academy** • 2708 W Peterson Ave
- **Lubavitch Girls High** • 2754 W Rosemont Ave
- **Minnie Mars Jamieson Elementary** • 5650 N Mozart St
- **NAES College** • 2838 W Peterson Ave
- **North Shore SDA Junior Academy** • 5220 N California Ave
- **Northside College Preparatory** • 5501 N Kedzie Ave
- **St Hilary Elementary** • 5614 N Fairfield Ave
- **St Philip Lutheran** • 2500 W Bryn Mawr Ave
- **Stuart G Ferst** • 6050 N California Ave
- **Telshe Yeshiva Chicago** • 3535 W Foster Ave
- **Victor V Neumann Alternative** • 2447 W Granville Ave
- **Yeshivas Tiferes Tzvi** • 6122 N California Ave

Supermarkets

- **Aldi** • 6220 N California Ave
- **Dominick's** • 5233 N Lincoln Ave

Of the bazillion tiny, unassuming Korean, Japanese, and Middle Eastern storefront restaurants peppering Peterson and Lincoln Avenues, Fondue Stube and Katsu stand out, as does Café Orange for its tentative nod at hipness—an unspeakable pretension in these parts. Local couples drink at Hidden Cove or Emerald Isle. Charcoal Delights has the best gyros this side of Greektown.

Coffee

- **Café Utjeha** • 5350 N Lincoln Ave
- **Dunkin' Donuts** • 5200 N Lincoln Ave
- **Dunkin' Donuts** • 5723 N California Ave
- **Starbucks** • 6075 N Lincoln Ave

Gyms

- **Curves (women only)** • 5360 N Lincoln Ave

Liquor Stores

- **California Food And Liquor** • 6343 N California Ave
- **Eden Liquor Store & Foods** • 5359 N Lincoln Ave

Nightlife

- **Emerald Isle** • 2537 W Peterson Ave
- **Hidden Cove** • 5338 N Lincoln Ave

Restaurants

- **Aztecas Mexican Taqueria** • 5421 N Lincoln Ave
- **Café Orange** • 5639 N Lincoln Ave
- **Charcoal Delights** • 3139 W Foster Ave
- **Fondue Stube** • 2717 W Peterson Ave
- **Garden Buffet** • 5347 N Lincoln Ave
- **IHOP** • 5929 N Lincoln Ave
- **Katsu** • 2651 W Peterson Ave
- **Pueblito Viejo** • 5429 N Lincoln Ave
- **Solga** • 5828 N Lincoln Ave
- **Sweet Collective** • 5333 N Lincoln Ave
- **Wolfy's** • 2734 W Peterson Ave
- **Woo Chon** • 5744 N California Ave

Shopping

- **Grazer's Gourmet** • 5333 N Lincoln Ave

Video Rental

- **Tom Video** • 5806 N Lincoln Ave

Bowmanville, Andersonville's low-rent sibling, has had a flirtation with gentrification, but the toniest residents are still the luminaries interred at Rosehill Cemetery, including Montgomery Ward, Richard Sears, Oscar Mayer, several Chicago mayors, and one Vice President (Charles Gates Dawes). At 350 acres, Chicago's largest cemetery barely leaves room for the car dealerships along Western Avenue.

$ Banks

- **Chase** • 6210 N Western Ave
- **Chase (ATM)** • Walgreens • 6236 N Western Ave
- **Citibank (ATM)** • 7-Eleven • 1750 W Foster Ave
- **Citibank (ATM)** • 7-Eleven • 5206 N Western Ave
- **Citibank (ATM)** • 7-Eleven • 6001 N Western Ave
- **North Community** • 5241 N Western Ave
- **TCF (ATM)** • 7-Eleven • 1750 W Foster Ave
- **TCF (ATM)** • 7-Eleven • 5206 N Western Ave
- **TCF (ATM)** • 7-Eleven • 6001 N Western Ave

Car Washes

- **Norwood 2 Hand Carwash** • 5462 N Damen Ave

Car Rental

- **Enterprise** • 5844 N Western Ave • 773-989-3390
- **Hertz** • 5534 N Western Ave • 773-506-2125

Gas Stations

- **Citgo** • 1840 W Peterson Ave
- **Citgo** • 5300 N Western Ave
- **Shell** • 5201 N Western Ave
- **Shell** • 6000 N Western Ave

o Landmarks

- **Rosehill Cemetery and Mausoleum** • 5800 N Ravenswood Ave

Pharmacies

- **Walgreens** • 6236 N Western Ave

Pizza

- **Delisi's Pizzeria** • 5806 N Western Ave
- **Fireside Restaurant & Lounge** • 5739 N Ravenswood Ave

Schools

- **Eliza Chappell Elementary** • 2135 W Foster Ave
- **Rogers Park Montessori** • 1800 W Balmoral Ave
- **Stone Scholastic Academy** • 6239 N Leavitt St

Map 36 • **Bryn Mawr / Bowmanville**

N

1

2

W Arthur Ave

N Clark St

W Loyola Ave

W Arthur Ave

N Rockwell St

N Maplewood Ave

N Campbell Ave

N Oakley Ave

N Bell Ave

N Leavitt St

N Hamilton Ave

N Hoyne Ave

N Seeley Ave

N Winchester Ave

N Ridge Ave

W Schreiber Ave

N Paulina St

W Schreiber Ave

2400W

N Ashland Ave

W Highland

33

W Devon Ave

34

W Highland Ave

W Highland Ave

WEST ROGERS PARK

N Paulina St

W Thome Ave

A

N Western Ave

W Rosemont Ave

W Thome Ave

W Thome Ave

Emerson Park

N Ravenswood Ave

N Hermitage Ave

W Glenlake Ave

W Thome Ave

N Artesian Ave

N Claremont Ave

W Granville Ave

N Carmen Ave

W Hood Ave

N Winchester Ave

N Wolcott Ave

Green Briar Park

W Glenlake Ave

N Hamilton Ave

N Seeley Ave

W Norwood St

N Hermitage Ave

N0009

W Peterson A

2400W

N0009

2000W

14

W Peterson Ave

Ridge Ave

N Ravenswood Ave

N Hermitage Ave

N Paulina St

35

W Thorndale Ave

W Thorndale Ave

37

W Ardmore Ave

W Rosehill Dr

1600W

W Ardmore

B

Rosehill Cemetery

W Edgewater Ave

W Victori

W Ardmore Ave

N0005

W Hollywood Ave

W Hollywood Ave

N Clark St

W Olive Ave

N Paulina St

W Bryn Mawr Ave

W Bryn Mawr Ave

W Gregory St

Lincoln Ave

N0009

W Catalpa Ave

N Damen Ave

N Campbell Ave

W Rascher Ave

W Rascher Ave

N Bowmanville Ave

N Hoyne Ave

N Winchester Ave

N Wolcott Ave

N Ravenswood Ave

N Ravenswood Ave

W Balmoral Ave

BOWMANVILLE

W Summerdale Ave

C

W Summerdale Ave

W Berwyn Ave

W Berwyn Ave

N Bell Ave

N Oakley Ave

W Farragut Ave

N Honore St

W Farragut Ave

N0005

W Foster Ave

N0005

N Ravenswood Ave

1600W

N Ashland Ave

41

W Foster Ave

39

2400W

N Clarmont Ave

N Western Ave

W Winona St

W Winona St

W Winona St

W Carmen Ave

Winnemac Park

1/4 mile

.25 km

More family and Fido friendly than uber-chic, the area that circles Rosehill Cemetery is largely residential with a sprinkling of serviceable restaurants and dive bars. Dependable Fireside Restaurant and Lounge with its coveted 4 am liquor license is the place to be when the 2 am bars close. Locals swear by artsy oddball Leadway Bar and Café.

Map

⊡ Coffee

- **Dunkin' Donuts** • 1954 W Peterson Ave
- **Dunkin' Donuts** • 6254 N Western Ave
- **Starbucks** • 2112 W Peterson Ave

⬤ Liquor Stores

- **Diala Grocery & Liquor** • 1935 W Foster Ave
- **Foster Food & Liquor** • 1900 W Foster Ave
- **L&M Food & Liquor** • 1968 W Peterson Ave

▼ Nightlife

- **Big Joe's 2 & 6 Pub** • 1818 W Foster Ave
- **Claddagh Ring** • 2306 W Foster Ave
- **Fireside Restaurant & Lounge** • 5739 N Ravenswood Ave
- **K's Dugout** • 1930 W Foster Ave
- **Leadway Bar & Café** • 5233 N Damen Ave
- **Mike's Ale House** • 5652 N Western Ave

⬤ Pet Shops

- **Four Paw Palace** • 2406 W Bryn Mawr Ave

⬤ Restaurants

- **Delisi's Pizzeria** • 5806 N Western Ave
- **Fireside Restaurant & Lounge** • 5739 N Ravenswood Ave
- **Greenhouse Inn** • 6300 N Ridge Ave
- **Max's Italian Beef** • 5754 N Western Ave
- **San Soo Gab San** • 5247 N Western Ave ⊚
- **Yes Thai** • 5211 N Damen Ave

⬤ Shopping

- **Target** • 2112 W Peterson Ave

Loyola

2

Loyola University (Lake Shore Campus)

PAGE 248

W Sheridan Rd

34

W Devon Ave

W Arthur Ave

W Schreiber Ave
W Schreiber Ave

N Ridge Ave

N Newgard Ave

N Wayne Ave

N Lakewood Ave

N Magnolia Ave

W Highland Ave
W Highland Ave

EDGEWATER

N Glenwood Ave

N Broadway St

W Rosemont Ave

N Kenmore Ave

N Sheridan Rd

Berger Park & Beach

N Ravenswood Ave

N Hermitage Ave

N Paulina St

N Clark St

N Greenview Ave

W Thome Ave
Emerson Park

A

W Thome Ave

W Granville Ave

Granville

W Hood Ave

W Glenlake Ave
W Glenlake Ave

EDGEWATER GLEN

N Winthrop Ave

3

W Norwood St

W Elmdale Ave

1600W

Senn Park

N Lakewood Ave

1200W

Thorndale

W Thorndale Ave

Lane Park & Beach

W Peterson Ave

N Hermitage Ave

N Paulina St

N Ridge Ave

N Clark St

W Thorndale Ave

W Rosedale Ave

3

MAGNOLIA GLEN

W Ardmore Ave

W Ardmore Ave

Rosehill Cemetery

36

W Victoria St

W Edgewater Ave

W Earls Ave

N Wayne Ave

N Magnolia Ave

W Victoria St

W Rosehill Dr

B

W Edgewater Ave

W Hollywood Ave

W Hollywood Ave

W Hollywood Ave

PAGE 226

Lincoln Park

N Paulina St

The Belle Shore Hotel Building

Bryn Mawr

2

W Bryn Mawr Ave

N Sheridan Rd

Edgewater Beach Apartments

W Bryn Mawr Ave
W Bryn Mawr Ave

14

N Wayne Ave

N Lakewood Ave

N Broadway St

41

W Gregory St

2

Philadelphia Church

W Catalpa Ave

W Rascher Ave
W Rascher Ave

W Catalpa Ave

N Winthrop Ave

N Kenmore Ave

P

ANDERSONVILLE

W Balmoral Ave

W Summerdale Ave

2

LAKEWOOD BALMORAL

2

Berwyn

W Berwyn Ave

N Wolcott Ave

N Ravenswood Ave

N Honore St

C

W Berwyn Ave

Swedish American Museum

Ann Sather Restaurant

W Farragut Ave

1600W

N Glenwood Ave

N Broadway St

1200W

W Berwyn Ave

39

N Ashland Ave

40

Foster Ave

Argyle

W Winona St

W Winona St

W Carmen Ave

W Carmen Ave

W Winnemac Ave

W Winnemac Ave

1/4 mile   .25 km

Andersonville and Edgewater are tranquil bastions for Chicago's "lakefront liberals." Besides beautiful residential areas and stroll-friendly commercial districts, Edgewater boasts the city's gay beach at Hollywood and the lakefront, not to mention the "lesbian Jewel." A'ville has gentrified, with swelling property taxes and encroaching chains, but its long-term denizens won't let it change quickly or quietly.

$ Banks

- **Bridgeview** • 1058 W Bryn Mawr Ave
- **Bridgeview** • 5345 N Sheridan Rd
- **Bridgeview** • 6041 N Clark St
- **Broadway** • 5960 N Broadway St
- **Chase** • 1055 W Bryn Mawr Ave
- **Chase** • 5715 N Broadway St
- **Chase** • 6009 N Broadway St
- **Chase (ATM)** • Walgreens • 5625 N Ridge Ave
- **Chase (ATM)** • Walgreens • 6125 N Broadway St
- **Chase (ATM)** • 6333 N Winthrop Ave
- **Chase (ATM)** • 5235 N Sheridan Rd
- **Citibank (ATM)** • 5340 N Clark St
- **First American (ATM)** • 5212 N Clark St
- **First Commercial** • 6033 N Sheridan Rd
- **Harris Trust & Savings (ATM)** • 6125 N Broadway St
- **North Community** • 5342 N Broadway St
- **North Side Federal Savings** • 5159 N Clark St
- **TCF** • 5343 N Broadway St
- **TCF** • 5516 N Clark St
- **TCF (ATM)** • 7-Eleven • 5623 N Clark St
- **TCF (ATM)** • Osco • 6150 N Broadway St
- **US** • 5340 N Clark St
- **Washington Mutual** • 5200 N Sheridan Rd
- **Washington Mutual** • 5531 N Clark St
- **Washington Mutual** • 5725 N Broadway St

⬤ Car Washes

- **Snappy Hand Car Wash** • 5961 N Ridge Ave
- **Super Spray Car Wash** • 5970 N Clark St
- **Superior Hand Car Wash** • 6147 N Broadway St

⬤ Car Rental

- **Enterprise** • 5313 N Sheridan Rd • 773-271-4500

⬤ Gas Stations

- **Clark Oil** • 1745 W Foster Ave
- **Marathon** • 5550 N Ashland Ave
- **Marathon** • 6262 N Clark St
- **Shell** • 5701 N Broadway St

○ Landmarks

- **Ann Sather** • 5207 N Clark St
- **The Belle Shore Hotel Building** • 1062 W Bryn Mawr Ave
- **Edgewater Beach Apartments** • 5555 N Sheridan Rd
- **Philadelphia Church** • 5437 N Clark St
- **Swedish American Museum** • 5211 N Clark St

⬤ Libraries

- **Edgewater Public Library** • 1210 W Elmdale Ave

℗ Parking

℞ Pharmacies

- **CVS** • 6150 N Broadway St
- **Dominick's** • 5235 N Sheridan Rd
- **Jewel-Osco** • 5343 N Broadway St ⊕
- **Jewel-Osco** • 5516 N Clark St ⊕
- **Walgreens** • 5625 N Ridge Ave ⊕
- **Walgreens** • 6125 N Broadway St

⬤ Pizza

- **Barry's Spot Pizza** • 5759 N Broadway St
- **Calo Pizzeria Restaurant** • 5343 N Clark St
- **Domino's** • 5912 N Clark St
- **Gino's North Pizzeria** • 1111 W Granville Ave
- **Homemade Pizza** • 5303 N Clark St
- **Pizza Mania** • 5777 N Ridge Ave
- **Pizzeria Aroma** • 1125 W Berwyn Ave
- **Primo Pizza** • 5600 N Clark St
- **Tedino's** • 5335 N Sheridan Rd

⬤ Schools

- **Helen C Peirce School of International Studies** • 1423 W Bryn Mawr Ave
- **Hyman G Rickover Navy Academy** • 5900 N Glenwood Ave
- **Jose J Marti Elementary** • 5126 N Kenmore Ave
- **Lake Shore** • 5611 N Clark St
- **Middle School Campus** • 5525 N Magnolia Ave
- **Northside Catholic Academy (St Gertrude Campus)** • 6216 N Glenwood Ave
- **Rogers Park Montessori (Thorndale)** • 1800 W Balmoral Ave
- **Sacred Heart** • 6250 N Sheridan Rd
- **Senn High** • 5900 N Glenwood Ave
- **St Gregory High** • 1677 W Bryn Mawr Ave
- **Stephen K Hayt Elementary** • 1518 W Granville Ave
- **Swift Elementary** • 5900 N Winthrop Ave
- **Trumbull Elementary** • 5200 N Ashland Ave

⬤ Supermarkets

- **Dominick's** • 5235 N Sheridan Rd
- **Dominick's** • 6009 N Broadway St
- **Edgewater Produce** • 5515 N Clark St
- **Jewel-Osco** • 5343 N Broadway St
- **Jewel-Osco** • 5516 N Clark St
- **True Nature Foods Community Market** • 6034 N Broadway St

No other neighborhood rewards a weekend afternoon ramble like Andersonville. Brunchers gorge on five-egg omelets at Pauline's, more precious fare at M. Henry, or Kopi, a crunchy café catering to backpackers, followed by casual shopping at independently-owned shops lining Clark Street. Catching an arty celluloid at Chicago Filmmakers is a popular hobby.

Coffee

- **A Taste of Heaven** • 5401 N Clark St
- **Coffee Chicago** • 5256 N Broadway St
- **Dunkin' Donuts** • 1127 W Bryn Mawr Ave
- **Dunkin' Donuts** • 6250 N Clark St
- **Dunkin' Donuts** • 6332 N Broadway St
- **Einstein Bros Bagels** • 5318 N Clark St
- **Icosium Kafe** • 5200 N Clark St
- **Kopi, A Traveler's Café** • 5317 N Clark St
- **Metropolis Coffee** • 1039 W Granville Ave
- **Pause** • 1107 W Berwyn Ave
- **Peacock Café** • 6014 N Broadway St
- **Screenz** • 5212 N Clark St
- **Starbucks** • 1070 W Bryn Mawr Ave
- **Starbucks** • 5300 N Clark St
- **Starbucks** • Dominick's •
  6009 N Broadway St
- **Trivoli Café** • 1147 W Granville Ave

Copy Shops

- **Edgraphx** • 5409 N Clark St
- **The UPS Store** • 1055 W Bryn Mawr Ave
- **The UPS Store** • 5315 N Clark St

Farmers Markets

- **Edgewater (Jun–Oct; Sat, 7 am–2 pm)** •
  N Broadway St & W Thorndale Ave

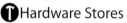Gyms

- **Cheetah Gym** • 5248 N Clark St
- **Cheetah Gym** • 5838 N Broadway St
- **Curves (women only)** •
  5339 N Sheridan Rd
- **Curves (women only)** •
  6118 N Broadway St

Hardware Stores

- **Cas Hardware Store** • 5305 N Clark St
- **Clarendon Electric & Hardware** •
  6050 N Broadway St
- **Marx Ace Hardware** • 5830 N Clark St

Liquor Stores

- **Buy Low Liquors** • 5201 N Clark St
- **Castle Wines & Spirits** •
  1128 W Thorndale Ave
- **Granville Liquors** •
  1100 W Granville Ave
- **In Fine Spirits** • 5418 N Clark St
- **J & H Food & Liquor** • 5652 N Clark St
- **Sun Liquors** • 1101 W Granville Ave

Movie Theaters

- **Chicago Filmmakers** • 5243 N Clark St

Nightlife

- **Charlie's Ale House** • 5308 N Clark St
- **Edgewater Lounge** • 5600 N Ashland Ave
- **Farraguts Tavern** • 5240 N Clark St
- **Granville Anvil** • 1137 Granville Ave
- **Joie de Vine** • 1744 W Balmoral Ave
- **Marty's Wine and Martini Bar** •
  1511 W Balmoral Ave
- **Moody's Pub** • 5910 N Broadway St
- **Ole St Andrew's Inn** • 5938 N Broadway St
- **Ollie's** • 1064 W Berwyn Ave
- **Pumping Company** •
  6157 N Broadway St
- **Simon's** • 5210 N Clark St
- **Sovereign** • 6202 N Broadway St
- **StarGaze** • 5419 N Clark St
- **@tmosphere** • 5355 N Clark St

Pet Shops

- **Fido Food Fair** • 5416 N Clark St
- **Ruff N'Stuff** • 5430 N Clark St
- **Scrub-A-Dub Dub** •
  1478 W Summerdale Ave

Restaurants

- **Alice and Friends Vegetarian Café** •
  5812 N Broadway St
- **Andie's** • 5253 N Clark St
- **Ann Sather** • 5207 N Clark St
- **Anteprima** • 5316 N Clark St
- **Ethiopian Diamond** •
  6120 N Broadway St
- **Flourish Bakery Café** • 1138
  W Bryn Mawr
- **Francesca's Bryn Mawr** •
  1039 W Bryn Mawr Ave
- **Hamburger Mary's** • 5400 N Clark St
- **Huey's Hot Dogs** • 1507 W Balmoral Ave
- **Icosium Kafe** • 5200 N Clark St
- **Indie Café** • 5951 N Broadway St
- **Jin Ju** • 5203 N Clark St
- **Kitty Moon** • 6237 N Clark St
- **La Fonda Latino** • 5350 N Broadway St
- **La Tache** • 1475 W Balmoral Ave
- **M Henry** • 5707 N Clark St
- **Moody's Pub** • 5910 N Broadway St
- **Pasticceria Natalina** • 5406 N Clark St
- **Pauline's** • 1754 W Balmoral Ave
- **Ras Dashen Ethiopian Restaurant** •
  5846 N Broadway St
- **Reza's** • 5255 N Clark St
- **Sabaidee** • 5359 N Broadway St

- **Standee's** • 1133 W Granville Ave ♲
- **Sushi Luxe** • 5204 N Clark St
- **Svea** • 5236 N Clark St
- **Tanoshii** • 5547 N Clark St
- **Taste of Lebanon** • 1509 W Foster Ave

Shopping

- **Alamo Shoes** • 5321 N Clark St
- **Andersonville Galleria** •
  5247 N Clark St
- **Blue Hydrangea** • 1113 W Berwyn Ave
- **Bon Bon** • 5410 N Clark St
- **Broadway Antique Market** •
  6130 N Broadway St
- **The Brown Elephant** • 5404 N Clark St
- **Cassona** • 5241 N Clark St
- **Early to Bed** • 5232 N Sheridan Rd
- **Edgewater Antique Mall** •
  6314 N Broadway St
- **Elda de la Rosa** • 5555 N Sheridan Rd
- **Erickson Jewelers** • 5304 N Clark St
- **Gethsemane Garden Center** •
  5739 N Clark St
- **Hip Fit** • 1513 W Foster Ave
- **Johnny Sprocket's** •
  1052 W Bryn Mawr Ave
- **Kate the Great Bookstore** •
  5550 N Broadway St
- **Middle East Bakery** • 1512 W Foster Ave
- **Paper Trail** • 5309 N Clark St
- **Presence** • 5216 N Clark St
- **Scout** • 5221 N Clark St
- **Soothe Your Senses Day Spa** •
  6260 N Broadway St
- **Surrender** • 5225 N Clark St
- **Toys Etcetera** • 5311N Clark St
- **Toys & Treasures** • 5311 N Clark St
- **True Nature Foods** • 6034 N Broadway St
- **Tulip Toy Gallery** • 1480 W Berwyn Ave
- **White Attic** • 5408 N Clark St
- **Wickstrom's Swedish Deli** •
  5247 N Clark St
- **Women & Children First** •
  5233 N Clark St

Video Rental

- **BJ Video** • 5552 N Broadway St
- **Blockbuster** • 5300 N Broadway St
- **Hollywood Video** • 6201 N Clark St
- **Mina's TV and Video** • 6137 N Clark St
- **National Video** • 1108 W Granville Ave
- **Ram Video & Electronics** •
  5845 N Clark St
- **Select Video** • 5358 N Clark St
- **Specialty Video** • 5307 N Clark St
- **Video Town** • 1127 W Thorndale Ave

Map 38 • **Ravenswood / Albany Park**

N

1   2

35

48

39

41

N Campbell Ave

N St Louis Ave

N Bernard Ave

N Kimball Ave

North Park College

N Christiana Ave

N Spaulding Ave

N Sawyer Ave

N Kedzie Ave

N Troy St

N Albany Ave

N Whipple St

N Sacramento Ave

N Richmond St

N Francisco Ave

N Mozart St

N California Ave

N Virginia Ave

N Fairfield Ave

N Fairfield Ave

N Washtenaw Ave

N Talman Ave

N Rockwell St

N Maplewood Ave

N Campbell Ave

N Artesian Ave

N Western Ave

N Maplewood Ave

N Rockwell St

N Maplewood Ave

N Campbell Ave

W Foster Ave

RAVENSWOOD

W Winona St

W Carmen Ave

W Carmen Ave

W Winnemac Ave

River Park

W Argyle St

LINCOLN SQUARE

W Argyle St

W Ainslie St

W Gunnison St

Ronan Park

W Gunnison St

North Branch Pumping Station

W Lawrence Ave

Gross Park

Albany Park Community Center

Kimball

Willis Building

Fish Furniture Co Building

Ronan Park Walking Trail

W Giddings St

W Leland Ave

W Leland Ave

Kedzie   Francisco   Rockwell   Western

Jacob Park

W Eastwood Ave

W Eastwood Ave

Ravenswood Manor Park

W Wilson Ave

W Windsor Ave

W Windsor Ave

3200W   2800W

W Sunnyside Ave

2400W

W Agatite Ave

W Pensacola Ave

Paradise

W Montrose Ave

HORNER PARK

W Pensacola Ave

W Cullom Ave

W Hutchinson St

W Hutchinson St

ALBANY PARK

Horner Park

W Berteau Ave

W Warner Ave

W Belle Plaine Ave

W Warner Ave

W Cuyler Ave

W Cuyler Ave

W Irving Park Rd

W Dakin St

California Park

W Byron St

W Berenice Ave

| 1/4 mile | .25 km |

Banks

- **Albany** • 3400 W Lawrence Ave
- **Charter One (ATM)** • 2900 W Montrose Ave
- **Chase** • 2959 W Irving Park Rd
- **Chase** • 4843 N Kedzie Ave
- **Chase (ATM)** • Walgreens • 3153 W Irving Park Rd
- **Chase (ATM)** • Walgreens • 4343 N Kedzie Ave
- **Citibank (ATM)** • 7-Eleven • 2800 W Irving Park Rd
- **LaSalle (ATM)** • Swedish Covenant Hospital • 5140 N California Ave
- **LaSalle (ATM)** • 3343 W Montrose Ave
- **TCF (ATM)** • 7-Eleven • 2800A W Irving Park Rd
- **TCF (ATM)** • Osco • 5158 N Lincoln Ave

Car Washes

- **Minute Man Car Wash** • 3218 W Irving Park Rd
- **Ruby Hand Car Wash** • 4334 N California Ave

Gas Stations

- **BP** • 2800 W Lawrence Ave
- **BP** • 3201 W Montrose Ave
- **Citgo** • 2816 W Irving Park Rd
- **Shell** • 5155 N Kimball Ave

Emergency Rooms

- **Swedish Covenant** • 5145 N California Ave

ₒLandmarks

- **Albany Park Community Center** • 3401 W Ainslie St
- **Fish Furniture Co Building** • 3322 W Lawrence Ave
- **North Branch Pumping Station** • Lawrence Ave & the Chicago River
- **Paradise** • 2916 W Montrose Ave
- **Ravenswood Manor Park** • 4626 N Manor Ave
- **River Park** • 5100 N Francisco Ave
- **Ronan Park Walking Trail** • 3000 W Argyle St
- **Willis Building** • 3221 W Lawrence Ave

Libraries

- **Albany Park Public Library** • 5150 N Kimball Ave

Pharmacies

- **CVS** • 5158 N Lincoln Ave
- **Walgreens** • 3153 W Irving Park Rd ⊚
- **Walgreens** • 4343 N Kedzie Ave
- **Walgreens** • 4801 N Lincoln Ave

Pizza

- **Angelo's Pizza & Restaurant** • 3026 W Montrose Ave
- **Boomer's** • 5035 N Lincoln Ave
- **Bravo International Pizzaria** • 3256 W Lawrence Ave
- **Golden Crust Pizzeria** • 4620 N Kedzie Ave
- **Little Caesar's Pizza** • 2501 W Lawrence Ave
- **Noli's Pizza** • 4839 N Kedzie Ave
- **Paisano's Pizza** • 5047 N Lincoln Ave
- **Papa Giorgio's** • 2604 W Lawrence Ave

Post Offices

- **US Post Office** • 2522 W Lawrence Ave

Schools

- **Albany Park Multicultural Academy** • 4929 N Sawyer Ave
- **Gateway to Learning** • 4925 N Lincoln Ave
- **Lawrence Hall Youth Services** • 4833 N Francisco Ave
- **Little Angels** • 5117 N Lincoln Ave
- **Little Fox Day** • 5014 N Lincoln Ave
- **Newton Bateman Elementary** • 4220 N Richmond St
- **North Park University** • 3225 W Foster Ave
- **North River Elementary** • 4416 N Troy St
- **Our Lady of Mercy** • 4416 N Troy St
- **Thomas J Waters Fine Arts Elementary** • 4540 N Campbell Ave
- **Von Steuben Metropolitan Science Center** • 5039 N Kimball Ave
- **William G Hibbard Elementary** • 3244 W Ainslie St

Supermarkets

- **Al-Khayyam Bakery and Market** • 4738 N Kedzie Ave
- **Aldi** • 2431 W Montrose Ave
- **Andy's Fruit Ranch** • 4733 N Kedzie Ave
- **Cermak Produce** • 4234 N Kedzie Ave
- **Clark Market** • 4853 N Kedzie Ave
- **Harvestime Foods** • 2632 W Lawrence Ave
- **Holy Land Grocery** • 4806 N Kedzie Ave
- **Sahar Meat Market** • Albany Plz Mall • 4829 N Kedzie Ave

Map 38

If you're hankering for halal meat or in the market to purchase a hookah, North Kedzie around Lawrence Avenue is a magnificent Middle Eastern melange of grocery stores and restaurants. If, on the other hand, you're hankering for any kind of nightlife, you'd do better to look elsewhere.

Coffee

- **Beans & Bagels** • 2601 W Leland Ave
- **Café Del Mundo** • 3152 W Irving Park Rd
- **Coffee Liberte** • 4807 N Spaulding Ave
- **Donut Doctor** • 3342 W Lawrence Ave
- **Dunkin' Donuts** • 3101 W Irving Park Rd
- **Dunkin' Donuts** • 4821 N Kedzie Ave
- **Jaafer Sweets** • Albany Plz Mall • 4825 N Kedzie Ave
- **Merle's Coffee House** • 4642 N Francisco Ave
- **Olympic Club** • 2615 W Lawrence Ave
- **Starbucks** • 4558 N Kedzie Ave

Copy Shops

- **Shree Printing Corporation** • 3011 W Irving Park Rd

Farmers Markets

- **Chicago World Market (Sun, 10 am–3 pm)** • 4540 N Campbell Ave

Gyms

- **Galter Lifecenter** • 5157 N Francisco Ave
- **Women's Workout World (women only)** • 2540 W Lawrence Ave

Hardware Stores

- **Jay's True Value** • 4608 N Kedzie Ave
- **Lincoln Square Hardware** • 4874 N Lincoln Ave

Liquor Stores

- **Buy Low Liquor Store** • 3360 W Montrose Ave
- **Cardinal Wine & Spirits** • 4905 N Lincoln Ave
- **Charlies Supermarket** • 2941 W Montrose Ave
- **David's Food & Liquor** • 3158 W Montrose Ave
- **Food & Liquors Express** • 2752 W Lawrence Ave
- **Foremost Liquor Store** • 4616 N Kedzie Ave
- **J&A Liquors** • 3213 W Lawrence Ave
- **Jerusalem Liquors** • 3133 W Lawrence Ave
- **Peacock Liquors** • 3056 W Montrose Ave
- **Prestige Liquors** • 3210 W Montrose Ave
- **Quick Stop** • 2901 W Irving Park Rd

Nightlife

- **Lincoln Square Lanes** • 4874 N Lincoln Ave
- **Montrose Saloon** • 2933 W Montrose Ave
- **Peek Inn** • 2825 W Irving Park Rd

Pet Shops

- **Ruff Haus Pets** • 4652 N Rockwell St

Restaurants

- **Al-Khaymeih** • 4742 N Kedzie Ave
- **Arun's** • 4156 N Kedzie Ave
- **Brasa Roja** • 3125 W Montrose Ave
- **Cousin's IV (Incredible Vitality)** • 3038 W Irving Park Rd
- **Dharma Garden Thai Restaurants** • 3109 W Irving Park Rd
- **El Huarachin Huarachon** • 3320 W Lawrence Ave
- **Great Sea Chinese Restaurants** • 3254 W Lawrence Ave
- **Golden Crust Italian Pizzeria** • 4620 N Kedzie Ave
- **Kang Nam** • 4849 N Kedzie Ave
- **Kitchen Chicago** • 4664 N Manor Ave
- **Lutz Continental Café** • 2458 W Montrose Ave
- **Manzo's Ristorante** • 3210 W Irving Park Rd
- **Nhu Lan** • 2612 W Lawrence Ave
- **Noon O Kabab** • 4661 N Kedzie Ave
- **Paradise** • 2916 W Montrose Ave
- **Penguin** • 2723 W Lawrence Ave
- **Pupuseria Las Delicias** • 3300 W Montrose Ave
- **Rockwell's Neighborhood Grill** • 4632 N Rockwell St
- **Salam** • 4636 N Kedzie Ave
- **Semiramis** • 4639 N Kedzie Ave
- **Thai Valley** • 4600 N Kedzie Ave

Shopping

- **Lincoln Antique Mall** • 3115 W Irving Park Rd
- **The Music Store** • 3121 W Irving Park Rd
- **Odin Tatu** • 3313 W Irving Park Rd
- **Rave Sports** • 3346 W Lawrence Ave
- **Sassy Boutique** • 3210 W Lawrence Ave
- **Scents & Sensibility** • 4654 N Rockwell St
- **Village Discount Outlet** • 3301 W Lawrence Ave
- **Village Discount Outlet** • 4027 N Kedzie Ave

Video Rental

- **AV Video Center** • 5153 N Lincoln Ave
- **Azteca Video** • 3308 W Montrose Ave
- **Bosna Video (Primarily Serbo-Croat)** • 2501 W Lawrence Ave
- **Hollywood Video** • 4246 N Kedzie Ave
- **V&K Video** • 4750 N Kedzie Ave

Map 39 · **Ravenswood / North Center**

N

1

2

W Berwyn Ave

W Farragut Ave

N Oakley Ave

N Damen

N Hoyne Ave

W Farragut Ave

N Ravenswood

W Farragut Ave

N Janssen Ave

Foster Ave

41

36

37

W Winona St

W Winona St

Winnemac Park

N Winchester Ave

N Wolcott Ave

W Carmen Ave

N Ravenswood Ave

W Carmen Ave

W Winnemac Ave

W Winnemac Ave

N Claremont Ave

A

W Argyle St

W Winnemac Ave

W Ainslie St

W Argyle St

N Clark St

N Bell Ave

N Hamilton Ave

W Argyle St

W Ainslie St

Lincoln Square

N Maplewood Ave

W Ainslie St

W Gunnison St

N Lincoln Ave

N Claremont Ave

LINCOLN SQUARE

N Hoyne Ave

N Seeley Ave

W Ainslie St

RAVENSWOOD

N Campbell Ave

N Artesian Ave

Rx

W Lawrence Ave

Ravenswood

W Giddings St

N Hamilton Ave

N Seeley Ave

4800N

N Winchester Ave

W Leland Ave

N Ravenswood Ave

N Ravenswood Ave

N Hermitage Ave

W Leland Ave

N Greenview Ave

W Leland Ave

Western

Damen

W Eastwood Ave

W Eastwood Ave

N Damen Ave

W Wilson Ave

B

W Wilson Ave

38

Old Town School of Folk Music

W Windsor Ave

W Sunnyside Ave

N Paulina Ave

40

N Maplewood Ave

N Artesian Ave

N Claremont Ave

Welles Park

W Agatite Ave

N Greenview Ave

Montrose

N Leavitt St

W Montrose Ave

2400W

N Western Ave

N Oakley Ave

N Bell Ave

W Montrose Ave

2000W

N Wolcott Ave

N Honore St

1600W

W Pensacola Ave

N Campbell Ave

W Pensacola Ave

W Hoyne Ave

W Pensacola Ave

W Pensacola Ave

W Cullom Ave

W Cullom Ave

W Cullom Ave

W Hutchinson St

W Hutchinson St

W Hutchinson St

W Hutchinson St

W Hutchinson

NORTH CENTER

N Claremont Ave

N Bell Ave

W Berteau Ave

W Berteau Ave

W Warner Ave

W Warner Ave

W Warner Ave

N Campbell Ave

C

W Belle Plaine Ave

W Cuyler Ave

Rx

W Cuyler Ave

W Cuyler Ave

W Cuyler Ave

St Benedict's Church

W Cuyler Ave

N Wolcott Ave

N Honore St

N Ravenswood Ave

Irving Park

N Janssen Ave

Revere Park

Rx

42

W Dakin St

N Bell Ave

N Hamilton Ave

N Seeley Ave

4000N

W Larchmont Ave

N Lincoln Ave

W Irving Park Rd

W Byron St

The Ravenswood area easily rivals Lincoln Park in price, and with good reason. Older, family-style, neighborhood living has prompted realtors to rename North Center the "St. Ben's" area (after St. Benedict's Church) to up the ante. Further north, Lincoln Square serves as a hub for European culture. Almost by default, this has become known as Chicago's Germantown with its quaint, village-esque strip and big Oktoberfest fun.

Banks

- **Albany** • 4400 N Western Ave
- **Bank of America (ATM)** • 1969 W Lawrence Ave
- **Bank of America (ATM)** • 4005 N Damen Ave
- **Bridgeview** • 4553 N Lincoln Ave
- **Charter One** • 4037 N Lincoln Ave
- **Charter One** • 4725 N Western Ave
- **Charter One (ATM)** • 2323 W Lawrence Ave
- **Chase** • 1825 W Lawrence Ave
- **Chase** • 4711 N Lincoln Ave
- **Chase (ATM)** • Walgreens • 2301 W Irving Park Rd
- **Chase (ATM)** • Walgreens • 4801 N Lincoln Ave
- **Chase (ATM)** • Bethany Methodist Hospital • 5025 N Paulina St
- **Citibank (ATM)** • 4400 N Western Ave
- **Citibank (ATM)** • 7-Eleven • 4631 N Western Ave
- **Community Bank of Ravenswood** • 2300 W Lawrence Ave
- **Corus** • 3959 N Lincoln Ave
- **Corus** • 4800 N Western Ave
- **First American (ATM)** • 4115 N Lincoln Ave
- **LaSalle (ATM)** • CVS • 4800 N Damen Ave
- **Lincoln Park Savings** • 1946 W Irving Park Rd
- **Lincoln Park Savings** • 2139 W Irving Park Rd
- **North Community** • 2000 W Montrose Ave
- **TCF** • Osco • 4051 N Lincoln Ave
- **TCF** • Jewel • 4250 N Lincoln Ave
- **TCF (ATM)** • 7-Eleven • 4631 N Western Ave
- **Washington Mutual** • 4000 N Lincoln Ave
- **Washington Mutual** • 4605 N Lincoln Ave

Gas Stations

- **Mobil** • 4000 N Western Ave
- **Mobil** • 4638 N Damen Ave
- **Shell** • 4346 N Western Ave

Emergency Rooms

- **Methodist Hospital of Chicago** • 5025 N Paulina St

Landmarks

- **Lincoln Square** • 4800 N Lincoln Ave
- **Old Town School of Folk Music** • 4544 N Lincoln Ave
- **St Benedict's Church** • 2215 W Irving Park Rd

Libraries

- **Sulzer Public Library** • 4455 N Lincoln Ave

Pharmacies

- **CVS** • 4051 N Lincoln Ave
- **CVS** • 4800 N Damen Ave
- **Walgreens** • 2301 W Irving Park Rd

Pizza

- **Apart Pizza Company** • 2205 W Montrose Ave
- **Chicago's Pizza** • 1919 W Montrose Ave
- **Giordano's of Lincoln Square** • 2010 W Montrose Ave
- **Pizza DOC** • 2251 W Lawrence Ave
- **Pizza Hut** • 2309 W Lawrence Ave
- **Stefano's** • 2124 W Lawrence Ave
- **Villa May Delicious Pizza** • 1834 W Montrose Ave

Post Offices

- **US Post Office** • 2011 W Montrose Ave

Schools

- **Adler** • 2239 W Lawrence Ave
- **James B McPherson Elementary** • 4728 N Wolcott Ave
- **John C Coonley Elementary** • 4046 N Leavitt St
- **Mary E Courtenay Language Arts Center** • 1726 W Berteau Ave
- **North Park Elementary** • 2017 W Montrose Ave
- **Old Town School of Folk Music** • 4544 N Lincoln Ave
- **Pilgrim Lutheran** • 4300 N Winchester Ave
- **Queen of Angels** • 4520 N Western Ave
- **Ravenswood Baptist Christian** • 4437 N Seeley Ave
- **Ravenswood Elementary** • 4332 N Paulina St
- **Roald Amundsen High** • 5110 N Damen Ave
- **St Matthias** • 4910 N Claremont Ave

Supermarkets

- **Deal$** • 4738 N Western Ave
- **Jewel-Osco** • 4250 N Lincoln Ave

Map 39 Ravenswood/North Center

Local hippysters shop at places like the Book Cellar, a cute bookshop cum wine café, at browse-friendly record store, Laurie's Planet of Sound, or quirky Quake Collectables. In the evening, the stretch of Lincoln Avenue that disects this area becomes a restaurant row with neighborhood and destination dining. From old standards such as Opart and Chicago Brauhaus, to hot new faces like Chalkboard, foodies will not go hungry.

 # Coffee

- **Beans & Bagels** • 1812 W Montrose Ave
- **Bourbon** • 4768 N Lincoln Ave
- **Café Marrakech Expresso** • 4747 N Damen Ave
- **Dunkin' Donuts** • 1743 W Lawrence Ave
- **Dunkin' Donuts** • 4010 N Western Ave
- **Dunkin' Donuts** • 4645 N Western Ave
- **The Grind** • 4613 N Lincoln Ave
- **Katerina's** • 1920 W Irving Park Rd
- **Perfect Cup** • 4700 N Damen Ave
- **Red Eye Café** • 4164 N Lincoln Ave
- **So Addicted** • 4805 N Damen Ave
- **Starbucks** • 1900 W Montrose Ave
- **Starbucks** • 4015 N Lincoln Ave
- **Starbucks** • 4553 N Lincoln Ave

Copy Shops

- **The UPS Store** • 4064 N Lincoln Ave

 # Farmers Markets

- **Lincoln Square**
  (Jun–Oct; Tues, 7 am–2 pm) •
  W Leland Ave & N Lincoln Ave
- **North Center**
  (Jun–Oct; Sat, 7 am–2 pm) •
  W Belle Plaine Ave & N Damen Ave

 # Gyms

- **Curves (women only)** •
  4351 N Lincoln Ave

Hardware Stores

- **Sears** • 1900 W Lawrence Ave

Liquor Stores

- **Best Buy Food & Liquor** •
  1832 W Montrose Ave
- **Bright** • 1628 W Lawrence Ave
- **Fine Wine Brokers (wine only)** •
  4621 N Lincoln Ave
- **Fox Liquors** • 4707 N Damen Ave
- **George's Liquors** • 1964 W Lawrence Ave
- **Houston Liquor & Foods** •
  1829 W Irving Park Rd
- **Leland Inn** • 4662 N Western Ave
- **Windy City Liquors** • 4959 N Damen Ave

 # Movie Theaters

- **Davis Theater** • 4614 N Lincoln Ave

 # Nightlife

- **Bowman's Bar and Grill** •
  4356 N Leavitt St
- **Celtic Crown Public House** •
  4301 N Western Ave
- **Chicago Brauhaus** • 4732 N Lincoln Ave
- **Daily Bar & Grill** • 4560 N Lincoln Ave
- **The Globe Pub** • 1934 W Irving Park Rd
- **Grafton Pub** • 4530 N Lincoln Ave
- **Huettenbar** • 4721 N Lincoln Ave
- **Jury's Food & Drink** • 4337 N Lincoln Ave
- **Katerina's** • 1920 W Irving Park Rd
- **Laschet's Inn** • 2119 W Irving Park Rd
- **The Long Room** • 1612 W Irving Park Rd
- **Margie's Pub** • 4145 N Lincoln Ave
- **O'Donovan's** • 2100 W Irving Park Rd
- **O'Lanagan's** • 2335 W Montrose Ave
- **The Rail** • 4709 N Damen Ave
- **Resi's Bierstube** • 2034 W Irving Park Rd
- **Wild Goose** • 4265 N Lincoln Ave

 # Pet Shops

- **Barking Lot (Dogs only)** •
  2442 W Irving Park Rd
- **Off the Leash** • 4955 N Damen Ave
- **Paws & Claws** • 5015 N Western Ave
- **Sit!** • 2316 W Leland Ave

Restaurants

- **Bad Dog Tavern** • 4535 N Lincoln Ave
- **Bistro Campagne** • 4518 N Lincoln Ave
- **Brioso** • 4603 N Lincoln Ave
- **Budacki's Drive-In** • 4739 N Damen Ave
- **Café 28** • 1800 W Irving Park Rd
- **Café Selmarie** • 4729 N Lincoln Ave
- **Chalkboard** • 4343 N Lincoln Ave
- **Chicago Brauhaus** • 4732 N Lincoln Ave
- **Diner Grill** • 1635 W Irving Pk Rd
- **Essence of India** • 4601 N Lincoln Ave
- **Feed the Beast** • 4300 N Lincoln Ave
- **First Slice Pie Café** •
  4401 N Ravenswood Ave
- **Glenn's Diner** • 1820 W Montrose Ave
- **Glunz Bavarian Haus** •
  4128 N Lincoln Ave
- **Golden Angel Restaurant** •
  4340 N Lincoln Ave
- **House of Wah Sun** • 4319 N Lincoln Ave
- **La Boca della Verita** • 4618 N Lincoln Ave
- **Lincoln Restaurant** • 4008 N Lincoln Ave
- **Los Nopales** • 4544 N Western Ave
- **Margie's Candies** • 1813 W Montrose Ave
- **Opart Thai House** • 4658 N Western Ave
- **Orange Garden** • 1942 W Irving Park Rd
- **Over Easy Café** • 4943 N Damen Ave
- **Pannenkoeken Cafe** •
  4757 N Western Ave
- **Pizza DOC** • 2251 W Lawrence Ave
- **Roong Petch** • 2209 W Montrose Ave
- **Smokin' Woody's** • 4160 N Lincoln Ave
- **Spacca Napoli** • 1769 W Sunnyside Ave
- **Sticky Rice** • 4018 N Western Ave
- **Tank Sushi** • 4514 N Lincoln Ave

 # Shopping

- **Architectural Artifacts** •
  4325 N Ravenswood Ave
- **Book Cellar** • 4736 N Lincoln Ave
- **The Cheese Stands Alone** •
  4547 N Western Ave
- **The Chopping Block** •
  4747 N Lincoln Ave
- **Different Strummer** • 4544 N Lincoln Ave
- **East Meets West** • 2118 W Lawrence Ave
- **European Import Center** •
  4752 N Lincoln Ave
- **Gallimaufry Gallery** • 4712 N Lincoln Ave
- **Glass Art & Decorative Studio** •
  4507 N Lincoln Ave
- **Griffins & Gargoyles Antiques** •
  2140 W Lawrence Ave
- **Hazel** • 1902 W Montrose Ave
- **Laurie's Planet of Sound** •
  4639 N Lincoln Ave
- **Margie's Candies** • 1813 W Montrose Ave
- **Merz Apothecary** • 4716 N Lincoln Ave
- **Patina** • 4907 N Damen Ave
- **Quake Collectables** • 4628 N Lincoln Ave
- **Timeless Toys** • 4749 N Lincoln Ave

 # Video Rental

- **Blockbuster** • 1958 W Irving Park Rd
- **Blockbuster** • 2301 W Lawrence Ave
- **Darkstar Video** • 4355 N Lincoln Ave
- **Lincoln Square Video (Yugoslavian)** •
  4725 N Lincoln Ave
- **Super Video** • 2055 W Irving Park Rd
- **Tom's Video** • 1830 W Wilson Ave

An uneasy truce exists in Uptown among Starbucks-hopping yuppies, grungy young artists, and perpetually-displaced poor. Condos pop up like pimples, while residents with an eye for neighborhood integrity and local flavor struggle to maintain the balance. The area between Argyle, Foster, Broadway, and Ashland, a.k.a. "SOFO," maintains the most diverse vibe and manageable rent.

$ Banks

- **American Metro** • 4878 N Broadway St
- **Bank of America (ATM)** •
  4620 N Broadway St
- **Bridgeview** • 4753 N Broadway St
- **Bridgeview** • 5117 N Clark St
- **Cathay Bank** • 4929 N Broadway St
- **Chase** • 1101 W Lawrence Ave
- **Chase** • 3956 N Sheridan Rd
- **Chase** • 5134 N Clark St
- **Chase (ATM)** • Walgreens •
  1500 W Wilson Ave
- **Citibank** • 4887 N Broadway St
- **Citibank (ATM)** • 7-Eleven •
  1425 W Montrose Ave
- **Citibank (ATM)** • 7-Eleven •
  4155 N Broadway St
- **First American (ATM)** • 3945 N
  Sheridan Rd
- **First American (ATM)** •
  1134 W Wilson Ave
- **First American (ATM)** •
  4000 N Southport Ave
- **First American (ATM)** •
  4800 N Sheridan Rd
- **First American (ATM)** • Amoco/BP •
  755 W Lawrence Ave
- **Harris Trust & Savings** •
  4531 N Broadway St
- **Harris Trust & Savings (ATM)** •
  1009 W Lawrence Ave
- **International Bank of Chicago** •
  5069 N Broadway St
- **LaSalle (ATM)** • 1145 W Wilson Ave
- **LaSalle (ATM)** • 4646 N Marine Dr
- **North Community** • 4701 N Clark St
- **TCF** • 1050 W Wilson Ave
- **TCF** • 4355 N Sheridan Rd
- **TCF (ATM)** • 7-Eleven •
  1425 W Montrose Ave
- **Washington Mutual** •
  4356 N Broadway St

🔴 Car Washes

- **Motor City Lube and Spa Detail** •
  939 W Irving Park Rd
- **Uptown Service Station** •
  4900 N Broadway St

⛽ Gas Stations

- **Amoco** • 755 W Lawrence Ave
- **Citgo** • 1530 W Lawrence Ave
- **Citgo** • 4000 N Clark St
- **Gas City** • 4070 N Clark St
- **Marathon** • 5156 N Broadway St

- **Shell** • 4800 N Ashland Ave
- **Uptown Service Station** •
  4900 N Broadway St

➕ Emergency Rooms

- **Louis A Weiss Memorial** •
  4646 N Marine Dr
- **Thorek** • 850 W Irving Park Rd

⭕ Landmarks

- **Aragon Ballroom** •
  1106 W Lawrence Ave
- **Graceland Cemetery** •
  4001 N Clark St
- **Green Mill Pub** • 4802 N Broadway St
- **St Augustine College** •
  1333 W Argyle St
- **Uptown Theatre** • 4816 N Broadway St

📖 Libraries

- **Bezazian Public Library** •
  1226 W Ainslie St
- **Uptown Public Library** •
  929 W Buena Ave

P Parking

℞ Pharmacies

- **CVS** • 845 W Wilson Ave
- **Jewel-Osco** • 4355 N Sheridan Rd
- **Walgreens** • 1500 W Wilson Ave
- **Walgreens** • 4025 N Sheridan Rd
- **Walgreens** • 4646 N Marine Dr

🍕 Pizza

- **Bo Jono's Pizzeria** •
  4185 N Clarendon Ave
- **CW Napkin** • 4443 N Sheridan Rd
- **Domino's** • 1415 W Irving Park Rd
- **Fornello Trattoria** •
  1011 W Irving Park Rd
- **Gigio's Pizzeria** • 4643 N Broadway St
- **Laurie's Pizzeria & Liquors** •
  5153 N Broadway St
- **Michael's Pizzeria & Sports Pub** •
  4091 N Broadway St
- **O-Tomat-O** • 4429 N Broadway St
- **Papa Romeo's Pizza** •
  1617 W Irving Park Rd
- **Pizza Factory** • 4443 N Sheridan Rd

- **Ranalli's Up North** •
  1522 W Montrose Ave
- **Rosati's Pizza** • 4863 N Broadway St
- **Uptown Pizza** • 1031 W Wilson Ave

✉ Post Offices

- **US Post Office** • 1343 W Irving Park Rd
- **US Post Office** • 4850 N Broadway St

🏫 Schools

- **A Step Ahead Learning Center** •
  4208 N Broadway St
- **Arai Campus** • 900 W Wilson Ave
- **Christopher House-Uptown DCC** •
  4701 N Winthrop Ave
- **Day School** • 800 W Buena Ave
- **Joan F Arai Middle** • 900 W Wilson Ave
- **John T McCutcheon Branch** •
  4850 N Kenmore Ave
- **Joseph Brennemann Elementary** •
  4251 N Clarendon Ave
- **Lakeview High** • 4015 N Ashland Ave
- **Lycee Francais de Chicago** •
  613 W Bittersweet Pl
- **McCutcheon Elementary** •
  4865 N Sheridan Rd
- **Park View Montessori** •
  640 W Irving Park Rd
- **Passages Elementary** •
  1447 W Montrose Ave
- **Prologue High** • 640 W Irving Park Rd
- **St Augustine College** •
  1333 W Argyle St
- **St Mary of the Lake Elementary** •
  4201 N Kenmore Ave
- **St Thomas of Canterbury** •
  4827 N Kenmore Ave
- **Stewart Elementary** •
  4525 N Kenmore Ave
- **Stockton CPC** • 4425 N Magnolia Ave
- **Stockton Elementary** •
  4420 N Beacon St
- **Truman College** • 1145 W Wilson Ave
- **Uplift Community High** •
  900 W Wilson Ave
- **Walt Disney Elementary** •
  4140 N Marine Dr
- **William C Goudy Elementary** •
  5120 N Winthrop Ave

🛒 Supermarkets

- **Aldi** • 4450 N Broadway St
- **Jewel-Osco** • 4355 N Sheridan Rd

Uptown's nightlife is lively, chock full of shiny new bars as well as reliable old stand-bys. Green Mill (famous for live jazz and Sunday night poetry slams) and Big Chicks (a favored, gay neighborhood bar with great art) have long drawn folks to Uptown. the new hotspots trickle down the lengths of Broadway, Clark, and Sheridan and range from the uber-cozy Dollop Coffee Co to the bumpin', always-packed Hopleaf.

☕ Coffee

- **City Coffee Emerald** • 3938 N Sheridan Rd
- **Corona's Coffee Shop** • 909 W Irving Park Rd
- **Dollop Coffee Co** • 4181 N Clarendon Ave
- **Dunkin' Donuts** • 5130 N Broadway St
- **Dunkin' Donuts** • 1441 W Montrose Ave
- **Dunkin' Donuts** • 4547 N Broadway St
- **New Chinatown Bakery & Coffee Shop** • 1019 W Argyle St
- **Starbucks** • 4600 N Magnolia Ave
- **Starbucks** • 4753 N Broadway St
- **Urban Tea Lounge** • 838 W Montrose Ave

📄 Copy Shops

- **Staples Copy & Print Centers** • 4610 N Clark St

🏋 Gyms

- **Bodyfit Athletic Club** • 4704 N Broadway St
- **Curves (women only)** • 1144 W Wilson Ave
- **Know No Limits** • 5121 N Clark St
- **World Gym** • 909 W Montrose Ave

🔧 Hardware Stores

- **Andersonville Hardware** • 5036 N Clark St
- **Crafty Beaver Home Center** • 1522 W Lawrence Ave
- **Uptown Ace Hardware** • 4654 N Broadway St

🍾 Liquor Stores

- **Foremost Liquors** • 1040 W Argyle St
- **GNS Food & Liquor** • 4092 N Broadway St
- **JJ Peppers Food Store** • 4800 N Broadway Rd
- **Laurie's Pizzeria & Liquors** • 5153 N Broadway St
- **Manhattan Liquors** • 4200 N Broadway St
- **Rayan's Discount Liquors** • 1532 W Montrose Ave
- **Sheridan Park Food & Liquor** • 1255 W Wilson Ave
- **Sheridan-Irving Liquor** • 3944 N Sheridan Rd

🎯 Nightlife

- **Bar on Buena** • 910 W Buena Ave
- **Big Chicks** • 5024 N Sheridan Rd
- **Carol's Pub** • 4659 N Clark St
- **Crew Bar & Grill** • 4804 N Broadway St
- **Green Mill Pub** • 4802 N Broadway St
- **Holiday Club** • 4000 N Sheridan Rd
- **Hopleaf** • 5148 N Clark St
- **Konak** • 5150 N Clark St
- **Max's Place** • 4621 N Clark St
- **Nick's Uptown** • 4015 N Sheridan Rd
- **The Spot** • 4437 N Broadway St

- **T's** • 5025 N Clark St
- **The Uptown Lounge** • 1136 W Lawrence Ave

🐾 Pet Shops

- **Soggy Paws** • 1148 W Leland Ave

🍴 Restaurants

- **Agami** • 4712 N Broadway St
- **Anna Maria Pasteria** • 4400 N Clark St
- **Café Lao** • 1007 W Argyle St
- **Café Too** • 4715 N Sheridan Rd
- **Deleece** • 4004 N Southport Ave
- **Demera** • 4801 N Broadway St
- **Furama** • 4936 N Broadway St
- **Hai Yen Restaurant** • 1055 W Argyle St
- **Hama Matsu** • 5143 N Clark St
- **JJ Fish & Chicken** • 4515 N Sheridan Rd
- **La Banh Mi Hung Phat** • 4942 N Sheridan Rd
- **Magnolia Café** • 1224 W Wilson Ave
- **Marigold** • 4832 N Broadway St
- **Palace Gate** • 4548 N. Magnolia
- **Pho Hoa** • 4925 N Broadway St
- **Riques** • 5004 N Sheridan Rd
- **Siam Noodle & Rice** • 4654 N Sheridan Rd
- **Silver Seafood** • 4829 N Broadway St
- **Sun Wah BBQ** • 1134 W Argyle St
- **TAC Quick** • 3930 N Sheridan Rd
- **Taqueria los Caminos de Michoacan** • 3948 N Sheridan Rd
- **Thai Pastry** • 4925 N Broadway St
- **Tweet** • 5020 N Sheridan Rd

🛍 Shopping

- **Angel Food Bakery** • 1636 W Montrose Ave
- **Eagle Leathers** • 5005 N Clark St
- **Foursided** • 5061 N Clark St
- **Play It Again Sports** • 3939 N Ashland Ave
- **Salvation Army Thrift Store** • 4315 N Broadway St
- **Shake Rattle and Read Book Box** • 4812 N Broadway St
- **Tai Nam Market Center** • 4925 N Broadway St
- **Tattoo Factory** • 4441 N Broadway St
- **Unique Thrift Store** • 4445 N Sheridan Rd
- **Uptown Bikes** • 4653 N Broadway St
- **Village Discount Outlet** • 4898 N Clark St
- **Wilson Broadway Mall** • 1114 W Wilson Ave
- **Wooden Spoon** • 5047 N Clark

📀 Video Rental

- **Banana Video** • 4923 N Clark St
- **Bankok Video & Grocery** • 4617 N Clark St
- **Blockbuster** • 4620 N Clark St
- **United Video** • 4519 N Sheridan Rd

It's official: Southern Avondale has now been designated "hot Avondale" by real estate developers. Certainly the sight of hipsters sipping coffee next to the blue collar regulars at Clara's is a clear indication that young artsy types have set their sights on the affordable spaces and ample parking to be found in this frontier neighborhood, as all points connected by the Blue Line are designated, eventually, for coolness.

💲 Banks

- **Bank of America** • 3260 W Belmont Ave
- **Chase** • 3227 W Addison St
- **Chase (ATM)** • Walgreens 2844 W Diversey Ave
- **Chase (ATM)** • Devry University •
  3300 N Campbell Ave
- **Chase (ATM)** • Walgreens 3302 W Belmont Ave
- **Citibank (ATM)** • 3611 N Kedzie Ave
- **Citibank (ATM)** • 7-Eleven • 3800 N Kedzie Ave
- **First American (ATM)** • 3201 W Diversey Ave
- **Harris Trust & Savings** • 2927 W Addison St
- **Harris Trust & Savings (ATM)** • 2550 W Addison St
- **LaSalle** • 3350 W Diversey Ave
- **North Community** • 2758 W Belmont Ave
- **TCF** • Jewel 3570 N Elston Ave
- **TCF (ATM)** • 7-Eleven • 3800 N Kedzie Ave
- **US** • 3611 N Kedzie Ave
- **Washington Mutual** • 3339 W Belmont Ave

🔴 Car Washes

- **123 Hand Car Wash** • 3635 N Kedzie Ave
- **Superior Performance II** • 2933 N Elston Ave

⊙ Car Rental

- **Enterprise** • 3029 N Kedzie Ave • 773-478-3310

℗ Gas Stations

- **BP** • 3201 W Addison St
- **Citgo** • 2920 N California Ave
- **Citgo** • 3001 W Belmont Ave
- **Marathon** • 2811 N Sacramento Ave
- **Marathon** • 3057 N Kedzie Ave
- **Shell** • 3159 W Addison St

○ Landmarks

- **Com-Ed Plant** • N California Ave & W Roscoe St

℞ Pharmacies

- **CVS** • 3411 W Addison St
- **Jewel-Osco** • 3572 N Elston Ave ⊚
- **Target** • 2939 W Addison St
- **Walgreens** • 3302 W Belmont Ave ⊚

🍕 Pizza

- **Little Caesar's Pizza** • 3135 W Addison St

✉ Post Offices

- **US Post Office** • 3750 N Kedzie Ave

🏫 Schools

- **A-Karrasel** • 3030 N Kedzie Ave
- **Albert G Lane Tech** • 2501 W Addison St
- **Avondale Elementary** • 2945 N Sawyer Ave
- **Carl Von Linne Elementary** •
  3221 N Sacramento Ave
- **DeVry Institute of Technology** •
  3300 N Campbell Ave
- **Gordon Technical High** • 3633 N California Ave
- **Grover Cleveland Elementary** • 3121 W Byron St
- **Logandale Middle** • 3212 W George St

🛒 Supermarkets

- **Jewel-Osco** • 3570 N Elston Ave

When encased meat emporium Hot Doug's relocated here to a stretch of California, local foodies took note. During lunch hour and on Saturdays, lines extend well beyond the doors for Doug's dogs and duck fat fries. Kuma's Corner offers heavy-metal themed burgers served by a well-inked staff, and Chief O' Neill's offers pub fare and live Celtic music.

Coffee

- **Dunkin' Donuts** • 3214 N Kimball Ave
- **Dunkin' Donuts** • 3310 W Addison St
- **Dunkin' Donuts** • 3427 W Diversey Ave
- **MoJoe's Hot House** • 2849 W Belmont Ave
- **Starbucks** • Target • 2939 W Addison St

Hardware Stores

- **Elston Ace Hardware** • 2825 W Belmont Ave
- **Home Depot** • 3500 N Kimball Ave
- **Kabbe True Value Hardware** • 2550 W Diversey Ave

Liquor Stores

- **American Way Liquor** • 3700 N Kedzie Ave
- **Discount Store** • 3457 N Albany Ave
- **JJ Peppers** • 3201 W Diversey Ave

Nightlife

- **Angie's Bar & Grill** • 3700 N Kedzie Ave
- **Chief O'Neill's** • 3471 N Elston Ave
- **Kuma's Corner** • 2900 W Belmont Ave
- **N** • 2977 N Elston Ave
- **Nelly's Saloon** • 3256 N Elston Ave
- **Small Bar** • 2956 N Albany Ave

Pet Shops

- **Belmont Feed (Birds only)** • 3036 W Belmont Ave
- **Pet A Cure** • 2949 W Diversey Ave
- **Pet Supplies Plus** • 3640 N Elston Ave

Restaurants

- **The Buffet Castle** • 3326 W Belmont Ave
- **Burrito House** • 3145 W Addison St
- **Chief O'Neill's** • 3471 N Elston Ave
- **Clara's** • 3159 N California Ave
- **Eat First Chinese Restaurant** • 3337 W Belmont Ave
- **Golden Rise Bakery** • 2957 W Diversey Ave
- **Hot Doug's** • 3324 N California Ave
- **IHOP** • 2818 W Diversey Ave ⊕
- **Kuma's Corner** • 2900 W Belmont Ave
- **La Finca** • 3361 N Elston Ave
- **Mr. Pollo** • 3000 W Belmont Ave
- **Sunshine Restaurant** • 3521 N Kedzie Ave
- **Taqueria Trespazada** • 3144 N California Ave
- **Zacatecas** • 2934 W Diversey Ave

Video Rental

- **Blockbuster** • 3951 N Kimball Ave

Map 42 • **North Center/Roscoe Village/West Lakeview**

Once a northside hipster enclave, rising prices and the proximity to Whole Foods have made Roscoe Village and West Lakeview ground-zero for the tan, fit, stroller-pushing/ dog-walking set. Roscoe Avenue, which was once a trolley route leading to long defunct Revierview Amusement Park, still holds its own for neighborhood restaurants, bars, and funky boutiques.

$ Banks

- **Chase** • 3531 N Western Ave
- **Chase** • 3868 N Lincoln Ave
- **Chase (ATM)** • Dominicks • 3350 N Western Ave
- **Chase (ATM)** • Walgreens • 1649 W Belmont Ave
- **Chase (ATM)** • Walgreens • 3358 N Western Ave
- **Citibank (ATM)** • 7-Eleven • 3801 N Western Ave
- **First American (ATM)** • 3636 N Western Ave
- **First American (ATM)** • 1700 W Diversey Pkwy
- **First American (ATM)** • 1900 W Belmont Ave
- **First American (ATM)** • 3601 N Western Ave
- **Harris Trust & Savings (ATM)** •
  3354 N Damen Ave
- **LaSalle** • 3944 N Western Ave
- **Lincoln Park Savings** • 3234 N Damen Ave
- **North Community** • 2800 N Western Ave
- **North Community** • 3401 N Western Ave
- **TCF** • Jewel • 3400 N Western Ave
- **TCF (ATM)** • 7-Eleven • 3801 N Western Ave
- **Washington Mutual** • 3348 N Western Ave

Car Washes

- **Ultra Sonic Car Wash** • 3650 N Western Ave

Car Rental

- **Enterprise** • 3844 N Western Ave • 773-539-5900

Gas Stations

- **BP/Amoco** • 3955 N Western Ave
- **Citgo** • 2401 W Diversey Ave
- **Marathon** • 3145 N Western Ave

o Landmarks

- **19th District Police Headquarters** •
  2452 W Belmont Ave

Libraries

- **Lincoln-Belmont Public Library** •
  1659 W Melrose St

Rx Pharmacies

- **CVS** • 2815 N Western Ave ☺
- **CVS** • 3944 N Western Ave ☺
- **Dominick's** • 3350 N Western Ave ☺
- **Jewel-Osco** • 3400 N Western Ave ☺
- **Walgreens** • 1649 W Belmont Ave
- **Walgreens** • 3358 N Western Ave

Pizza

- **Carreno's Pizzeria** • 1955 W Addison St
- **Pete's Pizza** • 3737 N Western Ave
- **Piazza Bella Trattoria** • 2116 W Roscoe St
- **Robey Pizza** • 1954 W Roscoe St

Police

- **19th District Police Headquarters** •
  2452 W Belmont Ave

Post Offices

- **US Post Office** • 3635 N Lincoln Ave

Schools

- **Alex Bell Elementary** • 3730 N Oakley Ave
- **Alexander Hamilton Elementary** •
  1650 W Cornelia Ave
- **Cardinal Bernardin Early Child** •
  1651 W Diversey Pkwy
- **Friedrich L Jahn Elementary** • 3149 N Wolcott Ave
- **George Schneider Elementary** • 2957 N Hoyne Ave
- **John L Audubon Elementary** • 3500 N Hoyne Ave
- **St Andrew Elementary** • 1710 W Addison St
- **St Benedict Elementary** • 3920 N Leavitt St
- **St Benedict High** • 3900 N Leavitt St
- **St Benedict Middle** • 3920 N Leavitt St

Supermarkets

- **Dominick's** • 3350 N Western Ave ☺
- **Jewel-Osco** • 3400 N Western Ave ☺
- **Paulina Meat Market** • 3501 N Lincoln Ave
- **Trader Joe's** • 3745 N Lincoln Ave

Map 42

Check out affordable art from up and comers at Sacred Art, and browse the hand-picked selection at "High Fidelity" lookalike Hard Boiled Records and Video. For night-life, sample handmade pasta and other seasonal, organic fare at Terragusto, then un-wind with a pint and sing along with the jukebox at laid-back rugby bar Black Rock.

Coffee

- **Dinkel's Bakery** • 3329 N Lincoln Ave
- **Dunkin' Donuts** • 1755 W Addison St
- **Dunkin' Donuts** • 3535 N Western Ave
- **MoJoe's Café Lounge** • 2256 W Roscoe St
- **Starbucks** • 1700 W Diversey Pkwy
- **Starbucks** • 2159 W Belmont Ave
- **Starbucks** • 3356 N Lincoln Ave
- **Su Van's Café and Bake Shop** • 3351 N Lincoln Ave
- **Thai Linda Café** • 2022 W Roscoe St

Copy Shops

- **FedEx Kinko's** • 3435 N Western Ave
- **Mail Box Plus** • 2248 W Belmont Ave

Farmers Markets

- **Roscoe Village (Jun–Oct; Sun, 7 am–2 pm)** • W Belmont Ave & N Wolcott Ave

Gyms

- **Curves (women only)** • 2037 W Roscoe St
- **Lakeview YMCA** • 3333 N Marshfield Ave

Hardware Stores

- **Community Home Supply** • 3924 N Lincoln Ave
- **Staubers Ace Hardware** • 3911 N Lincoln Ave

Liquor Stores

- **Armanetti Wine Shop** • 3530 N Lincoln Ave
- **Miller's Tap & Liquor Store** • 2204 W Roscoe St
- **Miska's Liquor** • 2156 W Belmont Ave
- **Pelly's Liquors** • 3444 N Lincoln Ave
- **R&S Liquor** • 2425 W Diversey Ave
- **West Lakeview Liquors** • 2156 W Addison St

Nightlife

- **Beat Kitchen** • 2100 W Belmont Ave
- **Black Rock** • 3614 N Damen Ave
- **Cody's Public House** • 1658 W Barry Ave
- **Four Moon Tavern** • 1847 W Roscoe St
- **Four Treys** • 1952 W Henderson St
- **G&L Fire Escape** • 2157 W Grace St
- **Hungry Brain** • 2319 W Belmont Ave
- **Martyrs'** • 3855 N Lincoln Ave

- **Mulligan's Public House** • 2000 W Roscoe St
- **Riverview Tavern & Grill** • 1958 W Roscoe St
- **Roscoe Village Pub** • 2159 W Addison St
- **Waterhouse** • 3407 N Paulina Ave
- **Xippo** • 3759 N Damen Ave

Pet Shops

- **Olly's Kingdom** • 2029 W Belmont Ave
- **Sam & Willy's** • 3405 N Paulina St

Restaurants

- **Costello Sandwich & Sides** • 2015 W Roscoe St
- **El Tinajon** • 2054 W Roscoe St
- **Kaze Sushi** • 2032 W Roscoe St
- **Kitsch'n on Roscoe** • 2005 W Roscoe St
- **La Mora** • 2132 W Roscoe St
- **Mrs Murphy and Sons** • 3905 N Lincoln Ave
- **Nazarlik** • 1650 W Belmont Ave
- **Piazza Bella Trattoria** • 2116 W Roscoe St
- **Sola** • 3868 N Lincoln Ave
- **T-Spot Sushi** • 3925 N Lincoln Ave
- **Terragusto** • 1851 W Addison St
- **Thai Linda Café** • 2022 W Roscoe St
- **Turquoise Restaurant on Roscoe** • 2147 W Roscoe St
- **Victory's Banner** • 2100 W Roscoe St
- **The Village Tap** • 2055 W Roscoe St
- **Volo Restaurant and Wine Bar** • 2008 W Roscoe St

Shopping

- **Antique Resources** • 1741 W Belmont Ave
- **Caravan Beads** • 3361 N Lincoln Ave
- **Father Time Antiques** • 2108 W Belmont Ave
- **Glam to Go** • 2002 W Roscoe St
- **Good Old Days Antiques** • 2138 W Belmont Ave
- **Lynn's Hallmark** • 3353 N Lincoln Ave
- **My Closet** • 3350 N Paulina St
- **Pleasure Chest** • 3436 N Lincoln Ave
- **Sacred Art** • 2040 W Roscoe St
- **Village Discount Outlet** • 2043 W Roscoe St

Video Rental

- **Blockbuster** • 1645 W School St
- **Blockbuster** • 3322 N Western Ave
- **Hard Boiled Records and Video** • 2010 W Roscoe St

Map 43 · **Wrigleyville / East Lakeview**

1

2

W Cuyler Ave

W Cuyler Ave

W Bittersweet Pl

N Kenmore Ave

W Irving Park Rd

40

Sheridan

W Dakin St

W Sheridan Rd

Hebrew Cemetery

N Alta Vista Ter

W Byron St

W Byron St

N Clark St

N Janssen Ave

N Lakewood Ave

N Racine Ave

A

N Ravenswood Ave

N Hermitage Ave

N Paulina St

N Marshfield Ave

N Ashland Ave

N Bosworth Ave

N Greenview Ave

N Janssen Ave

W Grace St

W Waveland Ave

N Wayne Ave

N Clifton Ave

N Seminary Ave

N Kenmore Ave

N Wilton Ave

N Fremont St

N Halsted St

N Broadway St

North Alta Vista Terrace

W Bradley Pl

P

W Patterson Ave

PAGE **269**

Wrigley Field

Addison

W Brompton Ave

N Reta Ave

WRIGLEYVILLE

W Addison St

4 $

Sheil Park

W Eddy St

W Cornelia Ave

W Cornelia Ave

W Newport Ave

W Newport Ave

W Newport Ave

N Elaine Pl

42

Paulina

Southport

44

W Roscoe St

1200W

W Henderson St

W Buckingham Pl

B

1600W

W Henderson St

N Racine Ave

N Lakewood Ave

N Clifton Ave

N Seminary Ave

N Kenmore Ave

N Sheffield Ave

N Wilton Ave

N Dayton St

W Aldine Ave

W School St

Southport Lanes

W Melrose St

N Greenview Ave

N Southport Ave

2000W

N Lakewood Ave

Belmont Ave

Belmont

2 $

3 $

Vic Theatre

N Orchard St

W California Ter

W Fletcher St

W Fletcher St

W Fletcher St

W Barry Ave

W Barry Ave

LAKEVIEW

N Wilton Ave

N Halsted St

W Barry Ave

W Nelson St

W Nelson St

W Nelson St

C

W Wellington Ave

Wellington

N Lincoln Ave

W Oakdale Ave

W Oakdale Ave

W Oakdale Ave

W Oakdale

N Ashland Ave

N Mildred Ave

W George St

N Burling St

N Orchard St

W Wolfram St

W Wolfram St

W Wolfram St

N Paulina St

N Marshfield Ave

N Bosworth Ave

N Greenview Ave

N Janssen Ave

2800W

N Wayne Ave

N Lakewood Ave

N Magnolia Ave

W Diversey Pkwy

29

W Diversey School Ct

N Seminary Ave

N Kenmore Ave

N Wilton Ave

Diversey

N Dayton St

N Burling St

W Diversey

W Schubert Ave

W Schubert Ave

1/4 mile

.25 km

W Drummond Pl

Pleasant, pretty streets belie atrocious traffic and parking, as well as the constant summertime disturbance of drunken Cubs fans roaming the streets and urinating in alleys and doorways. On the plus side, residents don't have to travel far for anything—tons of good restaurants, a variety of nightlife, the lakefront, and loads of services from groceries to video rentals cram into this youthful 'hood.

Banks

- **Bank of America** • 3215 N Lincoln Ave
- **Bank of America** • 963 W Belmont Ave
- **Bank of America (ATM)** • 945 W Belmont Ave
- **Bank of America (ATM)** • 3650 N Clark St
- **Bank of America (ATM)** • 3182 N Clark St
- **Bank of America (ATM)** • 3455 N Clark St
- **Bank of America (ATM)** • 3718 N Southport Ave
- **Bank of America (ATM)** • 948 W Addison St
- **Charter One (ATM)** • 958 W Diversey Pkwy • White Hen
- **Chase** • 1240 W Belmont Ave
- **Chase** • 2968 N Lincoln Ave
- **Chase** • 3335 N Ashland Ave
- **Chase** • 3730 N Southport Ave
- **Chase (ATM)** • 940 W Addison St
- **Citibank** • 3128 N Ashland Ave
- **Citibank (ATM)** • 7-Eleven • 1153 W Belmont Ave
- **Citibank (ATM)** • 7-Eleven • 3554 N Sheffield Ave
- **Citibank (ATM)** • 3753 N Clark St
- **Corus** • 3179 N Clark St
- **Corus** • 3604 N Southport Ave
- **First American** • 1345 W Diversey Pkwy
- **First American (ATM)** • 1001 W Belmont Ave
- **First American (ATM)** • 1153 W Addison St
- **First American (ATM)** • 1547 W Belmont Ave
- **First American (ATM)** • 2909 N Lincoln Ave
- **First American (ATM)** • 3100 N Lincoln Ave
- **First American (ATM)** • 3300 N Ashland Ave
- **First American (ATM)** • 3425 N Clark St
- **First American (ATM)** • 946 W Diversey Pkwy
- **First American** • 3166 N Clark St • Cesar's
- **Lakeside** • 2800 N Ashland Ave
- **LaSalle** • 3201 N Ashland Ave
- **LaSalle** • 3301 N Ashland Ave
- **LaSalle (ATM)** • 1060 W Addison St
- **LaSalle (ATM)** • 3650 N Clark St
- **North Community** • 1401 W Belmont Ave
- **North Community** • 3420 N Clark St
- **TCF** • Jewel • 2940 N Ashland Ave
- **TCF** • Jewel • 3630 N Southport Ave
- **TCF (ATM)** • Taco Bell • 1111 W Addison St
- **TCF (ATM)** • 7-Eleven • 1153 W Belmont Ave
- **TCF (ATM)** • 7-Eleven • 3554 N Sheffield Ave
- **TCF (ATM)** • Osco • 3637 N Southport Ave
- **Washington Mutual** • 3252 N Lincoln Ave
- **Washington Mutual** • 3500 N Clark St
- **Washington Mutual** • 3556 N Southport Ave

Car Washes

- **Quiroga's Detail & Hand Car Wash** • 3448 N Southport Ave

Car Rental

- **Enterprise** • 2900 N Sheffield Ave • 773-880-5001

Gas Stations

- **Amoco** • 1200 W Belmont Ave
- **BP** • 1355 W Diversey Pkwy
- **Citgo** • 3600 N Ashland Ave
- **Shell** • 1160 W Diversey Pkwy
- **Shell** • 2801 N Ashland Ave
- **Shell** • 3552 N Ashland Ave

Emergency Rooms

- **Advocate Illinois Masonic Medical Center** • 836 W Wellington Ave

Landmarks

- **North Alta Vista Terrace** • 3800 block of N Alta Vista Ter
- **Southport Lanes** • 3325 N Southport Ave
- **Vic Theatre** • 3145 N Sheffield Ave
- **Wrigley Field** • 1060 W Addison St

Parking

Pharmacies

- **CVS** • 3637 N Southport Ave
- **Jewel-Osco** • 2940 N Ashland Ave ♿
- **Walgreens** • 1001 W Belmont Ave
- **Walgreens** • 2835 N Sheffield Ave, Ste 505

Pizza

- **Art of Pizza** • 3033 N Ashland Ave
- **Bacci Pizzeria** • 950 W Addison St
- **Chicago's Pizza** • 3006 N Sheffield Ave
- **Chicago's Pizza & Pasta** • 3114 N Lincoln Ave
- **D'Agostino Pizzeria & Restaurant** • 1351 W Addison St
- **Gino's East** • 2801 N Lincoln Ave
- **Giordano's** • 1040 W Belmont Ave
- **Homemade Pizza Co** • 3430 N Southport Ave
- **La Gondola Pizzeria & Cucina Italiana** • 2914 N Ashland Ave
- **Leona's** • 3215 N Sheffield Ave
- **Papa Romeo's Pizza** • 926 W Diversey Pkwy
- **Philly's Best** • 907 W Belmont Ave
- **Pizza Capri** • 962 W Belmont Ave
- **Pizza Ria** • 3515 N Clark St
- **Pizza Rustica** • 3913 N Sheridan Rd
- **Pompeii Bakery** • 2955 N Sheffield Ave
- **Sapore di Napoli** • 1406 W Belmont Ave

Post Offices

- **US Post Office** • 3024 N Ashland Ave

Schools

- **Augustus H Burley Elementary** • 1630 W Barry Ave
- **Hawthorne Scholastic Academy** • 3319 N Clifton Ave
- **Horace Greeley Elementary** • 832 W Sheridan Rd
- **Inter-American Elementary** • 851 W Waveland Ave
- **James G Blaine Elementary** • 1420 W Grace St
- **John V LeMoyne Elementary** • 851 W Waveland Ave
- **Louis J Agassiz Elementary** • 2851 N Seminary Ave
- **St Alphonsus Academy** • 1439 W Wellington Ave
- **St Luke Academy** • 1500 W Belmont Ave

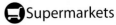 Supermarkets

- **Jewel-Osco** • 3630 N Southport Ave
- **Jewel-Osco** • 2940 N Ashland Ave ♿
- **Whole Foods Market** • 3300 N Ashland Ave

Map 43 • Wrigl

1

2

W Cuyler Ave
W Cuyler Ave
W Bittersweet Pl

W Irving Park Rd
40
Sheridan

W Dakin St

Hebrew
Cemetery

W Byron St
W Byron St
W Sheridan Rd

A

W Grace St

N Ashland Ave

W Waveland Ave

PAGE
269

Wrigley
Field

Addison

WRIGLEYVILLE

W Eddy St

W Brompton Ave

Shell
Park

W Cornelia Ave
W Cornelia Ave

42

W Newport Ave
W Newport Ave

Paulina
Southport
44

W Roscoe St
1200W
800W

B

W Henderson St
W Henderson St

W Buckingham Pl

W School St
W Aldine Ave

W Belmont Ave
Belmont

W Fletcher St
W Fletcher St
W Fletcher St
W California Ter

W Barry Ave
W Barry Ave

W Nelson St
W Nelson St

LAKEVIEW

W Wellington Ave
Wellington

W Oakdale Ave
W Oakdale Ave

C

W George St

W Wolfram St
W Wolfram St

W Diversey Pkwy
29
Diversey

W Schubert Ave

1/4 mile
.25 km

The Metro rocks this neighborhood while beautiful Music Box Theatre features art house films with a live organist on weekends. Spice lovers (and silverware haters) gnaw at Mama Desta's Red Sea Ethiopian restaurant. Wrigley bars cater to Cubs fans. For board games instead of baseball, head to the Newport Bar & Grill or Guthrie's Tavern.

Map 4

Coffee

- **Café Avanti** • 3714 N Southport Ave
- **Caribou Coffee** • 3240 N Ashland Ave
- **Cosi** • 1023 W Belmont Ave
- **Dunkin' Donuts** • 3000 N Ashland Ave
- **Dunkin' Donuts** • 3200 N Clark St
- **Einstein Bros Bagels** •
  3420 N Southport Ave
- **Einstein Bros Bagels** • 3455 N Clark St
- **Einstein Bros Bagels** • 933 W Diversey Pkwy
- **FIXX Coffee Bar** • 3053 N Sheffield Ave
- **The Julius Meinl Café** •
  3601 N Southport Ave
- **Mellow Grounds Coffee Lounge** •
  3807 N Ashland Ave
- **My Place for Tea** • 3210 N Sheffield Ave
- **Starbucks** • 1000 W Diversey Ave
- **Starbucks** • 1023 W Addison St
- **Starbucks** • 3045 N Greenview Ave
- **Starbucks** • 3184 N Clark St
- **Starbucks** • 3359 N Southport Ave

Copy Shops

- **FedEx Kinko's** • 3524 N Southport Ave ◎
- **The UPS Store** • 3105 N Ashland Ave
- **The UPS Store** • 3540 N Southport Ave

Farmers Markets

- **Southport Green Market (Jun–Oct; Sat,
  8 am–1 pm)** • 1420 W Grace St

Gyms

- **Chicago Fitness Center** •
  3131 N Lincoln Ave ◎
- **Curves (women only)** • 1409 W Addison St
- **Curves (women only)** • 2825 N Sheffield Ave
- **Lincoln Park Athletic Club** •
  1019 W Diversey Pkwy
- **Number One Gym** • 3232 N Sheffield Ave
- **XSport Fitness** • 3240 N Ashland Ave ◎

Hardware Stores

- **Ace Hardware** • 3921 N Sheridan Rd
- **Alhambra** • 3737 N Southport Ave
- **Klein True Value Hardware** •
  3737 N Southport Ave
- **Tenenbaum True Value Hardware** •
  1138 W Belmont Ave

Liquor Stores

- **1000 Liquors** • 1000 W Belmont Ave
- **Addison Liquors** • 932 W Addison St
- **Bel-Port Food & Liquor** •
  1362 W Belmont Ave
- **East Lake View Food & Liquor** •
  3814 N Clark St
- **Foremost Liquor Store** •
  3014 N Ashland Ave

- **Gilday Liquors** • 946 W Diversey Pkwy
- **Gold Crown Liquors Store** • 3425 N Clark St
- **Howards Wine Cellar (wine only)** •
  1244 W Belmont Ave
- **Que Syrah Fine Wines** •
  3726 N Southport Ave

Movie Theaters

- **Brew & View** • 3145 N Sheffield Ave
- **Music Box Theatre** • 3733 N Southport Ave

Nightlife

- **Bar Celona** • 3474 N Clark St
- **Berlin** • 954 W Belmont Ave
- **Bernie's** • 3664 N Clark St
- **Bottle Bar** • 950 W Wolfram St
- **Bourbon** • 3244 N Lincoln Ave
- **Bungalow Bar and Lounge** •
  1622 W Belmont Ave
- **Cooper's** • 1232 W Belmont Ave
- **Cubby Bear** • 1059 W Addison St
- **Elbo Room** • 2871 N Lincoln Ave
- **Fizz Bar and Grill** • 3220 N Lincoln Ave
- **Ginger Man Tavern** • 3740 N Clark St
- **Ginger's Ale House** • 3801 N Ashland Ave
- **Gunther Murphy's** • 1638 W Belmont Ave
- **Guthrie's Tavern** • 1300 W Addison St
- **Higgins' Tavern** • 3259 N Racine Ave
- **Improv Olympic** • 3541 N Clark St
- **Jack's Bar & Grill** • 2856 N Southport Ave
- **Justin's** • 3358 N Southport Ave
- **Lange's Lounge** • 3500 N Southport Ave
- **Lincoln Tap Room** • 3010 N Lincoln Ave
- **Metro** • 3730 N Clark St
- **Moxie** • 3517 N Clark St
- **Murphy's Bleachers** • 3655 N Sheffield Ave
- **Newport Bar & Grill** • 1344 W Newport Ave
- **Raw Bar** • 3720 N Clark St
- **Risque Café** • 3419 N Clark St
- **Schuba's** • 3159 N Southport Ave
- **Sheffield's** • 3258 N Sheffield Ave
- **Slugger's** • 3540 N Clark St
- **Smart Bar** • 3730 N Clark St
- **Sopo Lounge & Grill** •
  3418 N Southport Ave
- **Tai's Til 4** • 3611 N Ashland Ave
- **Ten Cat Tavern** • 3931 N Ashland Ave
- **Toons Bar** • 3857 N Southport Ave
- **Uncommon Ground Café** • 3800 N Clark St
- **Underground Lounge** • 952 N Newport Ave
- **Vida Lounge** • 1248 W George
- **Y*k-zies-Clark** • **3710 N Clark St**

Pet Shops

- **4 Legs** • 3809 N Clark St
- **Abby's Let's Pet (Dogs only)** •
  3404 N Ashland Ave
- **Petco** • 3118 N Ashland Ave

Restaurants

- **Ann Sather** • 929 W Belmont Ave
- **Blue Bayou** • 3734 N Southport Ave
- **Bolat** • 3346 N Clark St
- **Capt'n Nemos** • 3650 N Ashland Ave
- **Coobah** • 3423 N Southport Ave
- **Duck Walk** • 919 W Belmont Ave
- **Fixture** • 2706 N Ashland
- **Frasca** • 3358 N Paulina St
- **Golden Apple** • 2971 N Lincoln Ave ◎
- **Lucky's** • 3472 N Clark St
- **Mama Desta's Red Sea** • 3216 N Clark St
- **Matsu Yama** • 1059 W Belmont Ave
- **Matsuya** • 3469 N Clark St
- **Mia Francesca** • 3311 N Clark St
- **Mystic Celt** • 3443 N Southport Ave
- **Orange** • 3231 N Clark St
- **Panes** • 3002 N Sheffield Ave
- **Penny's Noodle Shop** • 3400 N Sheffield Ave
- **Pierogi Factory** • 1034 W Belmont Ave
- **PS Bangkok** • 3345 N Clark St
- **Rise** • 3401 N Southport Ave
- **Risque Café** • 3419 N Clark St
- **S&G** • 3000 N Lincoln Ave
- **Shiroi Hana** • 3242 N Clark St
- **Socca** • 3301 N Clark St
- **Tango Sur** • 3763 N Southport Ave
- **Twisted Spoke** • 3365 N Clark St
- **Wrigleyville Dog** • 3737 N Clark St
- **Violet** • 3819 N Southport Ave

Shopping

- **The Alley** • 3228 N Clark St
- **Bookworks** • 3444 N Clark St
- **Disgraceland** • 3338 N Clark St
- **Fashion Tomato** • 937 W Belmont Ave
- **Hollywood Mirror** • 812 W Belmont Ave
- **Izzy** • 3406 N Ashland Ave
- **J. Toguri Mercantile Co** • 851 W Belmont
  Ave
- **Krista K** • 3458 N Southport Ave
- **Leahy & LaDue Consignment** • 3753 N
  Southport Ave
- **Midwest Stereo** • 1613 W Belmont Ave
- **Namaskar Boutique** •
  3950 N Southport Ave
- **Never Mind** • 953 W Belmont Ave
- **Ragstock** • 812 W Belmont Ave
- **Strange Cargo** • 3448 N Clark St
- **Thousand Waves Spa** • 1212 W Belmont Ave
- **Trousseau** • 3543 N Southport Ave
- **Uncle Fun** • 1338 W Belmont Ave
- **Yellow Jacket** • 2959 N Lincoln Ave

Video Rental

- **Blockbuster** • 2803 N Ashland Ave
- **Nationwide Video** • 843 1/2 W Belmont Ave

A.K.A. Boystown due to its highly visable gay community, East Lakeview is home to Chicago's annual Pride Parade and the equally flamboyant Halsted Street Market Days. South of Belmont things tone down a bit, and brownstone and graystone condos are just as likely occupied by young (straight) married couples as by gays. Great shopping and active nightlife make parking in East Lakeview absolutely awful.

Banks

- **Bank of America (ATM)** • 3651 N Halsted St
- **Charter One** • 664 W Diversey Pkwy
- **Chase** • 3032 N Clark St
- **Chase** • 3714 N Broadway St
- **Chase (ATM)** • Walgreens • 2801 N Broadway St
- **Chase (ATM)** • Walgreens • 3046 N Halsted St
- **Chase (ATM)** • 3107 N Broadway St
- **Chase (ATM)** • Walgreens • 3201 N Broadway St
- **Chase (ATM)** • Walgreens • 3646 N Broadway St
- **Chase (ATM)** • Walgreens • 740 W Diversey Pkwy
- **Citibank (ATM)** • 7-Eleven • 3407 N Halsted St
- **Citibank (ATM)** • 7-Eleven • 3700 N Broadway St
- **Fifth Third** • 3601 N Broadway St
- **Fifth Third** • 640 W Diversey Pkwy
- **First American (ATM)** • 2830 N Broadway St
- **First American (ATM)** • 2924 N Broadway St
- **First American (ATM)** • 3000 N Clark St
- **First American (ATM)** • 3114 N Broadway St
- **First American (ATM)** • 3121 N Broadway St
- **First American (ATM)** • 3131 N Clark St
- **First American (ATM)** • Whole Foods • 3640 N Halsted St
- **First American (ATM)** • 3843 N Broadway St
- **First American (ATM)** • 521 W Diversey Pkwy
- **First American (ATM)** • 671 W Diversey Pkwy
- **Harris Trust & Savings** • 3601 N Halsted St
- **Harris Trust & Savings** • 558 W Diversey Pkwy
- **LaSalle** • 3051 N Clark St
- **LaSalle** • 538 W Diversey Pkwy
- **MidAmerica** • 3020 N Broadway St
- **North Community** • 3180 N Broadway St
- **North Community** • 3639 N Broadway St
- **North Community** • 742 W Diversey Pkwy
- **TCF** • Jewel • 3531 N Broadway St
- **TCF (ATM)** • Osco • 3101 N Clark St
- **TCF (ATM)** • 7-Eleven • 3407 N Halsted St
- **TCF (ATM)** • 7-Eleven • 3700 N Broadway St

Car Rental

- **Budget** • 3721 N Broadway St • 773-528-1770
- **Hertz** • 3151 N Halsted St • 773-832-1912

Gas Stations

- **Mobil** • 3901 N Broadway St
- **Shell** • 801 W Addison St

Emergency Rooms

- **St Joseph's** • 2900 N Lake Shore Dr

Landmarks

- **Belmont Harbor** • W Belmont Ave & N Lake Shore Dr
- **Belmont Rocks** • W Briar Pl at the lake
- **Dog Beach** • Northern tip of Belmont Harbor
- **The Giraffes** • N Elaine Pl & W Roscoe Ave
- **Totem Pole** • W Waveland Ave & N Belmont Harbor Dr

Libraries

- **John Merlo Public Library** • 644 W Belmont Ave

Parking

Pharmacies

- **CVS** • 3101 N Clark St
- **CVS** • 3033 N Broadway St
- **Jewel-Osco** • 3531 N Broadway St
- **Walgreens** • 2801 N Broadway St
- **Walgreens** • 3046 N Halsted St
- **Walgreens** • 3201 N Broadway St
- **Walgreens** • 3646 N Broadway St
- **Walgreens** • 740 W Diversey Pkwy

Pizza

- **Chili Mac's Pizza** • 3152 N Broadway St
- **Domino's** • 3103 N Clark St
- **Homemade Pizza** • 3314 N Broadway St
- **Nancy's Pizza** • 2930 N Broadway St
- **Pizza Paninos** • 3702 N Broadway St
- **Renaldi's Pizza Pub** • 2827 N Broadway St

Police

- **23rd District (Town Hall)** • 3600 N Halsted St

Post Offices

- **US Post Office** • 3170 N Sheridan Rd

Schools

- **Bernard Zell Ansche Emet Day** • 3760 N Pine Grove Ave
- **Chicago City Day** • 541 W Hawthorne Pl
- **Lake View Academy** • 716 W Addison St
- **Mt Carmel Academy** • 720 W Belmont Ave
- **Nettelhorst Elementary** • 3252 N Broadway St

Supermarkets

- **Jewel-Osco** • 3531 N Broadway St
- **Treasure Island** • 3460 N Broadway St

Map 44 · **East Lakeview**

Numerous dining options and a hopping bar scene (gay bars north of Belmont, Irish pubs south), make this area a hot destination for nightlife. Catch the latest arthouse film at Century Cinema. Roscoe's and Sidetrack are two cavernous gay clubs that really pack 'em in. If you are coming to East Lakeview, do yourself a favor and cab it. Taxis are abundant in these parts and it's a cinch to hail one at any hour.

Coffee

- **Argo Tea** • 3135 N Broadway St
- **Borders** • 2817 N Clark St
- **Cafe Latakia** • 3204 N Broadway St
- **Caribou Coffee** • 3025 N Clark St
- **Caribou Coffee** • 3300 N Broadway St
- **Caribou Coffee** • 3500 N Halsted St
- **Coffee & Tea Exchange** •
  3311 N Broadway St
- **Dunkin' Donuts** • 801 W Diversey Pkwy
- **House of Hookah** • 607 W Belmont Ave
- **Intelligentsia Coffee Roasters** •
  3123 N Broadway St
- **Red Hen Bread** • 500 W Diversey Pkwy
- **Starbucks** • 3358 N Broadway St
- **Starbucks** • 3845 N Broadway St
- **Starbucks** • 617 W Diversey Pkwy

Copy Shops

- **FedEx Kinko's** • 3001 N Clark St ⊕
- **Sir Speedy** • 2818 N Halsted St
- **The UPS Store** • 3023 N Clark St
- **The UPS Store** • 3712 N Broadway St

Farmers Markets

- **North Halsted Chicago Farmers Market
  (Jun–Oct; Sat, 7 am–2 pm)** •
  On Halsted St north of W Bradley Pl

Gyms

- **Bally Total Fitness** • 2828 N Clark St
- **Chicago Sweat Shop** • 3215 N Broadway St
- **Fitness Formula** • 3228 N Halsted St
- **Fitness Formula** • 3657 N Pine Grove Ave
- **New York Health Club** •
  3657 N Pine Grove Ave
- **Quads** • 3727 N Broadway St

Hardware Stores

- **Clark Street Ace Hardware** •
  3011 N Clark St
- **Edwards True Value Hardware** •
  2804 N Halsted St
- **Lehman's True Value Hardware** •
  3473 N Broadway St
- **Midtown True Value Hardware** •
  3130 N Broadway St

Liquor Stores

- **Apple Bite** • 2919 N Broadway St
- **Broadway Food & Liquor** •
  3158 N Broadway St
- **Eastgate Wine & Spirits** •
  446 W Diversey Pkwy
- **Gold Medal Liquors** • 3823 N Broadway St
- **The Gourmet Grape** • 3530 N Halsted St
- **Kafka Wine (wine only)** •
  3325 N Halsted St
- **Paradise Liquors** • 2934 N Broadway St
- **Sysha Food and Liquor** •
  702 W Diversey Pkwy
- **Valhalla** • 3317 N Broadway St

Movie Theaters

- **Landmark Century Centre Cinema** •
  2828 N Clark St

Nightlife

- **Bridget McNeill's** • 420 W Belmont Ave
- **Charlie's Chicago** • 3726 N Broadway St
- **Circuit** • 3641 N Halsted St
- **The Closet** • 3325 N Broadway St
- **Cocktail** • 3359 N Halsted St
- **Duke of Perth** • 2913 N Clark St
- **Friar Tuck** • 3010 N Broadway St
- **Hydrate** • 3458 N Halsted St
- **Kit Kat Lounge** • 3700 N Halsted St
- **Little Jim's** • 3501 N Halsted St
- **minibar** • 3341 N Halsted St
- **Monsignor Murphy's** •
  3019 N Broadway St
- **Roscoe's** • 3356 N Halsted St
- **Sidetrack** • 3349 N Halsted St
- **Spin** • 800 W Belmont Ave
- **Town Hall Pub** • 3340 N Broadway St
- **Wilde** • 3130 N Broadway St

Pet Shops

- **Paradise Pet Salon** • 3920 N Broadway St
- **Petco** • 3046 N Halsted St
- **Petsmart - Store** • 2832 N Broadway St
- **Scrub Your Pup** • 2935 N Clark St
- **Wigglyville** • 3337 N Broadway St

Restaurants

- **Adesso** • 3332 N Broadway St
- **Angelina Ristorante** • 3561 N Broadway St
- **Ann Sather** • 3411 N Broadway St
- **Arco de Cuchilleros** • 3445 N Halsted St
- **The Bagel** • 3107 N Broadway St
- **Baladoche** • 2905 N Clark St
- **Bobtail Soda Fountain** • 2951 N
  Broadway St
- **Chicago Diner** • 3411 N Halsted St
- **Clark Street Dog** • 3040 N Clark St ⊕
- **Cornelia's** • 750 W Cornelia Ave
- **Erwin, An American Café & Bar** •
  2925 N Halsted St
- **Firefly** • 3335 N Halsted St
- **Half Shell** • 676 W Diversey Pkwy
- **HB** • 3404 N Halsted St
- **Jack's on Halsted** • 3201 N Halsted St
- **Joy's** • 3257 N Broadway St
- **Koryo** • 2936 N Broadway St
- **La Creperie** • 2845 N Clark St
- **Las Mananitas** • 3523 N Halsted St
- **Mark's Chop Suey** • 3343 N Halsted St
- **New Tokyo** • 3139 N Broadway St
- **Ping Pong Restaurant** •
  3322 N Broadway St
- **Stella's Diner** • 3042 N Broadway St
- **Sura** • 3124 N Broadway St
- **Wakamono** • 3317 N Broadway St
- **Yoshi's Café** • 3257 N Halsted St

Shopping

- **Borderline** • 3333 N Broadway St
- **Century Mall** • 2828 N Clark St
- **Clothes Optional** • 2918 N Clark St
- **Cupcakes** • 613 W Briar Pl
- **Equinox** • 3401 N Broadway St
- **GayMart** • 3459 N Halsted St
- **He Who Eats Mud** • 3247 N Broadway St
- **P&L** • 2956 N Clark St
- **Pastoral Artisan Cheese, Bread & Wine** •
  2945 N Broadway St
- **Reckless Records** • 3161 N Broadway St
- **skinstinct** • 3343 N Broadway St
- **Spare Parts** • 2947 N Broadway St
- **Tulip Toy Gallery** • 3448 N Halsted St
- **Unabridged Books** • 3251 N Broadway St
- **Windy City Sweets** • 3308 N Broadway St

Video Rental

- **Blockbuster** • 3120 N Clark St
- **Broadway Video** • 3916 N Broadway St
- **Flicks DVD** • 650 W Cornelia Ave
- **Golden Video** • 3619 N Broadway St
- **Hollywood Video** • 2868 N Broadway St
- **Nationwide Video** • 3936 N Clarendon Ave
- **RJ's Video** • 3452 N Halsted St
- **Specialty Video** • 3221 N Broadway St
- **Windy City Video** • 3701 N Halsted St

1 mile

1 km

Essentials

If there's one thing you can count on in Northwest Chicago, it's that you can count on just about everything. Compared to other sections of the city, the Northwest is a bastion of stability. Most of the people and businesses have been around forever, and even typically transitory ethnic enclaves are fairly entrenched. This includes a crazy quilt of Eastern European, Middle Eastern, Korean, and Italian quarters, blocks, and streets. Northwest Chicago is blessed with an abundance of small parks and field houses, as well as a large hunk of forest preserve, giving much of the area a bucolic, suburban feel.

⊙Landmarks

- **The Admiral Theater** • 3940 W Lawrence Ave
- **Copernicus Center** • 5216 W Lawrence Ave
- **Eugene Field Park** • 5100 N Ridgeway Ave
- **Gompers Park** • 4222 W Foster Ave
- **Hanson Park Fieldhouse** • 5501 W Fullerton Ave

- **Harlem CTA Station** • N Harlem Ave & The Kennedy Expy
- **Logan Square Column** • 3100 W Logan Blvd
- **Superdawg Drive-In** • 6363 N Milwaukee Ave
- **Walt Disney House** • 2156 N Tripp Ave

Sundries / Entertainment

Northwest Chicago wears its blue-collar ethnic proclivities on its sleeve. Local shops and restaurants don't go out of their way to attract clientele outside of their own, and signs, menus, and even the staff at the area's abundant Korean and Eastern European businesses make little effort to communicate in English. (The same can be said for the clientele at many of the area's numerous, ostensibly English-speaking, corner taverns.) Adventuresome diners rise to the challenge—some of the city's best unsung gems are to be found here, including Thai vegan spot Amitabul and the Swedish Tre Kronor. Toss back authentic pints at the 5th Province Pub. Located in the Irish-American Heritage Center, it's only open on Friday and Saturday nights. Rosa's Lounge is a venerable, beloved Chicago jazz and blues venue.

☕Coffee

- **Café Prague** • 6710 W Belmont Ave
- **Cafeteria Marianao II** • 4825 W Armitage Ave
- **Caffé Italia** • 2625 N Harlem Ave
- **Capitol Café** • 2550 N Pulaski Rd
- **Dimaggio Bakery & Café** • 7326 W Lawrence Ave
- **Dk Café** • 6140 W Belmont Ave
- **Dunkin' Donuts** • 2337 N Cicero Ave
- **Dunkin' Donuts** • 2640 N Narragansett Ave
- **Dunkin' Donuts** • 3039 N Central Ave
- **Dunkin' Donuts** • 3359 N Harlem Ave
- **Dunkin' Donuts** • 3801 W Belmont Ave
- **Dunkin' Donuts** • 3843 N Cicero Ave
- **Dunkin' Donuts** • 3946 W Devon Ave
- **Dunkin' Donuts** • 4045 W Lawrence Ave
- **Dunkin' Donuts** • 4245 N Milwaukee Ave
- **Dunkin' Donuts** • 4359 N Pulaski Rd
- **Dunkin' Donuts** • 4644 W Diversey Ave
- **Dunkin' Donuts** • 4867 N Milwaukee Ave
- **Dunkin' Donuts** • 5000 N Irving Park Rd
- **Dunkin' Donuts** • 5050 N Cicero Ave
- **Dunkin' Donuts** • 5205 N Nagle Ave
- **Dunkin' Donuts** • 5650 N Fullerton Ave
- **Dunkin' Donuts** • 5949 N Higgins Rd
- **Dunkin' Donuts** • 5959 W Diversey Ave
- **Dunkin' Donuts** • 6001 N Addison St
- **Dunkin' Donuts** • 6200 W Belmont Ave
- **Dunkin' Donuts** • 6342 N Milwaukee Ave
- **Dunkin' Donuts** • 6408 W Irving Park Rd
- **Dunkin' Donuts** • 7156 N Harlem Ave
- **Dunkin' Donuts** • 7171 W Irving Park Rd
- **Dunkin' Donuts** • 7201 W Grand Ave
- **Dunkin' Donuts** • 7801 W Lawrence Ave
- **Edgebrook Coffee Shop** • 6322 N Central Ave
- **Euro Café** • 3435 N Harlem Ave
- **Euro Cappuccino** • 5759 W Belmont Ave
- **Flavors On Avers** • 4526 N Avers Ave
- **Gloria Jean's Coffee Bean** • 4202 N Harlem Ave
- **J Bean Coffee & Café** • 7221 W Forest Preserve Ave
- **Java Thai** • 4272 W Irving Park Rd
- **Jazz It Café** • 4202 W Irving Park Rd
- **Morning Grind** • 6701 N Olmsted Ave
- **Open Hearth Coffee Shop** • 5207 N Kimball Ave
- **Schlegl's Bakery & Café** • 3334 W Foster Ave
- **Starbucks** • Target • 2901 S Cicero Ave
- **Starbucks** • Target • 4104 N Harlem Ave
- **Starbucks** • 4159 W Peterson Ave
- **Starbucks** • 4365 W Irving Park Rd
- **Starbucks** • 5406 W Devon Ave
- **Starbucks** • 6312 N Nagle Ave

- **Starbucks** • 6451 W Diversey Ave
- **Starbucks** • Target • 6525 W Diversey Ave

🎬Movie Theaters

- **AMC Loews Norridge 10** • 4520 N Harlem Ave
- **LaSalle Bank Cinema** • 4901 W Irving Park Rd

🍸Nightlife

- **5th Province Pub** • Irish-American Heritage Ctr • 4626 N Knox Ave
- **Abbey Pub** • 3420 W Grace St
- **Babe's** • 4416 N Milwaukee Ave
- **The Burlington** • 3425 W Fullerton Ave
- **Edison Park Inn** • 6715 N Olmstead Ave
- **Emerald Isle** • 6686 N Northwest Hwy
- **Fantasy Lounge** • 4400 N Elston
- **Fischman Liquors** • 4780 N Milwaukee Ave
- **Flo's Algiers Lounge** • 5436 W Montrose Ave
- **Ham Tree** • 5333 N Milwaukee Ave
- **Hollywood Lounge** • 3301 W Bryn Mawr Ave
- **Jimmy Mack** • 5581 N Northwest Hwy
- **Moretti's** • 6727 N Olmsted Ave
- **New Polonia Club** • 6101 W Belmont Ave
- **Original Dugan's** • 6051 N Milwaukee Ave
- **Rosa's Lounge** • 3420 W Armitage Ave
- **Three Counties** • 5856 N Milwaukee Ave
- **Vaughan's Pub** • 5485 N Northwest Hwy
- **Weegee's Lounge** • 3659 W Armitage Ave

🍴Restaurants

- **Al Primo Canto** • 5414 W Devon Ave
- **Amitabul** • 6207 N Milwaukee Ave
- **Balanced Kitchen** • 6263 McCormick Blvd
- **Big Pho** • 3821 W Lawrence Ave
- **Birria Huentitan** • 4019 W North Ave
- **Blue Angel** • 5310 N Milwaukee Ave ⊚
- **Borincuba** • 3424 W Irving Park Rd
- **Brown Sack** • 3706 W Armitage Ave
- **Café con Leche** • 2714 N Milwaukee Ave
- **Carthage Café** • 3446 W Foster Ave
- **Chai Asian Bistro** • 4748 W Peterson Ave
- **Chiyo** • 3800 W Lawrence Ave
- **Chocolate Shoppe Ice Cream** • 5337 W Devon Ave
- **Don Juan** • 6730 N Northwest Hwy
- **Edgebrook Coffee Shop** • 6322 N Central Ave
- **El Cubanito** • 2555 N Pulaski Rd

- **Elliott's Seafood Grille & Chop House** • 6690 N Northwest Hwy
- **Fonda Del Mar** • 3749 W Fullerton Ave
- **Friendship Chinese Restaurant** • 2830 N Milwaukee Ave
- **Gale Street Inn** • 4914 N Milwaukee Ave
- **Gloria's Café** • 3300 W Fullerton Ave
- **Grota Smorgasborg** • 3112 N Central Ave
- **Halina's Polish Delights** • 5914 W Lawrence Ave
- **Hiromi's** • 3609 W Lawrence Ave
- **Joy Ribs** • 6320 N Lincoln Ave
- **La Villa Restaurant** • 3638 N Pulaski Rd
- **Mario's Café** • 5241 N Harlem Ave
- **Mayan Sol** • 3830 W Lawrence Ave
- **Mirabell** • 3454 W Addison St
- **Montasero's Ristorante** • 3935 W Devon Ave
- **Pollo Campero** • 2730 N Narragansett Ave
- **Red Apple** • 3121 N Milwaukee Ave
- **Ristorante Agostino** • 2817 N Harlem Ave
- **Sabatino's** • 4441 W Irving Park Rd
- **Seo Hae** • 3534 W Lawrence Ave
- **Shiraz** • 4425 W Montrose
- **Smak-Tak** • 5961 N Elston Ave
- **Smoque** • 3800 N Pulaski Rd
- **So Gong Dong Tofu House** • 3307 W Bryn Mawr Ave
- **Sol de Mexico** • 3018 N Cicero Ave
- **Super Pollo** • 3640 W Wrightwood Ave
- **Teresa II Polish Restaurants & Lounge** • 4751 N Milwaukee Ave
- **Trattoria Pasta D'Arte** • 6311 N Milwaukee Ave
- **Tre Kronor** • 3258 W Foster Ave
- **Via Veneto** • 6340 N Lincoln Ave
- **Zia's Trattoria** • 6699 N Northwest Hwy

🛍Shopping

- **Albany Office Supply** • 3419 W Lawrence Ave
- **American Science & Surplus** • 5316 N Milwaukee Ave
- **Fishguy** • 4423 N Elston Ave
- **Harlem Irving Plaza** • Irving Park Rd & Forest Preserve Dr
- **NY Shoes Imports** • 3546 W Lawrence Ave
- **Perfumes R' Us** • 3608 W Lawrence Ave
- **Rolling Stone Records** • 7300 W Irving Park Rd
- **Salvation Army Thrift Store** • 3837 W Fullerton Ave
- **Srpska Tradicija** • 3615 W Lawrence Ave
- **Sweden Shop** • 3304 W Foster Ave
- **Village Discount Outlet** • 4635 N Elston Ave

183

Greater Chicago · West

CRAGIN
HERMOSA
W Grand Ave
W Armitage Ave
LOGAN SQUARE
W North Ave
BUCKTOWN
WICKER PARK
64
90
94
48
W Grand Ave
WEST HUMBOLDT PARK
27
Bison Statues
Humboldt Park
21
Chicago
NOBLE SQUARE
N Austin Blvd
N Central Ave
N Laramie Ave
N Cicero Ave
HUMBOLDT PARK
W Division St
UKRAINIAN VILLAGE
N Ashland Ave
N Damen Ave
N Racine Ave
Dan Ryan Expy
N Clybourn Ave
NORTH AUSTIN
W Chicago Ave
50
WEST TOWN
49
EAST GARFIELD PARK
Conservatory-Central Park Drive
Chicago Center for Green Technology
23
Ashland
Austin Town Hall
Laramie
Garfield Park Conservatory
Engine 44 Firehouse Mural
Randolph Pl
Washington Blvd
Adams Ave
Austin
Central
Cicero
W Lake St
Pulaski
Kedzie
W Washington Blvd
NEAR WEST SIDE
W Ogden Ave
W Jackson Blvd
SOUTH AUSTIN
WEST GARFIELD PARK
Garfield Park
Delta Fish Market
Our Lady of Sorrows
California
Western
Medical Center
Racine
UIC-Halsted
Columbus Park
Cicero Stadium
PAGE 218
Eisenhower Expy
Austin
LAWNDALE
Cicero
290
Pulaski
Kedzie-Homan
TRI-TAYLOR
ILLINOIS MEDICAL DISTRICT
Polk
UNIVERSITY VILLAGE/ LITTLE ITALY
50
W Roosevelt Rd
25
Columbus Park Refectory
LITTLE VILLAGE
W Douglas Blvd
Douglas Park
18th
54th/Cermak
W 16th St
Central Park
W Ogden Ave
Western
Douglas Park
CICERO
Cicero
Pulaski
W Cermak Rd
Kedzie
California
Hoyne
BEART OF CHICAGO
PILSEN
34
W 26th St
Halsted
S Blue Island Ave
S Racine Ave
S Canalport Ave
S Throop St
4
12
W 26th St
Halsted
BRIDGEPORT
51
STICKNEY
W 31st St
MCKINGLEY PARK
Ashland
35th/Archer
W 35th St
52
Pershing Rd
Chicago Sanitary and Ship Canal
55
BRIGHTON PARK
W Pershing Rd
Stevenson Expy
ARCHER HEIGHTS
2
Union Stockyard Gate
15
W 43rd St
SLEEPY HOLLOW
W 47th St
W 43rd St
LE CLAIR COURTS
W 47th St
VITTUM PARK
53
W Archer Ave
W 51st St
Kedzie
Western
54
GAGE PARK
Pulaski
SHERMAN PARK
W 55th St
BACK OF THE YARDS
W Garfield Blvd
Chicago Midway
WEST ELSDON
W 59th St
ENGLEWOOD

1 mile   1 km

Essentials

Chicago's West Side retains a large part of the historic architecture yet to be infiltrated by massive condo developments, probably because there's not much demand for high-crime high-rises. The massive Garfield Park Conservatory offers many fresh breaths with its vast collection of foliage, and sits on one of four large parks, which include fishing lagoons, baseball diamonds, and even a golf course.

oLandmarks

- **Austin Town Hall** · 5610 W Lake St
- **Bison Statues at Humboldt Park** · 1400 N Sacramento Ave
- **Chicago Center for Green Technology** · 445 N Sacramento Blvd
- **Columbus Park Refectory** · Columbus Park, 500 S Central Ave
- **Delta Fish Market** · 228 S Kedzie Ave
- **Engine 44 Firehouse Mural** · 412 N Kedzie Ave
- **Garfield Park Conservatory** · 300 N Central Park Ave
- **Our Lady of Sorrows** · 3121 W Jackson Blvd
- **Union Stockyard Gate** · Exchange Ave & Peoria St

Sundries / Entertainment

The steadily gentrifying stretch of West Chicago Avenue is home to Black Beetle, a hotspot for hipsters as well as yuppies, and also hosts Tommy's Rock-n-Roll Café, where you can, seriously, purchase a guitar with a sandwich. For tastes south of the border, Mexican joints are all pretty much within walking distance from one another.

Coffee

- **Dunkin' Donuts** · 1345 N Pulaski Rd
- **Dunkin' Donuts** · 2477 S Archer Ave
- **Dunkin' Donuts** · 2801 S Kedzie Ave
- **Dunkin' Donuts** · 3528 S Leavitt St
- **Dunkin' Donuts** · 3910 S Archer Ave
- **Dunkin' Donuts** · 4302 S Ashland Ave
- **Dunkin' Donuts** · 4669 S Cicero Ave
- **Dunkin' Donuts** · 4701 S Kedzie Ave
- **Dunkin' Donuts** · 4800 W Lake St
- **Dunkin' Donuts** · 4957 S Central Ave
- **Dunkin' Donuts** · 5707 W North Ave
- **Dunkin' Donuts** · 6641 S Cicero Ave
- **Dunkin' Donuts** · 782 N Laramie Ave
- **Dunkin' Donuts** · 800 N Kedzie Ave
- **Humboldt Pie** · 1001 N California Ave
- **PR Cafeteria** · 1552 N Kedzie Ave
- **Starbucks** · 1940 W 33rd St
- **Starbucks** · 3350 W Roosevelt Rd
- **Starbucks** · Target· 4433 S Pulaski Rd
- **Starbucks** · 4701 S Cicero Ave
- **Tassili Café** · 4342 N Elston Ave
- **Tommy's Rock-n-Roll Café** · 2548 W Chicago Ave

Nightlife

- **Black Beetle** · 2532 W Chicago Ave
- **California Clipper** · 1002 N California Ave
- **Grandma Sally's** · 5225 W Madison
- **La Justicia** · 3901 W 26th St

Restaurants

- **Amarind's** · 6822 W North Ave
- **Bacchanalia Ristorante** · 2413 S Oakley Ave
- **Bruna's** · 2424 S Oakley Ave
- **CJ's Eatery** · 3839 W Grand Ave
- **Coco** · 2723 W Division St
- **Coleman's Hickory House** · 5754 W Chicago Ave
- **Depot** · 5840 W Roosevelt Rd
- **Edna's Restaurant** · 3175 W Madison St
- **El Salvador Restaurante** · 4125 S Archer Ave
- **Falco's Pizza** · 2806 W 40th St
- **Feed** · 2803 W Chicago Ave
- **Flying Saucer** · 1123 N California Ave
- **Haro** · 2436 S Oakley Ave
- **Humboldt Pie** · 1001 N California Ave
- **I. C. Y. Vegetarian Restaurant & Juice Bar** · 3141 W Roosevelt Rd
- **Ignotz** · 2421 S Oakley Ave
- **La Palma** · 1340 N Homan Ave
- **Lalo's** · 3515 W 26th St
- **Lindy's and Gertie's** · 3685 S Archer Ave
- **MacArthur's** · 5412 W Madison Ave
- **Maiz** · 1041 N California Ave
- **New Submarine Pier** · 4048 S Archer Ave
- **Taqueria Atotonilco** · 3916 W 26th St
- **Taqueria Los Comales** · 3141 W 26th St
- **Taqueria Los Gallos 2** · 4252 S Archer Ave
- **Taqueria Puebla Mexico** · 3625 W North Ave
- **TipsyCake** · 1043 N California Ave
- **Tommy's Rock-n-Roll Café** · 2548 W Chicago Ave

Shopping

- **Buyer's Flea Market** · 4545 W Division St
- **Family Dollar** · 5410 W Chicago Ave
- **Moo & Oink** · 4848 W Madison St
- **Village Discount Outlet** · 2514 W 47th St
- **Village Discount Outlet** · 4020 W 26th St

1

2

49

50

34

Pulaski

Central Park

54th/Cermak

Cicero

Kildare

W Cermak Rd

W 19th St

W Cullerton St

W 21st St

W Cermak Rd

19th St

W 1st St

W 21st St

W 22nd St

W 23rd St

W 23rd Pl

W 24th St

W 24th St

W 25th St

W Ogden Ave

S Trumbull Ave
S Saint Louis Ave
S Central Park Ave
S Millard Ave
S Lawndale Ave
S Ridgeway Ave
S Avers Ave
S Springfield Ave

S Harding Ave

W 26th St

W 26th St

W 26th St

W 27th St

W 28th St

W 30th St

W 31st St

A

W 27th St

W 28th St

W 29th St

S Austin Blvd

S 55th Ave
S 56th Ave
S 57th Ave
S 58th Ave

S 54th Ave
S 57th Ave
S 58th Ave

W 25th Pl

W 28th St

W 28th Pl

W 29th St

W 29th Pl

W 30th St

W 30th Pl

S Komar Ave
S Kolin Ave
S Kildare Ave
S Keeler Ave
S Tripp Ave

S Kostner Ave
S Kenneth Ave
S Kilbourn Ave

S Karlov Ave
S Kedvale Ave
S Keeler Ave

S Komensky Ave

Piotrowski
Park

W 34th St

W 35th St

CICERO

Harvey Ave
Lombard Ave

S 60th Ct
S 61st Ave

S 60th Ave
S 58th Ct

29th St

31st St

Edgewood Ave

33rd St

S 60th Ct
S 61st Ct

S 60th Ave
S 61st Ct

Harvey Ave

Custer Ave

W 31st Pl
W 32nd St
W 32nd Pl
W 33rd St

W Park Ave

S 52nd Ct
S 53rd Ct
S 54th Ct
S 55th Ct

S Laramie Ave
S 52nd Ave
S 53rd Ave

S Pulaski Rd

W 34th St

W 35th St

W 34th St

W 35th St

W 35th Pl

W 36th St

S Kostner Ave

Frontage Rd

B

36th St

37th St

W 34th St

S Austin Blvd

W 35th St

S Central Avenue

Custer Ave

S 60th Ct
S 61st Ct

S 60th Ave
S 61st Ct

Hawthorne Race Course

W 38th St

W Pershing Rd

W 41st St

STICKNEY

Cicero Ave

286

287

Chicago Sanitary and Ship Canal

55

W 40th St

W 42nd St

W 41st St

W 42nd Ave

S Hamlin Ave

S Saint Louis Ave

ARCHER HEIGHTS

S Drake Ave

W 42nd St

W 43rd St

W 44th St

LeClaire Courts

W 44th St

W 44th Pl

285

SLEEPY
HOLLOW

W 45th St

W 46th St

S Kolmar Ave

W 45th Pl

W 46th St

S Archer

LE CLAIR
COURTS

W 47th St

S Luna Ave
S Linder Ave
S Lotus Ave
S Long Ave
S Lorel Ave
S Lockwood Ave
S Laramie Ave
S Leclaire Ave
S Lamon Ave
S Leamington Ave
S Laporte Ave
S La Crosse Ave
S Lavergne Ave
S Lavel Ave

S Knox Ave
S Kilpatrick Ave
S Keating Ave

S Komensky Ave
S Karlov Ave
S Kedvale Ave

Archer
Park

W 48th St

W 49th St

W 50th St

S Springfield Ave
S Avers Ave
S Harding Ave

S Central Park Ave

S 47

W 50th St

53

Vittum Park

W 50th St

W 51st St

Pulaski

C

51st St

W 51st St

W 52nd St

W 53rd St

W 54th St

S Menard Ave
S Mason Ave
S Mayfield Ave
S Mason Ct

S Parkside Ave
S Mayfield Ave
S Menard Ave
S Massasoit Ave

S Major Ave
S Monitor Ave

VITTUM
PARK

W 53rd St

Archer Ave

W 52nd St

W 53rd St

W 54th St

W 55th St

S Kolin Ave
S Tripp Ave
S Keeler Ave
S Kildare Ave

S Kedvale Ave

Strohacker
Park

W 51st St

W 52nd Pl

W 53rd St

S Elsdon Ave
S Millard Ave

S Merrimac Ave
S Mobile Ave

S Austin Ave
S Moncolett Ave
S Meade Ave
S Moody Ave

W 56th St

W 57th St

Chicago Midway
Airport

PAGE
274

Airport Dr

W 55th St

W 55th Pl
W 56th St
W 56th Pl
W 57th St
W 57th Pl
W 58th St

WEST ELSDON

Pasteur
Park

Senaca
Park

Midway

1/2 mile

.5 km

Adlai E Stevenson Expy

ARCHER HEIGHTS

W 47th St

W 47th St

BACK OF THE YARDS

GARFIELD RIDGE

W Archer Ave

Pulaski

Kedzie

Western

W 51st St

Sherman Park

18

W 55th St

S Central Ave

PAGE 274

"The Body of Michigan Lake"

NELSON

Chicago Midway Airport

GAGE PARK

W 55th St

W Garfield Blvd

CLEARING

51

52

Midway

Midway Airport

W 59th St

Graffiti Mural

ENGLEWOOD

A

W 63rd St

Capital Cigar Store

CHICAGO LAWN

W 63rd St

WEST ENGLEWOOD

Ashland/ 63rd

S California Ave

WEST LAWN

Marquette Rd

MARQUETTE PARK

Halsted

W 65th St

53

BEDFORD PARK

Marquette Park

54

57

FORD CITY

W 71st St

S Cicero Ave

S Pulaski Rd

S Kedzie Ave

S Western Ave

S Damen Ave

S Ashland Ave

S Racine Ave

43

BURBANK

State Ave

W 79st St

ASHBURN

WRIGHTWOOD

WEST CHATHA

SCOTTSDALE

PARKVIEW

MARYCREST

GRESHAM

W 87th St

B

EVERGREEN PARK

Campbell House

William MR French H

S Central Ave

12 20

W 95th St

Bronzeville Children's Museum

Original Rainbow Cone

Edwin C Young Hous

Adams House

Frank Anderson Hou

Ridge Park

Oakdale Park

S Bell Ave

S Walden Pkwy

OAK LAWN

S Ridgeland Ave

Evans House

Karge House

Horton Mansion

Edward L Roberts House

294

W 99th St

TALLY'S CORNER

Bell Tower

McDonnell House

JB Condos Metra Stati

55

W 103rd Rd

Givens Irish Castle

Chambers House

103rd

Griffin Place M

McClember Ho

S Cicero Ave

S Pulaski Rd

MOUNT GREENWOOD

Burhans-Ellinwood Model House

Gately House

Harris House

Ridge Historical

Blackwelder House

Hopkinson House

Lackmore House

56

55

MOUNT GREENWOOD HEIGHTS

W 111th St

Beverly Arts Center

Ferguson House

Metra Station 111th

Arnett Chapel

C

W 115th St

Godspeed House

St. Walter Catholic Church

Bohn Park

Holy Name of Mary Church

Morgan Park Apostolic Church

ALSIP

W 119th St

S Kedzie Ave

S Western Ave

S Vincennes St

Dan Ryan Expy

59

Tri-State Tollway

Calumet Sag Rd

W 127th St

1 mile   1 km

Essentials

A corner of the city rich in history, diversity, and culture, the Southwest Side is home to Midway Airport, a host of historic residences, and the largest St. Paddy's Day parade outside the Emerald Isle. From the heavily Italian Clearing neighborhood to the Arab-American Marquette Park, and from affluent Beverly to impoverished Englewood, the Southwest Side is an enclave rich in family values and down-to-earth good folks.

oLandmarks

- **Adams House** • 9326 S Longwood Dr
- **Arnett Chapel, African Methodist Episcopal Church** • 11218 S Bishop St
- **Bell Tower Condos** • 10321 S Longwood Dr
- **Blackwelder Summerling House** • 10910 S Prospect Ave
- **The Body of Lake Michigan** • The ceiling near the security checkpoint at Midway Airport
- **Bohn Park** • 111th St & Prospect Ave
- **Bronzeville Children's Museum** • 9600 S Western Ave
- **Burhans-Ellinwood Model House** • 10410 S Hoyne Ave
- **Campbell House** • 9250 S Damen Ave
- **Capital Cigar Store** • 6258 S Pulaski Rd
- **Edward L Roberts House** • 10134 S Longwood Dr
- **Edwin C Young House** • 9215 S Pleasant Ave

- **Evans House** • 9914 S Longwood Dr
- **Ferguson House** • 10954 S Prospect Ave
- **Frank Anderson House** • 10400 S Pleasant Ave
- **Gately House** • 10655 S Hoyne Ave
- **Givens Irish Castle** • 10244 S Longwood Dr
- **Godspeed House** • 11216 S Oakley Ave
- **Graffiti Mural** • W 59th St & S Damen Ave
- **Harris House** • 10856 S Longwood Dr
- **Holy Name of Mary Church** • 1423 W 112th St
- **Hopkinson House** • 10820 S Drew St
- **Horton Mansion** • 10200 S Longwood Dr
- **Howe House** • 10208 S Wood St
- **JB Chambers House** • 10330 S Seeley Ave
- **Karge House** • 2035 W 99th St
- **Lackmore House** • 10956 S Prospect Ave
- **McCumber House** • 10305 S Seeley Ave
- **Metra 103rd/Washington Heights Rock Island District Branch Line Station** • 103rd St & Vincennes Ave

- **Metra Rock Island Main Line 111th St/Monterey Ave Station** • 111th St & Monterey Ave
- **Midway Airport** • 5700 S Cicero Ave
- **Morgan Park Apostolic Penecostal Church** • 11401 S Vincennes Ave
- **Morgan Park United Methodist Church** • 11030 S Longwood Dr
- **Oakdale Park** • 956 W 95th St
- **Original Rainbow Cone** • 9233 S Western Ave
- **Ridge Historical Society** • 10621 S Seeley Ave
- **Ridge Park** • 9625 S Longwood Dr
- **St Walter Catholic Church** • 11722 S Oakley Ave
- **Walter Burley Griffin Place** • W 104th Pl, Wood St to Prospect Ave
- **William MR French House** • 9203 S Pleasant Ave

Sundries/Entertainment

For a true Irish pub-hopping experience this side of the Atlantic, get your blarney on along Western Avenue between 103rd and 115th, give or take a couple blocks. Travelers who can't wait to shop can hop a bus along Cicero Avenue from Midway Airport to the Ford City Shopping Center, and follow it up with choice after choice of authentic blue-collar Southwest Side cuisine—burgers and beef (i.e. Top Notch Beefburger).

☕Coffee

- **Beverly Bakery** • 10528 S Western Ave
- **Beverly Bean** • 2734 W 111th St
- **Café Luna** • 1742 W 99th St
- **Dunkin' Donuts** • 10401 S Western Ave
- **Dunkin' Donuts** • 1431 W 95th St
- **Dunkin' Donuts** • 1614 W 59th St
- **Dunkin' Donuts** • 2340 W 52nd St
- **Dunkin' Donuts** • 3210 W 87th St
- **Dunkin' Donuts** • 3977 W Columbus Ave
- **Dunkin' Donuts** • 4612 W 59th St
- **Dunkin' Donuts** • 5448 S Pulaski Rd
- **Dunkin' Donuts** • 5931 S Kedzie Ave
- **Dunkin' Donuts** • 6100 S Western Ave
- **Dunkin' Donuts** • 6500 S Kedzie Ave
- **Dunkin' Donuts** • 6738 W Archer Ave
- **Dunkin' Donuts** • 6925 S Pulaski Rd
- **Dunkin' Donuts** • 7059 S Ashland Ave
- **Dunkin' Donuts** • 7547 S Paulina St
- **Dunkin' Donuts** • 7901 S Damen Ave
- **Dunkin' Donuts** • 7905 S Cicero Ave
- **Java Express** • 10701 S Hale Ave
- **M&R Coffee Depot** • 1955 W Monterey Ave
- **South Perk** • 6227 W 63rd St
- **Starbucks** • 8740 S Kedzie Ave

🎦Movie Theaters
- **AMC Ford City 14** • 7601 S Cicero Ave

▼Nightlife
- **Cork & Kerry** • 10614 S Western Ave
- **Groucho's** • 8355 S Pulaski Rd

- **Jeremy Lanigan's Irish Pub** • 3119 W 111th St
- **Keegan's Pub** • 10618 S Western Ave
- **Mrs O'Leary's Dubliner** • 10910 S Western Ave
- **Patrick's** • 6296 S Archer Ave
- **Sean's Rhino Bar** • 10330 S Western Ave

🍴Restaurants
- **Beverly Woods Restaurant** • 11532 S Western Ave
- **Birrieria de la Torre** • 6724 S Pulaski Rd
- **Bobak's** • 5275 S Archer Ave
- **Café 103** • 1909 W 103rd St
- **Fox's Beverly Restaurant and Pizza** • 9956 S Western Ave
- **Franconello's Italian Restaurant** • 10222 S Western Ave
- **Harold's Chicken Shack** • 7274 S Racine Ave
- **Hoe China Tea** • 4020 W 55th St
- **Janson's Drive-In / Snyder's Red Hots** • 9900 S Western Ave
- **Koda** • 10352 S Western Ave
- **Lagniappe** • 1525 W 79th St
- **Lume's** • 11601 S Western Ave
- **Nile** • 3259 W 63rd St
- **The Original Vito and Nick's Pizzeria** • 8433 S Pulaski Ave
- **Rhythm & Spice** • 2501 W 79th St
- **Sunugal** • 2051 E 79th St
- **Szalas** • 5214 S Archer Ave
- **Tatra Inn** • 6040 S Pulaski Rd
- **Top Notch Beefburger** • 2116 W 95th St
- **Uncle Joe's Jerk** • 10210 S Vincennes Ave
- **Veggie Bite** • 3031 W 111th St

🛍Shopping
- **African American Images Bookstore** • 1909 W 95th St
- **The Beverly Cigar Company** • 10513 S Western Ave
- **Beverly & Novelty Costume Shop** • 11626 S Western Ave
- **Beverly Records** • 11612 S Western Ave
- **Bobak's** • 5275 S Archer Ave
- **Borders Book, Music, Movies & Café** • 2210 W 95th St
- **Calabria Imports** • 1905 W 103rd St
- **County Fair** • 10800 S Western Ave
- **Ford City Shopping Center** • 7601 S Cicero Ave
- **Grich Antiques** • 10857 S Western Ave
- **Izzy Rizzy's House of Tricks** • 6356 S Pulaski Rd
- **Mr Peabody Records** • 11832 S Western Ave
- **Ms Priss** • 9915 S Walden Pkwy
- **My Sisters' Knits** • 9907 S Walden Pkwy
- **Optimo Hat** • 10215 S Western Ave
- **Village Discount Outlet** • 6419 S Kedzie Ave
- **Village Discount Outlet** • 7443 S Racine Ave
- **World Folk Music** • 1808 W 103rd St

W 44th St
W 45th St
W 46th St

285

55

Adlai E Stevenson Expy

S Central Ave

W 47th St
W 48th St
W 49th St
W 50th St

Archer
Park

W 51st St
W 51st Pl
W 52nd St
W 53rd St
W 54th St

A

287

Vittum Park

ARCHER HEIGHTS

Pulaski

S La Crosse Ave
S Lamon Ave
S Lapporte Ave
S Luverne Ave
S Lawler Ave
S Leamington Ave
S Lavergne Ave

S Knox Ave
S Kilpatrick Ave
S Keating Ave

S Lamon Ave
S Lorel Ave
S Lockwood Ave
S Long Ave
S Linder Ave
S Lotus Ave
S Luna Ave

51

W Archer Ave
W 53rd St

S Parkside Ave

W 52nd St
W 52nd Pl

S Springfield Ave
S Harding Ave

W Archer Ave

GARFIELD RIDGE

S Mayfield Ave
W 54th Pl

W 55th St

S Pulaski Rd

W 55th St
W 56th St

Nashville Ave
S Neenah Ave
S Mobile Ave
S Meade Ave
S Mulligan Ave
S Merrimac Ave
S Moody Ave
S Monitor Ave
S Mason Ave
S Austin Ave

S Mayfield Ave
S Mcvicker Ave
S Massasoit Ave
S Major Ave

WEST ELSON

S Kenton Ave

Pasteur
Park

W 56th St
W 57th St
W 58th St

Wentworth
Kinzie
Park

S Natoma Ave
S Normandy Ave
S Nordica Ave
S New England Ave
S Oak Park Ave
S Stevcastle Ave
S Sutherford Ave
S Stormundy Ave

Minuteman
Park

Chicago Midway
Airport

W 57th St
W 58th St

S Kolin Ave
S Kostner Ave
S Keeth Ave
S Keeler Ave
S Kildare Ave
S Tripp Ave

S Karlov Ave

W 59th St

S Kolmar Ave

W 59th St
W 60th St
W 60th Pl
W 61st St

S Nashville Ave
S Natchez Ave
S Nordica Ave
S Sayre Ave
S Nottingham Ave
S Neva Ave

W Archer Ave

Valley Forge
Park

Airport Dr

Midway

50

43

Nathan
Hale
Park

W 61st St
W 62nd St
W 63rd St

PAGE
274

W 62nd Pl

W 63rd St

WEST LAWN

W 63rd St

West
Lawn
Park

S Belt Circle Dr

W 63rd St
W 64th St
W 64th Pl
W 65th St

Lawler Park

W 63rd Pl
W 64th Pl
W 65th Pl
W 66th Pl
W 66th Pl

W 67th St

S Cicero Ave

W 67th St

B

W 66th Pl

W 68th St

W 68th St
W 69th St

W 69th Pl
W 70th St
W 70th Pl

S Octavia Ave

BEDFORD PARK

W 71st St
W 71st St
W 72nd St
W 72nd St
W 73rd St
W 73rd Pl
W 74th St
W 74th Pl
W 75th St

S Narragansett Ave
S Oak Park Ave

S Mason Ave

S Meade Ave

S Massasoit Ave

S Central Ave

S Linder Ave

S Leamington Ave

S Luclare Ave

Foringer Rd

W 70th Pl
W 72nd St
W 73rd St

W 71st St

S Kostner Ave

S Pulaski Rd

W 75th Pl
W 76th St
W 76th Pl
W Hayford St

Briartree Ln

W 76th Pl
W 76th Pl
W 77th St
W 77th Pl
W 78th St
W 78th St

S Natoma Ave
S Normandy Ave
S Nashville Ave
S New Castle Ave
S Oak Park Ave
S Rutherford Ave
S Mulligan Ave
S Merrimac Ave
S Melvina Ave
S Moody Ave
S Mobile Ave
S Meade Ave
S Mcvicker Ave
S Austin Ave
S Mason Ave
S Mayfield Ave
S Mansfield Ave
S Massasoit Ave
S Menard Ave
S Parkside Ave
S Major Ave
S Luna Ave
S Lotus Ave
S Linder Ave

S Lavergne Ave
S Lawler Ave
S La Crosse Ave
S Lamon Ave
S Lamor Ave

Rainey
Hancock
Park

W 78th Pl
W 78th Pl
W Myrick St

Bogan

79th St

79th St

S Kenton Ct
S Kenton Ave

SCOTTSDALE

W 80th St

W 80th Pl
W 81st Pl

S Nordica Ave
S Nera Ave

S Narragansett Ave
S Nashville Ave
S Natona Ave
S Natchez Ave
S Nordica Ave
S Neenah Ave
S New England Ave
S Oak Park Ave
S Rutherford Ave
S New Castle Ave
S Newland Ave
S Sayre Ave

S Mulligan Ave
S Mobile Ave
S Meade Ave
S Mcvicker Ave
S Melvina Ave
S Moody Ave
S Merrimac Ave

S Mason Ave
S Austin Ave
S Mayfield Ave

S Massasoit Ave
S Menard Ave

S Parkside Ave
S Major Ave

S Luna Ave
S Lotus Ave
S Lockwood Ave
S Long Ave
S Linder Ave

S Lamoir Ave
S Lararine Ave
S Lararine Ave

S Lavergne Ave
S Lawler Ave

C

W 79th St
W 80th St
W 80th Pl
W 81st St

BURBANK

W 81st Pl
W 82nd St
W 82nd Pl
W 83rd St

Scottsdale
Park

Durkin Center
Park

S Keating Ave
S Kolin Ave

W Crestline St
W 82nd St
W 82nd Pl

S Harlem Ave

W 84th St
W 84th Pl
W 85th St
W 85th Pl
W 86th St

W 83rd Pl
W 84th St

W 87th Pl
W 88th St
W 88th Pl

S Merrimac Ave
S Model Ave

S Mcvicker Ave

S Mason Ave
S Austin Ave

S Mayfield Ave

S Massasoit Ave

S Central Ave

S Menard Ave

S Parkside Ave
S Major Ave

S Lotus Ave
S Long Ave
S Linder Ave

S Lararine Ave
S Lawler Ave

S Lavergne Ave

Stevens Dr
S 53rd Ave

W 84th St
W 85th St
W 86th St

S Keating Ave
S Knox Ave

W 87th St

S Scottsdale Ave

W 83rd Pl

S Kildare Ave
S Keeler Ave
S Tripp Ave

S Kethelia Ave
S Kirkland St
S Keller Ave

S Kolmar Ave

S Kostner Ave
S Kedvale Ave
S Merrion Ln
S Kilbourn

55

W 87th St

W 89th St

1/2 mile   .5 km

Lake Michigan

1

2

INDIANA
ILLINOIS

E 51st St   51st   Hyde Park Blvd

Garfield   **Garfield**
Garfield Blvd

Washington
Park

Jackson
Park

W 55th St

E 59th St

E 63rd/
Cottage
Grove

63rd   **18**   **19**   **20**   E Hayes Dr

Halsted   E 63rd St

**WEST
WOODLAWN**

E Marquette Rd

69th   E 67th St   **WOODLAWN**

Oak Woods
Cemetery   SOUTH
SHORE   South Shore
Cultural Center

MANOR   E 71st St

58

ENGLEWOOD   E 74th St   GRAND
CROSSING   S Stony Island Ave   E 75th St

Auburn Park   **3**   E 75th St   **41**

E 76th St   New Regal
Theatre

CHATHAM   E 79th St   **2**   79th   SOUTH CHICAGO   E 79th St

HAMILTON
PARK

MARYNOOK   S Chicago Ave   S Yates Blvd   S South Shore Dr

57   **2**   STONY
ISLAND
PARK

E 83rd St

54   87th   E 87th St   Chicago
Skyway   S Commercial Ave   S Mackinaw Ave   Calumet River

BURNSIDE   CALUMET
HEIGHTS

94   WEST
CHESTERFIELD   PILL
HILL   **90**

PRINCETON   E 95th St   S Colfax Ave   E 95th St

Carter G Wooden
Regional
Library   95th/Dan Ryan   Chicago State
University   **12**   **20**

LONGWOOD
MANOR   Trinity United
Church of Christ   Robert S.
Abbott Park   GE GROVE
HEIGHTS   JEFFERY
MANOR

57   ROSEMOOR   S King Dr   Stony Island Ave   S Torrence Ave   SOUTH
DEERING

WASHINGTON
HEIGHTS   W 103rd St   E 103rd St   E 106th St   S Avenue O

Lilydale Progressive
Missionary Baptist   Hyde Park   S Ewing Ave   S Avenue O

FERNWOOD   **59**   Pullman
Clock
Tower   **60**

ROSELAND   E 111th St   Market   Palmer Hall
Park   Eggers
Woods

Lilydale First
Baptist Church   E 113th St   Lake Calumet

56   West Pullman
Elementary
School   E 115th St   Calumet River   **41**

W 119th St   S State St   S Halsted St   S Indiana Ave

WEST PULLMAN   West Pullman Park   Wolf Lake
Park

Cedar Park Cemetery
& Funeral Home   E 127th St   PULLMAN   Wolf Lake

W 127th St
Vermont Ave

GOLDEN
GATE   E 130th St   Chicago Skyway   Indianapolis Blvd   INDIANA
ILLINOIS

RIVERDALE   ALTGELD
GARDENS   Forest
Preserve   **912**

Little Calumet River   HEGEWISCH

1 mile   1 km

Essentials

The far South side still lives in the shadows of the abandoned steel mills that built this area, and along with the steel industry went the regional economy. Now that Chicago has been selected as the US bid to host the 2016 Olympic Games, however, developers are starting to speculate about this area's potential. Meanwhile, south central Chicago from Chatham southward comprises the comfortable middle-class area dubbed the "black bungalow belt." Here, strong community ties defy the Southside's rough-and-tumble reputation.

ₒLandmarks

- **Cedar Park Cemetary & Funeral Home** · 12540 S Halsted St
- **Chicago Skyway** · 8801 S Anthony St
- **Chicago State University** · 9501 S King Dr
- **Lilydale First Baptist Church** · 649 W 113th St
- **Lilydale Progressive Missionary Baptist Church** · 10706 S Michigan Ave
- **Market Hall** · E 112th St & Champlain Ave
- **New Regal Theatre** · 1645 E 79th St
- **Oak Woods Cemetery** · 1035 E 67th St
- **Palmer Park** · 201 E 111th St
- **Pullman Clock Tower** · 11141 S Cottage Grove Ave
- **Robert S Abbott Park** · 49 E 95th St
- **South Shore Cultural Center** · 7059 South Shore Dr
- **Trinity United Church of Christ** · 400 W 95th St
- **West Pullman Elementary** · 11941 S Parnell Ave
- **West Pullman Park** · 401 W 123rd St
- **Woodson Regional Library** · 3525 S Halsted St

Sundries/Entertainment

The Southside is home to one of the few African-American gay bars in Chicago: Jeffrey Pub in South Shore. Jazz legend Von Freeman, a remarkably youthful-looking octogenarian, jams every Tuesday night at New Apartment Lounge. Most of the area's barbeque shacks serve their take-out through bulletproof glass. For excellent, authentic soul food, go no further than Army & Lou's on E 75th Street. Vegetarians flock down the street to the always-bustling Soul Vegetarian East.

Coffee

- **Ali's** · 2704 E 75th St, #6
- **Dunkin' Donuts** · 120 W 87th St
- **Dunkin' Donuts** · 14 W 95th St
- **Dunkin' Donuts** · 150 W 63rd St
- **Dunkin' Donuts** · 207 W 79th St
- **Dunkin' Donuts** · 250 E 103rd St
- **Dunkin' Donuts** · 814 E 87th St
- **Dunkin' Donuts** · 8255 S Halsted St
- **Dunkin' Donuts** · 8753 S Stony Island Ave
- **Dunkin' Donuts** · 9802 S Halsted St
- **Spoon's Coffee Boutique** · 712 E 75th St
- **Starbucks** · 160 W 87th St
- **Starbucks** · 7101 S Stony Island Ave

Movie Theaters

- **ICE Chatham 14** · 210 87th St

Nightlife

- **Jeffrey Pub** · 7041 S Jeffery Blvd
- **New Apartment Lounge** · 504 E 75th St
- **Red Pepper's Masquerade Lounge** · 428 E 87th St
- **Reds** · 6926 S Stony Island Ave

Restaurants

- **Army & Lou's** · 422 E 75th St
- **Atomic Sub** · 6353 S Cottage Grove Ave
- **Barbara Ann's BBQ** · 7617 S Cottage Grove Ave
- **BJ's Market & Bakery** · 8734 S Stony Island Ave
- **Café Trinidad** · 557 E 75th St
- **Cal Harbor Restaurant** · 546 E 115th St
- **Captain Hard Times** · 436 E 79th St
- **Chatham Pancake House** · 700 E 87th St
- **Dat Old Fashioned Donut** · 8251 S Cottage Grove Ave
- **Helen's Restaurant** · 1732 E 79th St
- **Izola's** · 522 E 79th St
- **Lem's** · 311 E 75th St
- **Leon's Bar-B-Que** · 8249 S Cottage Grove Ave
- **Old Fashioned Donuts** · 11248 S Michigan Ave
- **The Parrot Cage** · 7059 S South Shore Dr
- **Phil's Kastle** · 3532 E 95th St ◌
- **Pupuseria El Salvador** · 3557 E 106th St
- **The Rib Joint** · 432 W 87th St
- **Seven Seas Submarine** · 11216 S Michigan Ave
- **Soul Queen** · 9031 S Stony Island Ave
- **Soul Vegetarian East** · 205 E 75th St
- **Tropic Island Jerk Chicken** · 1922 E 79th St
- **Uncle John's Barbecue** · 337 E 69th Pl
- **Vegetarian Fun Foods Surpreme** · 1702 E 87th St
- **Yassa African Caribbean** · 716 E 79th St

Shopping

- **African Hedonist** · 8501 S Cottage Grove Ave
- **Halsted Indoor Mall** · 11444 S Halsted St
- **Underground Afrocentric Bookstore** · 1727 E 87th St

A

B

C

Lake Michigan

Rainbow
Park

S South Shore Dr

E 79th St

Chicago Skyway
Service Area

Russell
Square
Park

SOUTH
CHICAGO

E 84th St

E 85th St

E 86th St

E 87th St

S Burley Ave

S Mackinaw Ave

Bessemer
Park

90

S Chicago Ave

PILL HILL

12 **20**   **60** E 95th St

E Foreman Dr

S Ewing Ave

Greater Chicago • South 59

LONGWOOD MANOR
Robichaux Park
95th/Dan Ryan

COTTAGE GROVE HEIGHTS

Oakdale Park
Euclid Park

WASHINGTON HEIGHTS

Smith Park

ROSEMOOR

Gately Park

Block Park

Fernwood Park

FERNWOOD

Hyde Park

PULLMAN

Palmer Park

ROSELAND

Lake Calumet

Morgan Field

WEST PULLMAN

White Park

West Pullman Park

Ford Fwy

Whistler Preserve

Carver Park

Crest Preserve

HEGEWISCH

ALTGELD GARDENS

Riverdale Park

Little Calumet River

1 mile
1 km

4

12 20 3 E 95th St E 94th St E Foreman Dr S Wilton Dr

58 E 96th St Calumet S Yeldon Dr
E 97th St Park
E 98th St E Grthy Dr

Veterans E 99th St S Avenue G
Memorial S Avenue H
Park E 100th St S Avenue J

E 101st St Chicago Skyway
E 103rd St E 102nd St 41 S Hwy 12

Trumbull E 104th St S Green Bay Ave S Indianapolis Ave
Park E 105th St S Avenue O

E 106th St S Avenue M

JEFFERY Wolfe Pig S Avenue O S Avenue C
MANOR Park S Avenue D
E 107th St S Avenue E
E 108th St S Avenue F

E 109th St

E 110th St SOUTH
DEERING

E 111th St

E 112th St

E 113th St

E 114th St Eggers
Woods

Rowen E 115th St
Park S Greenbay Ave

E 116th St

E 117th St

E 118th St Forsyth
Park

E 119th St

E 120th St

E 121st St Stewart St
Burton Ct
E 122nd St Roosevelt St

E 123rd St

E 124th St

Wolf Lake 124th St
Park
E 125th St College St

125th St
E 126th St
126th St

Wolf Lake 127th St

41 129th St

E 127th St ILLINOIS INDIANA

E 128th St S Avenue K

E 129th St S Avenue F

E 130th St Mann 133rd St 912
Park 134th St

HEGEWISCH S Avenue M

S Avenue N

E 134th St

E 135th St

E 136th St

E 137th St Burnham
Woods

Pulaski
Park

137th St
138th St

Lake Michigan

A

B

C

1 mile   1 km

Overview

Beverly Hills, best known simply as Beverly, is the stronghold of Chicago's heralded "South Side Irish" community. An authentic medieval castle, baronial mansions, rolling hills, and plenty of pubs compose Chicago's Emerald Isle of 39,000 residents.

Once populated by Illinois and Potawatomi Indian tribes, Beverly became home to clans of Irish-American families after the Great Chicago Fire. Famous residents include Andrew Greeley, Brian Piccolo, George Wendt, the Schwinn Bicycle family, and decades of loyal Chicago civil servants.

Proud and protective of their turf, these close-knit South Siders call Beverly and its sister community, Morgan Park, "the Ridge." The integrated neighborhood occupies the highest ground in Chicago, 30 to 60 feet above the rest of the city atop Blue Island Ridge.

Although the Ridge is just 15 miles from the Loop, most North Siders limit their visits south to just one day in March. The South Side Irish Parade marches down Western Avenue from 103rd to 115th Streets every year on the Sunday prior to St. Patrick's Day. The parade is the largest St. Patrick's Day celebration in the United States, and Chicago's South Siders are proud of this fact—don't dare confuse their parade with the lame one a week later in Chicago's downtown.

Most of the 200,000+ who gather on Western Avenue that day aren't there for the floats. Or the marching bands. Or the Irish dancers. They come for the Irish pubs. It's called a parade, but it's mostly a drink-a-thon. And if you want to participate, stay on the west side of Western. The area east of Western is dry.

But there is more than a 6-pack of reasons to visit Beverly. The Ridge Historic District is one of the country's largest urban areas on the National Register of Historic Places. Surprised, huh?

Architecture

Sadly, many Chicagoans are unaware of the rich architectural legacy on the city's far South Side. Beverly and Morgan Park encompass four landmark districts including the Ridge Historic District, three Chicago Landmark Districts, and over 30 Prairie Style structures.

Within approximately a nine-mile radius, from 87th Street to 115th Street and Prospect Avenue to Hoyne Avenue, one can view a vast collection of homes and public buildings representing American architectural styles developed between 1844 and World War II.

The 109th block of Prospect Avenue, every inch of Longwood Drive, and the Victorian train stations at 91st Street, 95th Street, 99th Street, 107th Street, 111th Street, and 115th Street are all great Chicago landmarks. Walter Burley Griffin Place on W 104th Street has Chicago's largest concentration of Prairie School houses built between 1909 and 1913 by Griffin, a student of Frank Lloyd Wright and designer of the city of Canberra in Australia.

Beverly Area Planning Association (BAPA) (11107 S Longwood Drive, 773-233-3100; www.bapa.org) provides a good architectural site map, plus events and shopping information for the district. History buffs might want to visit the Ridge Historical Society, open Tuesdays, Thursdays, and Sundays from 2 pm to 5 pm (10621 S Seeley Ave, 773-881-1675; www.ridgehistoricalsociety.org).

Culture & Events

The Beverly Arts Center is the epicenter of Ridge culture. The $8 million facility provides visual and performance art classes for all ages and hosts Chicago's only contemporary Irish film festival during the first week of March (2407 W 111th St, 773-445-3838; www.beverlyartcenter.org).

Historic Ridge homes open their doors to the public on the third Sunday of May for the annual Home Tour, Chicago's oldest such tour. Sites are chosen for their diverse architectural styles and historical significance. Tour hours are from 11 am to 5 pm and tickets can be purchased through BAPA or the Beverly Arts Center for $25 in advance or $30 the day of the event. All tours depart from the Beverly Arts Center by 3 pm and homes close promptly at 5 pm. Guided trolley tours are also offered for an additional $3. Contact BAPA at 773-233-3100 or www.bapa.org for more details.

Where to Eat

- **Café Luna**, 1742 W 99th St, 773-239-8990. Eclectic. Sink your teeth into their heart-healthy sandwiches and sinful desserts.
- **Franconello's**, 10222 S Western Ave, 773-881-4100. Italian. Perhaps the only pure Italians in Beverly making pasta dishes at this authentic Roma restaurant.
- **Janson's Drive-In**, 9900 S Western Ave, 773-238-3612. No indoor seating at this classic drive-thru.
- **Rainbow Cone**, 9233 S Western Ave, 773-238-7075. Ice cream. On summer nights more than 50 folks line up for sweet treats at this 76-year-old soda fountain.
- **Top Notch Beefburger**, 2116 W 95th St, 773-445-7218. Burgers really are top notch at this '50s-style grill.

Where to Drink

- **Lanigan's Irish Pub**, 3119 W 111th St, 773-233-4004. Anyone know where you can find a pint in Beverly? I've got quite a mean thirst.
- **Dubliner**, 10910 S Western Ave, 773-238-0784. One of the many Irish pubs lining Western Avenue.

Where to Shop

- **Bev Art Brewer and Winemaker Supply**, 10033 S Western Ave, 773-233-7579. Everything you need to brew and bottle it yourself.
- **Calabria Imports**, 1905 W 103rd St, 773-396-5800. Imported Italian gourmet foodstuffs.
- **Optimo Hat Co**, 10215 S Western Ave, 773-238-2999. Custom made men's hats.
- **World Folk Music Company**, 1808 W 103rd St, 773-779-7059. Instruments, sheet music, and lessons for budding Guthries and Baezs.

General Information

Address:	31st St & First Ave
	Brookfield, IL 60513
Phone:	708-485-0263
Website:	www.brookfieldzoo.org
Hours:	Open daily from 10 am–5 pm, and until 7:30 on Sundays from Memorial Day to Labor Day
Admission:	$11 adults, $7 children 3–11 & seniors, free for children two and under

Overview

While Lincoln Park Zoo is free, Brookfield offers a far more comprehensive wild animal experience with a strong emphasis on conservation education. 216 acres of creepy critters make for a memorable day trip. We'll skip the analogy with the Joliet Riverboat Casino.

Hamill Family Play Zoo

This interactive play area is part of a program to create a huge new wing of the zoo dedicated solely to kids. Great—just what a zoo needs: more kids. Children get to interact in a variety of ways, including donning costumes to play "zoo keeper" or "ring-tailed lemur," creating and frolicking in their own simulated habitats, planting seeds in the greenhouse, or spotting creepy insects in the outdoor bug path. Think a grownup would look silly dressed like a lemur? We want to play!

Regenstein Wolf Woods

The zoo's impressive wolf exhibit allows visitors to follow the progress of a small pack of endangered male wolves as they do the wolfy things wolves do. One-way glass allows spectators to get up close and personal with the wolves without freaking them out. So far, the mirrors have been 100% unsuccessful in detecting any wolf shoplifting.

Other Exhibits

Of course the zoo is full of exhibits, some more fascinating than others. Among them are the seasonal butterfly exhibit and the dragonfly marsh. Here are some other worthwhile sights:

- **Habitat Africa**: This is broken up into two sections: The Rainforest, with its zebras and African millipedes (heebie-jeebies), and The Savannah, with our favorite, the giraffes.

- **Dolphinarium**: Dolphin shows are scheduled at regular intervals two or three times a day (sometimes more during peak seasons and on weekends).

- **Tropic World**: Visit Kamba, the baby gorilla born in front of a captivated, slightly disgusted crowd of zoo visitors (mother Koola now knows how Marie Antoinette felt when she shared the delivery of her offspring with the French peasantry) and Bakari, the

newest addition to the Gorilla family, who was born to mother Binto in May '05.

- **Baboon Island**: Always a fun adventure, if for no other reason than to ogle certain colorful aspects of this animal's anatomy which we won't name (but it rhymes with "class," which we clearly don't have).

- **Bear Grottos**: Consider yourself lucky if you get a glimpse of these fascinating animals; this exhibit has unusual hours and is often unavailable.

- **Feathers and Scales: Birds and Reptiles**: We're pretty sure there are bats in there, but we've blocked the traumatic memory from our unstable minds. Enter at your own risk.

Eating at the Zoo

- **La Gran Cocina**: At the South American Marketplace. Walk-up stir-fry, chicken, pizza, and fruit.

- **Eco Café**: Near the Hamill Family Play Zoo. Brookfield Zoo teamed up with Whole Foods to create the Eco Café, offering yogurt, organic chips, and other healthy snacks. The green theme goes far beyond the menu, too. Much of the café's structure and function are of the tree-hugging sort.

- **Bocaditos**: Table service dining on the second floor of the South American Marketplace. Peruvian fare with a "familiar" twist (read: blanded down for white-bread palates).

- **Ituri Café**: Near the Habitat Africa playground. Walk-up food vendor with picnic tables.

- **Bear Gardens Café**: Watch bears watch you eat at this sandwich and pizza shop.

- **Nyani Lodge**: If watching monkeys throw feces at each other is your idea of a good dinnertime show, definitely check out this place.

How to Get There

By Car: From the Eisenhower or Stevens Expressway, exit at First Avenue. From there, signs will direct you the short distance to the zoo. Lot parking is $8.

By Train: From downtown Chicago, take the Burlington Northern Metra line to Zoo Stop/Hollywood Station.

By Bus: Pace buses 304 and 331 stop right at the zoo's gates.

If you're coming in from out of town, consider staying at a Holiday Inn, Doubletree Hotel, or Country Inn & Suites, all of which offer Brookfield Zoo packages, which include admission to Brookfield Zoo, admission to the Dolphin Show, admission to the Children's Zoo, 1 parking pass, and coupons for restaurants and gift shops. Details and booking information can be found on Brookfield Zoo's website, www.brookfieldzoo.org.

Lake Cook Rd

Marquette Rd

Hastings Ave

Main Entrance

Children's Learning Center

Botanic Garden Center

N

Chicago Botanic Garden

Bird Island

Gateway Visitor Center

McDonald Woods

Fruit & Vegetable Garden

The Crescent

Bulb Garden

Native Plant Garden

Heritage Garden

Aquatic Garden

Landscape Garden

The Esplanade

Rose Garden

Model Railroad Garden

Education Center

Dwarf Conifer

Japanese Garden

Arbor House

Circle Garden

The Greenhouses

English Walled Garden

English Oak Meadow

Waterfall Garden

Spider Land

McGinley Pavilion

Shroin House

Enabling Garden

Water Gardens

Lakeside Gardens

Sensory Garden

Great Basin

Skokie River

Carillon

Evening Island

Sun Evaluation Garden

Edens Expy

41

Skokie Blvd

Marsh Island

Prairie

Glencoe Golf Club

Henrici Dr

94

Prairie

Outdoor Classroom

Children's Garden

Share Evaluation Garden

33

34

General Information

Address:	1000 Lake Cook Rd, Glencoe, IL 60022
Phone:	847-835-5440
Website:	www.chicagobotanic.org
Hours:	Open 364 days, 8 am to sunset; closed Dec. 25
Admission:	Free

Overview

Occupying 385 acres, the serene and lovely Chicago Botanic Garden has been the backdrop for many a chi-chi wedding since they opened the gates in 1972. Both the Ikebana Society and Macy's sponsor flower shows throughout the year; check the events schedule at www.chicagobotanic.org to see what's going on when you're visiting. The Chicago Botanic Garden also offers lifestyle/wellness classes, including yoga and tai chi. Availability and times vary, so check the website or call for more information.

Nature

Twenty-three gardens and three prairie habitats make up the Botanic Garden. Among them are a specialized Japanese garden, a rose garden, a bulb garden, a greenhouse full of tropical vegetation, a waterfall garden, and several beds solely dedicated to indigenous plants and flowers.

Where to Eat

• **Garden Café:** Serves breakfast and café fare—salads, sandwiches, beer, and wine. Open 8 am–5 pm weekdays, 8 am–5:30 pm weekends, and open to 7 pm on Carillon Concert Mondays.

• **Garden Grille:** Grill being the operative word, serves burgers, dogs, and the like. Open for dinner from late May/early June to early September, 5:30 pm–8 pm, featuring a barbeque buffet and beer garden.

Note: Picnicking allowed in designated areas only.

How to Get to There

By Car: Take I-90/94 W (The Kennedy) to I-94 (The Edens) and US 41. Exit on Lake Cook Road, then go a half-mile east to the garden.

By Train: Take the Union Pacific North Line to Central (in Evanston), and catch the Pace bus 213 to Lake Cook and Nyoda, or take the same Metra train to Highland Park, and catch the Pace 473 to Lake Cook and Skokie. Easy Pace connections are also available from the Metra Glencoe stop. Buses don't run on Sundays and holidays.

By Bicycle: The Chicago Bikeway System winds through the forest preserves all the way up to the garden. Join it near the Billy Caldwell Golf Club at 6200 N Caldwell. A bicycle map is available on the Botanic Garden website.

Where to Stay

You can make an excursion of your visit to Ravinia and/or the Botanic Garden by booking a room at:

Renaissance Chicago North Shore (933 Skokie Blvd, Northbrook, 847-498-6500); **Residence Inn Chicago** (530 Lake Cook Rd, Deerfield, 847-940-4644); **Hyatt Deerfield** (1750 Lake Cook Rd, 847-945-3400); **Highland Park Courtyard** (1505 Lake Cook Rd, 847-831-3338).

Ravinia Festival

Address:	200 Ravinia Park Rd, Highland Park, IL 60035
Phone:	847-266-5100
Website:	www.ravinia.org
Hours:	June through mid-September, gates open three hours before concert time

Overview

Not to be outdone, the adjoining Ravinia Festival, the nation's oldest outdoor concert venue, has been hosting classical music concerts since 1904. The summer home of the CSO, Ravinia eventually added pop and jazz to their bill, including such notables as Janis Joplin, Aretha Franklin (a Ravinia regular), k.d. lang, Tony Bennett (also a regular), as well as top names from opera and world music.

The Pavilion—Those who are serious about the music experience pay a premium for one of the 3,200 seats in this covered, open-air pavilion, affording them a view of the stage and better acoustics.

The Lawn—Although you can't see the stage, great outdoor acoustics bring the concert to you on the lawn, where blanket rights come cheap—typically $10 a pop. Just add picnic.

The Martin Theatre—The only remaining building original to the Festival, the 1904 Martin Theatre now hosts Martinis at the Martin, a cabaret series celebrating the Great American Songbook.

Eating at Ravinia

Ravinia is well known for lawn picnickers who compete to outdo each other with elaborate spreads, including roll-up tables, table linens, candelabras, champagne, and caviar. For those less ambitious, Ravinia offers take-out sandwiches and picnic fare at The Gatehouse, burgers and dogs at Le Café, ice cream and other sweet treats at Carousel Ice Cream Shop, or you can make reservations to eat in at their fine-dining restaurant, Mirabelle. Wine, beer, and soft drinks are also available at concession stands throughout the park.

How to Get There

By Car: I-94 and I-294 have marked exits for Ravinia. Skip traffic back-ups on Lake Cook Road by exiting at Deerfield, Central, or Clavey Roads, and following directions to Park and Ride lots, which offer free parking and shuttle buses to Ravinia. The West Lot, Ravinia's closest parking spot, costs $15–$25 for parking and fills up early for the most popular concerts.

By Train: During festival season, the Union Pacific North Line offers the "Ravinia Special." For $5 round-trip, the train departs Madison and Canal at 5:50 pm, with stops at Clybourn, Ravenswood, Rogers Park, and Evanston, arriving at the Ravinia gates at 6:30 pm, and departing for the city 15 minutes after the concert's end.

Performances

The Cultural Center's free "LunchBreak" series provides downtown working stiffs with a welcome midday respite every weekday at 12:15pm.

Mondays: Classical Mondays featuring classical, chamber music and opera; in Preston Bradley Hall.

Tuesdays: Jazz, Blues and Beyond in Randolph Cafe.

Wednesdays: Dame Myra Hess Memorial Concerts featuring solo and ensemble performances of classical music showcasing young performers; in Preston Bradley Hall.

Thursdays: Daily Blend featuring acoustic pop, folk, country, and bluegrass; in Randolph Cafe.

Fridays: Music Without Borders featuring international music from around the globe; in Randolph Café.

Sunday Salon Series: Sundays, 3pm, Preston Bradley Hall. These weekly performances include long-time Chicago Cultural Center favorites, such as the Chicago chamber Orchestra, Classical Symphony Orchestra and the Protégé Philharmonic.

Call 312-FINE ART (312-346-3278) for information on frequently scheduled special programs.

Off-Loop theater productions appear regularly in the Center's Studio Theater, including the seasonal ShawChicago series featuring plays by Bernard Shaw on Saturdays, Sundays, and Mondays. Performances are free, but reservations are required (312-409-5605; www.shawchicago.org).

Art Galleries

A permanent exhibit in the Landmark Gallery, Chicago Landmarks Before the Lens is a stunning black-and-white photographic survey of Chicago architecture. Five additional galleries regularly rotate exhibits, showcasing work in many media by renowned and local artists. Tours of current exhibits are ongoing.

How to Get There

By Car: Travel down Michigan Avenue to Randolph Street. From Lake Shore Drive, exit at Randolph Street. For parking garages in the area, see Map 6.

By Train: From the Richard B. Ogilvie Transportation Center, travel east to Michigan Avenue on CTA buses 20, 56, 127, and 157. From Union Station, take CTA buses 60, 151, and 157 ($2.00, $1.75 with Chicago Card). From the Randolph Street station below Millennium Park, walk west across Michigan Avenue. For schedules contact the RTA Information Center (312-836-7000; www.rtachicago.com).

By L: Take the Green, Brown, Orange, Purple, or Pink Line to the Randolph stop ($2.00, $1.75 with Chicago Card). Walk east one block.

By Bus: CTA buses : 3, 145, 147, 151 stop on Michigan Avenue in front of the Cultural Center ($2.00, $1.75 with Chicago Card).

General Information

NFT Maps: 5, 6
Address: 78 E Washington St
Chicago, IL 60602
Phone: 312-744-6630
Website: www.chicagoculturalcenter.org
Hours: Mon–Thurs 8 am–7 pm, Fri 8 am–6 pm,
Sat 9 am–6 pm, Sun 10 am–6 pm,
and closed on holidays

Overview

The Chicago Cultural Center is the Loop's public arts center. Free—that's right, we said FREE—concerts, theatrical performances, films, lectures, and exhibits are offered daily. Admission to the Cultural Center and its art galleries are all free, too. Call 312-FINE ART (312-346-3278 for weekly event updates.

The building itself, constructed in 1897, is a neoclassical landmark featuring intricate glass and marble mosaics on its walls and grand stairways. Once the city's central public library, the Cultural Center boasts the world's largest Tiffany dome in Preston Bradley Hall. Free (there's that lovely word again) 45-minute architectural tours are held on Wednesdays, Fridays, and Saturdays at 1:15 pm. If you're interested in a guided group tour highlighting the building's history, call 312-744-8032 for more information. The building is also home to the Chicago Greeter Program, which allows visitors the opportunity to take a 2–3 hour walking tour with a chatty and knowledgeable guide around one of any number of neighborhoods throughout the city. Interested parties must book in advance at www.chicagogreeter.com. Surprise, surprise: it's free, as well.

General Information

NFT Map: 5
Address: 400 S State St
                Chicago, IL 60605
Phone: 312-747-4300
Website: www.chipublib.org

Overview

Harold Washington Library Center is the world's largest public library. Named after Chicago's first African-American mayor, the 756,640-square-foot neoclassical architectural monstrosity has over 70 miles of shelves storing more than 9 million books, microforms, serials, and government documents. Notable works of sculpture, painting, and mosaics liven up the building's ample wall space and open areas.

Harold Washington's popular library, containing current general titles and bestsellers, is easy to find on the ground floor. The library's audio-visual collection (including an impressive collection of books on tape as well as videos, DVDs, and popular music CDs) is also housed here. The second floor is home to the children's library, and the general reference library begins on the third floor where the circulation desks are located. Among the notable features of the library is the eighth floor Music Information Center housing sheet music and printed scores, 150,000 recordings, the Chicago Blues Archives, eight individual piano practice rooms, and a chamber music rehearsal room. The ninth floor Winter Garden, with its olive trees and soaring 100-foot high ceilings is a popular site for special events. If you have your sights set on getting hitched here, leave your priest or rabbi at home—the library's status as a civic building precludes religious services on its premises.

Frequent free public programs are held in the lower level's 385-seat auditorium, video theater, exhibit hall, and meeting rooms. Call 312-747-4649 for information on scheduled events. Additionally, the website houses a bbs (bulletin board system) for those participating in Chicago's "One City, One Book" reading club who want to discuss the latest selection.

Library hours are Monday through Thursday 9 am to 9 pm, Friday and Saturday 9 am to 5 pm, and Sunday 1 pm to 5 pm.

Research Services

To check the availability or location of an item, call Catalog Information at 312-747-4340 or search the library's Online Catalog on www.chipublib.org. Their Email Reference Service responds to information requests within two days. For faster answers to common research questions, check out the website's handy Virtual Library Service under Selected Internet Resources, then click on "Reference Shelf."

Computer Services

The Chicago Public Library's High Speed Wireless Internet System provides free access; all you need is a wireless enabled laptop computer, tablet PC, or PDA. The Library's network is open to all visitors free of charge and without filters. No special encryption settings, user names, or passwords are required.

The library's 96 computers with Internet access and 37 more with word processing, desktop publishing, graphic presentation, and spreadsheet applications are located on the third floor in the Computer Commons. Computer use is free and available on a first-come-first-served basis. You can reserve computers for up to one hour per day based on walk-in availability. For downloads, bring your own formatted disk or purchase one at the library for $2. Free laser printing is also provided. Operating hours are Monday through Thursday 9 am–8:30 pm, Friday and Saturday 9 am–4:30 pm, and Sunday 1 pm–4:30pm.

Thomas Hughes Children's Library

The 18,000-square-foot Thomas Hughes Children's Library on the second floor serves children through age 14. A British citizen and member of Parliament, Thomas Hughes was so taken by news of the tragic Chicago Fire that he started a book collection for Chicago. His collection resulted in the 8,000 titles that composed the first Chicago Public Library. In addition to more than 120,000 children's books representing 40 foreign languages, there is a reference collection on children's literature for adults. Twenty free computers, twelve with Internet connections, are also available. Children's programs are hosted weekly (312-747-4200).

Special Collections

The library's Special Collections & Preservation Division's highlights include: Harold Washington Collection, Civil War & American History Research Collection, Chicago Authors & Publishing Collection, Chicago Blues Archives, Chicago Theater Collection, World's Columbian Exposition Collection, and Neighborhood History Research Collection. The collections' reading room is closed Sunday.

How to Get There

By Car: The library is at the intersection of State Street and Congress Parkway in South Loop. Take I-290 E into the Loop. See Map 5 for area parking garages.

By L: The Brown, Purple, Orange, and Pink Lines stop at the Library Station. Exit the Red Line and O'Hare Airport Blue Line at Van Buren Station; walk one block south. Change from the Harlem/Lake Street Green Line to the northbound Orange Line at Roosevelt Road station; get off at Library Station ($2.00, $1.75 with chicago Card).

By Bus: CTA buses that stop on State Street in front of the library are the 2, 6, 29, 36, 62, 151, 145, 146, and 147.

Overview

Bordering the city to the north and surrounded by beautiful lakeshore scenery and affluent suburbs, Evanston may seem a world away. Truth be told, this town is only 12 miles from Chicago's bustling Loop. Spacious Victorian and Prairie Style homes with mini-vans and Mercedes parked on tree-lined streets overlook Lake Michigan and surround the quaint college town's downtown. Unlike other development-minded and sub-divided suburbs, Evanston still maintains a Chicago-esque feel and remains one of its most attractive bordering neighbors. Of course, Evanston residents still walk with their noses in the air and even charge their city neighbors to visit their beaches. We wonder what their tax base would look like without the city.

Once home to Potawatami Indians, Evanston was actually founded after the establishment of the town's most well-known landmark, Northwestern University. Plans for the school began in 1851, and after the university opened for business four years later, its founder John Evans (along with a bunch of other Methodist dudes) proposed the establishment of the city, and so the town was incorporated as the village of Evanston in 1863. Today, residents are as devoted to cultural and intellectual pursuits as the morally minded patriarchs were to enforcing prohibition.

The sophisticated, racially diverse suburb of over 74,000 packs a lot of business and entertainment into its 8.5 square miles. Superb museums, many national historic landmarks, parks, artistic events, eclectic shops, and theaters make up for the poor sports performances by Northwestern University's Wildcats in recent Big Ten football and basketball seasons.

Culture

Evanston has several museums and some interesting festivals that warrant investigation. Besides Northwestern's Block Museum of Art, the impressive Mitchell Museum of the American Indian showcases life of the Midwest's Native Americans (3001 Central St, 847-475-1030). The 1865 home of Frances E. Willard, founder of the Women's Christian Temperance Union and a women's suffrage leader, is located at 1730 Chicago Avenue (847-328-7500). Tours of the historic home are offered on the afternoons of every first and third Sunday of each month. Admission costs $5 for adults and $3 for children 12 and under.

Festivals & Events

- **May**: Evanston goes Baroque during Bach Week, 847-236-0452, www.bachweek.org.

- **June**: Fountain Square Arts Festival, 773-868-3010, and free Starlight Concerts hosted in many of the city's 80 parks through August, 847-448-8058

- **July**: Ethnic Arts Festival, 847-448-8260

- **September**: Town architectural walking tour, 312-922-3432, www.architecture.org.

- **December**: First Night, a city-wide arts celebration, rings in the New Year, 866-475-6483, www.firstnightevanston.org

Nature

Evanston is blessed with six public beaches open June 10th through Labor Day. Non-residents should remember their wallets to pay for beach passes. For hours, fees, and boating information, contact the City of Evanston's Recreation Division (847-866-2910; www.cityofevanston.org). The town's most popular parks (and there are nearly 90 of them) encircle its beaches: Grosse Point Lighthouse Park, Centennial Park, Burnham Shores Park, Dawes Park, and South Boulevard Beach Park. All are connected by a bike path and fitness trail. On clear days, Chicago's skyline is visible from Northwestern's campus. West of downtown, McCormick, Twiggs, and Herbert Parks flank the North Shore Channel. Bicycle trails thread along the shore from Green Bay Road south to Main Street. North of Green Bay Road is Peter N. Jans Community Golf Course, a short 18-hole, par 60 public links at 1031 Central Street (847-475-9173) and the Ladd Memorial Arboretum and Ecology Center, located at 2024 McCormick Boulevard (847-864-5181).

How to Get There

By Car: Lake Shore Drive to Sheridan Road is the most direct and scenic route from Chicago to Evanston. Drive north on LSD, which ends at Hollywood; then drive west to Sheridan and continue north. Near downtown, Sheridan becomes Burnham Place briefly, then Forest Avenue. Go north on Forest, which turns into Sheridan again by lakefront Centennial Park.

Parking: Watch how and where you park. The rules and regulations are strict and fiercely enforced. Remember…Evanston police do not have much to do.

By Train: Metra's Union Pacific North Line departing from the Richard B. Ogilvie Transportation Center in West Loop stops at the downtown Davis Street CTA Center station, 25 minutes from the Loop ($3.05 one-way). This station is the town transportation hub, where Metra and L trains and buses interconnect. For all Metra, L, and CTA bus schedules, call 312-836-7000; www.rtachicago.com.

By L: The CTA Purple Line Express L train travels direct to and from the Loop during rush hours ($2.00, $1.75 with Chicago Card). Other hours, ride the Howard-Dan Ryan Red Line to Howard Street, and transfer to the Purple Line for free.

By Bus: From Chicago's Howard Street Station, CTA and Pace Suburban buses service Evanston ($1.50 rush hours one-way; other, $1.25).

Additional Information
Chicago's North Shore Convention & Visitors Bureau 866-369-0011; www.visitchicagonorthshore.com

Evanston Public Library, 1703 Orrington Ave, 847-448-8600; www.epl.org

○Landmarks
· **Evanston Historical Society** · 225 Greenwood St
· **Light Opera Works** · 927 Noyles St

🍸Nightlife
· **1800 Club** · 1800 Sherman Ave
· **Bill's Blues Bar** · 1029 Davis St
· **Keg of Evanston** · 810 Grove St
· **Prairie Moon** · 1502 Sherman Ave
· **The Stained Glass Wine Bar** · 1735 Benson Ave
· **Tommy Nevin's Pub** · 1450 Sherman Ave

🍴Restaurants
· **Blind Faith Café** · 525 Dempster St
· **Buffalo Joe's** · 812 Clark St
· **Café Mozart** · 600 Davis St
· **Clarke's** · 720 Clark St
· **Dave's Italian Kitchen** · 1635 Chicago Ave
· **Dixie Kitchen and Bait Shop** · 825 Church St
· **Dozika** · 601 Dempster St
· **Hecky's Barbeque** · 1902 Green Bay Rd
· **Joy Yee's Noodle Shop** · 521 Davis St
· **Kafein Café** · 1621 Chicago Ave
· **Kansaku** · 1514 Sherman Ave

· **Las Palmas** · 817 University Pl
· **Lulu's Dim Sum and Then Sum** · 804 Davis St
· **Mt Everest** · 630 Church St
· **Narra** · 1710 Orrington Ave
· **Noodles & Company** · 930 Church St
· **Olive Mountain** · 610 Davis St
· **Pete Miller's Original Steakhouse** · 1557 Sherman Ave
· **Tapas Barcelona** · 1615 Chicago Ave
· **Trattoria Demi** · 1571 Sherman Ave
· **Unicorn Café** · 1723 Sherman Ave
· **Va Pensiero** · Margarita Inn· 1566 Oak Ave
· **Vive la Crepe** · 1565 Sherman Ave

🛍Shopping
· **Active Endeavors** · 901 Church St
· **Art & Science Hair Salon** · 811 Church St
· **Asinamali Women's Boutique** · 1722 Sherman Ave
· **Bookman's Alley** · 1712 Sherman Ave
· **Campus Gear** · 1717 Sherman Ave
· **Uncle Dan's Great Outdoors** · 700 Church St
· **William's Shoes** · 710 Church St

W Kinzie St

Carroll Dr

W Carroll Ave

N Homan Ave

N St Louis Ave

N Central Park Ave

W Fulton St

N Avers Ave

P

**Garfield Park
Conservatory**

W Fulton Blvd

Conservatory Dr

W Walnut St

Pulaski

N Pulaski Rd

N Harding Ave

**Gold Dome
Building**

**Conservatory
Central Park Drive**

W Lake St

N Hamilton Ave

W Maypole Ave

Kedz

W West End St

N McCrea Dr

Lagoon

P

W Maypole Ave

W Washington Blvd

Garfield

W Washington Blvd

MAP
49

W Warren Ave

W Warren Ave

Warren Dr

Park

W Madison St

S Pulaski Rd

S Springfield Ave

S Hamilton Blvd

S Woodard Dr

S Central Park Ave

S St Louis Ave

S Homan Ave

S Spaulding Ave

W Monroe St

Music Court Dr

W Monroe St

W Wilcox Ave

W Adams Ave

W Adams St

Independence Blvd

**Tennis
Courts**

W Jackson Blvd

W Jackson Blvd

S Christiana Ave

W Gladys Ave

S Trumbull Ave

W Van Buren St

W Fifth Ave

W Gladys Ave

S Millard Ave

S Fifth Ave

Pulaski

W Congress Pkwy

290

Dwight D Eisenhower Expy

W Harrison St

Overview

For a century now, the historic West Side has been home to an equally historic botanical gem—Garfield Park Conservatory. The mid 1990s saw major restoration efforts, along with the creation of The Garfield Park Conservatory Alliance, an organization that has raised money for various programs involving the Conservatory. The rest of the vast 185-acre park boasts fishing lagoons, a swimming pool, an ice rink, baseball diamonds, and basketball and tennis courts. Garfield Park's landmark Gold Dome Building houses a fitness center, a basketball court, and the Peace Museum.

Garfield and its sister parks—Humboldt Park (1400 N Sacramento Ave, 312-742-7549) and Douglas Park (1401 S Sacramento Ave, 773-762-2842)—constitute a grand system of sprawling green spaces linked by broad boulevards designed in 1869 by William Le Baron Jenney (better known as the "father of the skyscraper"). However, Jenney's plan didn't bear fruit until almost 40 years later (after the uprooting of corrupt park officials), when Danish immigrant and former park laborer Jens Jensen became chief landscape architect. In 1908, Jensen completed the parks and consolidated their three small conservatories under the 1.8-acre Garfield Park Conservatory's curvaceous glass dome, designed to resemble a "great Midwestern haystack."

Garfield Park Conservatory

Address: 300 N Central Park Ave
             Chicago, IL 60624
Phone: 773-746-5100
Website: www.garfield-conservatory.org
Hours: 9 am–5 pm daily; Thurs: 9 am–8 pm
Admission: FREE

One of the nation's largest conservatories, Garfield Park has six thematic plant houses with 1,000 species and more than 10,000 individual plants from around the world. Plants Alive!, a 5,000-square-foot children's garden, has touchable plants, a soil pool for digging, a Jurassic Park–sized bumble bee, and a two-story, twisting flower stem that doubles as a slide. School groups often book the garden for field trips, so call first to determine public access hours. Annual Conservatory events include the Spring Flower Show, Azalea/Camellia Show, Chocolate Festival, Summer Tropical Show, Chrysanthemum (Chicago's city flower) Show, and Holiday Garden Show. Call for program scheduling. Every weekend, seasonally, visitors can browse the open air Garfield Market featuring crafts, plants, and produce. There is a farmer's market at the park on Saturday mornings from June through October.

Fishing

Garfield Park's two lagoons at Washington Boulevard and Central Park Avenue and those at Douglas and Humboldt Parks are favorite West Side fishing holes. Seasonally, they are stocked with bluegill, crappie, channel catfish, and largemouth bass, along with an occasional unfortunate gang member. The fish here is perfect for those who need a little pollution with their protein. Kids can take free fishing classes at the park lagoons during the summer through the Chicago Park District (312-747-PLAY). Groups of ten kids or more fish every day of the week at a new location. You'll have to call in advance, as

groups are organized by appointment only. The program runs June 20–August 12, Mon–Fri, between 10 am and 4 pm.

Nature

The Chicago Park District leads free nature walks and has created marked trails with information plaques at the city's bigger parks, Garfield, Douglas, and Humboldt Parks included. Seasonally, visitors can view as many as 100 species of colorful butterflies at the formal gardens of the three parks. The parks' lagoons are officially designated Chicago "birding parks," so take binoculars. Picnics for 50 people or more, or tent set-up, require party-throwers to obtain permits issued by the Chicago Park District.

How to Get There

By Car: Garfield Park is ten minutes from the Loop. Take I-290 W; exit on Independence Boulevard and drive north. Turn east on Washington Boulevard to Central Park Avenue. Go north on Central Park Avenue two blocks past the Golden Dome field house and Lake Street to the Conservatory. A free parking lot is on the building's south side, just after Lake Street. Street parking is available on Central Park Avenue, Madison Street, and Washington Boulevard.

By L: From the Loop, take the Green Line west ($2, $1.75 with Chicago Card) to the Conservatory-Central Park Drive stop, a renovated Victorian train station at Lake Street and Central Park Avenue.

By Bus: From the Loop, board CTA 20 Madison Street bus westbound ($2, $1.75 with Chicago Card). Get off at Madison Street and Central Park Avenue. Walk four blocks north to the Conservatory.

Additional Information

Chicago Park District, 312-742-PLAY; www.chicagoparkdistrict.com

Nature Chicago Program—City of Chicago and Department of the Environment, 312-744-7606; www.cityofchicago.org

Chicago Ornithological Society, 312-409-9678; www.chicagobirder.org

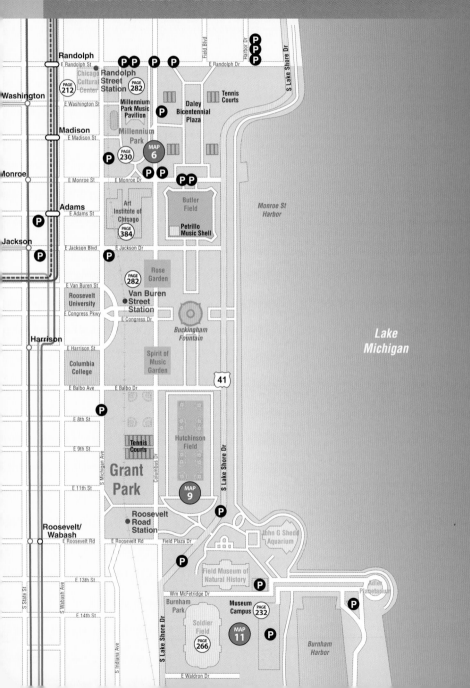

Overview

Grant Park, where grass meets glass, is Chicago's venerable "front lawn." Spanning the Lake Michigan shoreline from N Randolph Street to S Roosevelt Road and west to Michigan Avenue, it's safe to say there's not a more trafficked park this side of New York City's Central Park. Grant Park is a study in contrasts: on the one side featuring massive summer festivals (such as the annual homage to obesity known as Taste of Chicago) that turn the park into Chicago's dirty doormat; but during the rest of the year, a quiet place to relax, play, and count the number of panhandlers who ask if you can "help them out with a dollar."

The park's history can be traced back to 1835 when concerned citizens lobbied to prevent development along their pristine waterfront. Little did they know that when the State of Illinois ruled to preserve the land as "public ground forever to remain vacant of buildings" this meant for everyone, including the wealthy elite who were literally perched on the lofty balconies of the tawny palaces that lined the downtown shores of Lake Michigan. Be careful what you wish for, yes? Architect and city planner Daniel Burnham laid the groundwork for the park and made plans to erect museums, civic buildings, and general park attractions along the waterfront. This plan got somewhat sidetracked by the Great Chicago Fire of 1871. Interestingly enough, remaining debris from the fire was pushed into the lake and now forms part of the foundation for much of Grant Park and Chicago's famous shoreline. Chicagoans can thank local land-lover and legendary mail-order magnate Aaron Montgomery Ward for pressuring the State of Illinois in 1911 to preserve the land as an undeveloped open space.

Nature

Grant Park's lawns, gardens, lakefront, and bench-lined paths attract a mixed crowd of lunching office workers, exercise fanatics, readers, gawking tourists, homeless and not-so-homeless vagabonds, and just your run-of-the-mill idiots. South and north of famous Buckingham Fountain are the formal Spirit of Music Garden and Rose Garden, respectively. Near Daley Bicentennial Plaza (located on the park's north side) is the riotously colorful Wildflower Garden which is not to be missed during the time of the year when one can expect to see flowers in bloom. There are also a multitude of sculptures, ranging in form and style, strewn with abandon throughout the park, so expect to see art appreciators and imitators alike milling about as well.

Sports

Daley Bicentennial Plaza (337 E Randolph St, 312-742-7648) is equipped with a fitness center, skating rink, and 12 outdoor tennis courts. The courts are open year-round from 7 am to 10 pm on weekdays and from 8 am to 5 pm on weekends. Court time costs $7 per hour and there's a two-hour limit. Reservations are recommended and should be made well in advance. The skating rink is open daily from November to March for iceskating ($5 skate rental available) and open for free in-line skating the rest of the year. On the south end of the park, baseball diamonds and tennis courts are available on a first-come basis unless they are reserved for league play.

Buckingham Fountain

Buckingham Fountain is Grant Park's spouting centerpiece at the intersection of Congress Parkway and Columbus Drive, and was the original starting point of Route 66. Designed by Edward Bennett, the fountain is an homage to Lake Michigan and houses four statues that represent the Lake's four surrounding states (Illinois, Indiana, Michigan, and Wisconsin, ya big idiot). It has been showering onlookers with wind-blown spray since 1927 and, unfortunately, is notable for its role in the opening sequence of the sitcom *Married…with Children*. Today the water flows April through October from 8 am to 11 pm daily. For 20 minutes each hour the center basin jettisons water 150 feet into the air. Lights and music accompany the skyrocketing water display during evening hours. Food concessions and restrooms can be found nearby.

Festivals & Events

Chicagoans used to gather at the Petrillo Music Shell for free Grant Park Orchestra and Chorus concerts during the summer months. Now they go to the Jay Pritzker Pavilion in Millennium Park, located between Michigan and Columbus Avenues that, in and of itself, is worth a visit. Concerts take place June through August (312-742-7638; www.grantparkmusicfestival.com). You can't always pass up a free headliner concert at Grant Park's monstrous summer festivals. If at all possible, avoid the gut-to-gut feeding frenzy that is the Taste of Chicago. But if you must go, hit it on a weekday afternoon. We'll accept your "thank you" now; if you go on the weekend, you'll understand why. In mid-July through late-August, Grant Park hosts the Outdoor Film Festival, during which the city has free showings of classic movies in the middle of the park every Tuesday night. Come armed with blankets, food and drinks, and make sure you're not going to see the movie for the first time; the crowd of people can get pretty loud, and the enormous speakers echo. For a complete event schedule, contact the Mayor's Office of Special Events at 312-744-3315, or check out www.cityofchicago.org/specialevents.

How to Get There

By Car: Exits off Lake Shore Drive west to Grant Park are Randolph Street, Monroe Drive, Jackson Drive, Balbo Drive, and Roosevelt Road. Also, enter the park from Michigan Avenue heading east on the same streets. The underground East Monroe Garage is off Monroe Drive. Columbus Drive runs through Grant Park's center and has metered parking.

By Train: From the Richard B. Ogilvie Transportation Center, travel east to Michigan Avenue and Grant Park on CTA buses 14, 20, and 56 ($2, $1.75 with Chicago Card)). From Union Station, board CTA buses 60, 123, 151, and 157.

Metra trains coming from the south stop at the Roosevelt Road station on the south end of Grant Park before terminating at the underground Millennium Station at Randolph Street.

By L: Get off at any L stop in the Loop between Randolph Street and Van Buren Street ($2, $1.75 with Chicago Card). Walk two blocks east to Grant Park.

By Bus: CTA buses 13, 10 (weekends and daily in summer), 145, 146, 147, 151) stop along Michigan Avenue in front of Grant Park ($2, $1.75 with Chicago Card).

E 110th Pl

Clock Tower and
Factory Complex

E 111th St (Florence Dr)

**111th St
Pullman
Station**

Hotel
Florence

**Pullman
Park**

E 111th Pl

O

Historic
Pullman
Visitor
Center

**Arcade
Park**

E 112th St

Market
Hall

Greenstone
Church

E 112th St

Pullman
Stables

MAP
59

Historic
Pullman
Center

**Langley
Playground**

E 113th St

E 113th St

**Pullman
Elementary
School**

E 114th St

E 114th Pl

E 114th Pl

E 115th St

**115th St
Kensington
Station**

Dr Martin Luther King Jr Dr

S Vernon Ave

Cottage Grove Ave (Pullman Dr)

S Front Ave

Forrestville Ave

St Lawrence Ave

Champlain Ave

S Langley Ave (Fulton Ave)

S Ellis Ave

Overview

Although railroad magnate George Pullman's utopian community went belly-up, the Town of Pullman he founded 14 miles south of the Loop survives as a National Landmark Historic District. Built between 1880 and 1885, Pullman is one of America's first planned model industrial communities.

The "workers' paradise" earned Pullman humanitarian hoorahs, as well as a 6% return on his investment. Pullman believed that if laborers and their families lived in comfortable housing with gas, plumbing, and ventilation—in other words, livable conditions—their productivity would increase, as would his profits. Pullman was voted "the world's most perfect town" at the Prague International Hygienic and Pharmaceutical Exposition of 1896.

All was perfect in Pullman until a depression incited workers to strike in 1894, and the idealistic industrialist refused to negotiate with his ungrateful workers. While George Pullman's dream of a model community of indentured servitude died with him in 1897, hatred for him lived on. Pullman's tomb at Graceland Cemetery is more like a bomb shelter. To protect his corpse from irate labor leaders, Pullman was buried under a forest of railroad ties and concrete.

The grounds and buildings that make up Pullman went through most of the twentieth century stayed intact until 1998, when a man who heard voices in his head torched several of the site's primary buildings. Fortunately, die-hard Pullmanites have banded together to maintain the remaining structures, and for anyone interested in labor history or town planning, the city is worth a train or bus ride down from the Loop.

Architecture & Events

Architect Solon Beman and landscape architect Nathan Barrett based Pullman's design on French urban plans. Way back when, Pullman was made up of mostly brick rowhouses (95% still in use), several parks, shops, schools, churches, and a library, as well as various health, recreational, and cultural facilities.

Today, the compact community's borders are 111th Street (Florence Drive), 115th Street, Cottage Grove Avenue (Pullman Drive), and S Langley Avenue (Fulton Avenue). If you're interested in sightseeing within the historic district, we suggest you start at the Pullman Visitor Center (11141 S Cottage Grove Ave, 773-785-8901; www.pullmanil.org). There you can pick up free, self-guided walking tour brochures and watch an informative 20-minute film on the town's history. Call the center for additional specialty tour information and lecture details.

The annual House Tour on the second weekend in October is a popular Pullman event where several private residences open their doors to the public from 11 am to 5 pm on Saturday and Sunday ($17 in advance, $20 on day of event). May through October, the center also offers a ninety-minute Guided Walking Tour every first Sunday of the month at 1:30 pm ($5). Key tour sites include Hotel Florence, Greenstone Church (interior), Market Square, the stables, and the fire station.

Where to Eat

- **Seven Seas Submarine**, 11216 S Michigan Ave, 773-785-0550. Dine in or take out at this tiny sandwich shop.
- **Cal Harbor Restaurant**, 546 E 115th St, 773-264-5435. Omelettes, burgers, etc. at family grill.

Where to Drink

- **Pullman's Pub**, 611 E 113th St, 773-568-0264. Suds in a pre-Prohibition watering hole.

How to Get There

By Car: Take I-94 S to the 111th Street exit. Go west to Cottage Grove Avenue and turn south, driving one block to 112th Street to the Visitor Center surrounded by a large, free parking lot.

By Train: Metra's Electric Main Line departs from Millennium Station (underground) at Michigan Avenue between S Water Street and Randolph Street. Ride 30 minutes to Pullman Station at 111th Street ($3.05 one-way). Walk east to Cottage Grove Avenue, and head south one block to 112th and the Visitor Center.

By L: From the Loop, take the Red Line to the 95th Street station. Board CTA 111 Pullman bus going south ($2, $1.75 with Chicago Card.).

By Bus: CTA 4 bus from the Randolph Street Station travels south to the 95th Street and Cottage Grove stop. Transfer to 111 Pullman bus heading south ($2 with transfer).

Overview

Historic Jackson Park, named for Mary Jackson, original owner of the land and cousin to president Andrew Jackson, borders Lake Michigan, Hyde Park, and Woodlawn, and was, for a long time, an unused tract of fallow land. The 500-acre parcel was eventually transformed into a real city park in the 1870s thanks to Frederick Law Olmsted of Central Park fame. The Midway Plaisance connects Jackson to Washington Park.

Jackson Park experienced its 15 minutes of worldwide fame in 1893 when it played host to the World's Fair Columbian Exposition. Today, the Museum of Science and Industry and La Rabida Children's Hospital and Research Center occupy two of the former fair structures.

Until recently Jackson Park had gone to seed, but thanks to Mayor Daley's green thumb, the government has been pumping money into park rehabilitation projects and Jackson Park is reaping the benefits. Major improvements to the area's lakefront, bike path, athletic centers, and beaches have Jackson Park shimmering again.

Museum of Science and Industry

Address:	57th St & Lake Shore Dr
	Chicago, IL 60637
Phone:	773-684-1414
Website:	www.msichicago.org
Hours:	Mon–Sat 9:30 am–4 pm; Sun 11 am–4 pm
Admission:	$13 adults, ($12 for Chicagoans); $9 children ages 3–11, ($8.50 for Chicagoans); $12 seniors, ($11 for Chicagoans)

(Note: The Museum offers free admission on what would seem to be arbitrary days and hours vary month to month, so check the website regularly.)

The 1893 World's Fair Arts Palace is now home to the Museum of Science and Industry. The mammoth 350,000-square-foot bastion is one of the largest science museums in the world. Generations of Chicagoans and visitors have been wowed by a vast array of exhibits, including hatching baby chicks, *U-505* (the only World War II German submarine captured), and the Walk-Through Heart. The model railroad, another favorite exhibit, has been expanded to the now 3,500-square-foot *Great Train Journey*, which depicts the route from Chicago to Seattle. Other popular attractions include the fast-food toy exhibit, the coal mine, and the Fairy Castle.

Nature

Two lagoons surround Wooded Island, a.k.a. Paul H. Douglas Nature Sanctuary. Osaka Garden, a serene Japanese garden with an authentic tea house and entrance gate, sits at the island's northern tip. The ceremonial garden, like the golden replica of Statue of the Republic on Hayes Avenue, recalls the park's 1893 Exposition origins. The Chicago Audubon Society (773-539-6793; www.chicagoaudubon.org) conducts bird walks in the park. These sites and the Perennial Garden at 59th Street and Cornell Drive are also butterfly havens.

Sports

Back in the very beginning of the 20th century, the Jackson Park Golf Course was the only public course in the Midwest. Today, the historic 18-hole course is certified by the Audubon Cooperative Sanctuary and has beautiful wilderness habitats. (Or are those scruffy fairways?) Greens fees are $22.75 during the week and $25.75 on weekends (all rates are discounted for residents). A driving range is adjacent to the course (773-667-0524).

In the past six years, the city has spent over $10 million to improve fitness facilities in its parks, and the Jackson Park field house was the happy recipient of a much-needed face-lift. The swanky new weight room and gymnasium are open to adults weekdays from 9 am to 9:30 pm, and weekends from 9 am to 4:15 pm. The facilities are open to teens from 2 pm to 6 pm. Adult membership passes cost $50 for ten weeks and teens work out for free. From Hayes Drive north along Cornell Avenue are outdoor tennis courts, baseball diamonds, and a running track. Tennis courts are on the west side of Lakeshore Drive at 63rd Street. Jackson Park's beaches are at 57th Street and 63rd Street (water playground, too). Inner and Outer Harbors allow shore fishing (6401 S Stony Island Ave, 773-256-0903).

Neighboring Parks

North of Jackson Park at 55th Street and Lake Shore Drive is Promontory Point, a scenic lakeside picnic spot. Harold Washington Park, 51st Street and Lake Shore Drive, has a model yacht basin and eight tennis courts on 53rd Street.

To the west, 460-acre Washington Park (5531 S Martin Luther King Jr, 773-256-1248) has an outdoor swimming pool, playing fields, and nature areas. It's also worth stopping by to see Lorado Taft's 1922 Fountain of Time sculpture and the DuSable Museum of African-American History (740 E 56th Pl, 773-947-0600; www.dusablemuseum.org).

At 71st Street and South Shore Drive are South Shore Beach, with a harbor, bird sanctuary, and South Shore Cultural Center (7059 South Shore Dr, 773-256-0149). South Shore Golf Course is a nine-hole public course. Greens fees are $14.50 weekdays and $15.75 on weekends (312-245-0909).

How to Get There

By Car: From the Loop, drive south on Lake Shore Drive, exit west on 57th Street. From the south, take I-94 W. Exit on Stony Island Avenue heading north to 57th Drive. The museum's parking garage entrance is on 57th Drive. The Music Court lot is behind the museum. A free parking lot is on Hayes Drive.

By Bus: From the Loop, CTA buses 6 and 10 (weekends and daily in summer) stop by the museum ($2, $1.75 with Chicago Card).

By L: (the quickest way to get to Jackson Park)**:** Take the Green Line to the Garfield Boulevard (55th Street) stop ($2, 1.75 with Chicago Card); transfer to the eastbound 55 bus.

By Train: Sporadic service. From the Loop's Millennium Station at Randolph Street and Van Buren Street stations, take Metra Electric service ($2.05 one-way). Trains stop at the 55th, 56th, and 57th Street Station platform (may be under construction). Walk two blocks east. From the Richard B. Ogilvie Transportation Center, walk two blocks south to Union Station on Canal Street and catch CTA bus 1.

Overview

The largest of Chicago's 552 parks, Lincoln Park stretches 1,208 acres along the lakefront from the breeder cruising scene at the North Avenue Beach to the gay cruising scene at Hollywood Beach. The park boasts one of the world's longest bike trails, but thanks to an ever-increasing abundance of stroller-pushers, leashless dogs, and earbud-wearing roller-bladers, the path proves treacherous for cyclists and pedestrians alike. Nonetheless, sporty types and summertime dawdlers still find satisfaction indoors and out at Lincoln Park. Take a break from winter inside the Lincoln Park Conservatory, a tropical paradise full o' lush green plants no matter what the thermometer reads. Public buildings, including animal houses at the Lincoln Park Zoo, Café Brauer, Peggy Notebaert Nature Museum, and vintage beach bath houses, make the park as architecturally attractive as it is naturally beautiful.

Much of southern Lincoln Park is open green space populated by football, soccer, dog play, and barbeques. Paths shaded by mature trees lead to stoic statues. Until the 1860s, Lincoln Park was nothing more than a municipal cemetery filled with the shallow graves of cholera and smallpox victims, and it was concern about a public health threat that instigated the creation of the park. Although the city attempted to relocate all the bodies in the cemetery-to-park conversion of 1869, digging doggies may unearth more than picnickers' chicken bones.

Nature

In spring, bird watchers flock to Lincoln Park's ponds and nature trails. Addison Bird Sanctuary Viewing Platform north of Belmont Harbor overlooks five fenced-in acres of wetlands and woods. Birding programs around North Pond are run by the Lincoln Park Conservancy and the Chicago Ornithological Society (773-883-7275; www.friendslp.org). More than 160 species of birds have been identified at the 10-acre pond. Free guided walks are held on Wednesdays starting at 7:30 am. Bring binoculars and a canteen of coffee. The Fort Dearborn Chapter of the Illinois Audubon Society hosts free park and zoo bird walks (847-675-3622, www.illinoisaudubon.org). Migratory birds gather around the revamped 1889 Alfred Caldwell Lily Pool at Fullerton Parkway and North Cannon Drive. Next to the Conservatory, Grandmother's Garden and the more formal French-style garden across the street are favorites for both wedding party photos and the homeless during the warmer months.

Sports

Baseball diamonds on the park's south end are bordered by La Salle Drive and Lake Shore Drive, next to the newly renovated field house and NorthStar Eatery. Upgrades planned for the area include a running track, soccer field, and basketball and volleyball courts. Bicyclists and runners race along Lincoln Park Lagoon to the footbridge over Lake Shore Drive to North Avenue Beach, Chicago's volleyball mecca. To reserve courts and rent equipment, go to the south end of the landmark, boat-shaped bath house (312-742-3224). Just north of the bath house is a seasonal rollerblade rink and fitness club—the only place in the city that hosts outdoor yoga. North of Montrose Harbor on the North Wilson Drive lakefront is a free skateboard park.

The 9-hole Sydney R. Marovitz Public Golf Course (3600 Recreation Dr, 312-742-7930) hosts hackers year-round. Snail-slow play allows plenty of time to enjoy skyline views from this lakefront cow pasture, which is always crowded. You'll never see a golf cart on this course. Greens fees are $20 weekdays, $23 on weekends, and you can rent clubs for $10. Reserve tee times by calling 312-245-0909, or show up at sunrise. The starter sits in the northeast corner of the clock tower field house. For those who want to take it even more leisurely, check out the Diversey Miniature Golf Course (312-742-7929), which offers an 18-hole course complete with waterfalls and footbridges. Also nearby is the Diversey Golf Range (141 W Diversey Ave, 312-742-7929), open year-round (100 balls for $11.75, 50 balls for $8).

Four clay tennis courts, the last ones left in Chicago, are open 7 am–8 pm and cost $16 per hour (the 7 am–9 am early bird special costs $24); tennis shoes are required. For reservations and further information, call 312-742-7821. The free courts at Montrose are preferred by budget-conscious folks in the know.

Members of the Lincoln Park Boat Club row in Lincoln Park Lagoon. Rowing classes for the public are offered May through September (www.lpbc.net).

Whimsical, swan-shaped paddleboats at South Pond next to Café Brauer are as boring to paddle as you'd guess, but just try telling a kid that. Located at 2021 N Stockton Drive, this restored Prairie School national landmark houses seasonal restaurants and an upstairs ballroom and is a popular venue for weddings and other private functions. Fishermen frequent South Pond and the lagoon, as do a drove of self-entitled geese that would likely eat a truck-load of bread if you had it to give. Belmont, Montrose, and Diversey Harbors also allow shore fishing.

Lincoln Park Zoo

Address:	2200 N Cannon Dr
	Chicago, IL 60614
Phone:	312-742-2000
Website:	www.lpzoo.com
Hours:	Daily, 9 am–6 pm; animal buildings, 10 am–5 pm
	(call for special summer and weekend hours)
Admission:	FREE

Lions and tigers and bears and kids, oh my! We're not sure which scares us most. Established in 1868, Lincoln Park Zoo is the country's oldest free zoo, and while questions were raised in regards to nine animal deaths between 2005 and 2006, it still is a leader in wildlife conservation. National TV shows *Zoo Parade* and Ray Rayner's show *Ark in the Park* were filmed here. Look for some family (or, at least, in-law) resemblance at the cushy Regenstein Center for African Apes which opened in 2004, cost $26 million to build, and covers 29,000 square feet of living space. (Don't worry, it's supported by corporate sponsorships and private funds, not your tax dollars.) Come early and hear the white-cheek gibbons, the smallest of the ape family, mimic car alarms in their morning song to mark their territory. You may even catch one peeing off his tree before a captivated audience. Flanking the zoo's northwest side is the free Lincoln Park Conservatory, a fantastic source of oxygen renewal recommended for hangover sufferers. The new Pritzker Family Children's Zoo simulates a North American woods.

Peggy Notebaert Nature Museum

Address:	2430 N Cannon Dr
	Chicago, IL 60614
Phone:	773-755-5100
Website:	www.naturemuseum.org
Hours:	Mon–Fri 9 am–4:30 pm; Sat–Sun 10 am–5 pm
Admission:	*$9 adults, $7 seniors & students,*
	$6 children ages 3–12; Thursdays free

The Peggy Notebaert Nature Museum succeeds in making Illinois' level landscape interesting. The contemporary version of the 1857 Chicago Academy of Sciences, this hands-on museum depicts the close connection between urban and natural environments and represents global environmental issues through a local lens. A flowing water lab and flitting butterfly haven invite return visits. A must-see for anyone with a passion for taxidermy and/or *Silence of the Lambs*. You can also discover how pollutive you are in your everyday life—and how to change it—in their Extreme Greenhouse exhibit. Get back to nature with a full class and summer camp schedule.

Chicago History Museum

Address:	1601 N. Clark St & North Ave
	Chicago, IL 60614
Phone:	312-642-4600
Website:	www.chicagohistory.org
Hours:	Mon–Wed, Fri, Sat 9:30 am–4:30 pm;
	Thu 9:30 am–8 pm; Sun 12–5 pm
Admission:	$14 adults, $12 seniors & students,
	children under 12 free; Mondays free

The Chicago History Museum holds over 20 million primary documents relating to the history of the Chicago area. Exhibits about the city's pioneer roots, architecture, music, fashion, neighborhoods, windy politics, and oral histories breathe life into an otherwise dry history. Locals can access the excellent free research center (open Tuesday through Saturday) for genealogical information and housing history. Big Shoulders Café (312-587-7766) is an affordable, light lunch spot nearby.

Performances

Lincoln Park Cultural Center (2045 N Lincoln Park W, 312-742-7726) stages plays, theater workshops, and family-friendly performances year-round. Theater on the Lake (Fullerton Ave & Lake Shore Dr, 312-742-7529) performs nine weeks of alternative drama in summer. The newly renovated theater now hosts events throughout the calendar year, thanks to much-needed climate control improvements. Lincoln Park Zoo hosts outdoor summer concerts as well. Call the events hotline at 312-742-2283.

How to Get There

By Car: Lake Shore Drive exits to Lincoln Park are Bryn Mawr Avenue, Foster Avenue, Lawrence Avenue, Wilson Drive, Montrose Drive, Irving Park Parkway, Belmont Avenue, Fullerton Avenue, and North Avenue.

Free parking lots are at Recreational Drive near Belmont Harbor and Simonds Drive near Montrose Harbor. Paid lots are at North Avenue Beach, Chicago Historical Society, Lincoln Park Zoo, and Grant Hospital Garage. Stockton Drive and Cannon Drive have free street parking. A metered lot is on Diversey Parkway, next to the golf range.

By Bus: CTA buses 151, 156, 77, 146, and 147 travel through Lincoln Park ($2, $1.75 with Chicago Card). For schedules and fares, contact the RTA Information Center (312-836-7000; www.rtachicago.com).

By L: Get off the Red Line at any stop between Fullerton and Bryn Mawr avenues ($2, $1.75 with Chicago Card), then head one mile east. On the Brown Line, all stops between Sedgwick and Belmont are about a mile east of the park as well.

N

MAP
11

Michigan Ave

Indiana Ave

Prairie Ave

21st St

Calumet St

Mines Dr

Mor Dr

Lake Shore Dr

**Soldier Field
Parking Lot**

P

**Burnham
Park**

North Building

Level 4
  Meeting Rooms
  (N426-N427)
Level 3
  Exhibition Halls
Level 2
  Meeting Rooms
  (N226-N231)
Level 1
  Exhibition Halls C1, C2
  Meeting Rooms
  (N126-N140)

Lakeshore
Technology

E Cermak Rd (E 22nd St)

**Conference
Center**

Martin Luther King Dr

**Hyatt Parking
Garage**

P

Hyatt Hotel

**McCormick
Square**

**Parking
Garage A**

P

**Gate 4
South Building
Taxi Pick Up/Drop Off**

**McCormick Place West
Expansion Area**

24th St

**Gate 22
North Building
Taxi Pick Up/Drop Off**

South Building
Level 5
  Meeting Rooms (S501-S505)
Level 4
  Vista Room (S406)
  Meeting Rooms (S401-S405)
Level 3
  Exhibition Halls
  Grand Concourse
Level 2.5
  Food Court/Restaurant
  Shops & Services
  Metra Trains
Level 1
  Grand Ballroom (S100)
  Meeting Rooms
  (S101-S106)

E 24th Pl

E 25th St

55

Mines Dr

**Lakeside Center
(East Building)**

Level 4
  Meeting Rooms
  (E450-E451)
Level 3
  Exhibition Halls
  Meeting Rooms
  (E350-E354)
  Arie Crown Balcony
Level 2
  Exhibition Hall E
  Meeting Rooms
  (E250-E272)
  Arie Crown Theater
Level 1
  Offices

**Gate 30
Lakeside
Taxi Pick Up/Drop Off**

Fort Dearborn Dr

**Underground
Parking Lot C**

P

**Mercy
Hospital**

Mc 8th Dr

Parking Lot B

P

**Burnham
Park**

**Lake
Michigan**

41

General Information

NFT Map:	11
Mailing Address:	2301 S Lake Shore Dr
	Chicago, IL 60616
Phone:	312-791-7000
Website:	www.mccormickplace.com
South Building:	Exhibit Hall A; charter bus stop
North Building:	Exhibit Halls B and C;
	Metra train station
Lakeside Center:	Exhibit Halls D and E; 4,249-seat
	Arie Crown Theater (Level 2);
	underground parking garage

Overview

When it comes to the convention business, size matters. With 2.2 million square feet of exhibit space spread among three buildings, McCormick Place is the largest convention center in the country and the third largest in the world. The center hosts more than three million visitors every year for trade shows and public exhibitions in the South Building, North Building, and Lakeside Center (East Building), including the Chicago Auto Show. McCormick Place also includes the Arie Crown Theatre, second largest theatre in Chicago according to seating capacity, which holds a variety of plays, concerts, and seminars. The city's colossal cash cow has gotten bigger with the addition of a new $850 million West Building. A City of Chicago project ahead of time and on budget? Surely another sign that the apocalypse will be occuring soon. (For antonyms to "Chicago project completed ahead of time and on budget," see "Public Transportation – CTA – 'L' – Brown Line.") End times notwithstanding, the expansion added 460,000 square feet of exhibit space and 250,000 square feet of meeting rooms to the already gargantuan center.

McCormick Place's growth continues to bolster the rapid gentrification of South Loop, and with each expansion the complex's overall aesthetic appeal steadily improves. But despite major renovations, Chicagoans still refer to the complex as "the mistake on the lake." Mayor Daley called the black boxy behemoth the "Berlin Wall" that separates Chicagoans from their beloved lakefront.

Finding Your Way Around

Getting to McCormick Place is the easy part. Then you have to navigate the inside. The main entrance is off Martin Luther King Drive, next to the Hyatt Hotel. Here's how to crack the code names for meeting rooms and exhibit halls:

All meeting room locations start with E (Lakeside Center/East Building), N (North Building), or S (South Building). The first numeral represents the floor level, and the last two digits specify which room. Room numbers are never duplicated among the complex's three buildings.

Exhibit halls are named by consecutive letters starting with the South Building where Hall A (Level 3) is located. North Building houses Halls B (Level 3) and C (Level 1). Exhibit Halls D (Level 3) and E (Level 2) are in Lakeside Center.

Got all that?

Restaurants & Services

Connie's Pizza and McDonald's Express are in the North Building (Level 2). The Plate Room Food Court is in the Grand Concourse (Level 2.5 and 3), where Starbucks, shops, a shoe shine, and massage services are also located. (Aren't convention centers just *great*?) Business centers and ATMs are in the Grand Concourse (Level 2.5), North Building (Level 2), and Lakeside Center (Level 2). The new West Building expansion will have a large food court on the second floor. If you're totally lost, there are Visitor Information Centers in each building. Good luck finding them.

How to Get There

By Car: From the Loop, take Lake Shore Drive south; from the southeast, travel north on Lake Shore Drive. Signage to McCormick Place on Lake Shore Drive is frequent and clear. Parking garages are in Lakeside Center and the Hyatt. Lots are at 31st Street and Lake Shore Drive and at Martin Luther King Drive across from the South Building. Additional lots are north of McCormick Place at Burnham Harbor and Soldier Field.

By Bus: From the Loop, CTA buses 3 and 4 stop in front of the South Building. From Richard B. Ogilvie Transportation Center, take buses 124, 125, or 157 to Michigan Avenue; transfer to a southbound 3 or 4 ($2.00, $1.75 with Chicago Card). From Union Station, board eastbound bus 1 to Michigan Avenue; transfer to a southbound 3 or 4.

During major shows, countless charter buses circle downtown hotels, transporting conventioneers to McCormick Place for free. With the new express busway, charter buses travel from Randolph Street to the South Building in less than ten minutes. For schedules, check with the hotels and at McCormick Place information desks.

By Train: A Metra train ride from the Loop's Millennium Station at Randolph Street and Van Buren Street stations to the McCormick Place Station takes nine minutes ($1.85 one-way). Escalators to the train platform are on the west side of the Grand Concourse (Level 2.5).

E Benton Pl

N Beaubien Ct

N Stetson Ave

Millenium Station ●

E Randolph St

Harris Music & Dance Theater

Bike Garage

P

Chicago Cultural Center

PAGE 212

Wrigley Square

Boeing Gallery North

Chase Promenade North

Jay Pritzker Pavilion

E Washington St

P

N Garland Ct

N Michigan Ave

McCormick Tribune Plaza & Ice Rink

AT&T Plaza

Cloud Gate

Chase Promenade Central

Great Lawn

Columbus Dr

BP Pesdestrian Bridge

E Madison St

P

MAP 6

Crown Fountain

Boeing Gallery South

Chase Promenade South

Lurie Garden

P

E Monroe St

The Art Institute of Chicago

PAGE 384

Grant Park

PAGE 220

E Adams St

P

DePaul University (Loop Campus)

PAGE 244

E Jackson Dr

Overview

Only four years behind schedule (who's counting?) and hundreds of millions of dollars over budget (okay, this we counted), Millennium Park finally launched itself in late 2001 as the cultural epicenter Mayor Daley promised us it would be back in 1997. Even if it did take myriad stopgap funding measures resembling yesteryear Al Capone strong-arm tactics to eternally endow us with the AT&T Plaza, McCormick Tribune Plaza & Ice Rink, and the Chase Promenade, locals and tourists alike agree it was well worth it. Even, staunch, longtime local naysayers have come to acknowledge that, when all is said and done, the end result really is an amazing addition to Grant Park's northpoint and is, without a doubt, one of downtown Chicago's crowning jewels. The only remaining piece needed to complete the vision of this massive puzzle is the Chicago Art Institute Expansion Project, a $200 million addition designed by architect Renzo Piano. Tape cutting was originally planned for 2007, but the project is now scheduled to open in 2009. A delay on a Daley promise? Shocking.

Jay Pritzker Pavilion

The cornerstone of Millennium Park, without question, is the Pritzker Pavilion. It seems the whole park may have very well been conceived to give Frank Gehry's architectural masterpiece an appropriate setting. Spectacularly innovative, the pavilion's façade features immense stainless steel ribbons unfurling 40 feet into the sky. The pavilion's stage area is as big as Orchestra Hall across the street and can accommodate a 120-person orchestra and a 150-person choir. Seating for the free concert events includes a 4,000-seat terrace and an additional 95,000-square-foot lawn area that can accommodate 7,000 picnickers. A one-of-a-kind integrated sound system offers outdoor acoustics that rival the best in the world.

Harris Music & Dance Theater

Several dance and theatrical troupes share the 1,500-seat underground space behind Gehry's behemoth bandshell, including Hubbard Street Dance Chicago (not to be missed, but good luck getting tickets!), the Chicago Children's Choir, and the Jazz Institute of Chicago. Two underground parking garages flank the theater, and as with all parking in this area, it's first come/first served and a bit of a mess on the weekends.

Tickets and schedule available at www.harristheaterchicago.org

Nature & Sculpture

The park has several different defined spaces: Wrigley Square, with its neoclassical epistyle; the Chase Promenade, gearing up to house art fairs and ethnic festivals; and the AT&T Plaza, which is home to Anish Kapoor's 100-ton stainless steel jelly-bean sculpture, *Cloud Gate*. Flanking the skating rink to the south is the modernist Crown Fountain, which features two glass brick towers, 50 feet in height, with projected video images of the faces of actual Chicago residents. The Lurie Garden, a ridiculously conceptual assemblage of seasonal foliage, offers a beautiful public gathering space as well as more contemplative environments. The BP Bridge, a 925-foot-long winding bridge—Frank Gehry's first—connects Millennium Park to Daley Bicentennial Plaza just east of the park. Clad in brushed stainless steel panels, the BP Bridge complements the Pritzker Pavilion in function as well as design by creating an acoustic barrier for traffic noise. It's well worth the walk.

Sports

The 15,910-square-foot McCormick Tribune ice skating rink opens annually in November. Admission is free and skates are available for rental for $7. The park also houses a state-of-the-art, heated bicycle garage, which provides parking for 300 bikes, showers, a repair facility, and a café.

Dining

The 300-seat Park Grill (voted "Top 5 Best Burger in Chicago") overlooking the skating rink offers burgers, steaks, and salads year round. In the summer, carry-away grub is available from a variety of kiosks throughout the park.

How to Get There

No matter your mode of travel, approach the area around Millennium Park with patience and allow extra time. For train, L, and bus transportation recommendations, see our Grant Park or Art Institute sections. Metra's Randolph Street train station, servicing only south-bound trains, is located under Millennium Park.

If you choose to drive, underground parking is available in several areas. Access the Grant Park North Garage from Michigan Avenue. Enter Millennium Park Garage from the lower levels of Randolph Street and mid-level of Columbus Drive.

Grant Park

PAGE 220

41

Water Taxi Dock

E Roosevelt Rd

PO Underpass

S Columbus Dr

Main Entrance
Handicap Entrance

Shedd Aquarium

North Main Entrance

Group Entrance

Free Trolley Stop

The Field Museum

Handicap Entrance

Free Trolley Stop

South Main Entrance

Free Trolley Stop

Solidarity Dr
Solidarity Dr

Free Trolley Stop

North Entrance

Adler Planetarium

Group & Handicap Entrance

McFetridge Dr

Planetarium Lot

North Garage

Museum Campus Dr

Lynne White Dr

12th St Beach

Burnham Harbor

Soldier Field

PAGE 266

Northerly Island Park

Waldron Dr

MAP 11

S Prairie Ave

S Calumet Ave

18th St Station

S Lake Shore Dr

Waldron Garage

Burnham Park

Merrill C Meigs Field

Main Museum Visitor Entrance

E 18th St

South Lot

E Cullerton St

E 21st St

Lake Michigan

200E 300E

E Cermak Rd

S College Grove Ave

S Prairie Ave

S Calumet Ave

S Dr Martin L King Jr Dr

S Dr Martin L King Jr Dr

E 23rd St

23rd St McCormick Place Station

400E

Burnham Park

E 24th St

McCormick Place

PAGE 228

E 24th Pl

E 24th St

S Prairie Ave

E 25th St

Stevenson Expy

55

Overview

Museum Campus is the ultimate destination for educational field trips. South of Grant Park at the intersection of Roosevelt Road and Lake Shore Drive, Museum Campus's 57 acres of uninterrupted lakefront parkland connect three world-renowned Chicago institutions: The Field Museum, Shedd Aquarium, and Adler Planetarium & Astronomy Museum. You've got Mayor Daley to thank for all of this beautiful space; it was the bossman himself who championed the rerouting of Lake Shore Drive to create the Museum Campus, which opened in 1998. Chicagoans, take note: Although none of the museums that make up the museum campus are shouting from rooftops about it, all three offer reduced admission rates to locals. Be sure to ask for it.

The Field Museum

Address: 1400 S Lake Shore Dr
               Chicago, IL 60605
Phone: 312-922-9410
Website: www.fieldmuseum.org
Hours: Open daily 9 am–5 pm, except Christmas
Admission: $12 adults, $7 students & seniors,
               $7 children ages 4–11, discount for Chicagoans

The massive, Greek Revival-style museum constructed in 1921 houses over 20 million artifacts. From dinosaurs, diamonds, and earthworms to man-eating lions, totem poles, and mummies, there is just too much to savor in a single visit. In 2006, the museum introduced a new permanent exhibit called The Evolving Planet, featuring an interactive stroll through 4 billion years of evolution, from single-celled organisms through dinosaurs, hominids, and finally to human beings. Science: 1, Intelligent Design: 0. Another noteworthy permanent exhibit is Sue, the largest, most complete, and best preserved Tyrannosaurus Rex discovered to date. Complete with a half-smoked pack of Marlboros, since we now know that's what killed the dinosaurs. As with most museums, some temporary exhibits cost additional bucks on top of normal museum fees. Free museum tours are held weekdays at 11 am and 2 pm.

John G. Shedd Aquarium

Address: 1200 S Lake Shore Dr
               Chicago, IL 60605
Phone: 312-939-2438
Website: www.shedd.org
Hours: Memorial Day–Labor Day: Daily, 9 am–6 pm
               (Jun–Aug open 'til 10 pm on Thurs)
               Labor Day–Memorial Day: Mon–Fri: 9 am–5 pm;
               Sat–Sun: 9 am–6 pm. Closed Christmas
Admission: $23 adults ($17 Chicagoans), $16 seniors over 65
               and children under 11 ($12 Chicagoans)

Opened in 1929, the Beaux Arts-style aquarium's six wings radiate from a giant, circular coral reef tank. The museum features revolving exhibits with a special focus on marine ecology and preservation. Popular favorites include Wild Reef, where you can get up close and personal with the sharks. On Thursday evenings from mid-June through August, the Shedd hosts "Jazzin at the Shedd" from 5 to 10 pm, featuring live jazz, a light sit-down dinner with cocktails overlooking the downtown skyline, and full access to the aquarium until 10 pm.

Burnham Park

Burnham Park, the site of the 1933 Century of Progress exhibition, encompasses McCormick Place, Burnham Harbor, the former Merrill C. Meigs Airport (closed in a political coup by Mayor Daley

in 2003), and Soldier Field. A free skateboard park is located at Lake Shore Drive and 31st Street. The 12th Street Beach, especially popular with swimmers and divers because of the deep water east of the beach, is on Northerly Island. Other beaches are at 31st Street and 49th Street. Outdoor basketball courts are east of Lake Shore Drive around 35th Street and 47th Street. Fishing is welcome along Solidarity Drive and Burnham Harbor shore,. The wilderness Nature Area at 47th Street attracts butterflies and birds.

Adler Planetarium

Address: 1300 S Lake Shore Dr
               Chicago, IL 60605
Phone: 312-922-7827
Website: www.adlerplanetarium.org
Hours: 9:30 am–4:30 pm daily;
               First Friday of every month: 9:30 am–10 pm;
               Closed Thanksgiving and Christmas.
Admission: $19 for adults ($17 Chicagoans),
               $15 kids ages 4–17 ($14 Chicagoans),
               $17 seniors over 65 ($15 Chicagoans)

The Adler Planetarium & Astronomy Museum offers interactive exhibits explaining space phenomena and intergalactic events; its 2,000 historic astronomical and navigational instruments form the western hemisphere's largest collection. On the first Friday of every month, weather permitting, amateur astronomers young and old are invited to bring their own telescopes to the Planetarium lawns. Roving scientists offer tips and instructions on telescope usage and observational features. Chicago skyline views from the planetarium grounds are out of this world any day of the week, and are always worth the trip.

How to Get There

By Car: From the Loop, take Columbus Drive south; turn east on McFetridge Drive. From the south, take Lake Shore Drive to McFetridge Drive. Area parking lots are near Soldier Field, Field Museum, Adler Planetarium, and McCormick Place. All parking on Museum Campus costs $15 per day. Metered parking is available on Solidarity Drive.

By Bus: CTA buses 2, 6, 10, 12, 14, 127, 130, and 146 serve the area ($2 one-way, $1.75 with Chicago Card). For schedules and fares, contact the RTA Information Center at 312-913-3110; www.rtachicago.com.

By L: Ride the Orange, Red, or Green Lines to the Roosevelt Road stop ($2 one-way, $1.75 with Chicago Card). Walk east through the pedestrian underpass at Roosevelt Road.

By Train: From Richard B. Ogilvie Transportation Center, travel east on CTA bus 20 to State Street; transfer to the 146 ($2 one-way, $1.75 with Chicago Card). From Union Station take CTA bus 1, 126, or 151; transfer at State Street to the 10 or 146. From La Salle Street station, take the 146 ($2 one-way, $1.75 with Chicago Card). South Shore and Metra trains stop at the Roosevelt Road station.

By Trolley: Free trolleys travel to the Museum Campus from public transportation stations and some parking lots during the warmer months. See www.cityofchicago.org/transportation or call 1-877-CHICAGO for more details.

On Foot: Walk south through Grant Park past bobbing boats and the gushing Buckingham Fountain to the Museum Campus.

Water Taxis: Seasonally, water taxis operate between Navy Pier and Museum Campus (312-222-9328; www.shorelinesightseeing.com).

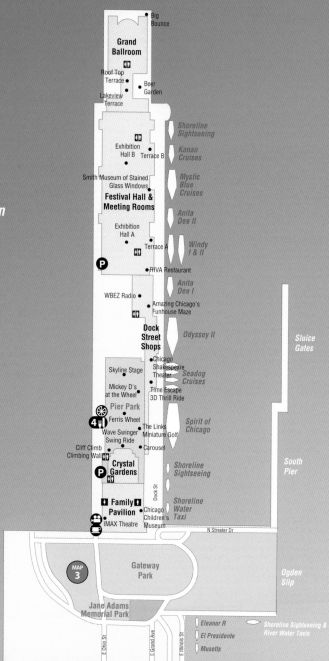

Big Bounce

Grand Ballroom

Roof Top Terrace

Beer Garden

Lakeview Terrace

Lake Michigan

Shoreline Sightseeing

Kanan Cruises

Exhibition Hall B

Terrace B

Mystic Blue Cruises

Smith Museum of Stained Glass Windows

Festival Hall & Meeting Rooms

Anita Dee II

Exhibition Hall A

Terrace A

Windy I & II

P

RIVA Restaurant

Anita Dee I

WBEZ Radio

Amazing Chicago's Funhouse Maze

Dock Street Shops

Odyssey II

Chicago Shakespeare Theater

Skyline Stage

Seadog Cruises

Mickey D's at the Wheel

Time Escape 3D Thrill Ride

Pier Park

Ferris Wheel

The Links Miniature Golf

Spirit of Chicago

Wave Swinger Swing Ride

Cliff Climb Climbing Wall

Carousel

Crystal Gardens

Shoreline Sightseeing

P

South Pier

Family Pavilion

Shoreline Water Taxi

IMAX Theatre

Chicago Children's Museum

N Streeter Dr

Sluice Gates

MAP 3

Gateway Park

Ogden Slip

Jane Adams Memorial Park

Eleanor R

El Presidente

Shoreline Sightseeing & River Water Taxis

Musetts

E Ohio St

E Grand Ave

E Illinois St

General Information

NFT Map:	3
Address:	600 E Grand Ave
	Chicago, IL 60611
Phone:	312-595-7437
Website:	www.navypier.com
Pier Hours:	Opens 10 am daily. Closing times of restaurants, shops, and attractions vary by season, holiday, and public exhibitions/events.
Skyline Stage:	1,500-seat outdoor performance pavilion in Pier Park, performances are May through September; 312-595-5022
IMAX Theatre:	312-595-5629
Free Fireworks:	Memorial Day to Labor Day, Wednesdays (9:30 pm) & Saturdays (10:15 pm). Free to the public.
WBEZ Radio:	National Public Radio's local station, 312-948-4600; www.wbez.org.
Exhibit Space:	Festival Hall, Lakeview Terrace, Ballroom Lobby, Grand Ballroom; 36 meeting rooms

Overview

A quintessential tourist trap, Navy Pier (a.k.a. the mall on the lake) is often avoided by real Chicagoans, who scoff at its self-consciously inoffensive blandness. Save for an occasional Skyline Stage concert, speed-boat ride, or high-end nosh at Riva, a trek to the pier is best reserved for those times when you have Grandma and a bevy of nieces and nephews in town, not to mention plenty of spending cash.

Opened to the public in 1916 as a municipal wharf, the pier has also done time as a) the University of Illinois at Chicago's campus, b) a hospital, c) a military training facility, d) a concert venue, and e) a white elephant. In 1989, the Metropolitan Pier and Exposition Authority invested $150 million to transform the crumbling pier into a peninsular entertainment-exhibition complex that attracts 8 million uninspired people a year. In addition to convention space, Navy Pier also houses two museums, the Shakespeare Theater, the Crystal Gardens, an outdoor concert pavilion, a vintage grand ballroom, a 15-story Ferris wheel, an IMAX Theatre, and, just for the hell of it, a radio station.

Chicago Shakespeare Theater

The Chicago Shakespeare Theater has a 510-seat, courtyard-style theater and a 180-seat studio theater that are Chicago's sole venues dedicated to performing wordsmith Willy's works. In addition to the season's plays, the theater produces Shakespeare "shorts" for younger patrons. A bookstore and teacher resource center are also on-site (312-595-5600; www.chicagoshakes.com).

Chicago Children's Museum

The Chicago Children's Museum features daily activities, a creative crafts studio, and 15 interactive exhibits ranging from dinosaur digs and waterworks to a toddler tree house, safety town, and construction zone. The museum is open Sunday–Wednesday and Friday 10 am to 5 pm, and Thursday and Saturday until 8 pm. Admission is $9 for adults and children, $8 for seniors, and Target First Free Mondays allow children 15 and under in free the first Monday of every month. Thursdays 5 pm to 8 pm are Kraft Free Family Nights, which means free admission for all. Dates vary. (312-527-1000; www.chichildrensmuseum.org).

Smith Museum of Stained Glass Windows

Smith Museum is the first stained-glass-only museum in the country. The 150 windows installed in the lower level of Festival Hall are mainly from Chicago-area buildings and the city's renowned stained glass studios. Windows representing over a century of artistic styles include works by Louis Comfort Tiffany, Frank Lloyd Wright, Louis Sullivan, and John LaFarge. The free museum is open during Pier hours (312-595-5024).

Getting There

By Car: From the north, exit Lake Shore Drive at Grand Avenue; proceed east. From the southeast, exit Lake Shore Drive at Illinois Street; go east. Three garages are on the Pier's north side, and plenty of parking lots are just west of Lake Shore Drive in Streeterville (Map 3).

By Bus: CTA buses 29, 65, 66, 120, 121, and 124 serve Navy Pier.

By L: Take the Green or Red Line to Grand Avenue ($2.00, $1.75 with Chicago Card). Board eastbound CTA Bus 29, or take the free trolley.

By Train: From Richard B. Ogilvie Transportation Center, take CTA buses 56 or 124. From Union Station, board bus 121.

By Trolley: Free, daily trolleys that typically run every 20 minutes travel between Navy Pier and State Street along Grand Avenue and Illinois Street. Pick-up points are indicated by "Navy Pier Trolley Stop" signs along the route.

By Boat: Seasonal water shuttles (one-way $3–13 adults, $3–6 kids) travel between Navy Pier and the Museum Campus and along the Chicago River to the Sears Tower (312-222-9328; www.shorelinesightseeing.com).

Pizza

· **Connie's Pizza** · 700 E Grand Ave

Coffee

· **Starbucks** · 600 E Grand Ave

Movie Theaters

· **Navy Pier IMAX Theatre** · 600 E Grand Ave

Restaurants

· **Bubba Gump Shrimp Co** · 700 E Grand Ave
· **Billy Goat Tavern** · 600 E Grand Ave
· **Capi's Italian Kitchen** · 700 E Grand Ave
· **Charlie's Ale House** · 600 E Grand Ave
· **Joe's Be-Bop Café & Jazz Emporium** · 700 E Grand Ave
· **Riva** · 700 E Grand Ave

General Information

Oak Park Visitors Bureau: 708-524-7800;
www.visitoakpark.com

Oak Park Tourist: www.oprf.com

Overview

You can thank Oak Park for Prairie Style architecture, *A Moveable Feast*, McDonald's, and, yes, *Tarzan*. The creators of each called this charming suburb their home: Frank Lloyd Wright, Ernest Hemingway, Ray Kroc, and Edgar Rice Burroughs, respectively.

Best known for its architectural gems and strong public schools, Oak Park (pop. 52,500) is a happy hunting ground for homebuyers seeking upscale, integrated living 10 miles from the Loop. Less impressed than most with his picture-perfect hometown, Hemingway famously described Oak Park as "a village of wide lawns and narrow minds."

Village trustees must still be smarting from Hemingway's crack because they publicize an official policy on maintaining diversity. The "diversity statement" sounds like some sort of disclaimer or a zealot's vision for heaven on Earth: "Ours is a community that encourages contributions of all citizens regardless of race, gender, ethnicity, sexual orientation, disability, religion …" —and indeed, Oak Park has quite a reputation as the place all the hip GLBT kids go when it's time to become hip GLBT parents.

Architecture

Oak Park harbors the nation's largest concentration of Frank Lloyd Wright buildings, 25 in the village and another 6 in neighboring River Forest. The village's must-see sites are located in a compact area bordered by Division Street, Lake Street, Forest Avenue, and Ridgeland Avenue. Designs by Wright, William Drummond, George W. Maher, John Van Bergen, and E. E. Roberts are represented throughout.

You can ground yourself in Prairie Style architectural principles at the brilliant Frank Lloyd Wright Home and Studio. Maintained by the Frank Lloyd Wright Preservation Trust, guided tours of the designer's personal space are offered weekdays at 11 am, 1 pm, and 3 pm and every twenty minutes on weekends between 11 am and 3:30 pm (951 Chicago Ave, 708-848-1976; www.gowright.org). Only 15 people are allowed per tour, and tickets can be purchased on the foundation's website or on-site (early arrival recommended) at a cost of $12 for adults, $10 for children 11–18 and seniors, and $5 for children 4–10. Worthwhile walking tours of the surrounding streets are also offered, and a combined $20 ticket ($10 for children 7–18 and seniors, and $5 for children 4–10) covers both the home-studio site and walking tour at a discount. Worth every penny.

Completed in 1908, Unity Temple (875 Lake St, 708-383-8873; www.unitytemple-utrf.org) was Wright's first commissioned public building; today it houses Oak Park's Unitarian-Universalist congregation. Unity Temple is open daily for self-directed tours and on weekends for guided visits ($8 for adults, $6 for students and seniors). Designed by George W. Maher, Historic Pleasant Home (217 S Home Ave, 708-383-2654; www.pleasanthome.org) aptly illustrates the architectural evolution from Victorian design to early Prairie Style with tours held Thursday through Sunday at 12:30 pm, 1:30 pm, and 2:30 pm ($5 adults, $3 children; Fridays "pay what you can").

The Oak Park Visitors Center offers maps and a PDA walking tour of the Ridgeland Historic District highlighting 15 of the area's Victorian "Painted Ladies" ($10 for adults, $5 for students and seniors) 10 am–3:30 pm daily. Call 708-524-7800, or visit www.visitoakpark.com for more information.

Culture & Events

Once a year in May, the public gets to snoop inside Wright-designed private residences during the popular Wright Plus Housewalk ($85). His home-studio and Robie House in Hyde Park (shuttle provided) are also included in the tour (708-848-3559; www.gowright.org).

Get your fill of he-man author Hemingway at the Ernest Hemingway Museum (200 N Oak Park Ave, 708-848-2222; www.hemingway.org), open Sunday through Friday 1 pm–5 pm, and Saturday 10 am–5 pm ($8 adults, $6 students and seniors). His birthplace, also included with the price of admission, is located just up the street at 339 N Oak Park Avenue. For a one-stop confab with both of Oak Park's favorite sons, stroll three blocks north and two west to the 600 block of N. Kenilworth Ave, where Wright's Balch House (611) stands across the street from the Prairie Style home (600) to which Hemingway's family moved when he was 5 years old.

Summer evenings, catch Shakespeare's works performed outdoors in Austin Gardens by the Oak Park Festival Theatre company (708-445-4440; www.oakparkfestival.com). The lush Oak Park Conservatory, originally built in 1929 to provide a place for all the exotic plants Oak Park residents collected on their travels abroad, is located at 615 Garfield Street (708-386-4700; www.oprf.com/conservatory; suggested $1 donation) and definitely worth a visit.

oLandmarks

- **Frank Lloyd Wright Home and Studio** • 951 W Chicago Ave

Nightlife

- **Avenue Ale House** • 825 S Oak Park Ave

Restaurants

- **Buzz Café** • 905 S Lombard Ave
- **Café Le Coq** • 734 Lake St
- **Cucina Paradiso** • 814 North Blvd
- **Jeruselum Café** • 1030 Lake St
- **Khyber Pass** • 1031 Lake St
- **Mama Thai** • 1112 W Madison St
- **Marion Street Grill** • 189 N Marion St
- **New Rebozo** • 1116 Madison St
- **Oak Park Abbey** • 728 Lake St
- **Pete's Red Hots** • 6346 W Roosevelt Rd
- **Petersen Ice Cream** • 1100 Chicago Ave
- **Philander's Oak Park** • Carlton Hotel • 1120 Pleasant St
- **Poor Phil's** • 139 S Marion St

Shopping

- **Antiques, Etc** • 125 N Marion St
- **Fly Bird** • 719 Lake St
- **Magic Tree Bookstore** • 141 N Oak Park Ave
- **Pumpkin Moon** • 1028 North Blvd

General Information

Address: 542 N Rte 21
             Gurnee, IL 60031
Phone: 847-249-4636
Website: www.sixflags.com/parks/greatamerica
Hours: Open May to October. Hours are generally
             10 am–10 pm, but vary by season.
             See website for specific hours and dates.
Entry: $54.99 adult fare, $34.99 for kids under 54", includes
             admission to both Six Flags and Hurricane Harbor.

Overview

Long lines, crappy food, hokey entertainment, and sun poisoning…if that isn't the stuff dreams are made of, then baby, we don't know what is.

Tickets

Reduced rates are available for advanced purchase through the website and via promotions throughout the season—look for discounted deals at Dominick's as well as on specially marked Coke cans. "The Flash" passes are available for impatient riders, offering 4 cuts in line for a mere $15 ($20 on weekends). If you want to come back for a second day, "twickets" are available at the park; the fee varies, but it's usually around $10 or $15. For die-hard thrill seekers, season passes offer the best deal at $94.99 apiece or $84.99 each for a family of four or more. Individual tickets and season passes can be purchased online at www.six-flagsticketing.com.

For the Kiddies

Camp Cartoon Network and Bugs Bunny National Park offer easy-going rides and games for tykes 54 inches and under, while Bugs, Yosemite Sam, and the rest amble around for photo ops. The double-decker classic kiddie ride Columbia Carousel, located just past the park's main entrance, may be too tame for young 'uns hopped up on funnel cake and Tweety-pops. New in 2007 is Wiggles World, inspired by Australian band The Wiggles. Characters Dorothy the Dinosaur, Captain Feathersword, Wags the Dog, and Henry the Octopus are available daily for photo-ops, meet-n-greets, and other humiliating activities you'll be forced to engage in for the sake of your children's fragile psyches. If your kids are a little older and more badass (but still too chickenshit to experience the real deal), take them on the Whizzer, mini-coaster and quintessential training wheels for every 'tween. Other rides the height-challenged set can get on include the Orbit, the Whirligig, the Ragin' Cajun, and the good old-fashioned Tilt-a-Whirl, spinning fun guaranteed to make your kids laugh and your stomach retch.

Thrill Rides

Every few years, Six Flags tries to outdo itself with a new, even more death-defying and harrowing ride. Most recently, this magnificent feat was accomplished with the opening of the Superman-Ultimate Flight ride. Passengers soar through the air head-first as though they were flying, nearly brushing the ground below them on the giant loop-de-loop. Other thrills include the Raging Bull "hyper-twister," where you drop at incredible degrees and speeds into subterranean depths. Batman The Ride allows your feet to dangle free, while riders remain standing, supported by a bicycle seat between the legs (men who desire children, be wary). We had serious misgivings about the decision to ride the Déjà Vu as we sat suspended, face-down, 120-something feet above the ground, secured only by a shoulder harness before dropping down at a 90-degree angle. Also try the equally frightening Vertical Velocity, V2 for short, which propels riders

backward and forward up a corkscrew at 70 mph in less than 4 seconds, suspended by the same paltry harness that barely staves off fatality in Déjà Vu. Meanwhile, the classic wooden American Eagle coaster offers vintage, but no-less-worrisome, rickety thrills. The Viper, newer and sexier cousin to the geriatric American Eagle, provides a similar timber ride, but with a 100% less chance of death than the Eagle. Shock Wave, also known as concussion-central, is no longer around, but try The Demon in its place if you're interested in forgetting your name and address. If you're feeling nostalgic, try Splashwater Falls, a blink-and-it's-over water ride in which a boat goes up a hill, around a curve, and down a big drop, soaking riders and bystanders on the overhead bridge/ride exit in the process. For 2008 they're introducing The Dark Knight (indoor roller coaster in complete darkness). Cool.

Hurricane Harbor Water Park

Opened in 2005, Great America's adjoining Hurricane Harbor water park introduced attractions such as "Skull Island," which press materials dub the thrill-evoking "world's largest interactive water play structure." How's that for screaming "fun?" There are also miles of water rides, including Hurricane Mountain, Vortex, and Typhoon (tube and bowl slides), and a splashing park for wee tots ("Mommy, why is the water yellow?"). The new and popular Tornado, a combination tube and bowl slide, allows four riders to experience spinning in the 60-foot-wide funnel together. An adventure river, Castaway Creek, offers both exciting adventures complete with geysers, as well as leisurely relaxation under waterfalls and mists. The park also features a 1,000+ gallon water drop that dumps itself upon unsuspecting visitors every ten minutes. Leave the Prada at home.

Fright Fest

Avoid the heat and long lines of the summer season and creep into the park during the month of October (mostly on weekends) among the Halloween-themed décor (last year, the Viper was dressed up as "Snakes on a Train," based on Samuel Jackson's recent "hit" movie) and scary music playing over the P.A. This is, by far, our favorite time to go and worth the price of a season pass for the convenience of just dropping by for a few thrills whenever the hell you feel like it (the park is open until midnight on most Saturday nights during Fright Fest). Water rides in the park are usually less crowded now, so take advantage of Splashwater Falls, Logger's Run, and Roaring Rapids (complete with blood-red water) to get the pasty white complexion and blue-tinged lip effect that will help you fit in since costumes aren't allowed.

Make a Night of It

Where to stay in Gurnee:
- **La Quinta Inn**, 5688 N Ridge Rd, 847-662-7600
- **Country Inn & Suites**, 5420 Grand Ave, 847-625-9700
- **Fairfield Inn**, 6090 Gurnee Mills Cir East, 847-855-8868
- **Grand Hotel & Suites**, 5520 Grand Ave, 847-249-7777
- **Hampton Inn**, 5550 Grand Ave, 847-662-1100

How to Get There

By Car: Take I-94 or I-294 west, exit at Grand Avenue. Be aware that traffic is very congested in July and August! Arrive extra early or extra late to beat the crowds.

By Train & Bus: Take the Metra Union Pacific North Line to Waukegan, where you can catch the Pace bus 565 to Great America. Note: Public transportation to Great America from the Ogilvie Transportation Center and Madison and Canal takes just over two hours each way.

General Information

www.skokie.org

Overview

When Skokie was first incorporated under the moniker Niles Centre in 1888, it was considered to be the rowdy neighbor of temperate Evanston due to the large number of taverns within its borders. By 1940, residents were clamoring for a name change and a PR facelift. In November of that year, the village was renamed Skokie after the nearby Skokie River and canals, which themselves were named after an old Native American word for "swampland." Personally, we'd be more attracted to a party town, but nonetheless, the facelift was a success. With the completion of the Edens Expressway in the 1950s, residential development in Skokie was booming.

A chunk of the growth comprised Eastern European refugees from World War II, many of whom were Jewish. It is estimated that between 1945 and 1955, 3,000 Jewish families resettled in Skokie. Synagogues and Jewish services followed, and the village soon developed a self-perpetuating reputation as a thriving Jewish enclave.

Skokie made international headlines in 1977–78 when it contested plans by the National Socialist Party of America, a branch of the American Nazi Party, to march on the village square. The NSPA was defended by the ACLU in a divisive case that brought the contest between free expression and freedom against hate speech into the international fore. As far as the NSPA was concerned, the decision to march in Skokie was an act of political manipulation. Chicago had denied the Nazis' right to march in SW Chicago's Marquette Park, which was the NSPA's home turf. The group then threatened to relocate their planned assembly to Skokie. When the Village of Skokie lost their bid to ban the march, Chicago finally conceded, allowing the Nazis to gather at Marquette Park in June 1978. A handful of Nazis showed up, countered by thousands of anti-Nazi protestors.

As if being the head of a neo-Nazi movement and threatening to march on the front lawns of concentration camp survivors doesn't already make you the world's biggest jackass/creep, NSPA leader Frank Collin secured the title in 1979 when he was arrested and incarcerated on child molestation charges.

Culture & Events

In 1988, an urban renewal project to restore the North Shore's decrepit Chicago River waterfront resulted in the two-mile Sculpture Park, an outdoor recreation area with walking paths, picnic areas, and featuring more than 72 sculptures by artists of local, national, and international renown (although, rubes that we are, we confess we haven't heard of any of 'em). The park, sandwiched between McCormick Blvd and the north branch of the Chicago River, runs the two miles from Touhy to Dempster.

Time travel through history at the Skokie Heritage Museum—an assemblage of historical photos, papers, and artifacts painstakingly gathered by the Skokie Historical Society. The museum, housed in a restored 1887 firehouse, also features the history of Skokie's firefighters. Behind the museum, an authentic 1840s log cabin relocated to this location allows kids a glimpse into the town's pioneer past.

Skokie is also home to the Holocaust Memorial of Illinois. Each year up to 15,000 local school kids visit this small but stirring exhibit of Jewish life before, during, and after the Holocaust. Fundraising efforts are underway for a much larger, grander space, capable of serving upward of 100,000 visitors annually.

Skokie Park District has many fairs up their sleeves, including a late-summer night's dream for kids. In the sticky heat of late-August, carnies set up for the Back-to-School Carnival. Backpack toting tots mingle with tweenies for a farewell-to-freedom bash (while parents openly celebrate with their "can't wait" grins). Running just one weekend, the summer ends with "a veritable smorgasbord" of rickety rides, corn dogs and the sickly sweet smell of elephant ears.

Every year in mid-May, the Skokie Festival of Cultures draws clog dancers, falafel hawkers, and accordion players from around the state for a weekend festival celebrating Skokie's diverse cultural heritage. The sulky loitering high-schoolers and fat ladies in track suits, on the other hand, are 100% local.

North Shore Center for the Performing Arts

Home to the Skokie Valley Symphony Orchestra, the Centre East Theater, and, most notably, the highly acclaimed Northlight Theater, the North Shore Center for the Performing Arts is a state-of-the-art performance venue. Touring artists perform here, world class theater (sometimes featuring ensemble members from Steppenwolf) is mounted here, and it's also a North Shore venue for exhibits and trade shows. Designed by architect Graham Gund in 1996, The North Shore Center for the Performing Arts has given Northeast Illinois culture seekers a reason to come to Skokie besides bagels and lox.

Where to Drink

Despite its alcohol-fueled history, Skokie is not really known as a place to imbibe socially. Young residents head to youthful watering holes in the vicinity of the Northwestern campus in formerly tee-totaling Evanston (will the ironies never end?). Meanwhile, local drunks hang out at anonymous corner taverns just like anywhere else. Retail workers, middle managers, and the secretarial set mingle and mate at the food and booze joints adjacent to Old Orchard.

Where to Eat

Old Orchard Shopping Center is filled with family-friendly chain options. Happily, Skokie still houses enough locally owned, independent restaurants to add interest and diversity to their dining scene. Folks travel from all over Chicagoland for local delis and kosher fare ever debating the superiority of Kaufman's v. New York Bagel and Bialy as THE place for a bagel and shmear.

How to Get There

By L: The Skokie Swift Yellow Line runs non-stop between the Howard Street Red Line terminus and the Skokie Dempster station at 5001 Dempster St. Trains run approximately every 10-15 minutes between 5 am and 10 pm.

By Car: Take the Edens Expressway (I-94), and exit at Dempster.

🎭 Movie Theaters

· **AMC Loews Gardens 1/6** · 175 Old Orchard Ctr

▶ Nightlife

· **Chammps** · 134 Old Orchard Ctr
· **Don's Fishmarket Tavern and Grill** · 9335 Skokie Blvd
· **Principal's Pub** · 4249 Main St

🍴 Restaurants

· **Barnum and Bagel** · 4700 Dempster St
· **Don's Fishmarket** · 9335 Skokie Blvd
· **El Tipico** · 3341 Dempster St
· **Grecian Kitchen Delights** · 3938 Dempster St
· **Hub's Ribs** · 3727 Dempster St
· **Hy Life Bistro** · 4120 Dempster St

Columbia College Chicago

1. Harold Washington Library
2. 18 E Congress Residence Hall
3. 33 E Congress Parkway Building
   -C-33
   -DanceAfrica Chicago
   -Center for Asian Arts & Media
4. University Center
5. Alexandroff Campus Center
   (Main Campus Building)
   -Museum of Contemporary Photography
6. Wabash Campus Building
   -Center for Black Music Research
7. South Campus Building
8. 1006 S Michigan Ave Building
9. 11th Street Campus
   -A&D Gallery
   -Getz, Classic, and New Studio Theater
10. Music Center
11. 1104 S Wabash Center
    -Center for Book and Paper Arts
    -Glass Curtain Gallery
    -Concert Hall
12. 11th & Wabash Sculpture Garden
13. Dance Center
14. Theater/Film Annex
15. Residence Center
16. 2 E 8th Residence Hall
17. 619 S. Wabash Building

General Information

NFT Maps:	8, 9, 11
Address:	600 S Michigan Ave
	Chicago, IL 60605
Phone:	312-663-1600
Website:	www.colum.edu
Event Information:	www.colum.edu/calendar

Overview

Named in honor of the World's Columbian Exposition, Columbia College Chicago first opened in 1890 as a women's speech academy. Over time, it has become one of America's most diverse private arts and media schools. It is best known for its film, television, and fiction departments, which turn out prominent professionals. Columbia alumni played key writing and production roles in *Barbershop*, *Real Women Have Curves*, *Analyze This*, *Schindler's List*, and *Leaving Las Vegas*. They win Emmy Awards (for art direction on *Alias*, special effects on *Star Trek: Enterprise*, animation on *Samurai Jack*, and cinematography on *Carnivale*). And they write acclaimed books (in addition to NFT); celebrated scribblers Joe Meno, Don DeGrazia, and Sam Weller all returned to Columbia's fiction writing department as faculty. Other programs include photography, dance, theater, music, art and design, journalism, fashion design, poetry, education, and management for the arts, entertainment, and media. Columbia's campus is the bustling South Loop, and its colorful student body immerse themselves in the city.

Tuition

As of 2007–08, full-time Columbia undergrads pay $18,094 a year in tuition and fees with an average on-campus residency cost of $12,018. For a bit more money, students have the option of staying in the DePaul, Roosevelt, and Columbia-shared University Center, a.k.a. "Super Dorm," the largest dormitory in the United States

Culture

Columbia College is one of Chicago's most esteemed cultural arts presenters; more than 300,000 visitors attend Columbia events each year. The college brings the DanceAfrica Chicago Festival to the city every fall and hosts a regular slate of innovative dance performances throughout the year. The Museum of Contemporary Photography is one of two fully accredited photography museums in the United States. The Chicago Jazz Ensemble, directed by trumpet virtuoso Jon Faddis, also makes its home at Columbia. The Story Week Festival of Writers, held in the spring, is among Chicago's top literary draws. The college brings in authors, editors, agents, and publishers for a week of readings, panels, and special events, such as "Read-Like-a-Rockstar" night at the Metro. Spring also brings Fashion Columbia and the Manifest Urban Arts Festival, celebrating graduate achievements. The college's galleries and theaters feature the work of students alongside notable outside artists.

- **Center for Book and Paper Arts**
  1104 S Wabash Ave, 2nd Fl
  312-344-6630
  www.colum.edu/centers/bpa

- **Museum of Contemporary Photography**
  600 S Michigan Ave
  312-663-5554
  www.mocp.org

- **A&D Gallery**
  619 S. Wabash Ave
  312-344-8687
  www.colum.edu/adgallery

- **Glass Curtain Gallery**
  1104 S Wabash Ave, 1st Fl
  312-344-6650

- **C-33**
  33 E Congress Pkwy
  312-344-7188

- **Dance Center**
  1306 S Michigan Ave
  312-344-8300
  www.dancecenter.org

- **Getz, Classic, and New Studio Theaters**
  72 E 11th St
  312-344-6126
  www.colum.edu/undergraduate/theater/calendar

- **Concert Hall**
  1014 S Michigan Ave
  312-344- 6240

- **DanceAfrica Chicago**
  33 E Congress Pkwy
  312-344-7070
  www.danceafricachicago.com

- **Center for Asian Arts & Media**
  29 E Congress Pkwy, 1st Fl
  312-344-7870
  www.asianartsandmedia.org

- **Center for Black Music Research**
  623 S Wabash Ave, Ste 600
  312-344-7559
  www.cbmr.org

- **Chicago Jazz Ensemble**
  600 S Michigan Ave
  312-344-6270
  www.chijazz.com

Department Contact Information

Undergraduate Admissions	312-344-7131
Graduate Admissions	312-344-7260
School of Fine and Performing Arts	312-344-7298
School of Media Arts	312-344-8220
School of Liberal Arts and Sciences	312-344-8217

Lincoln Park Campus

General Information

Lincoln Park Campus: Schmitt Academic Center
2320 N Kenmore Ave
Chicago, IL 60614-3298
Phone: 773-325-7000 x5700

Loop Campus: 1 E Jackson Blvd
Chicago, IL 60604
Phone: 312-362-8000

Website: www.depaul.edu

Suburban Campuses: University Center of Lake County
(Grayslake) 847-665-4000
Naperville: 312-476-4500/630-548-9378
Oak Forest: 312-476-3000/708-633-9091
O'Hare: 312-476-3600/847-296-5348
Rolling Meadows: 312-476-4800/847-437-9522

Overview

Established in 1898 by the Vincentian Fathers as a school for immigrants, DePaul has become the country's largest Catholic university (with over 23,000 students) and the biggest private educational institution in Chicago, offering 150 undergraduate and graduate programs of study. According to The Princeton Review's recent survey of college students nationwide, DePaul students rated as some of the happiest college students in the country; it must be all the bars near campus on Halsted Street and Lincoln Avenue.

Of the university's seven campuses in the Chicago area, the Lincoln Park and Loop campuses serve as the core locations. The highly acclaimed Theatre School, College of Liberal Arts and Sciences, School of Music, and School of Education hold down the 36-acre Lincoln Park campus amidst renovated historic homes on tree-lined streets. Popular student handouts include coffee shop The Bourgeois Pig (738 W. Fullerton), where students go to *actually* study, and English pub The Red Lion (2446 N. Lincoln), where students go to blow off studying. If you venture to the upstairs level at The Red Lion, you're likely to find a graduate class drinking pints while taking in a lecture, a welcome substitute for the juvenile-feeling desk/chair combo and bright lights of a classroom. The Red Lion is rumored to be haunted, but don't ask the waitresses about it; they don't know, and it annoys them.

DePaul's Loop Campus at Jackson Boulevard and State Street is where you'll find the College of Commerce, College of Law, and School of Computer Science, Telecommunications, and Information Systems. Nationally respected Kellstadt Graduate School of Business and DePaul's thriving continuing education program, the "School of New Learning," can also be found on the Loop Campus. The heart of the Loop campus is DePaul Center, located in the old Goldblatt Brothers Department Store, now grounded by a university-sanctioned Barnes and Noble. Most students in the Loop campus are adults, so popular hangouts include the Brown Line L, Red Line L, and Metra stations while they're all waiting for the train home. Prominent DePaul alumni include Chicago father-son mayors Richard M. Daley and his dad, the late Richard J. Daley; McDonald's Corporation's former CEO Jack Greenberg; Pulitzer Prize-winning composer George Perle; and actors Gillian Anderson and John C. Reilly.

Tuition

Each college has its own tuition; room and board costs depend on the residence facility and meal plan chosen. In the 2006–2007 academic year, undergraduate tuition for the College of Arts & Sciences was $22,900. Tuition for the School of Music and for the Theatre School cost about $27,100. Room and board cost between $6,500 and $9,200. Add on the cost of books, lab fees, and personal expenses, which can get pretty high depending on your bar tabs.

Sports

DePaul's Blue Demons men's basketball team teased Chicago with an NCAA Division I Championship in 2000, when the team appeared in its first tournament since 1992. Coach Dave Leitao, who took over in '02, planned to reinstate the Demons' winning record and almost succeeded in 2003. Almost. The team lost its chance at the title in the second round of the tournament and hasn't been making headlines since. The Blue Demons play at United Center (1901 W Madison St, 312-455-4500; www.unitedcenter.com) and Allstate Arena (6920 N Mannheim Rd in Rosemont, 847-635-6601; www.allstatearena.com). For tickets, call Ticketmaster at 312-559-1212, visit www.ticketmaster.com, go to the stadiums' box offices, or visit the DePaul Athletic Center box office (2323 N Sheffield Ave, 773-325-7526; www.depaulbluedemons.com).

Blue Demons' men's and women's teams include basketball, cross-country, soccer, tennis, and track & field. DePaul also has a men's golf team, as well as women's softball and volleyball squads. For stats and schedules, visit the Blue Demons' website, www.depaulbluedemons.com.

Culture on Campus

DePaul's vibrant Theatre School is the oldest of its kind in the Midwest. Founded in 1925 as the Goodman School of Drama, the school stages over 200 performances during its Showcase, Chicago Playworks, New Directors Series, and School Workshop seasons. The Theatre School Showcase performs contemporary and classic plays at its 1,325-seat Merle Reskin Theatre, a French Renaissance–style theater built in 1910 and located at 60 E Balbo Drive in the South Loop. The Chicago Playworks for Families and Young Audiences and the School of Music's annual opera are also performed at the Merle Reskin Theatre. For tickets ($8–$12), directions, and parking garage locations, call 312-922-1999 or go to theatreschool.depaul.edu. Take the Red Line to the Harrison Street or Jackson Street stops just southwest of the theater. CTA buses 29, 36, 151, and 146 also stop nearby. Check the Theatre School website for New Directors Series and School

Loop Campus

Workshop productions, theater locations, and ticket prices.

DePaul University Art Gallery is located in the John T. Richardson Library at 2350 N Kenmore Avenue (773-325-7506). Permanent collections of sculpture and oil paintings from local and international artists adorn the free gallery. A pay parking lot is located one block east of the library on N Sheffield Avenue. DePaul's John T. Richardson Library and Loop campus library in DePaul Center are open to the public year-round. Take plenty of change for the copy machines as check-out privileges are reserved for students and faculty.

Department Contact Information

Lincoln Park Campus Admissions Office	773-325-7500
Loop Campus Admissions Office	312-362-8300
College of Commerce	312-362-6783
College of Law	312-325-8701
Undergraduate College of Arts & Sciences	773-325-7310
Graduate College of Arts & Sciences	773-325-7315
John T Richardson Library	773-325-7862
Kellstadt Graduate School of Business	312-362-8000
Loop Campus Library	312-362-8433
School for New Learning	312-362-8001
School of Computer Science, Telecommunications and Information Systems	312-362-8381
School of Music	773-325-7260
Theatre School	773-325-7917

General Information

NFT Map:	13, 14
Main Campus:	3300 S Federal St
	Chicago, IL 60616
Phone:	312-567-3000
Website:	www.iit.edu

Overview

In the 19th century, when higher education was reserved for society's upper crust, meat magnate Philip Danforth Armour put his money to good use and funded an institution dedicated to students who wished to learn a variety of industrial arts. The Armour Institute carried his name until a merger with the engineering school Lewis Institute in 1940 changed the name to Illinois Institute of Technology. Over the next 40 years, the college continued to merge with other small technical colleges, resulting in the IIT we know today. The school is as notable for its Mies Van Der Rohe–designed campus as for its groundbreaking work in aeronautics research. The new student center, designed by Dutch architect Rem Koolhaas, includes a space-aged metallic tube through which the local L train travels.

Chicago-Kent College of Law, Stuart School Graduate School of Business, and the Institute of Design are based in the Loop. The Rice campus, in west suburban Wheaton, offers undergraduate continuing education and degree programs to working professionals. The National Center for Food Safety and Technology, located in the southwest suburbs, and the IIT Research Institute, housed in IIT's tallest building on its main campus in Bronzeville, are just two of the many research organizations IIT has incorporated since 1936 to serve various needs of private industry and government. IIT grants PhDs and other professional degrees in a vast array of areas including science, mathematics, engineering, architecture, psychology, design, business, and law. The interprofessional, technology-focused curriculum is designed to prepare the 6,400 students to become groundbreakers in an increasingly complex global workplace. IIT was recently named a "College of Distinction" by a new college guide honoring some of America's top educational institutions.

In June 2004, IIT's Research Institute Life Sciences Group was awarded $28 million in research funding. The prestigious award is among the largest ever received by IITRI for drug development.

Tuition

In the 2007–2008 academic year, undergraduate tuition cost $24,962. Room and board costs vary by residence but generally run between $7,000 and $10,000.

Sports

The IIT Scarlet Hawks are affiliated with the National Association of Intercollegiate Athletics Division I. Students can compete with other schools in baseball, basketball, cross-country, diving, soccer, swimming, and volleyball.

The 2004 swim season saw the Scarlet Hawks' third year head coach Rob Bond named NAIA Men's Swimming and Diving National Coach of the Year.

New Developments on Campus

The newest student residency, completed in 2003, is State Street Village. Located at State and 33rd Streets, the hall was designed by well-known Chicago-based architect Helmut Jahn. The German-born designer was named one of the Ten Most Influential Living American Architects by the American Institute of Architects (AIA) in 1991. Jahn, a graduate of IIT himself, created the six-building complex across the street from Van Der Rohe's masterful historical landmark, the S.R. Crown Hall. Jahn's new building brings student housing to a new level with poured-in-place concrete and glass-clad and corrugated stainless steel panels that reduce noise and vibrations from passing trains while simultaneously exhibiting a cutting-edge aesthetic. Currently underway is development of the $50 million University Technology Park on the main campus, to be built in phases over the next ten years. All of these fine developments can be taken in via an excellent 90-minute tour of the IIT campus, which costs a grand total of $5. You can take a tour the old-fashioned way (a.k.a. a real person leading you around) Monday through Saturday at 10AM and 1PM or borrow an iPod from the school and do a self-guided version. Get more details at http://mies.iit.edu/tours/ or by calling 312-567-5014.

Department Contact Information

Undergraduate Admissions	312-567-3025
Graduate Admissions	312-567-3020
Alumni Office	312-567-5040
Armour College of Engineering	312-567-3009
Center for Law and Financial Markets	312-906-6576
Center for Professional Development	630-682-6040
Chicago-Kent College of Law	312-906-5000
College of Architecture	312-567-3263
College of Science & Letters	312-567-3800
Keating Sports Center	312-567-3000
Institute of Business and Interprofessional Studies	312-567-3947
Institute of Design	312-595-4900
Institute of Psychology	312-567-3500
Stuart Graduate School of Business	312-906-6500
University Technology Park	312-567-3900

Loyola University (Lake Shore Campus)

Loyola University (Lake Shore Campus)

General Information

Lake Shore:	6525 N Sheridan Rd
	Chicago, IL 60626
Phone:	773-274-3000
Water Tower/Lewis	820 N Michigan Ave
Towers Campus:	Chicago 60611
Phone:	312-915-6000
Medical Center:	2160 S First Ave
	Maywood, IL 60153
Phone:	708-216-9000
Website:	www.luc.edu

Overview

Loyola University, one of the largest Jesuit universities in the United States, is known throughout the Midwest for its first-rate schools of business and law, as well as for its Medical Center (a well-respected research institution). It was originally established in 1870 as St. Ignatius College and was re-named in 1909. Approximately 15,000 students attend the university.

Lake Shore Campus, the largest campus of Loyola's four campuses, is on the lake in Rogers Park and houses the College of Arts & Sciences, the Graduate School, Niehoff School of Nursing, Mundelein College Adult Education Program, and Cudahy Library. The university's Water Tower campus downtown on Michigan Avenue is home to the Schools of Business, Education, Law, and Social Work and some College of Arts & Sciences courses. Loyola operates the Stritch School of Medicine and the Master's degree programs through the Niehoff School of Nursing at its suburban Maywood campus. The university also has a campus in Rome, one of the largest American campuses in Western Europe. Notable graduates include Sho Yano, who ranks first in the world with the highest known I.Q. Rumor has it this student also ranked dead last in dating and beer-chugging statistics.

Tuition

In the 2007–2008 academic year, undergraduate tuition cost $28,700. Room and board prices ranged from $6,670 to $14,360. Add on books, lab fees, and personal expenses. Graduate student tuition, fees, and expenses vary by college. It seems like a hefty sum, but Loyola University was ranked by U.S. News & World Report as one of the "best values" for a college education.

Sports

Loyola is the only school in Illinois to win a Division I National Championship basketball tournament, with the Loyola Ramblers taking the NCAA men's basketball championship in 1963. The Ramblers' most recent tournament appearance was in 1985. Unfortunately 22 years was not enough time to build another winning team as they fell short of an NCAA Tournament bid. But look out 2029…Go Ramblers! Catch them at the Joseph J. Gentile Center on the Lake Shore Campus. For tickets, visit the box office, call 773-508-9653, or go to http://loyolaramblers.cstv.com.

Loyola University has men's and women's basketball, cross-country, track, soccer, and volleyball teams. The women also have a softball squad. The men's volleyball team is ranked as one of the top ten in the nation.

Culture on Campus

Opened in October 2005, the new Loyola University Museum of Art (LUMA) became the new home of the famous Martin D'Arcy collection of Medieval, Renaissance, and Baroque art. Paintings by masters Tintoretto, Guercino, Bassano, and Stomer, plus sculpture, furniture, jewelry, decorative arts, and liturgical vessels, are part of the over 500-piece collection dating from 1150 to 1750. The museum, located at 820 N Michigan Avenue, is free on Tuesdays. Suggested general admission is $6, $5 for seniors, and free if you can pass for 14 and under. Hours: Tues: 10 am–8 pm; Wed–Sun: 10 am–5 pm. For more information, call 312-915-7600.

The university's Cudahy Library, Lewis Library at the Water Tower Campus, Science Library, Health Sciences Library, and Graduate Business School Library are all open to the public. Checkout privileges, however, are reserved for the university's students and faculty.

The Loyola University Theatre performs four classic dramas per year at the Kathleen Mullady Theatre (1125 W Loyola Ave, 773-508-3847) in the Centennial Forum/Mertz Hall building on the Lake Shore campus. Tickets cost $15 for the general public, $7 for seniors and students at other universities, and $5 for Loyola students. You can purchase tickets through the box office, which is open Monday through Friday, 3 pm–7 pm.

The Loyola Campus also offers a variety of media options for its students. Inside Loyola, Loyola Magazine and The Phoenix are available for readers, while WLUW exists for those students overwhelmed by textbooks, NFT Guides, or the newest issue of Jesuit Life International.

Department Contact Information

Undergraduate Admissions	773-915-6500
School of Continuing and Professional Studies	312-915-6501
College of Arts & Sciences	773-508-3500
School of Business Administration	312-915-6112
School of Education	312-916-6800
School of Law	312-915-7120
Stritch School of Medicine	708-216-3229
Niehoff School of Nursing	773-508-3249
Rome Center of Liberal Arts	800-344-7662
School of Social Work	312-915-7005
Graduate School of Business	312-915-6124
The Graduate School	773-508-3396
University Libraries	773-508-2658

1. Dearborn Observatory
2. Shanley Hall
3. Owen L Coon Forum
4. McCormick Auditorium
5. Theatre and Interpretation Center
6. Block Museum
7. Marjorie Ward Marshall Dance Center
8. John Evans Alumni Center
9. University Police
10. Business Office
11. Music Practice
12. Human Resources
13. Fielder Hillel Center
14. Family Institute
15. Engelhart Hall
16. Ford Motor Co Engineering Design Center
17. McCormick Tribune Center

Northwestern University (Evanston Campus)

General Information

Evanston Campus: 633 Clark St
Evanston, IL 60208
Phone: 847-491-3741

Chicago Campus: Abbot Hall
710 N Lake Shore Dr
Chicago, IL 60611
Phone: 312-503-8649

Website: www.northwestern.edu

Overview

Northwestern University, along with the University of Chicago, likes to think of itself as part of the "Ivy League of the Midwest." While this might seem a lofty moniker, the University is certainly the cream of the crop in the Big Ten Conference. Almost 18,000 full- and part-time students attend Northwestern's 11 schools, located in Evanston and downtown Chicago, a far cry from the 2 original faculty members and 10 students in attendance when the school opened in 1855. The University's name was derived from its founders' desire to service the citizens of the former Northwest Territory.

Founded in 1851, Northwestern University was established in Evanston by many of the same Methodist founding fathers of the town itself, including the founder of Chicago's Board of Trade. The 240-acre lakefront campus is bordered roughly by Lincoln Street to the north and extends south to Clark Street and west to Sheridan Road. The Evanston campus houses the Weinberg College of Arts and Sciences; McCormick School of Engineering and Applied Science; the Schools of Music, Communication, Education and Social Policy; the Graduate School; Medill School of Journalism; and J.L. Kellogg School of Management.

The university did a bit of branching out when it purchased land for the Chicago campus in 1920. Located on a 25-acre lot between the lake and Michigan Avenue in the Streeterville neighborhood, the Chicago campus houses the Schools of Law, Medicine, and Continuing Studies. Graduate school and Kellogg courses are also offered at the Chicago campus. Several excellent hospitals and medical research institutions affiliated with the university dominate the northern edge of Streeterville. The Robert H. Lurie Medical Research Center at Fairbanks Court and Superior Street, completed in 2004, has expanded the university's research abilities with nine floors of laboratory space. The new Prentice Women's Hospital was completed in late 2007, offering comprehensive women's and infants' health.

Tuition

In the 2007–2008 academic year, undergraduate tuition, books and fees cost $49,300, with room and board running about $10,700.00 per year. Graduate school tuition and fees vary by college.

Sports

Like all Big Ten Conference schools, Northwestern has football and basketball teams—but that's all we can really say of the Wildcats lately. There was more to talk about in the 1990s with back-to-back bowl appearances in the 1996 Rose Bowl (their first bowl appearance since winning in 1949) and the 1997 Citrus Bowl. After Nebraska de-clawed, skinned, and gutted the Wildcats at the 2000 Alamo Bowl, it seems the team has been licking its wounds. They made an appearance in, and lost, the 2003 Motor City Bowl against Bowling Green. 2007 looks okay with three patsies to start off the year, then it is all downhill once they begin conference play.

The Wildcats' home is Ryan Field at 1501 Central Avenue, about three blocks west of the Central Avenue stop on the elevated Purple Line. Basketball games are held at the Welsh-Ryan Arena behind the stadium. For tickets, call 847-491-2287. All sporting events are listed at www.nusports.com, where you can also purchase tickets online. Northwestern students can obtain free tickets to any game with the presentation of their WILDCARD ID.

Northwestern also has men's wrestling and baseball teams, plus men's and women's basketball, golf, soccer, tennis, and swimming and diving teams. Additionally, Wildcat women compete in cross-country, fencing, softball, field hockey, and volleyball, with a lacrosse team that's highly ranked, and a tennis team that competes nationally.

Culture on Campus

The Mary and Leigh Block Museum of Art on the Evanston campus (40 Arts Circle Dr; 847-491-4000; www.blockmuseum.northwestern.edu) has 4,000 items in its permanent collection, including Old Masters' prints, architectural drawings, contemporary photographic images, and modern sculpture. The Block is also home to the state-of-the-art Pick-Laudati Auditorium that hosts film festivals and contemporary classics, as well as different cinema series' and lectures throughout the year. Hours: Tues: 10 am to 5 pm; Wed–Fri: 10 am to 8 pm; weekends: noon–5 pm. Admission is always free.

The Pick-Staiger Concert Hall (50 Arts Circle Dr, 847-491-5441; www.pickstaiger.com), is not only the main stage for the university's musical performances, but it is also home to several professional performance organizations such as the Chicago Chamber Musicians, Symphony of the Shores, Chicago String Ensemble, Performing Arts Chicago, and others. Each year, Pick-Staiger Concert Hall also hosts the Segovia Classical Guitar Series and the Keyboard Conversations Series. Call 847-467-4000 to purchase tickets.

For the upper echelon student interested in art or vandalism, one can visit the famed "Rock" that students began defacing in the 1940s. "Go Cats!," "Rich Kids Can Tag As Well!" and "I'm wasting my parent's money!" have all made brief appearances.

Northwestern University also runs a student newspaper, The Daily Northwestern, and a student radio station, WNUR.

Department Contact Information

Undergraduate Admissions 847-491-7271
Graduate School (Evanston) 847-491-5279
Graduate School (Chicago) 312-503-8900
Weinberg College of Arts and Sciences 847-491-7561
Feinberg School of Medicine 312-503-8649
Kellogg School of Management 847-491-3300
Medill School of Journalism 847-467-1882
School of Communication 847-491-7023
School of Continuing Studies (Evanston) 847-491-5611
School of Education and Social Policy 847-491-8193
McCormick School of Engineering
   and Applied Science 847-491-5220
School of Law 312-503-3100
School of Music 847-491-7575

Colleges & Universities · **University of Chicago**

1. Laboratory for Astrophysics and Space Research
2. Astronomy and Astrophysics Center
3. Research Institutes
4. Biopsychological Research Center
5. Disciples Divinity House
6. Kovler Viral Oncology Laboratories
7. Ingleside Hall
8. Searle Chemical Laboratory
9. Jones Laboratory
10. Zoology
11. Hutchinson Commons
12. Reynolds Club
13. Statistics and Mathematics
14. Development Office- 5733 S University
15. Calvert House
16. Student Counseling and Resource Service
17. Human Development

18. Development Office- 5736 S Woodlawn
19. Nursery School- 5740 S Woodlawn
20. Nursery School- 5750 S Woodlawn
21. Abbott Memorial Hall
22. Goldblatt Pavillion
23. Armour Clincial Research
24. Goldblatt Memorial Building
25. McElwee Building
26. Gates-Blake Hall
27. Goodspeed Hall
28. Wieboldt Hall
29. Harper Memorial Library
30. Beecher Hall
31. Green Hall
32. Kelly Hall
33. Foster Hall
34. University High School
35. Orthogenic School
36. D'Angelo Law Library
37. Kane Center for Clinical Legal Education

General Information

NFT Map:	19
Mailing Address:	University of Chicago
	Administration Building
	5801 S Ellis Ave
	Chicago, IL 60637
Phone:	773-702-1234
Website:	www.uchicago.edu
Visitor's Center:	Ida Noyes Hall, 1st Fl
	1212 E 59th St
Phone:	773-702-9739
Guest Parking:	Lot located off Woodlawn Ave
	b/w 58th St and 59th St. Metered
	parking is available north of Ida Noyes Hall.

Overview

Located amidst the pleasant tree-lined streets of Hyde Park, the University of Chicago is a world-renowned research institution with a winning tradition in Nobel Prizes. Seventy-nine Nobel laureates have been associated with the university as faculty, students, or researchers. (Six of them are current faculty members, so get 'em while they're hot!) The university prides itself on its rigorous academic standards and top-ranked programs, while its students pride themselves on their scholarly devotion–traditionally shunning most overt displays of stereotypical collegiate debauchery.

While its business, law, and medical schools are reknown for cranking out brainy gurus with assembly line efficiency, the university also has a long alumni list filled with artists, writers, politicians, film directors, and actors. To name a few: Studs Terkel, Sara Paretsky, Carol Mosely-Braun, Kurt Vonnegut, Susan Sontag, David Auburn, John Ashcroft (well, you can't win 'em all), Ed Asner, Saul Bellow, Katharine Graham, Philip Glass, Saul Alinsky, Paul Goodman, Mike Nichols, and Second City improv theater founders Bernard Sahlins and Paul Sills.

Established in 1890, the University of Chicago was founded and funded by John D. Rockefeller. Built on 200 acres donated by Marshall Field and designed by architect Henry Ives Cobb, the university's English Gothic buildings of ivy-clad limestone ooze old money and intellectual achievements. Rockefeller described the university as "the best investment I ever made." We just hope parents footing the bill for their kids' education feel the same.

Tuition

The University of Chicago operates on a trimester schedule rather than the more common two-semester academic year. In the 2007–2008 academic year, an undergraduate student paid approximately $40,000 for tuition fees with an additional $11,139 for room and board. So if you add up all the books costs, lab fees, personal expenses...carry the one... that comes to around fifty grand a year. Costs for graduate students vary based on the school. Chicago has 13,000 students, 4,400 of them are undergraduates. About 2,000 of the graduate students attend classes at the downtown riverfront campus Gleacher Center (450 N Cityfront Plaza Dr, 312-464-8787; www.gleachercenter.com), where the popular Graham School of General Studies holds most of its continuing education classes.

Sports

A long time ago, the famous nickname "Monsters of The Midway" belonged to The University of Chicago's football team (not 'da Bears'), and the institution garnered football trophies right along with Nobel Prizes. The Maroons racked up seven Big Ten Football championships between 1899 and 1924, but the gridiron glory of yore faded and losing teams became the norm. The bleachers at Stagg field, where fans once flocked to witness athletic triumphs, earned more fame as the site where Enrico Fermi and university scientists split the atom on Dec. 2, 1942–four years later, president Robert Maynard Hutchins put in the university's walking papers from The Big Ten and abolished the football team. Perhaps this was a step towards prioritizing scholarly pursuits over athletic achievement, but the catastrophic results of the "controlled release of nuclear energy" might be to blame.

But the school hasn't totally abandoned sports. Varsity football, reinstated in 1969, is back and better than...well, it's back. Chicago is a member of the NCAA Division III UAA (University Athletic Association), a conference comprised of some of the nation's leading research institutions, and since 1990 has won team championships in men's basketball, women's cross country, football, men's and women's soccer, softball, men's indoor track & field, and wrestling.

Culture on Campus

Located at 5757 S. Woodlawn Avenue is Frank Lloyd Wright's residential ode to all things horizontal and structurally organic: The Robie House 708-848-1976; www.gowright.org). This Prairie Style masterpiece is considered one of the most important buildings in the history of American architecture, and with the exterior restoration phase recently completed on the $8-million dollar renovation, it once again appears fresh off the proverbial drafting board. (Adult tickets cost $12, children 7–18 and sentions pay $10, and if you want to adopt an art glass cabinet for restoration, its $20,000).

Two must-see but often overlooked free museums on campus are the Oriental Institute Museum (1155 E. 58th St., 773-702-9514; www. oi.uchicago.edu) and the Smart Museum of Art 5550 S. Greenwood Ave., 773-702-0200; www.smartmuseum.uchicago.edu). Showcasing ancient treasures from university digs since the 1900s (and yes, Indiana Jones did his undergraduate studies at U of C), the Oriental Institute houses permanent galleries devoted to ancient Egypt, Nubia, Persia, Mesopotamia, Syria, Anatolia, the ancient site of Megiddo, along with a rotation of special exhibits. The Smart Museum boasts a permanent collection of 10,000 fine art objects spanning five millenia of both Western and Eastern civilizations—so, yes, it'll be enough to look at for that afternoon you have to kill.

To satisfy the your inner cineaste, take in a picture show at Doc Films (Max Palevsky Cinema 1212 E 59th St, 773-702-8575; www.docfilms. uchicago.edu), the largest continuously running student film society in the nation. The screenings at their state-of-the-art theater range from foreign art house fare to documentaries to Hollywood classics, and feature companion lectures and Q&A with professors, actors, directors, and producers. If you're jonesing for a music fix, University of Chicago Presents is one of the city's landmark classical music presenters and features a variety of performances in the elegant, Victorian-style Mendel Hall.

The university's professional Court Theater is a nationally renowned, critically acclaimed theatre that provides fresh interpretations of classic dramas as well as more contemporary classics (5535 S Ellis Ave, 773-753-4472; www.courttheatre.org). Previous seasons have included productions of Edward Albee's Who's Afraid of Virginia Wolf, Tennessee Williams' The Glass Menagerie, August Wilson's Fences, and Tom Stoppard's Arcadia.

Department Contact Information

Log on to www.uchicago.edu/uchi/directories for a university directory and links to division and department web pages.

Undergraduate Student Admissions	773-702-8650
Biological Sciences	773-702-9000
Humanities	773-702-8512
Physical Sciences	773-702-7950
Social Sciences	773-702-8799
Divinity School	773-702-8200
Graduate School of Business	773-702-7743
Graduate Affairs	773-702-7813
Graham School of General Studies	773-702-1722
Harris Graduate School of Public Policy Studies	773-702-8401
Law School	773-702-9494
Pritzker School of Medicine	773-702-1939
School of Social Service Administration	773-702-1250

University of Illinois at Chicago

University of Illinois at Chicago

General Information

NFT Map: 26
Address: 1200 W Harrison St
          Chicago, IL 60680
Phone: 312-996-7000
Website: www.uic.edu

Overview

With over 25,000 students, the University of Illinois at Chicago (UIC) is the largest university in the city. Located on the Near West Side, UIC is ethnically diverse and urban to the core. It is a leading public research university and home to the nation's largest medical school.

Its legacy as a builder in Chicago, however, is a bit spotty. In the mid-1960s, the school leveled most of what was left of a vibrant Italian-American neighborhood to build its campus next to the Eisenhower Expressway. Today, UIC continues to consume city blocks south of Roosevelt Road in further developing the South Campus. The expansions have all but erased the colorful, landmark Maxwell Street flea market area (this bustling mess of market now takes place only on Sundays along nearby S Canal Street). The saving grace of this construction craze is that many of the original, ugly, cement slab structures are kissing the wrecking ball and being replaced with more inspired buildings. Even with the multi-million-dollar improvements, the campus is still fairly average; unless you're going to class or the doctor, a lone trip to UIC to see the Jane Addams Hull-House Museum is sufficient.

Tuition

For the 2007–2008 academic year, an Illinois resident undergraduate student's tuition and fees totaled $9,400; room and board cost $8,940 depending on the meal plan and type of housing. These figures do not include books, supplies, lab fees, or personal expenses.

Sports

Lately, the Division I Flames have been hot. The men's basketball team's first appeared in the NCAA Tournament in 1997, returning in 2002 and 2004 after winning the Horizon League Tournament. Additionally, the Flames women's gymnastics, tennis squad, and softball teams have all advanced to NCAA Tournament play in recent years.

Other Flames men's and women's teams include swimming & diving and cross-country/track & field. UIC also has men's tennis, gymnastics, baseball, and soccer, as well as women's basketball and volleyball. Basketball games and women's volleyball matches are played at the recently renovated UIC Pavilion at the corner of S Racine Avenue and Harrison Street. For tickets, call 312-413-8421, or visit www.uicflames.com.

Too bad the NCAA doesn't have a bowling tournament because UIC would be a strong contender. The campus has its own alley located at 750 S Halsted Street (312-413-5170) where the public is welcome to sling balls and swig beers with students.

Culture on Campus

Jane Addams Hull-House (800 S Halsted St, 312-413-5353; www.uic.edu/jaddams/hull), America's first settlement house, opened in 1889. The free museum documents the pioneering organization's social welfare programs that supported the community's destitute immigrant workers. Jane Addams was cool. Way cool. Museum hours are 10 am to 4 pm Tuesday through Friday and noon to 4 pm on Sunday, closed on Mondays and Saturdays.

Department Contact Information

All area codes are 312 unless otherwise noted.

Admissions and Records	996-4350
Graduate College	413-2550
College of Architecture & the Arts	996-5611
College of Applied Health Sciences	996-6695
College of Dentistry	996-1020
College of Business Administration	996-2700
College of Education	996-5641
College of Engineering	996-2400
College of Liberal Arts and Sciences	413-2500
College of Medicine	996-3500
College of Nursing	996-7800
College of Pharmacy	996-7240
School of Public Health	996-6620
College of Social Work	996-7096
College of Urban Planning and Public Affairs	413-8088
Office of Continuing Education	996-8025
University of Illinois Medical Center	800-842-1002

Continuing Education in Chicago

Whether you want to change careers or just your waistline, learn a foreign language or learn more about the one you already know, Chicago is a great city to channel your inner student.

Get to the point of the matter with fencing classes from the Chicago Athletic Association Fencers Club. Turn off the Food Network, and learn to do it yourself at Kendall College, The French Pastry School, or The Chopping Block. Learn to put your food down with style at the Flamenco Arts Center. Find out why laughter truly is the best medicine at The Second City Training Center or Comedy Sportz. Run away and join the circus after trapeze classes from The Flying Gaonas. And discover that you really can teach an old dog new tricks at AnimalSense.

Continuing Education And Professional Development

Chicago School of Massage Therapy, www.csmt.com, 866-267-8482, 17 N State St, 5th Fl, 60602

The French Pastry School, www.frenchpastryschool.com, 312-726-2419, 226 W Jackson Blvd, 60606

Kendall College, www.kendall.edu, 866-667-3344, 900 N Branch St, 60622

Pacific College of Oriental Medicine, www.pacificcollege.edu, 888-729-4811, 3646 N Broadway, 2nd Fl, 60613

Roosevelt University, www.roosevelt.edu, 312-341-3500, 430 S Michigan Ave, 60605

School of the Art Institute of Chicago, www.saic.edu, 312-629-6100, 37 S Wabash, 7th Fl, 60603

School of Continuing Studies at Northwestern University, www.scs.northwestern.edu, 312-503-6950, 399 E Chicago Ave, 60611

A Little Bit Of Everything

AnimalSense, www.animalsense.com, 773-275-3647, various locations.

The Discovery Center, www.discoverycenter.cc, 773-348-8120, 2940 N Lincoln Ave, 60657

Gallery 37 Center for the Arts, www.g37centerforthearts.org, 312-744-8925, 66 E Randolph St, 60602

Motorcycle Riding School, www.motorcyclelearning.com, 773-968-7433, 1400 N Halsted St, 60622

Ride Chicago Motorcycle School, www.ride-chicago.com, 773-334-4998, 5215 N Ravenswood Ave

Writers The Loft, www.thewritersloft.com, 773-348-4116, 1450 W Waveland Ave, 60613

Arts And Lifestyle

Chicago Bauhaus Academy (woodworking and furniture design), www.chicagobauhaus.org, 773-761-0418, 6525 N Clark St, 60626

Comedy Sportz, www.comedysportzchicago.com, 773-549-8080, 5100 N Ravenswood Ave, 60640

Fire Arts Center of Chicago, www.firearts.org, 773-329-9908, 1907 N Mendell St, 60622

Glass Frog Studio, www.glassfrogstudio.com, 773-523-8933, 3509 S Wolcott Ave, 60609

Lillstreet Art Center, www.lillstreet.com, 773-769-4226, 4401 N Ravenswood Ave, 60640

Mudhouse Studio, www.mudhousestudio.com, 773-975-7522, 3841 N Ashland Ave, 60613

Old Town School of Folk Music, www.oldtownschool.org, 773-728-6000, 4544 N Lincoln Ave, 60625

Palette & Chisel Academy of Fine Art, www.paletteandchisel.org, 312-642-4400, 1012 N Dearborn, 60610

The Screenwriters Group, www.screenwritersgroup.com, 773-665-8500, 1803 W Byron St, 60613

The Second City Training Center, www.secondcity.com, 312-664-4032, 1616 N Wells St, 60614

WoodSmyth's (woodworking classes), www.woodsmythschicago.com, 773-477-6482, 1835 W School St, 60657

Athletics And Dance

All About Dance, www.allaboutdance.org, 773-572-8701, 2214 N Clark St, 60614

Chicago Athletic Association Fencers Club, www.caafc.com, 312-644-4880, 441 N Wabash, 60611

Chicago Sailing Club, www.chicagosailing.com, 773-871-7245, 2712 N Campbell Ave, 60647

Flamenco Arts Center, www.flamencoartscenter.com, 773-868-4130, 3755 N Western Ave, 60618

The Flying Gaonas, www.flyinggaonastrapeze.com, 773-398-9881.

JABB Gym, www.jabbboxing.com, 312-733-5222, 410 N Oakley Blvd, 2nd Flr, 60612

Latin Street Dancing, www.laboriqua.com, 312-427-2572, 540 N La Salle St, 5th Fl, 60610

The School of Ballet Chicago, www.balletchicago.org, 312-251-8838, 218 Wabash St, 3rd Fl, 60604

Together We Tri (triathalon training), www.togetherwetri.com, 866-889-3874

Food And Wine

BIN 36, www.bin36.com, 312-755-9463, 339 N Dearborn, 60610; 847-808-9463

Calphalon Culinary Center, www.calphalonculinarycenter.com, 312-529-0100, 1000 W Washington St, 60607

The Chopping Block, www.thechoppingblock.net, 773-472-6700, 4747 N Lincoln Ave; 312-644-6360, The Merchandise Mart Plaza, Ste 107, 60654.

Fox & Obel, www.fox-obel.com, 312-410-7301, 401 E Illinois St, 60611

Just Grapes, www.justgrapes.net, 312-627-9463, 560 W Washington Blvd, Ste 100, 60661

Sur La Table Culinary Center, www.surlatable.com, 312-337-0600, 52-54 E Walton St, 60611

Foreign Languages

Alliance Francaise de Chicago, www.afchicago.com, 312-337-1070, 810 N Dearborn St, 60610

Instituto Cervantes Chicago, www.chicago.cervantes.es, 312-335-1996, 31 W Ohio St, 60610

Italidea, www.italidea.org, 500 N Michigan Ave, Ste 1450, 312-832-4053, 60611

General Information

Chicagoland Bicycle Federation:	9 W Hubbard St, Ste 402, 312-427-3325; www.biketraffic.org
Chicago Park District:	www.chicagoparkdistrict.com; 312-742-PLAY
Chicago Cycling Club:	www.chicagocyclingclub.org; 773-509-8093
	(Organized weekend rides April through October)
Chicago Transit Authority:	www.transitchicago.com
DOT Bikes Website:	www.chicagobikes.org

Overview

Despite the environmental and physical benefits, and Mayor Daley's efforts to make Chicago streets more hospitable to pedallers, bike riders are still seen by most drivers as a road nuisance and the designated bike lanes on streets such as Milwaukee, King Drive, and Elston are a joke—illegal passing lanes are more like it (and they tend to be a good place for a biker to get "doored" by a parked car). Furthermore, designated lakefront bike paths are anything but: a sunny Saturday morning guarantees a path that is crowded with headphone-wearing roller bladers, leashless dogs, and shoulder-to-shoulder stroller pushers—not exactly the place to practice for a Lance Armstrong-like debut. Nonetheless, every year thousands of Chicagoans choose to take their lives into their hands by taking it to the street in hopes that the city will become more bike-friendly. Events like the annual Bike the Drive in May (no cars on Lake Shore Drive for a whole morning!) and services like the state-of-the-art bike parking garage in Millennium Park (complete with showers!) indicate that things are improving—and locking your bike to a rack for free sure beats paying for valet parking in many neighborhoods.

If you are a cyclist in Chicago, bear in mind that bicycles, like other vehicles of the roads, are subject to the same laws and rights as drivers. You might feel like the only biker in the city who comes to a full stop at a corner, but fastidiously sticking to the laws is a good way to make a case for drivers to accept bikers. This includes the right to take a lane and the obligation to hand signal for turns. It goes without saying that you should always ride defensively (but don't bike on sidewalks: you can be ticketed). Helmets are still optional, but you'd have to have a pretty thick head to tempt fate without one. The same goes for an adequate assortment of chains and u-locks. Bike thievery is rampant in every neighborhood in the city. The police department now offers a bike registration service so you'll have legal recourse if you stumble upon your stolen bike on eBay.

Bikes Onboard Mass Transit

Bicycles are permitted (free) on all L trains at all times except 7 am–9 am and 4 pm–6 pm on weekdays. Use the accessible turnstile or ask an attendant to open an access gate. Don't try to take your bike through the tall steel gates—it will get stuck! Only two bikes per carriage are allowed, so check for other bikes before you get on. Bikes are only permitted on CTA buses equipped with front exterior bike racks, such as the 63rd Street, 72 North Avenue, 75th Street, and 65 Grand buses. If your bike is the first to be loaded, lower the rack and place it in position with the front wheel facing the curb. If there is already a bike on the rack, place your bike's rear wheel toward the curb. If two bikes are already loaded, wait for the next bus. On Metra commuter trains, bikes are allowed to travel free of charge in off-peak hours. There is a maximum number of bikes allowed per rail car (it varies by line—check the Metra website for your planned route), so follow the conductor's instructions if he or she asks you to board a different car.

Bike Shops	Address	Phone	Map
Kozy Cyclery	219 W Erie St	312-266-1700	2
Sport Mart	620 N La Salle Dr	312-337-6151	2
Bike Chicago	600 E Grand Ave	312-595-9600	3
Mission Bay Multi Sports	738 W Randolph St	312-466-9111	4
Cycle Bike Shop	1465 S Michigan Ave	312-987-1080	11
Wheels & Things	5210 S Harper Ave	773-493-4326	19
Art's Cycle	1652 E 53rd St	773-363-7524	20
Rapid Transit Cycle Shop	1900 W North Ave	773-227-2288	21
Quick Release Bike Shop	1527 N Ashland Ave	773-871-3110	22
Working Bikes Cooperative	1125 S Western Ave	312-421-5048	23
Boulevard Bikes	2535 N Kedzie Blvd	773-235-9109	27
Upgrade Cycle Works	1130 W Chicago Ave	312-226-8650	24
Irv's Bike Shop	1725 S Racine Ave	312-226-6330	26
Oscar Wastyn Cycles	2634 W Fullerton Ave	773-384-8999	27
Kozy Cyclery	1451 W Webster Ave	773-528-2700	29
Cycle Smithy	2468 1/2 N Clark St	773-281-0444	30
Performance Bicycle Shop	2720 N Halsted St	773-248-0107	30
Village Cycle Center	1337 N Wells St	312-751-2488	31
Yojimbo's Garage	1310 N Clybourn Ave	312-587-0878	31
Roberts Cycle	7054 N Clark St	773-274-9281	34
Uptown Bikes	4653 N Broadway St	773-728-5212	40
On The Route Bicycles	3146 N Lincoln Ave	773-477-5066	43
Johnny Sprocket's	3001 N Broadway	773-244-1079	44
Kozy Cyclery	3712 N Halstead St	773-281-2263	44
Sports Authority	3134 N Clark St	773-871-8500	44
Edgebrook Cycle & Sport	6450 N Central Ave	773-792-1669	46

Billiards

The city's affluent "nesters" may be more interested in big-screen TVs than pool tables these days. But you'd rather mix your pleasure with strategy, a convivial game of billiards is still a fine way of turning strangers into friends… not to mention learning the angles above the angles above the angles. Many bars, from the seedy to the swanky, have a table or four. Chicago is also home to a good number of establishments that cater specifically to pool sharks. Have a good one, and don't get hustled.

The game's popularity goes in cycles. It spiked in the '80s thanks largely to *The Color of Money*, a pool-themed film starring Paul Newman and Tom Cruise, part of which was shot at **Chris's Billiards (Map 48)**. With two-dozen tables, no booze and no nonsense, this Jefferson Park institution remains the most credible spot among Chicago's seasoned players, although it sometimes intimidates newcomers. (We wouldn't call it "sleazy," but we wouldn't eat off the floor, either.) **Uno Billiards (Map 38)** is an oasis of seediness in the otherwise upscale Albany Park area. The equipment's not in tip-top shape, but cut this place and it bleeds character. **Chicago Billiards (Map 35)** is also a hike from downtown, but it's a more family-oriented room with a full food menu. If you're looking for snooker, a billiards variation wildly popular in Britain, they've got the hook-up here.

Somewhat hipper environs can be found at **City Pool Hall Food & Spirits (Map 1)**, a well-kept room also noted for its delectable burgers, and **Pressure Billiards & Café (Map 37)**, which boasts regulation tournament tables and, on weekends, one of the city's least hack-prone standup comedy nights. If racking the balls ever gets seriously trendy again, you can bet that the folks at **G Cue Billiards (Map 24)** will be the first to know. Professional player Tom Karabatsos runs this two-level lounge, which accommodates more hangers-out than pool purists. If the massive video screens don't take your eye off the eight ball, the young, smartly dressed clientele might. The pub grub is adequate. The mixed drinks are weak. Some of our sources report nasty experiences with the staff (and not the good kind of nasty experiences, either).

For an even more gloriously inauthentic pool adventure, you can usually find a table at one of Chicago's bowling alleys. **Diversey-River Bowl (Map 42)** may be better known for its blacklights and throbbing pop soundtrack, but for those who can't shoot straight sober, it's got a game room with a full-service bar. It's open 'til 3 am on weekends. **Waveland Bowl (Map 42)** has tables all night, every night, though there's often a wait, and it's hard to focus when high school and college kids keep distracting us with their air hockey and their Dance Dance Revolution. **Southport Lanes (Map 43)** is a mite classier, with lovely Brunswick tables in a welcoming back area.

A few major music venues also have tables, where musicians can be found relieving their road-warrior angst between sound checks. Show up early at the Double Door or the Empty Bottle (See Nightlife Map 21), and you might get to hustle the people who wrote your favorite song.

Billiards	Address	Phone	Fee	Map
City Pool Hall Food & Spirits	640 W Hubbard St	312-491-9690	$12 per hour	1
G Cue Billiards	157 N Morgan St	312-850-3170	$14 per hour	24
Seven Ten Lanes	2747 N Lincoln Ave	773-549-2695	$12 per hour	29
Chicago Billiards	5544 N Kedzie Ave	773-866-9924	$10 per hour	35
Lincoln Billiards	5334 N Lincoln Ave	773-728-1553	$10 per hour	35
Pressure Billiards & Café	6318 N Clark St	773-743-7665	$10 per hour	37
Uno Billiard	3112 W Lawrence Ave	773-267-8166	$10 per hour	38
Waveland Bowl	3700 N Western Ave	773-472-5900	$8-$15 per hour	42
Southport Lanes	3325 N Southport Ave	773-472-6600	$20 per hour	43
Chris's Billiards	4637 N Milwaukee Ave	773-286-4714		48

Bowling

Bowling is supposed to be the most blue-collar of all sports, so in the City of Big Shoulders, you'd expect comb-overs, beer frames, unfashionable wrist guards, and visible plumber's cracks to abound. In the '90s, several local alleys jazzed it up for the teenagers with rock music and late-night fog-and-light shows, and we can live with that. Lately, however, the trend is toward atmosphere-conscious boutique spots that treat strikes and spares as an afterthought. These are nice places to take a date, but we're a little scared when so-called bowling alleys advertise "small plates."

But if you're intrigued by the idea of high-end lounges that mash-up retro kitsch with modern glam, head to **10 Pin-Strike Bar Bowl & Grille (Map 2)**, where you can sip a trend-'tini on a cushy couch with an urban professional crowd. And the upscale, Hollywood-themed chain, **Lucky Strike Lanes (Map 3)**, is a good place to kill time if you're waiting to catch a movie at the adjacent AMC River East.

If you prefer not to define your bowling experience as "sophisticated" or "cutting edge," we recommend **Lincoln Square Lanes (Map 38)**, the city's only second-floor alley, which has been open since 1918. Climb a flight of stairs above the Ace Hardware store and you'll get twelve lanes with old-school wood floors, live blues and rockabilly music on weekends, and a balcony from which to watch the action. Other good choices for an authentic Chicago bowling adventure include **Diversey-River Bowl (Map 42)**, where there's an eclectic mix of league fanatics and hipster rockers ordering bottles of Bud shaped like bowling pins, or the only-slightly-grungy **Waveland Bowl (Map 42)**, which has been open 24 hours a day, seven days a week since 1969.

And for a place that successfully incorporates "the real deal" with truly modern sensibilities, head to the **Timber Lanes (Map 39)**, where a "Big Lebowski" poster hovers over lane one amidst wood-paneled walls, an Elvis pinball machine, and a mammoth bar. It debuted in 1945 and has since become home to men's, women's, mixed, gay and lesbian, and Chicago Braille Center blind leagues. They've also hosted full-contact, Mexican-wrestling style bowling with Los Diablos Guapos, and nude nights (although shoes were still required) with the Windy City Naturists.

Bowling	Address	Phone	Fee	Map
Seven Ten Lanes	1055 E 55th St	773-347-2695	$16 per hour per lane, $2 shoes	19
Waveland Bowl	3700 N Western Ave	773-472-5900	$1.50-$6 per game. $4 shoes	42
Southport Lanes	3325 N Southport Ave	773-472-6600	Mon-Thurs: $20 per hr per lane, $2 shoes	43
Fireside Bowl	2648 W Fullerton Ave	773-486-2700	$3.50 per game or $20 per hour, $2 shoes	27
10 Pin-Strike Bar Bowl & Grille	330 N State St	312-644-0300	$6.95 game, $3.95 Shoes	2
Diversey-River Bowl	2211 W Diversey Pkwy	773-227-5800	Mon-Thurs: $19-32 per hr per lane, $3 shoes	42
Habetler Bowl	5250 N Northwest Hwy	773-774-0500	$4 per game for adults, $3.50 shoes	W
Lincoln Square Lanes	4874 N Lincoln Ave	773-561-8191	$4 game, $3 shoes	38
Lucky Strike Lanes	322 E Illinois St	312-245-8331	$5.95 game, $3.95 shoes	3
Seven Ten Lanes	2747 N Lincoln Ave	773-549-2695	$20 per hr per lane, $2 shoes	29
Timber Lanes	1851 W Irving Park Rd	773-549-9770	$2.50 per game, $2 shoes	39

Weather permitting, golfers can tee up all year round in Chicago. The Chicago Park District offers six public courses open daily, dawn to dusk. At **Jackson Park's (South)** premier 18-hole facility, the scenery alone will make you forget the bustle of the city. The nine-hole **Sydney R. Marovitz (Waveland) Golf Course (43)** is usually busy, but it has great views of the lake. And **Robert A. Black's (Map 34)** nine-hole, 2,339-yard, par-33 layout was designed by the renowned Dick Nugent. In addition, the park district operates three driving ranges and three learning centers, including one for juniors at **Douglas Park**.

The Forest Preserve District of Cook County offers 10 public courses in and around the city. **Indian Boundary's (Northwest)** huge fairways and fast-moving greens make for fun play and golfers often catch glimpses of visiting deer. At **Edgebrook (Northwest)**, bordered by mature trees along the Chicago River, the signature fifth hole—a 93-yard par three with an elevated green—offers a serious test of skill. Just 10 minutes from downtown, **Bill Caldwell's (Northwest)** sharply undulating greens make it a great place to play a quick nine.

And, for a real urban golf experience, the privately owned **Harborside International**, host to some Illinois PGA events, offers two tricky 18-hole, Scottish-links courses open to the public in season. Private courses in the city include the **Beverly**, **Ridge**, and **Ridgemoor** country clubs and **Riverside Golf Club**. However, if you want to see Tiger Woods play, you'll have to head out to the suburbs; the PGA tour visits clubs like Cog Hill in southwest Lemont and the members-only Medinah Country Club in the western 'burbs.

Golf Courses

	Address	Phone	Map	Weekdays	Weekends
The Green at Grant Park	352 E Monroe St	312-987-1818	06		
Robert A Black Golf Course	2045 W Pratt Blvd	312-742-7931	34	$16.25	$17.75
Sydney R Marovitz Golf Course	3600 N Recreation Dr	312-742-7930	43	$20	$23
Bill Caldwell Golf Course	6200 N Caldwell Ave	773-792-1930	NW	$17.10	$19.26
Edgebrook Golf Course	6100 N Central Ave	773-763-8320	NW	$24	$28
Indian Boundary Golf Course	8600 W Forest Preserve Ave	773-625-9630	NW	$28	$30
Columbus Park Golf Course	5701 W Jackson Blvd	312-746-5573	W	$14.50	$15.75
Marquette Park Golf Course	6700 S Kedzie Ave	312-245-0909	SW	$15.25	$16.50
Harborside International Golf Center	11001 S Doty Ave	312-782-7837	S	$80	$92
Jackson Park Golf Course	63rd St & Lake Shore Dr	773-667-0524	S	$22.75	$25.75
South Shore Country Club	7059 S South Shore Dr	773-256-0986	S	$14.50	$15.75
Peter N Jans Community Golf Course	1031 Central St	847-475-9173	Evanston	$17	$23
The Glen Club	2901 W Lake Ave, Glenview	847-724-7272	N/A	$125–$165	$135–$165
Glencoe Park District Course	621 Westley Rd, Glencoe	847-835-0250	N/A	$38	$47
Winnetka Park District Course	1300 Oak St, Winnetka	847-501-2050	N/A	$40	$46

Driving Ranges

	Address	Phone	Map	Fees
Diversey Driving Range	141 W Diversey Dr	312-742-7929	3	$11/100 balls, $2 clubs
Marquette Park Golf Course	6700 S Kedzie Ave	312-747-2761	SW	$7.50/60 balls
Harborside International Golf Center	11001 S Doty Ave	312-782-7837	S	$10/100 balls
Jackson Park Golf Course	63rd St & Lake Shore Dr	773-667-0524	S	Small bucket $6, large bucket $9 (no fee for clubs)

General Information

Chicago Park District: www.chicagoparkdistrict.com
312-742-PLAY (7528)

Chicagoland Bicycle
Federation: www.chibikefed.org
312-427-3325

Chicago Area Runner's
Association: www.cararuns.org
312-666-9836

Overview

Greater Chicago offers more than 250 recreational off-road paths that allow bikers, skaters, walkers, and joggers to exercise without worrying about vehicular traffic—now if only we could get dogs off the paths! In addition to recreational paths in the city's parks, designated off-street trails line the Lakefront, North Shore Channel, North Branch Trail along the Chicago River, Burnham Greenway, and Major Taylor Trail.

Lakefront Trail

Chicago has one of the prettiest and most accessible shorelines of any city in the US—this is the 500-pound gorilla of recreational paths in Chicago. Use one of Lake Shore Drive's over/underpasses (generally available every half mile or so) and you'll discover 15 miles of bathing beaches and over 20 miles of bike paths—just don't anticipate being able to train for the Tour de France during summer weekends, when the sheer number of people makes it impossible to bike along the path at faster than a snail's pace. But thanks to Burnham and Bennett's 1909 "Plan for Chicago," at least we can count on the shoreline remaining non-commercial, with great cycling, jogging, blading, skating, and swimming opportunities for all.

Major Taylor Trail

If you've ever wanted to take in a slice of Chicago's southwestern-most corner (and let's face it, who hasn't?), try the six-mile bike route that begins at Dawes Park at 81st and Hamilton Streets near Western Avenue. The route incorporates an abandoned railroad right-of-way and runs to the southeast through Beverly and Morgan Park, ending up at the Cook County Forest Preserve near 130th and Halsted Streets. The trail was named in honor of cycling legend Marshall "Major" Taylor, one of the first African-American cyclists, who lived out the final years of his life in a YMCA in Chicago.

North Branch Trail

To access the northern end of the trail, take Lake Cook Road to the Chicago Botanic Garden, located east of I-94. You can also start from any of the forest preserves as the path winds southward. To access the southern end of the trail in Chicago, take Milwaukee Avenue to Devon Avenue and head a short way east to the Caldwell Woods Preserve. The North Branch winds along the Chicago River and the Skokie Lagoons, but unlike most of the other trails, this one crosses streets, so be careful and look out for cars as you approach. Still, it represents a great way to get out of the city—and if you make it all the way to the Botanic Garden, admission is free as you won't have to pay for parking!

Burnham Greenway

The 11-mile stretch of the Burnham Greenway, which extends from 104th Street on the city's south side all the way down to Lansing in the south suburbs, has undergone major work over the past few years. The trail has a bit of a checkered past (the former railroad right-of-way was once cited for major pollution), but current paving projects make it a good bet for biking, skating, and pedestrians. Expect to find all of northern Illinois' major ecosystems, from wetlands to prairies to a Ford Motor plant in close proximity to one another.

North Shore Channel Trail

This trail follows the North Shore Channel of the Chicago River from Lawrence Avenue through Lincolnwood, Skokie (where you'll find a bizarre sculpture park lining the trail), and Evanston to Green Bay Road at McCormick Boulevard. Not all of the seven miles of the trail are paved bike paths and you'll have to switch back and forth between path and street. Skokie recently paved the trail segment between Oakton and Howard Streets, but there are still many missing links in the route, much to the chagrin of Friends of the Chicago River (FOCR), who are trying to extend and improve the Channel Trail. The Green Bay Trail branches off to the north from the North Shore Channel Trail and will take you past multimillion dollar houses, cute suburban downtowns, and the Ravinia Festival.

Chicago Park District

Many of the parks under the jurisdiction of the Chicago Park District have paths dedicated to cycling, jogging, walking, rollerblading, and skating. The Chicago Area Runner's Association is so committed to lobbying for runners' rights that it successfully petitioned to have the Lincoln Park running paths plowed and salted through the winter so they could continue their running activities (though prepare to find water fountains that are shut off and bathrooms that are locked). This calls into question the sanity of such masochistic dedication, but we can only assume that the entire year is needed to prepare for the Chicago Marathon, held annually in October. Check out the chart on the facing page to determine Chicago Parks that designate jogging/walking and cycling/skating paths.

Park District—North Region	Address	Phone	Jog/Walk	Bike/Skate	Map
Brooks Park	7100 N Harlem Ave	773-631-4401	■		45
Emmerson Park	1820 W Granville Ave	773-761-0433	■		36
Eugene Field Park	5100 N Ridgeway Ave	773-478-9744		■	48
Oz Park	2021 N Burling St	312-742-7898	■		30
Peterson Park	5801 N Pulaski Rd	312-742-7584	■		46
Portage Park	4100 N Long Ave	773-685-7235	■		48
River Park	5100 N Francisco Ave	312-742-7516		■	38
Shabbona Park	6935 W Addison St	773-685-6205	■		47
Warren Park	6601 N Western Ave	773-262-6314	■	■	33
Frank J Wilson Park	4630 N Milwaukee Ave	773-685-6454	■		48
Winnemac Park	5100 N Leavitt St	312-742-5101	■		39

Park District—Central Region	Address	Phone	Jog/Walk	Bike/Skate	Map
Columbus Park	500 S Central Ave	773-287-7641	■	■	49
Douglas Park	1401 S Sacramento Ave	773-762-2842	■	■	50
Dvorak Park	1119 W Cullerton St	312-746-5083	■		26
Humboldt Park	1400 N Sacramento Ave	312-742-7549	■	■	50
Riis Park	6100 W Fullerton Ave	312-746-5363	■	■	47
Rutherford Sayre Park	6871 W Belden Ave	312-746-5368	■		47
Union Park	1501 W Randolph St	312-746-5494	■		24

Park District—Southwest Region	Address	Phone	Jog/Walk	Bike/Skate	Map
Bogan Park	3939 W 79th St	773-284-6456	■		53
Cornell Square Park	1809 W 50th St	312-747-6097	■		54
Hayes Park	2936 W 85th St	312-747-6177	■		54
LeClaire Courts/Hearst Community	5120 W 44th St	312-747-6438	■		53
Mt Greenwood Park	3724 W 111th St	312-747-6564	■		55
Rainey Park	4350 W 79th St	773-284-0696	■		53
Senka Park	5656 S St Louis Ave	312-747-7632	■		54
Sherman Park	1301 W 52nd St	312-747-6672	■		54
Avalon Park	1215 E 83rd St	312-747-6015	■		57
Bradley Park	9729 S Yates Ave	312-747-6022	■		60
Gately Park	810 E 103rd St	312-747-6155	■		59
Hamilton Park	513 W 72nd St	312-747-6174	■		57
Lake Meadows Park	3117 S Rhodes Ave	312-747-6287	■	■	14
Meyering Playground Park	7140 S Martin Luther King Dr	312-747-6545	■		57
Palmer Park	201 E 111th St	312-747-6576	■		59
Rosenblum Park	8050 S Chappel Ave	312-747-6649	■		60
Washington Park	5531 S Martin Luther King Dr	773-256-1248	■	■	57

Park District—Lakefront Region	Address	Phone	Jog/Walk	Bike/Skate	Map
Calumet Park	9801 S Ave G	312-747-6039	■		60
Jackson Park	6401 S Stony Island Ave	773-256-0903	■	■	58
Lincoln Park	2045 Lincoln Park West	312-742-7726	■	■	30
Loyola Park	1230 W Greenleaf Ave	773-262-8605	■	■	34
Rainbow Park & Beach	3111 E 77th St	312-745-1479		■	58

Sports · **Skating**

General Information

Chicago Park District: 312-742-PLAY (7529);
                          www.chicagoparkdistrict.com

Overview

Due to the temperature extremes that Chicago experiences, its residents can enjoy both ice skating and inline skating at various times of the year. Ice skating can be a fun, free, winter activity if you have your own skates, and if you don't, many rinks rent them. Skateboarding is also a popular pastime and a number of parks throughout the city are equipped with skating facilities.

Inline Skating

Similar to bike riding, inline skating in Chicago serves dual purposes. If you plan on strapping on the blades to get from A to B, be super-careful navigating the streets. As it is, Chicago drivers tend to have difficulty seeing cyclers, and chances are they won't notice you until you've slammed into their open car door. Wear protective gear whenever possible, especially a helmet, and learn to shout loudly so that people can anticipate your approach. If recreational skating is more your speed, check out the Recreational Paths page for cool places to skate. If you'd like to join the hundreds of summer skaters out there, and you don't have your own gear, the following places offer skate rental: Londo Mondo, 1100 N Dearborn St at W Maple St, 312-751-2794; Bike Chicago at Navy Pier, 312-755-0488. Hourly rates range from $7 to $10, while daily rates are from $20 to $35.

Skate Parks

If what you're after is a phat jam session, grab your blades or board and a couple of buddies and head down to the magnificent Burnham Skate Park (east of Lake Shore Drive at 31st St, 312-747-2200). With amazing grinding walls and rails, vert walls, and banks, Burnham Park presents hours of fun and falls. Less intense but equally fun are the two skate parks with ramps, quarter pipes, and grind rails. One can be found at West Lawn Park (4233 W 65th St, 773-284-2803) the other at Oriole Park (5430 N Olcott Ave, 773-631-6197).

Ice Skating

The long-running and popular Skate on State was canceled due to the opening of two new ice rinks: the McCormick Tribune Ice Rink at Millennium Park and the Midway Plaisance ice rink.

The rink at Millennium Park is a beautiful place to skate during the day or evening, with Chicago's glorious skyline in the background. And after the ice melts, the area plays host to al fresco dining and entertainment in the summer months. Located at 55 North Michigan Avenue, enter on the east side of Michigan Avenue between Monroe Drive and Randolph Street. Parking is available for $10 at the Grant Park North Garage. (Enter from Michigan Avenue median at Washington or Madison Streets.) Entry is free, skate rental is $7, and if you have your own and want them sharpened there's a $5 fee (312-742-5222; www.millenniumpark.org).

The Olympic-sized skating rink and warming house complex at Midway Plaisance is the alternative to Millennium Park. Located at 59th and Woodlawn Avenue, entry is $5 ($4 for kids) and skate rentals cost $3. During the summer, the facility is used for rollerskating and other entertainment (312-745-2470).

Other ice skating rinks are located seasonally at:

McFetridge Sports Complex (year-round) · 3843 N California Ave, 773-478-2609 (admission is $4 for kids under 12 years, $5 for adults + $3 skate rental)

Daley Bicentennial Plaza Rink · 337 E Randolph St, 312-742-7650 (free admission + $4 rental)

McKinley Park · 2210 W Pershing Rd, 312-747-5992 (free admission + $5 rental)

Mt. Greenwood Park · 3721 W 111th St, 312-747-6564 (free admission + $5 rental)

Navy Pier Ice Rink · 600 E Grand Ave, 312-595-5100 ($12 admission + rental)

Riis Park · 6100 W Fullerton Ave, 312-746-5735 (free admission + $5 rental)

The Rink (roller skating) · 1122 E 87th St, 773-221-2600 ($1)

Rowan Park · 11546 S Avenue L, 773-646-1967 (free admission + $5 rental)

Warren Park · 6601 N Western Ave, 773-761-8663 ($4 admission + $4 rental)

West Lawn Park · 4233 W 65th St, 773-284-2803 (free admission + $5 rental)

Gear

If you're after skateboard gear, check out Air Time Skate Boards at 3317 N Clark St, 773-472-6868 and Uprise Skateboard Shop at 1820 N Milwaukee Ave, 773-342-7763.

For skating equipment, Air Time; (above) also does inline skates, as does Londo Mondo which has two locations: 1100 N Dearborn Street at W Maple St, 312-751-2794; and 2148 N Halsted St, 773-327-2218.

For all your ice skating needs, try the Skater's Edge store in the McFetridge Sports Complex (3843 N California Ave, 773-463-1505). They deal in hockey skates and other equipment as well as inline skates and accessories such as sequined dresses!

General Information

General Park Info: 312-742-PLAY
Department of Beaches and Pools: 312-742-5121

The Chicago Park District offers several indoor and outdoor pools, ten of which are equipped with ramps or lifts for disability access. At the top of our list is the 500-person-capacity outdoor wonderment at **Washington Park (Map 18)**, a 50-meter pool that's connected to a large, oval, side pool where fountains spray into a zero-depth entrance. Even better—it's got a 36-foot, theme-park-style water slide. It's overrun with kids during open swim periods, but grown folks like the designated lap times, water aerobics classes, and adult swims.

We also like the 30-meter outdoor pool at **River Park (Map 38)**, an Albany Park spot that boasts a diving well, a spacious deck with lounge chairs and umbrella tables, and an interactive kids' water playground. And when the weather gets cold, there's great lap swimming at the Ida Crown Natatorium at **Eckhart Park (Map 24)**. What's a natatorium? It's a pool inside its own building, and this one looks like it might have been designed by Eero Saarinen, but it wasn't.

All outdoor pools are free for the summer (Memorial Day-Labor Day). During the year, all lap swim fees for indoor pools are for 10-week sessions ($20 before 9 am; $10 after 9 am), and recreational and family swims are free. Get a complete list of facilities and register for aquatic exercise, diving, lifeguard, underwater hockey, and water polo classes at http://chicagoparkdistrict.com.

Outdoor Pools

	Address	Phone	Map
Wentworth Gardens Park	3770 S Wentworth Ave	312-747-6996	13
Taylor Park	41 W 47th St	312-747-6728	15
Washington Park	5531 S MLK Dr	773-256-1248	18
Pulaski Park	1419 W Blackhawk St	312-742-7559	22
Union Park	1501 W Randolph St	312-746-5494	24
Dvorak Park	1119 W Cullerton St	312-746-5083	26
Wrightwood Park	2534 N Greenview Ave	312-742-7816	29
River Park	5100 N Francisco Ave	312-742-7516	38
Chase Park	4701 N Ashland Ave	312-742-7518	40
McFetridge Sports Center (California Park)	3843 N California Ave	773-478-2609	41
Hamlin Park	3035 N Hoyne Ave	312-742-7785	42

Indoor Pools

	Address	Phone	Map
McGuane Park	2901 S Poplar Ave	312-747-7463	12
Dyett Recreational Center	513 E 51st	312-745-1211	16
Clemente Park	2334 W Division St	312-742-7466	21
Eckhart Park/Ida Crown Natatorium	1330 W Chicago Ave	312-746-5553	24
Harrison Park	1824 S Wood St	312-746-5491	25
Sheridan Park	910 S Aberdeen St	312-746-5369	26
Stanton Park	618 W Scott St	312-742-9553	31
Mather Park	5941 N Richmond St	312-742-7501	35
Welles Park	2333 W Sunnyside Ave	312-742-7511	39
Gill Park	833 W Sheridan Rd	312-742-5807	43

While we admit we're suckers for any sport that includes the word "love" in its scoring system, we try not to think of the significance that it means "zero" in tennis talk. Find love and more at these Chicago tennis courts.

All tennis courts (except Daley Bicentennial Plaza in Grant Park, Diversey Park, Chase Park, California Park, and Waveland Park) are free and open to the public on a first-come-first-served basis. Courts are open daily—check each park for individual hours. 312-742-7529 (general info); 773-256-0949 (Lake Front Region Office).

Tennis Courts

	Address	Phone	Fees	Map
Grant Park	331 E Randolph St	312-742-7648		6
Daley Bicentennial Plaza	337 E Randolph St	312-742-7648	$7/hr; reservations required	6
Roosevelt Park	62 W Roosevelt Rd	312-742-7648		8
Mandrake Park	900 E Pershing Rd	312-747-7661		12
McGuane Park	2901 S Poplar Ave	312-747-7463		12
Armour Square Park	3309 S Shields Ave	312-747-6012		13
Ellis Park	707 E 37th St	312-746-5962		14
Fuller Park	331 W 45th St	312-747-6144		15
Taylor Park	41 W 47th St	312-747-6728		15
Metcalfe Park	4134 S State St	312-747-6728		16
Kenwood Community Park	1330 E 50th St	312-747-6286		17
Washington Park	5531 S Martin Luther King Dr	773-256-1248		18
Nichols Park	1355 E 53rd St	312-747-2703		19
Clemente Park	2334 W Division St	312-742-7466		21
Union Park	1501 W Randolph St	312-746-5494		24
Harrison Park	1824 S Wood St	312-746-5491		25
Sheridan Park	910 S Aberdeen St	312-746-5369		26
Jonquil Park	1023 W Wrightwood Ave	N/A		29
Oz Park	2021 N Burling St	312-742-7898		30
Lake Shore Park	808 N Lake Shore Dr	312-742-7891		32
Lerner Park	7000 N Sacramento Ave	N/A		33
Rogers Park	7345 N Washtenaw Ave	773-262-1482		33
Indian Boundary Park	2500 N Lunt Ave	773-742-7887		33
Warren Park	6601 N Western Ave	773-262-6314		33
Loyola Park	1230 W Greenleaf Ave	773-262-8605		34
Pottawattomie Park	7340 N Rogers Ave	773-262-5835		34
Touhy Park	7348 N Paulina St	773-262-6737		34
Legion Park at the Chicago River	W Peterson Ave to W Foster Ave at the Chicago River	N/A		35
Green Briar Park	2650 W Peterson Ave	773-761-0582		35
Mather Park	5941 N Richmond St	312-742-7501		35
Emmerson Playground Park	1820 W Granville Ave	773-761-0433		36
Senn Park	1550 W Thorndale Ave	N/A		37
Horner Park	2741 W Montrose Ave	773-478-3499		38
River Park	5100 N Francisco Ave	N/A		38
Welles Park	2333 W Sunnyside Ave	312-742-7511		39
Chase Park	4701 N Ashland Ave	312-742-7518	$5/hr	40
Revere Park	2509 W Irving Park Rd	773-478-1220		41
Brands Park	3259 N Elston Ave	773-478-2414		41
McFetridge Sports Center (California Park)	3843 N California Ave	773-478-2609	$16-$24/hr	41
Hamlin Park	3035 N Hoyne Ave	312-742-7785		42
Lincoln Park-Waveland Tennis Center	W Waveland Ave & N Lake Shore Dr	312-742-7674	$7/hr; reservations required	44
Lincoln Park-Diversey Tennis Center	2800 N Lake Shore Dr	312-742-7821	$16/hr; reservations must be made in person	44

Volleyball Courts

Hoops The Gym • 312-850-4667, 1001 W Washington Blvd
State-of-the-art court rentals. 24/7.

Lincoln Park/North Avenue Beach • 312-742-7529 (reservations and price information)
101 courts—12 are always open to the public. Much league play and reserved courts.
Office hours: Mon–Fri: 1 pm–9 pm; Weekends: 8 am–5 pm.

Lincoln Park/Montrose Beach • 312-742-5121
45 courts allotted on a first-come-first-served basis. League play in the evening.

Jackson Park/63rd Street Beach • 312-742-4847
Four free courts — first-come-first-served.

Yoga

	Address	Phone	Website	Map
Ab-Sutra Yoga Studio	821 W Superior St	312-235-6984	www.ab-sutra.com	1
Siddha Yoga Meditation Center	770 N Halsted St	312-738-2798	www.siddhayogachicago.org	1
Yoga Circle	401 W Ontario St	312-915-0750	www.yogacircle.com	1
Bikram Yoga	219 W Chicago Ave	312-255-9642	www.bikramcitychicago.com	2
Lakeshore Athletic Club	441 N Wabash Ave	312-644-4880	www.lsac.com	2
Yoga Now	742 N LaSalle St, Ste 201	312-280-9642	www.yoganowchicago.com	2
Lakeshore Athletic Club	333 E Ontario St	312-944-4546	www.lsac.com	3
Adia Yoga	555 W Madison St	312-902-2040	www.adiayoga.com	4
Soham Yoga	55 E Washington St	312-409-1416	www.sohamyoga.com	5
Dahn Yoga	332 N Michigan Ave	312-263-9642	www.dahnyoga.com	6
Lakeshore Athletic Club	211 N Stetson Ave	312-616-9000	www.lsac.com	6
Enso Studio	719 S State St	312-427-3676	www.ensostudio.com	8
Adia Yoga	1936 S Michigan Ave	312-326-2979	www.adiayoga.com	11
Core Studio	1505 S Michigan Ave	312-922-1680	www.corestudiochicago.com	11
Three Pillars Wellness Center	1516 E 53rd St	773-363-7607	www.3pillars.org	19
Bikram Yoga's College of India	1344 N Milwaukee Ave	773-395-9150	www.bycic.com	21
Global Yoga & Wellness Center	1823 W North Ave	312-719-6227	www.globalyogacenter.com	21
Nature Yoga Sanctuary	2021 W Division St	773-227-5720	www.natureyoga.com	21
Moksha Yoga Center	700 N Carpenter St	312-942-9642	www.mokshayoga.com	24
Nirvana Yoga	1151 W Jackson Blvd	312-829-9642		24
Sana Vita Studio	1357 W Grand Ave	312-829-8482	www.sanavitastudio.com	24
Soulistic Studio and Spa	805 N Milwaukee Ave, Ste 200	312-226-7685	www.soulisticstudiospa.com	24
Yoga Skills	310 S Racine Ave	773-908-7074	www.yogaskills.com	24
Stellaria Natural Health	2755 W Logan Blvd	773-486-3797	www.stellarianaturalhealth.com	27
Temple of Kriya Yoga	2414 N Kedzie Blvd	773-342-4600	www.yogakriya.org	27
Yoga Bound	1753 N Damen Ave	773-395-2929		28
Harmony Mind Body Fitness	1962 N Bissell St	773-296-0263	www.harmonybody.com	29
Lakeshore Athletic Club	1320 W Fullerton Ave	773-477-9888	www.lsac.com	29
Yogaview	2232 N Clybourn Ave	773-883-9642	www.yogaview.com	29
Bikram Yoga's College of India	2736 A N Clark St	773-348-9642	www.bycic.com	30
Dahn Yoga	2732 N Clark St	773-755-9566	www.dahnyoga.com	30
Flow Inc Pilates + Yoga	2248 N Clark St	773-975-7540	www.flowchicago.com	30
Exhale Mind Body Spa	945 N State St	312-753-6500	www.exhalespa.com	32
Yoga State	850 N Lake Shore Dr	312-503-9642	www.yogastate.com	32
Blue Beryl Dharma Center	1741 W Columbia Ave	773-262-8191	www.lamalobsang.com	34
Sweet Magic Studio	6960 N Sheridan Rd	773-764-6488	www.yogakareena.com	34
Sivananda Yoga Vedanta Center	1246 W Bryn Mawr Ave	773-878-7771	www.sivananda.org/chicago	37
Yoga Now	5852 N Broadway St	773-561-9642	www.yoganowchicago.com	37
Bloom Yoga Studio	4663 N Rockwell St	773-463-9642	www.bloomyogastudio.com	38
Ki Workshop	4512 N Lincoln Ave	773-934-4216	www.kiworkshop.com	39
Om on the Range Yoga Studio	3759 N Ravenswood Ave	773-525-9642	www.omontherange.net	42
Spirit Rising Yoga	3717 N Ravenswood Ave	773-975-9754	www.spiritrisingyoga.com	42
Sweet Pea's Studio	3717 N Ravenswood Ave	773-248-9642	www.sweetpeasstudio.com	42
Chicago Yoga Center	3047 N Lincoln Ave	773-327-3650	www.yogamind.com	43
Healing Earth Resources	3111 N Ashland Ave	773-327-8459	www.healingearthresources.com	43
Moksha Yoga Center	3334 N Clark St	773-975-9642	www.mokshayoga.com	43
Namaskar Boutique	3950 N Southport Ave	773-472-0930	www.namaskarchicago.com	43
The Peace School	3121 N Lincoln Ave	773-248-7959	www.peaceschool.org	43

General Information

NFT Map:	11
Address:	1410 S Museum Campus Dr
	Chicago, IL 60605
Phone:	312-235-7000
Lost & Found:	312-235-7202
Website:	www.soldierfield.net
Box Office:	847-615-BEAR (2327)
Bears Website:	www.chicagobears.com
Ticketmaster:	312-559-1212;
	www.ticketmaster.com

Overview

Like many Bears fans, the "new" Soldier Field is big, burly, and visually abrasive, especially the pre-game tailgaters in the parking lots. Plans began for its building in 1919 as a memorial to American soldiers who died in the wars. It officially opened on October 9th, 1924 (the 53rd anniversary of the Chicago Fire) as Municipal Grant Park Stadium. Renamed and dedicated in 1925, Soldier Field eventually became a key installment in the multi-million dollar Lakefront Improvement Plan for the Chicago shoreline between Navy Pier and McCormick Place. An estimated $365 million went towards the renovation of the 63,000-seat stadium, which opened in time for the 2003-2004 NFL Season and debuted on ABC's *Monday Night Football*. Improved Solider Field amenities include 60% more seating on the sidelines, three times as many concessions stands (400), several cozy meeting nooks throughout the stadium, two 82 x 23-foot video screens, a 100,000-square-foot lounge/entertainment facility, and twice as many bathrooms (although you'd never know it judging by the lines). Critics debate whether the expanded structure resembles a giant toilet-bowl or a flying saucer. (Voters Decide: Toilet Bowl Wins in a Landslide!) And since the Bears made it all the way to the Super Bowl in 2007, we expect Bears fans to increase exponentially in bigness, burliness, and visual-abrasiveness.

How to Get Tickets

Contact Ticketmaster to purchase individual game tickets. Season tickets are nearly impossible to come by within the next ten years as a recent bid by a staff member has him 2,876th in line. The best way to get great seats (other than by having them left to you in a will) is to work with a licensed ticket broker. Fans marked their territory early in 2004 by purchasing a one-time Permanent Seat License (PSL), and in exchange for paying big premiums to help cover construction expenses, PSL holders are promised first choice of ticket seating each year. Of the stadium's 63,000 seats, 27,500 are PSL zones, and the remaining 33,500 are non-licensed seats in the stadium's higher altitudes. A $100 per-seat, non-refundable deposit is required to get on a season ticket waiting list. The deposit will be applied to the first year of non-PSL season tickets, and you can find an application on the Bears website.

How to Get There

By Car: From the north or south, take Lake Shore Drive; follow the signs to Soldier Field. For parking lots, exit at E McFetridge, E Waldron, E 14th Boulevard, and E 18th Drive. From the west, take I-55 E to Lake Shore Drive, turn north, and follow the signs. Travel east on I-290, then south on I-90/94 to I-55; get on I-55 E to Lake Shore Drive.

Parking lots surrounding Soldier Field cost $15 on non-event days, including the new underground North Parking Garage. Rates rise on game days. Call the Standard Parking Customer Service Hotline with questions (312-583-9153). Two parking and game-day tailgating lots are located south of Waldron Drive. There are also lots on the Museum Campus off McFetridge Drive and near McCormick Place off 31st Street and E 18th Street.

By Train: On game days, CTA Soldier Field Express bus 128 runs non-stop between the Ogilvie Transportation Center and Union Station to Soldier Field. Service starts two hours before the game, runs up to 45 minutes before kickoff, and up to 45 minutes post-game.

By L: Take the Red, Orange, or Green Lines to the Roosevelt station stop. Either board eastbound CTA bus 12 or the free Green Trolley to the Museum Campus, and then walk south to Soldier Field. Walking from Roosevelt station would take approximately 15 minutes...an alternate to waiting for the bus.

By Bus: CTA buses 12, 127, and 146 stop on McFetridge Drive near Soldier Field. Contact the RTA Information Center for routes and schedules at 312-836-7000 or online at www.rtachicago.com.

By Trolley: The Green Trolley travels along Michigan Avenue, Washington Street, Canal Street, and Adams Street to the Museum Campus. From there, you can walk south to the field. For routes and schedules, visit www.cityofchicago.org/transportation.

General Information

NFT Map: 13
Address: 333 W 35th St
Chicago, IL 60616
General Info: 312-674-1000
Ticket Sales: 866-SOX-GAME
Website: www.whitesox.com

Overview

Both of Chicago's major league ballparks are named for corporations (one famous for gum, the other famous for cell phones) but the similarities end there. Any White Sox fan will tell you: tourists pay big bucks to watch ivy grow in the little place on the North Side, real baseball fans head to see the White Sox play at US Cellular Field.

Straddled by the Bridgeport and Bronzeville neighborhoods on Chicago's south side, US Cellular Field opened in 1991 to replace the old Comiskey Park. The new park was built for $167 million—a relative bargain even in 1991. Cost-cutting meant altering the original design, though, and not for the better. What the park lacks in beauty, it makes up for with its friendly staff, terrific sightlines, and fabulous food—perennially rated among the best in Major League Baseball. Meat-eaters: Follow your nose to the grilled onions and say "Polish with." Better yet, say "Polish witt." You'll get a sublimely good Polish sausage smothered in caramelized onions. Come hungry on Thursdays: Ball Park Franks are $1 and Best's kosher hot dogs are $2.50 each at select concession stands during all Thursday home games.

Look around and you'll notice that most Sox fans do enjoy their food at the ballpark—not many anorexics or bulimics in this crowd. And if you're hoping to hear about fashion, or business deals, or coffee shops, this ain't the place. Fans here talk about baseball. They love the game, and they love the team that FINALLY brought a World Series trophy to Chicago in 2005.

Nancy Faust, the hardest-working (and most creative) organist in baseball, has been the official White Sox organist since 1970 and still plays day games. And Roger Bossard—an obsessive-compulsive turf guru who consults to sports franchises around the world—maintains one of the most beautiful, truest playing real-grass surfaces in all of sports. Bill Veeck's scoreboard explodes with fireworks at each home run, and street musicians serenade fans as they head to the red line or the parking lot after games. It's all just about perfect.

How to Get Tickets

Purchase tickets through the team's website (www.whitesox.com) or at the US Cellular Field Box Office (weekdays:10am–6pm, weekends:10am–4pm).Children shorter than the park's turnstile arm (approximately 36 inches) are admitted free, but must share your seat. Best

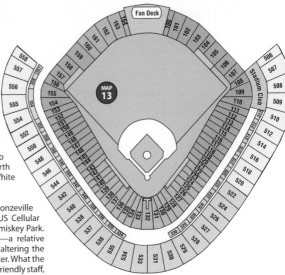

Ballpark bargain: Half-Price tickets available for all regular seats (except Premium Lower Box) on Monday home games. Check the website for Value Days schedules.

How to Get There

By Car: US Cellular Field is located at the 35th Street exit off the Dan Ryan Expressway. Take I-90/94, stay in the local lanes, and exit at 35th Street. If you possess a prepaid green parking coupon or plan on paying cash for parking ($18), exit at 35th Street. Follow signs to "Sox Parking" at lots E, F, and L on the stadium's south side. Fans with red, prepaid season parking coupons exit at 31st Street, and follow signs for "Red Coupons" to lots A, B, and C just north of the stadium. If the 35th Street exit is closed due to heavy traffic, which is often the case on game days, proceed to the 39th Street exit; turn right for "Sox Parking" and left for "Red Coupons." The handicapped parking and stadium drop-off area is in Lot D, west of the field and accessible via 37th Street.

By Bus: CTA buses 24 and 35 stop closest to the park. Others stopping in the vicinity are the 29, 44, and 39. Armies of cops surround the venue on game days because the neighborhood is rough, especially at night.

By L: Ride the Red Line to the Sox-35th Street stop just west of the ballpark. Another good option, especially heading north after the game, is the Green Line. The 35th-Bronzeville-IIT (Illinois Institute of Technology) Station is a little longer walk that the Sox 35th Street stop, but always less crowded.

General Information

NFT Map: 23
Address: 1901 W Madison St
                Chicago, IL 60612
Phone: 312-455-4500
Website: www.unitedcenter.com
Ticketmaster: 312-559-1212;
                www.ticketmaster.com
Chicago Bulls: 312-455-4000
Bulls Website: www.bulls.com
Chicago Blackhawks:
                312-455-7000
Blackhawks Website:
                www.chicagoblackhawks.com

Overview

The commanding crown of Chicago's developing West Town District, the United Center is home to both the NHL's Blackhawks and the NBA's Bulls. This ultra-high-tech stadium is also a theater, convention hall, and premier concert arena. Opened in 1994, the $175 million stadium was privately funded by deep-pocketed Blackhawks owner William Wirtz and penny-pinching Bulls majority owner Jerry Reinsdorf (a privately funded and owned stadium—what a concept!) and built to replace the beloved but aging Chicago Stadium. The Bulls have had trouble recapturing both the winning record and popularity they experienced during the Michael Jordan era; however, they still manage to sell out most of their home games. And just in case you forget whose "house" this is, the impressive statue of Michael Jordan located in front of the main entrance to the United Center is there to remind you.

Although it's been some time since the Blackhawks won the Stanley Cup (1961), the team enjoys unwavering support from its boisterous fans who relish games against their long-standing rivals, the St. Louis Blues. The Blackhawks' prior trips to the playoffs (2001–2002 season) and the lack of a season at all in 2004–2005 resulted in record attendance (but unfortunately not a record performance) for the 2006 season. Coach Dennis Savard, is now at the reins of this storied franchise and hopes to heat things up on the ice once again in 2009. Chicago Blackhawks fans are some of the more loyal in the NHL and will show up for 2009 in full battle gear. Suffice to say, nothing short of bringing home the Stanley Cup will do for this team and their devout fans. Even for non-hockey fans, a Blackhawks game is well worth the trip just to experience the unique and traditional way these fans approach the National Anthem. There is no silence here; instead, fans yell and cheer wildly to honor the USA.

How to Get Tickets

Book tickets over the phone or online with Ticketmaster, by United Center mail order, or visit the United Center box office at Gate 4. Box office hours are Monday to Saturday, 11 am to 6 pm. For Bulls and Blackhawks season tickets and group bookings call the phone numbers above.

How to Get There

By Car: From the Loop, drive west on Madison Street to United Center. From the north, take I-90/94 and exit at Madison Street; head west to the stadium. From the southwest, take I-55 N to the Damen/Ashland exit; head north to Madison Street. From the west, take I-290 E to the Damen Avenue exit; go north to Madison Street.

Parking lots surround United Center, as do countless cops. General public parking is in Lot B on Warren Boulevard (cars, $15–31; limo, RV, and bus parking, $25). Lot H on Wood Street is closest to the stadium and is reserved for VIPs. Disabled parking is in Lots G and H on Damen Avenue.

By L: Take the Forest Park Branch of the Blue Line to the Medical Center-Damen Avenue Station. Walk two blocks north to United Center.

By Bus: CTA bus 19 United Center Express is the most intelligent and safest choice. In service only on event and game days, this express bus travels from Chicago Avenue south down Michigan Avenue, then west along Madison Street to the United Center. Michigan Avenue stops are at Chicago Avenue, Illinois Street, and Randolph Street. On Madison Street, stops are at State Street, Wells Street, and Clinton Street ($1.75 one-way). Service starts two hours before events and continues for 45 minutes after events. CTA bus 20 also travels Madison Street beginning at Wabash Avenue and has "owl service."

General Information

NFT Map:	43
Address:	1060 W Addison St
	Chicago, IL 60613
Cubs Box Office Phone:	773-404-2827
Tickets.com:	800-THE-CUBS (843-2827)
Lost & Found:	773-404-4185
Website:	www.cubs.com

Overview

In 2009, Wrigley Field will play host to the Chicago Cubs for the 94th year. Unfortunately, it has been even longer since the team has claimed a title. Built in 1914 and originally known as Weeghman Park, the stadium was renamed Wrigley Field in 1926 to honor chewing gum mogul and former Cub owner William Wrigley, Jr. It is the second-oldest ball park in Major League Baseball (Boston's Fenway Park—1912) and is a refreshing throwback to simpler times. Ivy-strewn walls, a Merion Bluegrass and clover field, and a manual scoreboard transcend both time and technology during this age of artificial playing surfaces and high-tech super stadiums. The glow from night game lights warms the hearts of most North Chicago locals who aren't game attendees. On the other side of the fence, Wrigleyville activists have lobbied to limit the amount of time the lights are burning, in an attempt to limit their neighborhood's party reputation, to stop drunks peeing in alleyways, and to protect their over-inflated property values.

Wrigley Field has been the site of some of baseball's most historic moments: Ernie Banks' 500th career home run in 1970, Kerry Wood's twenty strikeouts in 1998, and Sammy Sosa's sixty home runs in 1998, 1999, and 2001. The Cubs haven't won a World Series title since their back-to-back wins over Detroit in 1907 and 1908, and haven't appeared in the Fall Classic since 1945, yet this loveable losing team has one of the most impressive attendance records in Major League Baseball. Of course, most patrons pay no attention to the game as an outing to Wrigley has become an opportunity to drink beer and "be seen." Every year, faithful fans claim this is their year…but 2009 looks to be no better. Regardless of whether the Cubs win or lose, they still get to call "The Friendly Confines" home. Nostalgia for the "old school" landmark ballpark has many fans challenging recent proposals to expand Wrigley Field.

How to Get Tickets

Individual game tickets can be purchased from the Cubs' website, by calling 800-843-2827, or in person at some Chicagoland Tickets.com outlets (if you're hanging out in Indiana or Wisconsin). You can also buy tickets at the Wrigley Field Box Office, open weekdays from 8 am to 6 pm and weekends from 9 am to 4 pm. You can usually score discount tickets to afternoon games Monday through Thursday in April, May, and September, or by waiting around the ballpark until the game starts. Especially when they are in the typical six-game losing skid. Children aged two and up require tickets.

How to Get There

By Car: If you must… Remember the old days when Wrigleyville hillbillies used to let you park on their front lawns for five bucks? Well, today traffic on game days is horrendous, and parking prices are sky-high. Post-game spill-out from local bars and dozens of mindless cab drivers freeze traffic as police do their best to prevent drunken revelers from stumbling into the streets. From the Loop or south, take Lake Shore Drive north; exit at Irving Park Road, and head west to Clark Street; turn south on Clark Street to Wrigley Field. From the north, take Lake Shore Drive to Irving Park Road; head west to Clark Street, and turn south. From Chicago's West Side, take I-290 E or I-55 N to Lake Shore Drive, then follow directions above. From the northwest, take I-90 E and exit at Addison Street; travel east three miles. From the southwest side, take I-55 N to I-90/94 N. Exit at Addison Street; head east to the park.

Street parking around Wrigley Field is heavily restricted and nearly impossible. The Cubs operate a garage at 1126 W Grace Street. Purchase parking passes through the mail or at the Wrigley Field Box Office. On game nights, tow trucks cruise Wrigleyville's streets nabbing cars without a resident permit sticker. Park smart at the DeVry Institute, and catch CTA bus 154/Wrigley Express to and from the park. ($6 covers parking and roundtrip shuttle per carload.)

By L: Riding the Howard/Dan Ryan Red Line used to be the fastest and easiest way to get to Wrigley Field ($2.00 one-way). It is still easy but recent CTA overhauls, due to mismanagement, embezzlement and general misbehavior have greatly reduced service and increased wait time. Get off at the Addison Street stop one block east of the field.

By Bus: CTA buses 22, 8, and 152 stop closest to Wrigley Field ($2.00 one-way). For routes and schedules, visit www.rtachicago.com.

Every time the Olympics hit your TV screen, you say to yourself, "Geez. This spring, I will really do it! I will get in shape, by gum!" And are you bored with the gym scene? Do you want to make new friends? Chicago has many opportunities to get out and meet new people in its multitudinous leagues and training clubs. Though we were voted the 2006 Fattest City in America by Men's Fitness magazine (taking over the top spot from Houston, the champ in 2001, 2002, and 2005), you wouldn't know it from the number of sports opportunities available to area residents.

General Tips

If you're interested in finding a specific league or group for a particular sport, a good place to start is *Chicago Athlete* magazine. This free publication is available online at www.chicagoaa.com and is on hand at many of the downtown athletic clubs and the Chicago Department of Tourism. You can look at the site to see which places carry it.

If you're a beginner, before you go spending a ton of money on your sport of choice, check out the Chicago Park District's website to see if they offer something near you on the cheap. They offer loads of clubs, training groups, and classes on a wide range of sports from archery to weightlifting to yoga. Their handy online program guide lets you search by age group, parks, program type, or zip code. The latter is particularly handy if you don't know where to find your local park district building. Check out their site for an excellent starting point for many sports teams and clubs.

Multiple Sports Leagues and Clubs

Chicago Sport and Social Club (www.chicagosportandsocialclub.com) is the mother of all of the Windy City leagues. Offering volleyball, basketball, football, floor hockey, soccer, dodge ball, dance, bowling, running, kickball, yoga, softball, rock climbing, kayaking, tennis, boot camp and boxing fitness, and even bar games (such as euchre, darts, and pool), this league has it all. Even if you're not interested in joining, you can watch the league's be-thonged hardbodies spike the ball around every summer at Oak Street Beach or vicariously take in an aerobics class while you burn your hide to a crisp.

If you're interested in something a little more (how do we put this?) *queer* in your sports experience, then join the Chicago Metropolitan Sports Association (www.chicagomsa.com). This non-profit is the largest gay and lesbian sports organization in the Midwest. Offering badminton, bowling, flag football, soccer, co-ed and women's softball, tennis, and volleyball, this league is the best place to meet other queer jocks for pick-ups (games and otherwise) and fun in the sun. Again, if you're not interested in playing, it's fun to watch. The games take place along the lakefront. Check their website for more information and game times.

Running

By far, most of the area sports groups and clubs are focused on running. We're not sure why that is, but if you're training for a running event, say, the Chicago Marathon or your first 5K, Chicago Area Runner's Association (www.cararuns.org) has you covered. This organization is for all levels of runners—from the seasoned marathoner to the amateur looking to begin running for the first time. With group runs, clinics, training programs, and a monthly newsletter, this organization has it all for anyone wanting to feel the gravel beneath their New Balances, the wind in their hair, and the lakefront gnats in their teeth.

Triathlon

Want to "tri" something a little more involved? How about a triathlon? The city offers tons of opportunities to get involved with this swim-bike-run race. These clubs run the gamut from volunteer-driven organizations to professional training for a fee. Check out Chicago Endurance Sports (www.chicagoendurancesports.com), Chicago Tri Club (www.chicagotriclub.com), Lakeview YMCA Triathlon Club (www.lakeviewymca.org/proTriathlon.html), or Together We Tri (www.togetherwetri.com). With any of these groups, you can expect to join a group that will tailor your workouts to your needs, find a supportive team environment, attend clinics on transitions and the individual sports, and get a training schedule that you can use on your non-group workout days.

Rugby

If rugby's your game, then Chicago has opportunities to join in the fun and violence. Two women's teams dominate the Chicago scene—North Shore Women's Rugby (www.northshorerugby.com) and Chicago Women's Rugby (www.cwrfc.com). For the men, Chicago offers more opportunities: Chicago Griffins Rugby Club (www.chicagogriffins.com), Chicago Lions Rugby Football Club (www.chicagolions.com), Lincoln Park Rugby Football Club (www.lprfc.com), and the South Side Irish Rugby (www.southsideirishrugby.com).

Miscellaneous

If you're interested in swimming, the Central Masters Swimming Association website has everything you're looking for. Check them out at www.chicagomasters.com. If soccer is more your thing, see the Chicago Area Soccer Association at the League Republic's website (www.leaguerepublic.com/soccer.jsp). While their site is less than user-friendly, you can click on "league search" in the upper right-hand corner of the page and type "Chicago" into the search engine. From there, you can find all of the teams you might want to join. Want to rollerblade? Get Inline... Chicagoland is the club for you! Check 'em out at www.getinlinechicagoland.com.

Whether you're an amateur or a seasoned veteran, Chicago offers many opportunities to get out there and become a jock! Check out these options, and have some fun while getting healthier.

General Information

Address:	10000 W O'Hare
	Chicago, IL 60666
Phone:	773-686-2200 / 800-832-6352
Website:	www.ohare.com
Ground Transportation:	773-686-8040
Lost & Found:	773-894-8760
Parking:	773-686-7530
Traveler's Aid:	773-894-2427
Police:	773-686-2385
Customs Information:	773-894-2900

Overview

O'Delay might be a more fitting name for O'Hare, although Beck might take exception to such a name change. What else can we say about one of the world's busiest airports? To its credit, O'Hare, located in one of the country's most unpredictable weather zones, serves more than 190,000 travelers daily. While the airport is located just 17 miles northwest of the Loop, it's wise to leave the better part of a day to locate and arrive at your departure gate. Commuter traffic, airline snafus, parking, security checks, snowstorms, airport construction, and roadwork can make traveling from O'Hare as pleasurable as a migraine. In the event that you do get to your gate early, take advantage of the free Wi-Fi available to download some relaxing meditation tunes. Also, keep in mind if you're taking a red-eye flight that most eateries and shops are closed at night and early morning, so bring your own grub and entertainment, just don't bring it in an eyedropper or stored in the sole of your shoe.

Expansion spells relief, according to Mayor Daley, who is pushing a controversial $6.6-billion plan designed to double O'Hare's capacity and secure its "busiest" title for the rest of the 21st century. The plan calls for building another runway, reconfiguring the other seven, building an additional entrance on the airport's west side, and spending millions soundproofing area homes and schools. Recently political opposition has thrown up hefty lawsuits to block legislation that would cement the deal into federal law.

Meanwhile, the rest of us are stuck in traffic, in line, on the runway, etc…

How to Get There

By Car: If you must drive, pack aspirin in your glove compartment along with your favorite CDs because the crawl down the Kennedy will probably be the most grueling part of your entire trip. To be on the safe side, allow over an hour just for the drive (more during rush hours). From the Loop to O'Hare, take I-90 W. From the north suburbs, take I-294 S. From the south suburbs, take I-294 N. From the west suburbs, take I-88 E to I-294 N. Get off all of the above highways at I-190, which leads you directly to the airport. All of the major routes have clear signage, easily legible when you're moving at a snail's pace.

Parking: O'Hare Airport's parking garage reflects its hometown's passion for sports. All levels of the Main Parking Garage are "helpfully" labeled with Chicago sports teams' colors and larger-than-life logos (Wolves, Bulls, Blackhawks, White Sox, Bears, and Cubs). Annoying elevator muzak whines each team's fight song. If this isn't enough to guide you to your car, we can't help you, because the garage's numbering-alphabetical system is more aggravating than the tinny elevator tunes.

How to Get There—*continued*

If you're parking for less than three hours, go to Level 1. Parking costs $4 for the first 3 hours, $10 for up to 4 hours, and a deterring $50 per day. Overnight parking close to Terminals 1, 2, and 3 on Levels 2 through 6 of the garage or in outside lots B and C costs $30 a day. For flyers with cash to burn, valet parking is available on Level 1 of the garage for $10 per hour or $45 per day (8–24 hours). Parking in the International Terminal 5's designated Lot D costs $3 per hour for the first two hours and $2 per hour thereafter; the daily rate is $30; $50 for five days. Incoming international passengers always disembark in Terminal 5 (even if the airline departs from another terminal) because passengers must clear customs.

Long-term parking lots are Economy Lots E ($16), F ($9), and G ($13). From Lot E, walk or take the free shuttle to the free Airport Transit System (ATS) train station servicing all terminals. From Lot G, the shuttle will take you to the ATS stop in Lot E. Budget-conscious frequent flyers may want to purchase a prepaid Lot E "ExpressLane Parking" windshield tag for hassle-free, speedy departure from the airport.

By Bus: CTA buses 220 and 330 stop at the airport. If you're not near either of those bus lines, your best bet is to take your nearest bus line north or south to one of the O'Hare Blue Line train stations. The CTA also offers a special door-to-door service to and from the airport for Chicago-area residents and out-of-towners needing extra assistance. Call 312-663-4357 for additional information.

By Train: The odds of the Metra's schedule conveniently coinciding with your flight time are only slightly better than those of the Bulls winning the championship this year. The Wisconsin North Central Line departs Union Station for Antioch with a stop at the O'Hare Transfer station five times

a day, starting in the afternoons on weekdays only ($3.30 one-way). Travel time is 30 minutes.

By L: We recommend the Blue Line as the best transportation method if you don't have several large bags or dependents in tow. The train runs between downtown Chicago and O'Hare 24 hours a day every 8 to 10 minutes ($2 one-way or $1.75 with Chicago Card). Travel time from the Loop is 45 minutes. The train station is on the lowest level of the airport's main parking garage. Walk through the underground pedestrian tunnels to Terminals 1, 2, and 3. If you're headed for the International Terminal 5, walk to Terminal 3 and board the free Airport Transit System (ATS) train.

By Cab: Join the cab queue at the lower level curb-front of all terminals. There are no flat rates, as all of the cabs run on meters, but you probably won't have to spend more than $40. Some cab companies servicing O'Hare include American United, 773-262-8633; Flash Cab, 773-878-8500; Jiffy Cab, 773-487-9000; Yellow Cab, 312-808-9130; and Dispatch, 312-829-4222. Beware if you're traveling to certain suburbs, though. Fare rules allow cabbies to raise your fare for these routes by 50%! Ask what the fare will be when you enter the cab.

By Kiss & Fly: The Kiss & Fly is a convenient drop-off and pick-up point for "chauffeurs" who want to avoid the inevitable chaos at the terminal curb-side. Flyers should leave enough time for the ATS transfer to their terminals. The Kiss & Fly zone is off Bessie Coleman Drive. Take I-190 to the International Terminal exit to Bessie Coleman Drive. Turn left at the light and follow Bessie Coleman Drive north to the Kiss & Fly entrance and ATS stop.

By Shuttle: Continental Airport Express (773-247-1200 or 888-2-THEVAN) provides a daily shuttle service between O'Hare and downtown Chicago from 6 am until 11:30

pm with departures approximately every 10–15 minutes. Shuttles stop at all major downtown hotels. Tickets cost $25 one-way ($46 return) for individuals, $18 per person ($34 return) for pairs going to the same destination and returning together, and $14 per person ($27 return) for three or more going to the same downtown destination and returning together. Shuttle ticket counters are located in the baggage claim areas of Terminal 1 by Door 1E and Terminal 3 at Door 3E; however, shuttles pick up passengers at Terminals 1, 2, 3, and 5. If you haven't pre-purchased a ticket at a counter, have cash ready for the driver.

Omega Airport Shuttle offers hourly service between O'Hare and Midway beginning around 7 am each day 'til about 11:45 pm and between Hyde Park and O'Hare from 5 am to 11:45 pm. The shuttle leaves from the International Terminal's outside curb by Door 5E and from the airport's Bus Shuttle Center in front of the O'Hare Hilton Hotel by Door 4. Allow at least an hour for travel time between the airports and expect to pay $17 for a one-way fare. Omega also has over 20 pickup and drop-off locations on the South Side serving O'Hare and Midway Airports. (773-734-6688; www.omegashuttle.com).

By Limousine: Sounds pricey, but depending on where you're going and how many people you are traveling with, it may be cheaper to travel by limo than by cab or shuttle. Advance reservations recommended. Limo services include O'Hare-Midway Limousine Service, 312-558-1111 (or 800-468-8989 for airport pick-up), www.ohare-midway.com; and My Chauffeur/American Limo, 847-376-6100, www.mychauffeurchicago.com.

Airlines

Airline	Terminal	Phone
Aer Lingus	5	888-474-7424
Aero Mexico	5	800-237-6639
Air Canada	2	888-247-2262
Air Canada Jazz	2	888-247-2262
Air France	5	800-237-2747
Air India	5	800-621-8231
Air Jamaica	5	800-523-5585
Alaska Airlines	3	800-252-7522
Alitalia	5	800-223-5730
All Nippon	1, 5	800-235-9262
America West	2	800-843-9322
American Airlines:		800-443-7300
Domestic	3	
International	3 dep/5 arr	
American Eagle	3	800-433-7300
Asiana Airlines	5	800-227-4262
Austrian Airlines	5	800-843-0002
British Airways	5	800-247-9297
BMI British Midland	5	800-788-0555
Cayman Airways	5	800-422-9626
Continental Airlines	2	800-525-0280
Delta Airlines	3	800-221-1212
El Al	5	800-223-6700
Iberia Airlines	3 dep/5 arr	800-772-4642
Japan Airlines JAL	5	800-525-3663

Airline	Terminal	Phone
JetBlue	2	800-538-2583
KLM Royal Dutch Airlines	5	800-225-2525
Korean Air	5	800-438-5000
LOT Polish Airlines	5	212-789-0970
Lufthansa	1 dep/5 arr	800-645-3880
Mexicana Airlines	5	800-531-7921
Northwest Airlines:		
Domestic	2	800-225-2525
International	2	800-447-4747
Pakistan International Airlines	5	800-221-6024
Royal Jordanian	5	800-223-0470
Scandinavian Airlines (SAS)	5	800-221-2350
South African Airways	5	800-521-4845
Spirit Airlines	3	800-772-7117
Swiss International Airlines	5	877-359-7947
TACA Airlines	5	800-400-8222
Ted Airlines	1	800-225-5833
Turkish Airlines	5	800-874-8875
United Airlines:		800-241-6522
Domestic/International dep	1, 2	
International arr	5	
United Express	1, 2	800-241-6522
US Airways	2	800-428-4322
USA 3000	5	877-872-3000
Virgin Atlantic	5	800-821-5438

Car Rental

Alamo • 560 Bessie Coleman Dr., 800-327-9633/773-694-4646
Avis • 10000 Bessie Coleman Dr, 800-331-1212/ 773-825-4600
Budget • 580 Bessie Coleman Dr, 800-527-0700/773-894-1900
Dollar • O'Hare Intl Arpt, 800-800-4000/866-434-2226

Enterprise • 4025 Mannheim Rd, 800-867-4595/847-928-3320
Hertz • 10000 Bessie Coleman Dr, 800-654-3131/773-686-7272
National • 560 Bessie Coleman Dr, 800-227-7368/773-694-4646
Thrifty • 3901 N Mannheim Rd, 847-928-2000

Hotels

All shuttles to airport hotels depart from the Bus Shuttle Center in front of the O'Hare Hilton Hotel in the center of the airport.

Best Western • 10300 W Higgins Rd, 847-296-4471
Clarion • 5615 N Cumberland Ave, 773-693-5800
Courtyard • 2950 S River Rd, 847-824-7000
Crown Plaza • 5440 N River Rd, 847-671-6350
Days Inn • 1920 E Higgins Rd, 847-437-1650
Comfort Inn • 2175 E Touhy Ave, 847-635-1300
DoubleTree • 5460 N River Rd, 847-292-9100
Embassy Suites • 5500 N River Rd, 847-678-4000
Four Points Sheraton • 10249 W Irving Park Rd, 847-671-6000
Hampton Inn • 3939 N Mannheim Rd, 847-671-1700
Hawthorn Suites • 1251 American Ln, 847-706-9007
Hilton • O'Hare Intl Arprt, 773-686-8000
Holiday Inn • 10233 W Higgins Rd, 847-954-8600
Hotel Sofitel • 5550 N River Rd, 847-678-4488

Hyatt Regency • 9300 W Bryn Mawr Ave, 847-696-1234
Hyatt Rosemont • 6350 N River Rd, 847-518-1234
La Quinta Inn • 1900 E Oakton St, 847-439-6767
Marriott Suites • 6155 N River Rd, 847-696-4400
Marriott Hotel • 8535 W Higgins Rd, 773-693-4444
Ramada Plaza • 5615 N Mannheim Rd, 773-693-5800
Residence Inn • 7101 Chestnut St, 847-375-9000
Sheraton Suites • 6501 N Mannheim Rd, 847-699-6300
InTown Suites • 2411 Landmeier Rd, 847-228-5500
Super 8 • 2951 Touhy Ave, 847-827-3133
Travelodge • 3003 Mannheim Rd, 847-296-5541
Westin • 6100 N River Rd, 847-698-6000
Wyndham • 6810 N Mannheim Rd, 847-297-1234

General Information

Address:	5757 S Cicero Ave
	Chicago, IL 60638
Phone:	773-838-0600
Website:	www.midwayairport.org
Police:	773-838-3003
Parking:	773-838-0756
Customs:	773-948-6330

Overview

Located just ten miles southwest of downtown Chicago is Midway—one of the fastest-growing airports in the country serving 47,000 passengers daily. Considered the city's outlet mall of airports, Midway primarily provides service from budget carriers like Southwest Airlines and ATA. On the positive side, it is an easy alternative to the nightmare named O'Hare. Plus the bars for pre-flight entertainment aren't as crowded.

Expect Midway to gain altitude in national airport rankings with the recent completion of its $793 million terminal development. After ten years of planning and construction, the new features include a swank new terminal building, new concourses, a 3,000-space parking facility, food court, retail corridor, and a customs facility to facilitate international flights. In 2003, Concourses G and H were demolished to allow for the expansion of Concourse B. All the changes have upped Midway's jet gate count from 29 to 43.

Superstitious travelers beware of flying December 8th. On this date in 1972, a Boeing 737 crashed into a residential area during landing. In 2005, exactly 33 years later another Boeing slid off the runway in a landing attempt on December 8. Spooky.

How To Get There

By Car: From downtown, take I-55 S. From the northern suburbs, take I-290 S to I-55 N. From the southern suburbs, take I-294 N to I-55 N. From the western suburbs, take I-88 E to I-294 S to I-55 N. Whether you're traveling north or south along I-55, look for the Cicero Avenue/South/Midway Airport exit.

By Bus: CTA buses 55, 59, and 63 all run from points east to the airport. Take the Green Line or the Red Line to the Garfield Station and transfer to bus 55 heading west ($1.75 one-way including transfer). If you're coming from the south on the Red Line, get off at the 63rd Street stop and take bus 63 westbound ($1.80 one-way). Other buses that terminate at the airport include 54B, 379, 382, 383, 384, 385, 386, 831, and 63W.

By L: A 30-minute train ride on the Orange Line is the most convenient and cost-effective method for travel between the Loop and Midway Airport ($2, $1.75 with Chicago Card). The Orange Line's first train departs from Midway Station (last stop on the line's southern end) for the Loop at 3:55 am daily and 5:35 am on Sundays and holidays. The first train of the day from the Loop's Adams/Wabash Station at 4:29 am arrives at Midway at 4:54 am, well in advance of the airport's first early bird flight. The last train from Midway to the Loop departs at 12:56 am and arrives at 1:23 am. The final Midway-bound owl train departs from the Adams/Wabash stop around 1:29 am, arriving at Midway by 1:53 am. Trains run every five to seven minutes during rush hours, ten minutes most other times, and fifteen minutes late evenings. We recommend that wee-hours travelers stay alert at all times.

By Cab: Cabs depart from the lower level of the main terminal and are available on a first-come-first-served basis. There are no flat rates (all cabs run on meters), but you can plan on paying around $25 to get to the Loop. Some cab companies servicing Midway include American United, 773-262-8633; Flash Cab, 773-878-8500; Flash Dispatch, 773-561-1444; Jiffy Cab, 773-487-9000; and Yellow Cab, 312-808-9130.

By Shuttle: Continental Airport Express (773-247-1200 or 888-2-THEVAN) travels between Midway and downtown and some northern suburban locations from 6 am until 10:30 pm. Shuttles depart every 15 minutes and make stops at all major downtown hotels. Tickets cost $20 one-way ($36 roundtrip) for individuals, $14 per person for pairs going to the same destination ($26 roundtrip), and $12 per person for three or more going to the same downtown destination ($22 roundtrip). The ticket counter and loading zone are in the terminal's lower level across from the baggage claim area by door LL3. To calculate a shuttle fare to north suburb locations, use the online fare calculator at www.airportexpress.com.

Omega Airport Shuttle (773-483-6634; www.omegashuttle.com) offers service leaving every 45 minutes or so between Midway and O'Hare beginning around 7 am each day with the final shuttle departing around 10 pm. Allow at least an hour for travel time between the airports and expect to pay $16 one-way. Contact Omega for information on more than 20 pickup locations on the South Side, to confirm schedules, to make reservations, and to prearrange home pickups.

By Limousine: Sounds pricey, but depending on where you're going and how many people you are traveling with, it may be cheaper to travel by limo than by cab or shuttle. Advance reservations recommended. Limo services include O'Hare-Midway Limousine Service, 312-558-1111 (or 800-468-8989 for airport pick-up), www.ohare-midway.com; and My Chauffeur/American Limo, 847-376-6100, www.americanlimousine.com

Parking

Short-term parking is on the first floor. Parking is free for the first ten minutes, then $4 for 30 minutes to an hour. Add an additional $2 for every hour thereafter, up to $50 for 24 hours. Levels 4, 5, and 6 have the same rates for short-term parking, but the prices level off after four hours so that it only costs $36 per day. If you're planning on parking for a while, the best option is the economy lot for $14 a day on Cicero Avenue at 55th Street, a quarter-mile away. Allow extra time to take the free shuttle between the lot and the terminal.

A new 6,300-space economy parking garage opened in December 2005 at the northwest corner of 55th Street and Laramie Avenue. Rates start at $2 for the first hour, $5 for the first two hours, and $12 for two to 24 hours.

Airlines

Concourse A

Air Midwest	800-637-2247
Air Tran	800-825-8538
ComAir	800-927-0927
Delta	800-221-1212
Frontier	800-432-1359
Northwest	800-225-2525
Southwest	800-435-9792
Ted/United Express	800-225-5833

Concourse B

ATA	800-225-2995
Southwest	800-435-9792

Concourse C

American	800-433-7300
Continental/ Continental Express	800-525-0280

Car Rental

Alamo	800-327-9633	Enterprise	800-566-9249
Avis	800-331-1212	Hertz	800-654-3131
Budget	800-527-7000	National	800-227-7368
Dollar	800-800-4000	Thrifty	800-527-7075

Hotels

Best Western • 8220 S Cicero Ave, 708-497-3000
Fairfield Inn • 6630 S Cicero Ave, 708-594-0090
Hampton Inn • 6540 S Cicero Ave, 708-496-1900
Hilton • 9333 S Cicero Ave, 708-425-7800
Holiday Inn Express • 6500 S Cicero Ave, 708-458-0202
Marriott Midway • 6520 S Cicero Ave, 708-594-5500
Courtyard Midway • 6610 S Cicero Ave, 708-563-0200
Sleep Inn • 6650 S Cicero Ave, 708-594-0001

General Information

Mailing address:
Chicago Transit Authority
Merchandise Mart Pl, 7th Fl
PO Box 3555
Chicago, IL 60654

Phone: 312-664-7200
CTA information: 888-YOUR CTA (968-7282)
Website: www.transitchicago.com

Overview

Once you figure out its complicated card system, CTA service will, eventually, get you relatively close to where you need to go (most of the time), and sometimes the city's trains and buses are even on schedule!

For location-to-location CTA directions and schedules, we honestly and without irony, recommend the useful CTA trip planner at tripsweb.rtachicago.com. It allows you to plan your course by either estimated departure times or planned arrival times.

Fares and Fare Cards

The city's tiered, pain-in-the-ass approach to fare payment makes it more expensive to pay with cash and easier to pay with cards. They don't call Chicago the city that works your nerves for nothing.

In a nutshell, you must use a card to ride the L train or to transfer. You can use a card or pay cash on the bus, but you cannot transfer with a cash purchase. Furthermore, cash fares are $2 per each leg of the journey, whereas card fares are $1.75 and an additional 25 cents for up to three more transfers within two hours (the transfer rate is deducted from your card on the next leg of your journey).

The easiest way to get around all this gobbledygook? Just buy a visitor's pass.
• 1-Day Visitor Pass for $5
• 2-Day Visitor Pass for $9
• 3-Day Visitor Pass for $12
• 5-Day Visitor Pass for $18

Visitor passes give you unlimited rides on all CTA buses, L trains and PACE (suburban) buses, but CTA Visitor Passes are not valid on Metra (commuter railroad) trains.

Your visitor pass activates the first time you use it—it's good for the number of consecutive days shown on the front of the card. Example: a 3-day pass is valid for 72 hours from the first time you insert it into the card reader on el turnstiles or inside the bus. At that point the expiration date and time will be printed on the back of the card.

Here's a breakdown on the benefits, limitations, and rules for fare methods..

Cash: Cash fares are $2 and only available on city buses. You must use a fare card to ride the L. You cannot buy a transfer with a cash fare. Each leg of the journey will cost $2 ($1 for applicable reduced-fare passengers). To pay with cash, insert bills or change into the money eater inside the bus. You must use exact change. No change will be given.

Fare Card: You can purchase the standard paper fare card at any L station from the big blue fare card machines. Fare cards can be purchased in any amount (fare minimum is $1.75) and used on the bus or L. Fares are $1.75, plus 25 cents to transfer. Purchasing a fare card is easy—insert the amount of money you want on your card into the money-eater (whether it will actually accept your crinkly or faded dollar bills or spit them back out at you is entirely another matter), and push the "vend" button. Your card will pop out of the slot (at roughly waist level) below the money eater. Lost or stolen fare cards are not replaceable. Money can be added at any fare card machine. To use a fare card, insert it into the card reader on CTA turnstiles or inside the bus (next to the bus money-eater). No change is given from CTA fare card machines.

Chicago Card: The Chicago Card can be purchased online (allow about a week for delivery) or at participating Jewel and Dominick's grocery store locations and some currency exchanges (go to their website for addresses of participating vendors). Chicago cards can be purchased for predetermined amounts ($10, $20) or for specific amounts. Balances can be checked, and Chicago Cards can be reloaded at CTA Fare card machines. Touch the card to the Chicago Card sensor, enter your reload amount into the money eater, and retouch your card to the sensor until the readout says, "Thank you." Do not forget to retouch your card to the sensor after adding money, or the money will not be added to your card. There is a 10% bonus for every increment of $20 added to your card—for $20, you get a $2 bonus, for $40, a $4 bonus and so on. To use the Chicago Card, simply press it against the sensor at the turnstile or on the bus. Lost or stolen Chicago Cards can be replaced, with their remaining value, for $5 if you chose the option to register the card (optional card registration is free, so why not?).

Chicago Plus Card: The Chicago Plus card is like the Chicago Card except for a few key differences. Registration of the Chicago Plus card is mandatory. Card balances can only be checked and/or have money added (credit card only) online or by calling CTA customer service. With the Chicago Plus card, you have the option of choosing pay-as-you-go or purchasing a monthly pass. You must have an e-mail address to use a Chicago Plus card. Like the regular Chicago Card, there is a $5 fee to replace your Chicago Card Plus if it is lost or stolen.

Pass Back Option: At any time, you can share your CTA card with up to six other people traveling with you by passing the card back over the turnstile. The full fare for each rider will be deducted from your card.

Reduced Fares: Reduced fares are available for qualified passengers—people with disabilities, senior citizens, and children under 12. Regular cash fare for kid's ages 7–11 is $1. Children under age 7 ride free.

Go to the CTA website for more information about reduced fare applicability at www.transitchicago.com.

CTA Buses

CTA's buses cart about one million sweaty, crabby passengers around Chicago and its surrounding suburbs everyday; the fleet is the second-largest public transportation system in the US. CTA's 152 bus routes mirror Chicago's efficient grid system. The majority of CTA routes run north-south or east-west, and in areas where the streets are numbered, the bus route is usually the same as the street.

Recently, the entire CTA bus fleet has been overhauled to comply with ADA accessibility standards. The result is that now all buses kneel, that is, they tilt to make the first step less steep. All buses are equipped with wheelchair lifts and secure wheelchair seating. Additionally, as a boon to the

visually impaired and those too busy gawking at Chicago's skyscrapers to read the signs on the front of each bus, all buses clearly and loudly announce the bus number and direction at every stop.

Bus Stops: CTA stops are clearly marked with blue and white signs displaying the name and number of the route, as well as the final destination. Most routes operate from the early morning until 10:30 pm. Night routes, called "Night Owls," are identified on bus stop signage by an owl picture. Owl service runs approximately every half-hour through the night.

Fares: Buses accept exact fare only for individual rides. A regular one-way cash fare is $2. Transfers are not available with cash fares. Bus fares can also be paid with CTA fare cards or Chicago and Chicago Plus cards. In this case, the fare is $1.75, plus 25 cents for up to two transfers within two hours. The transfer fee will be charged at the next leg of your journey. You must always insert your fare card into the card machine, or press your Chicago Card on the sensor — even for the free transfer. No money will be deducted for the third leg of a journey after a transfer has been purchased (within the two hour limit).

Bicycles Onboard: Designated CTA buses are equipped with bike racks mounted on front grills to carry up to two bikes. Generally speaking, CTA bike buses are those that travel to lakefront beaches, like the 63rd Street, the #72 North Avenue buses, #77 Belmont, or the #92 Foster Avenue bus. Additional buses with bike racks are often added during summer months or for special events.

Loading your bike onto a CTA bus:
• If your bike is the first to be loaded, lower the rack and place it in position with the front wheel facing the curb.
• If there is already a bike on the rack, place your bike's rear wheel toward the curb.
• If two bikes are already loaded and the rack is full; wait for the next bus.

Transit · The L

Blue Line O'Hare, Forest Park, Cermak
Brown Line Ravenswood
Green Line Lake, Ashland/63rd, East 63rd
Pink Line Douglas Branch
Orange Line Midway
Purple Line Evanston Shuttle and Express
Purple Line Express Weekday rush hours only
Red Line Howard, Dan Ryan
Yellow Line Skokie Swift
Free train connections at station

Lake Michigan

Inset

○ Elevated train lines
Ⓣ Free train connections at station
Ⓣ-Ⓣ Walk between stations for free connection

Overview

Whether traveling underground, on street level, or above the sidewalk, Chicagoans refer to their elevated rapid transit system as the "L." (Though some prefer to call it the "Smell.") No matter which one you choose, either name says Chicago as loud and clear as the high-pitched whine, guttural grumble, and steely grind of the train itself. L tracks lasso Chicago's heart, creating The Loop, where five of the seven L lines ride side-by-side above the pulsating business and financial district.

L trains make 1,452 trips each day and serve 143 stations in the Chicago Metropolitan Area. The numerous track delays and stalls in service are a burden to thousands of daily commuters. Nonetheless, due to the general directness of the L routes, easy station-to-station transfers, and the difficulties of parking (especially near popular destinations such as Grant Park and Wrigley Field), the benefits of L transportation usually outweigh the discomforts and inconveniences.

Fares

The standard full fare on CTA trains is $2 ($1.75 with Chicago Card). A 25¢ transfer allows two additional rides within two hours of issuance. Transfer rates are automatically deducted from your fare card when reused within the time limit. Transferring within the rail network is free at determined, connected transfer stations.

To ride the L, you need a farecard. Read the CTA Overview for a thorough discussion on the merits of each fare card option, or go to the CTA website at www.transitchicago.com.

Frequency of Service

CTA publishes schedules that say trains run every 3 to 12 minutes during weekday rush hours and every 6 to 20 minutes all other times. Nice idea, but the truth is service can be irregular, especially during non-rush hours, after-hours, and in bad weather. While the system is relatively safe late at night, stick to stations in populated areas as much as possible. Buses with Owl Service may be better options in the wee hours.

L Lines

Blue Line: Comprising the O'Hare, Forest Park, and Cermak branches traveling west, O'Hare and Forest Park run 24-hours, while Cermak is operational only on weekdays.

Pink Line: Last year Chicago's newest rail line took over the blue line route from the loop to 54th and Cermak.

Red Line: Runs north-south from the Howard Street station down to the 95th Street/Dan Ryan station; operates 24-hours.

Brown Line: Starts from the Kimball Street station and heads south with service to the Loop and sometimes just to Belmont Avenue. On weekdays and Saturdays, the first Loop-bound train leaves Kimball Street at 4:01 am; the last train to leave the Loop is at 12:18 am. Sunday service begins at: 4 am and ends at 11:40 pm. After that, take the Red Line to Belmont Avenue, and transfer to the Brown Line where the last train leaves at 2:25 am (12:55 am on Sundays). The Brown Line also runs between Kimball Street and Belmont Avenue from 4 am to 2:04 am weekdays and Saturdays; and from 5:01 am to 2:04 am on Sundays. Countdown to a new Brown: The 4-year Brown Line station renovation project is underway and the agonizing delays have already begun. At present, most of the affected stations are west of Western Avenue. Check the CTA website for the latest station closings.

Orange Line: Travels from Midway Airport to the Loop and back. Trains depart from Midway beginning at 3:55 am weekdays and Saturdays, and at 7 am on Sundays; the last train leaves the Loop for the airport at 1:29 am daily.

Green Line: Covers portions of west and south Chicago. The Harlem/Lake Street branch travels straight west. The Ashland Avenue/63rd Street and E 63rd Street/Cottage Grove branches go south and split east and west. Depending on the branch, service begins around 4 am weekdays with the last trains running around 1 am. Weekend schedules vary.

Purple Line: Shuttles north-south between Linden Place in suburban Wilmette and Howard Street, Chicago's northernmost station. Service starts at 4:35 am and ends at 12:55 am weeknights, 1:45 am on weekends, and 12:55 am Sundays. Weekdays, an express train runs between Linden Place and the Loop between 6:25 am and 10:10 am and then again between 2:55 pm and 6:15 pm. At all other times, take the **Purple Line Express** to the Howard Street station, and transfer to the Red Line to reach the Loop.

Yellow Line: Runs between the north suburban Skokie station and Chicago's Howard Street station on weekdays from 4:50 am to 10:18 pm. On weekends, take CTA bus 97 from Skokie station to Howard Street and catch the Red Line to the Loop.

Bicycles

Bicycles ride free and are permitted onboard at all times except weekdays from 7 am to 9 am and 4 pm to 6 pm. Only two bikes are allowed per car, so survey the platform for other bikes and check out the cars as they pull into the station for two-wheelers already onboard. When entering a station, either use the turnstile, or ask an attendant to open the gate. Don't try to take your bike through the tall steel gates—it WILL get stuck!

PACE Suburban – Chicago Buses

Pace buses serve over 35 million passengers in the Chicago suburbs and some parts of the city. With 240 routes covering 3,446 square miles, Pace provides a vital transportation service to commuters traveling between suburbs, within suburbs, to Metra train stations, and into the city. Buses usually run every 20–30 minutes, and service stops by mid-evening. Special express service is offered to Chicago-area entertainment and cultural venues. Contact Pace for specific bus route and schedule information (847-364-PACE; www.pacebus.com).

Park-n-Ride Stations: Pace has 11 Park-n-Ride stations located throughout Pace's six-county coverage area (check the Pace website for locations).

Fares: Pace fares cost $1.50 for regular service and $1.25 for local or feeder service. Transfers are $.25 for regular service. The one-way fare on express routes 355, 426, 835, and 855 costs $3. CTA Transit Cards may be used on Pace buses. Pace offers discounts for students, children, seniors, and disabled riders, as well as several bus pass package purchase options. Pass options include the Pace 30-Day Commuter Club Cards (CCC), which allows unlimited Pace rides for $50. A combined Pace/CTA 30-day unlimited pass costs $75 and can be used on all Pace buses and CTA trains and buses. The PlusBus Sticker (sold by Metra with a Metra Monthly Train Pass) costs $30 and allows unlimited Pace bus use.

Greyhound Buses

Greyhound is the rock-bottom traveler's best friend. The bus line offers dirt-cheap fares, the flexibility drifters prefer, basic station amenities (i.e. dirty toilets and vending machines that steal your money), and the gritty, butt-busting experience of traveling America's scenic blue-line highways and rural byways with some colorful characters.

Tips on riding "the Dog" out of town:
- Pack your own toilet paper and Wet Ones.
- Air freshener, deodorant, a pillow, and earplugs make being bused more bearable.
- Pack a cooler. Then padlock it.
- Charge your iPod. Seriously.
- Bring a cushion.
- Get your shots.

Stations: Greyhound's main train station is south of Union Station at 630 W Harrison St in West Loop (312-408-5800). CTA buses 60, 125, 156, and 157 make stops near the terminal. The closest L stop is on the Blue Line's Forest Park Branch at the Clinton Street Station on Congress Parkway. Additional Chicago-area Greyhound stations are located within L train stations: 14 W 95th St in the Red Line's 95th Street/Dan Ryan Station (312-408-5999), and 5800 N Cumberland Ave on the Blue Line's O'Hare Branch in the Cumberland Station (773-693-2474). The general aura of the Chicago Greyhound Station is one of seediness and squalor. Keep your belongings with you at all times.

Shipping Services: Greyhound Package Xpress offers commercial and personal shipping services and is available at all three Chicago bus stations. Packages are held at the station for pick-up. The main terminal in th South Loop also houses a UPS shipping office that provides door-to-door package delivery.

Fares: Tickets can be purchased on the phone or online with a credit card, or at a station with cash, travelers' checks, or credit cards.

Regular fare pricing applies for both individual advance ticket sales and minutes-before-departure sales. Tickets can be used for travel to the designated destination on any day or at any departure time. Because Greyhound does not reserve seats, boarding occurs on a first-come-first-served basis, so get in line at the boarding zone for a choice seat. However, Greyhound's bark is bigger than its bite—if a significant number of passengers turn out for the same bus, Greyhound rolls another bus, or two, or three out on the spot. Good dog.

Children under 12 receive 40% discounts off of regular fares, seniors 62 and older receive 5% discounts, military members receive 10% discounts, and patients of Veteran's Administration Hospitals receive a 25% discount. Other discounts are available online. The cost for an individual return ticket is always deeply discounted if it is purchased at the same time as a departure ticket.

Tickets purchased three days in advance earn a half-price companion ticket (no age restrictions). Passengers accompanying someone with a disability always ride at a reduced rate.

Megabus.com

Roll over Greyhound, there's a new dog in town, and a cheaper one at that! Megabus.com is the Midwest's answer to the East Coast Chinatown buses. An import from the UK, these buses travel between most major Midwest cities, including Minneapolis, Detroit, Milwaukee, St. Louis, Cleveland, Indianapolis, and Pittsburgh! That's not a comprehensive list, and they are always adding more cities as demand increases, so check back.

Fares: And that brings us to the best part about Megabus, which is that the ticket prices are determined by how far in advance you buy your tickets, how popular the route is, and what day of the week you travel on. If your Fairy Godmother is on your side, it is possible that you could take a round-trip bus to, say, Kansas City, for TWO DOLLARS. That's right, these bus fares go as low as $1 each way. Of course, as the service becomes more popular, the fares go up. And if you're like us, you don't buy your fares months ahead of time, which adds to the cost. But even so, most fares don't go too much higher than $20 each way. Still a sweet deal, even by Greyhound standards.

Stations: Megabus doesn't have stations, per se. But you'll see the line snaking outside Union Station as you approach. Union Station in downtown Chicago is the arrival and departure stop for all buses out of Chicago. Park yourself at the east side of South Canal Street, between Jackson Blvd and Adams Street, and try to get there early. It's first come, first serve seating.

Megabus doesn't run as frequently as Greyhound, but for lapses in service, you can always check in on its umbrella company, Van Galder, which is in turned owned by the corporate bus superpower Coach USA (www.coachusa.com/vangalder or call 800-747-0994 (toll free) or 608-752-5407). Van Galder is a touch more expensive, but its routes are more frequent and more comprehensive.

Other important logistics: You can order your Megabus ticket online (www.megabus.com/us) or call for a reservation (877-GO-2-MEGA) up to 45 days in advance. You can only bring one piece of luggage (up to 50 pounds) to stow under the bus and one small carry-on. No bikes allowed. Megabus is more or less wheelchair accessible, just make sure you call and let them know, and they can accommodate you.

Zone

	A
	B
	C
	D
	E
	F
	G
	H
	I
	J
	K
	M

UP-N   **Metra/Union Pacific North Line**
Chicago (OTC) to Kenosha, WI

UP-NW   **Metra/Union Pacific Northwest Line**
Chicago (OTC) to Harvard & McHenry

UP-W   **Metra/Union Pacific West Line**
Chicago (OTC) to Geneva

MD-N   **Metra/Milwaukee District North Line**
Chicago (Union Station) to Fox Lake

MD-W   **Metra/Milwauvkee District West Line**
Chicago (Union Station) to Elgin/Big Timber

NCS   **Metra/North Central Service**
Chicago (Union Station) to Anitioch

BNSF   **Metra/Burlington Northern Santa Fe**
Chicago (Union Station) to Aurora

ME   **Metra Electric**
Chicago (Randolph St Station) to University Park

HC   **Metra/Heritage Corridor**
Chicago (Union Station) to Joliet

SWS   **Metra/South West Service**
Chicago (Union Station) to Orland Park

RI   **Metra/Rock Island District**
Chicago (LaSalle St Station) to Joliet

SS   **Metra/South Shore**
Chicago (Randolph St Station) to South Bend, IN

General Information

Metra Address:	Metra Passenger Services
	547 W Jackson Blvd
	Chicago, IL 60661
Phone:	312-322-6777
Website:	www.metrarail.com
Metra Passenger Service:	312-322-6777
South Shore Metra Lines:	800-356-2079
RTA Information Center:	312-836-7000;
	www.rtachicago.com

Overview

With a dozen lines and roughly 495 miles of track overseen by the RTA, Metra does its best to service Cook, DuPage, Lake, Will, McHenry, and Kane counties with 230 stations scattered throughout the city and 'burbs. The rails, emanating from four major downtown stations, are lifelines for commuters traveling to and from the Loop.

The good news for Metra is that ridership is strong; the sheer multitude of folks who live in the suburbs but work in the city (and hate to deal with rush hour a-holes) means that Metra will always have a job. The bad news for riders is that parking at popular stations is difficult, if not impossible, and most people don't live close enough to Metra stations to walk. In an attempt to resolve its parking issues, Metra is purchasing land surrounding many suburban stations and constructing new parking facilities. Check out the website, www.metrarail.com, for updates on development plans.

Loop Stations

There are four major Metra train stations in the Loop from which 12 train lines emanate. Here's a chart to help clear up any possible confusion:

Station	Line
Richard B. Ogilvie T.C.	Union Pacific Lines
Union Station	Milwaukee District Lines
	North Central Service
	Southwest Service
	Burlington Northern
	Heritage Corridor
	Amtrak
LaSalle Street Station	Rock Island Line
Randolph Street Station	South Shore Railroad
(Millennium Station)	Metra Electric—Branches:
	Main Line, South Chicago,
	Blue Island

Fares

Depending on the number of Metra zones you traverse, one-way, full-fare tickets cost between $2.15 and $8.05. To calculate a base one-way fare, visit www.metrarail.com/Data/farechk.html. Tickets may be purchased through a ticket agent or onboard the train (with a $2 surcharge if the ticket windows were open at the time you boarded the train). There is no reserved seating.

Metra offers a number of reasonably priced ticket packages, including a Ten-Ride Ticket (which saves riders 15% off of one-way fares) and a Monthly Unlimited Ride Ticket (the most economical choice for commuters who use Metra service daily). If your commute includes CTA and/or Pace bus services, consider purchasing the Link-Up Sticker ($36) for unlimited connecting travel on CTA and Pace buses. Metra's Weekend Pass costs $5 and includes unlimited rides on Saturday and Sunday, with the exception of the South Shore route. You can buy all the aforementioned tickets in person, through the mail, or online at www.metrarail.com/TBI/index.html.

Children under age seven ride free. Children ages 7–11 ride for half-price on weekdays and for free on the weekends. Children ages 12–17 ride for half-price on weekends. Full-time grade school or high school students are eligibile to receive 50% off the cost of regular one-way fares. Senior citizens/disability fares are approximately half of the regular fare. US Military Personnel in uniform also ride Metra for half-price. Anyone wearing capri pants after Labor Day will be charged double.

Wendella RiverBuses

Spring through fall, commuters can get to North Michigan Avenue quickly on a Wendella RiverBus plying the Chicago River during rush hours, leaving from Transportation Center at the dock on the northwest corner of Madison Street. RiverBuses run daily from April 1 through November 29. The trip takes nine minutes one-way. The first boat leaves the train station dock at 7 am; the last boat departs from the dock at 400 N Michigan Avenue, at the base of the Wrigley Building at 7 pm. The fare is $2 one-way. Discounted Monthly and Ten-Ride fares are also available (312-337-1446; www.wendellariverbus.com).

Baggage & Pets

While Metra may be "the way to really fly," Metra's restrictions on baggage are more stringent than those of most airlines, though they now allow bicycles on weekday off-peak hours and on weekends (details on the "Bikes on Trains" program are divulged at metrarail.com/Special_Promotions/bikes_on_trains.html). Skis, golf clubs, non-folding carts, water buffaloes, and other large luggage items can never be transported on trains. Pets, with the exception of service animals, are also prohibited aboard trains.

General Information

Loop Station Address:	Millennium Station at Randolph Street
	151 E Randolph St
	Underground at N Michigan
	Ave & E Randolph St
	Chicago, IL 60601
Phone:	312-782-0676
Lost & Found:	219-874-4221 x205
Website:	www.nictd.com

Overview

Although the historic South Shore train lines were built in 1903, they still get you from the Loop to Indiana's South Bend Airport in just 2.5 hours. The Northern Indiana Commuter Transportation District (NICTD) oversees the line and its modern electric trains, which serve as a vital transportation link for many northwest Indiana residents working in the Loop.

The South Shore's commuter service reflects its Indiana ridership. Outbound heading from the Loop, there are limited stops before the Hegewisch station, close to the Indiana state line. When traveling by train to Chicago's South Side, you're better off on an outbound Metra Electric Line train departing from the Randolph Street Station (see Metra page). Taking a trip on the South Shore is a rather cheap form of post-industrial voyeurism, as a complete round-trip from the Loop all the way to South Bend can be had for around $20. Along the way you will pass by dozens of antiquated factories, one of the longest stretches of sand-dunes in the Great Lakes region, and, of course, oh-so charming Gary, Indiana.

Fares

Regular one-way fares can be purchased at the stations (with cash or personal check) or on the train (cash only). Ticket prices vary with distance traveled. Tickets purchased onboard the train cost $1 more if the station's ticket windows were open at the time of departure.

Special South Shore fares and packages include commuter favorites: 10-Ride and 25-Ride tickets and the Monthly Pass which is good for unlimited travel. These can be purchased in person at stations staffed with ticket agents, station vending machines, and via the mail. Senior citizens/disability fares offer savings for persons aged 65 and older with valid identification and for disabled passengers. Students with school identification qualify for student fares, including reduced one-way tickets and discounted 25-Ride Tickets good for travel during weekdays. Youth fares include free passage for infants under two years (who must sit in a paying passenger's lap) and half off a regular fare for children aged two to 13 years. Family fares are available on weekends and holidays as well as off-peak times on weekdays. Each fare-paying adult (minimum age 21) may take up to two children (age 13 and under) with them free of charge. Additional children will be charged the reduced youth fare. There are no published fare discounts for military personnel.

Baggage & Pets

Any accompanying baggage must be placed in the overhead racks. No bicycles are permitted onboard. Apart from small animals in carry-on cages, the only pets allowed onboard are service dogs accompanied by handlers or passengers with disabilities. Animals must not occupy seats.

General Information

Amtrak Reservations:	1-800-USA-RAIL (872-7245)
Website:	www.amtrak.com
Union Station:	225 S Canal St
	Chicago, IL 60606
Phone:	312-322-6900

Overview

The best city in America for riding the rails, Chicago hubs Amtrak's 500-station national railroad network, which covers every state but Alaska, Hawaii, South Dakota, and Wyoming. Departing from Union Station, Amtrak trains head west to Los Angeles, San Francisco, Portland and Seattle; east to Washington, D.C., New York City and Boston; north to Milwaukee and Minneapolis; and south to New Orleans and San Antonio, Texas.

Fares

Amtrak offers affordable fares for regional travel, with travel times comparable to flying when you factor in today's early airport check-ins. Their prices can't compete with airfares on longer hauls, but just as airlines offer deeply discounted fares, so does Amtrak. Ask sales agents about special fares and search Amtrak's website for the best deals. (Booking in advance does present some savings.) We recommend the website, as callers risk being on hold longer than it takes to ride a train from Chicago to Los Angeles.

Amtrak offers special fares year-round for seniors, veterans, students, children under 16, and groups of two or more traveling together. The "Hot Deals" page on Amtrak's website lists sale fares. Amtrak has also hooked its cars up with plenty of travel partners to create interesting "Amtrak Vacations" packages, including air-rail deals, whereby you rail it one way and fly back the other—attractive for long-distance travel.

The prices listed below are approximate, likely to change and don't include upgrades like sleeper cars. Check with Amtrak for updates.

Service

Someday, high-speed rail may come to the Midwest. Meanwhile, only a lucky few can claim to have arrived on time when traveling the longer routes on Amtrak, so tell whoever is picking you up you'll call them on your cell phone when you get close.

Pack food for your ride, as dining-car fare is mediocre and pricey. On the upside, Amtrak's seats are comfortable and roomy; some have electric sockets for computer hookups; bathrooms are in every car; and the train is almost always clean.

And you don't have to travel light. Your ticket lets you carry on two bags and check three, each weighing up to 50 pounds. Check an additional three bags and items such as bicycles, golf bags, baby strollers, musical instruments, and skis with handling fees of $5 to $10 each. Amtrak's default liability for checked baggage tops out at $500, so if your designer duds are worth more than that you'll want to ante up for extra coverage. Weapons; large, sharp objects; corrosive or dangerous chemicals; and the like are all prohibited, just like on planes; check for current regs before you pack.

Within Illinois and to Missouri: Amtrak's Illinois Service trains travel to 28 downstate cities from Chicago daily: "The Illinois Zephyr" and "The Carl Sandburg" travel to Quincy (on the Mississippi); "Illini Service" and "The Saluki" roll between Chicago and Carbondale; "The Lincoln Service" goes through corn and soybean country to St. Louis; and "The Ann Rutledge" heads to Kansas City. Also running daily, "The Southwest Chief" stops in Kansas City five hours into its trip to Albuquerque and Los Angeles; the fare runs about $85 one way. "The City of New Orleans" makes a number of downstate stops, too.

To Milwaukee and Minneapolis: Frequent enough for commuters, "Hiawatha Service" runs seven trains daily to Sturtevant, Wis. (near Racine); Milwaukee's Mitchell Airport; and downtown Milwaukee, leaving Chicago about every two hours and stopping en route in suburban Glenview. The 90-minute trip costs $21 each way (a good alternative to driving on busy weekends and rush hours). "Hiawatha Service" accepts RTA Transit Checks. En route to the Northwest, "The Empire Builder" also stops in Milwaukee, as well as Minneapolis; it takes some eight and a half hours to reach the Twin Cities, with one-way fare about $92.

To Michigan: Skip scary driving through the "Snow Belt" by taking the train. Three lines offer daily service to the Winter Water Wonderland: "The Pere Marquette" heads to Grand Rapids; "The Blue Water" takes passengers to Port Huron; and "The Wolverine" goes to Ann Arbor and Detroit, among other places. The ride to the Motor City takes about six hours and costs $27 to $48 one-way.

To the East Coast: "The Capitol Limited" runs daily through Cleveland and Pittsburgh to Washington, D.C., an 18-hour trip, while "The Cardinal" takes 28 hours to get to New York via Indianapolis, Cincinnati, Philadelphia, and Washington three days a week. The "Lake Shore Limited" passes through Albany, N.Y., and goes to New York City (21 hours) and Boston (24 hours). One-way tickets to the Eastern Seaboard cost between $80 and $150.

To Seattle or Portland: The "Empire Builder" takes passengers to Seattle and Portland and everywhere in between. With the journey to Seattle taking around 44 hours, we definitely recommend dropping some additional dollars on a sleeper car. One-way fare costs between $140 and $250.

To San Francisco: You'll spend two solid days and then some riding the rails during the 52-hour journey on the "California Zephyr" to San Francisco (Emeryville). The fare costs roughly $175 to $230 one-way. The "Zephyr" passes through Denver, Salt Lake City, and Sacramento, and makes a host of small-town America stops along the way.

To Los Angeles: You'll have plenty of time to study your map to the Hollywood stars on the "Southwest Chief," which departs for L.A. daily via Albuquerque, takes almost 42 hours, and costs $200 to $250 one-way.

To San Antonio: The mighty "Texas Eagle" doesn't exactly glide to the Alamo. It stops at 40 cities on its way from the Midwest to the Southwest. The 32-hour trip will cost around $117.

To New Orleans: The train Chicago's Steve Goodman made famous, "The City of New Orleans," runs from Chicago via Memphis to The Big Easy in roughly 20 hours. The fare runs about $100 to $180 one-way. Good morning, America, how are you?

Union Station

210 S Canal St at E Adams St and E Jackson Blvd ·
312-655-2385 · www.chicagounionstation.com

An innovation for both design and travel, Chicago's Union Station is the "Grand Dame" of rail service in a city once considered to be the undisputed rail center of the United States. Designed by the architects Graham, Anderson, Probst, and White and built between 1913 and 1925, Union Station is a terminus for six Metra lines and a major hub for Amtrak's long-distance services. In its peak (1940s), this local transportation treasure handled as many as 300 trains and 100,000 passengers on a daily basis. While today's volume is just half that, this monumental station stands as the last remaining grand station still in use in the City of Chicago and was given landmark status in 2002. Most commuters don't take the time to gaze skyward when rushing through the Great Hall of Union Station (who really has the time to stop and assess their surroundings beyond that of their intended use?), but by not doing so, they are missing something special. Take the time to look up at the magnificent light-swathed ceiling and maybe then it will become clear why Union Station's ornate Great Hall is considered one of the United States' great interior public spaces. Union Station is also a premiere location for formal functions as it annually plays host to a multitude of private affairs and black-tie gatherings.

Both Metra's and Amtrak's train services are on the Concourse Level (ground floor) of the station. This level is then further divided into the North Concourse and South Concourse. Although not always adequately staffed, there is an information desk located between the concourses on this level. And while there is signage throughout Union Station, the many escalators, stairways, and multiple entrances/exits can make navigating the block-long building somewhat of a challenge.

Ticket Windows: The easiest way to get to Metra ticket agents is to enter Union Station at the Clinton Street entrance near East Jackson Boulevard and go down into and through the Grand Hall. Metra's ticket agents will be on your left in the North Concourse. Metra's ticket office is open weekdays 6 am–11pm, Saturday 6:30 am–11pm, and Sunday 7 am–11 pm. Metra Lines that terminate at Union Station are Milwaukee District East and West Lines, North Central Service, Burlington Northern Santa Fe, Heritage Corridor, and South West Service.

To get to the Amtrak action, enter Union Station off Canal Street, take the escalator down into the Grand Hall, and turn left. Amtrak's attractive, vintage ticket agent desk straddles the two concourses and is open daily 6 am–10 pm. Amtrak's waiting rooms and baggage claim are in the South Concourse. For more detail on Amtrak service, call 800-872-7245 or visit www.amtrak.com

Services: On the Mezzanine/Street Level, there is a plethora of convenience stores, newsstands, and eateries. ATMs are located in both concourses on this level. One particular stop of note for contrarian travelers should be the in-house bar appropriately called, "The Snuggery". It's a pretty snug fit, and one can find errant Amtrak employees here, along with a revolving cast of grey-flannel suit types.

Public Transportation: The closest L stop to Union Station is Clinton Street on the Blue Line, which stops two blocks south of the station. The Orange, Brown, and Purple lines stop three blocks east of the station at the Quincy stop on Wells Street. CTA buses 1, 151, 157, and 125 all stop at Union Station. Most commuters heading to work in the Loop enter and exit the station from the Madison Street, Adams Street, and Jackson Boulevard doorways where cabs line up.

Richard B. Ogilvie Transportation Center

500 W Madison St at S Canal St · 312-496-4777

Built in 1911 and known locally as the North Western or Madison Street Station, the Metra's Union Pacific Lines originate from the Richard B. Ogilvie Transportation Center. Where Union Station is about form and function, Ogilvie focuses solely on function. Overtly stark and sterile, the tall, smoky-glass-and-green-steel-girder building replaced what was once a classic grand train station similar to the ornate, Beaux Arts-inspired Union Station. Though most of the historic fixtures have been removed, some of the original clocks remain and serve as a reminder of earlier days. Even though promised renovations of the unused historic sub-level areas have yet to come to fruition (it is hoped that the empty space under the tracks can be turned into 120,000 square feet of shops and restaurants), this highly trafficked station remains quite active. Roughly 40,000 passengers pass through the Richard B. Ogilvie Transportation Center on a daily basis.

Ticket Windows: Metra's ticket office is on the Upper Level, across from the entrance to the train platform and is open 5:30 am–12:40 am Monday–Saturday, and 7 am–12:40 am Sundays. ATMs can be found on the Upper Level at Citibank and next to the currency exchange. Public phones are also by the currency exchange in the southeast corner of the Upper Level.

Services: Loads of junk food options are available on the Street Level food court, which also serves as a make-shift waiting room for commuters. If you want healthier fare, try the Rice Market and Boudin Sourdough Bakery on the east side of the building. There is available shopping about if you're killing time or wanting to pick up a last-minute gift. An interesting and annoying amenity footnote: the only restrooms in the station are on the Street Level, which is a LONG escalator ride from the train platform. There are no plans for this to change until the proposed renovations are completed, so it's best to "go before you go."

Public Transportation: The closest L station is the Green Line's Clinton Street stop at Lake Street, several blocks north of the station. CTA buses 20, 56, and 157 board at Washington and Canal Streets and travel to North Michigan Avenue and the Loop. Coming from the Loop, take the same bus lines west across Madison Street. If you're after a cab, you'll find other like-minded commuters lining up in front of the main entrance on Madison Street between Canal and Clinton Streets.

Millennium Station

151 E Randolph St at N Michigan Ave · 312-322-7819

Nicknamed the "Triple S" (South "Start" Station), the Millennium Station serves Metra's three electric commuter rail lines in Chicago (Main Line, South Chicago Branch, Blue Island Branch) in addition to several diesel lines. The underground station, centrally located in the Loop, services up to 100,000 commuters daily. This is also the station where the South Shore Line to South Bend, Indiana originates. Schedules for all are somewhat sporadic except during weekday rush hour commutes. The Van Buren Street Station also serves both the Metra Electric and South Shore lines and is located at East Jackson Boulevard and Van Buren Street (312-322-6777). When planning train travel from the Randolph Street and Van Buren Street stations, it's best to verify schedules and stops with the RTA Information Center (312-836-7000; www.rtachicago.com) before committing to a travel plan.

Ticket Windows: Enter the Millennium Station at East Randolph Street and North Michigan Avenue. The ticket office is immediately visible upon descending the steps off Michigan Avenue or entering via the Pedway, which tunnels around the Loop and east under Michigan Avenue, ending at the station. Ticket office hours are 6 am–10:20 pm daily. The waiting room is open 5 am–12:50 am daily.

Services: Recently a few shops finally opened in this station, including an outpost of a certain very, very large coffee chain and a couple of regrettably bland retail offerings. On an upbeat note, the bathrooms are rather clean, which is a most welcome find in the Loop.

Public Transportation: Millennium Station is served by CTA buses 56, 151, 157 and on days when there are events at the United Center, express bus 19 becomes available. A little over one block west of the train station in the Loop is the Randolph Street L station, serviced by the Orange, Green, Purple, and Brown lines.

LaSalle Street Station

414 S La Salle St at E Congress Pkwy · 312-322-8957

The La Salle Street Station, located underneath the Chicago Stock Exchange, serves the Metra Rock Island District Line's passengers. This former behemoth of a station has been greatly reduced in both size and stature, handling roughly 15,000 commuters daily. The service has 11 main line stops and 10 south suburban stops on its way to Joliet.

Ticket Windows: Enter the station off LaSalle Street, take the escalator one floor up, and walk through the slim corridor to an open-air area where the tracks are. To your right you'll see the ticket office. Agents are on duty 7 am–8 pm weekdays, 10:30 am–6:30 pm on Saturday, and closed on Sunday.

Services: There are no shops to speak of at the LaSalle Street Station, but there is a waiting room is open 6 am–12 am daily.

Public Transportation: The Blue Line's La Salle Street stop at Congress Parkway and the Orange, Purple, and Brown lines' La Salle Street stop at Van Buren Street drop L riders right in front of the train station. CTA buses 6 and 146 stop near the station, as well.

Transit • **Free Trolleys**

Shopping Daily 10 am-6 pm
Metra/Navy Pier Daily 10 am-6 pm
Metra/Museums Daily 10 am-6 pm
Lincoln Park/Metra Daily 10 am-6 pm
Lincoln Park/Navy Pier Daily 10 am-6 pm
Navy Pier Sun-Thurs 10 am-11 pm
Fri-Sat 10 am-1am
Lincoln Park Shuttle Weekends and
Holidays 10 am-6pm

If you want to mingle with the tourists at top sightseeing and shopping destinations like Michigan Avenue, State Street, and Navy Pier, the city of Chicago makes transit easy with free "trolley" service. Most trolley-buses run every 20 minutes from 10 or 10:30 am to early evening from Memorial Day weekend through Labor Day weekend and at selected holidays. Some lines may run on weekends only (check map for specific line hours). Daily free trolley service between Navy Pier and State Street along Grand Avenue and Illinois Street runs all year round during Pier hours.

The color-coded trolley routes dovetail with CTA bus routes and make stops at major Loop L stations and Metra stations. Trolley stops are identified by graphic, color-coded signs. Because fare-based trolley companies also roam the streets, be sure to look for the "Free Trolley" sign in the front window. You don't need a ticket to ride; just hop on and off as you please. However, the lines can be long at peak times, so don't wait until the kids get cranky to head home.

For more information, contact: 877-244-2246; www.cityofchicago.org/transportation

Lake Michigan

Diversey Harbor

North Pond

Lincoln Park

Lincoln Park Lagoon

South Pond

South Pond

W Diversey Ave
W Diversey Pkwy
W Diversey Pkwy

W Schubert Ave
W Schubert Ave

W Drummond Pl
W Drummond Pl

W Wrightwood Ave

W Deming Pl
W Deming Pl

W St James Pl
W Roslyn Pl

W Arlington Pl
W Arlington Pl

W Fullerton Pkwy
E W Fullerton Pkwy
W Fullerton Pkwy

W Kemper Pl

W Belden Ave

W Grant Pl

W Webster Ave

W Dickens Ave

W Armitage Ave

W Wisconsin St

W Menomonee St

W Willow St
W Willow St
W Willow St

W St Paul Ave

W Eugenie St

W Concord Pl
W Concord Ln

W Concord Pl

W Lutz Pl
W Weed St

W Concord Pl

W North Ave
E North Ave

W Burton Pl
W Burton St
E Burton Pl

W Weed St

W Blackhawk St

W Eastman St

W Schiller St
W Schiller St
E Schiller St

N Halsted St

N Mildred Ave
N Dayton St
N Burling St
N Orchard St

N Pine Grove Ave
N Hampden Ct
N Lehmann Ct

N Wrightwood Ave

N Sheffield Ave

N Clark St

N Lakeview Ave

N Commonwealth Ave

N Lincoln Ave

N Geneva Ter

N Hudson Ave

N Howe St

N Fremont St
N Edward Ct
N Burling St
N Pearl Ct
N Orchard St

N Orleans St

N Mohawk St
N Hudson Ave
N Sedgwick St

N Cleveland Ave
N Fern Ct
N Hudson Ave

N Lincoln Park W

N Orleans St

N Crilly Ct
N Crilly Ct

N Meyer Ct
N St Michaels Ct

N North Park Ave

N Orleans St

N Wieland St

N Vine St

N Dayton St

N Bissell St

N Ridge Dr
N Ridge Dr

N Cannon Dr

N Stockton Dr

N Fremont St
N Burling St
N Frontier Ave

N Larrabee St

N LaSalle St
N Sandburg Ter
N Germania Ter

N Clark St

N Dearborn Pkwy
N State Pkwy
N Astor St

Lincoln Park

41

MAP 29
MAP 30
MAP 22
MAP 31
MAP 32

General Information

City of Chicago Department of Transportation (DOT)
Non-Emergency/
24-Hour Road Conditions Phone: 311
Street Closings Hotline: 312-787-3387
Website: www.cityofchicago.org

Illinois Department of Transportation (IDOT)
Phone: 217-782-7820
IDOT Traffic Hotline: 312-368-4636
Website: www.dot.state.il.us/news.html
Chicago Skyway Bridge: 312-747-8383
Road Conditions: 800-452-4368
WBBM-AM 780:   Traffic updates every eight
                             minutes

Orientation

Anyone who says baldness is hereditary has never found him/herself in a Chicago traffic jam, pulling out his/her hair to pass the time and calm the nerves. We highly recommend taking public transportation whenever possible, especially since Chicago has such strong bus and rail systems. But if you must drive in the city, Chicago's grid system makes it relatively easy to navigate.

The intersection of State and Madison Streets in the Loop serves as the base line for both Chicago's street and house numbering system. Running north and south is State Street—the city's east/west dividing line. Madison Street runs east and west and divides the city into north and south. Street and building numbers begin at "1" at the State and Madison Streets intersection and numerically increase going north, south, east, and west to the city limits. Street signs will let you know in what direction you're heading. The city is divided into one-mile sections, or eight square blocks, each with a consecutively higher series of "100" numbers. For example, Western Ave, sitting at 2400 W, is further west than Ashland Ave, located at 1600 W. In addition, Chicagoans numerically refer to street locations such as Irving Park Road as "40 hundred north" rather than "four thousand north."

Buildings with even number addresses are on the north and west sides of streets; odd numbers sit on the south and east sides. Chicago's diagonal streets also follow the grid numbering system, most of which receive north or south addresses. East-west streets north of Madison are named, as in Fullerton or Belmont; south of Madison they are generally numbered, as in 31st or 79th, with several major streets being named. Once you get out of the city limits, good luck. Often times you will find that our suburban friends like to refer to the same road by two different names. Roads will also magically turn into something different for no apparent reason. And sometimes they don't bother putting up street signs at all.

Bridge Lift Season

While bridges spanning the Chicago River contribute to the city's architectural fame, they also serve as a major source of traffic congestion. Boating season demands that bridges lower and rise, so as to allow Chicago's elite access to Lake Michigan in their sailboats. Chicago's bridge lift season runs from early April until June. Each month has designated lift days. Lifts generally begin at 9:30 am and affect the entire

downtown area between 11:30 am and 1 pm. During May, more lifts are scheduled on Saturdays between 2 pm and 4 pm. The schedule intensifies on holiday weekends to include evening rush hours. Check out the DOT's website for detailed schedules.

Snow Routes

Failure to efficiently handle city snow removal seals the re-election fate of Chicago's mayors. The Department of Streets and Sanitation manages the ice and snow removal on Chicago's streets. Over 280 salt spreaders/plows cruise 607 miles of arterial streets divided into 245 designated snow routes. Parking is automatically restricted on these routes when snow is piled at least two inches on the pavement. Unfortunately, the two-inch snow routes are a crap-shoot. Tow trucks will enforce these restrictions by their own rules, it seems. On a snow route, you will either find your car gone or buried by a passing plow. Safety dictates you keep your car off of these routes even if only an inch and a half are predicted. Priority arteries also restrict parking daily from 3 am until 7 am between December 1 and April 1, whether or not snow is present (though so far this relatively new rule has not been strictly enforced).

Major Expressways and Tollways

While the city's grid system is logical, the interstate highway system feeding into the city is confusing for those who don't travel it often. Chicago has free expressways and tollways which require paying a fee. The expressways are generally referred to by their names, such as "The Kennedy" or "The Eisenhower." When venturing into Indiana, one can experience the Chicago Skyway, a stretch of elevated road that connects I-94 and the Indiana Toll Road that soars 120 feet above the Calumet River. When using the tollways, which includes the Skyway, I-PASS speeds up the process and can be purchased through the Illinois State Toll Highway Authority by calling 800-824-7277.

DMVs

The Illinois Department of Motor Vehicles (DMV) is one of life's unavoidable hassles. But you'd be pleasantly surprised to see how many of your car-related responsibilities (like renewing your driver's license, getting vehicle registrations, etc.) can be completed online (www.dmv.org). Unless you're British and enjoy standing in line for hours. Visit the website, or call 312-793-1010 for more information.

Chicago DMVs	Map	Hours
100 W Randolph St	5	Mon–Fri: 8 am–5 pm
69 W Washington St, Concourse Level	5	Mon–Fri: 8 am–5 pm
17 N State St, Ste 1000	5	Mon–Fri: 8 am–4:30 pm
5401 N Elston Ave	46	Mon–Tues: 8:30 am–5 pm; Wed: 10 am–7 pm; Thurs–Fri: 8:30 am–5 pm
9901 S Martin Luther King Dr	59	Mon–Tues: 8:30 am–5 pm; Wed: 10 am–7 pm; Thurs–Fri: 8:30 am–5 pm
5301 W Lexington Ave	49	Tues: 9 am–7 pm; Wed–Fri: 8 am –5:30 pm; Sat: 8 am–12 pm

General Information

Office of the City Clerk—Parking Permits

Mailing Address:	City Hall
	121 N La Salle St, Rm 107
	Chicago, IL 60602
Phone:	312-744-6861
Hours:	Weekdays, 8 am–5 pm
Website:	www.chicityclerk.com

Department of Revenue (DOR)—Parking Ticket Payments

Mailing Address:	PO Box 88298
	Chicago, IL 60680-1298
Phone:	312-747-4747
Website:	www.cityofchicago.org/revenue
Parking Ticket Assistance & "Boot" Inquiries:	312-744-PARK (7275)
Auto Pound Headquarters: (for towed vehicles)	312-744-4444
City Non-Emergency Phone:	311

City Stickers

Residents of Chicago who own motor vehicles (see "sadomasochist" at www.wikipedia.org) must have an annually renewed city sticker for their cars, which can be purchased from the Office of the City Clerk through the mail (by returning the renewal application you've received in the mail), in person at one of their offices, or online. Stickers may also be purchased at local currency exchanges, but you might get charged extra there. New residents are required to purchase their sticker in person with a proof of residency at one of the offices within 30 days of their move-in date. A four-passenger vehicle sticker for long-time residents costs $75, while new residents get a price cut at $37. Senior citizens are also eligible for discounts, but they check IDs, so don't pretend you're over 50; they'll find out you're lying. After March 1st of each year, half-year stickers are available at half-price for new city residents or current residents who've recently purchased a car. For more information on office locations and pricing, call 312-742-9200 or visit the City Clerk's website.

Residential Zone Permit Parking

If you're lucky enough to find a parking spot, you still need to put a permit on your car. Chicago's Residential Parking Permit program reserves street parking during peak parking hours for neighborhood residents and those who provide a service to the residents. Cars in violation of this ordinance will be ticketed. Take that, suckers. Permits cost $25 annually and are available through the Office of the City Clerk via mail, online, and in person. Applicants must have a valid Chicago City Sticker and an Illinois State license plate. One-day guest passes may also be purchased and distributed by qualified residents. Fifteen 24-hour passes cost $5 per pack at a two-pack limit, so choose your guests wisely and frugally. Check out the City Clerk website or call 312-744-5346 for more information.

Parking Tickets

The Department of Revenue (DOR) handles the payment of parking tickets. You can pay parking tickets by mail, online, or in person; scribbling curse words on it, ripping it up, and throwing it at the mailbox does not count as "paying" it, according to the stingy DOR. For the addresses and hours of payment processing and hearing facilities, see the DOR website.

Three or more unpaid tickets guarantees a metal, yellow surprise fitted to your car tire; yep, say hello to the boot. Ten or more tickets and the entire car is encased in molybdenum steel. If violations aren't paid within 24 hours of booting, your vehicle will be towed…maybe. In addition to the boot fee, towing, and storage fees must be paid to retrieve your car from a City Auto Pound. If your car is towed due to a boot, contact the City of Chicago's Ticket Help Line (312-744-7275). All payments for outstanding parking ticket debt must be made to a DOR Payment Center, not at the pound. The city has two payment plans available for motorists with large ticket fines. The General Payment Plan requires either a deposit of $500 or 25% of your parking debt (whichever is greater) in addition to all outstanding boot, towing, and storage fees. If you qualify for the Hardship Parking Payment Plan, you can make a deposit of $250 or 25% of your debt, whichever is lower. If either of these cases applies to you, we also suggest you stop parking in Chicago and find another means of travel, since you apparently can't handle the responsibility. Visit the DOR website for further requirements.

Auto Pounds

To locate your towed vehicle, contact the City of Chicago Auto Pound Headquarters (312-744-4444). There are six auto pounds in addition to the O'Hare Auto Pound (10000 W O'Hare at Remote Lot E, 773-694-0990).

For a standard vehicle, the towing fee is a hefty $150 plus a $10 per day storage fee for the first five days, $35 per day thereafter. Fees can be paid at the pound; they accept cash, cashier's checks, VISA, MasterCard, Discover, American Express, and first-born children. No arms or legs, please.

Failure to claim vehicles or request a hearing within 21 days of notification can result in your convenient mode of transportation being sold or destroyed and, even then, you still owe the city for the outstanding fines. In that case, see the rest of the Transit section for alternate ways of navigating your way through Chicago.

Important note: "Minor" street repairs and construction are common occurrences on Chicago streets, during which signs should be posted on nearby trees or parking meters stating that parking is temporarily prohibited. If you park there, you will be towed. If you parked there on purpose despite seeing the signs, well, you deserve it. If you parked there on accident, we feel for you, so read on for our tips on how to not look like a panicky idiot while trying to find your car. First of all, don't bother contacting the city pound. They will have no idea what you're talking about! Save yourself the embarrassment of reporting your car stolen, and call the number posted on the sign where your car was parked. Chances are it was kindly moved to another location so as to allow workers to continue with important road improvements, but it may not have officially been moved by the city of Chicago. Operators should be able to track it down using your license plate number since city code mandates that the kindly moving of a car must be reported within a few hours, whether it be by the city or the other parking powers that be. Otherwise, you can always walk around your neighborhood aimlessly searching for your car, but we don't recommend it. We've only been successful doing that once or twice, and, anyway, it just turned out that we forgot where we parked after a night of heavy drinking.

Legend:
- Sky Walk
- Underground Walkway
- Under Construction / Proposed

1. 25 E Washington Street
2. 1 N State Street
3. 139 N Wabash Avenue
4. Hyatt Regency Chicago
5. Swissotel Chicago
6. Stouffer Riviere Hotel
7. 200 N Dearborn Apartments
8. 77 W Wacker Drive
9. 201 N Clark Street
10. City Hall/County Building
11. State of Illinois Center
12. 69 W Washington Street
13. Richard J Daley Center
14. 1 N Dearborn St
15. Chicago Cultural Center
16. Prudential Center
17. 303 E Wacker Drive
18. The Sporting Club
19. Columbus Plaza
20. Illinois Center
21. Boulevard Towers
22. Dirksen Federal Building
23. 203 N LaSalle Street
24. 150 N Michigan Avenue
25. Carson Pirie Scott & Co

While a number of cold-weather cities are known for their above-ground walkways, Chicago is known for its Pedway, a 40-block network of tunnels and overhead bridges that connects important public, government, and private sector buildings with retail stores, major hotels, rapid transit stations, and commuter rail stations. A subterranean city with shops, restaurants, services, and public art works, the Pedway is a welcome alternative to navigating trafficked intersections on foot and walking outdoors in Chicago's frigid winters. The underground walkway system is open 24 hours; however, access to a number of the buildings is limited after standard business hours. The first Pedway links were built in 1951 to connect the State Street and Dearborn Street subways at Washington Street and Jackson Boulevard. Today, Chicago's Pedway continues to grow as city government and the private sector cooperate to expand it. Those planning on making a subterranean trip to experience the Pedway in its glory would do well to click on over to www.spiegl.org/pedway/pedway.html for a map of the whole lair.

As a city renowned for both Al Capone and architecture, Chicago has something to suit all tastes. (And that's before you've even hit the restaurants.) Chicago has continued to steal the limelight with its originality, most lately styling itself as a green city and prospective Olympic host. Here's our pick of some of the headline grabbing landmarks, alongside some of the more understated and unusual offerings.

Legacy Architecture

Early skyscrapers such as the **Monadnock Building (Map 5)** can be found in the Loop, alongside other noteworthy structures like Adler and Sullivan's historic **Auditorium Building (Map 6)**. Contrast these with Midwest native **Frank Lloyd Wright's Home and Studio (Oak Park)** in the suburb of Oak Park, whose famous Prairie style can also be seen at the **Robie House (Map 19)** on the city's south side. Jump forward a couple of decades and German Mies van der Rohe arrives on the scene, with his dictum "less is more." Trek over to the **Illinois Institute of Technology (IIT) (Map 13)** to really immerse yourself in his spare glass and steel structures. Chicago is also home to a triumvirate of quirky Bertrand Goldberg masterpieces—**Marina Towers (Map 2)**, which graces the cover of Wilco's *Yankee Hotel Foxtrot*, **River City (Map 7)**, and the **Raymond Hilliard Apartments (Map 10)**.

Great New Architecture

IIT is also the site of some fab new architecture, such as starchitect Rem Koolhaas's incredible **McCormick Tribune Campus Center (Map 14)**, which literally encases the L in a tube, and Helmut Jahn's **State Street Village (Map 14)**. Back downtown, you can monitor the construction of Santiago Calatrava's **Chicago Spire (Map 3)**, pushing out the new **Trump International Hotel and Tower (Map 2)** to become the country's tallest building. Expect a flurry of activity as momentum for Chicago's 2016 Olympic bid gathers pace.

Green Landmarks

Sustainability is worn as a badge of immense pride these days and nowhere more so than in this city. Mayor Daley is the green guru, practicing what he preaches with the installation of the **City Hall Green Roof (Map 5)**. Elsewhere the **Chicago Center for Green Technology (West)** aims to spread the word, offering free public programs in a state of the art facility — and best of all, it can be reached by public transportation.

Outdoor Spaces

Chicago's status as a green city got off to a good start, thanks to some forward-thinking chaps. By advocating the lakefront as a place for recreation, they've left a wonderful legacy. Highlights are **Lincoln Park (Parks & Places)** with the free **Lincoln Park Zoo (Map 30)**) to the north and **Jackson Park (Parks & Places)** (site of the 1893 World's Columbian Exposition) to the south. Central **Grant Park (Parks & Places)** is home to the **Buckingham Fountain (Map 9)**, and offers festivals throughout the warmer months. And don't forget the harbors. **Belmont Harbor (Map 44)** is home to the Chicago Yacht Club Sailing School, while **The Point at Diversey (Map 30)** provides a fabulous view of the city from the north. Within the downtown itself, outdoor spaces include **Daley Plaza (Map 5)** (you saw it in the movie *The Lake House*),

which offers free lunchtime cultural events. Outside of the city limits, **Garfield Park Conservatory (Parks & Places)** is a jewel in a barren landscape.

Public Artwork

Better described as a work of art rather than simply an outdoor space, **Millennium Park (Parks & Places)** is not to be missed. Legendry architect Frank Gehry has conjured up another of his steel creations with the **Jay Pritzker Pavilion (Map 6)** (an open air venue offering complimentary concerts), while British and Spanish artists have stolen the show with **Cloud Gate (Map 6)** (otherwise known as The Bean) and **The Crown Fountain (Map 6)** (a.k.a. kiddies' pool). Another heavy concentration of public artwork is found in the Loop, with the **Joan Miro Sculpture (Map 5)** and Alexander Calder's **Flamingo (Map 5)** being amongst the high profile pieces. How often do children get the chance to slide down a Picasso?

Lowbrow Landmarks

Chicago has its share of more unassuming sights too, including the mysterious **Totem Pole (Map 44)** along the lakefront and **Agora (Map 9)**, an army of headless metal people. Also easy to miss is the amazing artwork **The Body of Lake Michigan (Southwest)**. Look up as you go through the security checkpoint at Midway airport; it's quite impressive. Out to the south west is the **Union Stockyard Gate (West)**, a reminder of the days referred to in Carl Sandburg's line "Hog Butcher for the world." You can then go sample some meat—the infamous cheezboiger—at the unpretentious **Billy Goat Tavern (Map 3)**.

Overrated Landmarks

With the nickname "The Windy City" derived from the hot air dispensed by earlier politicians, the city also has its fair share of overrated landmarks. The amazingly hideous new **Soldier Field (Map 11)** fits the bill perfectly. If there were flying saucers in classical civilization, they would look something like this. Also registering on the ugly scale is the **James R. Thompson Center (Map 5)**. Enough said. However, the prize for most over-hyped attraction must go to **Navy Pier (Parks & Places)** with its wall-to-wall tourists and mediocre eateries. Consider yourself warned.

Underrated Landmarks

On the other hand, Chicago has a lot of well-kept secrets worth exploring. Home to a large collection of art glass by Louis Comfort Tiffany, the **Chicago Cultural Center (Map 5)** and **Macy's (Map 5)** on State Street both have spectacular domes. Continuing on the glass theme, the **American Windows (Map 6)** by Marc Chagall are another treat often overshadowed by the heavy-weight impressionist collection at the **Art Institute (Map 6)**. Another find is **The Newberry Library (Map 32)**, which sits quietly on Washington Square Park, but boasts a hive of activity inside: classes, concerts, and lectures. As for the Hyde Park area, check out the **University of Chicago (Map 19)** and its **Oriental Institute Museum (Map 19)**. You'll also find the **Nuclear Energy Sculpture (Map 19)** by Henry Moore, which commemorates the first nuclear reaction which took place here.

Map 1 · River North / Fulton Market District

The Blommer Chocolate Co	600 W Kinzie St · 312-226-7700	Opened in 1939. Eventually became the largest commercial chocolate manufacturer in the US.

Map 2 · Near North / River North

Courthouse Place	54 W Hubbard St	This Romanesque-style former courthouse has witnessed many legendary trials.
Marina Towers	300 N State St	Bertrand Goldberg's riverside masterwork. Love the parking.
Merchandise Mart	222 Merchandise Mart Plz · 312-527-7600	Houses furniture showrooms and a small mall.
Rock 'N Roll McDonald's	600 N Clark St · 312-664-7940	Glitzy take on fast food fodder.
Sotheby's	215 W Ohio St · 312-396-9599	Renowned auction house. We bid $5.
Trump International Hotel and Tower	330 N Wabash Ave · 312-822-0690	Chicago's very own bit of glitz, brought to us by The Donald.

Map 3 · Streeterville / Mag Mile

Billy Goat Tavern	430 N Michigan Ave · 312-222-1525	Cheezborger! Cheezborger!
Chicago Spire	400 N Lake Shore Dr	Proposed 2000 foot tower, due to break ground in summer 2007.
Museum of Contemporary Art	220 E Chicago · 312-280-2660	Party down on First Fridays. Get in for free on Tuesdays.
Tribune Tower	435 N Michigan Ave · 312-222-2116	Check out the stones from famous buildings around the world including a real-life rock from the moon!
Wrigley Building	400 N Michigan Ave	Monument to chewing gum.

Map 4 · West Loop Gate / Greek Town

Dugan's Drinking Emporium	128 S Halsted St · 312-421-7191	Sports bar in Greektown. Fantastic beer garden and favorite cop hangout.
Union Station	200 S Canal St · 312-322-4269	Built in 1925, the architecture is not to be missed!

Map 5 · The Loop

Chicago Board of Trade	141 W Jackson Blvd · 312-435-3590	The goddess Ceres tops this Deco monolith.
Chicago Board Options Exchange	400 S La Salle St · 312-786-5600	The world's largest options market.
Chicago Cultural Center	78 E Washington St · 312-744-6630	The spot for free lectures, exhibits, concerts, and movies.
Chicago Mercantile Exchange	20 S Wacker Dr · 312-930-1000	Economics at work in polyester jackets.
Chicago Stock Exchange	440 S La Salle St · 312-663-2222	The second-largest stock exchange in the country.
City Hall Green Roof	121 N LaSalle St	First green roof on a municipal building. Cool.
Daley Civic Plaza	50 W Washington St · 312-443-5500	Home of a Picasso sculpture, a Christmas tree ceremony, and many alfresco lunches.
Flamingo	219 S Dearborn St	Alexander Calder's fabulous red flamingo.
The Four Seasons	70 W Madison St	Mosaic by Marc Chagall—you know, the one who did all those flying people.
Harold Washington Public Library	400 S State St · 312-747-4300	The world's largest public library building; nearly 100 works of art on every floor.
James R Thompson Center	100 W Randolph St	Lots of glass combined with the colors red, silver and blue. Ghastly!
Joan Miro Sculpture	69 W Washington St	Part of the Loop's outdoor public artwork program.
Macy's	111 N State St · 312-781-1000	Folks are still mourning the passing of Marshall Fields. Luckily the clock and Tiffany dome remain.
Monadnock Building	53 W Jackson Blvd · 312-922-1890	Claim to fame: world's largest office building when completed in 1893.
Monument with Standing Beast	100 W Randolph St	Jean DuBuffet sculpture. Looks like melted snow.
Quincy L Station	220 S Wells St	Restored to its original glory.
Rookery Building	209 S La Salle St · 312-553-6150	Take a peek inside at Frank Lloyd Wright's spectacular remodelled interior.
Sears Tower	233 S Wacker Dr · 312-875-9696	Currently the tallest building in the US, with a cool skydeck.

Map 6 • The Loop / Grant Park

American Windows	111 S Michigan Ave • 312-443-3600	Spectacular stained glass by Marc Chagall.
Art Institute of Chicago	111 S Michigan Ave • 312-443-3600	World-class art museum.
Auditorium Building	430 S Michigan Ave • 312-431-2354	Designed by Louis Sullivan; on National Register of Historic Places.
Cloud Gate	Millennium Park	Much-photographed sculpture, affectionately known as "the bean."
The Crown Fountain	N Michigan Ave b/w E Madison St & E Monroe Dr	Captivating modern take on traditional fountain, swarming with kids.
Fine Arts Building	410 S Michigan Ave • 312-427-7602	The country's first artists' colony, converted from a Studebaker carriage plant in 1898.
Jay Pritzker Pavilion	Millennium Park	Frank Gehry signature steel structure, offering free outdoor concerts.
Prudential Building	1 Prudential Plz	Classic '50s skyscraper.
Santa Fe Building	224 S Michigan Ave	Home to the world-renowned Chicago Architecture Foundation.
Symphony Center	220 S Michigan Ave • 312-294-3000	Classical music headquarters.

Map 7 • South Loop / River City

Maxwell Street Market (Sun, 7 am–3 pm)	Canal St b/w Taylor St & Roosevelt Rd • 312-922-3100	Outdoor bazaar where you can shop for dish soap or bicycle parts while grazing at authentic taco stands.
Old Post Office	404 W Harrison St	This massive, vacant edifice straddling I-90/94 and I-290 is a benchmark for traffic reports.
River City	800 S Wells St	A fluid cement design experiment built by architect Bertrand Goldberg in the '80s; considered a flop, but actually brilliant.
US Postal Distribution Center	433 W Harrison St • 312-983-8391	The city's main mail routing center, employing over 6,000 people and operating 24 hours a day.

Map 8 • South Loop / Printers Row / Dearborn Park

Columbia College Center for Book & Paper Arts	1104 S Wabash Ave • 312-344-6630	Two galleries feature changing exhibits of handmade books, paper, letterpress, and other related objects.
Former Elliot Ness Building	618 S Dearborn St	If he sends one of yours to the hospital, you send one of his to the morgue…
Old Dearborn Train Station	47 W Polk St	Turn-of-the-century train station with a lighted clocktower visible for several blocks. Al Capone took a train to prison from here.
Pacific Garden Mission	646 S State St • 312-922-1462	America's oldest continuously-operating rescue mission with free showings of long running radio drama Unshackled!

Map 9 • South Loop / South Michigan Ave

Agora	S Michigan Ave & E Roosevelt Rd	If you've ever wanted to see 106 headless metal people, here's where you can.
Buckingham Fountain	Columbus Dr & E Congress Pkwy	Built of pink marble; inspired by Versailles.
Chicago Hilton and Towers	720 S Michigan Ave • 312-922-4400	Check out the frescoes in the lobby; sneak a kiss in the palatial ballroom.
John G Shedd Aquarium	1200 S Lake Shore Dr • 312-939-2435	Marine and freshwater creatures from around the world are on view in this 1929 Classical Greek-inspired Beaux Arts structure.
Johnson Publishing Headquarters	820 S Michigan Ave • 312-322-9200	Largest African-American-owned publishing company, home of Ebony and Jet magazines.
Spirit of Music Garden	601 S Michigan Ave	Where the city struts during Chicago SummerDance.

Map 10 • East Pilsen / Chinatown

Chinatown Gate	S Wentworth Ave & W Cermak Rd	Built in 1976. The characters on the gate read "The world belongs to the people."
Chinatown Square	S Archer Ave	Restaurants, bakeries, gift stores, and herb shops.
On Leong Merchants Association Building	2216 S Wentworth Ave • 312-328-1188	1926 building inspired by architecture of the Kwangtung district of China. Now the home of the Pui Tak Center.
Ping Tom Memorial Park	300 W 19th St • 312-747-7661	Park with Chinese landscape elements.
Raymond Hilliard Apartments	2111 S Clark St • 312-225-3715	Another Bertrand Golberg gem going from subsidized senior housing to mixed-income residential.

Map 11 • South Loop / McCormick Place

Adler Planetarium & Astronomy Museum	1300 S Lake Shore Dr • 312-922-7827	Depression era wonder that thrilled millions at 1933 Century of Progress Exposition.
America's Courtyard	South of Adler Planetarium on the lakefront	A spiral of stones that echoes both the Milky Way and ancient structures. Designed by Denise Milan and Ary R. Perez.
The Chicago Daily Defender	2400 S Michigan Ave • 312-225-5656	Founded in 1905, it was the country's most influential black newspaper through the '50s. Still in operation, but much-diminished.
Chicago Legends	2109 S Wabash Ave • 312-326-0300	Boasts R&B and hip-hop programming, not particularly open-minded toward hip-hop patrons.
Clarke House	1827 S Indiana Ave	Built in 1836 by an unknown architect, this Greek Revival-style home has been relocated twice and is now an official Chicago landmark.
The Field Museum	1400 S Lake Shore Dr • 312-922-9410	Go to see Sue, world's largest known T. Rex; stay for the jam-packed halls of vaguely macabre taxidermy.
Hillary Rodham Clinton Women's Park and Gardens of Chicago	S Prairie Ave, b/w 18th St & 19th St	A garden from a former first lady.
Hyatt Regency McCormick Place	2233 S Dr Martin L King Jr Dr • 312-567-1234	The only hotel attached to the city's main convention center.
McCormick Place	2301 S Lake Shore Dr • 312-791-7000	Hard to miss.
National Vietnam Veterans Art Museum	1801 S Indiana Ave • 312-326-0270	Features art about the war created by Vietnam veterans from all sides of the conflict.
Northerly Island Park	Lakefront, south of Adler Planetarium	Greenspace now encompassing former site of Meigs Field airport.
Quinn Chapel, African Methodist Episcopal Church	2401 S Wabash Ave • 312-791-1846	Built in 1892, this Victorian Gothic-style church houses Chicago's oldest African-American congregation.
Second Presbyterian Church	1936 S Michigan Ave • 312-225-4951	Reconstructed in 1900 by Howard Van Doren Shaw, this ponderous Gothic Revival-style church has stained glass by Tiffany.
Soldier Field	425 E McFetridge Dr • 312-747-1285	Once on the National Register of Historic places, this renovated monster is home to Da Bears.
The Wheeler Mansion	2020 S Calumet Ave • 312-945-2020	This Second Empire-style mansion now houses a boutique hotel for high-end travelers.
Willie Dixon's Blues Heaven Foundation	2120 S Michigan Ave • 312-808-1286	Former Chess Records studio. Tours, exhibits, workshops, and performances.

Map 12 • Bridgeport (West)

Library Fountain	W 34th St & Halsted St	Pretty water.
McGuane Park	2901 S Poplar Ave • 312-747-7463	A park for playing.
Monastery of the Holy Cross	3111 S Aberdeen St • 773-927-7424	Have your breakfast served by monks in this bed and breakfast monastery.
St Mary of Perpetual Help	1039 W 32nd St	Built in the 1880s, this was the first Polish Roman Catholic Church in the US to be consecrated.
Wilson Park	S May St & W 34th Pl	A nice respite in the middle of the city.

Map 13 • Bridgeport (East)

Illinois Institute of Technology	31st to 35th St, b/w Dan Ryan Expy & Michigan Ave • 312-567-3000	Mies van der Rohe designed campus. Jewel in the crown? Crown Hall of course.
Old Neighborhood Italian American Club	3031 S Shields Ave • 312-326-6420	Founded by Angelo LaPietra, a former high-ranking Chicago mobster, after his release from Leavenworth.
Richard J Daley House	3536 S Lowe Ave	Childhood home of Mayor Richard J. Daley.

Map 14 • Prairie Shores / Lake Meadows

Black Metropolis Convention & Tourism Council	3501 S King Dr, Ste 1E • 773-373-2865	Information central for questions on everything Bronzeville.
Bronzeville Bed & Breakfast	3911 S Dr Martin L King Jr Dr • 773-373-8081	Fine lodging in the old Goldblatt mansion.
Chicago Bee Building	3647 S State St	Formerly the HQ of the *Chicago Bee* Newspaper; now offices.
Chicago Bee Public Library	3647 S State St • 312-747-6872	Originally home of black newspaper, *Chicago Bee*.
Douglas Tomb	E 35th St & Lake Park Ave	Resting place of Lincoln's nemesis, overlooking tracks of Illinois Central railroad and the subdivision he founded. The entrance is on the east side of Lake.
Dunbar Park	S Indiana Ave & E 31st St	Dunbar High's girl's softball team plays here.

Early Chicago Defender Building	3435 S Indiana Ave	Originally an 1899 synagogue, was home of *Chicago Defender* from 1920–1940.
Eighth Regiment Armory	3533 S Giles Ave	First armory built in US for black regiment, 1914–1918, now a Chicago public high school.
Griffin Funeral Home	3232 S King Dr • 312-842-2422	Site of Civil War era Camp Douglas, with Civil War museum, founder forefather drilled there.
Ida B Wells / Barnett Home	3624 S King Dr	Former home of the journalism and civil rights pioneer.
IIT Student Housing	3303 S State St • 312-808-9771	Supercool housing for this iconic institute.
Interesting Benches	S Dr Martin L King Jr Dr b/w E 33rd St & E 35th St	13 artists created these 24 unique bench sculptures. Sit on them.
McCormick Tribune Campus Center	3201 S State St	Student center wrapped around the L. Wow!
Monument to the Great Northern Migration	S Dr Martin L King Jr Dr & E 26th St	Statue by Alison Sarr depicts a man with a briefcase atop a pile of old shoes. Represents the journey of African Americans from the south.
Olivet Baptist Church	3101 S King Dr • 312-538-0124	Church with a longstanding tradition of civil rights organizing ranging from abolitionist and feminist mass meetings to Black Panther Party programs.
Overton Hygenic Building	3619 S State St	Former headquarters of foremost producer of black cosmestics.
St James Catholic Church	2929 S Wabash Ave • 773-534-9281	Traditional community caretaking that included caring for Confederate POWs at Camp Douglas
Sunset Café	315 E 35th St	One of Chicago's earliest and most legendary jazz venues.
Supreme Life Insurance Company Head Office	3501 S King Dr	Built in 1921 and remodeled in 1950, this former major black insurance company enoys new life as a mixed commercial structure.
Victory Monument	35th St & King Dr	Early postwar tribute to WWI's black Eighth Regiment of the Illinois National Guard that served as part of the US 370th Infantry in France.
Wabash Avenue YMCA	3763 S Wabash Ave	Since 1913 provided housing and job training for new black arrivals from the South, where the Association for the Study of Negro Life and History, the first group devoted to black studies, was founded in 1915.

Map 16 · Bronzeville

Corpus Christi Church	4920 S King Dr • 773-285-7720	Built in 1921 for a predominately Irish parish that rapidly evolved into a predominately black parish.
Drexel Fountain	S Drexel Blvd & E Oakwood Blvd	The city's oldest remaining fountain.
Harold Washington Cultural Center	4701 S King Dr • 773-373-1900	Beautiful homage to the late mayor; it's a jaw-dropping technology & arts center.
Jamaican Consulate/ Jamaican Market Place	4655 S King Dr, Ste 104 • 773-624-092	A bit of Kingston on the Old South Side.
Liberty Baptist Church	4849 S King Dr • 773-268-6757	An afrocentric 1958 Go-Go styled temple considered King's original Chicago workshop.
Provident Hospital	500 E 51st St • 312-527-2000	Now county controlled, this century old hospital was the first to train black doctors and nurses and the site of the first successful open heart surgery.
Robert S Abbott Home	4742 S King Dr	Former home of *Chicago Defender* founder.
Steelife Gallery	4655 S King Dr • 773-538-4773	House of art that inspires the people.

Map 17 · Kenwood

Drexel Square Park	Drexel Blvd, from 51st St to 39th St	Victorian gem boasting city's oldest suriving fountain donated by prominent banking family.
Little Black Pearl Art & Design Center	1060 E 47th St • 773-285-1211	Offers visual arts classes, a swanky art café, and a gallery.
Louis Farrakhan Home	4855 S Woodlawn Ave	Well-guarded home of the leader of the Nation of Islam.
Rainbow/PUSH Coalition Headquarters	930 E 50th St • 773-373-3366	Originally the 1924 home of KAM Isaiah Israel, Chicago's oldest Jewish congregation, with late 1940s addition.
South Kenwood Mansions	b/w S Dorchester Ave, S Ellis Ave, E Hyde Park Blvd, & E 47th St	Built in the early 1900s by wealthy businessmen looking to flee the cramped North Side. Once in a state of disrepair, the mansions have (mostly) been rehabbed and are still the Jewels of the South Side.

Map 18 · Washington Park

Aquatic Center & Refectory	5531 S Martin Luther King Jr Dr · 773-256-1248	Designed by Daniel Burnham's firm, the Refectory now holds locker rooms for the Aquatic Center and its 36-foot waterslide.
DuSable Museum of African-American History	740 E 56th Pl · 773-947-0600	Founded in 1961 and dedicated to preserving and honoring African-American culture. The oldest non-profit institution of its kind.
Former Home of Jesse Binga	5922 S Dr Martin L King Jr Dr	Home of nation's first African-American banker.
Washington Park	5531 S Martin Luther King Dr · 773-256-1248	A sprawling 367-acre park with beautiful lagoons and fields. Check out the "Fountain of Time" sculpture in the southeast corner of the park.

Map 19 · Hyde Park

Frederick C Robie House	5757 S Woodlawn Ave	Designed by Frank Lloyd Wright; renovations proceeding, stay tuned.
Midway Plaisance Park & Skating Rink	S Ellis Ave & S University Ave, from E 59th St to E 60th St · 312-747-0233	Olympic-sized outdoor skating rink.
Nichols Park	1300 E 55th St	Home of the Parrots of Hyde Park.
Nuclear Energy Sculpture	5600 S Ellis Ave	Birthplace of the Atomic Age.
Oriental Institute Museum	1155 E 58th St · 773-702-9514	Educate yourself.
Rockefeller Memorial Chapel	5850 S Woodlawn Ave · 773-702-2100	Built in 1928, this English Gothic styled cathedral contains one of the world's largest carillons.
University of Chicago	S University Ave & E 57th St · 773-702-1234	A pretty spot for wandering on the south side.

Map 20 · East Hyde Park / Jackson Park

Osaka Garden/Wooded Island	Just south of the Museum of Science and Industry, b/w the West and East Lagoons	A Japanese garden in the middle of Jackson Park—why not?
Promontory Point Park	5491 S Shore Dr	Picnic with a view.

Map 21 · Wicker Park / Ukrainian Village

Coyote Building	1600 N Milwaukee Ave	This 12-story Art Deco building was constructed in 1929 and is currently a shrine to actor Peter Coyote.
Crumbling Bucktown	1579 N Milwaukee Ave	Structural icon visible from miles away; nucleus of Around the Coyote Arts Festival.
Division Street Russian Bath	1916 W Division St · 773-384-9671	Treat yourself to an old-school day at the spa, complete with Swedish massages and a granite heating room.
Flat Iron Building	1579 N Milwaukee Ave	This distinct triangular-shaped building is a part of the Chicago Coalition of Community Cultural Centers and houses artist studios.
Holy Trinity Orthodox Cathedral and Rectory	1121 N Leavitt St · 773-486-6064	Designed by Louis Sullivan to look like a Russian cathedral.
Wicker Park	Pierce St & Hoyne St	The homes in this district reflect the style of Old Chicago.

Map 22 · Noble Square / Goose Island

House of Crosses	1544 W Chestnut St	Eccentric owners have covered the property with hundreds of wooden crosses.
Morton Salt Elston Facility	Elston Ave & Blackhawk St	Has a painting of the famous salt girl, and, hey: acres of salt!
Nelson Algren Fountain	Division St & Ashland Blvd	Has a recent controversial addition.
North Avenue Bridge	W North Ave	Wretched traffic jams; river view.
Polish Museum of America	984 N Milwaukee Ave · 773-384-3352	Right-to-life painting on the side.
Pulaski Park/Pulaski Fieldhouse	Blackhawk St & Cleaver St	Has an outdoor swimming pool.
St Stanislaus Kostka Church	1351 W Evergreen Ave · 773-278-2470	One of the oldest in Chicago.
Weed Street District	b/w Chicago River & Halsted St	Several bars and clubs in one area. Party on.

Map 23 · West Town / Near West Side

First Baptist Congregational Church	1613 W Washington Blvd · 312-243-8047	Can seat 2000 people and houses one the largest totally enclosed organs in the country. There's a joke here somewhere.
Metropolitan Missionary Baptist Church	2151 W Washington Blvd · 312-738-0053	An attempt to find an appropriate design for the then-new Christian Science religion. Sold to Baptists in 1947.

Ukrainian Cultural Center	2247 W Chicago Ave · 773-384-6400	A gathering place to share and celebrate Ukrainian culture. Yeah!
Ukrainian National Museum	2249 W Superior St · 312-421-8020	Museum, library, and archives detail the heritage, culture, and people of Ukraine.
United Center	1901 W Madison St · 312-455-4500	Statue of His Airness still draws tourists.

Map 24 · River West / West Town

Eckhart Park/Ida Crown Natatorium	1330 W Chicago Ave · 312-746-5553	One of two swimming pools in the area.
Harpo Studios	1058 W Washington Blvd · 312-591-9222	Home of the Oprah Winfrey Show.
Jackson Boulevard Historic District	W Jackson Blvd & W Adams St b/w S Ashland Ave & S Laflin St	Amazingly, this cluster of preserved late-nineteenth century mansions survives in this declining area.

Map 25 · Illinois Medical District

18th St L station	W 18th St & S Paulina St	Gateway to Pilsen features colorful murals celebrating Mexican culture.
Bowler Row Houses	2148 W Bowler St	Historical row houses that have survived the wrecking ball.
Oakley Row Houses	801 S Oakley Ave	Italianate row houses that date back to 1870's.
Vietnam Survivors Memorial	815 S Oakley Ave	Privately funded memorial was erected by Vets.

Map 26 · University Village / Little Italy / Pilsen

National Italian American Sports Hall of Fame	1431 W Taylor St	How many Italian American sports stars do you know? DiMaggio is right out front.

Map 27 · Logan Square

Illinois Centennial Monument	3100 W Logan Blvd	Every city needs an obelisk or two…
Logan House	2656 W Logan Blvd	Renowned for over-the-top holiday décor.

Map 28 · Bucktown

Margie's Candies	1960 N Western Ave · 773-384-1035	The Beatles ate here.

Map 29 · DePaul / Wrightwood / Sheffield

Biograph Theater	2433 N Lincoln Ave · 773-348-4123	Site of gangster John Dillinger's infamous death in 1934; currently closed for renovation.
Cortland Street Drawbridge	1440 W Cortland St	Built in 1902 by John Ernst Erickson, this innovative leaf-lift bridge changed the way the world built bridges, and vice versa.
McCormick Row House District	W Chalmers Pl, W Belden Ave, & W Fullerton Pkwy	Quaint example of late 19th-century urban planning and architecture.
Pumpkin House	1052 W Wrightwood Ave	A Halloween spectacle of lighted pumpkins.

Map 30 · Lincoln Park

Dewes Mansion	503 N Wrightwood Ave · 773-477-3075	Ornate historic home done in the German Baroque style and built in 1896.
Kauffman Store and Flats	2312 N Lincoln Ave	One of the oldest existing buildings designed by Adler and Sullivan. It's amazing that its characteristic features have survived.
Lincoln Park Boat Club	N Cannon Dr & Fullerton Pkwy · 773-549-2628	Paddling, rowing, and sculling since 1910.
Lincoln Park Conservatory	2391 N Stockton Dr · 312-742-7736	The place to warm up in those brutal Chicago winters.
Lincoln Park Cultural Center	2045 N Lincoln Park W · 312-742-7726	Programming in visual arts for all ages.
Lincoln Park Zoo	N Cannon Dr, south of W Fullerton Pkwy · 312-742-2000	Oldest free zoo in the U.S.
Midwest Buddhist Temple	435 W Menomonee St	Enter their annual haiku contest.
Oz Park	2021 N Burling St	You're not in Kansas anymore.
Peggy Notebaert Nature Museum	2430 N Cannon Dr · 773-755-5100	An oasis for adults and kids to reconnect with nature by playing with wildflowers and butterflies.
The Point at Diversey	Lakefront at Diversey Harbor	One of the best views of the skyline. Ever.
Theurer-Wrigley House	2466 N Lakeview Ave	Early Richard E. Schmidt (and maybe Hugh H.G. Garden) based on late-Italian Renaissance architecture.
Waterlily Pond	Fullerton, just west of the zoo entrance	You might forget you're in a city.

Map 31 · Old Town / Near North

Steppenwolf Theatre	1650 N Halsted St · 312-335-1650	The one John Malkovich, Gary Sinise, and co. started.

Map 32 · Gold Coast / Mag Mile

Charnley-Persky House	1365 N Astor St · 312-915-0105	Louis Sullivan and Frank Lloyd Wright designed this national historic landmark. Go look before it becomes a CVS.
John Hancock Building	875 N Michigan Ave	Zone out the tourists, and focus in on the prettiest view of the city.
Lake Shore Drive Apartments	860 Lake Shore Dr	Less is more—by Mies van der Rohe.
The Newberry Library	60 W Walton St · 312-943-9090	There's plenty on offer at this humanities library.
Old Playboy Mansion	1340 N State Pkwy	You have no idea what happened here.
Water Tower Place and Park	845 N Michigan Ave · 312-440-3165	Huge shopping—6 floors—Marshall Field's…er, Macy's.

Map 33 · West Rogers Park

Bernard Horwich JCC	3003 W Touhy Ave · 773-761-9100	Community center with programming for kids/adults, pool/fitness center, senior center, and sports leagues.
Croatian Cultural Center	2845 W Devon Ave · 773-338-3839	A place where families can relax, socialize and congregate. Intended to benefit the Croatian community in Chicago (duh).
High Ridge YMCA	2424 W Touhy Ave · 773-262-8300	Community center with programming for kids/adults, summer activities, child care programs, sport teams, and a pool.
India Town	W Devon Ave, near Washtenaw Ave	Features Indian and Pakistani shops, grocery stores, restaurants, and more.
Indian Boundary Park	2500 W Lunt Ave · 773-742-7887	Petting zoo, tennis courts, chess tables, ice rink, skate park, batting cages, spray pool, with seasonal community center classes.
Rogers Park/West Ridge Historical Society	7344 N Western Ave · 773-764-4078	Photos/memorabilia/historical documents of the community's history detailing its ethnic diversity.
Thillen's Stadium	Devon & Kedzie Ave	16 softball fields. Features little league baseball and various other games and benefits.
Warren Park	6601 N Western Ave · 773-262-6314	Seasonal free entertainment, pony rides, ethnic food festivals, amusement park rides, arts and crafts, winter sledding hill, baseball diamond, picnic pavilions, and dog play areas.

Map 34 · East Rogers Park

Angel Guardian Croatian Catholic Church	6346 N Ridge Ave · 773-262-0535	1905 red-brick Romanesque church. Turn-of-the-century German stained glass windows by Franz Mayer and F. X. Zettler.
Robert A Black Golf Course	2045 W Pratt Blvd · 312-742-7931	The newest Chicago Park District course. 2,300-yard, par 33 layout for all skill levels.

Map 35 · Arcadia Terrace / Peterson Park

Lincoln Avenue Motels	N Lincoln Ave b/w W Foster Ave & W Devon Ave	Seedy vice dens with cool vintage signs are falling prey to the wrecking ball.

Map 36 · Bryn Mawr / Bowmanville

Rosehill Cemetery and Mausoleum	5800 N Ravenswood Ave	Chicago's historical glitterati entombed among unsurpassed sculpture and architecture.

Map 37 · Edgewater / Andersonville

Ann Sather	5207 N Clark St · 773-271-6677	Heavenly cinnamin rolls and swedish meatballs.
The Belle Shore Hotel Building	1062 W Bryn Mawr Ave	Former homes of roaring 1920s nightlife, now historic landmarks restored to their former glory as apartments.
Edgewater Beach Apartments	5555 N Sheridan Rd	The big pink building symbolizing the end of the lakeshore bike path.
Philadelphia Church	5437 N Clark St · 773-728-5106	Complete with can't-miss neon sign.
Swedish American Museum	5211 N Clark St · 773-728-8111	Everything you want to know about Swedish culture, which is more than you thought.

Map 38 · Ravenswood / Albany Park

Albany Park Community Center	3401 W Ainslie St · 773-509-5650	Local community center at SW corner of Ainslie and Kimball.
Fish Furniture Co Building	3322 W Lawrence Ave	Striking 1931 Art Moderne building with fish motif, currently houses Interstate Blood Bank.
North Branch Pumping Station	Lawrence Ave & the Chicago River	With its 1930s Art Deco facade, it seems like something prettier should be happening than North Side sewage pumping…
Paradise	2916 W Montrose Ave · 773-588-1989	It's a sushi restaurant. It's a beauty shop. It's a sauna ($12, unlimited time). It's Paradise. Of course, it's a neighborhood landmark.
Ravenswood Manor Park	4626 N Manor Ave	It's just a tiny triangle wedged between the non-elevated L and several streets, but it's ground zero for garden sales, neighborhood associations, dogs, kids, and community activity.
River Park	5100 N Francisco Ave	More than 30 acres of park, including one of the few city canoe launches.
Ronan Park Walking Trail	3000 W Argyle St	These boots are made for…walking!
Willis Building	3221 W Lawrence Ave	1924 Renaissance Revival building designed by Jens Jensen.

Map 39 · Ravenswood / North Center

Lincoln Square	4800 N Lincoln Ave	A virtual tour through a European-style neighborhood.
Old Town School of Folk Music	4544 N Lincoln Ave · 773-728-6000	Northern expansion of beloved Chicago institution. Classes and concert venue.
St Benedict's Church	2215 W Irving Park Rd · 773-588-6484	The namesake of the St. Ben's neighborhood.

Map 40 · Uptown

Aragon Ballroom	1106 W Lawrence Ave · 773-561-9500	One of the better smaller music venues in the city.
Graceland Cemetery	4001 N Clark St · 773-525-1105	Chicago's famous buried in a masterpiece of landscape architecture.
Green Mill Pub	4802 N Broadway St · 773-878-5552	Chicago legend… And birthplace of the poetry slam.
St Augustine College	1333 W Argyle St · 773-878-8756	Episcopalian bilingual training school occupying original headquarters of Essanay Studios, where Chaplin, Broco Billy, and Swanson made films before moving to Southern CA.
Uptown Theatre	4816 N Broadway St	An acre of seats in a magic city.

Map 41 · Avondale / Old Irving

Com-Ed Plant	N California Ave & W Roscoe St	What's that humming sound in Avondale? Must be this ginormous electrical plant.

Map 42 · North Center / Roscoe Village / West Lakeview

19th District Police Headquarters	2452 W Belmont Ave · 312-744-5983	Going to "Western & Belmont" is synonymous for being in deep sh#*.

Map 43 · Wrigleyville/ East Lakeview

North Alta Vista Terrace	3800 block of N Alta Vista Ter	London-style row houses with Edwardian elegance.
Southport Lanes	3325 N Southport Ave · 773-472-6600	Four hand-set lanes. Eat a Honeymooner while you wait.
Vic Theatre	3145 N Sheffield Ave · 773-472-0449	Drink, watch films, and take in an occasional band at this old theatre.
Wrigley Field	1060 W Addison St · 773-404-CUBS	Charm-filled and crumbling ballpark that remains indifferent to wins or losses on the field.

Map 44 · East Lakeview

Belmont Harbor	W Belmont Ave & N Lake Shore Dr	Home to the Chicago Yacht Club sailing school.
Belmont Rocks	W Briar Pl at the lake	Popular lakefront hangout.
Dog Beach	Northern tip of Belmont Harbor	Fun and frolic with your pup.
The Giraffes	N Elaine Pl & W Roscoe Ave	Iconic public art.
Totem Pole	W Waveland Ave & N Belmont Harbor Dr	Where did it come from? Why is it there? Nobody knows.

Northwest

The Admiral Theater	3940 W Lawrence Ave	Built in 1928, this former vaudeville theater is now a well-known "gentlemen's club."
Copernicus Center	5216 W Lawrence Ave • 773-777-9184	Jefferson Park's cultural hub.
Eugene Field Park	5100 N Ridgeway Ave • 773-478-9744	Features a 1928 Tudor Revival fieldhouse, the Eugene Field Cultural Center (home of the Albany Park Theater Project).
Gompers Park	4222 W Foster Ave • 773-685-3270	Large riverfront park.
Hanson Park Fieldhouse	5501 W Fullerton Ave	Very old fieldhouse with WWII barracks.
Harlem CTA Station	N Harlem Ave & The Kennedy Expy	One of the more "el"egant stations.
Logan Square Column	3100 W Logan Blvd	It's just like Paris, yet different.
Superdawg Drive-In	6363 N Milwaukee Ave	Everyone knows the Superdog and his sexy girlfriend.
Walt Disney House	2156 N Tripp Ave	Where old Walt learned to ride his bike.

West

Austin Town Hall	5610 W Lake St	115-year-old former town hall; now a public recreation building.
Bison Statues at Humboldt Park	1400 N Sacramento Ave	Meet up by the Bison.
Chicago Center for Green Technology	445 N Sacramento Blvd • 312-746-9642	A green center for this self-styled green city.
Columbus Park Refectory	Columbus Park, 500 S Central Ave	Historic refectory now available for weddings and other fetes.
Delta Fish Market	228 S Kedzie Ave	Defunct fish fry-up features live blues in its parking lot.
Engine 44 Firehouse Mural	412 N Kedzie Ave	When kids do it, it's called graffiti.
Garfield Park Conservatory	300 N Central Park Ave	Tropical oasis in the midst of the urban jungle.
Our Lady of Sorrows	3121 W Jackson Blvd	Unsung treasure built in the late 19th century.
Skokie Northshore Sculpture Park	McCormick Blvd b/w Touhy Ave & Dempster St • 847-679-4265	Culture in the 'burbs. No joke.
Union Stockyard Gate	Exchange Ave & Peoria St	This limestone gate marks the place that made Chicago "hog butcher to the world."

Southwest

Adams House	9326 S Longwood Dr	A 1901 Frank Lloyd Wright gem.
Arnett Chapel, African Methodist Episcopal Church	11218 S Bishop St • 773-238-0670	One of oldest black congregations in historically black Morgan Park.
Bell Tower Condos	10321 S Longwood Dr	Built in 1916 for 13th Church of Christ Science, retains many of original architectural features including mother-of-pearl stained glass.
Blackwelder Summerling House	10910 S Prospect Ave	Built in sections from 1865 to 1873, was once Morgan Park's social center and home to Morgan Park's first village president, Isaac Blackwelder.
The Body of Lake Michigan	The ceiling near the security checkpoint at Midway Airport	Please remove your shoes. And look up.
Bohn Park	111th St & Prospect Ave	Originally known as Depot Park and sometimes called the Commons, features street lamps from 1893 World's Columbian Exposition.
Bronzeville Children's Museum	9600 S Western Ave • 708-636-9504	The romper room for learning black history for kids of all ages.
Burhans-Ellinwood Model House	10410 S Hoyne Ave	One of two 1917 models designed by Wright for a subdivision of prefabricated American-System Built Houses.
Campbell House	9250 S Damen Ave	An 1896 Tudor designed for the founder of the John H. Vanderpoel Collection.
Capital Cigar Store	6258 S Pulaski Rd	World's most conspicous cigar-store Indian.
Edward L Roberts House	10134 S Longwood Dr	An 1892 Queen Anne, now St. Barnabas's rectory, built by a lumber-milling magnate to exhibit decorative architectural details from his catalogue.
Edwin C Young House	9215 S Pleasant Ave	Robust Queen Anne with tower, front porch, and portcochiere.
Evans House	9914 S Longwood Dr	A 1908 Prairie Style gem designed by Frank Lloyd Wright.
Ferguson House	10954 S Prospect Ave	An 1873 Italianate beauty; built for the manager of Lancaster Fire Insurance.
Frank Anderson House	10400 S Pleasant Ave	Elegant Renaissance house now the residence of Chicago State University's president.

Gately House	10655 S Hoyne Ave	A 1927 neo-classical, recalling classical revival mansions of English Regency. Was home of founder of Gately's People Store based in Roseland.
Givens Irish Castle	10244 S Longwood Dr	Seminal grand dame of the mansion district in the original Beverly Hills.
Godspeed House	11216 S Oakley Ave	Farmhouse built in 1876 for the Rev. Thomas Goodspeed, pastor of Morgan Park Baptist Church and professor at Baptist Theological Seminary.
Graffiti Mural	W 59th St & S Damen Ave	An example of when it's public "art" not public "nuisance."
Harris House	10856 S Longwood Dr	A 1906 hilltop Tudor built for the founder of Rotary International.
Holy Name of Mary Church	1423 W 112th St · 773-238-6800	Opened in 1947, Morgan Park's oldest black parish.
Hopkinson House	10820 S Drew St	Italianate built for real estate dealer, landscaped by parks landscape architect Jens Jensen.
Horton Mansion	10200 S Longwood Dr	An 1890 Colonial Revival built for the founder of Chicago Bridge & Iron.
Howe House	10208 S Wood St	An 1881 Stick Style designed for one of area's oldest residents by a family friend, Daniel H. Burnham.
JB Chambers House	10330 S Seeley Ave	A 1871 blend of Gothic, Italianate, and French Empire styles.
Karge House	2035 W 99th St	A 1926 Spanish Colonial, known for distinctive stone block construction with ornate block detailing and medallions with scuplted Indian heads.
Lackmore House	10956 S Prospect Ave	Built 1801–1872 by relative of the area's first settler, DeWitt Lane.
McCumber House	10305 S Seeley Ave	A 1911 Colonial Revival once used as a Marshall Field & Co. Showcase House.
Metra 103rd/Washington Heights Rock Island District Branch Line Station	103rd St & Vincennes Ave	Refurbished handsome late Victorian gem that originally served the village of Washington Heights.
Metra Rock Island Main Line 111th St/ Monterey Ave Station	111th St & Monterey Ave	A restored at-grade Victorian gem from early 1892, built to replace 1870 station, after Rock Island railroad expanded its suburban service.
Midway Airport	5700 S Cicero Ave	World's Busiest Airport…in 1932. Today a place to fly and land cheaply, surrounded by tiny bungalows filled with various Eastern European types.
Morgan Park Apostolic Penecostal Church	11401 S Vincennes Ave · 773-239-9586	One of oldest black congregations in Morgan Park.
Morgan Park United Methodist Church	11030 S Longwood Dr · 773-238-2600	Early Prairie School treasure along the Blue Island Ridge.
Oakdale Park	956 W 95th St · 312-747-6569	A post-WWII greenspace with oak-shaded walking trails.
Original Rainbow Cone	9233 S Western Ave	People line up day and night in the summer.
Ridge Historical Society	10621 S Seeley Ave · 773-881-1675	Blue Island Ridge history is preserved in the old Walgreen mansion.
Ridge Park	9625 S Longwood Dr · 773-779-0007	Fieldhouse houses John H. Vanderpoel Art Association, comprising 600 pieces dedicated to renowed instructor at Art Institute of Chicago.
St Walter Catholic Church	11722 S Oakley Ave · 773-779-1515	Half-century-old Catholic community with modern approach to traditional values.
Walter Burley Griffin Place	W 104th Pl, Wood St to Prospect Ave	Largest concentration of Prairie Style homes in Chicago, built from 1910–1914.
William MR French House	9203 S Pleasant Ave	An 1894 Colonial Revival mansion built for the first director of the Art Institute of Chicago; sculpture by brother David Chester French.

South

Carter G Woodson Regional Library	9525 S Halsted St · 312-747-6900	Named for the "Father of Black History," houses Vivian Harsh black history collection.
Cedar Park Cemetery & Funeral Home	12540 S Halsted St · 773-785-8840	Final resting place where deer, geese, and other wildlife play in peace.
Chicago Skyway	8801 S Anthony St · 312-747-8383	Soar 125 feet over the southside on this thrilling overpass!
Chicago State University	9501 S King Dr · 773-995-2000	Metropolitan Chicago's oldest public university.
Lilydale First Baptist Church	649 W 113th St · 773-785-1976	Another cultural anchor for Roseland's historically black community.
Lilydale Progressive Missionary Baptist Church	10706 S Michigan Ave · 773-785-8623	Serving the historically black community on Roseland's northern end since the end of WWI.
Market Hall	E 112th St & Champlain Ave	George M. Pullman built colonnaded apartments surrounding a prototype shopping mall in 1893 to house friends visiting the World's Columbian Exposition.
New Regal Theatre	1645 E 79th St	80-year-old former movie-house.
Oak Woods Cemetery	1035 E 67th St	Former Mayor Washington and civil rights activist Ida B. Wells rest here.
Palmer Park	201 E 111th St · 312-747-6576	Created in 1904 to intergrate social services with recreation for congested tenement districts. Features three WPA-comissioned murals by James Edward McBurney.
Pullman Clock Tower	11141 S Cottage Grove Ave · 773-785-8901	This beacon of Pullman can be seen from far and wide.
Robert S Abbott Park	49 E 95th St · 312-737-6100	Created in 1949 to serve the rapidly growing black community near 95th St & Michigan Ave; one of first parks named after a prominent African American.
South Shore Cultural Center	7059 South Shore Dr · 773-747-2536	A glittering pearl on the south lakefront.
Trinity United Church of Christ	400 W 95th St · 773-962-5650	Where US Senator Barack Obama worships.
West Pullman Elementary	11941 S Parnell Ave · 773-535-5500	Mammoth 1894 structure featuring Romanesque stylings.
West Pullman Park	401 W 123rd St · 312-727-7090	A 1915 greenspace created to Americanize an industrializing community.

Evanston

Evanston Historical Society	225 Greenwood St · 847-475-3410	Explore Evanston's history. Closed Monday and Tuesday.
Light Opera Works	927 Noyles St · 847-869-6300	26 seasons of musical theater. Hmmmm.

Oak Park

Frank Lloyd Wright Home and Studio	951 W Chicago Ave · 708-848-1976	See the drafting room where the Prairie Style was created. Inspiring.

Useful Phone Numbers

City Board of Elections	312-269-7900
State Board of Elections	217-782-4141
ComEd	800-334-7661
Peoples Gas Billing	312-240-4350
Peoples Gas Emergencies	312-240-7001
Drivers Licensing Facilities	312-793-1010
Office of Mayor Richard Daley	312-744-5000
Governor's Office	312-814-2121
General Aldermanic Information	312-744-3081

Helpful Websites and Local Blogs

Angie's List • www.angieslist.com
Membership-driven site rating local contractors and other services. Great for home repair, caterers, etc.
Centerstage Chicago • www.centerstagechicago.com
Chicago's original online guide.
Citysearch Chicago • www.chicago.citysearch.com
Restaurants, clubs, etc.
City of Chicago • http://egov.cityofchicago.org
Helpful all-purpose guide to city services.
The Chicagoist • www.chicagoist.com
Local news/events blog.
The Chicago Blog • http://pressblog.uchicago.edu
Publicity news from the University of Chicago Press, including book reviews, press releases, and "intelligent commentary."
Chicago City Clerk • www.chicityclerk.com
Renew your city sticker online!
Chicago Recycling • www.chicagorecycling.org
All the scoop on where to dispose of your junk.
Cook County Assessor • www.cookcountyassessor.com
Research properties and tax assessments.
Cook County Tresurer • www.cookcountytreasurer.com
Pay your property tax online and download forms
Daily Candy • www.dailycandy.com/chicago
Sign up to get info on deals and steals on fashion, food and fun in the city.
Gaper's Block • www.gapersblock.com
A popular Chicago web-publication detailing local news, fun events, and cool places in the city.
Metromix • www.metromix.com
City guide put out by the Trib.
My Open Bar • http://chi.myopenbar.com
Daily updates on where to drink for free or cheap throughout the city
Not For Tourists • www.notfortourists.com
Duh.
Pitchfork Media • www.pitchforkmedia.com
Cool indie music site and sponsors of the grooviest music fest ever.
Spacefinder • www.chireader.com/spacefinder
The source for apartment rentals.

Taxi Cabs

Checker	312-243-2537
American United	773-248-7600
Flash Cab	773-898-8500 or 773-561-4444
Yellow Cab	800-829-4222

We're Number One!!!

World's Busiest Airport: O'Hare International
World's Largest Public Library: Harold Washington Library
World's Largest Aquarium: Shedd Aquarium
World's Largest Free Public Zoo: Lincoln Park Zoo
World's Largest Modern Art Museum:
Museum of Contemporary Art
Worlds Largest Commercial Office Building:
Merchandise Mart, 222 Merchandise Mart Plaza
World's Longest Street: Western Avenue
World's Busiest Roadway: The Dan Ryan Expressway
World's Largest Food Festival: Taste of Chicago

Chicago Timeline

1779: Jean-Baptiste Point du Sable establishes Chicago's first permanent settlement.
1803: U.S. Army constructs Fort Dearborn. It is destroyed during conflicts with Native Americans in 1812 and rebuilt in 1816.
1818: Illinois is admitted into the union.
1833: Chicago incorporates as a town of 350 people, bordered by Kinzie, Des Plaines, Madison, and the lakefront.
1837: Chicago incorporates as a city. The population is 4,170. Ogden becomes the city's first mayor.
1851: Northwestern University is founded.
1856: Fort Dearborn is demolished.
1860: Republican Party nominates Abraham Lincoln for president at Chicago's first political convention.
1865: Merry Christmas! Union Stockyards open on Christmas Day.
1869: Water tower is completed.
1871: Great Chicago Fire!
1885: World's first "skyscraper," the 9-story Home Insurance building, goes up on La Salle Street.
1886: Haymarket Riots. Eight Chicago policemen are killed.
1889: Jane Addams opens Hull House.
1892: World's first elevated trains begin operation.
1893: Columbia Exposition celebrates 400th anniversary of Columbus's discovery of America.
1907: Chicago physicist Abraham Michelson is first American to win Nobel Prize.
1910: Original Comiskey Park opens.
1914: Wrigley Field opens.
1927: $750,000 donated to city to build fountain in honor of Clarence Buckingham.
1929: John G. Shedd presents Shedd Aquarium as a "gift to the Chicago People."
1930: Adler Planetarium opens through a gift from Max Adler.
1930: Merchandise Mart built by Marshall Field.
1931: Chicagoan Jane Addams becomes first woman to win Nobel Peace Prize.
1931: Al Capone sent to prison for 11 years for evading taxes.
1934: John Dillinger shot by FBI outside Biograph Theater.
1955: O'Hare International Airport opens.
1958: End of the line: Last streetcar in Chicago stops operating.
1968: Democratic National Convention riots.
1971: Chicago Union Stock Yards are closed.
1974: Sears Tower is completed.
1983: Harold Washington elected first black mayor.
1995: A heat wave contributed to the death of over 700 Chicagoans.
1997: City Council absolves Mrs. O'Leary's cow of blame for Great Chicago Fire.
1998: Six-peat! Chicago Bulls win their sixth world championship in eight years.
2003: Four-peat! Richard M. Daley re-elected for historic fourth term!
2005: White Sox win World Series; Cubs fans heard weeping from miles away.
2007: Chicago piched as US bid for 2016 Olympics.

25 Essential Chicago Movies

Northside 777 (1948)
Man with the Golden Arm (1955)
Raisin in the Sun (1961)
Medium Cool (1969)
The Sting (1973)
Blues Brothers (1980)
Risky Business (1983)
Ferris Bueller's Day Off (1986)
Adventures in Babysitting (1987)
Planes, Trains and Automobiles (1987)
The Untouchables (1987)
Backdraft (1991)
Candyman (1992)
The Fugitive (1993)
Hoop Dreams (1994)
Mission: Impossible (1996)
My Best Friend's Wedding (1997)
High Fidelity (2000)
Save the Last Dance (2000)
What Women Want (2000)
Barbershop (2002)
Road to Perdition (2002)
The Company (2003)
Chicago (2002)
Batman Begins (2005)
The Weatherman (2005)

Overview

WGN is the classic Chicago TV station. Its radio affiliate at 720 AM *is* Chicago talk radio. WGN isn't a bad place to find intelligent conversation, particularly through the long-running "Extension 720" program hosted by Milt Rosenberg. **WXRT** is the city's independent rock station—one of the few remaining stations still free from the smothering embrace of Clear Channel Communications. Their Sunday morning Beatles Brunch with host Terri Hemmert (a Chicago institution in her own right) is heaven for fans of the Fab Four. In general the station is a little heavy on the white-boy blues (think Clapton and Stevie Ray Vaughan) and crunchy rock ala Dave Matthews and Hootie—if that's your thing. Midway down the dial, alt-music station **Q101's** morning host Mancow Muller is a more immature version of Howard Stern—less sex, more body secretions. In terms of print media, we'll put it this way: the **Tribune** appeals to Cubs fans, while the **Sun-Times** is favored by White Sox fans. **Time Out** is the latest alt entertainment weekly to come to Chicago and the **Reader** is the essential paper for slacker job seekers and apartment hunters. The *Reader* also is known for its investigative pieces that take on everything from the daily life of dogcatchers to the seamy world of local politics.

Television

	CLTV	(Cable)			
2	WBBM	(CBS)	26	WCIU	(the U)
5	WMAQ	(NBC)	32	WFLD	(Fox)
7	WLS	(ABC)	38	WCPX	ION Television
9	WGN	(CW)	44	WSNS	(Telemundo)
11	WTTW	(PBS)	23	WFBT	(Brokered—ethnic)
20	WYCC	(PBS)	50	WPWR	(My 50)
23	WWME	(Me TV)	60	WXFT-TV	(Telefutura)
			66	WGBO	(Univision)

Print

Chicago Defender	200 S Michigan Ave, Suite 1700	312-225-2400	Black community newspaper.
Chicago Free Press	3845 N Broadway St, 2nd Fl	773-868-0005	Gay community news.
Chicago Innerview Magazine	1849 S. Blue Island Avenue	312-850-3635	Free monthly music mag previewing bands coming to concert in town.
Chicago Magazine	435 N. Michigan Ave., Suite 1100	312-222-8999	Upscale glossy mag.
Chicago Reader	11 E Illinois St	312-828-0350	Free weekly with listings.
Chicago Reporter	332 S Michigan Ave	312-427-4830	Investigative reporting on issues of race, poverty, and social justice.
Chicago Sun-Times	350 N. Orleans St, 10th Fl	312-321-3000	One of the big dailies.
Chicago Tribune	435 N Michigan Ave	312-222-3232	The other big daily.
Crain's Chicago Business	360 N Michigan Ave	312-649-5411	Business news.
CS	200 W Hubbard	312-274-2500	Free monthly upscale Chicago lifestyle mag.
Daily Herald	155 E Algonquin Rd, Arlington Hts	847-427-4300	Suburban news.
Daily Southtown	6901 W 159th St, Tinley Pk	708-633-6700	News for southsiders.
Ebony	820 S Michigan Ave	312-322-9200	National glossy about African Americans.
Hoy Chicago	435 N Michigan Ave # 22	312-527-8400	Daily Spanish-language newspaper
Hyde Park Herald	1435 E. Hyde Park Boulevard	773-643-8533	Local for Hyde Parkers.
Korea Times	3720 W Devon Ave	847-626-0388	Daily Korean-language newspaper.
La Raza	6001 N Clark St	773-273-2900	Hispanic community paper.
Lerner-Booster-Skyline	7331 N Lincoln Ave, Lincolnwood	847-329-2000	Conglomeration of neighborhood papers.
N'Digo	19 N Sangamon	312-822-0202	Black community weekly.
Newcity	770 N Halsted Ave	312-243-8786	Alternative free weekly.
The Onion	47 W Division St	312-751-0503	Local listings in AV Club insert.
Punk Planet	4229 N. Honore	773-248-7172	Independent music and culture zine.
Red Eye	435 N Michigan Ave	312-222-4970	Commuter-targeted offshoot of the *Trib* for 20- and 30-somethings.
Time Out Chicago	247 S State St	312-924-9555	Glossy arts and entertainment weekly.
Today's Chicago Woman	150 East Huron	312-951-7600	Weekly for working women.
UR Chicago	4043 N Ravenswood	773-404-1497	Free monthly local entertainment mag.
Venuszine	2000 N. Racine, suite 3400	773-327-9790	Subscription based mag on both local and national culture and music.
Windy City Times	5443 N. Broadway	773-871-7610	Gay-targeted news weekly.

Public Radio

AM		
560	WIND	Talk
620	WTMJ	News/Talk
	no longer exists	
720	WGN	Talk
780	WBBM	Talk
820	WCSN	Religious
850	WAIT	Standards
890	WLS	News/Talk
1000	WMVP	Sports
1110	WMBI	Religious
1280	WBIG	Talk
1390	WGCI	Gospel
1450	WVON	Talk (Black- oriented)
1490	WPNA	Polish
1510	WWHN	Gospel
1570	WBEE	Jazz

FM		
88.1	WCRX	Columbia College
88.5	WHPK	U of Chicago
88.7	WLUW	Loyola U
89.3	WNUR	Northwestern
90.1	WMBI	Christian
90.0	WDCB	Jazz
91.5	WBEZ	National
93.1	WXRT	Rock
93.9	WLIT	Adult Contemporary
94.7	WZZN	Oldies
95.1	WIIL	Rock
95.5	WNUA	Smooth jazz
95.9	WKKD	Rock
96.3	WBBM	Dance
97.9	WLUP	Rock
98.7	WFMT	Classical
99.5	WUSN	Country

99.9	WRZA	Variety Hits
	(Nine FM)	(also includes WDEK
	92.5 & WKIE 92.7)	
100.3	WNND	Adult Contemporary
101.1	WKQX	Modern Rock
101.9	WTMX	Adult Contemporary
102.7	WVAZ	Urban Contemporary
103.1	WXXY	80s
103.5	WKSC	Top 40
104.3	WJMK	Jack FM
105.1	WOJO	Spanish
105.9	WCKG	Adult Contmeporary
106.7	WYLL	Christian
107.5	WGCI	Urban Contemporary

22 Essential Chicago Books

Native Son, by Richard Wright.
Gripping novel about a young black man on the South Side in the '30s.

Neon Wilderness, by Nelson Algren.
Short story collection set in Ukrainian Village and Wicker Park.

One More Time, by Mike Royko.
Collection of Royko's *Tribune* columns.

The Boss: Richard M. Daley, by Mike Royko.
Biography of the former Mayor.

The Jungle, by Upton Sinclair.
Gritty look at the life in the meat-packing plants.

Adventures of Augie March, by Saul Bellow.
More Chicago in the '30s.

V.I. Warshawsky, by Sara Paretsky.
Mystery series firmly rooted in Chicago landscape.

50 Years at Hull House, by Jane Addams.
Story of the Near West Side.

Secret Chicago, by Sam Weller.
Off-the-beaten path guidebook.

Ethnic Chicago, by Melvin Holli & Peter D'A. Jones.
Insider's guide to Chicago's ethnic neighborhoods.

House on Mango Street, by Sandra Cisneros.
Short story collection about a Latina childhood in Chicago.

Our America: Life and Death on the South Side of Chicago, by Lealan Jones, et al.
Life in the Chicago Projects as told by two schoolchildren.

The Coast of Chicago, by Stuart Dybek.
Short stories of Chicago denizens.

Hairstyles of the Damned, by Joe Meno.
Teen angst and punk rock in '80s Chicago.

Never a City So Real: A Walk in Chicago, by Alex Kotlowitz.
Modern reflection on the city of big shoulders.

American Pharaoh: Mayor Richard J. Daley, by Adam Cohen and Elizabeth Taylor.
Recent work that explores the life and works of Hizzoner the First.

Studs Lonigan, by James T. Farrell.
Growing up gritty and Irish in Washington Park, circa the early 20th century.

Chicago: The Second City, by A. J. Liebling.
Legendary *New Yorker* columnist and curmudgeon comes to the Windy City, gives it a new sobriquet, and tells all.

A Guide to Chicago's Murals, by Mary Lackritz Gray.
Murals, murals, and more murals.

The Pig and the Skyscraper, by Marco D'Eramo.
Wandering Italian sociologist comes to Chicago and explores the wide world of capitalism through Chicago's radical history, skyscrapers, and meat-processing plants.

The Devil in The White City by Erik Larson
Account of Chicago serial killer H.H. Holmes and the 1893 Chicago World's Fair.

Chicago Then and Now (Then & Now Thunder Bay) by Elizabeth McNulty
Explores Chicago's transformation and progression as a city.

From May to September, every corner of the city is hopping with all manner of block parties, church carnivals, neighborhood festivals, and all-out hootenanny. Contact the Mayor's Office of Special Events for a complete list of the city's 100+ festivals.

Event	When & Where	Description
Chinese New Year	Sunday after the Chinese New Year (late-January or mid-February), Chinatown	2009 is the year of the Ox. Celebrate!
Chicago Auto Show	Early February, McCormick Place	The nation's largest auto show celebrates its 100th year.
Uplift! Chicago (formerly Expo For Today's Black Woman)	Friday to Sunday, first weekend of May, McCormick Place East, 2301 S Lake Shore Dr	This faith-based event, started in 1993, is undergoing an "evolution." www.upliftchicago.com
St Patrick's Day Parade	Saturday prior to St Paddy's, Columbus Ave, Balbo to Randolph	The Chicago River turns green. On purpose.
Chicago Flower Show	Mid-March, Navy Pier	Escape from winter.
Chicago Latino Film Festival	Early April, various venues	20+-year-old festival screens the best in local and international Latino film. www.latinoculturalcenter.org/Filmfest
Great Chicago Places & Spaces	Weekend in Mid-May, various venues	An architectural love-fest with dozens of free tours around the city.
Bike Chicago	May-September, various venues	More than 100 events including "Bike the Drive" and the midnight LATE Ride.
Printers Row Book Fair	Second weekend in June, Dearborn St, b/w Harrison St & Balbo Dr	Watch for Booksellers Gone Wild, coming soon to pay-per-view.
Andersonville Midsommarfest	Second weekend in June, Clark St, b/w Foster & Balmoral Aves	Ain't it Swede?
Taste of Chicago	Last week in June, first week in July, Grant Park	Why go to a restaurant when you can eat standing up in the hot sun in a crowd?
Country Music Fest	Last weekend in June, Grant Park	Annual Lakeside hoe-down. www.cityofchicago.org/specialevents
Gay Pride Parade	Last Sunday in June, Halsted/Broadway Sts b/w Halsted & Grace Sts	400,000 of the city's gay community and their fans take it to the streets. www.chicagopridecalendar.org
Beverly Arts Fair	Third week in June, Beverly Arts Center, 2407 W 111th St	Family fun in Beverly.
Juneteenth Celebration	Third Saturday in June, 79th & Stony Island	African-American Pride celebration includes parade, music, and lots of barbecue at Rainbow Beach.
57th Street Art Fair	First week in June, 57th & Kimbark	Oldest juried art fair in the Midwest. www.57thstreetartfair.org
Jeff Fest	Late June, Jefferson Park	Neighborhood festival of guys named Jeff. Okay, just kidding. It's Jefferson Park—get it?"
Bronzeville House Tours	Late June, 3402 S King Dr	The best way to peek into Chicago's African- American history.
Gospel Music Festival	First weekend in June, Grant Park	As much about the soul food as the music.
Chicago Blues Festival	Second weekend in June, Grant Park	Drawing the top names in blues for 21 years.
Old Town Art Fair	Mid-June, 1800 N Orleans St, Menominee St, Lincoln Ave	Arts and crafts.
Independence Eve Fireworks	July 3, Grant Park	Real fireworks occur when a million spectators try to leave Grant Park.
Chicago Hip-Hop Heritage Month	July 1-31, various venues	Where "New Beat" culture celebrates its past, present, and future. www.chihiphop.org.
Venetian Night	Third weekend in July, Monroe Harbor	Wow! Decked out boats!

Event	When & Where	Description
Outdoor Film Festival	Tuesdays, Mid-July to mid-August, Grant Park	Classic movies, a carafe of vino, and KFC. Life is good.
Rock Around the Block	Second weekend in July	Lots of street-festival-quality live music. Expect Bumpus and Underwater People.
Taste of Logan Square	Mid-August, Fullerton & Kedzie	It tastes cement-y.
Korean Street Festival	Mid-July, 3200–3400 W Bryn Mawr	One-stop shopping for your bibimbap, juk, and kimbap.
Fiesta Del Sol	Last weekend in July, Cermak Rd, b/w Throop & Morgan Sts	One of the most festive of the fests.
Bud Billiken Parade	Second Saturday in August, King Dr	World's biggest African-American parade. www.budbillikenparade.com
Black Harvest International Film & Video Festival	First two weeks of August, Gene Siskel Film Center, 164 N State St	Where the substance and form of black filmmaking knows no boundaries.www.siskelfilmcenter.org.
Northalsted Market Days	Second weekend in August, Halsted St b/w Belmont Ave & Addison St	See Gay Pride Parade. Add beer and live music. http://www.northalsted.com/daze.htm
Air and Water Show	Third weekend in August, lakefront	The Stealth Bombers never fail to thrill.
Viva Chicago Latin Music Fest	Last weekend in August, Grant Park	Salsa under the stars.
Taste of Polonia	Last weekend in August, 5200 W Lawrence Ave	Polka and kielbasa! Heaven! Pierogies! Paradise!
Gold Coast Art Fair	Early August, Wells St	Fine arts in a fancy neighborhood.
Summer Dance	August, Grant Park	Kick up your heels under the stars. Free lessons, and free DJs on Wednesday nights. http://egov.cityofchicago.org/SummerDance/
African Festival of the Arts	Friday to Sunday, Labor Day weekend, Washington Park, 5531 S King Dr	Last and biggest major afrocentric expo of the year. www.africainternationalhouse.org.
Celtic Fest	Second weekend in September, Grant Park	Clog dance in the bonny heath.
German-American Fest	Early September, Lincoln & Leland	Oktoberfest in Lincoln Square. Bring your own leiderhosen.
World Music Festival	Late September, Grant Park	Music acts from around the world, plus beer.
57th St Children's Book Fair	Late September, b/w Kimbark & Dorchester Aves	Lots of kids. Lots of books.
Chicago International Film Festival	October, various locations	Worthy display of the best in international cinema. www.chicagofilmfestival.org
Chicagoween	Mid to Late October, Daley Plaza	Daley Plaza becomes Pumpkin Plaza with trick-or-treating, pumpkin carving, and storytellers.
Halloween Parade	Halloween, Halsted b/w Belmont & Addison	Flamboyant Boystown costume extravaganza.
Tree Lighting	Day after Thanksgiving, Daley Plaza	Decking the halls by City Hall.
Mag Mile Lights Festival	Saturday evening before Thanksgiving, Michican Ave	Festive celebration of obligatory consumption.
Thanksgiving Parade	Thanksgiving Day morning, 8:30 am, State St	8:30 am? Yeah, as if.
Christkindlmarket	Thanksgiving Day–December, Daley Plaza	A German village appears for traditional Christmas shopping, food, and songs.

*All dates subject to change. For more up-to-date information and a schedule of neighborhood festivals, contact the Mayor's Office of Special Events at www.cityofchicago.org/specialevents.

With 13,705 sworn-in police officers, Chicago's crime incidence keeps dropping. Index crime numbers are the lowest in every category since 1984.

Statistics	2007	2006	2005	2004	2003	2002
Murders	443	467	447	448	599	651
Criminal Sexual Assault	1,593	1,537	1,618	1,678	1,836	2,024
Robbery	15,412	15,868	15,961	15,914	17,328	18,530
Aggravated Assault and Battery	17,414	17,463	17,934	18,746	19,812	22,905
Burglary	24,719	24,196	25,298	24,425	25,151	25,613
Theft	82,418	84,007	83,235	93,245	97,921	97,468
Motor Vehicle Theft	18,567	21,806	22,491	22,803	22,729	25,098
Arson	705	713	683	782	947	1,016

Departments

Departments	Address	Phone	Map
1st District (Central)	1718 S State St	312-745-4290	11
9th District (Deering)	3501 S Lowe Ave	312-747-8227	13
21st District (Prairie)	300 E 29th St	312-747-8340	14
2nd District (Wentworth)	5101 S Wentworth Ave	312-747-8366	15
13th District (Wood)	937 N Wood St	312-746-8357	21
12th District (Monroe)	100 S Racine Ave	312-746-8309	24
14th District (Shakespeare)	2150 N California Ave	312-744-8290	27
18th District (Near North)	1160 N Larrabee St	312-742-5870	31
24th District (Rogers Park)	6464 N Clark St	312-742-5907	34
20th District (Foster)	5400 N Lincoln Ave	312-742-8714	35
19th District Police Headquarters	2452 W Belmont Ave	312-744-5983	42
23rd District (Town Hall)	3600 N Halsted St	312-744-8320	44

Chicago hospitals are as varied and interesting as the citizens they serve. Although you don't have to go far to find medical facilities in this city, finding quality medical care is another story.

The Illinois Medical District on the near southwest side is one of the largest healthcare centers in the world. Here you will find the brand-new **Stroger (Map 25)** hospital (basically the infamous Cook County Hospital with a facelift), home to the nation's first and oldest trauma unit. It is by far the busiest hospital in the area and serves a large and mostly indigent population. Unless you are in danger of certain demise, avoid Stroger's emergency department since waits of up to 12 hours for a non-life-threatening reason may bore you to death. The medical campus is also home to the **University of Illinois at Chicago (Map 25)**, **Rush University Medical Center (Map 25)**, and several smaller hospitals.

On the north side, your best bet is to go to **Advocate Illinois Masonic Medical Center (Map 43)** for anything serious or **St. Joseph's Hospital (Map 44)** where you might get a room with a view of Lake Michigan. **Northwestern Memorial Hospital (Map 3)** is also a good choice if you are closer to downtown and/or if you have really good insurance. They also house several hospitals in the same campus, and if you break your neck craning to look up at all the pretty skyscrapers in the Streeterville 'hood, they have a first-rate spinal cord unit.

On the south side, the **University of Chicago (Map 19)** hospitals are second to none. A large and imposing set of buildings set in a somewhat dubious neighborhood, the hospital has a first-rate children's emergency department, world-renowned staff, and an excellent reputation. Park on the street at your own risk—the garage may be expensive, but so is replacing your car stereo.

Emergency Rooms	Address	Phone	Map
Northwestern Memorial	251 E Huron St	312-926-2000	3
Mercy	2525 S Michigan Ave	312-567-2000	11
Michael Reese	2929 S Ellis Ave	312-791-2000	14
Provident	500 E 51st St	312-572-2000	16
University of Chicago	5841 S Maryland Ave	773-702-1000	19
University of Chicago Children's	5721 S Maryland Ave	773-702-1000	19
St Elizabeth's	1431 N Claremont Ave	773-278-2000	21
St Mary of Nazareth	2233 W Division St	312-770-2000	21
John H Stroger	1900 W Polk St	312-864-7203	25
Rush University Medical Center	1650 W Harrison St	312-942-5000	25
St Anthony's	2875 W 19th St	773-484-1000	25
University of Illinois Medical Center	1740 W Taylor St	312-355-4000	25
VA Medical Center	820 S Damen Ave	312-569-8387	25
Children's Memorial	2300 Children's Plz	773-880-4000	30
Lincoln Park	550 W Webster Ave	773-883-2000	30
Swedish Covenant	5145 N California Ave	773-878-8200	38
Methodist Hospital of Chicago	5025 N Paulina St	773-271-9040	39
Louis A Weiss Memorial	4646 N Marine Dr	773-878-8700	40
Thorek	850 W Irving Park Rd	773-525-6780	40
Advocate Illinois Masonic Medical Center	836 W Wellington Ave	773-975-1600	43
St Joseph's	2900 N Lake Shore Dr	773-665-3000	44

Other Hospitals	Address	Phone	Map
Rehabilitation Institute of Chicago	345 E Superior St	312-238-1000	3
Kindred Chicago-Lakeshore	6130 N Sheridan Rd	773-381-1222	37
Kindred	2544 W Montrose Ave	773-267-2622	38
Neurologic & Orthopedic Institute	4501 N Winchester Ave	773-250-0000	39
Chicago Lakeshore	4840 N Marine Dr	773-878-9700	40

Post Offices	Address	Phone	Map
US Post Office	222 Merchandise Mart Plz	312-321-0233	2
US Post Office	540 N Dearborn St	312-644-3919	2
US Post Office	227 E Ontario St	312-642-3576	3
US Post Office	168 N Clinton St	312-906-8557	4
US Post Office	100 W Randolph St	312-263-2686	5
US Post Office	211 S Clark St	312-427-0016	5
US Post Office	233 S Wacker Dr	312-876-1024	5
US Post Office	5 S Wabash Ave	312-427-0016	5
US Post Office	200 E Randolph St	312-861-0473	6
US Post Office	358 W Harrison St	312-692-6128	7
US Post Office	433 W Harrison St	800-275-8777	7
US Post Office	2345 S Wentworth Ave	312-326-6440	10
US Post Office	2035 S State St	312-225-0218	11
US Post Office	4101 S Halsted St	773-247-0731	15
US Post Office	4601 S Cottage Grove Ave	773-924-6658	16
US Post Office	700 E 61st St	773-493-1712	18
US Post Office	1526 E 55th St	773-324-0896	19
US Post Office	956 E 58th St	773-324-1807	19
US Post Office	1635 W Division St	773-278-2069	22
US Post Office	116 S Western Ave	312-243-2560	23
US Post Office	1859 S Ashland Ave	312-733-4750	26
US Post Office	2339 N California Ave	773-489-2855	27
US Post Office	2405 N Sheffield Ave	773-929-7041	29
US Post Office	2368 N Clark St	773-549-2728	30
US Post Office	2500 N Clark St	773-477-9372	30
US Post Office	2643 N Clark St	773-525-5965	30
US Post Office	875 N Michigan Ave	312-644-0485	32
US Post Office	1723 W Devon Ave	773-743-2650	34
US Post Office	7056 N Clark St	773-764-8154	34
US Post Office	7617 N Paulina St	773-743-2830	34
US Post Office	2522 W Lawrence Ave	773-561-3330	38
US Post Office	2011 W Montrose Ave	773-472-1314	39
US Post Office	1343 W Irving Park Rd	773-327-0345	40
US Post Office	4850 N Broadway St	773-561-1720	40
US Post Office	3750 N Kedzie Ave	773-539-6210	41
US Post Office	3635 N Lincoln Ave	773-404-0980	42
US Post Office	3024 N Ashland Ave	773-248-8495	43
US Post Office	3170 N Sheridan Rd	773-244-0444	44

The Chicago Public Library System has 75 branches serving Chicago citizens. Much to the delight of many Windy City book-borrowers, the city has recently constructed several new branches and renovated over 55 existing neighborhood branches with the help of a huge capital improvement program.

With the **Harold Washington Library (Map 5)** as their anchor, two regional libraries, **Sulzer Regional Library (Map 39)** in Lincoln Square and the Southwest side's **Woodson Library (Map 59)**, serve as backup reference and research collections. It is worth noting that Harold Washington Library has a few stand-out exhibits, including one of the history of the blues in the city and, of course, one on the man himself, Chicago's first African-American mayor. Neighborhood branches are geared towards the communities they serve: **Chinatown (Map 10)** has an impressive collection of Asian studies material and literature, the **Rogers Park (Map 34)** branch features a significant Russian-language selection, and Boystown's **John Merlo (Map 44)** collection houses a considerable offering of gay literature and studies. Many of the smaller branches have a decent selection of juvenile materials as well as career guidance and adult popular literature (and Internet access). Architecturally, some of the more interesting branches include the **Chicago Bee (Map 14)** branch, the former newspaper headquarters that serves as a neighborhood landmark for Bronzeville, and the historic Pullman (Parks & Places) branch, specializing in the history of the Pullman district. Chicago's first library branch, the neo-classical **Blackstone (Map 17)**

library, is named after the Stockyards magnate. Families and schools should take advantage of the Chicago Public Library System's "Great Kids Museum Passports" available only to adult Chicago residents with a valid library card. You can check out any of their free passports using your library card just like you would any other item, and the loan is good for one week. The pass entitles entry for up to 8 people to any one of the eleven participating cultural institutions in the city. If you don't have access to a library card, you can still partake in a bit of book-love by checking out one of the many free lectures or readings that take place at the Harold Washington Library and the galaxy of branch outposts throughout the year. Before visiting Chicago, visitors can also peruse some of the nice digital exhibits the Library has created at www.chipublib.org/digital/digital.html. Here they will find tributes to the late, great Mayor Harold Washington and some interesting exhibits on the history of the city's sewer system (well, interesting for us, at least). For more information, call your local library or visit the general website at www.chipublib.org.

Chicago also has many excellent research libraries and university libraries, one of which is the independent **Newberry Library (Map 32)**, established in 1887. It shelves rare books, manuscripts, and maps, and hosts the raucous annual Bughouse Square debates in late July. Chicago's universities and colleges generally welcome the public to their libraries during specified hours, but it's best to call first and check.

Library	Address	Phone	Map
Albany Park Public Library	5150 N Kimball Ave	312-744-1933	38
Asher Library-Spertus Institute	610 S Michigan Ave	312-322-1749	9
Bessie Coleman Public Library	731 E 63rd St	312-747-7760	18
Bezazian Public Library	1226 W Ainslie St	312-744-0019	40
Blackstone Public Library	4904 S Lake Park Ave	312-747-0511	17
Bucktown/Wicker Park Public Library	1701 N Milwaukee Ave	312-744-6022	28
Budlong Woods Public Library	5630 N Lincoln Ave	312-742-9590	35
Canaryville Public Library	642 W 43rd St	312-747-0644	15
Chicago Bee Public Library	3647 S State St	312-747-6872	14
Chinatown Public Library	2353 S Wentworth Ave	312-747-8013	10
Daley Public Library	3400 W Halsted St	312-747-8990	13
Eckhart Park Branch	1330 W Chicago Ave	312-746-6069	24
Edgewater Public Library	1210 W Elmdale Ave	312-744-0718	37
Hall Public Library	4801 S Michigan Ave	312-747-2541	16
Harold Washington Public Library	400 S State St	312-747-4300	5
Humboldt Park Public Library	1605 N Troy St	312-744-2244	27
John Merlo Public Library	644 W Belmont Ave	312-744-1139	44
King Public Library	3436 S Dr Martin L King Jr Dr	312-747-7543	14
Library of Columbia College	624 S Michigan Ave	312-344-7900	9
Lincoln Park Public Library	1150 W Fullerton Ave	312-744-1926	29
Lincoln-Belmont Public Library	1659 W Melrose St	312-744-0166	42
Logan Square Public Library	3030 W Fullerton Ave	312-744-5295	27
Lozano Public Library	1805 S Loomis St	312-746-4329	26
Mabel Manning Public Library	6 S Hoyne Ave	312-746-6800	23
Malcolm X College Library	1900 W Van Buren St	312-850-7000	23
Midwest Public Library	2335 W Chicago Ave	312-744-7788	23
Near North Public Library	310 W Division St	312-744-0991	31
The Newberry Library	60 W Walton St	312-943-9090	32
Northtown Public Library	6435 N California Ave	312-744-2292	33
Rogers Park Public Library	6907 N Clark St	312-744-0156	34
Roosevelt Public Library	1101 W Taylor St	312-746-5656	26
Sulzer Public Library	4455 N Lincoln Ave	312-744-7616	39
The Swedenborg Library	77 W Washington St, Rm 1700	312-346-7003	5
University of Chicago Harper Memorial Library	1116 E 59th St	773-702-7959	19
University of Illinois at Chicago Library	801 S Morgan St	312-996-2726	26
Uptown Public Library	929 W Buena Ave	312-744-8400	40
Woodson Library	9525 S Halstead St	312-747-6900	49

The last FedEx drop in Chicago is at 10 pm at O'Hare Airport. Get off the Kennedy at Manheim Road South. Go to Irving Park Road and head west to the first light. Make a right on O'Hare Cargo Area Road. FedEx's address is Building 611, O'Hare Cargo Area Road (800-463-3339; www.FedEx.com).

*=Pick-up time, pm; WSC=World Service Center

Map 1 • River North / Fulton Market District

Self-Service	400 W Erie St	7:30 PM
Self-Service	600 W Chicago Ave	7:30 PM
Self-Service	401 W Superior St	7 PM
Self-Service	445 W Erie St	7 PM
Self-Service	770 N Halsted St	7 PM
Self-Service	430 W Erie St	6 PM

Map 2 • Near North / River North

FedEx Kinko's	444 N Wells St	9:30 PM
FedEx Kinko's	350 N Clark St	9 PM
FedEx Kinko's	222 Merchandise Mart Plz	9 PM
Self-Service	444 N Wells St	8:45 PM
Self-Service	77 W Wacker Dr	8 PM
Self-Service	205 W Wacker Dr	8 PM
Self-Service	311 W Superior St	8 PM
Self-Service	414 N Orleans St	8 PM
Self-Service	54 W Hubbard St	8 PM
Self-Service	56 W Illinois St	8 PM
Self-Service	330 N Wabash Ave	8 PM
Self-Service	420 N Wabash Ave	8 PM
Self-Service	223 W Erie St	7:45 PM
Self-Service	225 W Wacker Dr	7:30 PM
Self-Service	308 W Erie St	7:30 PM
Self-Service	343 W Erie St	7:30 PM
Self-Service	515 N State St	7:30 PM
Self-Service	730 N Franklin St	7:30 PM
Self-Service	405 N Wabash Ave	7:30 PM
Self-Service	640 N La Salle St	7:30 PM
Self-Service	1 E Wacker Dr	7:15 PM
Self-Service	35 E Wacker Dr	7 PM
Self-Service	55 W Wacker Dr	7 PM
Self-Service	211 W Wacker Dr	7 PM
Self-Service	320 W Ohio St	7 PM
Self-Service	20 W Kinzie St	7 PM
Self-Service	215 W Superior St	7 PM
Self-Service	300 N State St	7 PM
Self-Service	1 W Superior St	7 PM
Self-Service	1 E Erie St	7 PM
Self-Service	65 E Wacker Dr	6:30 PM
Self-Service	540 N Dearborn St	6:30 PM
Self-Service	325 N Wells St	6 PM

Map 3 • Streeterville / Mag Mile

Self-Service	401 N Michigan Ave	8 PM
Self-Service	211 E Chicago Ave	8 PM
Self-Service	233 E Erie St	8 PM
Self-Service	737 N Michigan Ave	8 PM
Self-Service	541 N Fairbanks Ct	8 PM
Self-Service	633 N St Clair St	8 PM
Self-Service	676 N St Clair St	8 PM
Self-Service	211 E Ontario St	7:30 PM
Self-Service	444 N Michigan Ave	7:30 PM
Self-Service	625 N Michigan Ave	7:30 PM
Self-Service	645 N Michigan Ave	7:30 PM
Self-Service	333 E Ontario St	7:30 PM
Self-Service	251 E Huron St	7:30 PM
Self-Service	150 E Huron St, #160	7:30 PM
Self-Service	400 N Michigan Ave	7:30 PM
Self-Service	505 N Lake Shore Dr	7:30 PM
Self-Service	430 N Michigan Ave	7:15 PM
Self-Service	142 E Ontario St	7 PM
Self-Service	401 E Illinois St	7 PM
Self-Service	440 N McClurg Ct	7 PM
Self-Service	455 E Illinois St	7 PM
Self-Service	676 N Michigan Ave	7 PM
Self-Service	474 N Lake Shore Dr	7 PM
Self-Service	360 N Michigan Ave	7 PM
Self-Service	512 N McClurg Ct	6:30 PM
FedEx Kinko's	540 N Michigan Ave	6 PM
Self-Service	540 N Michigan Ave	6 PM
Marcel Pack & Ship	680 N Lake Shore Dr	5 PM

Map 4 • West Loop Gate / Greek Town

Self-Service	500 W Madison St	9 PM
FedEx Kinko's	127 S Clinton St	8:45 PM
Self-Service	127 S Clinton St	8:45 PM
Self-Service	300 S Riverside Plz	8:30 PM
FedEx Kinko's	608 W Lake St	8 PM
Self-Service	550 W Washington Blvd	8 PM
Self-Service	608 W Lake St	8 PM
Self-Service	555 W Madison St	8 PM
Self-Service	10 S Riverside Plz	7:30 PM
Self-Service	222 S Riverside Plz	7:30 PM
Self-Service	833 W Jackson Blvd	7:30 PM
Self-Service	100 N Riverside Plz	7 PM
Self-Service	120 S Riverside Plz	7 PM
Self-Service	2 N Riverside Plz	7 PM
Self-Service	820 W Jackson Blvd	7 PM
Self-Service	850 W Jackson Blvd	7 PM
Self-Service	322 S Green St	7 PM
Self-Service	547 W Jackson Blvd	7 PM
Self-Service	600 W Jackson Blvd	7 PM
Self-Service	641 W Lake St	7 PM
Self-Service	550 W Jackson Blvd	7 PM
Self-Service	500 W Monroe St	6:30 PM
Self-Service	619 W Jackson Blvd	6:30 PM
Self-Service	168 N Clinton St	6 PM
Self-Service	130 S Jefferson St	6 PM
Self-Service	730 W Randolph St	6 PM
Self-Service	651 W Washington Blvd	5:30 PM
Self-Service	216 S Jefferson St	5:30 PM

Map 5 • The Loop

FedEx Kinko's	200 W Jackson Blvd	9 PM
FedEx Kinko's	227 W Monroe St	9 PM
FedEx Kinko's	111 W Washington St	9 PM
FedEx Kinko's	2 N LaSalle St	9 PM
Self-Service	333 W Wacker Dr	9 PM
Self-Service	171 N Clark St	8:30 PM
Self-Service	123 N Wacker Dr	8:30 PM
Self-Service	233 S Wacker Dr	8:30 PM
FedEx Kinko's	6 W Lake St	8 PM
FedEx Kinko's	29 S La Salle St	8 PM
FedEx Kinko's	55 E Monroe St	8 PM
Self-Service	6 W Lake St	8 PM
Self-Service	100 W Monroe St	8 PM
Self-Service	111 W Jackson Blvd	8 PM
Self-Service	175 W Jackson Blvd	8 PM
Self-Service	111 S Wacker Dr	8 PM
Self-Service	225 W Washington St	8 PM
Self-Service	30 S Wacker Dr	8 PM
Self-Service	1 N Franklin St	8 PM
Self-Service	1 S Wacker Dr	8 PM
Self-Service	10 S Wacker Dr	8 PM
Self-Service	125 S Wacker Dr	8 PM
Self-Service	150 N Wacker Dr	8 PM
Self-Service	150 S Wacker Dr	8 PM
Self-Service	20 N Wacker Dr	8 PM
Self-Service	200 S Wacker Dr	8 PM
Self-Service	200 W Madison St	8 PM
Self-Service	205 W Randolph St	8 PM
Self-Service	230 W Monroe St	8 PM

Map 5 • The Loop—*continued*

Self-Service	303 W Madison St	8 PM
Self-Service	71 S Wacker Dr	8 PM
Self-Service	210 S Clark St	8 PM
Self-Service	203 N LaSalle St	8 PM
Self-Service	200 N LaSalle St	8 PM
Self-Service	222 N LaSalle St	8 PM
Self-Service	120 N LaSalle St	8 PM
Self-Service	30 N LaSalle St	8 PM
Self-Service	134 N LaSalle St	8 PM
Self-Service	10 S LaSalle St	8 PM
Self-Service	190 S LaSalle St	8 PM
Self-Service	115 S LaSalle St	8 PM
Self-Service	208 S LaSalle St	8 PM
Self-Service	311 S Wacker Dr	7:45 PM
Self-Service	180 N Wabash Ave	7:30 PM
Self-Service	105 W Madison St	7:30 PM
Self-Service	135 S La Salle St	7:30 PM
Self-Service	407 S Dearborn St	7:30 PM
Self-Service	21 S Clark St	7:30 PM
Self-Service	36 S Wabash Ave	7:30 PM
FedEx Kinko's	101 N Wacker Dr	7 PM
FedEx Kinko's	400 S LaSalle St	7 PM
Self-Service	203 N Wabash Ave	7 PM
Self-Service	70 E Lake St	7 PM
Self-Service	100 W Randolph St	7 PM
Self-Service	1 N State St	7 PM
Self-Service	25 E Washington St	7 PM
Self-Service	33 N Dearborn St	7 PM
Self-Service	29 E Madison St	7 PM
Self-Service	55 W Monroe St	7 PM
Self-Service	30 W Monroe St	7 PM
Self-Service	29 S La Salle St	7 PM
Self-Service	11 E Adams St	7 PM
Self-Service	55 E Jackson Blvd	7 PM
Self-Service	53 W Jackson Blvd	7 PM
Self-Service	401 S State St	7 PM
Self-Service	191 N Wacker Dr	7 PM
Self-Service	200 W Adams St	7 PM
Self-Service	200 W Monroe St	7 PM
Self-Service	29 N Wacker Dr	7 PM
Self-Service	300 S Wacker Dr	7 PM
Self-Service	309 W Washington St	7 PM
Self-Service	101 N Wacker Dr	7 PM
Self-Service	10 S Dearborn St, Ste 4800	7 PM
Self-Service	20 S Clark St	7 PM
Self-Service	247 S State St	7 PM
Self-Service	100 N LaSalle St	7 PM
Self-Service	11 S LaSalle St	7 PM
Self-Service	3660 N Lake Shore Dr	7 PM
Self-Service	1 E Jackson Blvd	6:30 PM
Self-Service	55 E Monroe St	6 PM
Self-Service	209 S La Salle St	6 PM
Self-Service	131 S Dearborn St	6 PM
Self-Service	140 S Dearborn St, Ste 109	6 PM
Self-Service	230 S Dearborn St	5:45 PM
Self-Service	219 S Dearborn St	5:30 PM
Self-Service	77 W Jackson Blvd	5 PM

Map 6 • The Loop / Grant Park

FedEx Kinko's	225 N Michigan Ave	9 PM
FedEx Kinko's	34 S Michigan Ave	9 PM
FedEx Kinko's	130 E Randolph St	9 PM
Self-Service	150 N Michigan Ave	8 PM
Self-Service	200 E Randolph St	8 PM
Self-Service	300 E Randolph St	8 PM
Self-Service	333 N Michigan Ave	8 PM
Self-Service	200 S Michigan Ave	8 PM
Self-Service	224 S Michigan Ave	8 PM
Self-Service	332 S Michigan Ave	8 PM
Self-Service	30 N Michigan Ave	8 PM
Self-Service	8 S Michigan Ave	7:30 PM
FedEx Kinko's	111 E Wacker Dr	7 PM
Self-Service	111 E Wacker Dr	7 PM
Self-Service	307 N Michigan Ave	7 PM
Self-Service	155 N Michigan Ave	7 PM
Self-Service	310 S Michigan Ave	7 PM
Self-Service	430 S Michigan Ave	7 PM
Self-Service	180 N Michigan Ave	7 PM
Self-Service	20 N Michigan Ave	7 PM
Self-Service	233 N Michigan Ave	6 PM
Self-Service	200 E Randolph St	4 PM

Map 8 • South Loop / Printers Row / Dearborn Park

FedEx Kinko's	700 S Wabash Ave	8:45 PM
Self-Service	700 S Wabash Ave	8:45 PM
Self-Service	47 W Polk St	8 PM
Self-Service	536 S Clark St	7:30 PM
Self-Service	800 S Wells St	7:30 PM
Self-Service	542 S Dearborn St	7 PM
Self-Service	600 S Federal St	7 PM
Self-Service	819 S Wabash Ave	5 PM

Map 10 • East Pilsen / Chinatown

FedEx Kinko's	1242 S Canal St	8 PM
Self-Service	1242 S Canal St	8 PM
Self-Service	329 W 18th St	7:30 PM

Map 11 • South Loop / McCormick Place

Self-Service	1455 S Michigan Ave	7 PM
Self-Service	2035 S State St	5 PM

Map 12 • Bridgeport (West)

Self-Service	970 W Pershing Rd	6 PM

Map 13 • Bridgeport (East)

Self-Service	710 W 31st St	6 PM
Self-Service	3300 S Federal St	6 PM

Map 14 • Prairie Shores / Lake Meadows

Chicago Computer Club	329 E 35th St	6PM
Self-Service	10 W 35th St	6 PM

Map 19 • Hyde Park

FedEx Kinko's	1315 E 57th St	7 PM
Self-Service	1525 E 53rd St	7 PM
Self-Service	1554 E 55th St	7 PM
Self-Service	1155 E 60th St	7 PM
Self-Service	5801 S Ellis Ave	7 PM
Self-Service	1315 E 57th St	7 PM
Self-Service	E 57th St & S University Ave	7 PM
Self-Service	5841 S Maryland Ave	6:45 PM
Self-Service	1126 E 59th St	6:30 PM
Self-Service	956 E 58th St	6:30 PM
Self-Service	E 59th St & S Kimbark Ave	6:30 PM

Map 20 • East Hyde Park / Jackson Park

Post Link	1634 E 53rd St	5 PM

Map 21 • Wicker Park / Ukrainian Village

FedEx Kinko's	1800 W North Ave	8:45 PM
Self-Service	1800 W North Ave	8:45 PM
Self-Service	1520 N Damen Ave	7 PM
Myoffice	2136 W Division St	6 PM
Copy Max	1573 N Milwaukee Ave	6 PM

Map 22 • Noble Square / Goose Island

FedEx Kinko's	875 W Division	9:30 PM
Self-Service	935 W Chestnut St	7:30 PM
Self-Service	939 W North Ave	7 PM
Self-Service	1467 N Elston Ave	7 PM
Self-Service	1608 N Milwaukee Ave	7 PM
Self-Service	848 W Eastman St	6:45 PM

Map 23 • West Town / Near West Side

Self-Service	1700 W Van Buren St	7 PM
Self-Service	2023 W Carroll Ave	7 PM
Self-Service	265 N Western Ave	6:30 PM
Packaging & Shipping	2002 W Chicago Ave	6 PM
Self-Service	1812 W Hubbard St	5:30 PM

Map 24 • River West / West Town

Self-Service	400 N Noble St	7 PM
Self-Service	1500 W Carroll Ave	6:30 PM
Self-Service	1030 W Chicago Ave	5 PM
Pak Mail	1461 W Chicago Ave	4 PM

Map 25 • Illinois Medical District

Self-Service	1725 W Harrison St	7 PM
Self-Service	840 S Wood St	7 PM
Self-Service	820 S Damen Ave	6 PM
Self-Service	715 S Wood St	4 PM

Map 26 • University Village / Little Italy / Pilsen

Self-Service	1100 W Cermak Rd	7 PM
Self-Service	1201 W Harrison St	6:30 PM
Self-Service	851 S Morgan St	5:30 PM
Windy City Pack & Ship	1100 W Cermak Rd, Ste B423	3 PM

Map 28 • Bucktown

Self-Service	1829 W Fullerton Ave	7:30 PM
Self-Service	2349 N Elston Ave	7 PM
Self-Service	2211 N Elston Ave	6 PM

Map 29 • DePaul / Wrightwood / Sheffield

FedEx Kinko's	2300 N Clybourn Ave	8:45 PM
FedEx Kinko's	2300 N Clybourn Ave	8:45 PM
Self-Service	2300 N Clybourn Ave	8:45 PM
Self-Service	2000 N Racine Ave	7 PM
Self-Service	2323 N Seminary Ave	7 PM
Self-Service	1918 N Mendell St	6 PM
Self-Service	990 W Fullerton Ave	5:30 PM
Self-Service	1117 W Wisconsin St	4:15 PM

Map 30 • Lincoln Park

Self-Service	802 W Belden Ave	7:15 PM
Self-Service	1749 N Wells St	7 PM
Self-Service	2500 N Clark St	7 PM

Map 31 • Old Town / Near North

Self-Service	900 N Franklin St	8 PM
Self-Service	213 W Institute Pl	7:30 PM
Self-Service	820 N Orleans St	7:30 PM
Self-Service	1350 N Wells St	7 PM
Self-Service	1333 N Kingsbury St	7 PM
Cleaners Mail Comp	900 N Kingsbury St	5:30 PM

Map 32 • Gold Coast / Mag Mile

FedEx Kinko's	875 N Michigan Ave	9 PM
FedEx Kinko's	1201 N Dearborn St	8:45 PM

Self-Service	1201 N Dearborn St	8:45 PM
Self-Service	100 E Walton St	7:30 PM
Self-Service	919 N Michigan Ave	7:30 PM
Self-Service	1 E Delaware Pl	7:30 PM
Self-Service	900 N Michigan Ave	7 PM
Self-Service	980 N Michigan Ave	7 PM
Self-Service	1165 N Clark St	6:30 PM
Self-Service	875 N Michigan Ave	6:30 PM
Self-Service	844 N Rush St	6 PM
Global Postal & Shipping	1151 N State St	5 PM

Map 33 • West Rogers Park

Self-Service	7555 N California Ave	7:15 PM
Unik Technic Corporation	2337 W Devon Ave	7 PM

Map 34 • East Rogers Park

Self-Service	1723 W Devon Ave	7 PM
Self-Service	6355 N Broadway St	6:30 PM
Self-Service	7056 N Clark St	6 PM

Map 37 • Edgewater / Andersonville

Self-Service	5419 N Sheridan Rd	7:30 PM
Bedmar Courier Express	5655 N Clark St	7 PM
Postal Mart	5250 N Broadway St	5 PM

Map 38 • Ravenswood / Albany Park

Self-Service	2522 W Lawrence Ave	7 PM

Map 39 • Ravenswood / North Center

Self-Service	1807 W Sunnyside Ave	7:30 PM
Self-Service	4619 N Ravenswood Ave	7:10 PM
Self-Service	1700 W Irving Park Rd	6:45 PM
Self-Service	4001 N Ravenswood Ave	6:30 PM
Remesas Montrose	1924 W Montrose Ave	6 PM
Self-Service	4043 N Ravenswood Ave	6 PM

Map 40 • Uptown

Self-Service	4753 N Broadway St	7 PM
Self-Service	4850 N Broadway St	6:30 PM

Map 41 • Avondale / Old Irving

Self-Service	2704 W Roscoe St	7 PM
Self-Service	3611 N Kedzie Ave	7 PM
Self-Service	3401 N California Ave	7 PM
Self-Service	2630 W Bradley Pl, #2650	6:30 PM
Self-Service	3500 N California Ave	4:30 PM

Map 42 • North Center / Roscoe Village / West Lakeview

FedEx Kinko's	3435 N Western Ave	8 PM
Self-Service	3435 N Western Ave	8 PM
Self-Service	1800 W Larchmont Ave	7:30 PM
Self-Service	3717 N Ravenswood Ave	7 PM
Mailbox Plus	2248 W Belmont Ave	6 PM

Map 43 • Wrigleyville / East Lakeview

FedEx Kinko's	3524 N Southport Ave	8 PM
Self-Service	3524 N Southport Ave	8 PM
Self-Service	1300 W Belmont Ave	7:30 PM
Self-Service	3024 N Ashland Ave	6 PM

Map 44 • East Lakeview

FedEx Kinko's	3001 N Clark St	8 PM
Self-Service	3001 N Clark St	8 PM
Self-Service	2800 N Sheridan Rd	7 PM
Postal Place	3304 N Broadway St	6:30 PM
Steve Rozells Postal Plus	559 W Diversey Pkwy	6 PM

Chicago's lesbian and gay communities are a diverse, politically influential presence within the city. Just look to the pride pylons lining North Halsted Street, the city's officially recognized gay district, as well as the numerous city politicians who vie for a prime spot in the city's annual gay pride parade that attracts over 400,000 spectators and participants on the last Sunday in June. Also in East Lakeview (a.k.a. Boystown), the North Halsted Street Market Days function as a second gay pride celebration, but this time all the gays' funky straight friends are invited. A recent host to the International Gay Games, Chicago vies for the top seat among America's most eclectic gay communities.

Chicago's gay and lesbian community has also carved out a niche in the more residential and low-key Andersonville neighborhood. Anchored by the venerable Women & Children First bookstore, Clark Street, Andersonville's main drag, is a queer corridor of gay and gay-friendly shops, restaurants, and nightlife. Unlike Boystown, which is dominated by, well, boys, Andersonville is known for its female-friendly vibe. Every June, Chicago's lesbians take it to the streets in the annual Dyke March, trouncing, stomping, and twirling through Andersonville on the Saturday before the "official" gay pride parade.

Gay life in Chicago is not just limited to Halsted Street and Andersonville though, nor is it relegated to a few summer street fairs. From Edgewater to South Shore to Humbolt Park, gays and lesbians have become visible entities in many of Chicago's far-reaching 'hoods, notwithstanding the hundreds who live quietly in domestic bliss from Edison Park to Pullman.

With such a diverse array of lesbigay life thriving in the city, it's no wonder that the city's lesbigay offerings are equally diverse. Whether your interests are activism or acupuncture, draperies or drag kings, literature, liturgies, or leather bars, or some combination of the above, you can find your niche in Chicago.

Publications/Media

Pick up a copy of the following publications, log onto a website, or tune in to find out what's happening around town, from the current political headlines to the hottest clubs. Gay rags can be found in gay-friendly book stores, cafés, bars, shops, and gay friendly transit stops.

The Field Guide to Gay and Lesbian Chicago • by Kathie Bergquist and Robert McDonald. This comprehensive guide to gay and lesbian life in Chicago is available at bookstores everywhere.

Windy City Times • www.wctimes.com • Gay and Lesbian news weekly—check this site for a calendar of events.

Identity • www.identitychicago.com • A cross-cultural GLBT monthly, focusing on race, gender, and culture published by Windy City Media Group.

OUT! Guide • Comprehensive GLBT resource guide with listings for services including therapists, carpenters, real estate brokers, accounting services, social services, restaurants, and much, much more. Indispensable!

Chicago Free Press • www.chicagofreepress.com • Weekly publication with features on political issues, arts, culture, spiritual life, entertainment, and resource lists.

Gay Chicago • www.gaychicagomag.com • One of the city's oldest gay publications, with events listings, columns, news, astrology, and reviews. Male-focused.

Chicago Gay and Lesbian Chamber of Commerce www.glchamber.org Charged with developing gay and lesbian businesses, the chamber also hosts events for gay and lesbian professionals.

Boystown Chicago www.boystownchicago.com/ A message board, event calendar, and columnist spot for the gay and lesbian community.

Chicago Pride www.chicagopride.com Another site with the gay happenings across Chicago.

Boi • www.boimagazine • Heavily advertising-based guide to the club scene for circuit boys.

Dyke Diva • www.dykediva.com • An online guide, for gals, of Chicago events and happenings.

Windy City Radio • Tune in Sunday nights, 11 pm–midnight, on WCKG, 105.9 FM, or tune in online at www.windycityradio.com anytime.

Think Pink at WLUW Radio • www.wluw.org • Queer radio every Tuesday 6:30–8 pm.

Pink Magazine www.pinkmag.com/chicago/ Best for its listing of gay friendly businesses and restaurants.

Arts & Culture

Women & Children First Books • 5233 N Clark St 773-769-9299 • This 27-year-old lesbian resource in Andersonville is the largest feminist bookstore in the world. Hosts events and discussions regularly.

Unabridged Books • 3251 N Broadway St 773-883-9119 • Largest gay selection in the city, located in the heart of Boystown. You will find a well-annotated book selection, as well as calendars and magazines.

Gerber/Hart Gay and Lesbian Library and Archives • 1127 W Granville St • 773-381-8030 This amazing library houses more than 10,000 books, magazines, newspapers, and videos. Regularly hosts both gay and lesbian book discussion groups. For special events including readings and screenings, check the website at www.gerberhart.org.

Barbara's Bookstore • 1110 N Lake St, Oak Park • 708-848-9140 • Gay-friendly bookstore with a large selection of gay and lesbian fiction and non-fiction titles.

Seminary Cooperative Bookstore 5757 University Ave • 773-752-4381 Located in Hyde Park, this bookstore has sections on GLBT studies.

57th Street Books · 1301 E 57th St · 773-684-1300
Another Hyde Park bookstore with a strong GLBT
section.

Specialty Video · 3221 N Broadway St · 773-248-3434;
5307 N Clark · 773-878-3434
Huge selection of gay and lesbian videos and DVDs.
Dirty movies in the back.

Chicago Filmmakers · 5243 N Clark St · 773-293-1447 ·
Sponsors of Reeling, the Chicago Lesbian and Gay
International Film Festival.

Chicago Lesbian & Gay International Film Festival ·
www.chicagofilmmakers.org/reeling · Movies by and
about LGBT.

Facets Multimedia · 1517 W Fullerton Ave
773-281-9075 · Large selection of gay arthouse films.

About Face Theatre · 773-784-8565
Roving gay & lesbian theater company.

Bailiwick Repertory Theater · 1229 W Belmont Ave ·
773-883-1090 · Sponsors annual Gay Pride theater
festival.

Theatre Building · 1225 W Belmont Ave ·
773-327-5252 · Many gay theatre productions are
mounted here.

Aldo Castillo Gallery · 233 W Huron St · 312-327-2563 ·
Fine arts gallery with lesbigay latino/a bent.

Woman Made Gallery · 685 N Milwaukee Ave
312-738-0400 · www.womanmade.org
Regularly features lesbian artists.

Las Manos Gallery · 5220 N Clark St · 773-728-8910 ·
Lesbian-owned and -operated, regularly features gay
and lesbian artists.

Literary Exchange · PO Box 438583 · 773-509-6881 ·
Black lesbian writers' group publishes the 'zine
Literary Express.

Blithe House Quarterly · www.blithe.com ·
Online gay & les literary journal published in Chicago.

Artemis Singers · PO Box 578296 · 773-764-4465 ·
Lesbian-feminist chorus.

Chicago Gay Men's Chorus · 3540 N Southport Ave,
PO Box 333 · 773-296-0541 · www.cgmc.org ·
The name says it all. Mounts fun, campy annual
Christmas concert.

Windy City Gay Chorus · 3023 N Clark St
773-404-WCGC· www.windycitysings.org ·
Sponsors four different gay choruses, including
UNISON and The Slickers.

Lakeside Pride Freedom Band ·
www.lakesidepride.org · 773-381-6693
Chicago's gay & lesbian marching band. Doesn't
every city have one?

Homolatte · www.homolatte.com ·
Bi-monthly queer spoken word and acoustic music
series with writers and musicians, hosted by Out
Music 2005 Artist of the Year Scott Free.

4 + 1 Productions · www.4plus1.org

Sports & Recreation

Chi-Town Squares · 5315 N Clark St · 773-339-6743 ·
Gay and lesbian square dancing—what else?

Chicago Metropolitan Sports Association ·
www.chicagomsa.com · 312-409-7932
Organizes all varieties of gay and lesbian competitive
athletics: bowling, softball, etc.

Chicago Smelts · 3712 N Broadway St · 312-409-4974 ·
www.chicagosmelts.org · Gay & lesbian swim club.

Frontrunners/Frontwalkers ·
www.frfwchicago.org · 312-409-2790
Weekly LBG running and walking group sponsors
annual "Proud to Run" race.

Windy City Rodeo · 312-409-3835 · www.ilgra.com ·
Rope 'em up, rough riders.

Thousand Waves Spa · 1212 W Belmont
773-549-0700 · www.thousandwavesspa.com ·
Women-only spa offers herb wraps and massages
along with jacuzzi, steam room, and sauna.

Windy City Athletic Association · www.wcaa.net
773-327-WCAA · Also organizes gay and lesbian
competitive sports.

Social Groups/Organizations

Affinity: Advocates for African-American Lesbians ·
www.affinity95.org · 773-324-0377

Men of All Colors Together (MACT) · PO Box 408922,
60640 · 312-409-6916

Amigas Latinas Lesbianas/Bisexuales ·
www.AmigasLatinas.org · 312-409-5697

Association of Latin Men for Action (ALMA) ·
2855 N Lincoln Ave · www.almachicago.org ·
773-929-7688

Asians & Friends, Chicago · www.afchicago.org ·
312-409-1573

P-FLAG · Parents & Friends of Lesbians and Gays ·
www.pflag.org

**COLAGE Chicago · Children of Lesbians and Gays
Everywhere** · www.colage.org/Chicago · 773-548-3349

Chicagoland Bisexual Network ·
www.bisexual.org/g/chicagoland

Chicago Gender Society · PO Box 578005, 60657 ·
708-863-7714 · www.chicagogender.com

Political Groups/Activism

Equality Illinois · 3712 N Broadway St, #125, 60613 ·
773-477-7173 · www.equalityillinois.org

Human Rights Campaign Chicago · 800-777-4723

Oak Park Area Lesbians/Gays · 947 Garfield St ·
708-848-0273

Stonewall Democrats · 1830 S Michigan Ave ·
773-573-8838 · www.illinoisstonewall.org

Illinois Gender Advocates · 47 W Division
312-409-5489 · www.genderadvocates.org

Religious Services

AIDS Pastoral Care Network · 1501 S California,
60608 · 773-257-6425

319

Archdiocesan Gay and Lesbian Outreach (AGLO)
711 Belmont Ave, #106, 60657 ·
www.aglochicago.org · 773-525-3872
Roman Catholic

Broadway United Methodist Church
3344 N Broadway St · 773-348-2679 · Reconciling

Center for Spiritual Living · 3036 N Ashland, 60657·
773-248-5683 · www.chicagocsl.org · Science church

Church of the Open Door · 5954 S Albany Ave, 60629 ·
773-778-3030 · Black LGBT church

Congregation Or Chadash · 656 W Barry Ave, 60657 ·
773-271-2148 · www.orchadash.org · LGBT synagogue

Dignity Chicago · www.dignitychicago.org
312-458-9438 · LGBT Catholic

Good Shepherd Parish and Christ the Redeemer
MCC · 7045 N Western Ave, 60645 · 773-275-7776
Non-denominational

Integrity/Chicago · PO Box 3232, Oak Park, 60303 ·
773-348-6362 · Episcopal, meets 3rd Friday for
Eucharist/reception

Lake Street Church of Evanston · 607 Lake St, Evanston ·
847-864-2181 · www.lakestreet.org ·
Inside/Out GL group

Pilgrim Congregational Church · 460 Lake St, Oak Park ·
708-848-5860 · www.afterhours.com · Actively
inclusive

Resurrection MCC · 5757 S University Ave, 60637 ·
773-288-1535 · Non-demominational

Vajrayana Buddhist Center · 3534 N Hoyne Ave, 60618 ·
773-529-1862

Jewish Family Community Service 5150 Golf Rd
312-357-4619

St. Paul's United Church of Christ, 2336 N Orchard St
773-348-3829

New Spirit Community Church (Oak Park)
542 S. Scoville 708-848-5460

Health Center & Support Organizations

Haymarket Center 932 W. Washington Street
312-226-7984

Horizons Community Services
www.horizonsonline.org ·
The Midwest's largest lesbian, gay, bisexual, and
transgendered social service agency.
· **Lesbian and Gay Help Line** · 773-929-HELP
(6 pm until 10 pm)
· **The Crisis Hotline/Anti-Violence Project**
773-871-CARE
· **Legal Services** · 773-929-HELP
legal@horizonsonline.org
· **Mature Adult Program** · 773-472-6469 x245
perryw@horizonsonline.org
· **Psychotherapy Services** · 773-472-6469 x261
sarag@horizonsonline.org
· **Youth Services** · 773-472-6469 x252

premp@horizonsonline.org

Illinois State HIV/AIDS/STD Hotline
772-AID-AIDS

AIDS Foundation of Chicago ·
411 Wells St, Ste 300, Chicago, IL 60607 ·
312-922-2322 · www.aidschicago.com
A charitable foundation, not a direct service provider.

AIDSCARE · 212 E Ohio, 5th Fl, Chicago, IL 60611
773-935-4663

GLAAD Chicago · PO Box 46343, Chicago, IL 60614 ·
773-871-7633

PFLAG Chicago · PO Box 11023, Chicago, IL 60611 ·
773-472-3079

Howard Brown Health Center · 4025 N Sheridan Rd ·
773-388-1600 · General counseling as well as
anonymous, free AIDS-testing and GLBT Domestic
Violence Counseling and Prevention Program. Also
provides general practitioner care for men and
women, on a sliding fee scale.

Lesbian Community Cancer Project ·
Howard Brown Health Center · 773-561-4662 ·
Support and resources for lesbians with cancer. Free
quit-smoking clinics.

AA – New Town Alano Club · 909 W Belmont Ave,
2nd Fl · 773-529-0321 · Gay and lesbian AA, CA, OA,
ACOA, Coda, etc.

Support Groups · Many support groups exist for men,
women, and families in Chicago. Call Howard Brown
or Horizons for referrals.

Center on Halstead · 3640 N Halsted, 60613 ·
773-472-6469 · www.centeronhalsted.org · Opening
in 2007, this will be one of the country's largest and
most advanced LGBT Community Centers. Will have a
Whole Foods in the space.

Chicago House · 1925 N Clybour Ave Ste 401 ·
773-248-5200 · www.chicagohouse.org · Homeless
shelter for people living with HIV/AIDS.

Bath Houses

Steamworks · 3246 N Halsted St (773) 929-6080
If you're shy check out 'lights out' night every other
Thursday.

Man's Country · 5015 N Clark St 773-878-2069
www.manscountrychicago.com Bath house, private
rooms, hot strippers.

Erotica

Banana Video · 4923 N Clark St 2nd Fl 773-561-8322

Bijou · 1363 N Wells St 800-932-7111

Cupid's Treasures · 3519 N Halstead St 773-348-3884

The Ram · 3511 ½ N Halstead St 773-525-9528

Bars & Clubs

Gay

- **3160** · 3160 N Clark St · 773-327-5969 ·
  Piano and cabaret bar.
- **Anvil** · 1137 W Granville St · 773-973-0006
  Leather/Levis old-school joint, very local.
- **Bucks Saloon** · 3439 N Halsted St · 773-525-1125
  Typical gay watering hole.
- **Cell Block** · 3702 N Halsted St · 773-665-8064
  Leather bar.
- **Charlie's** · 3726 N Broadway St · 773-871-8887
  Country & Western, with traditional dancing after 2.
- **Chicago Eagle** · 5015 N Clark St · 773-728-0050
  Leather bar with back room.
- **Hunter's** · 1932 E Higgins Rd, Elk Grove Village
  847-439-8840 · Dance/video bar in the 'burbs
- **Jackhammer**· 6406 N Clark St (773) 753-5772
  www.jackhammer-chicago.com
  Far north, without the Boystown attitude.
- **Little Jim's** · 3501 N Halsted St · 773-871-6116
  Neighborhood bar, 4 am license.
- **Lucky Horseshoe** · 3169 N Halsted St · 773-404-3169
  Male dancers.
- **Manhandler** · 1948 N Halsted St · 773-871-3339
  Country & Western.
- **North End** · 3733 N Halsted St · 773-477-7999
  A welcoming gay sports bar.
- **Nutbush** · 7201 W Franklin St, Forest Park
  708-366-5117 · Video bar in the 'burbs.
- **Second Story Bar** · 157 E Ohio St · 312-923-9536 ·
  Streeterville hideout.
- **Sidetrack** · 3349 N Halsted St · 773-477-9189 ·
  Huge video bar, women welcome.
- **Touché** · 6412 N Clark St · 773-465-7400 ·
  Far North leather bar.

Lesbian

- **The Closet** · 3325 N Broadway St · 773-477-8533
  4 am license, men welcome.
- **Chix Mix** · www.chixmixproductions.com
  Roving women's dance parties.
- **Club Intimus** · 312 W Randolph St · 312-901-1703
  Roving women's dance party. Call for info.
- **Lost & Found** · 3058 W Irving Park Rd · 773-463-7599 ·
  Old-school women's bar with door buzzer and
  billiards.
- **DiChano's** · 201 155th St, Calumet City · 708-891-3980 ·
  4 am license, entertainment sometimes. Formerly
  known as The Patch.
- **StarGaze** ·5419 N Clark St · 773-561-7363 ·
  Restaurant, dancing, Salsa nights.
- **Temptations** · 10235 W Grand Ave, Franklin Park ·
  847-455-0008 · Entertainment and dancing in the
  land of the big hair.

Both

- **Atmosphere** · 5355 N Clark St · 773-784-1100
  Neighborhood bar, dancing.
- **Berlin** · 954 W Belmont Ave · 773-348-4975 ·
  Mixed dance clubs. Women-only nights every first
  and third Wednesday.
- **Big Chicks** · 5024 N Sheridan Rd · 773-728-5511
  Mostly men with free bbq/buffet every Sunday.
- **Circuit/Rehab** · 3641 N Halsted St · 773-325-2233 ·
  Big nightclub. Women's nights on some Fridays.
- **Club Escape** · 1530 E 75th St · 773-667-6454
  Mixed dance venue, some entertainment.
- **Cocktail** · 3359 N Halsted St · 773-477-1420
  Watch male dancers, sip cocktails.
- **Escapades** · 6301 S Harlem Ave · 773-229-0886
  4 am license, dancing, videos.
- **Gentry on Halsted** · 3320 N Halsted St
  773-348-1053 · Cabaret shows, piano bar.
- **Hydrate** · 3458 N Halsted St · 773-975-9244
  Mostly guys but girl friendly.
- **Jeffrey Pub** · 7041 S Jeffrey Blvd. · 773-363-8555
  4 am, Southside institution, dancing.
- **Pour House** · 103 155th St, Calumet City ·
  708-891-3980 · 4 am, dancing.
- **Roscoe's** · 3356 N Halsted St · 773-281-3355
  Mostly men, cavernous, dancing, videos, café.
- **Scot's** · 1829 W Montrose Ave · 773-528-3253
  Mostly men, friendly neighborhood bar.
- **Spin Nightclub** · 800 W Belmont Ave
  773-327-7711 · Mostly men, dancing.
- **T's Bar & Restaurant** · 5025 N Clark St · 773-784-6000 ·
  Not gay-exclusive, *very* gay-friendly. Bar food.
- **Lakeview Broadcasting Company** (LBC) ·
  3542 N Halsted 773-857-2444
  Along the gay strip in Boystown, very gay friendly

Serving the nation's busiest convention center, most Chicago hotels are designed for business travelers, complete with expense-account prices. Even a modest downtown room can be outrageously steep.

Livin' Large: For a special urban splurge, book a suite at one of Chicago's palace hotels, such as the **Ritz-Carlton (Map 32)**, **Four Seasons (Map 32)**, or **Peninsula (Map 2)**. Hip travelers will want to stay at one of downtown's two **W (Maps 3, 5)** hotels, the **Sofitel (Map 32)**, **Hotel 71 (Map 2)**, or the **Hard Rock Hotel (Map 6)**, located in the vintage Union Carbide building on Michigan Avenue.

Livin' Boutique: Another lodge located in a historic landmark, the **Hotel Burnham (Map 5)** is a lovely boutique hotel near the heart of Chicago's theater district. Burnham and its Kimpton Hotel Group sister, **Hotel Allegro (Map 5)**, also in the theater district, feature free wine receptions every evening for hotel guests. **Hotel Blake (Map 8)** on Printer's Row offers boutique-type amenities with handsome rooms, although the views can leave a bit to the imagination.

Livin' Cheap: Steer budget-conscious out-of-town guests toward the **Travelodge Downtown (Map 8)**. It's not eye candy, but the location (just off Michigan Avenue, between Millennium Park and the Museum Campus) makes it quite a deal.

Around the corner at the **Congress Plaza Hotel (Map 9)**, picketers have been toting their placards for years. The Hotel Workers Union is on strike pending serious concessions from the management, and their dispute does not seem to be cooling. The strike has hurt business, which has cut prices—let your conscience be your travel agent, and brace yourself for heckling should you book here (and remember that Upton Sinclair would *not* approve.)

Good values can also be had away from downtown. **City Suites (Map 43)**, and its "Neighborhood Inns of Chicago" partners, **The Majestic (Map 44)**, and **Willows (Map 44)**, in Chicago's Lakeview and Lincoln Park neighborhoods, offer small hotel charm at reasonable rates. If those are still above your station, **Heart o' Chicago Motel (Map 37)** is skipping distance from the Edgewater White Castle and a short walk from the vivacious Andersonville strip. **Sheffield House (Map 43)**, once a transient hotel, offers spare, cheap rooms, appealing to backpacking European travelers and frugal Cubs fans—it's a pop fly's distance from Wrigley Field.

B&Bs: Compared to cities of similar expanse, Chicago doesn't offer much by way of B&B's. **The Wheeler Mansion (Map 11)**, near McCormick Place, is luxurious and antique-filled, with fireplaces, custom baths and bedding, and ridiculously high ceilings. The more modest **Wicker Park B&B (Map 21)** dishes up a good breakfast—the owners also own the nearby Alliance bakery, where morning sweets are baked fresh daily. **The Flemish House B&B (Map 32)** is on a quiet, tree-lined lane, a calm refuge from the Rush Street and Oak Street Beach hullabaloo. **The Old Town Bed and Breakfast (Map 4)**, run by the friendly and eccentric Serritella family, features stylish bedrooms and a common area with a grand piano, formal dining room, and deluxe gourmet kitchen available for guests to use—it's where a John Cheever character would bunk.

Livin' Real Cheap: There are also three youth hostels in Chicago open to the public with rates as low as $15 a night for card-carrying International Youth Hostel members. For deals, Hot Rooms is a Chicago-based reservation service offering low-rates on undersold rooms: www.hotrooms.com.

Map 2 · Near North / River North

		Phone	Pricing
Amalfi Hotel	20 W Kinzie St	312-395-9000	189
Best Western Inn	125 W Ohio St	312-467-0800	119
Comfort Inn & Suites	15 E Ohio St	312-894-0900	96
Conrad Chicago	521 N Rush St	312-645-1500	215
Courtyard by Marriott	30 E Hubbard St	312-329-2500	149
Embassy Suites Hotel	600 N State St	312-943-3800	149
Four Points	630 N Rush St	312-981-6600	145
Hampton Inn	33 W Illinois St	312-832-0330	139
Hilton Garden Inn	10 E Grand Ave	312-595-0000	169
Holiday Inn	350 W Mart Center Dr	312-836-5000	119
Holiday Inn Express Magnificent Mile	640 N Wabash Ave	312-787-4031	104
Homewood Suites	40 E Grand Ave	312-644-2222	149
Hotel 71	71 E Wacker Dr	312-346-7100	234
House of Blues Hotel	333 N Dearborn St	312-245-0333	189
The James	616 N Rush St	312-337-1000	219
Ohio House Motel	600 N Lasalle St	312-943-6000	95
Peninsula Chicago Hotel	108 E Superior St	312-337-2888	525
Riverpark Motel & Suites	19 E Ohio St	312-787-4900	49
Wacker Hotel	111 W Huron St	312-787-1386	70
Westin River North Chicago	320 N Dearborn St	312-744-1900	199

Map 3 · Streeterville / Mag Mile

The Affinia Chicago	166 E Superior St	312-787-6000	149
Allerton Crowne Plaza	701 N Michigan Ave	312-440-1500	129
Best Western Inn	162 E Ohio St	312-787-3100	89
Courtyard Magnificent Mile	165 E Ontario St	312-573-0800	159
Embassy Suites Lakefront	511 N Columbus Dr	312-836-5900	159
Fairfield Inn	216 E Ontario St	312-787-3777	189
Holiday Inn	300 E Ohio St	312-787-6100	153
InterContinental Chicago	505 N Michigan Ave	312-944-4100	152
Marriott	540 N Michigan Ave	312-836-0100	149
Omni Chicago Hotel	676 N Michigan Ave	312-944-6664	199
Park Hyatt Hotel	800 N Michigan Ave	312-335-1234	375
Radisson Hotel	160 E Huron St	312-787-2900	89
Red Roof Inn	162 E Ontario St	312-787-3580	80
Sheraton Hotel & Towers	301 E North Water St	312-464-1000	149
W Chicago Lakeshore	644 N Lake Shore Dr	312-943-9200	225
Wyndham Chicago	633 N St Clair St	312-573-0300	107

Map 4 · West Loop Gate / Greek Town

Crowne Plaza Metro	733 W Madison St	312-829-5000	157
New Jackson Hotel	768 W Jackson Blvd	312-372-8856	40
Old Town Bed and Breakfast	1442 N Park Ave	312-440-9268	185

Map 5 · The Loop

Buckingham Athletic Club Hotel	440 S La Salle St	312-663-8910	155
Hampton Inn Majestic Theater District	22 W Monroe St	312-332-5052	159
Hilton Palmer House	17 E Monroe St	312-726-7500	151
Hotel Allegro	171 W Randolph St	312-236-0123	199
Hotel Burnham	1 W Washington St	312-782-1111	219
Hotel Monaco	225 N Wabash Ave	312-960-8500	219
Renaissance Chicago Hotel	1 W Wacker Dr	312-372-7200	219
Silversmith Hotel & Suites	10 S Wabash Ave	312-372-7696	239
W Chicago City Center	172 W Adams St	312-332-1200	220

Map 6 · The Loop / Grant Park

Fairmont Hotel	200 N Columbus Dr	312-565-8000	239
Francine Manilow	233 E Wacker Dr	312-938-0129	199
Hard Rock Hotel	230 N Michigan Ave	312-345-1000	199
Hyatt Regency Chicago Hotel	151 E Wacker Dr	312-565-1234	159
Manilow Tower Suites	175 N Harbor Dr	312-540-1380	250/night 3 night min.
Swissotel Chicago	323 E Wacker Dr	312-565-0565	219

General Information · **Hotels**

Map 7 · South Loop / River City

		Phone	Pricing
Holiday Inn	506 W Harrison St	312-957-9100	102
Intown Suites	350 W Roosevelt Rd	630-941-9075	219

Map 8 · South Loop / Printers Row / Dearborn Park

Blake Hotel	500 S Dearborn St	312-986-1234	109
Ho Jo Inn	720 N La Salle St	312-664-8100	99
Hostelling International	24 E Congress Pkwy	312-692-1560	27
Travelodge	65 E Harrison St	312-427-8000	89

Map 9 · South Loop / South Michigan Ave

Best Western Grant Park Hotel	1100 S Michigan Ave	312-922-2900	83
Chicago Hilton and Towers	720 S Michigan Ave	312-922-4400	109
Congress Plaza Hotel	520 S Michigan Ave	312-427-3800	69
Essex Inn	800 S Michigan Ave	312-939-2800	119

Map 11 · South Loop / McCormick Place

Hyatt Regency McCormick Place	2233 S Dr Martin L King Jr Dr	312-567-1234	179
The Wheeler Mansion	2020 S Calumet Ave	312-945-2020	230

Map 12 · Bridgeport (West)

Benedictine Bed and Breakfast	3111 S Aberdeen St	773-927-7424	145

Map 14 · Prairie Shores / Lake Meadows

Amber Inn	3901 S Michigan Dr	773-285-1000	69
Bronzeville Bed & Breakfast	3911 S Dr Martin L King Jr Dr	773-373-8081	175
Zanzibar Motel 5	453 E Pershing Rd	773-373-6100	53

Map 16 · Bronzeville

Jacks House	5020 S Michigan Ave	773-536-1640	60

Map 17 · Kenwood

Ramada Inn Lake Shore	4900 S Lake Shore Dr	773-288-5800	119

Map 18 · Washington Park

Long Hotel	5615 S Prairie Ave	773-288-6973	140 weekly
Mystic Hotel & Restaurant	5522 S Indiana Ave	773-493-5028	70

Map 20 · East Hyde Park / Jackson Park

Wooded Isle Suites	5750 S Stony Island Ave	773-288-5578	141

Map 21 · Wicker Park / Ukrainian Village

Wicker Park Inn B&B	1329 N Wicker Park Ave	773-486-2743	95

Map 22 · Noble Square / Goose Island

House of Two Urns B&B	1239 N Greenview Ave	773-235-1408	165

Map 24 · River West / West Town

Rosemoor Hotel	1622 W Jackson Blvd	312-243-2900	40

Map 26 · University Village / Little Italy / Pilsen

Marriott	625 S Ashland Ave	312-491-1234	209

Map 27 · Logan Square

Milshire Hotel	2525 N Milwaukee Ave	773-384-7611	46
North Hotel	1622 N California Ave	773-278-2425	80

Map 30 · Lincoln Park

Arlington House International Hostel	616 W Arlington Pl	773-929-5380	79
Belden Stratford Hotel	2300 N Lincoln Park W	773-281-2900	119
China Doll	738 W Schubert Ave	773-525-4967	245
Covent Hotel	2653 N Clark St	773-549-3399	125 weekly
Parkview Hotel	1816 N Clark St	312-664-3040	169
Windy City Urban Inn	607 W Deming Pl	773-248-7091	115

Map 31 • Old Town / Near North

		Phone	Pricing
Marshall Hotel	1232 N La Salle Dr	312-664-3080	50

Map 32 • Gold Coast / Mag Mile

Ambassador East	1300 N State Pkwy	312-787-3700	109
Drake Hotel	140 E Walton St	312-787-2200	175
Flemish House	68 E Cedar St	312-664-9981	155
Four Seasons Hotel Chicago	120 E Delaware Pl	312-280-8800	390
Hilton - The Drake	140 E Walton Pl	312-943-6678	159
Hilton Suites	198 E Delaware Pl	312-664-1100	159
Hotel Indigo	1244 N Dearborn St	312-787-4980	149
Mark Twain Hotel	111 W Division St	312-642-7150	115 weekly
Millenium Knickerbocker	163 E Walton St	312-751-8100	89
Raffaello Hotel	201 E Delaware Pl	312-943-5000	149
Residence Inn	201 E Walton St	312-943-9800	159
Ritz Carlton Hotel	160 E Pearson St	312-266-2343	390
Seneca Hotel	200 E Chestnut St	312-787-8900	99
Sofitel Water Tower	20 E Chestnut St	312-324-4000	215
Sutton Place Hotel	21 E Bellevue Pl	312-266-2100	170
Talbot Hotel	20 E Delaware Pl	312-944-4970	179
Tremont	100 E Chestnut St	312-751-1900	89
Westin	909 N Michigan Ave	312-943-7200	169
Whitehall Hotel	105 E Delaware Pl	312-944-6300	135

Map 33 • West Rogers Park

Exel Inns Of Chicago	2881 W Touhy Ave	847-803-9400	64

Map 34 • East Rogers Park

Super 8 Motel	7300 N Sheridan Rd	773-973-7440	89

Map 35 • Arcadia Terrace / Peterson Park

Apache Motel	5535 N Lincoln Ave	773-728-9400	50
Diplomat Motel	5230 N Lincoln Ave	773-271-5400	52
Guest House Motel	2600 W Bryn Mawr Ave	773-561-6811	50
Lincoln Inn	5952 N Lincoln Ave	773-784-1118	45
Lincoln Motel	5900 N Lincoln Ave	773-561-3170	50
Riverpark Motel & Suites	6060 N Lincoln Ave	773-539-4800	58
Summit Motel	5308 N Lincoln Ave	773-561-3762	55

Map 37 • Edgewater / Andersonville

The Ardmore House	1248 W Ardmore Ave	773-728-5414	99
Chicago Lodge	920 W Foster Ave	773-334-5600	85
Heart O' Chicago Motel	5990 N Ridge Ave	773-271-9181	89

Map 40 • Uptown

Dolins Louis	4700 N Racine Ave	773-561-1741	35

Map 43 • Wrigleyville/ East Lakeview

Ambers Hotel	1632 W Belmont Ave	773-248-1740	47
Bellwood Hotel	1409 W Diversey Pkwy	773-404-6000	58
City Suites Hotel	933 W Belmont Ave	773-404-3400	109
Diplomat Hotel	3208 N Sheffield Ave	773-549-6800	50
Sheffield House	3834 N Sheffield Ave	773-248-3500	61

Map 44 • East Lakeview

Abbott Hotel	721 W Belmont Ave	773-248-2700	75
Belair Hotel	424 W Diversey Pkwy	773-248-4000	80
Best Western	3434 N Broadway St	773-244-3434	120
Days Inn	644 W Diversey Pkwy	773-525-7010	77
Inn at Lincoln Park	601 W Diversey Pkwy	773-348-2810	79
Majestic Hotel	528 W Brompton Ave	773-404-3499	109
Willows	555 W Surf St	773-528-8400	109

Chicago is a kid's kind of town. From sandy beaches and leafy parks to diverse downtown museums, concerts, and suburban attractions, Chicago's options for family fun are non-stop—just like your kids.

The Best of the Best

The best part about Chicago family-style is that lots of stuff is free...or practically free. Great entertainment and educational venues keep cash in parents' pockets for school supplies, groceries, gas, and an occasional adult night out.

- **Top Park:** Lincoln Park (Lake Shore Dr & North Ave, 312-742-2000; www.lpzoo.com). From an expansive sandy beach, baseball diamonds, basketball courts, and bike paths to grassy meadows, fishing lagoons, museums, and the nation's oldest free zoo, Lincoln Park promises a full day of outdoor activity.

- **Generations of Amusement:** Kiddieland (8400 W North Ave, Melrose Park, 708-343-8000; www. kiddieland.com). Before Disney and Six Flags, there was Kiddieland, one of the nation's oldest family-owned and operated amusement parks. Many of the more than 30 rides and attractions are original to this wholesome, 80-year-old icon of fun including the jelly-bean-colored bumper cars, carousel, swirling tea cups, and "Little Dipper" rollercoaster. Thrill-seeking 'tweens scream on the "Log Jammer" and high-flying "Galleon." Kids need more steam? Free Pepsi served all day. Unlimited rides for $21.50 admission fee (ages six and up); $18.50 (ages 3–5, seniors); free under age two; discounted admission after 5 pm. Open April–October. Call for seasonal schedule.

- **Spellbinding Story Time:** Lincoln Park Zoo (2200 N Cannon Dr, 312-742-2000; www.lpzoo.com). Donning safari khakis and pith helmet, Professor Bonnie spins adventurous tales and sings for preschoolers at the *Farm-in-the-Zoo*. Wildly popular, this story hour is the toughest ticket in town. Arrive early to secure admission (donation suggested). At the free *Second Sunday Stories*, children's book authors read their works about life on the farm followed by activities and tours of the *Farm-in-the-Zoo*. Call for schedule.

- **Slickest Sledding Hill:** Soldier Field Lakefront Park (312-742-7529; www.chicagoparkdistrict.com). The best part of the Soldier Field's pretty 17-acre park is the free, giant sledding hill with frozen lake views. BYO ride and bundle up for frigid lakefront winds. In warmer months, check out the Children's Garden.

- **Coolest Ice Rink:** McCormick Tribune Ice Rink in Millennium Park (55 N Michigan Ave, 312-742-7529; www.chicagoparkdistrict.com). Skate hand-in-hand in the shadow of architectural landmark buildings lining the Mag Mile. Open daily, admission is free to the 16,000-square-foot rink; skate rental available and warming room on-site.

- **Best-Kept Secret:** Chicago Public Library's "Kraft Great Kids Museum Passport" (Main Branch at 400 S State St, 312-747-4300 and branches city-wide; www. chipublib.org). Families can't afford not to know about the passports—on loan for one week at a time, they provide family members with free admission to over a dozen of Chicago's premier (read: pricey) cultural institutions, including the biggies at the Museum Campus plus the Art Institute, Peggy Notebaert Museum, and Chicago History Museum (formerly the Chicago Historical Society). Available only to Chicago Public Library card-carrying adult Chicago residents. See website for participating institutions and details.

- **Railroad Shop That Rocks:** Berwyn's Toy Trains & Models (7025 Ogden Ave, Berwyn, 708-484-4384). A roundhouse of activity where engineers of all ages can play at the many display train tables and enjoy a charming, 7-by-14-foot tooting layout in the back, Keep with the transportation theme and stop by Berwyn's *Spindle*, a massive sculpture just two miles south on Cermak and Harlem—it's an enormous desk organizer, skewering eight de-commissioned cars. For real.

- **WOW Waterparks:** (312-742-7529; www.chicagopark district.com). The Chicago Park District operates over 20 free waterparks with arching jets, umbrella sprays, pipe falls, and bubble jets in Chicago's neighborhood parks and beaches. All facilities open daily in summer 11 am to 8 pm.

- **Best Beach:** North Avenue Beach (1600 North Ave, 312-742-7529; www.chicagoparkdistrict.com). From swimming, spiking volleyballs, and kickboxing to sunbathing and sipping sun-downers, this expansive beach on Lake Michigan rivals any on the California coast. The tug-boat shaped beach house has locker facilities and rents volleyball equipment, roller blades, and bikes. On the upper deck is Castaways restaurant and ice cream parlor. There's also a full outdoor fitness center with weights and spin cycles plus a roller blade rink for pick up hockey under the summer sun.

- **Sensational Soda Fountain:** Margie's Candies (1960 N Western Ave, 773-384-1035). Celebrating 85 years of scoop, this old-fashioned ice cream parlor serves yummy frozen treats like soda fountains of yesteryear. Kids who flash report cards with an A get a free ice cream cone.

- **A Child's Choice Bakery:** Sweet Mandy B's (1208 W Webster Ave, 773-244-1174). Trendy and tasty, this cheery bakery's kid confections include awesome cupcakes, chunky whoopee pies, and whimsical cut-out frosted cookies. Signature sweet: "Dirt Cups"—a cake, crushed Oreo cookie, and whipped cream combo crawling with psychedelic gummy worms.

- **Coolest Family Concerts:** Joe Segal's Jazz Showcase (59 W Grand Ave, 312-670-2473; www.jazzshowcase. com). Hipster kids and jiving parents and grandparents hang out at this swank, serious jazz club's Sunday 4 pm matinee performances where top musicians jam. Non-alcoholic beverages and snacks served. Discount adult admission; children under 12 free. All Ages Blue Chicago Show (736 N Clark St, 312-661-1003; www. bluechicago.com) on Saturday nights from 8 pm to 3 am where families rock to the Gloria Shannon Blues Band in the basement of the Blue Chicago store. Adult admission $8; kids under age 11 free. No alcohol or smoking allowed. Jammin' at the Zoo (Lincoln Park Zoo, Lake Shore Dr & North Ave, 312-742-2000; www.lpzoo.com) once a month during the summer, shows starting at 7 pm. Serving the needs of cross-generational rock aficionados, previous concerts have featured They Might Be Giants, Collective Soul and The Gin Blossoms. Adult admission $20; kids pay half that.

- **Flying High:** Mayor Daley's Kids and Kites Festival (Alternating lakefront locations, 312-744-3315; www. cityofchicago.org/specialevents). Every spring and fall, the Windy City lives up to its blow-hard reputation, lifting kids' spirits and kites to new heights along the lakefront. Kite flying professionals and instructors help enthusiasts of all ages construct kites and fly them for free. Complimentary kite kits provided or bring your own. Free family entertainment, crafts, and storytelling on-site.

- **Not So Little League:** Chicago White Sox FUN damentals Field (U.S. Cellular Field, 333 W 35th St, 312-674-1000; www.whitesox.com). Little sluggers age three and up play ball in a 15,000-square-foot field of their own within the White Sox's home park. While junior trains, parents spy the pro game going on below from the new, kid-friendly interactive baseball diamond and skills area perched above the left-field concourse. Budding all-stars hone their pitching, batting, and base-running techniques under the sharp eyes of college and pro coach-instructors from the year-round Chicago White Sox Training Academy in Lisle. Batter yet, it's all free with ball-park admission.

- **Masterpiece Portraits:** Classic Kids (917 W Armitage Ave, 773-296-2607; 566 Chestnut St, Winnetka, 847-446-2064). Pricey but priceless photos from this studio capture your kid at his or her model best. Pay a $300 sitting fee plus cost for handcrafted prints and treasure your tyke forever.

- **Weirdest City Sight:** Chicago River runs green (Chicago River downtown along Wacker Dr). No, it's not algae or bile, but bio-degradable green dye. Every St. Patrick's Day, the city turns the Chicago River emerald green like the Incredible Hulk.

- **Parents' Parking Dream:** Little Parkers Program, Standard Parking Garages (888-700-7275; www. standardparking.com). Select garages downtown specially equip families for road trips home with puzzles, crayons, and coloring books. Family-friendly garage amenities include spacious bathrooms with diaper-changing stations. Some rent family videos to monthly parkers. Participating garages: Grant Park North Garage, 25 N Michigan Ave; East Monroe Garage, 350 E Monroe St; Chicago Historical Society Garage, 1730 N Stockton Dr; Huron-St. Claire Self Park near Northwestern Memorial Hospital; Erie-Ontario Self Park in Streeterville neighborhood; and 680 N Lake Shore Dr Self Park.

- **Finest Family Festival:** Tall Ships (312-744-3370; www.cityofchicago.org/specialevents). Ahoy there, matey! In early August, over 25 old-world sailing vessels drop anchor along the lakeshore at Navy Pier, DuSable Harbor, and the Chicago River filling the skyline with billowing sails. There are daily deck tours ($10 boarding fee) as well as free entertainment and fireworks.

- **Kudos Kids' Theatre:** Marriott Theatre for Young Audiences (Marriott Lincolnshire Resort, 10 Marriott Dr, Lincolnshire, 847-634-0200; www.marriotttheatre. com). Not a bad seat in the house at this intimate arena theater where actors welcome pint-sized audience participation and roam the aisles interacting with kids. Post-performance, the actors conduct Q&A answering kids' theatrical questions. Family productions run year-round. Tickets $12 per person; free parking.

- **Oscar Performances:** Children's International Film Festival (city-wide, 773-281-9075; www.cicff.org). For over two weeks each fall, Chicago's theater venues feature hundreds of witty, ingenious long- and short-form children's movies from around the world, some created by kids. Filmmakers, directors, and animators teach seminars for movie-lovers of all ages.

- **Hippest Halloween Happening:** Chicago Symphony Orchestra's Hallowed Haunts Concert (220 S Michigan Ave, 312-294-3000; www.cso.org). Skeletons rattle and ghosts boogie to classical morbid music at the Chicago Symphony Orchestra's creepy family concert featuring hair-raising Romantic-Era pieces and medieval chants. Come in costume to the concert and ghoulish pre-performance party. Tickets: $7–$45.

- **Perfect Pumpkin Patch:** Sonny Acres Farm (29 W 310 North Ave, West Chicago, 630-231-9515; www.sonnyacres.com). During October, the Feltes family homestead has it all for fall: jack-o-lanterns for carving, homemade pies, decorative Thanksgiving and Halloween displays, and a killer costume shop. Kids love the mountains of pumpkins, crunchy caramel apples, scary hay rides, youngster carnival rides, and haunted barns (one for tiny tikes and another for blood-thirsty teens). Free farm admission and parking; purchase tickets for attractions.

- **Fields of Dreams:** Of course Wrigley Field, but a family outing at the venerable ballpark amounts to a month's down payment on a mini van. For $10 or less per ticket, take the family to the 'burbs' farm league games at pristine ballparks complete with entertainment, eats, and fireworks: Kane County Cougars (34W002 Cherry Ln, Geneva, 630-232-8811; www.kccougars.com) and Shaumburg Flyers (1999 S Springinsguth Rd, Schaumburg, 847-891-2255; www.flyersbaseball.com).

- **No-Flab Family Workout:** Tri-Star Gymnastics' Family Fun Night (1401 Circle Ave, Forest Park, 708-771-7827; www.tri-stargym.org). Families bounce on trampolines, swing on bars, tumble across mats, and climb ropes together at Tri-Star's warehouse-sized gymnastic training facility. Held from 4:30 pm to 5:30 pm on Saturday nights during the school year, admission is $5 per child and parents get in free. Parental supervision (no more than two kids per adult) and signed waiver required.

- **Musical Marathon Encounter:** Chicago Symphony Orchestra's Day of Music (220 S Michigan Ave, 312-294-3333; www.cso.org). A free live music marathon lasting eight hours held each fall. In addition to the world-renowned Chicago Symphony Orchestra, hear the city's top musicians perform classical, jazz, blues, world music, plus lively family entertainment. For year-round family concert performances, check out the orchestra's Kraft Matinee Series.

- **Horse'n Around:** Arlington Park Race Track's Family Day (2200 W Euclid Ave, Arlington Heights, 847-385-7500; www.arlingtonpark.com). From mid-May through mid-September it's a sure bet you'll win big with the kids on a Sunday afternoon at the horse races. Wild West, luau, and circus-themed family activities surround the seriously fun thoroughbred racing action at this swank, clean track. Pony rides, face painters, and petting zoo on-site. From noon to 4 pm, attend the free Junior Jockey Club events (847-870-6614) including educational equine care talks and behind-the scenes track tours (children 12 and under).

- **Brightest Christmas Lights:** Cuneo Museum and Gardens' Winter Wonderland Holiday Light Festival (1350 N Milwaukee Ave, Vernon Hills, 847-362-3042; www.cuneomuseum.org). The largest drive-through Christmas display in Northern Illinois twinkles with millions of lights creating dazzling holiday scenes. Superhero and storybook light sculptures dance in the woods. Festival runs first Friday after Thanksgiving through New Year's weekend from 6 pm to 10 pm. Admission per car is $10 on weekends, $5 weekdays.

- **Winter Blahs Buster:** Fantasy Kingdom (1422 N Kingsbury St at Evergreen St, 312-642-5437; www.fantasykingdom.org). When Chicago's plunging temps prevent playground play, take tykes to this warehouse-turned-play-space magic kingdom to blow off steam. Kids clamor through a giant castle fitted with slides and tunnels (socks required) while donning Camelot costumes for dress-up fun. $12 per child.

- **Shadiest Theme Park:** Pirate's Cove (901 Leicester Rd, Elk Grove Village, 847-437-9494; www.elkgroveparks.org). On the other hand, when Chicago's soaring temps make playing outdoors as appealing as a trip down the Styx, hit this blessedly small-scale, low-tech theme park. Your (10-and-under) mateys will scramble up the Smugglers Cove, ride a rope-and-pulley griffin, and paddle around a wee lagoon, all while you actually keep cool in this heavily-shaded treasure. Great low-cost birthday party site. $6 for residents, $8 for nonresidents.

Rainy Day Activities

Art Institute of Chicago, 111 S Michigan Ave, 312-443-3600; www.artic.edu. While kids find the doll house–sized Thorne Miniature Rooms and shiny medieval armor very cool, they also discover artistic expression from around the world at the Kraft Education Center. Interactive exhibitions introduce children to art from other cultures, time periods, and world-wide geographic regions. "Edutaining" art books and masterpiece puzzles in the children's library reinforce visual learning. Free kids' programs and drawing workshops are also held throughout museum galleries. Admission is free on Tuesdays (however, donation strongly suggested); children under 5 always free.

Cernan Earth and Space Center, Triton College Campus, 2000 Fifth Ave, River Grove, 708-456-0300, ext. 3372; www.triton.edu/cernan. Named after Apollo astronaut Eugene Cernan, a native Chicagoan and the last man on the moon, this cozy planetarium's intimate dome theater features kids' star programs ($5), earth and sky shows, and laser light shows. Monthly sky watch and lectures hosted. Mini space-related museum (free admission) and great celestial gift shop.

Chicago's Museum Campus, 1200–1400 S Lake Shore Dr. The closest you'll come to an educational amusement park. Dinosaurs, live sharks, giant mechanical insects, ancient mummies, and exploding stars are just a handful of adventures your kids will encounter on the lakefront's brainy peninsula home to the Field Museum (312-922-9410; www.fieldmuseum.org), Adler Planetarium & Astronomy Museum (312-922-7827; www.adlerplanetarium.org), and John G. Shedd Aquarium (312-939-2438; www.shedd.org). Check with each institution for its free admission days and special family programs.

Diversey River Bowl, 2211 W Diversey Pkwy, 773-227-5800; drbowl.com. Families, couples, and serious bowlers mix it up at this upbeat city alley. Decent grilled food served and full bar on-site. Wednesday through Sunday nights at 8 pm, glow-in-the-dark bowling known as Rock 'n Bowl goes well past the little one's bedtime but is fun for teens with chaperones.

DuPage Children's Museum, 301 N Washington St, Naperville, 630-637-8000; www.dupagechildrensmuseum.org. The 45,000-square-foot museum loaded with hands-on, action-packed exhibits keeps pre-schoolers with nano-second attention spans exploring until exhaustion.

Exploritorium, 4701 Oakton St, Skokie, 847-674-1500, x2700; www.skokieparkdistrict.org. From finger paints and water games to costumes and a multi-storied jungle gym, this facility tuckers tykes out. The climbing gym outfitted with twisting ropes, tubes, and tunnels even brings out the Tarzan in parents. Miniscule admission fee; free for Skokie adult residents and kids under 3.

Federal Reserve Bank of Chicago Visitors' Center, 230 S LaSalle St, 312-322-5322; www.chicagofed.org. The buck stops here where kids learn the power of pocket change through hands-on and computerized exhibits explaining the Fed's role in managing the nation's money. Kids love the rotating, million-dollar cube of cash and $50,800 coin pit. Sneak a peak into the vault stocked with $9 million, trace our country's currency history, and learn how to identify fake bills. Free admission. Open weekdays 9 am–4 pm; free guided tours on Mondays at 1 pm.

Garfield Park Conservatory, 300 N Central Park Ave, 312-746-5100; www.garfield-conservatory.org. Kids really dig Plants Alive!, the free, landmark Conservatory's 5,000-square-foot greenhouse blooming with child-friendly vegetation. Kids climb a two-story twisting daisy stem that doubles as a slide and come nose-to-stinger with a Jurassic-sized bumble bee. Attend story-telling, plant seeds, and dig in the soil pool.

Kohl Children's Museum of Greater Chicago, 2100 Patriot Blvd, Glenview, 847-832-6600; www.kohlchildrensmuseum.org. Kids climb the rigging of a pirate ship, "ride" an L train, meander through mazes, and push mini carts through a fully stocked grocery store.

Mitchell Museum of the American Indian, 2600 Central Park Ave on Kendall College Campus, Evanston, 847-475-1030; www.mitchellmuseum.org. From real teepees and dug-out canoes to bow-and-arrows and tom-toms, this compact sensory museum's engaging hands-on exhibits and craft sessions teach kids about the rich Native American life and culture. During the school year, sessions are offered semi-monthly on Saturdays, and on Tuesdays, Wednesdays, and Thursdays in summer. All programs held from 10:30 am to noon.

Museum of Science and Industry, 57th St at S Lake Shore Dr, 773-684-1414; www.msichicago.org. The ultimate hands-on learning experience for families, this massive museum is a tsunami of scientific exploration. Favorite kid exhibits are the 3,500 square-foot The Great Train Story model railroad, the United Airlines jet, a walk-through human heart, a working Coal Mine, and the Idea Factory workshop packed with gears, cranks, and water toys. OMNIMAX Theater on-site. Call for free day schedule.

Navy Pier, 600 E Grand Ave, 312-595-7437; www.navypier.com. A mega-sized free entertainment emporium jutting into Lake Michigan, Navy Pier has an IMAX Theater and tons of carnival-like attractions. The renowned Shakespeare Theater performs kid-friendly shorts of Willy's works. The 57,000-square-foot Chicago Children's Museum has 15 permanent engaging exhibits for toddlers to pre-teens (312-527-1000; www.chichildrensmuseum.org). Museum admission free on Thursday nights from 5 pm to 8 pm.

Oak Brook Family Aquatic Center, 1450 Forest Gate Rd, Oak Brook, 630-990-4233; www.obparks.org. Wet, wild fun for the whole family at this splashy indoor aquatic facility. They've got a zero-depth pool and slide for tadpoles as well as an Olympic-sized pool for bigger fish. Special swim events include watery holiday-themed parties, arts and crafts, water sports days, and dive-in movie nights where you can watch a family flick from your inflatable raft.

Peggy Notebaert Nature Museum, 2430 N Cannon Dr, 773-755-5100; www.naturemuseum.org. Kids delight in Butterfly Haven, a soaring tropical greenhouse habitat, home to hundreds of exotic winged beauties from around the world. The Children's Gallery replicates prairie and wetland habitats. Hands-on, free scientific activities and animal feedings always scheduled. Chicago residents enjoy a $1 discount on admission fee. On Thursdays, admission is free; however donations are strongly suggested.

Pelican Harbor Indoor/Outdoor Aquatic Park, 200 S Lindsay Ln, Bolingbrook, 630-739-1700; www. bolingbrookparks.org. Chicago area's only indoor/ outdoor waterpark open year-round. Kids zip down six thrilling water slides (one 75-foot tall), float on inner tubes, and plunge into the diving well. There is a large zero-depth pool for little swimmers, lap pool, sand volleyball, whirlpool, and concessions.

Shops at Northbridge, 520 N Michigan Ave, 312-327-2300; www.westfield.com/northbridge. The entire third floor is not only lined with child apparel, toy, and accessory stores, but has The LEGO Store with play stations and a spacious LEGO building zone. Best part is parents don't have to clean up those blasted colored blocks!

Spertus Museum of Judaica, 618 S Michigan Ave, 312-322-1700; www.spertus.edu/museum. The Children's ARTiFACT Center recreates an impressive archeological site where kids dig up artifacts from ancient Middle East civilizations and experiment with writing in Cuneiform. Free admission on Fridays; all-inclusive, $10 family pass sold the rest of the week.

Wonder Works, 6445 W North Ave, Oak Park, 708-383-4815; www.wonder-works.org. About half a mile west of Chicago's city limits, this modest children's museum is far more accessible for many city families than the Chicago Children's Museum at Navy Pier and boasts the triple advantages of being low-cost ($5 admission + free street parking), low-key, and packed with friendly volunteers. Usually closed on Mondays and Tuesdays, Wonder Works often makes an exception for school holidays (call to confirm, though).

Outdoor *and* Educational

Fresh air family fun venues that work your kids' muscles and minds pack the city and suburbs. Here are some of the best:

Brookfield Zoo, First Ave & 31st St, Brookfield, 708-485-0263; www.brookfieldzoo.org. Chicago's largest zoo, spanning 216 wooded acres, is home to over 2,500 animal residents from around the world. Hamill Family Play Zoo and the Children's Zoo offer interactive programs on animal antics and opportunities to pet kid-friendly creatures babysat by helpful docents. Several dolphin shows daily. Family and child educational classes offered, plus summer camps and special holiday events. Explore the woodsy Indian Lake district where a life-sized dinosaur "lives." Open daily. Admission is free October through March on Tuesdays and Thursdays and January through February on Saturdays and Sundays.

Cantigny Park, 1 S 151 Winfield Rd, Wheaton, 630-668-5161; www.cantignypark.com. The 15-acre complex named after a World War I battle is home to the First Division Museum showcasing the history of the famed U.S. Army's 1st Infantry Division and *Chicago Tribune* founder's Robert R. McCormick Mansion Museum. After clamoring over the cannons, kids can stop to smell the flowers blooming in the manicured gardens. Family programs and concerts scheduled year-round. Park opens Tuesday through Sunday 9 am to sunset; museum is open 9 am–4 pm. Park and museum admission free; car parking fee, $7 Monday to Friday, and $8 on the weekends. Nearby is the top-rated, public Cantigny Golf Course (630-668-3323) offering junior golf instruction and a 9-hole Youth Links Course

Chicago Botanic Garden, 1000 Lake Cook Rd, Glencoe, 847-835-5440; www.chicagobotanic.org. Open daily, admission is free to this 385-acre living preserve with more than 1.2 million plants rooted in 23 gardens, three tropical greenhouses, three natural habitats, eight lagoons, and bike paths. Kids love the winding, willow-branch tunnel in the Children's Garden where they can dig for worms and plant seeds. On Monday nights in summer, picnickers listen to the resonating chimes of carillon bell concerts on Evening Island. Late May through October, come for the Jr. Railroad where model trains puff through a garden of America's best loved landmarks (exhibit admission charged); in early December, make sure to check out the Reindog Parade (think bassets with antlers), with or without a Fido of your own.

Cuneo Museum and Gardens, 1350 Milwaukee Ave, Vernon Hills, 847-362-3042; www.cuneomuseum.org. Kids romp through the 75-acre wooded estate's formal gardens, animal sanctuaries, and deer park surrounding a palatial Italianate mansion. Open Tuesday–Sunday 10 am–5 pm; $5 grounds admission fee; mansion tours cost $12 for adults, $7 for children.

Fermi National Accelerator Laboratory, Kirk Rd & Pine St, Batavia, 630-840-3351; www.fnal.gov. Release energy outdoors biking, hiking, and rollerblading the nature trails at the nuclear plant's 680-acre campus. Rare species of butterflies, plants, birds, and baby buffalos live on the rural grounds. Guided prairie tours offered in summer. Picnickers welcome and lake fishing available. Open daily; admission free. Kids power up their nuclear knowledge at the Leon M. Lederman Science Education Center learning about nature's secrets and how the universe began. Admission free; open weekdays. Fermilab physicists conduct behind-the-scenes lab tours and Q&A with guests the first weekend of every month.

Graceland Cemetery, Clark St & Irving Park Blvd, 312-922-3432. Eerie and educational, the famous 119-acre necropolis built in 1860 is a national architectural landmark filled with palatial mausoleums, haunting headstones, and reportedly disappearing angelic statues marking the graves of Chicago's rich, famous, and infamous. The Chicago Architecture Foundation's (www.architecture.org) spine-chilling cemetery tour is a drop-dead Halloween family favorite.

Grosse Point Lighthouse, Sheridan Rd & Central St, Evanston, 847-328-6961; www.grossepointlighthouse.net. The pretty grounds surrounding the charming, white, tapering lighthouse built in 1873 and fairy-tale stone cottage are open year-round. Tours of both structures are offered weekends June through September for children aged 8 and up. A wooded trail twists down a grassy slope to the isolated Lighthouse Landing Beach.

Tempel Lipizzans Farm, Wadsworth Rd & Hunt Club Rd, Wadsworth, 847-623-7272; www.tempelfarms.com. Trained in the centuries-old tradition of the Spanish Riding School in Vienna, dancing, white Lipizzaner stallions fly through the air performing fancy four-footed feats. Performances are Wednesdays and Sundays, June through August. Tours of the historic stables offered year-round.

Lambs Farm, 14245 W Rockland Rd, Libertyville, 847-362-4636; www.lambsfarm.org. Over 40 years old, this is Chicagoland's favorite farmyard, a non-profit residential farm for persons with developmental disabilities. Animal petting zoo, mini-golf, and vintage carousel open in season. Year-round feel-good family events include an old-fashioned Breakfast with Santa, Easter Brunch, fall festival, and more. Shops and kid-friendly country restaurant open Tuesday through Sunday.

Lincoln Park Zoo, 2200 N Cannon Dr, 312-742-2000; www.lpzoo.com. The nation's oldest free zoo hasn't rested on its laurels—come see the up-to-date Ape House, Regenstein African Journey habitat, and North American animal exhibit at the Pritzker Family Children's Zoo. Kids love the graceful giraffes, lumbering elephants, and giant hissing Madagascar cockroaches. Additional family favorites are the Farm-in-the-Zoo, lion house, sea lion pool, and old-fashioned carousel (summer). Call for information on family programs including the ever popular Night Watch where families sleep over at the zoo!

Morton Arboretum, 4100 Illinois Rte 53, Lisle, 630-968-0074; www.mortonarb.org. Forests, meadows, gardens, and wetlands cover 1,700 acres of this outdoor tree and plant museum with paved roads and 14 miles of trails for hiking and biking. Kids particularly dig the Children's Adventure Garden and Maze. Overall, a great place to tromp around and picnic. Food service on-site. Guided tours and kid/family nature classes offered year-round. Favorite family fall activities include leaf collecting and the "Scarecrow Trail." Open daily. Discounted admission on Wednesdays.

Naper Settlement, 523 S Webster St, Naperville, 630-420-6010; www.napersettlement.org. Kids experience life on the Midwestern prairie of the past at this re-creation of a 19th-century agrarian community. Working blacksmith shop, post office, and school house manned by costumed interpreters. The living history village's seasonal programs cater to kids with games, pony rides, and entertainment.

North Park Village Nature Center, 5801 N Pulaski Rd, 312-744-5472; www.cityofchicago.org/environment. You'll think you're a hundred miles west of the city at this 46-acre rolling woods and wetlands where deer roam and owls screech. Nature paths throughout. Admission free; open year-round. Popular week-long EcoExplorers summer camps for kids aged five to 14 years also offered.

Sears Tower Skydeck, 233 S Wacker Dr, 312-875-9696; www.theskydeck.com. OK, so only a pane of glass separates your baby from the sky blue. But the Knee-High Chicago kids' exhibit is worth the parental panic. Interactive displays tell tales of Chicago from a bird's eye view. A touch-and-talk computer explains city landmarks.

Classes

Many of the city's fine cultural institutions have stellar, kid-focused curricula and host popular summer camps. Chicago and suburban park districts offer solid sports instruction, dance, and crafts classes. But private specialty schools also instruct many pint-sized prodigies. Here are some of the most popular and pedigreed organizations:

Academy of Movement and Music, 605 Lake St, Oak Park, 708-848-2329. This 34-year-old school offers popular dance and movement classes. The cool, creative Boys Production class for guys ages five to nine focuses on high-energy body movement practically applied to mini-manly visual arts projects, including mazes, puzzles, murals, sculptures, and machinery.

Alliance Francaise, 810 N Dearborn St, 312-337-1070; www.afchicago.com. Cultivating everything French in Chicagoans of all ages since 1897, this institution breeds petite Francophiles through intense language classes, camps, and cultural programs.

Bubbles Academy, 1504 N Fremont St, 312-944-7677; www.bubblesacademy.com. Yoga for youngsters taught with a creative twist in an open, airy studio.

Dennehy School of Irish Dance, 2555 W 111th St, 773-881-3990; www.dennehydancers.com. A South Side Irish institution, Dennehy has churned out high-stepping Irish dancers for over forty years. Its most-famous pupil so far is egomaniac, foot-pounding Michael Flatley of stage hits *Riverdance* and *Lord of the Dance*.

Flavour Cooking School, 7401 W Madison St, Forest Park, 708-488-0808; www.flavourcookingschool.com. Kids learn to really stir it up from scrambled eggs and lasagna to stir-fry and California cuisine at this cozy cooking school and culinary cookware shop. Class content determined by chefs' ages: Kitchen Helpers (age 4–6); Young Chefs (age 7–11); Sous Chefs (age 12+). Kids' summer cooking camps are also offered.

Gallery 37, 66 E Randolph St, 312-744-8925. Spearheaded by Maggie Daley, as in Mayor Richie's wife, Gallery 37's creative curriculum provides 14- to 21-year-old Chicago residents with educational on-the-job training in the visual, literary, media, culinary, and performing arts. Under the direction of professional artists, apprentices are paid while creating art projects throughout the city such as bench-painting, sculpture, play-writing, and multicultural dance. Eight-week summer program and limited programming during school year. Applications required.

Illinois Rhythmic Gymnastics Center, 636 Ridge Rd, Highland Park, 847-831-9888; www.ilrhythmicgymnastics.com. This top flexible factory turns out more national and Olympic gymnastic team members than any other in the country.

Language Stars, locations city-wide, 866-557-8277; www.languagestars.com. Children aged one through 10 are instructed in foreign language through play-based immersion.

Lou Conte Dance Studio, 1147 W Jackson Blvd, 312-850-9766; www.hubbardstreetdance.org. The dance studio of esteemed Hubbard Street Dance Chicago offers killer classes for teens (aged 11 to 14) in hip-hop, tap, jazz, ballet, African, modern, and more. Also teaches children and teen dance classes through the new, thriving Beverly Arts Center (2407 W 111th St, 773-445-3838; beverlyartcenter.org).

Merit School of Music, 38 S Peoria St, 312-786-9428; www.meritmusic.org. This tuition-free conservatory provides economically disadvantaged youth with excellent instruction in playing classical and jazz instruments. An answer to the public school system's sad arts education cuts.

Music Institute of Chicago, 1490 Chicago Ave, Evanston, 847-905-1500; www.musicinst.com. Students of all ages flock to this esteemed school specializing in the Suzuki Method for many instruments. Group and private instruction in string, wind, brass, and percussion instruments offered.

Old Town School of Folk Music, 4544 N Lincoln Ave & 909 W Armitage Ave, 773-728-6000; www.oldtownschool.org. Opened in 1957, this is Chicago's premier all-American music center specializing in lessons on twangy instruments. The school is best known for its Wiggleworms music movement program catering to the under-five folk. Engaging teen curriculum in music, theater, dance, and art is also offered. Kids' concerts—actually, all concerts—rock.

Ruth Page Center for the Arts, 1016 N Dearborn St, 312-337-6543; www.ruthpage.com. Prima ballerina classes for beginners to advanced students offered at this fine school whose graduates dance for the American Ballet Theatre, the New York City Ballet, and professional companies world-wide.

Second City Training Center, 1616 N Wells St, 312-664-3959; www.secondcity.com. Sign up your bucket of laughs for famed Second City's improvisational classes. Hilarious kids ages 4–12 attend hour-long sessions on Saturdays. Teen improv program is also offered.

Sherwood Conservatory of Music, 1312 S Michigan Ave, 312-427-6267; www.sherwoodmusic.org. Over-a-century-old Sherwood Conservatory specializes in the Suzuki Method for children ages three to 12 in cello, violin, viola, flute, piano, harp, and guitar. Also teaches classes at the South Side's Beverly Arts Center (2407 W 111th St, 773-445-3838; beverlyartcenter.org).

The Chopping Block, 4747 N Lincoln Ave, 773-472-6700; www.thechoppingblock.net. The Lincoln Square neighborhood store and kitchen complex of this sophisticated culinary store hosts cooking classes for kids ages 7–12 two times a week. Four-day cooking camp for two hours a day held in summers.

Tri-Star Gymnastics, 1401 Circle Ave, Forest Park, 708-771-7827; www.tri-stargym.org. This women-run gym pumps out gymnastic champs ages 18 months through teens. Flexing its muscle since 1987, the not-for-profit center offers caring instruction for boys and girls in gymnastics, tumbling, and trampoline. The center is home to a GIJO Team (Junior Olympics) and USGA Teams.

Shopping Essentials

Designer duds, high-style child furniture, imaginative toys, and kids' tunes—Chicago stores have it all for newborns to teens. Here's just a sampling of the top shops:

- **Alamo Shoes** • 5321 N Clark St • 773-334-6100; 6548 W Cermak Rd, Berwyn • 708-795-818 • Experienced staff for toddler shoe fittings.
- **American Girl Place** • 111 E Chicago Ave • 312-943-9400 • Dolls and books.
- **Bearly Used** • 401 Linden Ave, Wilmette • 847-256-8700 • Fab deals on duds and furniture.
- **Building Blocks Toy Store** • 3306 N Lincoln Ave • 773-525-6200 • Old-fashioned, brain-building toys.
- **Carrara Children's Shoes** • 2506 ½ N Clark St • 773-529-9955 • Tot soles from Italy.
- **Children in Paradise** • 909 N Rush St • 312-951-5437 • Personable kids' bookseller.
- **Cut Rate Toys** • 5409 W Devon Ave • 773-763-5740 • Discounted favorites.
- **Disney Store** • 717 N Michigan Ave • 312-654-9208 • Princess paraphernalia and Mouse gear.
- **Fly Bird** 719 Lake St, Oak Park 708-383-3330 Off-beat furnishings, fashion and toys from baby to adult
- **Forest Bootery** • 492 Central Ave, Highland Park • 847-433-1911; 284 E Market Sq, Lake Forest • 847-234-0201 • Great but pricey shoe store.
- **Galt Toys + Galt Baby** • 900 N Michigan Ave • 312-440-9550; 2012 Northbrook Court, Northbrook • 847-498-4660 • High-end toy store and baby supplies.
- **Gymboree** • 835 N Michigan Ave • 312-649-9074 • Designer preemie and kids' clothes.
- **Kozy's Bike Shop** • 601 S LaSalle St • 312-360-0020 • Everything for biking families.
- **LMNOP** • 2570 N Lincoln Ave • 773-975-4055 • Hip, fun kids' clothes.
- **Land of Nod** • 900 W North Ave • 312-475-9903 (stores also in Oak Brook Center and Northbrook Court) • Cute kids' furniture.
- **Lazar's Juvenile Furniture** • 6557 N Lincoln Ave, Lincolnwood • 847-679-6146 • Tried-and-true children's furniture store.
- **Little Strummer** • 909 W Armitage Ave • 773-751-3410 • Kids' tunes.
- **Madison and Friends** • 940 N Rush St • 312-642-6403 • Designer clothes.
- **Magic Tree Bookstore** 141 N Oak Park Ave, Oak Park 708-848-0770 Friendly and expert independent booksellers.
- **Mini Me** • 900 N Michigan Ave • 312-988-4011 • European designer clothes.
- **Oilily** • 520 N Michigan Ave • 312-527-5747 • Colorful patterned kids' clothes.
- **Pottery Barn Kids** • 2111 N Clybourn Ave • 773-525-8349 (stores also in Oak Brook Center, Old Orchard Center, and Deer Park Town Center) • Furnishings for the completely coordinated kid's boudoir.
- **Psycho Baby** • 1630 N Damen Ave • 773-772-2815 • Funky kids' clothes.
- **Pumpkin Moon** • 1028 North Blvd, Oak Park • 708-524-8144 • Funky, vintage toys.
- **Red Balloon Company** • 2060 Damen Ave • 773-489-9800 • Toys, clothes, furniture.
- **The Right Start** • 2121 N Clybourn Ave • 773-296-4420 • Baby equipment galore.
- **Shops at Northbridge** • 520 N Michigan Ave • 312-327-2300 • Entire third floor is kids' clothing, toys, and accessories, including Nordstrom.
- **The Second Child** • 954 W Armitage Ave • 773-883-0880 • Gently used designer clothes.
- **Timeless Toys** • 4749 N Lincoln Ave • 773-334-4445 • Old-fashioned, hand-crafted toys.
- **Toyscape** • 2911 N Broadway St • 773-665-7400 • Toys galore.
- **Uncle Fun** • 1338 W Belmont Ave • 773-477-8223 • Hilarious novelties and vintage tin wind-up toys.
- **U.S. Toy–Constructive Playthings** • 5314 W Lincoln Ave, Skokie • 847-675-5900 • Educational toys favored by teachers.

Where to go for more information

Chicago Parent Magazine • www.chicagoparent.com

Oaklee's Guide for Chicagoland Kids • www.oakleesguide.com

Dog Parks, Runs and Beaches

Make no bones about it, Chicago is a dog's kind of town. More than 750,000 canines live and play in the Windy City. Dogs socialize and exercise their owners daily at designated Dog-Friendly Areas (DFAs), shady parks, and sprawling beaches.

Dog-Friendly Areas

DFAs are off-leash areas reserved just for canines. Amenities vary by park but often include: doggie drinking fountains; agility equipment; wood chips, pea pebble, and asphalt surfaces; "time out" fenced-in areas for shy or overexcited dogs; trash receptacles and doggie bags for, well, not take-out; and bulletin boards and information kiosks to post animal lovers' announcements.

DFAs are managed jointly by the neighborhoods' dog owners' councils and the Chicago Park District. These spaces are essential to the happiness of Chicago dogs and their owners, as police are notorious for dealing out hefty fines and even arresting dog owners who fail to clean up after or leash their dogs. But at the DFA, canines run free and poop where they please. Just remember to clean up after your pooch, ensure that your dog is fully immunized, de-wormed, licensed, and wearing ID tags. There are limits on how many pups one person can bring at once and please no puppies under four months, dogs in heat, dogs with the name "Killer," or children under 12.

- **Challenger Park**, 1100 W Irving Park Rd (Map 40)
  Nestled next to a cemetery and under the EL tracks, this relatively new DFA has plenty of amenities and neighborhood action. Avoid at all costs during Cubs games.

- **Churchill Field Park**, 1825 N Damen Ave (Map 28)
  This triangular space next to the train tracks is covered with pea gravel and asphalt and many abandoned tennis balls (Golden Retrievers can't get enough).

- **Coliseum Park**, 1466 S Wabash Ave (Map 11)
  Long, narrow, and fenced-in park where dogs race the overhead trains. Nothing to write home about, but, hey, it's legal.

- **Hamlin Park**, 3035 N Hoyne Ave at Wellington Ave (Map 42)
  Located in the shady southwest corner, this active L-shaped park appeals to tennis-ball chasers and fetching owners.

- **Margate Park**, 4921 N Marine Dr (Map 40)
  Called "Puptown" by the Uptown canine-loving community, this beloved DFA is usually packed with doggone fun. Locals are diligent about keeping the pea gravel picked up.

- **Noethling (Grace) Park**, 2645 N Sheffield Ave (Map 29)
  Dogs and owners from the Lincoln Park area love to hang out at the "Wiggley Field" dog run—Chicago's first pooch park. Wiggley's got a doggy obstacle course, an asphalt surface, drinking fountain, "time out" area, and info kiosk.

- **Ohio Place Park**, N Orleans St and W Ohio St (Map 2)
  Next to the I-90/94 exit ramp, this fenced-in strip of concrete flanked by bushes isn't pretty, but a dog can play fetch here without a leash. Careful: As the lot is not a Chicago Park District facility, it is not double-gated.

- **River Park**, 5100 N Francisco Ave (Map 38)
  The city's newest DFA.

- **Walsh Playground Park**, 1722 N Ashland Ave (Map 29)
  A 4,500-square-foot park with a small off-leash area for fetching with pea gravel and shade.

- **Wicker Park**, 1425 N Damen Ave (Map 21)
  Popular pooch as well as dog owner pick-up park. Often packed with dog-walkers wrangling fleets of frisky canines.

Creating a DFA takes a serious grass-roots effort spearheaded by the neighborhood's dog owners. They must organize themselves to get the community to bow to their desires through site surveys and three community meetings and raise one-half of the funds needed to build the DFA. Most importantly, they must unleash the support of their alderman, police precinct, and park district. For information on DFAs, call the Park District at 312-742-7529. Chicago's Dog Advisory Work Group, DAWG, (312-409-2169) also assists neighborhood groups in establishing DFAs

Top Dog Parks and Beaches

Leashed dogs and well-behaved owners are welcome in most of Chicago's parks and on its beaches, except during the height of swimming season when the sands are off-limits. Here are some local canines' top picks.

- **Calumet Park and Beach (9800 South)**
  A 200-acre beach and park getaway in the city with tennis courts, baseball fields, basketball courts, water fun, and plenty of parking.

- **Dog Beach (3200 N Lake Shore Dr)**
  This crescent of sand at the north corner of Belmont Harbor is separated from the bike path by a fence, making it an unofficial dog sand box. But the water is dirty, and the police do ticket, so it's not the most ideal dog-frolicking area.

- **Horner Park (2741 W Montrose Ave)**
  Dog heaven with lots of trees, grass, squirrels to chase, and other pups to meet, particularly after work.

- **Lincoln Park (2045 Lincoln Park W)**
  Paws down, the best dog park in town for romping, fetch, and Frisbee. Unofficial "Bark Park" where pet lovers congregate is a grassy area between Lake Shore Dr and Marine Dr.

- **Montrose/Wilson Avenue Beach (MonDog) (4400 North)**
  The city's only legal off-leash beach, MonDog is perfect for pooches to practice dogpaddling. Lake water is shallow and the beachfront is wide.

- **Ohio Street Beach and Olive Park (400 N Lake Shore Dr)**
  The perfect combo for cross-training canines: Olive Park's fenced-in grassy areas for running and neighboring Ohio Street Beach's calm waters for swimming.

- **Promontory Point (5491 South Shore Dr)**
  Radical run for daring, buff dogs that dive off the scenic picnic area's rocks into the deep water below.

- **Sherman Park (1301 W 52nd St)**
  The best place in the city for a Victorian-style stroll over picturesque bridges and through lagoons.

More Doggie Information

Chicago's canine community keeps up to sniff on doggie doings through *Chicagoland Tails Magazine*, www.chicagolandtails.com and the Chicago Canine website, www.chicagocanine.com. The definitive local resource for all things dog is Margaret Littman's book *The Dog Lover's Companion to Chicago* (Avalon Travel Publishing).

Self-Storage / Van and Truck Rentals

Self-Storage Locations

	Address	Phone	Map
Metro Self Storage	465 N Desplaines St	312-243-2222	1
Public Storage	362 W Chicago Ave	312-266-0170	1
Self Storage 1	360 N Union Ave	312-733-1122	1
Self Storage	1601 S Canal St	312-421-0082	10
South Loop Self Storage	1601 S Federal St	312-674-9807	10
U-haul	419 E 25th St	312-326-2860	11
Public Storage	1414 S Wabash Ave	312-427-4835	11
Safeguard Self Storage	1353 S Wabash Ave	312-431-1400	11
Public Storage	3659 S Ashland Ave	773-247-0444	12
U-Store-It	345 N Western Ave	312-421-0200	23
U-haul	2647 N Western Ave	773-227-3489	28
Storage Mart	2647 Western Ave	773-227-2195	28
Public Storage	1916 N Elston Ave	773-227-3357	29
Self Storage 1	2001 N Elston Ave	773-276-9000	29
U-haul Center Lincoln Park	1200 W Fullerton Ave	773-935-0620	29
U-Store-It	1840 N Clybourn Ave	312-255-9900	29
Public Storage	1129 N Wells St	312-951-8803	31
Storage Mart	1015 N Halsted St	312-787-0001	31
Public Storage	2101 W Howard St	773-262-1161	33
Public Storage	5643 N Broadway St	773-784-2299	37
Public Storage	5733 N Broadway St	773-878-0906	37
U-haul	4055 N Broadway St	773-871-7155	40
Public Storage	4072 N Broadway St	773-404-8181	40
Public Storage	4430 N Clark St	773-989-1098	40
Public Storage	2835 N Western Ave	773-772-7535	42
Self Storage 1	3839 N Sheffield Ave	773-477-6000	43

Van and Truck Rentals

		Address	Phone	Map
Penske	East Bank Storage	730 W Lake St	312-466-1290	4
Penske	Dumore Supplies	2525 S Wabash Ave	312-949-6260	11
U-Haul	Downtown Lock Box	1333 S Wabash Ave	312-939-2040	11
U-haul	Storage Today	419 E 25th St	312-326-2860	11
U-Haul	East Bank Storage	1200 W 35th St	773-847-2351	12
U-Haul	Car One Auto Repair	3042 S Quinn St	312-842-5022	12
U-Haul	Pro Tech Auto Repair	3700 S Ashland Ave	773-523-0444	12
Budget	Clark Accutech	444 W 26th St	312-225-1769	13
U-Haul	Value Food Center	344 E 63rd St	773-752-5749	18
U-Haul	Noah Supermarket	5539 S Michigan Ave	773-955-0938	18
U-Haul	Hyde Park Self Storage	5155 S Cottage Grove Ave	773-256-1793	19
Penske	Elite Truck Rental	265 N Western Ave	312-942-1001	23
U-Haul	Better Methods Supply	1948 W Fulton St	312-738-0225	23
U-Haul	A&C Moving Solutions	431 N Wolcott Ave	312-850-2014	23
Budget	Fleet Services	1005 W Huron St	312-226-3073	24
U-Haul	A&A Automobile Service	1352 W Lake St	312-850-3382	24
Budget	Automotriz Monterrey	2000 S Western Ave	773-847-6989	25
U-Haul	Quick Oil	2928 W Armitage Ave	773-227-6432	27
Budget	Moving Chicago	2241 N Elston Ave	773-252-0298	28
U-Haul	Sunshine Movers &Truck Rental	2323 N Damen Ave	773-772-3920	28
U-haul	Storage Today	2647 N Western Ave	773-227-3489	28
U-Haul	Branch Location	1200 W Fullerton Ave	773-935-0620	29
U-Haul	Storagemart	1015 N Halsted St	312-587-1667	31
U-Haul	Factory Muffler Complete Auto	3055 W Devon Ave	773-338-7610	33
Budget	Chicago Moves Truck Rental	5450 North Western Ave	773-539-8044	36
U-Haul	Lite Site	1610 W Highland Ave	773-465-0475	37
Budget	Chicago Moves Truck Rental	2955 W Montrose Ave	773-539-8044	38
U-haul	Center Uptown	4055 N Broadway St	773-871-7155	40
U-Haul	Volume Plastics	2631 W Barry Ave	773-583-3418	41
U-Haul	M&W Appliances Whse	3161 N Elston Ave	773-478-0616	41
U-Haul	Penas Grease & Oil	3715 N Western Ave	773-583-4658	42
U-Haul	Cubs Park Service Station	3648 N Clark St	773-935-6688	43
Budget	Branch Location	3721 N Broadway St	773-528-1770	44

General Information • Internet & Wi-Fi

Internet

		Phone	Map
Panera Bread	501 S State St	312-922-1566	8
Windy City Cyber Café	2246 W North Ave	773-384-6470	21
Efebos Internet Café	1640 S Blue Island Ave	312-633-9212	26
Panera Bread	2070 N Clybourn Ave	773-325-9035	29
Office Mart	2801 W Touhy Ave	773-262-3924	33
Screenz	5212 N Clark St	773-334-8600	37
Ignite Center	3171 N Clybourn Ave	773-404-7033	42
Panera Bread	616 W Diversey Pkwy	773-528-4556	44
Panera Bread	6059 N Lincoln Ave	773-442-8210	NW

Wi-Fi

		Phone	Map
Caribou Coffee	600 N Kingsbury St	312-335-0576	1
Cosi	55 E Grand Ave	312-321-1990	2
Caribou Coffee	500 W Madison St	312-463-1130	4
Bean Addiction	555 W Madison St	312-474-9140	4
Caribou Coffee	10 S La Salle St	312-609-5108	5
Argo Tea	16 W Randolph St	312-553-1551	5
Lavazza	27 W Washington St	312-977-9971	5
Cosi	28 E Jackson Blvd	312-939-2674	5
Cosi	33 N Dearborn St	312-727-0290	5
Intelligentsia Coffee & Tea	53 W Jackson Blvd	312-253-0594	5
Caribou Coffee	55 W Monroe St	312-214-0852	5
Lavazza	134 N La Salle St	312-977-9701	5
Argo Tea	140 S Dearborn St	312-553-1551	5
Caribou Coffee	200 N La Salle St	312-223-1606	5
Cosi	203 N La Salle St	312-368-4400	5
Cosi	230 W Monroe St	312-782-4755	5
Cosi	230 W Washington St	312-422-1002	5
Caribou Coffee	311 W Monroe St	312-920-9746	5
Cosi	116 S Michigan Ave	312-223-1061	6
The Coffee Beanery	150 N Michigan Ave	312-781-9970	6
Caribou Coffee	41 E 8th St	312-786-9205	8
Panera Bread	501 S State St	312-922-1566	8
Caribou Coffee	800 S Wabash Ave	312-786-9205	8
Café Au Lait	1900 S State St	312-225-3940	11
Bridgeport Coffeehouse	3101 S Morgan St	773-247-9950	12
Hidden Pearl Café	1060 E 47th St	773-285-1211	17
Third World Café	1301 E 53rd St	773-288-3882	19
Istria Café	1520 E 57th St	773-955-2556	19
Einstein Bros Bagels	5706 S University Ave	773-834-1018	19
Argo Tea	5758 S Maryland Ave	773-834-0366	19
Barista Café	852 N Damen Ave	773-489-2010	21
Café Ballou	939 N Western Ave	773-342-2909	21
Filter	1585 N Milwaukee Ave	773-227-4850	21
Alliance Bakery	1736 W Division St	773-278-0366	21
Letizia's Natural Bakery	2144 W Division St	773-342-1011	21
Windy City Cyber Café	2246 W North Ave	773-384-6470	21
Coffee on Milwaukee	1046 N Milwaukee Ave	773-276-3200	22
Atomix	1957 W Chicago Ave	312-666-2649	23
Muse Café	817 N Milwaukee Ave	312-850-2233	24
West Gate Coffeehouse	924 W Madison St	312-829-9378	24
Sip Coffee House	1223 W Grand Ave	312-563-1123	24
Bialy's Café	1421 W Chicago Ave	312-733-7165	24
Swim Café	1357 W Chicago Ave	312-492-8600	24
Café Jumping Bean	1439 W 18th St	312-455-0019	26
Mi Cafetal	1519 W 18th St	312-738-2883	26
Efebos Internet Café	1640 S Blue Island Ave	312-633-9212	26
Kristoffer's Café & Bakery	1733 S Halsted St	312-829-4150	26
Coffee Beanery	2158 N Damen Ave	773-278-4200	28
Panera Bread	2070 N Clybourn Ave	773-325-9035	29
Bean Café	2235 N Sheffield Ave	773-325-4577	29
Savor the Flavor	2545 N Sheffield Ave	773-883-5287	29
Ambrosia Café	1963 N Sheffield Ave	773-404-4450	29
Bourgeois Pig Café	738 W Fullerton Ave	773-883-5282	30
Cosi	2200 N Clark St	773-472-2674	30
Caribou Coffee	2453 N Clark St	773-327-9923	30
Argo Tea	2485 N Clark St	773-733-4231	30
Argo Tea	819 N Rush St	312-951-5302	32
Ennui Café	6981 N Sheridan Rd	773-973-2233	34
Café Utjeha	5350 N Lincoln Ave	773-907-8853	35
Metropolis Coffee	1039 W Granville Ave	773-764-0400	37
Pause	1107 W Berwyn Ave	773-334-3686	37
Trivoli Café	1147 W Granville Ave	773-338-4840	37
Screenz	5212 N Clark St	773-334-8600	37
Coffee Chicago	5256 N Broadway St	773-784-1305	37
Red Eye Café	4164 N Lincoln Ave	773-327-9478	39
Perfect Cup	4700 N Damen Ave	773-989-4177	39
Café Marrakech Expresso	4747 N Damen Ave	773-271-4541	39
So Addicted	4805 N Damen Ave	773-561-3210	39
Urban Tea Lounge	838 W Montrose Ave	773-907-8726	40
Corona's Coffee Shop	909 W Irving Park Rd	773-529-1886	40
Nick's on Wilson	1140 W Wilson Ave	773-271-1155	40
Dollop Coffee	4181 N Clarendon Ave	773-755-1955	40
MoJoe's Hot House	2849 W Belmont Ave	773-596-5637	41
MoJoe's Café Lounge	2256 W Roscoe St	773-388-1236	42
Ignite Center	3171 N Clybourn Ave	773-404-7033	42
Cosi	1023 W Belmont Ave	773-868-1227	43
My Place for Tea	3210 N Sheffield Ave	773-525-8320	43
Caribou Coffee	3240 N Ashland Ave	773-281-3362	43
Mellow Grounds Coffee Lounge	3807 N Ashland Ave	773-528-2877	43
House of Hookah	607 W Belmont Ave	773-348-1550	44
Panera Bread	616 W Diversey Pkwy	773-528-4556	44
Caribou Coffee	3025 N Clark St	773-529-6366	44
Intelligentsia Coffee Roasters	3123 N Broadway St	773-348-8058	44
Argo Tea	3135 N Broadway St	773-248-3061	44
Café Latakia	3204 N Broadway St	773-929-6667	44
Caribou Coffee	3300 N Broadway St	773-477-3695	44
Caribou Coffee	3500 N Halsted St	773-248-0799	44
Panera Bread	6059 N Lincoln Ave	773-442-8210	NW
Open Hearth Coffee Shop	5207 N Kimball Ave	773-279-9686	NW
J Bean Coffee & Café	7221 W Forest Preserve Ave	708-583-2245	NW
Euro Café	3435 N Harlem Ave	773-286-8544	NW
Caffe' Italia	2625 N Harlem Ave	773-889-0455	NW
Humboldt Pie	1001 N California Ave	773-342-4743	W
Café Luna	1742 W 99th St	773-239-8990	SW
Spoon's Coffee Boutique	712 E 75th St	773-874-3847	S
Café Mozart	600 Davis St	847-492-8056	Evanston

Bowling and Billiards

		Phone	Map
Waveland Bowl	3700 N Western Ave	773-472-5900	42

Copy Shops

		Phone	Map			Phone	Map
FedEx Kinko's	444 N Wells St	312-670-4460	2	FedEx Kinko's	1800 W North Ave	773-395-4639	21
FedEx Kinko's	127 S Clinton St	312-559-1324	4	FedEx Kinko's	2300 N Clybourn Ave	773-665-7500	29
FedEx Kinko's	29 S La Salle St	312-578-8520	5	FedEx Kinko's	3524 N Southport Ave	773-975-5031	43
24 Seven Copies	222 N La Salle St	312-704-0247	5	FedEx Kinko's	3001 N Clark St	773-528-0500	44
FedEx Kinko's	1242 S Canal St	312-455-0920	10				

Delivery & Messengers

	Address	Phone	Map
Deadline Express	449 N Union Ave	312-850-1200	1
On The Fly Courier	131 N Green St	312-738-2154	4

Gyms

	Address	Phone	Map
XSport Fitness	230 W North Ave	312-932-9100	31
XSport Fitness	3240 N Ashland Ave	773-529-1461	43
Chicago Fitness Center	3131 N Lincoln Ave	773-549-8181	43

Locksmiths

	Phone		Phone
Safemasters	312-627-8209	Aabbitt	312-719-8200
Gateway Locksmith	800-964-8282	A-ABC 24-hour Locksmith	773-772-3930
Five Star Lock & Key	773-778-2066	A-AAround the Clock	800-281-5445
Always Available	773-478-1960		

Pharmacies

		Phone	Map			Phone	Map
Walgreens	641 N Clark St	312-587-1416	2	Walgreens	1601 N Wells St	312-642-4008	31
Walgreens	757 N Michigan Ave	312-664-8686	3	Walgreens	1200 N Dearborn St	312-943-0973	32
Walgreens	111 S Halsted St	312-463-9142	4	CVS	1201 N State Pkwy	312-640-2842	32
Dominick's	1 N Halsted St	312-279-8861	4	Walgreens	7510 N Western Ave	773-764-1765	33
Walgreens	501 N Roosevelt Rd	312-492-8559	7	Walgreens	3019 W Peterson Ave	773-728-6254	35
Jewel-Osco	1224 S Wabash Ave	312-663-4646	8	Jewel-Osco*	5343 N Broadway St	773-334-2083	37
Dominick's	1340 S Canal St	312-850-3915	10	Jewel-Osco	5516 N Clark St	773-784-7348	37
Walgreens	316 W Cermak Rd	312-791-0392	10	Walgreens	5625 N Ridge Ave	773-989-7546	37
Dominick's	3145 S Ashland Ave	773-247-2633	12	Walgreens	3153 W Irving Park Rd	773-588-9196	38
Walgreens	3405 S Dr MLK Jr Dr	312-326-4058	14	CVS*	4051 N Lincoln Ave	773-871-2611	39
Walgreens	1554 E 55th St	773-667-1177	19	Jewel-Osco	3572 N Elston Ave	773-583-9858	41
CVS*	2427 W Chicago Ave	773-342-6060	23	Dominick's	3350 N Western Ave	773-929-8910	42
Walgreens	1931 W Cermak Rd	773-847-5781	25	Jewel-Osco*	3400 N Western Ave	773-327-1204	42
Walgreens	2001 N Milwaukee Ave	773-772-2370	28	CVS*	3944 N Western Ave	773-279-7600	42
Dominick's	2550 N Clybourn Ave	773-935-5777	28	Jewel-Osco*	2940 N Ashland Ave	773-871-8242	43
Dominick's	959 W Fullerton Ave	773-248-0049	29	CVS*	3033 N Broadway St	773-883-6141	44
Walgreens	1520 W Fullerton Ave	773-929-6968	29	Walgreens	3046 N Halsted St	773-325-0413	44
CVS	1714 N Sheffield Ave	312-640-5161	29	CVS Pharmacy	3101 N Clark St	773-477-3333	44
Dominick's	424 W Division St	312-274-1299	31	Walgreens	3201 N Broadway St	773-327-3591	44

Store is open 24 hours, but the prescription counter closes at 10 pm.

Plumbers

	Phone		Phone
Sunrise Plumbing & Sewer	773-960-6462	Emergency Response	773-736-3247
Sears HomeCentral	773-737-3580	Apex Plumbing & Sewer	773-477-7714
Roto-Rooter	800-438-7686	Action Plumbing & Sewer	773-376-6666
O'Bannon Plumbing & Sewer (Southside)	773-862-5112	A-AAAA Plumbing & Sewer	773-282-2878
O'Bannon Plumbing & Sewer (Northside)	773-486-5748	A Metro Plumbing & Sewer Service	877-872-3060
FPS	773-268-4604	A Better Man Plumbing & Sewer	773-286-9351

Restaurants

		Phone				Phone	
Plymouth Restaurant	327 S Plymouth Ct	312-362-1212	5	San Soo Gab San	5247 N Western Ave	773-334-1589	36
				Standee's	1133 W Granville Ave	773-743-5013	37
White Palace Grill	1159 S Canal St	312-939-7167	7	IHOP	2818 W Diversey Ave	773-342-8901	41
Room 21	2110 S Wabash Ave	312-328-1198	11	Golden Apple	2971 N Lincoln Ave	773-528-1413	43
Kevin's Hamburger Heaven	554 W 39th St	773-924-5771	13	Clark Street Dog	3040 N Clark St	773-281-6690	44
				Blue Angel	5310 N Milwaukee Ave	773-631-8700	NW
Hollywood Grill	1601 W North Ave	773-395-1818	28	Izola's	522 E 79th St	773-846-1484	S
Tempo	6 E Chestnut St	312-943-4373	32	Phil's Kastle	3532 E 95th St	773-734-9591	S
Deluxe Diner	6349 N Clark St	773-743-8244	34				

Overview

Chicago is widely regarded as a world-class food destination, and rightly so, we say. Midwestern stereotypes of super sports fans inhaling Italian beef and hot links notwithstanding, Chicago is a goldmine for foodies whether they be searching for culinary nirvana at one of the city's big name, high price gastro-palaces where you have to wait weeks, or even months, to get a seat, or at one of the myriad mom–and–pop neighborhood spots where you may be the only English speaker in the place and you know the best dishes aren't always on the menu.

In the past decade, Chicago's adventuresome appetite has come to life. After an era of complacency, during which the city's top dining emporiums basically rested on their laurels, a whole new school of Chicago restaurant has come to the fore. Once fueled by students of the masters: Bayless, Trotter, Gordon Sinclair, and so on, the Chicago dining renaissance is already in its second or third generation, and now the students of the students, those who honed their skills at places like Trio and Tru, are taking the reins as they charge into Chicago's culinary future.

And anyways, you gotta problem with hot links?

What follows is a breakdown of some of our favorite spots, old and new. Of course, with every new restaurant opening, there is likely another one closing. Therefore, we offer this caveat: phone first.

That's Chicago

Some restaurants are more than just places to grab a bite. They're defining institutions of the city. The original **Billy Goat Tavern (Maps 3, 5, 24)** is known to baby boomers as the birthplace of John Belushi's "cheezeboiga" skit, but Chicagoans appreciate it as the dank watering hole where reporters from the Tribune and Sun–Times would once gather after work to talk shop. Today it's mostly frequented by wide–eyed tourists who play at slumming it. "The true originator of Chicago-style pizza" is a title claimed by nearly every pizza shack in town. Of the lot, **Pizzeria Uno's (Map 2)** claim seems the most legit—their recipe dates back to 1943. Other Chicago pizza institutions include **Lou Malnati's (Map 2)** and **Gino's East (Maps 2, 43)**. Equally important is the Chicago Dog—that is, a hot dog on a steamed bun "dragged through the garden" with a virtual salad on top—onions, relish, tomatoes, pickle spears, sport peppers, mustard (no ketchup, thank you very much), and a dash of celery salt. Post–pub dogs at **Weiner's Circle (Map 30)** are a Lincoln Park right-of-passage—the servers are infamous for their saucy attitudes. On the Northwest side, **Superdawg (West)** is a landmark. The vintage dog spot offers classic drive–in (not drive–thru) service. **Manny's Coffeeshop (Map 7)** in the South Loop is where local politicos go to make

deals over meals (breakfast or lunch). For dinner they head to Taylor Street's **Rosebud (Map 2)** for homestyle Italian. Finally, two Chicago institutions put the city on the international culinary radar. **Frontera Grill (Map 2)** packs 'em in for creative and upscale Mexican fare in a festive environment. For a more subdued experience, **Charlie Trotter's (Map 30)** pushes the culinary envelope with its own exquisite creations.

The New Garde

Homaru Canto, who wet his feet at Charlie Trotter's, and Grant Achatz, hailing from Trio, push the food frontiers with their high–concept, scientific approach to haute cuisine. Canto's **MOTO (Map 24)** and Achatz's **Alinea (Map 30)** follow a global trend of clever (and pricey) deconstructions and reconceptions of such mundane ideas as peanut butter and jelly or a margarita with chips and salsa. Meanwhile, does Shawn McClain aspire to be the next Rich Melman? He garnered raves with his Asian–inspired menu at **Spring (Map 21)**, and then wowed veggie lovers with his second venture, **Green Zebra (Map 24)**. Now McClain takes on meat at Printer's Row's **Custom House (Map 8)**. What's next: a retro–styled diner or a pan–Latin party room?

Trendspotting: Comfort Food

Maybe it's a counter-reaction to all of the scientifically complex fusion food spawned in Chicago in the past how many years, but if restaurant trends are any sign, Chicagoans are turning back to homespun comforts big-time. Hot new spots like **Chalkboard (Map 39)**, **Anteprima (Map 37)**, **Old Town Brasserie (Map 31)**, **Table 52 (Map 32)**, and **Room 21 (Map 11)** focus on the classics with a comfort twist—like Chalkboard's grilled bleu cheese on brioche with tomato soup bisque, or Antiprima's homemade pastas. Global comfort food is big, too. Chicagoans are eating more pho (Vietnamese noodle soup pronounced "fuh"), pupusas, stews, and such than ever before, and turning to family-owned restaurants with food like mama made it—if mama was Julia Child. Duck fat, anyone? Slather it on. Braised veal cheeks? Keep 'em coming.

By the same token, bakeries and sweet shops are on the upsurge (Chicago waistlines are sure to follow). Folks are lining up for cupcakes at shops like **Swirlz (Map 30)**, **Molly's (Map 30)**, the aptly named **Cupcakes (Map 44)**, or other decadent baked treats such as the lovingly crafted Sicilian fare at **Pasticceria Natalina (Map 37)**, or the heavenly **Flourish Bakery Café (Map 37)**.

Chicago's Best Dining Bets

Hey Big Spender

If you've got an expense account burning a hole in your pocket, or it's time to dazzle the future in–laws, here are some of Chicago's spendiest options. **Charlie Trotter's**

(Map 30) is the classic big bucks splurge–if you really want to go for it, reserve the kitchen table. Other classic spends include **Everest (Map 5)**, **Nomi (Map 3)**, and **Les Nomades (Map 3)**. **Tru (Map 3)** is renowned for its caviar staircase; **Spiaggia (Map 32)** for it's gorgeous lake view. For something a little more, um, unusual, Chef Homaro Canto's **Moto (Map 24)** and Grant Achatz's **Alinea (Map 30)** are known for pushing culinary frontiers with their clever, high-concept approaches to haute cuisine. On the other, neanderthal end of the spectrum, die-hard carnivores empty their wallets at Chicago classics **Morton's (Map 32)**, **David Burke's Primehouse (Map 2)**, or **Gene & Georgetti (Map 2)**.

Where Top Chefs Go to Eat
Lula (Map 27) and **Schwa (Map 22)**.

Hey Cheapskate
Of course, you don't have to spend a fortune to eat well in Chicago. Cheap taquerias, hot dog stands, and corner grills abound in Chicago. For a more unique meal, without breaking the bank, we recommend **Sticky Rice (Map 39)** Thai. This super delicious and authentic BYOB Thai spot features such exotic specialties as friend caterpillars and ant-egg omelets along with the usual curry and noodle dishes–all prepared amazingly well, and nothing on the menu tops ten bucks. For a cheap date, **La Creperie (Map 44)** is loaded with low-price charm. This 40-year-old French classic has the shabby look of Parisian authenticity, a gorgeous outdoor patio, and free live French music on Thursday evenings.

Pizza Pizza Pizza
Chicago's a pizza city, and classic spots such as **Pizzeria Uno (Map 2)** and **Lou Malnati's (Maps 2, 21, 29)** attract tourists and suburbanites in droves. Meanwhile, **Candlelite (Map 33)** in Roger's Park has been serving fresh, hot pies to the local community for decades. Another neighborhoodie, **Pete's Pizza (Map 42)**, specializes in cracker-crisp crust and sweet sauce. **Golden Crust (Map 38)** is a family spot in Albany Park that's open (and delivers) very late. **Art of Pizza (Map 43)** has won numerous awards and acclaim for its scrumptious deep disher. Thin-crust European-style pizzas have taken Chicago by storm. **Pizza D.O.C. (Map 39)**, Chicago's wood-fired pizza pioneer still packs 'em in for excellent, classic pies. Nearby **Spacca Napoli (Map 39)** gives the wood-fired pizza a Neapolitan twist. **Piece (Map 21)** offers precious pies to the Wicker Park crowd, and **Coalfire (Map 24)** is what the name implies— Chicago's first coal-fired pizza joint.

Vegging Out in Chicago
The phrase "vegetarian Chicago" has often seemed oxymoronic, but just as more mainstream restaurants are introducing more veggie items than the token pasta or risotto, so have more bona–fide vegetarian restaurants been appearing on our beefy shores.

Chicago Diner (Map 44) and **Heartland Café (Map 34)** (which does serve some meat) are the crunchy, old–school standard bearers. New spots include Roger's Park's **Lake Side Café (Map 34)**, the Turkish–turned raw food **Cousin's Incredible Vitality (Map 38)**, and **Alice and Friends Vegetarian Restaurant (Map 37)**, home of the mock meat. **Karyn's (Map 30)** in Lincoln Park attracted such a following for its raw food menu that Karyn opened **Karyn's Cooked (Map 2)** in Old Town. On Devon, **Mysore Woodlands (Map 33)** serves vegetarian food from southern India, while **Arya Bhavan (Map 33)** specializes in Indian vegetarian food from the north and south. **Amitabul (Northwest Chicago)** does Vegan Thai on the Northwest side, and **Soul Vegetarian East (South Chicago)** in the Southside Chatham neighborhood. For upscale vegetarian, try the **Green Zebra (Map 24)**. In Logan Square, down–to–earth scenester spot **Lula (Map 27)** is known for being particularly vegetarian friendly. For a very special night, choose the fixed–price vegetarian tasting menus at **Arun's (Map 38)** or **Charlie Trotter's (Map 30)**. Finally, vegetarians and non–vegetarians alike line up for breakfasts served by followers of Sri Chimnoy at Roscoe Village's popular **Victory's Banner (Map 42)**.

Poor Man's Steak and Other Meaty Matters
Lots of Northsiders swear that the best burgers in Chicago are grilled at **Moody's Pub (Map 37)**, while Southsiders contendthat Beverly's **Top Notch Beefburger (Southwest)** takes the honors. Avondale's **Kuma's Corner (Map 41)** is giving both of these old time burger places a run for their money with their hard rock-themed burgers, kobe beef sliders, and the classic Kuma burger, topped with a fried egg. If, on the other hand, you like your meat served on the bone with tangy sauce, head to the **Gale Street Inn (Northwest)** in Jefferson Park, street–festival mainstay **Robinson's (Maps 4, 30)**, Southside stalwart **Leon's Barbeque (South)**, or Logan Square's **Calvin's BBQ (Map 27)**. For encased meats, Chicago has no lack of options—just follow the Vienna Beef signs. For something different, try encased exotic meats such as ostrich or wild boar at **Hot Doug's (Map 41)**, a destination stop for top chefs from around the world. On weekends, they feature french fries cooked in duck fat (and lines out the door).

Soul Food and Southern Cooking
We say soul food is the most American of American cuisines. On the south side, you can't go wrong with **Army & Lou's (South)**—it's a Chicago legend. **Valois (Map 19)** serves no frills, cafeteria–style soul food. **Ms Lee's Good Food (Map 18)** offers gut–busting Southern food for carry–out only, or bring your family and eat in at **Captain Hard Times Dining (South)**. **Soul Queen (South)** cafeteria may have seen better days, but history is written in the photos on the walls. On the west side, stuff yourself silly at **Edna's** on Madison

(West). For Cajun food, try Chicago breakfast staple **Wishbone (Maps 24, 42)** or Jimmy Banno's famous **Heaven on Seven (Maps 3, 5)**. **Dixie Kitchen and Bait Shop (Map 19, Evanston)** serves up soul and Cajun, as does Bronzeville's **Negro League Café (Map 16)**.

Passport to Good Eating

Culinarily, you can travel the world and never leave Chicago. While some of Chicago's dining emporiums fly high on the local radar, we have a soft spot for the ramshackle storefronts where the home cooking's happening. Here's a grab bag list of our favorite ethnic eats:

African: **Mama Desta's Red Seas (Map 43)**, **Ethiopian Diamond (Map 37)**, **Ras Dashen (Map 37)**, **Bolat (Map 43)**, **Demera (Map 40)**

Caribbean: **Calypso Café (Map 19)**, **La Palma (West)**, **Coco (West)**, **Tropic Island Jerk Chicken (South)**, **Café Bolero (Map 27)**, **Café Central (Map 24)**, **Ja'Grill (Map 29)**

Chinese: **Phoenix Café (Map 10)**, **Evergreen (Map 10)**, **Furama (Map 40)**, **Double Li (Map 10)**, **Three Happiness (Map 10)**

Cuban: **Café 28 (Map 39)**, **Café LaGuardia (Map 28)**

Eastern European: **Red Apple (Northwest)**, **Sayat Nova (Map 3)**, **Adria Mare (Map 37)**, **Pierogi Factory (Map 43)**

English / Irish: **Red Lion Pub (Map 29)**, **Chief O'Neill's (Map 41)**, **Mrs. Murphy and Sons (Map 42)**, **Grafton Pub (Map 39)**

French: **Café Matou (Map 28)**, **Bistro Campagne (Map 39)**, **La Tache (Map 37)**, **Avec (Map 4)**, **La Creperie (Map 44)**, **Café Bernard (Map 30)**, **Bistrot Margot (Map 31)**

German: **Mirabell (Northwest)**, **Chicago Brauhaus (Map 39)**, **Glunz Bavarian Haus (Map 39)**

Greek: **Costa's (Map 4)**, **Santorini (Map 4)**, **Athena (Map 4)**

Indian: **Mysore Woodlands (Map 33)**, **Udupi Palace (Map 33)**, **Arya Bhavan (Map 33)**, **Viceroy of India (Map 33)**

Italian: **Ignotz (West)**, **Brunas (West)**, **Angelina (Map 44)**, **Anteprima (Map 37)**, **A Tavola (Map 23)**, **Vinci (Map 30)**, **The Village (Map 5)**

Japanese: **Tank Sushi (Map 39)**, **Agami (Map 40)**, **Mirai Sushi (Map 21)**, **Katsu (Map 35)**, **Chiyo (Northwest)**, **Tanoshii (Map 37)**

Korean: **Jin Ju (Map 37)**, **San Goo Gap San (Map 36)**, **Hama Matsu (Map 40)**, **So Gong Dong Tofu House (Northwest)**, **Kang Nam (Map 38)**, **Solga (Map 35)**, **Woo Chon (Map 35)**, **Jin Ju (Map 37)**

Mexican: **Nuevo Leon (Map 26)**, **Tecatilan (Map 23)**, **Taqueria Trespasada (Map 41)**, **Las Palmas (Map 21, Evanston)**, **Maiz (West)**, **Los Nopales (Map 39)**, **La Finca (Map 41)**, **El Huarachin Huarachon (Map 38)**

Middle Eastern: **Semiramis (Map 38)**, **Noon O' Kebab (Map 38)**, **Taste of Lebanon (Map 37)**, **Turquoise (Map 42)**, **Fattoush (Map 30)**, **Café Suron (Map 34)**

North African: **Tizi Melloul (Map 2)**, **Couscous (Map 26)**, **Icosium Kafe (Map 37)**

Nuevo Latino: **Cuatro (Map 11)**, **Carnivale (Map 1)**, **DeCero (Map 24)**

Scandinavian: **Tre Kroner (Northwest)**, **Svea (Map 37)**

South American: **Brasa Roja (Map 38)**, **El Nandu (Map 27)**, **Lito's Empanadas (Map 30)**, **Pupuseria Las Delicias (Map 38)**

Spanish: **Arco de Cuchlleros (Map 44)**, **Azucar (Map 27)**

Thai: **Amarind's (West)**, **Opart (Map 39)**, **Thai Valley (Map 38)**, **Arun's (Map 38)**, **Sticky Rice (Map 39)**, **Indie Café (Map 37)**

Vietnamese: **Pho Hoa (Map 40)**, **Café Lao (Map 40)**, **Fan Si Pan (Map 24)**, **Nhu Lan (Map 38)**

Breakfast

Okay, so you're one of those annoying people who manages to be up, dressed, and ready to go before noon. Good for friggin' you. Why don't you get out of my face and go eat at one of these popular breakfast /brunch spots: **Sweet Maple Café (Map 26)**, **Orange (Map 8, 43)**, **Over Easy Café (Map 39)**, **Ina's (Map 24)**, **Flo (Map 24)**, **Yolk (Map 9)**, **Pannenkoeken Café (Map 39)**, or **Tweet (Map 40)**.

Diners

Because sometimes you just want a cup of joe and a patty melt. We recommend: **Salt and Pepper Diner (Maps 29, 43)**, **Nookie's Tree (Map 44)**, **Ramova Grill (Map 13)**, **Salonica Grill (Map 19)**, **Clara's (Map 41)**, **Lou Mitchell's (Map 4)**, **Manny's Coffee Shop (Map 7)**, **Hollywood Grill (Map 28)**, **The Golden Apple (Map 43)**, **The Golden Angel (Map 39)**, and, last but in no way least, **The S&G (Map 43)**, a.k.a. Sam and George's.

Foodies on the Web

Need a recommendation?

Both professional food critics and the vox populi weigh in on the popular restaurant sites of the Chicago Reader (www.chicagoreader.com) and the Chicago

Tribune's Metromix (www.metromix.com). Both offer search categories, so you can find places by location, price, type of cuisine, etc. If you're going somewhere off–the–beaten path, however, be sure to phone first— Metromix, in particular, often seems to be out–of–date.

Chicago Magazine's food editors will deliver the latest Chicago food gossip directly to your inbox every week or so, along with chef interviews, links, and whatever food ephemera amuses them. Subscribe to Dish for free at the Chicago Magazine website (www.chicagomagazine.com):

Professional chefs and passionate lay folk chat about both the latest hot spots and hidden neighborhood gems on the LTH Forum (www.lthforum.com). The foodie debates, all in the spirit of fun, can get raucous, and sometimes even local celebrity chefs enter the fore to throw down. A warning: Regular posting on the LTH Forum is a tell-tale sign of your descent down the slippery slope of food geekdom.

Key: $: Under $10 / $$: $10–$20 / $$$: $20–$30 / $$$$: $30–$40 / $$$$$: $40+
* : Does not accept credit cards. / † : Accepts only American Express. / † †: Accepts only Visa and Mastercard
Time listed refers to kitchen closing time on weekend nights.

Map 1 • River North / Fulton Market District

Name	Address	Phone	Price	Time	Description
Carnivale	702 W Fulton St	312-850-5005	$$$	11:30 pm	Authentic, soulful Latin fusion cuisine.
Iguana Café	517 N Halsted St	312-432-0663	$	2 am	Internet cafe with bagels and such.
Japonais	600 W Chicago Ave	312-822-9600	$$$	11:30 pm	Elegant, way-upscale Asian.
La Scarola	721 W Grand Ave	312-243-1740	$$	11 pm	Authentic Italian in a super-close atmosphere.
Powerhouse	215 N Clinton St	312-928-0800	$$$$$	10:30 pm	Unpretentious fine-dining menu.
Reza's	432 W Ontario St	312-664-4500	$$$	12 am	Huge portions of Persian fare.
Scoozi!	410 W Huron St	312-943-5900	$$	10 pm	Once-trendy Italian has had its day.
Timo	464 N Halsted St	312-226-4300	$$$	11 pm	Eclectic eating in funky atmosphere.
Tony Rocco's River North	416 W Ontario St	312-787-1400	$$	11:30 pm	Italian home cooking and broasted chicken.
Zealous	419 W Superior St	312-475-9112	$$$$	10 pm	Over-the-top gourmet from Trotter protégé.

Map 2 • Near North / River North

Name	Address	Phone	Price	Time	Description
1492 Tapas Bar	42 E Superior St	312-867-1492	$$	2 am	Tasty tapas in River North graystone.
A Mano	335 N Dearborn St	312-629-3500	$$$	11 pm	Hand-tossed thin pizzas.
Aigre Doux	230 W Kinzie St	312-329-9400	$$$	11 pm	Husband and wife team pair up to offer creative, upscale comfort food like sticky toffee pudding with Devonshire cream.
Avenues	108 E Superior St	312-573-6754	$$$$$	10:30 pm	Sophisticated menu with a view.
Ballo	445 N Dearborn St	312-832-7700	$$$	12:30 am	Loud and clubby. Nonetheless, Italian food here is actually decent.
Ben Pao	52 W Illinois St	312-222-1888	$$	11 pm	Upscale Chinese spot.
Blue Water Grill	520 N Dearborn St	312-777-1400	$$$	12 am	Menu highlighting seasonal ingredients and seafood.
Brasserie Jo	59 W Hubbard St	312-595-0800	$$$	11 pm	Swanky French.
Brett's Kitchen	233 W Superior St	312-664-6354	$	4 pm	Charming breakfast and sandwich stop.
Café Iberico	739 N La Salle St	312-573-1510	$	1:30 am	Shoulder-to-shoulder tapas joint.
Chicago Chop House	60 W Ontario St	312-787-7100	$$$$$	11:30 pm	Old-school steaks meet old-school politicos and similar characters.
Club Lago	331 W Superior St	312-951-2849	$$	11 pm	Generous servings of basic Italian.
Crofton on Wells	535 N Wells St	312-755-1790	$$$	11 pm	Pushing the envelope with some top regional cuisine.
Cyrano's Bistrot & Wine Bar	546 N Wells St	312-467-0546	$$	10:30 pm	Steak frites!
David Burke's Primehouse	616 N Rush St	312-660-6000	$$$$$	12 am	Aged steaks by former Smith & Wollensky VP.
Frontera Grill	445 N Clark St	312-661-1434	$$	11 pm	Rick Bayless's famous cantina—expect to wait awhile.
Fulton's on the River	315 N La Salle St	312-822-0100	$$$$	11 pm	Best. Oysters. In. Chicago.
Gaylord Fine India Cuisine	678 N Clark St	312-664-1700	$	10 pm	Indian buffet.
Gene & Georgetti	500 N Franklin St	312-527-3718	$$$$$	12 am	Big steaks.
Gino's East	633 N Wells St	312-943-1124	$$	11 pm	Legendary deep dish pizza since 1966.
Graze	35 W Ontario St	312-255-1234	$	12 am	Sharing is hard with food this good.
Keefer's	20 W Kinzie St	312-467-9525	$$$	11:30 pm	French-influenced steakhouse.
Kevin	9 W Hubbard St	312-595-0055	$$$	10:30 pm	Promising new fusion.
Kinzie Chophouse	400 N Wells St	312-822-0191	$$$	11 pm	Neighborhood steak house.
Klay Oven	414 N Orleans St	312-527-3999	$$	10 pm	Upscale Indian buffet.

Arts & Entertainment • **Restaurants**

Key: $: Under $10 / $$: $10–$20 / $$$: $20–$30 / $$$$: $30–$40 / $$$$$: $40+
* : Does not accept credit cards. / † : Accepts only American Express. / † †: Accepts only Visa and Mastercard
Time listed refers to kitchen closing time on weekend nights.

Map 2 • Near North / River North— *continued*

Lawry's The Prime Rib	100 E Ontario St	312-787-5000	$$$	11 pm	Carnivore's delight.
Le Lan	749 N Clark St	312-280-9100	$$$$	11pm	Heavenly Pan-Asian.
Lou Malnati's Pizzeria	439 N Wells St	312-828-9800	$	12 am	Famous in a city famous for pizza.
Maggiano's Little Italy	516 N Clark St	312-644-7700	$$	11 pm	Gut-busting family-style Italian.
Mr Beef	666 N Orleans St	312-337-8500	$*	5 pm	Get your Italian beef fix at this tried-and-true Chicago classic.
Nacional 27	325 W Huron St	312-664-2727	$$$	11 pm	Pan-Latin supper club with dance floor. Babaloo!
Naha	500 N Clark St	312-321-6242	$$$$	10 pm	Mediterranean-inspired luxury.
Osteria Via Stato	620 N State St	312-642-8450	$$$$	11 pm	Menu-oriented Italian. Fancy, but reasonably priced.
Pizzeria Uno	29 E Ohio St	312-321-1000	$	1 am	Legendary Chicago pizza.
Quartino	626 N State St	312-698-5000	$$$	12 am	Trendy Italian small plates and house-cured salami.
Redfish	400 N State St	312-467-1600	$$	12 am	Fun Cajun; free beads and good drinks.
Rosebud on Rush	720 N Rush St	312-266-6444	$$	12 am	A branch of Chicago's legendary, old-school Italian.
Roy's	720 N State St	312-787-7599	$$$	10 pm	Pretty Hawaiian contemporary cuisine.
Ruth's Chris Steak House	431 N Dearborn St	312-321-2725	$$$$	11:30 pm	Consistent steak chain.
Shanghai Terrace	108 E Superior St	312-573-6744	$$$$	11 pm	The city's most extravagant Chinese restaurant.
Shaw's Crab House & Blue Crab Lounge	21 E Hubbard St	312-527-2722	$$$$	11 pm	A seafood destination.
Smith & Wollensky	318 N State St	312-670-9900	$$$$	11 pm	Chicago branch of New York steak emporium.
Sullivan's Steakhouse	415 N Dearborn St	312-527-3510	$$$$	11 pm	Another upscale steakhouse.
Sushi Naniwa	607 N Wells St	312-255-8555	$$	11 pm	Quality sushi. Great outdoor.
Tizi Melloul	531 N Wells St	312-670-4338	$$$	11 pm	Exotic setting for Moroccan tangines.
Topolobampo	445 N Clark St	312-661-1434	$$$$	10:30 pm	Standard bearer for upscale Mexican.
Vermillion	10 W Hubbard St	312-527-4060	$$$	11 pm	Indian-Latin fusion—what next?
Vong's Thai Kitchen	6 W Hubbard St	312-644-8664	$$	11 pm	Thai with a satisfying kick.
Wildfire	159 W Erie St	312-787-9000	$$	11 pm	Fun, trendy American.

Map 3 • Streeterville / Mag Mile

Bandera	535 N Michigan Ave	312-644-3524	$$	11 pm	Lunch above Mag Mile.
Billy Goat Tavern	430 N Michigan Ave	312-222-1525	$*	2 am	Cheezboiga; no fries, chips; pepsi, no coke.
Capital Grille	633 N St Clair St	312-337-9400	$$$$	11 pm	Macho steak and zin.
Copperblue	580 E Illinois St	312-527-1200	$$$$	11:30 pm	Contemporary American in chic locale yet not crazy pretentious.
D4 Irish Pub & Café	345 E Ohio St	312-624-8385	$$$	1 am	Upscale Irish pub with a copy of the Book of Kells.
De La Costa	465 E Illinois St	312-321-8930	$$$$	12 am	Buzz-worthy upscale pan-Latin.
Emilio's Tapas Sol y Nieve	215 E Ohio St	312-467-7177	$$$	12 am	One of the nicest branches of the local tapas chain.
Fox & Obel Café	401 E Illinois St	312-379-0112	$$	9 pm	Creative café grub with gourmet ingredients from next-door market.
Grand Lux Café	600 N Michigan Ave	312-276-2500	$$$	12 am	A Mag Mile vittle and view indulgence. Go ahead, be a tourist!
Heaven on Seven	600 N Michigan Ave	312-280-7774	$$	11 pm	Cajun grub and cocktails.
Hot Diggity Dogs	251 E Ohio St	312-943-5598	$*	8 pm	Walk-up chicawga dawgs.
Indian Garden	247 E Ontario St	312-280-4910	$$	10:30 pm	Good veggie options.
Kamehachi	240 E Ontario St	312-587-0600	$$	12 am	Old school sushi spot.
Les Nomades	222 E Ontario St	312-649-9010	$$$$$	10 pm	Deluxe haute cuisine.
Nomi	800 N Michigan Ave	312-239-4030	$$$$$	10 pm	Deluxe French fusion.
Sayat Nova	157 E Ohio St	312-644-9159	$$	10 pm	Armenian.
Tru	676 N St Clair St	312-202-0001	$$$$$	11:30 pm	Dazzling contemporary cuisine.
Volare	201 E Grand Ave	312-410-9900	$$$	11 pm	Casual Italian.
Wave	644 N Lake Shore Dr	312-255-4460	$$	11 pm	Trendy W Hotel gruberie is making a…you guessed it.

Map 4 • West Loop Gate / Greek Town

Athena	212 S Halsted St	312-655-0000	$$$	1 am	Goddess Athena-inspired outdoor and indoor.
Avec	615 W Randolph St	312-377-2002	$$	1 am	Small plates, big flavors, chefs' hangout. 'Nuff said.
Blackbird	619 W Randolph St	312-715-0708	$$$$	11:30 pm	Chic les plus ultra.
Butter	130 S Green St	312-666-9813	$$$$	11 pm	As in "smooth as…" at this upscale eatery.

Costa's	340 S Halsted St	312-263-9700	$$$	12 am	Greece at its warmest. Have the octopus.
Dine	733 W Madison St	312-602-2100	$$$	11 pm	Martinis and comfort food at the Crowne Plaza.
Extra Virgin	741 W Randolph St	312-474-0700	$$	12 am	Italian wine bar/small plates.
Gold Coast Dogs	225 S Canal St	312-258-8585	$*	10 pm	Gotta have the dogs.
Greek Islands	200 S Halsted St	312-782-9855	$$$	1 am	Greek Heaven—not to be missed.
J&C Inn	558 W Van Buren St	312-663-4114	$$$	2 pm	Dingy outside—best sandwiches in town inside.
Lou Mitchell's	565 W Jackson Blvd	312-939-3111	$*	3 pm	Rub shoulders with local pols at this legendary grill.
Meli	301 S Halsted St	312-454-0748	$	3 pm	Brunch spot makes us wanna challah.
N9ne	440 W Randolph St	312-575-9900	$$$	12 am	Toast marshmallows at the table at this ultra-trendy contemporary spot.
Nine Muses	315 S Halsted St	312-902-9922	$$$	2 am	Brick bars and backgammon.
Parthenon	314 S Halsted St	312-726-2407	$$$	12 am	Creators of flaming saganaki!
Pegasus Restaurant and Taverna	130 S Halsted St	312-226-3377	$$$	12:45 am	Rooftop garden—Chicago secret!
Red Light	820 W Randolph St	312-733-8880	$$$$	12 am	Fusion of Asian dishes in a oriental atmosphere.
Robinson's No 1 Ribs	225 S Canal St	312-258-8477	$	7:30 pm	Dress down and dig in.
Rodity's	222 S Halsted St	312-454-0800	$$$	1 am	Greek lamb since 1972.
Santorini	800 W Adams St	312-829-8820	$$$	1 am	Fish, shellfish, and roasted chicken. Yum.
Sepia	123 N Jefferson St	312-441-1920	$$$$	10:30 pm	Contemp. American with flare.
Starfish	804 W Randolph St	312-997-2433	$$	11:30 pm	Flamboyant sushi place.
Sushi Wabi	842 W Randolph St	312-563-1224	$$$	12 am	Self-consciously chic sushi.

Map 5 · The Loop

Atwood Café	1 W Washington St	312-368-1900	$$$	11 pm	High tea with contemporary flair.
Billy Goat Tavern	330 S Wells St	312-554-0297	$*	4 pm	Grubby cheezboiga joint made famous by John Belushi.
Everest	440 S La Salle St	312-663-8920	$$$$$	10 pm	Classic fine dining experience with a knock-out view.
Gold Coast Dogs	17 S Wabash Ave	312-578-1133	$*	7 pm	Onion, sport peppers, pickle spear, tomato, celery salt, mustard.
Gold Coast Dogs	159 N Wabash Ave	312-917-1677	$*	6 pm	Classic dog joint.
Hannah's Bretzel	180 W Washington St	312-621-1111	$	6 pm	Homemade pretzels and organic lunch fare.
Heaven on Seven	111 N Wabash Ave	312-263-6443	$$	5 pm	Cajun Chicago classic. Closed for dinner.
La Cantina Enoteca	71 W Monroe St	312-332-7005	$$	12 am	Casual Italian with seafood specialty.
La Rosetta	70 W Madison St	312-332-9500	$$	9 pm	Family-style Italian.
Lockwood	17 E Monroe St	312-917-3404	$$$$	10 pm	Fine Dining at the Palmer House.
Nick's Fishmarket & Grill	51 S Clark St	312-621-0200	$$$	11 pm	Power lunch.
Oasis Café	21 N Wabash Ave	312-558-1058	$$	5 pm	Middle Eastern hideout inside of a jewelry store.
Plymouth Restaurant	327 S Plymouth Ct	312-362-1212	$	24-hrs	24-hour diner with bar and grill.
Russian Tea Time	77 E Adams St	312-360-0000	$$$	12 am	Rich food. Richer interior. Copious amounts of vodka.
Trattoria No 10	10 N Dearborn St	312-984-1718	$$$	10 pm	Elegant Italian.
The Village	71 W Monroe St	312-332-7005	$$	1 am	Quaint, casual Italian looks like a village.
Vivere	71 W Monroe St	312-332-4040	$$$	11 pm	Dated Italian luxury.

Map 6 · The Loop / Grant Park

Aria	200 N Columbus Dr	312-444-9494	$$$$	11 pm	Artistic, creative pan-global grub.
Artist's Café	412 S Michigan Ave	312-939-7855	$$†	11 pm	Sit at the counter. They've got the chattiest waiters in town.
Bennigan's	150 S Michigan Ave	312-427-0577	$$	1:30 am	The busiest Bennigan's in the world! Yetch.
China Grill	230 N Michigan Ave	312-334-6700	$$$$$	11 pm	Les So Very Tres.
The Gage	24 S Michigan Ave	312-372-4243	$$	12 am	Drink the luck o' the Irish.
The Green at Grant Park	352 E Monroe St	312-987-1818	$$	9.30 pm	Did you make a birdie? Celebrate with a cocktail on the patio.
Park Grill	11 N Michigan Ave	312-521-7275	$$$	10:30 pm	Contemporary American cooking in Millenium Park.

Map 7 · South Loop / River City

Bake for Me	608 W Roosevelt Rd	312-957-1994	$	2 pm	Good coffee and pastries.
Manny's Coffee Shop	1141 S Jefferson St	312-939-2855	$	8 pm	Famous deli—popular with politicians.
White Palace Grill	1159 S Canal St	312-939-7167	$	24-hrs	An ode to grease, and some fine omelettes to boot.

Key: $: Under $10 / $$: $10–$20 / $$$: $20–$30 / $$$$: $30–$40 / $$$$$: $40+
* : Does not accept credit cards. / † : Accepts only American Express. / † † : Accepts only Visa and Mastercard
Time listed refers to kitchen closing time on weekend nights.

Map 8 • South Loop / Printers Row / Dearborn Park

Amarit	600 S Dearborn St	312-939-1179	$$	11 pm	Pretty good Thai.
Blackie's	755 S Clark St	312-786-1161	$	10 pm	A famous burger, lesser-known best breakfast in South Loop on Fri, Sat, Sun.
Cafe Mediterra	728 S Dearborn St	312-427-2610	$	9 pm	Grab coffee, a kebab, or a wrap at this BYOB.
Custom House	500 S Dearborn St	312-523-0200	$$$$	10 pm	Shaun McClain does steak house.
Eleven City Diner	1112 S Wabash Ave	312-212-1112	$$	12 am	Traditional Jewish deli.
Hackney's	733 S Dearborn St	312-461-1116	$$	11:30 pm	A specialty burger and onion loaf; a north shore legend since 1939.
Orange	75 W Harrison St	312-447-1000	$$	3 pm	Precious, overpriced, but coffee-to-go is cheap.
South Loop Club	701 S State St	312-427-2787	$††	2 am	Very casual bar/restaurant with surprisingly good kitchen.
SRO	610 S Dearborn St	312-360-1776	$$	8 pm	Great kitchen boasting Chicago's #1 Turkey Burger.
Tamarind	614 S Wabash Ave	312-379-0970	$$	11 pm	Sushi and Pan-Asian; sake-based "fruitinis."
Trattoria Caterina	616 S Dearborn St	312-939-7606	$$	9 pm	A little touch of Italy, and a great value for Italian cuisine.

Map 9 • South Loop / South Michigan Ave

Kitty O'Shea's	720 S Michigan Ave	312-294-6860			Irish bartenders and beer, boring food.
Oysy	888 S Michigan Ave	312-922-1127	$$$	11 pm	Chic, industrial sushi setting.
Spertus Cafe	610 S Michigan Ave	312-322-1718	$	7 pm	Prepackaged Puck at the Spertus museum.
Yolk	1120 S Michigan Ave	312-789-9655	$$	3 pm	Bright, clean brunch spot with eggs o'plenty.

Map 10 • East Pilsen / Chinatown

Chi Cafe	2160 S Wentworth Ave	312-842-9993	$	12 am	Crowd-pleasing Pan-Asian.
Double Li	228 W Cermak Rd	312-842-7818	$$	10 pm	Authenic Schezuan in nondescript space.
Emperor's Choice	2238 S Wentworth Ave	312-225-8800	$	12 am	Start with seafood; finish with tea.
Evergreen	2411 S Wentworth Ave	312-225-8898	$	12 am	More upscale than most Chinatown grub.
Happy Chef Dim Sum House	2164 S Archer Ave	312-808-3689	$	2 am	Entrees priced to try several dishes.
Joy Yee's Noodle Shop	2159 S China Pl	312-328-0001	$$	10:30 pm	Huge portions of Korean and Chinese, plus bubble tea.
Lao Sze Chuan Spicy City	2172 S Archer Ave	312-326-5040	$	12 am	Authentic Chinese dishes plus great evening karaoke.
Penang	2201 S Wentworth Ave	312-326-6888	$	1 am	Malaysian favorites.
Phoenix	2131 S Archer Ave	312-328-0848	$	11 pm	The best Chinese breakfast in town.
Three Happiness	209 W Cermak Rd	312-842-1964	$	24-hrs	Long waits for dim sum.
Won Kow	2237 S Wentworth Ave	312-842-7500	$	12 am	Cheap, tasty dim sum.

Map 11 • South Loop / McCormick Place

Carolina Caramel Room for Dessert	1511 S State St	312-922-5007		12 am	Enjoy a slice of gourmet cake in a chill atmosphere.
Chef Luciano	49 E Cermak Rd	312-326-0062	$††	7 pm	Walk-in restaurant with eclectic entrees; Italian/African/Cajun influences.
Chicago Firehouse Restaurant	1401 S Michigan Ave	312-786-1401	$$$$	10:30 pm	Transformed Chicago firehouse complete with pole and fine dining.
Cuatro	2030 S Wabash Ave	312-842-8856	$$$	11 pm	Trendy atmosphere for pan-Latin grub.
Gioco	1312 S Wabash Ave	312-939-3870	$$$	12 am	Great Italian dining.
Kroll's	1736 S Michigan Ave	312-235-1400	$$	11 pm	Chicago outpost of Green Bay grill. Packers Backers better watch their backs.
La Cantina Grill	1911 S Michigan Ave	312-842-1911	$$	11 pm	Comfy Mexican with no surprises.
NetWorks	2231 S Dr Martin L King Jr Dr	312-567-1234	$$	10 pm	Contemporary American with a focus on Chicago specialties.
Opera	1301 S Wabash Ave	312-461-0161	$$$	12 am	Theatrical Asian grub.
Room 21	2110 S Wabash Ave	312-328-1198	$$$$		Over the top classic American.
Triad	1933 S Indiana Ave	312-225-8833	$$$	12 am	Guess what? Another sleek sushi lounge.
Zapatista	1307 S Wabash Ave	312-435-1307	$$	11 pm	Fancified Mexican food in big, loud environment.

Map 13 • Bridgeport (East)

Carb^uan	300 W 26th St	312-225-3200	$	11 pm	So what if they use gas? The food is still delicious.
Franco's Ristorante	300 W 31st St	312-225-9566	$$	10 pm	Family-style Italian near Sox park.
Freddie's Pizza & Pasta Parlor	701 W 31st St	312-808-0149	$	11 pm	Italian ice, beef sandwiches, and appropriate attitude.
Gio's	2724 S Lowe Ave	312-225-6368	$	9 pm	BYO Italian deli with groceries.
Kevin's Hamburger Heaven	554 W 39th St	773-924-5771	$*	24-hrs	Hamburgers and milkshakes.
Metropolis Rotisseria	924 W Armitage Ave	773-868-9000	$$	9:30 pm	Chicken shack next to the train tracks.
Pancho Pistola's	700 W 31st St	312-225-8808	$$	12 am	Two words: Eggs and beans.
Phil's Pizza	3551 S Halsted St	773-523-0947	$	1:30 am	Pizza-rific.
Ramova Grill	3510 S Halsted St	773-847-9058	$*	5 pm	Old-school diner.
Schaller's Pump	3714 S Halsted St	773-376-6332	$*	10pm	Try the steak sandwiches and hash browns.
Stages	657 W 31st St	312-225-0396	$	10pm	Fuel up at this diner attached to a gas station.
Wing Yip Chop Suey	537 W 26th St	312-326-2822	$*	9 pm	Nader bumper sticker on window.

Map 14 • Prairie Shores / Lake Meadows

Blue Sea Restaurant	427 E Pershing Rd	773-285-3325	$*	12 am	Fast food and carry out.
Chicago Rib House	3851 S Michigan Ave	773-268-8750	$	1 am	It is named like that for a reason. All-day lunch.
Hong Kong Delight	327 E 35th St	312-842-2929	$$	10 pm	Not quite like being there, but close enough.
Pearl's Place	3901 S Michigan Ave	773-285-1700	$	7:45 pm	Mama's soul food at a snail's pace.
Wings Around the World	321 E 35th St	312-326-6930	$	11:30 pm	Wings cooked 50 ways.

Map 16 • Bronzeville

Ain't She Sweet	4532 S Cottage Grove Ave	773-373-3530	$	6 pm	Fresh, hearty sandwiches, yummy treats and uncompromised service.
Barbara's	353 E 51st St	773-624-0087	$*	6 pm	Soul breakfast and lunch.
Blue 47	4655 S King Dr	773-536-6000	$$$	10:15 pm	Buppie hotspot, overpriced with stingy portions, but great bar.
Harold's Chicken Shack	108 E 47th St	773-285-8362	$*	4 am	It may say #7 but it is #1 around here.
Harold's Chicken Shack	307 E 51st St	773-373-9016	$*	4 am	Fries, bread, and chicken.
Negro League Caf^ua	301 E 43rd St	773-536-7000	$$$	2 am	Where black baseball history stokes up a new Bronzeville Renaissance.
Sweet Potatoes Caf^ua	501 E 47th St	773-536-5555	$	10 pm	Soul food like your auntie makes, but not better than grandma's. The sweet potato pie is as it should be, finger-licking and fattening.

Map 17 • Kenwood

Fung's Chop Suey	1400 E 47th St	773-924-2328	$*	10:30 pm	When you're thinking delivery.
Kenny's Ribs & Chicken	1461 E Hyde Park Blvd	773-241-5550	$	2 am	Cheap and good to go.
Lake Shore Caf^ua	4900 S Lake Shore Dr	773-288-5800	$$	10 pm	Basic hotel food.
Original Pancake House	1517 E Hyde Park Blvd	773-288-2323	$*	5 pm	A pancake style for every person.

Map 18 • Washington Park

Ms Lee's Good Food	205 E Garfield Blvd	773-752-5253	$*	11 pm	Soul food carry-out by ex-Gladys' Luncheonette.
Rose's BBQ Chicken	5426 S State St	773-268-3401	$*	1 am	Don't mind the floor, it's the sauce.

Map 19 • Hyde Park

Bonjour Caf^ua Bakery	1550 E 55th St	773-241-5300	$	7 pm	Have a pastry and be seen.
C'Est Si Bon	5225 S Harper Ave	773-363-4123	$$	4 pm	Go for Sunday Brunch.
Calypso Caf^ua	5211 S Harper Ave	773-955-0229	$$	11 pm	Good Caribbean. Great drinks.
Cedars Mediterranean Kitchen	1206 E 53rd St	773-324-6227	$$	10 pm	Great food, horrible service.
Chant	1509 E 53rd St	773-324-1999	$$$††	12 am	Upscale Asian for Hyde Parkers.
Daley's Restaurant	809 E 63rd St	773-643-6670	$$*	9 pm	The mayor ought to try this place.
Dixie Kitchen and Bait Shop	5225 S Harper Ave	773-363-4943	$$	11 pm	A little taste of the South.
Hyde Park Gyros	1368 E 53rd St	773-947-8229	$*	10 pm	Gyros and Fried Mushrooms-yum!
Kikuya Japanese Restaurant	1601 E 55th St	773-667-3727	$$	9:30 pm	Best sushi in the neighborhood.
La Petite Folie	1504 E 55th St	773-493-1394	$$$$	10 pm	The only haute cuisine in the neighborhood. Expensive and worth it.
Maravilla's Mexican Restaurant	5211 S Harper Ave	773-643-3155	$	11 pm	Cheap, good Mexican. Stinging salsa. Open real late.
Medici on 57th	1327 E 57th St	773-667-7394	$	12 am	The essence of life at U of C.
Mellow Yellow	1508 E 53rd St	773-667-2000	$	11 pm	Comfort food for morning and night.
Nathan's	1372 E 53rd St	773-288-5353	$	10 pm	A Taste of Jamaica.
Noodles Etc	1460 E 53rd St	773-947-8787	$	10 pm	More collegiate than the original.

Arts & Entertainment · **Restaurants**

Key: $: Under $10 / $$: $10–$20 / $$$: $20–$30 / $$$$: $30–$40 / $$$$$: $40+
*: Does not accept credit cards. / †: Accepts only American Express. / † †: Accepts only Visa and Mastercard
Time listed refers to kitchen closing time on weekend nights.

Map 19 • Hyde Park—continued

Ribs 'n' Bibs	5300 S Dorchester Ave	773-493-0400	$	1 am	Finger lickin'. Wear the bib.
Salonica	1440 E 57th St	773-752-3899	$*	9:30 pm	Where to go the morning after.
Thai 55 Restaurant	1607 E 55th St	773-363-7119	$	10 pm	Good Americanized Thai.
Valois	1518 E 53rd St	773-667-0647	$*	10 pm	See Your Food.

Map 20 • East Hyde Park / Jackson Park

Café Corea	1603 E 55th St	773-288-1795	$	9 pm	Cozy Café.
Morry's Deli	5500 S Cornell Ave	773-363-3800	$*	7:45 pm	Good on the go.
Nile Restaurant	1611 E 55th St	773-324-9499	$	9 pm	Varied Middle Eastern.
Orly's Café	1660 E 55th St	773-643-5500	$	10 pm	Stick to the Mexican. Have a margarita.
Piccolo Mondo	1642 E 56th St	773-643-1106	$$	9:30 pm	Best Italian in the area.
Siam Thai Cuisine	1639 E 55th St	773-324-9296	$	10 pm	More Thai in Hyde Park.
Snail's Thai Cuisine	1649 E 55th St	773-667-5423	$	10 pm	Great Hyde Park Thai.

Map 21 • Wicker Park / Ukrainian Village

Bin Wine Café	1559 N Milwaukee Ave	773-486-2233	$$	1 am	Casual swirl and nosh.
Bite	1039 N Western Ave	773-395-2483	$	11:30 pm	Eat here, then Empty your Bottle next door.
Blue Line Club Car	1548 N Damen Ave	773-395-3700	$$	2 am	Mix a diner with a Martini club and here you go.
Bluefin	1952 W North Ave	773-394-7373	$$$	12 am	Upscale, trendy sushi bar.
Bob San	1805 W Division St	773-235-8888	$$$$	12:30 pm	Youthful sushi joint.
The Bongo Room	1470 N Milwaukee Ave	773-489-0690	$	2:30 pm	Great breakfast spot, expect to wait on weekends.
Cold Comfort Café & Deli	2211 W North Ave	773-772-4552	$$	4 pm	Freshly made deli sandwiches; groceries.
Earwax	1561 N Milwaukee Ave	773-772-4019	$$*	12 am	Wicker Park staple and eclectic health food mecca.
Feast	1616 N Damen Ave	773-772-7100	$$$	11 pm	Popular for Sunday brunch.
Flash Taco	1570 N Damen Ave	773-772-1997	$*	5 am	Cheap late-night tacos.
Handlebar	2311 W North Ave	773-384-9546	$$	12 am	Bicycle-themed (largely) vegetarian restaurants decorated with off-duty messengers.
Jerry's	1938 W Division St	773-235-1006	$$	2 am	Jerry's knows good sandwiches, and isn't afraid to... make them.
Las Palmas	1835 W North Ave	773-289-4991	$	12 pm	Great al fresco dining and atrium seating.
Letiza's Natural Bakery	2144 W Division St	773-342-1011	$	11 pm	Addictive sweets and savory fare that holds its own
Mas	1670 W Division St	773-276-8700	$$	11:30 pm	Stylish Latin cooking, dinner only.
Milk & Honey	1920 W Division St	773-395-9434	$	4 pm	Heaven for breakfast.
Mirai Sushi	2020 W Division St	773-862-8500	$$	11 pm	Chic dining and good sushi.
People Lounge	1560 N Milwaukee Ave	773-227-9339	$$	2 pm	Traditional tapas with international groove.
Picante	2016 W Division St	773-328-8800	$*	2:30 am	Very very very very very small taqueria.
Piece	1927 W North Ave	773-772-4422	$$	12:30 am	Designer pizza joint.
Smoke Daddy	1804 W Division St	773-772-6656	$	1 am	Barbecue and blues.
Spring	2039 W North Ave	773-395-7100	$$$$	10:30 pm	Vogue, overpriced Asian-inspired seafood by Shaun McClain.
Su-Ra	2257 W North Ave	773-276-9450	$$	10:30 pm	Contemporary spin on classic Korean.
Sultan's Market	2057 W North Ave	773-235-3072	$*	9 pm	Cheap Middle Eastern, groceries.
Thai Lagoon	2322 W North Ave	773-489-5747	$$	11 pm	Great Thai, funky atmosphere.
Thai Village	2053 W Division St	773-384-5352	$	10 pm	Cheap, tasty, and great outdoor seating.
Tre Via	1575 N Milwaukee Ave	773-227-7990	$$$	1 am	Ambitious Italian with many comfort-food options.

Map 22 • Noble Square / Goose Island

Buenos Aires Forever	939 N Ashland Ave	773-486-8081	$$	11 pm	Argentine cuisine in a casual storefront setting. BYOB.
Corosh	1072 N Milwaukee Ave	773-235-0600	$$	1 am	Italian and pub fare, great patio.
El Barco Mariscos Seafood	1035 N Ashland Blvd	773-486-6850	$$	12 am	Outdoor seating, terrific ceviche.
La Pasadita	1132 N Ashland Ave	773-384-6537	$	3 am	Muy deliciosa, muy casual. Prime after-hours hot-spot.
Luc Thang	1524 N Ashland Blvd	773-395-3907	$	11 pm	Thai with Chinese and Vietnamese touches.
NYC Bagel	1001 W North Ave	312-274-1278	$	5 pm	NY-style deli, best egg salad in the city.

Name	Address	Phone	$	Time	Description
Podhalanka	1549 W Division St	773-486-6655	$	8 pm	Authentic Polish hole-in-the-wall with potato pancakes, buttery pierogies and more.
Sangria Restaurant and Tapas Bar	901 W Weed St	312-266-1200	$$	2 am	Specialty sangria and contemporary tapas in bright, lively room.
Schwa	1466 N Ashland Ave	773-252-1466	$$$$	10:30 pm	Innovative fine dining with a hipster vibe.
Usagi Ya	1178 N Milwaukee Ave	773-292-5885	$$	1 am	Affordable sushi.

Map 23 · West Town / Near West Side

Name	Address	Phone	$	Time	Description
A Tavola	2148 W Chicago Ave	773-276-7567	$$$	10:30 pm	Upscale Italian charm in an intimate setting.
The Bleeding Heart Bakery	2018 W Chicago Ave	773-278-3638	$	7 pm	Pastry with a purpose.
China Dragon Restaurant	2008 W Madison St	312-666-3766	$$*	10:30 pm	Dependably fantastic Chinese.
Old Lviv	2228 W Chicago Ave	773-772-7250	$*	8 pm	Eastern European buffet.
Sunrise Café	2012 W Chicago Ave	773-276-8290	$	3 pm	Good coffee, good breakfast puts a smile on the face.
Takie Outit	2132 W Chicago Ave	773-252-1880	$	10:30 pm	Dim sum in the tum tum.
Tecatlitan Restaurant	1814 W Chicago Ave	773-384-4285	$	2 am	Popular family-style, Mexican restaurant.

Map 24 · River West / West Town

Name	Address	Phone	$	Time	Description
Amelia's Mexican Grille	1235 W Grand Ave	312-421-2000	$$	11 pm	OK food, outside seating can get quite noisy.
Aroma	941 W Randolph St	312-492-7889	$	11 pm	Busy Thai Restaurants serving up the yummies. They do delivery.
Avenue M	695 N Milwaukee Ave	312-243-1133	$$$$	2 pm	High-end steaks and chops.
Bella Notte	1374 W Grand Ave	312-733-5136	$$$$	11:30 pm	Romantic, Italian, and schmoozy.
Bombon Café	38 S Ashland Ave	312-733-8717	$	8 pm	Upscale tortas in a bright sunny setting!
Breakfast Club	1381 W Hubbard St	312-666-3166	$$*	3 pm	Brunch and then some.
Burger Baron	1381 W Grand Ave	312-733-3285	$	8:30 pm	Burgers and beer for the Everyman.
Butterfly Sushi Bar and Thai Cuisine	1156 W Grand Ave	312-563-5555	$$	11 pm	Cute BYOB sushi storefront in the East Village.
Café Central	1437 W Chicago Ave	312-243-6776	$$	9 pm	Tasty Puerto Rican cuisine, diner décor, and vintage neighborhood photos.
Cannella's on Grand	1132 W Grand Ave	312-433-9400	$$$$	11 pm	Nice-ish Italian for this strip of Grand.
Carmichael's Chicago Steak House	1052 W Monroe St	312-433-0025	$$$$	12 am	Great steaks in a vintage style dining room.
Chicago Chocolate Café	847 W Randolph St	312-738-0888	$	12 am	Hot chocolate served five ways.
Coalfire	1321 W Grand Ave	312-226-2625	$$	11 pm	Chicago's first coal-fired pizza.
DeCero	814 W Randolph St	312-455-8114	$$$	11 pm	Made-to-order tacos, fresh fruit cocktail, Mexican heaven.
Fan Si Pan	1618 W Chicago Ave	312-738-1405	$$$	9 pm	Extra-fresh Vietnamese and Laotian food.
Flo	1434 W Chicago Ave	312-243-0477	$$	11 pm	Mexican-influenced breakfast in a relaxed atmosphere.
Follia	953 W Fulton St	312-243-2888	$$$	11 pm	Swanky, upscale Italian.
Green Zebra	1460 W Chicago Ave	312-243-7100	$$$$	11 pm	Innovative and mostly vegetarian, by Spring's Shawn McClain.
Habana Libre	1440 W Chicago Ave	312-243-3303	$$	11 pm	BYOB plantain paradise.
Hacienda Tecatlitlan	820 N Ashland Blvd	312-243-6667	$$	12 am	Beautiful, authentic interior with amazing margaritas.
Ina's	1235 W Randolph St	312-226-8227	$$$	9 pm	Special occasion breakfasts. Try the scrapple—it's better than it sounds.
Jerry's Sandwiches	1045 W Madison St	312-563-1008	$	6 pm	Fresh and slightly gourmet concoctions.
La Sardine	111 N Carpenter St	312-421-2800	$$	10 pm	Tuesdays fixed price for $20!
Marche	833 W Randolph St	312-226-8399	$$$	12 am	Theatrical French brasserie dining.
May Street Market	1132 W Grand Ave	312-421-5547	$$$	11 pm	American / Global fusion with foam and such.
Misto	1118 W Grand Ave	312-226-5989	$$$$	11 pm	Contemporary Italian cuisine, but more popular bar.
Moto	945 W Fulton Market	312-491-0058	$$$$	11 pm	Conceptual laboratory food creations.
Otom	951 W Fulton Market	312-491-5804	$$$	12 am	Moto's cheaper, less scientific neighbor.
Salerno's Pizza and Pasta	1201 W Grand Ave	312-666-3444	$	11 pm	Tony Soprano would be proud, and full.
Silver Palm	768 N Milwaukee Ave	312-666-9322	$$$	2 am	Dine in a 1940s train car on upscale American food.
Sushi X	1136 W Chicago Ave	312-491-9232	$$	12 am	Speakeasy sushi bar with fish so fresh they swim to your plate. BYOB.
Swim Café	1357 W Chicago Ave	312-492-8600	$	6 pm	Fresh, homemade breakfast and lunch fair with aquatic theme.
Twisted Spoke	501 N Ogden Ave	312-666-1500	$	3 am	Famous for serving smut movies and eggs simultaneously.
Vinnie's Sandwich Shop	1204 W Grand Ave	312-738-2985	$	5 pm	No frills, handy for construction workers.

Key: $: Under $10 / $$: $10–$20 / $$$: $20–$30 / $$$$: $30–$40 / $$$$$: $40+
* : Does not accept credit cards. / † : Accepts only American Express. / † † : Accepts only Visa and Mastercard
Time listed refers to kitchen closing time on weekend nights.

Map 24 • River West / West Town—continued

Vivo	838 W Randolph St	312-733-3379	$$$$	12 am	Restaurants Row's first residence of Italian dining.
West Town Tavern	1329 W Chicago Ave	312-666-6175	$$$	10 pm	Upscale comfort food.
Windy City Café	1062 W Chicago Ave	312-492-8010	$	4 pm	Small town diner feel and menu, grab a booth.
Wishbone	1001 W Washington Blvd	312-850-2663	$$	10 pm	Comfort food, comfort folks.

Map 25 • Illinois Medical District

Carnitas Uruapan Restaurant	1725 W 18th St	312-226-2654	$*	5 pm	Carnitas muy necesitas.
Damenzo's	2324 W Taylor St	312-421-1142	$	1 am	Pizza, pizza puffs, small bar.
El Charco Verde	2255 W Taylor St	312-738-1686	$	10 pm	A Mexican favorite.
Ferrara Bakery	2210 W Taylor St	312-666-2200	$	6 pm	Serving Italian pastries since 1908.
Lu-lu's Hot Dogs	1000 S Leavitt St	312-243-3444	$*	1 am	Dog's popular with local med students.
TJ's Family Restaurant	1928 W Cermak Rd	773-927-3349	$*	10 pm	Neighborhood diner.

Map 26 • University Village / Little Italy / Pilsen

Al's Number 1 Italian Beef	1079 W Taylor St	312-226-4017	$*	1 am	Where's the beef? Right here.
Carm's Beef and Snack Shop	1057 W Polk St	312-738-1046	$*	11 pm	Italian subs and sausages.
Chez Joel	1119 W Taylor St	312-226-6479	$$$	11 pm	Delicious French cuisine in Little Italy.
Couscous	1445 W Taylor St	312-226-2408	$$	9:30 pm	Middle Eastern and Maghrebin Cuisine. Unique falafel.
De Pasada	1519 W Taylor St	312-243-6441	$	12 pm	Inexpensive, good quality Mexican--friendly staff.
Demitasse	1066 W Taylor St	312-226-7669	$	3 pm	Delightful breakfast spot.
Francesca's	1400 W Taylor St	312-829-2828	$$	11 pm	Loud, bustling dining room.
Franconello's Italian Restaurant	1301 S Halsted St	312-421-1301	$	10:30 pm	UIC outpost of Beverly Italian.
Golden Thai	1509 W Taylor St	312-733-0760	$	10 pm	Always busy, but there's better Thai out there.
Japonica	1422 W Taylor St	312-421-3288	$$	11 pm	Sushi ventures into Little Italy.
Kohan Japanese Restaurant	730 W Maxwell St	312-421-6254	$$	10 pm	Sushi for UIC students.
La Cebollita	1723 S Ashland Ave	312-492-8443	$*	10 pm	Gorditas, sopas, to dine-in or carry out.
La Vita	1359 W Taylor St	312-491-1414	$$$	11 pm	Date-spot for northern Italian.
May Street Café	1136 W Cermak Rd	312-421-4442	$	10:30 pm	Inexpensive, super casual pan-Latin.
Mundial-Cocina Mestiza	1640 W 18th St	312-491-9908	$$	10 pm	Lovingly-prepared, family-owned Mexican.
New Rosebud Café	1500 W Taylor St	312-942-1117	$	11:30 pm	Popular with the United Center crowd.
Nuevo Leon	1515 W 18th St	312-421-1517	$*	4 am	Real-deal Mexican grub in Pilsen.
Pizza Tango	1013 W 18th St	312-421-2111	$	10 pm	Argentinean-style thin crust pizza.
Playa Azul	1514 W 18th St	312-421-2552	$$*	12 am	Seafood a la Mexicaine.
Steak 'n Egger	1174 W Cermak Rd	312-226-5444	$	24-hrs	24-hour comfort food.
Sweet Maple Café	1339 W Taylor St	312-243-8908	$	2 pm	Super-homey breakfast, homemade biscuits.
Taj Mahal	1512 W Taylor St	312-226-6546	$$	10 pm	Affordable Indian.
Taqueria Los Comales	1544 W 18th St	312-666-2251	$*	1 am	Mexican fast food in cheerful environment.
Taylor Street Taco Grill	1412 W Taylor St	312-850-9717	$	10 pm	On the cheaper end, but not bad.
Tuscany	1014 W Taylor St	312-829-1990	$$	11 pm	Elegant Taylor Street Italian.
WOW Café & Wingery	717 W Maxwell St	312-997-9969	$	12 am	N'awlins wing joint with a plethora of sauces.

Map 27 • Logan Square

Azucar	2647 N Kedzie Ave	773-486-6464	$$	2 am	Clubby tapas spot.
Bonsoiree Café and Delicacies	2728 W Armitage Ave	773-486-7511	$$	10 pm	This new spot is all about cozy seating and creative catering.
Borinquen Restaurant	1720 N California Ave	773-227-6038	$	12 am	Order a jibarito—a steak sandwich between two plantain slices.
Buona Terra Ristorante	2535 N California Ave	773-289-3800	$$	11 pm	Logan Square shmoozy Italian.
Café Bolero	2252 N Western Ave	773-227-9000	$$	12 am	Tasty Cuban fare.
Caliente	2556 W Fullerton Ave	773-772-4355	$$	11 pm	Heat up the night, or morning, with Pan-Latin eats and a BYOB policy.
Calvin's BBQ	2540 W Armitage Ave	773-342-5100	$$	10 pm	Chef Calvin Woods' fresh, wholesome, spiced home-style cooking.
Choi's Chinese Restaurant	2638 N Milwaukee Ave	773-486-8496	$$	9 pm	Good, fresh Chinese food.
Dunlay's on the Square	3137 W Logan Blvd	773-227-2400	$$	11 pm	American food and sports viewing.
El Cid	2115 N Milwaukee Ave	773-252-4747	$	1 am	Authentic Mexican for the masses.
El Nandu	2731 N Fullerton Ave	773-278-0900	$$	12 am	Argentinian delicacies mixed with music.
El Pollo Loco	2715 N Milwaukee Ave	773-394-5626	$*	10 pm	Lots to cluck about with this cheap flame-grilled chicken.

Fat Willy's Rib Shack	2416 W Schubert Ave	773-782-1800	$$	11 pm	Finger-lickin' ribs and brisket.
Hachi's Kitchen	2521 N California Ave	773-276-8080	$$	12 am	Locals rave over this Logan Square sushi spot.
Johnny's Grill	2545 N Kedzie Blvd	773-278-2215	$	10 pm	Diner food for the grunge crowd.
Lula Café	2537 N Kedzie Blvd	773-489-9554	$$	10 pm	Pan-ethnic nouveau for hipsters.
Mama's Apple	2139 N Milwaukee Ave	773-252-2807	$	11 pm	Mama's in the kitchen cooking up Latin comfort food.
Sai Mai	2532 N California Ave	773-276-8424	$	11:30 pm	Tasty Thai comes at the right price at this BYOB eatery.
Taqueria Moran	2226 N California Ave	773-235-2663	$	10 pm	Stand apart marinated pork tacos.

Map 28 · Bucktown

Arturo's Tacos	2001 N Western Ave	773-772-4944	$	10 pm	Taqueria boasts cheap eats and a boisterous crowd
Bluebird	1749 N Damen Ave	773-486-2473	$$$	2 am	Should be called the bacon bird.
Café Laguardia	2111 W Armitage Ave	773-862-5996	$$	11 pm	Cuban food like you wouldn't believe.
Café Matou	1846 N Milwaukee Ave	773-384-8911	$$$	11 pm	Fantastic French food, dodgy locale.
Club Lucky	1824 W Wabansia Ave	773-227-2300	$$	12 am	Italian retro-styled joint.
Coast Sushi Bar	2045 N Damen Ave	773-235-5775	$$	12 am	BYOB sushi.
Hollywood Grill	1601 N North Ave	773-395-1818	$	24-hrs	24-hour Wicker Park dive.
Honey 1 BBQ	2241 N Western Ave	773-227-5130	$$	12 am	BBQ cooked in a big ole smoker. Yum.
Hot Chocolate	1747 N Damen Ave	773-489-1747	$$	12 am	Much more than just hot chocolate.
Il Covo	2152 N Damen Ave	773-862-5555	$$$	11 pm	Italian spot with upstairs lounge.
Irazu	1865 N Milwaukee Ave	773-252-5687	$*	9:30 pm	Hipsters and bikers gather 'round for Central American staples.
Jane's	1655 W Cortland St	773-862-5263	$$$	11 pm	Good-for-you gourmet.
La Bonita	2165 N Western Ave	773-486-7340	$$$$	11 pm	Haute tamales in cantina ambience.
Le Bouchon	1958 N Damen Ave	773-862-6600	$$	12 am	Affordable, crowded French.
Margie's Candies	1960 N Western Ave	773-384-1035	$	11 pm	Immense ice cream concoctions.
Meritage Café & Wine Bar	2118 N Damen Ave	773-235-6434	$$$$	12 am	Great food, great domestic wine list. A real neighborhood restaurant.
Rinconcito Sudamericano	1954 W Armitage Ave	773-489-3126	$$	10 pm	Yummy South American food.
Rio's D'Sudamerica	2010 W Armitage Ave	773-276-0170	$$$$	12 am	Swanky South American for date nights.
Riverside Deli & Café	1656 W Cortland St	773-278-3354	$$*	5 pm	Great deli, with awesome Sunday brunch.
Silver Cloud Club & Grill	1700 N Damen Ave	773-489-6212	$$	12 am	A mac & cheese and meat-loaf kind of place.
Takashi	1952 N Damen Ave	773-772-6170	$$$	10:30 pm	Japanese fusion by James Beard Award winning chef.
Think Café	2235 N Western Ave	773-394-0537	$$$	11 pm	Gourmet Italian—reasonable prices.
Vella Café	1912 N Western Ave	773-489-7777	$$	7 pm	Wholesome (and tasty) breakfast and lunch spot.

Map 29 · DePaul / Wrightwood / Sheffield

Ambrosia Café	1963 N Sheffield Ave	773-404-4450	$	3 am	Smoothies and hookahs? Huh.
Goose Island Brewing Company	1800 N Clybourn Ave	312-915-0071	$	1 pm	Pub grub at its best.
Green Dolphin Street	2200 N Ashland Ave	773-395-0066	$$$$	11 pm	Live jazz club and contemporary American.
Ja' Grill	1008 W Armitage Ave	773-929-5375	$$	11 pm	Fun, authentic Jamaican in Lincoln park? Go figure.
John's Place	1200 W Webster Ave	773-525-6670	$$	11 pm	Healthy comfort food.
Metropolis	2009 N Bissell St	773-868-9000	$*	9:30 pm	Try the frozen bananas (with or without nuts).
Minnies	1969 N Halsted St	312-943-9900	$	2 am	Mini-burgers and mini-sandwiches served hot or cold.
Red Lion Pub	2446 N Lincoln Ave	773-348-2695	$	12 am	It's haunted!
Sai Café	2010 N Sheffield Ave	773-472-8080	$$$	12 am	Traditional sushi place.
Salt & Pepper Diner	2575 N Lincoln Ave	773-525-8788	$*	4 pm	Cheap breakfasts in an area with few such options.
Shine & Morida	901 W Armitage Ave	773-296-0101	$$	11 pm	Chinese and Japanese all-in-one.
State	935 W Webster Ave	773-975-8030	$$$	12 am	Flashy service-oriented spot with concierge service.
Sweet Mandy B's	1208 W Webster Ave	773-244-1174	$	10 pm	Picture-perfect sweet shoppe.
Taco & Burrito House	1548 W Fullerton Ave	773-665-8389	$*	5 am	Super-cheap burrito shack, open very late.
Tsuki	1441 W Fullerton Ave	773-883-8722	$$	12 am	It was bound to happen: tapas + sushi.
Twisted Lizard	1964 N Sheffield Ave	773-929-1414	$$	12 am	Yuppie Mexican.
Vosges Haut Chocolat	951 W Armitage Ave	773-296-9866	$	8 pm	Gourmet chocolates.

Map 30 · Lincoln Park

Alinea	1723 N Halsted St	312-867-0110	$$$$$	10 pm	Conceptual experiments in fine dining.
Austrian Bakery & Deli	2523 N Clark St	773-244-9922	$	8:30 pm	Low-carb diets are so over. Celebrate here.

Key: $: Under $10 / $$: $10–$20 / $$$: $20–$30 / $$$$: $30–$40 / $$$$$: $40+
* : Does not accept credit cards. / † : Accepts only American Express. / † † : Accepts only Visa and Mastercard
Time listed refers to kitchen closing time on weekend nights.

Map 30 • Lincoln Park—continued

Boka	1729 N Halsted St	312-337-6070	$$$	12 am	Ambitious menu, swank décor.
Brick's Chicago	1909 N Lincoln Ave	312-255-0851	$$	9 pm	Thin-crust pizza and Trappist ales hold sway here.
Café Ba-Ba-Reeba!	2024 N Halsted St	773-935-5000	$$$	12 am	Noisy, bustling tapas joint.
Café Bernard	2100 N Halsted St	773-871-2100	$$	11:30 pm	Charming French.
Charlie Trotter's	816 W Armitage Ave	773-248-6228	$$$$$	10:30 pm	World-famous nouvelle cuisine.
Crepe & Coffee Place	2433 N Clark St	773-404-1300	$	10 pm	Serious crepe lovers.
Dunlay's	2600 N Clark St	773-883-6000	$$$	11 pm	Casual traditional american dinner spot.
Emilio's Tapas	444 Fullerton Pkwy	773-327-5100	$$$	12 am	One of the first tapas joints n Chicago.
Ethel's Chocolate Lounge	819 W Armitage Ave	773-281-0029	$	11 pm	I'm guessing... Chocolate?
Fattoush	2652 N Halsted St	773-327-2652	$$	11 pm	Nicely priced Middle-East nosh.
Frances' Deli	2552 N Clark St	773-248-4580	$	8 pm	Inventive deli.
Geja's Café	340 W Armitage Ave	773-281-9101	$$$	12:30 am	Romantic fondue with live flamenco.
Hai Yen	2723 N Clark St	773-868-4888	$$	10 pm	Little Vietnam favorite swanked up for Lincoln Park.
Hema's Kitchen II	2411 N Clark St	773-529-1705	$$	11 pm	Almost as good as original on Devon.
Hey Sushi	2630 N Clark St	773-248-3900	$$	12 am	Clubby sushi spot.
Karyn's	1901 N Halsted Ave	312-255-1590	$$	10 pm	The queen of raw food.
Landmark	1633 N Halsted St	312-587-1600	$$$$	2 am	Cavernous club restaurant for Lincoln Parkers and the Steppenwolf crowd.
Lito's Empanadas	2566 N Clark St	773-857-1337	$	9 pm	He don't make no burritos.
Molly's Cupcakes	2536 N Clark St	773-883-7220	$	10 pm	Build your own cupcake at this school-themed bakery.
Mon Ami Gabi	2300 N Lincoln Park W	773-348-8886	$$$	11 pm	French bistro.
Nookies	1746 N Wells St	312-337-2454	$*	9:45 pm	Inventive omelettes with some strong coffee.
Nookies, Too	2114 N Halsted St	773-327-1400	$	12 am	Inventive omelettes with some strong coffee.
North Pond	2610 N Cannon Dr	773-477-5845	$$$$	10 pm	Earthy contemporary American.
O' Fame	750 W Webster Ave	773-929-5111	$$	11 pm	Nice, neighborhood casual Italian.
Original Pancake House	2020 N Lincoln Park W	773-929-8130	$$*	4 pm	Breakfast-y grill.
Piattini	934 W Webster Ave	773-281-3898	$$	11 pm	Italian tapas.
PS Bangkok	2521 N Halsted St	773-348-0072	$	11 pm	Popular Thai with delivery.
Red Rooster	2100 N Halsted St	773-929-7660	$$$	11:30 pm	Inauspicious entrance, with authentic France beyond.
Robinson's No 1 Ribs	655 W Armitage Ave	312-337-1399	$*	10 pm	Down home ribs in Lincoln Park.
Salvatore's Ristorante	525 W Arlington Pl	773-528-1200	$$$	10 pm	Cute neighborhood Italian.
Sedgwick's Bar & Grill	1935 N Sedgwick St	312-337-7900	$	12 am	Home-style breakfast buffet.
Sushi O Sushi	346 W Armitage Ave	773-871-4777	$$	11 pm	Newly remodeled fresh seafood.
Sushi Para II	2256 N Clark St	773-477-3219	$$	10:30 pm	A.Y.C.E. sushi that's good. No, really.
Swirlz Cupcakes	705 W Belden Ave	773-404-2253	$	7 pm	Gourmet cupcakes, including gluten-free options.
Taco Burrito Palace #2	2441 N Halsted St	773-248-0740	$*	5 am	Speedy Mexican.
Tilli's	1952 N Halsted St	773-325-0044	$$	11 pm	Cute staff and good food.
Toro	2546 N Clark St	773-348-4877	$$	11 pm	Worth the wait for raw fish lovers
Twin Anchors	1655 N Sedgwick St	312-266-1616	$$	12 am	Sinatra came for the ribs and stayed for the drinks and atmosphere.
Vinci	1732 N Halsted St	312-266-1199	$$$	11:30 pm	Homemade pasta raises the bar.
Wiener's Circle	2622 N Clark St	773-477-7444	$*	5:30 am	Classic dogs served with a generous helping of sass.

Map 31 • Old Town / Near North

Bistrot Margot	1437 N Wells St	312-587-3660	$$$$	11 pm	Great date place.
Chic Café	361 W Chestnut St	312-873-2032	$$	8 pm	Gourmet prix fixe by culinary students.
Dinotto Ristorante	215 W North Ave	312-202-0302	$$	12 am	Everyone's a regular at this neighborhood Italian joint.
Fireplace Inn	1448 N Wells St	312-664-5264	$$$	1:30 am	Popular spot to watch sports.
Fresh Choice	1534 N Wells St	312-664-7065	$*	10 pm	Sandwich and smoothie king.
Garlic and Chili	1232 N La Salle Dr	312-255-1717	$	9:30 pm	Off the beaten track and located next to the transient motel, it's a hidden gem.
Kamehachi	1400 N Wells St	312-664-3663	$$$	1:30 am	Sushi favorite with upstairs lounge.
Kiki's Bistro	900 N Franklin St	312-335-5454	$$$$	10 pm	Stylish French.
Las Pinatas	1552 N Wells St	312-664-8277	$$	12 am	Festive atmosphere, fantastic food.
Mangia Roma	1623 N Halsted St	312-475-9801	$$	10:30 pm	Casual Roman spot with pizza.
Michael's	101 W North Ave	312-642-5246	$	24-hrs	Classic diner, great sundaes.
Mizu	315 W North Ave	312-951-8880	$$	10:30 pm	Sushi and skewered meats with dipping sauces.
MK	868 N Franklin St	312-482-9179	$$$$	10 pm	Very stylish.

O'Brien's	1528 N Wells St	312-787-3131	$$$	12:30 pm	Best outdoor in Old Town.
Old Jerusalem	1411 N Wells St	312-944-0459	$$	11 pm	Cheap, good food.
Old Town Brasserie	1209 N Wells St	312-943-3000	$$$	1:30 am	Classic French comfort food in cozy room.
Salpicon	1252 N Wells St	312-988-7811	$$	11 pm	Colorful Mexican with tequila tastings.
Topo Gigio Ristorante	1516 N Wells St	312-266-9355	$$$	11 pm	Crowded reliable Italian. Big outdoor.
Wells on Wells	1617 N Wells St	312-944-1617	$$	2 am	Two words: pretzel buns.

Map 32 • Gold Coast / Mag Mile

Ashkenaz	12 E Cedar St	312-944-5006	$	7 pm	Chicago's true Jewish deli.
Bistro 110	110 E Pearson St	312-266-3110	$$$	11 pm	Popular Sunday jazz brunch.
Bistrot Zinc	1131 N State St	312-337-1131	$$	11 pm	Quiet elegance.
Café des Architectes	20 E Chestnut St	312-324-4063	$$$	10 pm	French Mediterranean with late kitchen.
Café Spiaggia	980 N Michigan Ave	312-280-2750	$$	10:30 pm	More casual and less pricey than its Spiaggia forebear.
Cape Cod Room	140 E Walton Pl	312-787-2200	$$$$	11 pm	Over-the-top nautical décor.
Carmine's	1043 N Rush St	312-988-7676	$$$	12:30 am	Crowded and pricey Italian.
Fornetto Mei	107 E Delaware Pl	312-944-6300	$$$	10 pm	Authentic pizza. Deep dish lovers stay away.
Gibson's Steakhouse	1028 N Rush St	312-266-8999	$$$$$	12 am	If you love steak, get a reservation.
Hugo's Frog Bar & Fish House	1024 N Rush St	312-640-0999	$$$	12 am	Hearty seafood.
Il Mulino New York	1150 N Dearborn St	312-440-8888	$$$$$	11 pm	Top NYC Italian with top NYC prices.
Le Colonial	937 N Rush St	312-255-0088	$$$	12 am	Indochine comes to the Second City. Very nice.
Le Petit Paris	260 E Chestnut St	312-787-8260	$$$$	10 pm	Shhh! Don't tell anyone about this Gallic hideaway!
McCormick & Schmick's	41 E Chestnut St	312-397-9500	$$$$	12 am	Seafood chain that outdoes itself on portions and taste.
Morton's of Chicago	1050 N State St	312-266-4820	$$$$$	11 pm	The steakhouse standard.
Original Pancake House	22 E Bellevue Pl	312-642-7917	$$*	5 pm	The apple waffle/pancake is right!
Pane Caldo	72 E Walton St	312-649-0055	$$$$	11 pm	Tucked-away genius Italian trattoria.
Pump Room	1301 N State Pkwy	312-266-0360	$$$$$	12 am	Chicago old-school tradition. Dress code.
Sarah's Pastries & Candies	11 E Oak St	312-664-6223	$	10 pm	Decadent cakes and other goodies,
Spiaggia	980 N Michigan Ave	312-280-2750	$$$$$	10:30 pm	One of Chicago's best—gorgeous lake view and Italian cuisine.
Table Fifty-Two	52 W Elm St	312-573-4000	$$$	10 pm	Upscale southern food by Oprah's ex-chef.
Tavern on Rush	1031 N Rush St	312-664-9600	$$$$	1 am	Summer mainstay, American menu.
Tempo	6 E Chestnut St	312-943-4373	$$*	24-hrs	24/7 patio seating and huge menu.
Tsunami	1160 N Dearborn St	312-642-9911	$$$	11:30 pm	Sushi and sake in a club-like atmosphere.

Map 33 • West Rogers Park

Afghan Restaurant	2818 W Devon Ave	773-262-8000	$	2 pm	Afghan gyro for "hunger", whole baby goat for "starving."
Annapurna	2608 W Devon Ave	773-764-1858	$	11 pm	Vegetarian fast food.
Arya Bhavan	2508 W Devon Ave	773-274-5800	$$	11 pm	Northern Indian all-vegetarian.
Ben Tre	3146 W Touhy Ave	773-465-3011	$	9 pm	Comfy Vietnamese comfort food.
Café Montenegro	6954 N Western Ave	773-761-2233	$*	12 am	Greek-accented coffeeshop.
Candlelite	7452 N Western Ave	773-465-0087	$	2 am	Rogers Park pizza institution, with cocktails.
Chopal	2240 W Devon Ave	773-338-4080	$	11pm	When you need a kebob—late.
Ghandi India Restaurant	2601 W Devon Ave	773-761-8714	$$	11 pm	Family-style North and South Indian fare.
Good Morgan Kosher Fish Market	2948 W Devon Ave	773-764-8115	$$*	2 am	Fish market/restaurant in the Devon kosher strip.
Hashalom	2905 W Devon Ave	773-465-5675	$*	9 pm	Israeli/Moroccan, kosher, BYOB, closed Sat/Sun.
Hema's Kitchen	6406 N Oakley Ave	773-338-1627	$$	11 pm	Indian comfort food.
Indian Garden	2546 W Devon Ave	773-338-2929	$$	10:15 pm	Get your tandoori here.
Mysore Woodland's	2548 W Devon Ave	773-338-8160	$$	10 pm	One of teh better Indian spots in this strip.
Siam Pasta	7416 N Western Ave	773-274-0579	$	11 pm	Bangkok home cookin'.
Sukhadia's	2559 W Devon Ave	773-338-5400	$	9:30 pm	Indian sweet maker and caterer.
Tiffin	2536 W Devon Ave	773-338-2143	$$	10:30 pm	Most upscale Indian restaurant on Devon, yet moderately priced.
U Lucky Dawg	6821 N Western Ave	773-274-3652	$*	11 pm	Famous hot dog joint. Breakfast, lunch, and dinner, outdoor seating.
Udupi Palace	2543 W Devon Ave	773-338-2152	$	9:30 pm	Pure vegetarian Indian food, low-fat, not too spicy.
Uru-Swati	2629 W Devon Ave	773-62-5280	$	10pm	Vegetarian fast food and snacks.
Viceroy of India	2520 W Devon Ave	773-743-4100	$$	10:30 pm	Popular Indian restaurant, vegetarian options.

Key: $: Under $10 / $$: $10–$20 / $$$: $20–$30 / $$$$: $30–$40 / $$$$$: $40+
* : Does not accept credit cards. / † : Accepts only American Express. / † † : Accepts only Visa and Mastercard
Time listed refers to kitchen closing time on weekend nights.

Map 34 • East Rogers Park

Name	Address	Phone	Price	Time	Description
A&T Grill	7026 N Clark St	773-274-0036	$	9 pm	Classic diner-grill.
Buffalo Joe's	1841 W Howard St	773-764-7300	$*	11 pm	Wings and fast food carryout spot, with a soul food flava.
Caf^ua Suron	1146 W Pratt Blvd	773-465-6500	$$$	11 pm	Lebanese fine dining. BYOB.
Capt'n Nemos	7367 N Clark St	773-973-0570	$	7 pm	Free soup sample while you wait at this always jovial local sandwich chain.
Caribbean American Bakery	1539 W Howard St	773-761-0700	$	8 pm	Jamaican bakery featuring meat pies, pastries, and jerk chicken for carryout.
Dagel & Beli Shop	7406 N Greenview Ave	773-743-2354	$	10 pm	Dyslexic sandiwches.
Deluxe Diner	6349 N Clark St	773-743-8244	$*	24-hrs	Retro-styled greasy spoon.
El Famous Burrito	7047 N Clark St	773-465-0377	$*	1 am	Best greasy burrito in Chicago.
Ennui Café	6981 N Sheridan Rd	773-973-2233	$*	12 am	We would write something but we can't muster the passion.
Ghareeb Nawaz	2032 W Devon Ave	773-761-5300	$*	12 am	Indo-Pakistani lunch counter on the east side of the strip.
Grande Noodles and Sushi Bar	6632 N Clark St	773-761-6666	$$	10 pm	Damn fine pot stickers.
Heartland Café	7000 N Glenwood Ave	773-465-8005	$$	11 pm	Brown rice, socialist newspapers, and vegetarian tidbits reign here.
La Cazuela Mariscos	6922 N Clark St	773-338-5425	$	10 pm	Taqueria specializing in seafood.
Lake Side Café	1418 W Howard St	773-262-9503	$$	9 pm	Vegetarian restaurant specializing in organic grub.
Morseland	1218 W Morse Ave	773-764-8900	$$$	2 am	Rogers Park café with ambitious fare.
Panini Panini	6764 N Sheridan Rd	773-761-4110	$$*	10 pm	Italian cafe for Loyola student.
Quesadillas y Mariscos Dona Lolis	6924 N Clark St	773-761-5677	$*	10 pm	Authentic quesadillas and gorditas with interesting ingredients.
Taste of Peru	6545 N Clark St	773-381-4540	$	12 am	Barebones spot for cheap. authentic Peruvian food.
Thai Spice	1320 W Devon Ave	773-973-0504	$	11 pm	Look beyond the grim exterior for freshly prepared Thai.
Tickie's Belizean Cuisine	7605 N Paulina St	773-973-3919	$	8 pm	Authentic Caribbean food in cheerful storefront across from the Howard L.

Map 35 • Arcadia Terrace / Peterson Park

Name	Address	Phone	Price	Time	Description
Aztecas Mexican Taqueria	5421 N Lincoln Ave	773-506-2052	$	12 am	Standard Mexican fare.
Café Orange	5639 N Lincoln Ave	773-275-5040	$$	2 am	Korean and Japanese fare with a hip vibe and occasional karaoke.
Charcoal Delights	3139 W Foster Ave	773-583-0056	$	11 pm	Great gyros to go.
Fondue Stube	2717 W Peterson Ave	773-784-2200	$$	12 am	Fun fondue!
Garden Buffet	5347 N Lincoln Ave	773-728-1249	$	11 pm	Korean/Japanese with huge buffet and sushi bar.
IHOP	5929 N Lincoln Ave	773-769-1550	$	12 am	It's an IHOP for pete's sake. What else do you need to know?
Katsu	2651 W Peterson Ave	773-784-3383	$$$	10 pm	Familiar, family sushi place.
Pueblito Viejo	5429 N Lincoln Ave	773-784-9135	$$	2:20 am	Adorable Columbian village-theme with live music on weekends.
Solga	5828 N Lincoln Ave	773-728-0802	$$$	11 pm	Korean BBQ with charcoal grill.
Sweet Collective	5333 N Lincoln Ave	773-293-0888	$	6 pm	It's the homemade ice cream, stupid.
Wolfy's	2734 W Peterson Ave	773-743-0207	$	9 pm	Dine in and carry out dogs, burgers, and such.
Woo Chon	5744 N California Ave	773-728-8001	$	12 am	Authentic Korean BBQ. Brusque but oddly fun service.

Map 36 • Bryn Mawr / Bowmanville

Name	Address	Phone	Price	Time	Description
Delisi's Pizzeria	5806 N Western Ave	773-784-6320	$	10:30 pm	Chicago memorabilia, great pizza and complimentary Tootsie Rolls.
Fireside Restaurant & Lounge	5739 N Ravenswood Ave	773-561-7433	$$	3 am	Cajun-tinged barfood and late kitchen.
Greenhouse Inn	6300 N Ridge Ave	773-273-4182	$$	2:30 pm	Church and bridge groups meet for homemade soups.
Max's Italian Beef	5754 N Western Ave	773-989-8200	$$*	7 pm	Chicago institution; home of the pepper-and-egg sandwich.
San Soo Gab San	5247 N Western Ave	773-334-1589	$$	24-hrs	Do-it-yourself Korean barbeque at 4 am.
Yes Thai	5211 N Damen Ave	773-878-3487	$	10:30 pm	Noodles and curries in a cozy atmosphere.

Map 37 • Edgewater / Andersonville

Alice and Friends Vegetarian Café	5812 N Broadway St	773-275-8797	$$$	10 pm	Veggie to vegan.

Andie's	5253 N Clark St	773-784-8616	$$	11:30 pm	Fresh Middle Eastern in airy atmosphere.
Ann Sather	5207 N Clark St	773-271-6677	$	2 pm	Heavenly cinnamin rolls and swedish meatballs.
Anteprima	5316 N Clark St	773-506-9990	$$$	11 pm	This cozy A-Ville Italian just feels right.
Ethiopian Diamond	6120 N Broadway St	773-338-6100	$$$	11 pm	Visit for jazz on Fridays.
Flourish Bakery Café	1138 W Bryn Mawr	773-271-2253	$	9 pm	Three words—red velvet cake.
Francesca's Bryn Mawr	1039 W Bryn Mawr Ave	773-506-9261	$$	11 pm	Dined in an SRO before?
Hamburger Mary's	5400 N Clark St	773-784-6969	$$	11 pm	Flamboyant burger joint popular with families and The Gays.
Huey's Hot Dogs	1507 W Balmoral Ave	773-293-4800	$*	8 pm	Fast, friendly dogs and burgers.
Icosium Kafe	5200 N Clark St	773-271-5233	$	10 pm	It's crepe-tastic!
Indie Café	5951 N Broadway St	773-561-5577	$$	10:30 pm	Thai and sushi. Yummy and cheap.
Jin Ju	5203 N Clark St	773-334-6377	$$$	11 pm	Upscale Korean.
La Fonda Latino	5350 N Broadway St	773-271-3935	$$	9:30 pm	Real tasty pan-Latin.
La Tache	1475 W Balmoral Ave	773-334-7168	$$	11 pm	Neighborhood French bistro.
M Henry	5707 N Clark St	773-561-1600	$$	2:30 pm	Stylish brunch option in Andersonville.
Moody's Pub	5910 N Broadway St	773-275-2696	$	2 am	Burgers only, but the best.
Pasticceria Natalina	5406 N Clark St	773-989-0662	$	8 pm	Friggin' amazing sicilian pastries and sweets.
Pauline's	1754 W Balmoral Ave	773-561-8573	$*	3 am	Weekend breakfast hotspot; try the famous five-egg omelette, if you must.
RAS Dashen Ethiopian Restaurant	5846 N Broadway St	773-506-9601	$$	11 pm	Traditional Ethiopian comfort food; vegan-friendly.
Reza's	5255 N Clark St	773-561-1898	$$	12 am	Many Persian options, leftovers for lunch the next day.
Sabaidee	5359 N Broadway St	773-506-0880	$*	8:30 pm	Homemade sausages and other Laotian specialties.
Standee's	1133 W Granville Ave	773-743-5013	$	24-hrs	Loyola students and others congregate here for diner fare.
Sushi Luxe	5204 N Clark St	773-334-0770	$$	11 pm	Upscale sushi, fancy cocktails, and wretched service.
Svea	5236 N Clark St	773-275-7738	$*	3:30 pm	Adorable, tiny Swedish diner.
Tanoshii	5547 N Clark St	773-878-6886	$$	12 am	Order from the chef for innovative sushi.
Taste of Lebanon	1509 W Foster Ave	773-334-1600	$*	7:30 pm	Dongy room, rock-bottom prices, above-average Mid-east fare.

Map 38 • Ravenswood / Albany Park

Al-Khaymeih	4742 N Kedzie Ave	773-583-0999	$	11 pm	Lebanese eatery with better-than-average vegetarian appetizers.
Arun's	4156 N Kedzie Ave	773-539-1909	$$$$$	10:30 pm	Worldwide rep for four-star prix fixe Thai.
Brasa Roja	3125 W Montrose Ave	773-866-2252	$$	10 pm	Friendly Columbian place specializing in flame-roasted chicken.
Cousin's IV	3038 W Irving Park Rd	773-478-6868	$$	11:30 pm	Overcooking not a prob at this raw restaurant.
Dharma Garden Thai Restaurants	3109 W Irving Park Rd	773-588-9140	$	10 pm	Thai vegetarian and seafood dishes. Karaoke some evenings.
El Huarachin Huarachon	3320 W Lawrence Ave	773-267-3926	$*	10 pm	Crazy good homestyle Mexican.
Golden Crust Italian Pizzeria	4620 N Kedzie Ave	773-539-5860	$	2 am	Honkin' portions of the Italian-American comfort food of yore.
Great Sea Chinese Restaurants	3254 W Lawrence Ave	773-478-9129	$$	10:30 pm	Otherwise basic Chinese locally famous for its hot wings.
Kang Nam	4849 N Kedzie Ave	773-539-2524	$$	10:30 pm	Could be the best Korean BBQ in town. Crazy excellent.
Kitchen Chicago	4664 N Manor Ave	773-463-0863	$	2 pm	Café food: soup, sandwiches, sweets.
Lutz Continental Café	2458 W Montrose Ave	773-478-7785	$$	10 pm	If Grandma was German, she would serve these pastries.
Manzo's Ristorante	3210 W Irving Park Rd	773-478-3070	$$	1:30 am	Do not miss the Sunday buffet. Tasty, plentiful and cheap Italian.
Nhu Lan	2612 W Lawrence Ave	773-878-9898	$	8 pm	Vietnamese sandwich shop.
Noon O Kabab	4661 N Kedzie Ave	773-279-8899	$	11 pm	Bring a doggie bag for day-after lunch.
Paradise	2916 W Montrose Ave	773-588-1989	$$*	10:30 pm	Competent sushi connected to a Korean spa.
Penguin	2723 W Lawrence Ave	773-271-4924	$	10 pm	High-fat, authentic Argentine ice cream (empanadas and pizza, too, but go straight for dessert).
Pupuseria Las Delicias	3300 W Montrose Ave	773-267-5346	$	10 pm	Corn meal fritters stuffed with joy.
Rockwell's Neighborhood Grill	4632 N Rockwell St	773-509-1871	$	11 pm	Familiar bar food and brunchtime favorites in a friendly atmosphere.
Salam	4636 N Kedzie Ave	773-583-0776	$*	10 pm	Home of the 19-cent falafel.
Semiramis	4639 N Kedzie Ave	773-279-8900	$$	10 pm	Lebanese with great value to quality ratio. Try the sumac fries.
Thai Valley	4600 N Kedzie Ave	773-588-2020	$*	10 pm	BYOB Thai restaurant with lunch specials.

Key: $: Under $10 / $$: $10–$20 / $$$: $20–$30 / $$$$: $30–$40 / $$$$$: $40+
* : Does not accept credit cards. / † : Accepts only American Express. / † † : Accepts only Visa and Mastercard
Time listed refers to kitchen closing time on weekend nights.

Map 39 • Ravenswood / North Center

Bad Dog Tavern	4535 N Lincoln Ave	773-334-4040	$$	12 am	Food, fireplace, and folk music.
Bistro Campagne	4518 N Lincoln Ave	773-271-6100	$$	10:30 pm	Organic French fare in a cozy room.
Brioso	4603 N Lincoln Ave	773-989-9000	$$	11 pm	Lively neighborhood spot for tasty Mexican.
Budacki's Drive-In	4739 N Damen Ave	773-561-1322	$	8 pm	Artery clogging late-night eats.
Café 28	1800 W Irving Park Rd	773-528-2883	$$	10:30 pm	Trendy Cuban.
Café Selmarie	4729 N Lincoln Ave	773-989-5595	$$	11 pm	Bright clean, bakery/cafe with wine and beer.
Chalkboard	4343 N Lincoln Ave	773-477-7144	$$$	10 pm	Inventive spin on comfort classics.
Chicago Brauhaus	4732 N Lincoln Ave	773-784-4444	$$	12 am	Live German music in beerhouse atmosphere.
Diner Grill	1635 W Irving Pk Rd	773-248-2030	$*	24-hrs	Home to the infamous "Slinger." Motto: Eat it here, leave it somewhere else.
Essence of India	4601 N Lincoln Ave	773-506-0002	$$	10:30 pm	Traditional northern Indian food, fancier than Devon St.
Feed the Beast	4300 N Lincoln Ave	773-588-4280	$$	11 pm	Affordable Italian food.
First Slice Pie Café	4401 N Ravenswood Ave	773 506 1719	$$*	6 pm	Upscale café benefiting the hungry in more ways than one.
Glenn's Diner	1820 W Montrose Ave	773-506-1720	$$	9 pm	Fish-focused American fare.
Glunz Bavarian Haus	4128 N Lincoln Ave	773-472-4287	$$	11 pm	Weiner schnitzel and beer.
Golden Angel Restaurant	4340 N Lincoln Ave	773-583-6969	$*	24-hrs	24-hour diner.
House of Wah Sun	4319 N Lincoln Ave	773-477-0800	$	11:30 pm	Chinese/Cantonese/Mandarin eatery.
La Boca della Verita	4618 N Lincoln Ave	773-784-6222	$$	11 pm	Cozy Italian café.
Lincoln Restaurant	4008 N Lincoln Ave	773-248-1820	$$	11 pm	Old-school family joint. Been there forever.
Los Nopales	4544 N Western Ave	773-334-3149	$$	10 pm	Creative, cheap Mexican BYOB.
Margie's Candies	1813 W Montrose Ave	773-348-0400	$	11 pm	Ridiculously decadent sundaes and homemade confections.
Opart Thai House	4658 N Western Ave	773-989-8517	$	10:45 pm	Local favorite for fresh Thai. BYOB.
Orange Garden	1942 W Irving Park Rd	773-525-7479	$$	10 pm	Over seventy years of Cantonese cooking.
Over Easy Café	4943 N Damen Ave	773-506-2605	$	3 pm	Bright breakfast spot.
Pannenkoeken Café	4757 N Western Ave	773-769-8800	$	3 pm	It's like having dessert for breakfast!
Pizza DOC	2251 W Lawrence Ave	773-784-8777	$$	11 pm	Popular spot for wood-fired pizzas. Early for families, later for dates.
Roong-petch Restaurant	2209 W Montrose Ave	773-509-0007	$	10 pm	Vegetarians get their own special menu.
Smokin' Woody's	4160 N Lincoln Ave	773-880-1100	$$	11 pm	Ribs 'n' wings 'n' other sticky eats.
Spacca Napoli	1769 W Sunnyside Ave	773-878-2420	$$	10 pm	Neapolitan styles pizza in Ravenswood.
Sticky Rice	4018 N Western Ave	773-588-0133	$	12 am	No frills storefront serves amazing Thai for cheap!
Tank Sushi	4514 N Lincoln Ave	773-769-2600	$$	11:30 pm	Fresh sushi with Latin flair.

Map 40 • Uptown

Name	Address	Phone	Price	Time	Description
Agami	4712 N Broadway St	773-506-1845	$$$	2 am	Swanky sushi.
Anna Maria Pasteria	4400 N Clark St	773-506-2662	$$	11 pm	Cute, neighborhood Italian, casual date spot.
Café Lao	1007 W Argyle St	773-275-5092	$*	11pm	Straighforward, well-executed Vietnamese.
Café Too	4715 N Sheridan Rd	773-275-0626	$	9 pm	Uptown café provides job training for the homeless.
Deleece	4004 N Southport Ave	773-325-1710	$$	11 pm	Ambitious global fare in cute storefront.
Demera	4801 N Broadway St	773-334-8787	$$	4 pm	Neighborhood Ethiopian.
Furama	4936 N Broadway St	773-271-1161	$$	10 pm	Dim sum with karaoke.
Hai Yen Restaurant	1055 W Argyle St	773-561-4077	$$	10:30 pm	Chinese and veggie pho.
Hama Matsu	5143 N Clark St	773-506-2978	$$$	10:30 pm	Japanese and Korean fare.
JJ Fish & Chicken	4515 N Sheridan Rd	773-275-3474	$*	9 pm	Fried catfish, perch and okra…a heart attack waiting to happen.
La Banh Mi Hung Phat	4942 N Sheridan Rd	773-878-6688	$*	6pm	Savory Vietnamese sandwiches.
Magnolia Café	1224 W Wilson Ave	773-728-8785	$$	11:30 pm	American bistro.
Marigold	4832 N Broadway St	773-293-4653	$$$	11 pm	Tasty, but is it that much better than take-out?
Palace Gate	4548 N. Magnolia	773-769-1793	$$	10pm	True blue Ghanaian grub.
Pho Hoa	4925 N Broadway St	773-784-8723	$	11pm	Vietnamese soup for beginners and veterans alike.
Riques	5004 N Sheridan Rd	773-728-6200	$	11 pm	Inexpensive and creative Mexican BYOB.
Siam Noodle & Rice	4654 N Sheridan Rd	773-769-6694	$	9:30 pm	Damn fine Thai food.

Silver Seafood	4829 N Broadway St	773-784-0668	$	1 am	Asian delights from the sea.
Sun Wah BBQ	1134 W Argyle St	773-769-1254	$$	9 pm	Notable for the barbequed ducks hanging in the window.
TAC Quick	3930 N Sheridan Rd	773-327-5253	$$	11 pm	Cheap and delicious. Thai-language menu available for the adventurous.
Taqueria los Caminos de Michoacan	3948 N Sheridan Rd	773-296-9709	$	5 am	No ambiance, bad Mexican soap operas, incredibly delicious regional Mexican food.
Thai Pastry	4925 N Broadway St	773-784-5399	$	11 pm	Free pastry with every order!
Tweet	5020 N Sheridan Rd	773-728-5576	$$	10:30 pm	Gourmet food without pretension.
Unique so Chique	4600 N Magnolia Ave	773-561-0324	$	6 pm	Where else can you get an honest afternoon tea?

Map 41 • Avondale / Old Irving

The Buffet Castle	3326 W Belmont Ave	773-267-6688	$	10:30 pm	Smorgasbord, Chinese-style. MSG a plenty.
Burrito House	3145 W Addison St	773-279-9111	$	2 am	At least they're open late.
Chief O'Neill's	3471 N Elston Ave	773-583-3066	$	10 pm	Excellent traditional pub fare.
Clara's	3159 N California Ave	773-539-3020	$*	4 pm	Ultimate cheap greasy spoon.
Eat First Chinese Restaurant	3337 W Belmont Ave	773-588-7071	$	11 pm	No dining room to speak of, but super-fast delivery of standard Chinese.
Golden Rise Bakery	2957 W Diversey Ave	773-772-7620	$	7 pm	Find organic bread, ice cream and Fair Trade coffee at this bakery.
Hot Doug's	3324 N California Ave	773-279-9550	$*	4 pm	Super popular gourmet hot dogs and duck fat fries.
IHOP	2818 W Diversey Ave	773-342-8901	$	24-hrs	It's an IHOP.
Kuma's Corner	2900 W Belmont Ave	773-604-8769	$$	2 am	Heavy metal bar and grill with famous burgers and lots of ink.
La Finca	3361 N Elston Ave	773-478-4006	$	10 pm	Friendly, family run servicable Mexican and margaritas.
Mr. Pollo	3000 W Belmont Ave	773-509-1208	$	9 pm	South American chicken joint. Get a guanabana shake.
Sunshine Restaurant	3521 N Kedzie Ave	773-267-1578	$	3 pm	Grill grub.
Taqueria Trespazada	3144 N California Ave	773-539-4533	$*	2 am	Tasty, cheap tacos and salsas—no atmosphere.
Zacatecas	2934 W Diversey Ave	773-278-4828	$	3 am	Taqueria. Typical.

Map 42 • North Center / Roscoe Village / West Lakeview

Costello Sandwich & Sides	2015 W Roscoe St	773-929-2323	$	9 pm	Yummy baked sandwiches.
El Tinajon	2054 W Roscoe St	773-525-8455	$$	10 pm	Good, cheap Guatemalan. Great mango margaritas.
Kaze Sushi	2032 W Roscoe St	773-327-4860	$$	11:30 pm	Innovative, gourmet sushi.
Kitsch'n on Roscoe	2005 W Roscoe St	773-248-7372	$$	10 pm	Clever retro food and tiki bar. Friendly staff.
La Mora	2132 W Roscoe St	773-404-4555	$$	11 pm	Neighborhood Mediterranean-influenced Italian fare.
Mrs Murphy and Sons	3905 N Lincoln Ave	773-248-3905	$$$	11 pm	Fancy Irish food: An oxymoron, or reality? Decide for yourself here.
Nazarlik	1650 W Belmont Ave	773-327-5800	$*	10:30 pm	Unpretentious, family-style Turkish
Piazza Bella Trattoria	2116 W Roscoe St	773-477-7330	$$$	11 pm	Neighborhood Italian.
Sola	3868 N Lincoln Ave	773-327-3868	$$$	10:30 pm	Contemporary American with Polynesian flair.
T-Spot Sushi	3925 N Lincoln Ave	773-549-4500	$$	11 pm	Good sushi and tea in small Euro-fancy room. BYOB.
Terragusto	1851 W Addison St	773-248-2777	$$	9:30 pm	Italian market with café.
Thai Linda Café	2022 W Roscoe St	773-868-0075	$$	9:45 pm	Standard-issue neighborhood Thai.
Turquoise Restaurant on Roscoe	2147 W Roscoe St	773-549-3523	$$	12 am	Fresh and creative Middle-Eastern fare.\
Victory's Banner	2100 W Roscoe St	773-665-0227	$	3 pm	Vegetarian brunch served by toga-clad Sri Chimnoy followers.
Volo Restaurant and Wine Bar	2008 W Roscoe St	773-348-4600	$$$	12 am	New American small plates with swirl.

Map 43 • Wrigleyville / East Lakeview

Ann Sather	929 W Belmont Ave	773-348-2378	$	3 pm	Warm, family friendly ambience, Swedish comfort food.
Blue Bayou	3734 N Southport Ave	773-871-3300	$$	11 pm	New Orleans-themed, in case you couldn't guess.
Bolat	3346 N Clark St	773-665-1100	$$	11 pm	West African cuisine - try the okra with rice.
Capt'n Nemos	3650 N Ashland Ave	773-929-7687	$	9 pm	Great sandwiches and yummy soup.
Coobah	3423 N Southport Ave	773-528-2220	$$	2 am	Trendy Latin spot near Music Box.
Duck Walk	919 W Belmont Ave	773-665-0455	$	11 pm	Your basic Thai, cheap but good.
Fixture	2706 N Ashland	773-248-3331	$$	12 am	Small plates and big wine list.
Frasca	3358 N Paulina St	773-248-5222	$$	11 pm	European-style pizza with a cozy wine bar and outdoor seating.

355

Arts & Entertainment · **Restaurants**

Key: $: Under $10 / $$: $10–$20 / $$$: $20–$30 / $$$$: $30–$40 / $$$$$: $40+
* : Does not accept credit cards. / † : Accepts only American Express. / † † : Accepts only Visa and Mastercard
Time listed refers to kitchen closing time on weekend nights.

Map 43 • Wrigleyville / East Lakeview—*continued*

Golden Apple	2971 N Lincoln Ave	773-528-1413	$	24-hrs	24-hour greasy hangover food. Once featured on This American Life.
Lucky's	3472 N Clark St	773-549-0665	$	3 am	They put fries IN the sandwich. Genius.
Mama Desta's Red Sea	3216 N Clark St	773-935-7561	$$	11:30pm	No forks at this authentic Ethiopian restaurant.
Matsu Yama	1059 W Belmont Ave	773-327-8838	$$	12 am	Lovely, fresh sushi.
Matsuya	3469 N Clark St	773-248-2677	$$	11:30 pm	One of the best on Sushi Row.
Mia Francesca	3311 N Clark St	773-281-3310	$$	11 pm	Contemporary Italian date place.
Mystic Celt	3443 N Southport Ave	773-529-8550	$$	2 am	Irish pub-style restaurant. Awesome Irish eggrolls.
Orange	3231 N Clark St	773-549-4400	$$	2 pm	Super stylish brunches.
Panes	3002 N Sheffield Ave	773-665-0972	$	10 pm	Homemade sandwiches, muffins, cookies, and brownies.
Penny's Noodle Shop	3400 N Sheffield Ave	773-281-8222	$$	10:30 pm	Pad thai, pad see ew, popular place for a lite lunch.
Pierogi Factory	1034 W Belmont Ave	773-325-1015	$	9 pm	Open late to preempt your hang over.
PS Bangkok	3345 N Clark St	773-871-7777	$	11:30pm	Popular neighborhood Thai that delivers.
Rise	3401 N Southport Ave	773-525-3535	$$	11:30 pm	Sushi nightspot.
Risque Café	3419 N Clark St	773-525-7711	$$$*	2 am	Tangy barbecue and over 300 craft beers.
S&G	3000 N Lincoln Ave	773-935-4025	$	24-hrs	Cop hangout with chintzy decorating and fake plants. In other words, we love it.
Shiroi Hana	3242 N Clark St	773-477-1652	$$	10:30 pm	Standard sushi spot.
Socca	3301 N Clark St	773-248-1155	$$	11 pm	Tasty, satisfying Mediterannean.
Tango Sur	3763 N Southport Ave	773-477-5466	$$	11:30 pm	Vegetarian's vision of hell: big juicy Argentine steaks.
Twisted Spoke	3365 N Clark St	773-525-5300	$	1 am	Plays porn and serves eggs late night on weekends, slow service.
Violet	3819 N Southport Ave	773-327-0234	$$	7 pm	Precious cafe fare.
Wrigleyville Dog	3737 N Clark St	773-296-1500	$*	4 am	Post Metro stop for chili-cheese fries.

Map 44 • East Lakeview

Adesso	3332 N Broadway St	773-868-1516	$$	11:30 pm	Italian comfort food.
Angelina Ristorante	3561 N Broadway St	773-935-5933	$$$	11 pm	Casual, romantic Italian.
Ann Sather	3411 N Broadway St	773-305-0024	$	3 pm	Airy branch of local comfort food chain.
Arco de Cuchilleros	3445 N Halsted St	773-296-6046	$$$	12 am	Intimate tapas; great sangria.
The Bagel	3107 N Broadway St	773-477-0300	$	11 pm	Great deli fare.
Baladoche	2905 N Clark St	773-880-5090	$	11 pm	Don't call them waffles.
Bobtail Soda Fountain	2951 N Broadway St	773-880-7372	$	11 pm	Norman Rockwell would be proud.
Chicago Diner	3411 N Halsted St	773-935-6696	$$	11 pm	A vegetarian institution.
Clark Street Dog	3040 N Clark St	773-281-6690	$*	3 am	Late night hot dogs and cheese fries.
Cornelia's	750 W Cornelia Ave	773-248-8333	$$	11 pm	Tres Gay Boystown ski lodge / cabaret lounge.
Erwin, An American Café & Bar	2925 N Halsted St	773-528-7200	$$$$	10 pm	Elegant.
Firefly	3335 N Halsted St	773-525-2505	$$	1 am	Upscale neighborhood joint.
Half Shell	676 W Diversey Pkwy	773-549-1773	$$$*	11:30 pm	Casual raw bar.
HB	3404 N Halsted St	773-661-0299	$$	10:30 pm	Nice date spot for upscale comfort food.
Jack's on Halsted	3201 N Halsted St	773-244-9191	$$$$	11:30 pm	Great wine list.
Joy's	3257 N Broadway St	773-327-8330	$$	11 pm	Standard noodles, soup, or fried rice; impressively simple.
Koryo	2936 N Broadway St	773-477-8510	$$	11 pm	Upscale Korean.
La Creperie	2845 N Clark St	773-528-9050	$$	11 pm	Live French music. Shabby, but cute.
Las Mananitas	3523 N Halsted St	773-528-2109	$$*	12 am	Forgettable ffod, lethal margaritas.
Mark's Chop Suey	3343 N Halsted St	773-281-9090	$	11 pm	The BEST eggrolls.
New Tokyo	3139 N Broadway St	773-248-1193	$$	10:45 pm	Reasonably priced sushi and BYOB at this cozy Japanese spot.
Ping Pong Restaurant	3322 N Broadway St	773-281-7575	$$$	12 am	Always busy BYO, hit or miss Asian fusion.
Stella's Diner	3042 N Broadway St	773-472-9040	$	10 pm	Can you say diner?
Sura	3124 N Broadway St	773-248-7872	$$	2 am	Classy Thai bistro with funky swinging chairs in the bar.
Wakamono	3317 N Broadway St	773-296-6800	$$	11:30 pm	Sushi and Japanese small plates.
Yoshi's Café	3257 N Halsted St	773-248-6160	$$$	11 pm	Franco-Japanese fusion.

Northwest

Al Primo Canto	5414 W Devon Ave	773-631-0100	$$$$	10 pm	"Endless feast" of terrific Brazillian food.
Amitabul	6207 N Milwaukee Ave	773-774-0276	$$	10 pm	Buddha-inspired Korean Vegan.
Balanced Kitchen	6263 N McCormick Blvd	773-463-1085	$$	7 pm	No meat, dairy, or wheat. Why live?
Big Pho	3821 W Lawrence Ave	773-866-2015	$*	10pm	Vietnamese comfort food in a bowl.
Birria Huentitan	4019 W North Ave	773-276-0768	$*	24-hrs	Cheap late night eats and huge burritos.
Blue Angel	5310 N Milwaukee Ave	773-631-8700	$	24-hrs	Chicago's only stunt-flier-themed 24-hour diner.
Borincuba	3424 W Irving Park Rd	773-866-2822	$$	8 pm	Home-cooking from Cuba and Puerto Rico.
Brown Sack	3706 W Armitage Ave	773-661-0675	$*	7 pm	Pick up gourmet sandwiches and amazing malts or milkshakes.
Café con Leche	2714 N Milwaukee Ave	773-289-4274	$*	8 pm	Huevos con chorizo and a quick cup of joe start the morning right.
Carthage Café	3446 W Foster Ave	773-539-9004	$$	3 am	Hook up with a hookah and taste exotic Tunisian specialtes.
Chai Asian Bistro	4748 W Peterson Ave	773-481-0008	$	10 pm	Good by any standard. Great for the Northwest side.
Chiyo	3800 W Lawrence Ave	773-267-1555	$$$	12 am	Order their 7-course kaiseki menu a few days in advance. Otherwise, opt for the sukiyaki.
Chocolate Shoppe Ice Cream	5337 W Devon Ave	773-763-9778	$*	11 pm	Ice cream shop on acid.
Don Juan	6730 N Northwest Hwy	773-775-6438	$$	11 pm	Popular Mexican spot.
Edgebrook Coffee Shop	6322 N Central Ave	773-792-1433	$*	2 pm	Old-school homemade diner grub.
El Cubanito	2555 N Pulaski Rd	773-235-2555	$*	5 pm	Yummy Cuban sammiches.
Elliott's Seafood Grille & Chop House	6690 N Northwest Hwy	773-775-5277	$$$	11pm	Grilling steaks and seafood for 70 years.
Fonda Del Mar	3749 W Fullerton Ave	773-489-3748	$$	11 pm	Stylish Mexican food minus the price tag.
Friendship Chinese Restaurant	2830 N Milwaukee Ave	773-227-0970	$$	10:30 pm	Classy Chinese.
Gale Street Inn	4914 N Milwaukee Ave	773-725-1300	$$$	10:30 pm	Classy ribs 'n' jazz joint.
Gloria's Café	3300 W Fullerton Ave	773-342-1050	$$	9 pm	Columbian comfort food and cafe fare.
Grota Smorgasborg	3112 N Central Ave	773-622-4677	$$	10 pm	All-you-can-eat chow in medieval-feeling banquet hall.
Halina's Polish Delights	5914 W Lawrence Ave	773-205-0256	$*	9 pm	Tiny authentic Polish diner.
Hiromi's	3609 W Lawrence Ave	773-588-6764	$	2 am	Phillipino and Japanese food. Tagalong karaoke (English on request).
Joy Ribs	6320 N Lincoln Ave	773-509-0211	$$	12 pm	Korean BBQ done one better with a zingy marinade.
La Villa Restaurant	3638 N Pulaski Rd	773-283-7980	$$	1:30 am	Neighborhood family-friendly eatery.
Mario's Café	5241 N Harlem Ave	773-594-9742	$	2:30 am	Need a quick Bulgarian fix? Mario's is the place.
Mayan Sol	3830 W Lawrence Ave	773-539-4398	$$*	10 pm	Upscale Central American and South American cuisine.
Mirabell	3454 W Addison St	773-463-1962	$$	11 pm	Adorable German tavern.
Montasero's Ristorante	3935 W Devon Ave	773-588-2515	$$	10 pm	Don't be surprised to find an envelope full of unmarked bills in the toilet tank.
Pollo Campero	2730 N Narragansett Ave	773-622-6657	$	10 pm	Guatemalan fried-chicken chain.
Red Apple	3121 N Milwaukee Ave	773-588-5781	$	9:30 pm	Polish comfort food. Is there any other kind?
Ristorante Agostino	2817 N Harlem Ave	773-745-6464	$$	11 pm	Elegant date place for impeccable Italian.
Sabatino's	4441 W Irving Park Rd	773-283-8331	$$	12:30 am	Romantic date place.
Seo Hae	3534 W Lawrence Ave	773-539-2444	$$	10 pm	No frills family-owned Korean place.
Shiraz	4425 W Montrose Ave	773-777-7275	$$	10 pm	Try a Koobideh at this Persian spot.
Smak-Tak	5961 N Elston Ave	773-763-1123	$	9 pm	Great pierogis on a penny budget.
Smoque	3800 N Pulaski Rd	773-545-7427	$$	10 pm	BYOBBBQ!
So Gong Dong Tofu House	3307 W Bryn Mawr Ave	773-539-8377	$$	10 pm	Yummy Korean tofu soup spot.
Sol de Mexico	3018 N Cicero Ave	773-282-4119	$$$	10 pm	Creative, upscale Mexican food in a dressed-up taqueria.
Super Pollo	3640 W Wrightwood Ave	773-278-9227	$	9:30 pm	Cheap, delicious Puerto Rican.
Teresa II Polish Restaurants & Lounge	4751 N Milwaukee Ave	773-283-0184	$$*	11 pm	Clean your plate or Teresa will scold you.
Trattoria Pasta D'Arte	6311 N Milwaukee Ave	773-763-1181	$$	11 pm	Upscale, creative Italian.
Tre Kronor	3258 W Foster Ave	773-267-9888	$$	10 pm	Swedish institution.
Via Veneto	6340 N Lincoln Ave	773-267-0888	$$$	11 pm	Trattoria food in a banquet hall body.
Zia's Trattoria	6699 N Northwest Hwy	773-775-0808	$$$	11pm	Edison Park's version of swanky.

West

Amarind's	6822 W North Ave	773-889-9999	$$	10 pm	People drive from all over for awesome Thai food.
Bacchanalia Ristorante	2413 S Oakley Ave	773-254-6555	$$*	11 pm	Cozy Italian spot.
Bruna's	2424 S Oakley Ave	773-254-5550	$$	11 pm	Cozy old-school Italian.

357

Key: $: Under $10 / $$: $10–$20 / $$$: $20–$30 / $$$$: $30–$40 / $$$$$: $40+
* : Does not accept credit cards. / † : Accepts only American Express. / † † : Accepts only Visa and Mastercard
Time listed refers to kitchen closing time on weekend nights.

West—*continued*

CJ's Eatery	3839 W Grand Ave	773-292-0990	$$	9 pm	Diner meets soul food meets south of the border.
Coco	2723 W Division St	773-384-4811	$$$	1 am	Upscale contemporary and classic Puerto Rican.
Coleman's Hickory House	5754 W Chicago Ave	773-287-0363	$	3 am	Killer chicken and ribs at dirt cheap prices.
Depot	5840 W Roosevelt Rd	773-261-8422	$	10 pm	Lovingly homemade diner classics
Edna's Restaurant	3175 W Madison St	773-638-7079	$	7 pm	Best soul food on the west side.
El Salvador Restaurante	4125 S Archer Ave	773-579-0405	$$*	9 pm	Pupusas and more.
Falco's Pizza	2806 W 40th St	773-523-7996	$	1:30 am	Popular casual Italian spot.
Feed	2803 W Chicago Ave	773-489-4600	$$*	10 pm	Tasty grilled chicken.
Flying Saucer	1123 N California Ave	773-342-9076	$$	10 pm	Creative diner fare at hipster hangout.
Haro	2436 S Oakley Ave	773-847-2400	$$	1 am	The small plate madness is spreading!!!
Humboldt Pie	1001 N California Ave	773-342-4743	$	10 pm	Spacious, eccentric coffeehouse and pizza place.
I.C.Y. Vegetarian Restaurant & Juice Bar	3141 W Roosevelt Rd	773-762-1090	$	11pm	Veggie diner fare.
Ignotz	2421 S Oakley Ave	773-579-0300	$$*	11 pm	Northern Italian in cozy setting.
La Palma	1340 N Homan Ave	773-862-0886	$	8 pm	Authentic Puerto Rican grub at no-frills cafeteria.
Lalo's	3515 W 26th St	773-522-0345	$$	10 pm	Local chain popular for their margaritas.
Lindy's and Gertie's	3685 S Archer Ave	773-927-7807	$	12 am	Local chili and ice-cream chain.Try the chili-ice-cream sundae.
MacArthur's	5412 W Madison Ave	773-261-2316	$*	9 pm	Sweet potatoes, collard greens, and grits, cafeteria style.
Maiz	1041 N California Ave	773-276-3149	$*	10 pm	Homemade corn masa antojito heaven.
New Submarine Pier	4048 S Archer Ave	773-890-4733	$*	10 pm	Best subs on this side of town.
Taqueria Atotonilco	3916 W 26th St	773-762-3380	$*	11 pm	Quick, friendly eat-in or take-out hangover cure-all.
Taqueria Los Comales	3141 W 26th St	773-247-0977	$*	5 am	Stop for excellent tacos on your way home from jail.
Taqueria Los Gallos 2	4252 S Archer Ave	773-254-2081	$*	12am	Homestyle food from Jalisco.
Taqueria Puebla Mexico	3625 W North Ave	773-772-8435	$*	9 pm	Authentic Mexican from the Puebla region.
TipsyCake	1043 N California Ave	773-384-4418	$$$	6 pm	Sumptuous cakes.
Tommy's Rock-n-Roll Café	2548 W Chicago Ave	773-486-6768	$	4 pm	Homemade donuts, sandwiches, and guitars.

Southwest

Beverly Woods Restaurant	11532 S Western Ave	773-233-7700	$$$	8 pm	Banqueting traditional in original Beverly Hills.
Birrieria de la Torre	6724 S Pulaski Rd	773-767-6075	$*	10pm	Soup, soup, oh Mexican soup...
Bobak's	5275 S Archer Ave	773-735-5334	$	9 pm	A melange of Polish buffet and supermarket, Chicago style.
Café 103	1909 W 103rd St	773-238-5115	$$$	10 pm	Finally, fine-dining in Beverly.
Fox's Beverly Restaurant and Pizza	9956 S Western Ave	773-239-3212	$$	10 pm	Sweet sauce + crispy thin crust = the southside's best pizza.
Franconello's Italian Restaurant	10222 S Western Ave	773-881-4100	$$	11 pm	Peek-a-boo with the chefs in the exhibition kitchen as they crank out old-world class.
Harold's Chicken Shack	7247 S Racine Ave	773-783-9499	$*	2 am	Stand out branch of local chicken chain.
Hoe China Tea	4020 W 55th St	773-284-2463	$	9:30 pm	Come for the fruity cocktails.
Janson's Drive-In / Snyder's Red Hots	9900 S Western Ave	773-238-3612	$*	10 pm	No indoor seating at this classic drive-thru.
Koda	10352 S Western Ave	773-445-5632	$$$	11 pm	No surprises in this servicable Beverly Bistrot.
Lagniappe	1525 W 79th St	773-994-6375	$$	8 pm	Like a trip to N'Awlins but with better food.
Lume's	11601 S Western Ave	773-233-2323	$	3:45 pm	Where the beautiful people breakfast and lunch 'til evening.
Nile	3259 W 63rd St	773-434-7218	$	11pm	Possibly the best Middle Eastern grub in Chicago.
The Original Vito and Nick's Pizzeria	8433 S Pulaski Rd	773-735-2050	$$*	11 pm	Da pizza's all dat matters here, kay?
Rhythm & Spice	2501 W 79th St	773-476-5600	$	10pm	Order the jerk chicken, duh.
Sunugal	2051 E 79th St	773-721-5600	S	10:30 pm	Friendly Sengalese for cheap.
Szalas	5214 S Archer Ave	773-582-0300	$$$	11 pm	Outrageously campy decor!
Tatra Inn	6040 S Pulaski Rd	773-582-8313	$	8 pm	Eastern European smorgasbord.

Top Notch Beefburger	2116 W 95th St	773-445-7218	$*	8:30 pm	Burgers and fries in 50's environment—very Happy Days.
Uncle Joe's Jerk	10210 S Vincennes Ave	773-779-9966	$	8 pm	Beverly Plaza location, where jerk salad is to slay for.
Veggie Bite	3031 W 111th St	773-239-4367	$	10 pm	Vegan fast food. Budget, belly, and bovine friendly.

South

Army & Lou's	422 E 75th St	773-483-3100	$$	10 pm	Southside soul food.
Atomic Sub	6353 S Cottage Grove Ave	773-684-2602	$*	3 pm	Watch out, the bomb has hit!
Barbara Ann's BBQ	7617 S Cottage Grove Ave	773-651-5300	S*	12 am	Better than average 'cue and links.
BJ's Market & Bakery	8734 S Stony Island Ave	773-374-4700	$	9 pm	Popular sunday soul food buffet.
Café Trinidad	557 E 75th St	773-846-8081	$$	9 pm	Great seafood options like curry crab and red snapper.
Cal Harbor Restaurant	546 E 115th St	773-264-5435	$*	6 pm	Omelettes, burgers, etc. at family grill.
Captain Hard Times	436 E 79th St	773-487-2900	$$$	12 am	Southside date destination.
Chatham Pancake House	700 E 87th St	773-874-0010	$	3 pm	Cheap, hearty breakfast.
Dat Old Fashioned Donut	8251 S Cottage Grove Ave	773-723-1002	$*	10 pm	Krispy Kreme, eat your heart out.
Helen's Restaurant	1732 E 79th St	773-933-9871	$*	7 pm	Southern cafeteria with downhome cooking.
Izola's	522 E 79th St	773-846-1484	$$	24-hrs	Homey southern food in 24-hour diner.
Lem's	311 E 75th St	773-994-2428	$*	2 am	The gold standard of BBQ joints.
Leon's Bar-B-Que	8249 S Cottage Grove Ave	773-488-4556	$*	3 am	Southside BBQ fixture.
Old Fashioned Donuts	11248 S Michigan Ave	773-995-7420	$	6 pm	Donuts as an art form.
The Parrot Cage	7059 S South Shore Dr	773-602-5333	$$$	10 pm	Fine dining brought to you by Washburne College culinary students.
Phil's Kastle	3532 E 95th St	773-734-9591	$*	24-hrs	50s soda shop with prices to match.
Pupuseria El Salvador	3557 E 106th St	773-374-0490	$	7 pm	Addictive Central American stuffed griddle patties.
The Rib Joint	432 W 87th St	773-651-4108	$	12:45 am	What else? Ribs, of course!
Seven Seas Submarine	11216 S Michigan Ave	773-785-0550	$*	8 pm	Dine in or take out at this tiny sandwich shop.
Soul Queen	9031 S Stony Island Ave	773-731-3366	$	12 am	Inexpensive comfort food.
Soul Vegetarian East	205 E 75th St	773-224-0104	$$	11 pm	Vegetarian soul food? SVE pleases even the skeptics.
Tropic Island Jerk Chicken	1922 E 79th St	773-978-5375	$	11 pm	Caribbean carry-out.
Uncle John's Barbecue	337 E 69th Pl	773-892-1233	$*	10 pm	Heavenly bbq for takeout only.
Vegetarian Fun Foods Supreme	1702 E 87th	773-734-6321	$*	10pm	Veggie fast food dive
Yassa African Caribbean	716 E 79th St	773-488-5599	$$	10 pm	Lots of vegetarian options at this Sengalese spot.

Evanston

Blind Faith Café	525 Dempster St	847-328-6875	$$	10 pm	Vegetarian. Healthy, fiber-filled fare for the Birkenstock set. Food so earthy, you'll need to floss the dirt from your teeth.
Buffalo Joe's	812 Clark St	847-328-5525	$*	12 am	Kick-ass wings and more!
Café Mozart	600 Davis St	847-492-8056	$	11 pm	Wireless Internet, leopard couch, snarky staff.
Clarke's	720 Clark St	847-864-1610	$	2 am	Inexpensive sandwiches and omelettes.
Dave's Italian Kitchen	1635 Chicago Ave	847-864-6000	$$	10:45 pm	Family pizza joint with a killer wine list.
Dixie Kitchen and Bait Shop	825 Church St	847-733-9030	$$	11 pm	Hot cornmeal johnnycakes, fried green tomatoes, corn fritters, North Carolina pulled pork and black eyed peas. Lawd!
Dozika	601 Dempster St	847-869-9740	$$	10 pm	Pan-Asian cuisine. Expensive, but nice variety.
Hecky's Barbeque	1902 Green Bay Rd	847-492-1182	$$	10 pm	It's the sauce that's the boss.
Joy Yee's Noodle Shop	521 Davis St	847-733-1900	$$	10:30 pm	Pricey, trendy "bubble tea" specialists.
Kafein Café	1621 Chicago Ave	847-491-1621	$	2 am	Open 'til 2 am on weeknights and 3 am on weekends, perfect for those late-night cram sessions.
Kansaku	1514 Sherman Ave	847-864-4386	$$$	10pm	Chic but approachable sushi.
Las Palmas	817 University Pl	847-328-2555	$$	11 pm	High-priced margaritas; fresh Mexican fare.
The Lucky Platter	514 Main St	847-869-4064	$$	10 pm	Unique comfort food complimented by David Lynch-esque folk art décor.
Lulu's Dim Sum and Then Sum	804 Davis St	847-869-4343	$$	11 pm	Best Pad Thai in Evanston. Huge portions, reasonably priced.
Mt Everest	630 Church St	847-491-1069	$$$	10 pm	Nepalese and Indian food with lunch buffet.

Key: $: Under $10 / $$: $10–$20 / $$$: $20–$30 / $$$$: $30–$40 / $$$$$: $40+
* : Does not accept credit cards. / † : Accepts only American Express. / † †: Accepts only Visa and Mastercard
Time listed refers to kitchen closing time on weekend nights.

Evanston—*continued*

Mustard's Last Stand	1613 Central St	847-864-2700	$*	10:30 pm	Legendary hot dog institution.
Narra	1710 Orrington Ave	847-866-8700	$$$$	10 pm	Unpretentious fine dining in the Hotel Orrington.
Noodles & Company	930 Church St	847-733-1200	$$	10 pm	Thai noodles, pasta, even mac and cheese!
Olive Mountain	610 Davis St	847-475-0380	$$	10:30 pm	Middle Eastern specialties.
Pete Miller's Original Steakhouse	1557 Sherman Ave	847-328-0399	$$$$$	1:30 am	American. Beef bubbas stake out this joint.
Tapas Barcelona	1615 Chicago Ave	847-866-9900	$$$	11 pm	Spanish. Lick your fingers with friends over tasty tapas and sangria.
Trattoria Demi	1571 Sherman Ave	847-332-2330	$$	10 pm	Good Italian food in a cozy setting.
Unicorn Café	1723 Sherman Ave	847-332-2312	$*	12 am	Quaint and reasonably priced.
Va Pensiero	1566 Oak Ave	847-475-7779	$$$$$	10 pm	Italian. Classy, romantic supper club offering over 250 Italian wines. A "pop the question" kind of place.
Vive la Crepe	1565 Sherman Ave	847-570-0600	$$	10pm	Cute psuedo-French place for a cheap date.

Oak Park

Buzz Café	905 S Lombard Ave	708-524-2899	$	9 pm	Neighborhood-centric, good food, quirky art, live story-telling, and music. Nuff said!
Café Le Coq	734 Lake St	708-848-2233	$$$$	10 pm	French Bistro wows Oak Park foodies, just down the street from many of Oak Park's sites.
Cucina Paradiso	814 North Blvd	708-848-3434	$$$	10:30 pm	Italian. Fork-twirling Oak Parkers come a-datin' at this friendly pasta place and bar.
Jeruselum Café	1030 Lake St	708-848-7734	$$	11 pm	Terrific Middle Eastern food, with an extensive juice bar.
Khyber Pass	1031 Lake St	708-445-9032	$$	10 pm	Indian. Taxi drivers and curry-loving locals fill up on lunch and dinner buffets.
Mama Thai	1112 W Madison St	708-386-0100	$$	10 pm	Inexpensive, charming, and delicious.
Marion Street Grill	189 N Marion St	708-383-1551	$$$	10 pm	Inviting, upscale restaurant featuring fresh seafood, steaks, and chops. Impressive wine list.
New Rebozo	1116 Madison St	708-445-0370	$$$	10:30 pm	Best Mexican in town with a delicious upscale tweak to the specials.
Oak Park Abbey	728 Lake St	708-358-8840	$$	11 pm	Small plates have struck Oak Park and continue to spread!
Pete's Red Hots	6346 W Roosevelt Rd	708-383-6122	$*	12 am	Fast food at its finest. Best fries ever.
Petersen Ice Cream	1100 Chicago Ave	708-386-6131	$$	10 pm	American. Comfort food and silky ice cream make this diner a popular destination.
Philander's Oak Park	1120 Pleasant St	708-848-4250	$$$$	11:30 pm	Seafood. Marine cuisine served in handsome atmosphere; nightly, fishtail to live jazz.
Poor Phil's	139 S Marion St	708-848-0871	$$	1 am	Popcorn is free; popcorn shrimp isn't.

Navy Pier

Bubba Gump Shrimp Co	700 E Grand Ave	312-252-4867	$$	12 am	Navy Pier tourist trap.
Capi's Italian Kitchen	700 E Grand Ave	312-276-0641	$$	10 pm	Hand-tossed brick oven pizza.
Joe's Be-Bop Café & Jazz Emporium	700 E Grand Ave	312-595-5299	$$$	10 pm	Live jazz and Southern food from the owners of Jazz Showcase.
Riva	700 E Grand Ave	312-644-7482	$$$	11 am	Touristic fine dining on the Pier.

Skokie

Barnum and Bagel	4700 Dempster St	847-676-4466	$	9 pm	Eat-in deli popular with families.
Don's Fishmarket	9335 Skokie Blvd	847-677-3424	$$$	11 pm	Popular seafood restaurant features "Shrimp Extravaganza", "Crabfest", and "Lobsterfest."
El Tipico	3341 Dempster St	847-676-4070	$$	11:30 pm	Skokie's favorite margarita and burrito joint.
Grecian Kitchen Delights	3938 Dempster St	847-677-5507	$	9 pm	Mostly carryout with good value Greek Chicken.
Hub's Ribs	3727 Dempster St	847-673-9409	$	12 am	Nothing kosher or vegetarian-friendly about this local bbq favorite.
Hy Life Bistro	4120 Dempster St	847-674-2021	$$$*	9 pm	Kosher restaurant that is vegetarian-friendly.
Kabul House	3320 Dempster St	847-763-9930	$$	10 pm	One of Chicagoland's few Afghani restaurants.
Kaufman's Deli	4905 Dempster St	847-677-9880	$	8 pm	This is THE deli that people return to. Best bagels in the Midwest.
Papillon	5111 Brown St	847-763-1322	$$$	10 pm	French fine dining in downtown Skokie.
Pita Inn	3910 Dempster	847-677-0211	$	12 am	Local favorite for cheap, speedy falafel and shawerma.
Ruby of Siam	9420 Skokie Blvd	847-675-7008	$$	11 pm	Authentic and appealing Thai food.
Shallots Bistro	4741 Main St	847-677-3463	$$$$	10 pm	Kosher fine dining—closed Fridays and Saturdays

Chicago is a city of neighborhoods, and as such, we are a city of great little neighborhood taverns. These are the places where the beer you drink is on tap, the bartender throws a basket of pretzels in front of you when you grab your stool, and on any given weekday between 5 and 7 you're likely to see the same sad sacks you see every night, stealing precious time between the bossman and the kids. And then there's the jukebox. The best ones feature all your favorite bar songs, from Hank Williams to The Cars, Blondie to Sly and the Family Stone, and "My Way" sung in Polish or Korean just for the hell of it.

Dive Bars

Rub shoulders with the characters from a Nelson Algren story at any of the following joints: **Cal's (Map 5)** in the South Loop attracts local winos along with shaggy looking roadies and local slummers from the nearby University Center. In Old Town, the **Old Town Ale House (Map 31)** was once voted best dive bar in the country by someone-mumblemumble-we-forget-who. In Rogers Park, **The Lamp Post (Map 34)** has long drawn a friendly crowd of boozy locals.

Arty Crowd

Young urban arty types have carved out their kitsch-embracing niches at Ukrainian Village and Wicker Park spots such as **Club Foot (Map 21)**, **The Gold Star Bar (Map 21)**, **The Inner Town Pub (Map 21)**, **Lava Lounge (Map 21)**, **Rainbo Club (Map 21)**, and **Small Bar (Map 21)**, while their Pilsen and River West brethren drink their PBR at **Skylark (Map 26)** and **The Fulton Lounge (Map 24)**, respectively. On the west side, **The California Clipper (West Chicago)** appeals to today's rat pack wannabes, and on the north side, get drunk with happy hipsters and local punters at **The Village Tap (Map 42)**, **The Long Room (Map 39)**, and **the Edgewater Lounge (Map 37)**.

South Side

Bridgeport denizens cheer on the home team at neighborhood spot **Schaller's (Map 13)**. Further south, University of Chicago Poindexters have been sipping suds at **The Woodlawn Tap (Map 19)** and **The Cove (Map 20)** since the ivy was only neigh high.

Live Music

Some of Chicago's best live music venues are also neighborhood spots. **The Velvet Lounge (Map 11)**, in the near south side, is a legendary avant-garde jazz dive of the old school tradition. **Katerina's (Map 39)**, on an unassuming stretch of Irving Park in North Center, features regular live gypsy music along with local acts. In the West Village, the **Empty Bottle (Map 21)** is the place to catch touring indie bands. Further west, **Rosa's Lounge (Northwest Chicago)** is a friendly venue for live blues. Catch jazz legend Von Freeman jamming at **Chatham's New Apartment Lounge (South Chicago)** every Wednesday night, or live jazz any night of the week at **Uptown's Green Mill Lounge (Map 40)**. In the northwest side, **The Abbey Pub (Northwest)** features everything from alternative rock acts like The Breeders and Peaches, to singer-songwriter showcases and burlesque. If you want to put some twang in your thang, alt-country acts from the Bloodshot Records label regularly perform at **Bucktown's Hideout (Map 29)**.

Shake a Tailfeather

In Chicago, even the best place to get your groove on is often the one right around the corner. Despite the concentration of huge, dazzling and super expensive high-concept nightclubs in River North and River West, (which are typically the domains of tourists and suburbanites), many local folk prefer smaller, friendlier, more intimate, and cheaper local options to catch Saturday (or Monday, or Thursday) night fever. In Lincoln Park, **Neo (Map 30)** attracts children of the Eighties and their wannabes with retro dance tunes ranging from goth to new wave. Legendary gay bar **Berlin (Map 43)**, in Lakeview, draws a pansexual crowd for their ever-rotating array of theme nights. In the East Village, **Sonotheque (Map 24)** is the place to catch the latest beats.

Shout Outs

Of course, sometimes a neighborhood lounge becomes so popular that it starts to attract folks from outside its zip code range. **Delilah's (Map 29)** in Lincoln Park draws aging punkers from all over the city for their excellent punk rock jukebox, occasional celebrity guest dj's, and great selection of scotches. And speaking of selections, the selection of Belgian beers at Andersonville's **Hopleaf (Map 40)** is hard to beat, and so are the crowds who mass there. Finally, a couple honorable shout-outs to **Michelle Fire's Big Chicks (Map 40)**, a welcoming gay club in Uptown featuring Michelle's outstanding original artwork collection, and **Chief O'Neill's (Map 41)**, an Avondale pub with live Irish music, great pub grub, and loads of craic.

Map 1 • River North / Fulton Market District

Emmit's Irish Pub & Eatery	495 N Milwaukee Ave	312-563-9631	An old-school Chicago establishment.
Funky Buddha Lounge	728 W Grand Ave	312-666-1695	See and be seen at this trendy live music lounge.
The Motel Bar	600 W Chicago Ave	312-822-2900	Hotel bar without the hourly rates!
Rednofive & Fifth Floor	440 N Halsted St	312-733-6699	Two levels of existence: downstairs=dancing, upstairs=posing.
Richard's Bar	491 N Milwaukee Ave	312-733-2251	Old man bar good for starter drinks.

Map 2 • Near North / River North

Andy's	11 E Hubbard St	312-642-6805	Old-school jazz…a Chicago legend.
Bin 36	339 N Dearborn St	312-755-9463	Wineology 101.
Blue Frog Bar & Grill	676 N La Salle Dr	312-943-8900	Chutes and Ladders, Howdy Doody, and Karaoke.
Brehon Pub	731 N Wells St	312-642-1071	Irish pub, lots of TVs for Masterpiece Theater…uh, sports.

Gentry	440 N State St	312-836-0933	A piano bar is one of the many features of this multi-themed gay club.
Green Door Tavern	678 N Orleans St	312-664-5496	A Chicago landmark; old-school classic.
Howl at the Moon	26 W Hubbard St	312-863-7427	Late-night dinner and pianists who encourage patrons to sing.
Martini Park	151 W Erie St	312-640-0577	Trendy, cavernous spot with a long martini list.
Martini Ranch	311 W Chicago Ave	312-335-9500	Martinis and after-work mingling.
Ontourage	157 W. Ontario	312-573-1470	Fat chance getting near any of the celebrities who come here.
Pippin's Tavern	806 N Rush St	312-787-5435	Old union haunt = lots of beer.
Pops for Champagne	601 N State St	312-266-POPS	Jazz and champers.
Redhead Piano Bar	16 W Ontario St	312-640-1000	Snug piano bar favorite of the area.
Rockwell Lounge	710 N Clark St	312-787-2675	Posh champagne and caviar club.
Rossi's Liquors	412 N State St	312-644-5775	A dive in the best sense of the word.
Sound Bar	226 W. Ontario	312-787-4480	High-end bells and whistles dance club with tough door.
Spy Bar	646 N Franklin St	312-587-8779	Basement club, house music, fashionable crowd, pricey drinks.
Streeter's Tavern	50 E Chicago Ave	312-944-5206	Ritzy dive bar for students and tourists.
Swirl Wine Bar	111 W Hubbard St	312-828-9000	Nibble upstairs on Pan-Asian food, and recline downstairs to lounge.
Vision	640 N Dearborn St	312-266-1944	Attached to Excalibur; a modern alternative to the oxygen bar.

Map 3 · Streeterville / Mag Mile

Billy Goat Tavern	430 N Michigan Ave	312-222-1525	Cheezboiga; no fries, chips; pepsi, no coke.
Dick's Last Resort	435 E Illinois St	312-836-7870	Between Mardi Gras and Hell.
Reagle Beagle	160 E Grand Ave	312-755-9645	Relive the 80s at this cozy bar & grill.
Timothy O'Toole's Pub	622 N Fairbanks Ct	312-642-0700	Irish sports bar with tons of TV space.

Map 4 · West Loop Gate / Greek Town

| Dylan's | 118 S Clinton St | 312-876-2008 | Unpretentious West Looper with grub. |
| Snuggery Saloon & Dining Room | 225 S Canal St | 312-441-9334 | Commuter bar inside Union Station. |

Map 5 · The Loop

Cal's	400 S Wells St	312-922-6392	Dictionary definition of "dump" that draws grungy rockers and neighborhood drunks.
Exchequer Pub	226 S Wabash Ave	312-939-5633	Loop location for the working class.
Manhattans	415 S Dearborn St	312-957-0460	Tired of martini bars? Try small but fun Manhattans.
Miller's Pub	134 S Wabash Ave	312-263-4988	A Loop tradition.
Petterino's	150 N Dearborn St	312-422-0150	Go to church on Sunday, then cabaret here on Monday.

Map 6 · The Loop / Grant Park

| Houlihan's | 111 E Wacker Dr | 312-616-FOOD | Trendy, semi-obnoxious sports bar. |

Map 8 · South Loop / Printers Row / Dearborn Park

Buddy Guy's Legends	754 S Wabash Ave	312-427-0333	One of the oldest blues clubs in Chicago, and the hardest to get a drink in.
George's Cocktail Lounge	646 S Wabash Ave	312-427-3964	Columbia students and faculty quaff in this dive between classes.
Kasey's Tavern	701 S Dearborn St	312-427-7992	108-year-old neighborhood oasis.
South Loop Club	701 S State St	312-427-2787	There's something creepy about this place.
Tantrum	1023 S State St	312-939-9160	Tucked-away, nicely appointed bar that attracts a lively South Loop following.

Map 9 · South Loop / South Michigan Ave

| Kitty O'Shea's | 720 S Michigan Ave | 312-294-6860 | Cool Irish spot…may turn your hair green. |
| Savoy Bar and Grill | 800 S Michigan Ave | 312-939-1464 | Serious drinking in a kooky '50s hotel; early morning breakfast. |

Map 11 · South Loop / McCormick Place

The Chicago Legends	2109 S Wabash Ave	312-326-0300	25-and-over cocktail lounge / nightclub.
Reggie's	2105 S State St	312-949-0120	Record store, all-age live music venue, and sports bar & grill all in one place.
Velvet Lounge	67 E Cermak Rd	312-791-9050	Raw, gritty jazz haven.
Wabash Tap	1233 S Wabash Ave	312-360-9488	South Loop, no ties, relax-after-work joint.

Map 13 · Bridgeport (East)

Cobblestone's Bar and Grill	514 W Pershing Rd	773-624-3630	Keep it down during a Sox game.
Jimbo's Lounge	3258 S Princeton Ave	312-326-3253	Walk in with a Cubs hat…we dare you!
Schaller's Pump	3714 S Halsted St	773-376-6332	Neighborhood Sox bar with grub.

Map 16 • Bronzeville

Jokes & Notes	4641 S King Dr	773-373-3390	Upscale comedy/jazz club on fire, with stainless steel bar.

Map 19 • Hyde Park

Seven Ten Lanes	1055 E 55th St	773-347-2695	1920s décor in Hyde Park haven.
Woodlawn Tap & Liquor Store	1172 E 55th St	773-643-5516	U of Chicago legend.

Map 20 • East Hyde Park / Jackson Park

Bar Louie	5500 S South Shore Dr	773-363-5300	Corporate chain martini bar.
The Cove	1750 E 55th St	773-684-1013	Down-and-outers meet life-of-the-minders.

Map 21 • Wicker Park / Ukrainian Village

Beachwood Inn	1415 N Wood St	773-486-9806	Atari, potato chips and basement-price beers.
Between Boutique Café & Lounge	1324 N Milwaukee Ave	773-292-0585	Home of the beer martini.
Borderline	1954 W North Ave	773-278-5138	When you really shouldn't have one more, but you do anyway, you have it here.
Club Foot	1824 W Augusta Blvd	773-489-0379	Cool rock bar, cheap drinks, and DJs every night.
Davenport's	1383 N Milwaukee Ave	773-278-1830	Once legendary skanker bar, now yuppy fern bar. Whattya gonna do?
Debonair Social Club	1575 N Milwaukee	773-227-7990	Friendly and glam go hand in hand in this hipster club.
Double Door	1572 N Milwaukee Ave	773-489-3160	Top local and national alt-rock acts.
Empire Liquors	1566 N Milwaukee Ave	773-278-1600	Eclectic DJs and overflow crowds.
Empty Bottle	1035 W Western Ave	773-276-3600	Avant-garde jazz and indie rock. Smells like cat.
Estelle's Café & Lounge	2013 W North Ave	773-782-0450	Lat time we were here a girl puked on my shoes and no one cared.
Gold Star Bar	1755 W Division St	773-227-8700	Hear the Cars and Cash in under an hour.
Happy Village	1059 N Wolcott Ave	773-486-1512	Ping pong inside, lush beer garden outside—a divey gem.
Inner Town Pub	1935 W Thomas St	773-235-9795	Wicker Park art dorks.
Innjoy	2051 W Division St	773-394-2066	WP Scene-ster place for drinking and local acts.
Jun Bar	2050 W Division	773-486-6700	Casual lounge with house music on weekends.
Lava Lounge	1270 N Milwaukee Ave	773-342-5282	Former dive bar has reopened as a swank club.
Phyllis' Musical Inn	1800 W Division St	773-486-9862	Divey hot-spot for local music acts.
Pontiac Café	1531 N Damen Ave	773-252-7767	Redneck Bingo on Sundays!
Rainbo Club	1150 N Damen Ave	773-489-5999	Cool-kid mecca and favorite hang of local celeb John Cusack. Enough said.
Rodan	1530 N Milwaukee Ave	773-276-7036	Ultra modern lounge—video mirrors in the bathrooms.
Small Bar	2049 W Division St	773-772-2727	Small is the new big at this hipster-cool, cozy hang.
Subterranean Cabaret & Lounge	2011 W North Ave	773-278-6600	Semi-cool music spot.
Vintage Wine Bar	1942 W Division St	773-772-3400	Way-cool retro-look wine bar with solid wine list.
The Violet Hour	1520 N Damen Ave	773-252-1500	Speakeasy that makes perfect drinks. Get there early.

Map 22 • Noble Square / Goose Island

Crobar	1543 N Kingsbury St	312-266-1900	Club creatures come for the music, tourists come for the creatures.
Exit	1315 W North Ave	773-395-2700	Ooohhh. Dark and scary. Eighties punk/goth throwback.
Hot Shots	1440 N Dayton St	312-654-8204	Romanian music.
Joe's	940 W Weed St	312-337-3486	Huge sports bar and music venue for national bands and drunk people.
Republic	1520 N Fremont St	312-787-1130	Meet Trixie and Chad at this enormous club.
Zentra	923 W Weed St	312-787-0400	Image is everything. National DJ acts, fashionable crowd, and hookahs.

Map 23 • West Town / Near West Side

Cleo's	1935 W Chicago Ave	312-243-5600	Hooray for Wing Night Mondays.
Darkroom	2210 W Chicago Ave	773-276-1411	No flash is necessary; artsy crowd, electro music, and industry parties.
Guess Hookah	1829 W Chicago Ave	312-666-8801	Weekend DJ's, BYO but buy your tobacco in the shop.
High Dive	1938 W Chicago Ave	773-235-3483	Ranch fries, comfy booths and Bird Machine band posters.
Sak's Ukrainian Village Restaurant	2301 W Chicago Ave	773-278-4445	One of the few bastions of the old country remaining in the Village.
Tuman's	2159 W Chicago Ave	773-782-1400	Revived local legend. Cheap beer and comfort food.

Map 24 • River West / West Town

Betty's Blue Star Lounge	1600 W Grand Ave	312-243-8778	Where hipsters get drunk and f*ck.
Cobra Lounge	235 N Ashland Ave	312-226-6300	Live bands, DJ, and no TVs.
Fulton Lounge	955 W Fulton Market	312-942-9500	Hip but laid back, cool music, outside seating.
J Patricks	1367 W Erie St	312-243-0990	Irish flags, beers, and accents.
Jak's Tap	901 W Jackson Blvd	312-666-1700	From the good folks who brought us the Village Tap.

Juicy Wine Company	694 N Milwaukee Ave	312-492-6620	Find hard-to-find wines, meats and cheeses at this wine bar.
Mahoney's Bar & Grill	551 N Odgen Ave	312-733-2121	Hard-core sports bar.
Matchbox	770 N Milwaukee Ave	312-666-9292	Chicago's smallest bar…bar none.
Relax Lounge	1450 W Chicago Ave	312-666-6006	This classic fifties-style lounge offers spiked milkshakes.
Sonotheque	1444 W Chicago Ave	312-226-7600	Super sleek: the design, the crowd, the music.
Stanley's Kitchen & Tap on Racine	324 S Racine Ave	312-433-0007	Sunday brunch here includes a bloody mary bar and Southern fare.
Tasting Room	1415 W Randolph St	312-942-1313	Swank, low-key wine bar.
Twisted Spoke	501 N Ogden Ave	312-666-1500	$2 Jim Beams served by suicide girls and free porn on Saturday nights.
Victor Hotel	311 N Sangamon St	312-773-6900	Vintage lounge with dramatic decor.

Map 26 • University Village / Little Italy / Pilsen

Bar Louie	1321 W Taylor St	312-633-9393	Generally good music and decent entrees.
Bevi Amo Wine Bar	1358 W Taylor St	312-455-8255	Good selection, if a bit pricey.
Hawkeye's Bar & Grill	1458 W Taylor St	312-226-3951	Quality bar food (including the healthy side).
The Illinois Bar & Grill	1421 W Taylor St	312-666-6666	Great greasy food and burgers.
Junior's Sports Lounge	724 W Maxwell St	312-421-2277	Sports bar with upscale pretensions.
Skylark	2149 S Halsted St	312-948-5275	Hip hangout for Pilsen arty crowd.

Map 27 • Logan Square

Fireside Bowl	2648 W Fullerton Ave	773-486-2700	No longer a punk rock venue, it's just bowling now.
Ronny's	2101 N California Ave	n/a	Garage rock lounge with a microwave.
Streetside Café	3201 W Armitage Ave	773-252-9700	Micro-brews, DJs spin smooth house, ample ambiance.
Tini Martini	2169 N Milwaukee	312-269-2900	Velvet ropes in this stretch of Milwaukee? Give me a break.
Two Way Lounge	2928 W Fullerton Ave	773-227-5676	This downright rugged bar offers cheap Old Style.
Whirlaway	3224 W Fullerton Ave	773-276-6809	Old Style, old couches, and a truly eclectic jukebox.
The Winds Café	2657 N Kedzie Blvd	773-489-7478	Neighborhood bar smack dab in the middle of the 'hood.

Map 28 • Bucktown

Cans	1640 N Damen Ave	773-227-2277	Canned beers galore! Loud crowd, loud music, great hot wings!
Charleston Tavern	2076 N Hoyne Ave	773-489-4757	Yuppie dive.
Cleo's	2048 W Armitage Ave	773-227-6700	Cruisy neighborhood spot.
Cortland's Garage	1645 W Cortland St	773-862-7877	Garage-themed bar for wanna-be grease monkeys.
Danny's Tavern	1951 W Dickens Ave	773-489-6457	Hipster house bar with candlelit alcoves.
Darwin's	1935 N Damen Ave	773-252-8530	Evolve in this great little dive bar.
Gallery Cabaret	2020 N Oakley Ave	773-489-5471	Hip dive bar with local acts, attracts plenty of wannabe barflies.
Green Eye Lounge	2403 W Homer St	773-227-8851	Microbrews within crawling distance of the Blue Line Western stop.
Lemmings	1850 N Damen Ave	773-862-1688	Lite Brite works of art.
The Liar's Club	1665 W Fullerton Ave	773-665-1110	Only sometimes overly hipster, otherwise rad music and good times.
The Map Room	1949 N Hoyne Ave	773-252-7636	Global theme mixed with the occasional free buffet.
The Mutiny	2428 N Western Ave	773-486-7774	All bands start somewhere…unfortunately it's here.
Northside Bar & Grill	1635 N Damen Ave	773-384-3555	Popular Wicker Park pick-up bar.
Quenchers Saloon	2401 N Western Ave	773-276-9730	Crowded on the weekends, but ultra comfy couches and free popcorn.

Map 29 • DePaul / Wrightwood / Sheffield

The (Prop) House	1675 N Elston Ave	773-486-2086	In the middle of an industrial area; house beats resonate.
Deja Vu	2624 N Lincoln Ave	773-871-0205	Rock-themed 4 am bar for the messy college crowd.
Delilah's	2771 N Lincoln Ave	773-472-2771	Punk rock dive specializing in scotch.
Gin Mill	2462 N Lincoln Ave	773-549-3232	Ever see a college kid drink gin?
The Grand Central	950 W Wrightwood Ave	773-832-4000	Hip but not hipster.
Green Dolphin Street	2200 N Ashland Ave	773-395-0066	Big band and jazz venue that serves late-night dinner and vibrations.
Hideout	1354 W Wabansia Ave	773-227-4433	Haven for alt-country and other quirky live tune-age.
Hog Head McDunna's	1505 W Fullerton Ave	773-929-0944	Lincoln Parksy music spot…for the not so musically inclined.
Irish Eyes	2519 N Lincoln Ave	773-348-9548	…are often crying.
Kincade's	950 W Armitage Ave	773-348-0010	Happy-hour sports bar.
Local Option	1102 W Webster Ave	773-348-2008	Neighborhood hole-in-the-wall and proud of it.
Nic and Dino's Tripoli Tavern	1147 W Armitage Ave	773-477-4400	Quality bar food.
Red Lion Pub	2446 N Lincoln Ave	773-348-2695	It's haunted, but don't ask the waitresses; they don't know.
Rose's Lounge	2656 N Lincoln Ave	773-327-4000	DePaul dive chock full of tchotchkes and cheap beer.
Webster Wine Bar	1480 Webster Ave	773-868-0608	Perfect place for "getting to know you" while enjoying flights and pairings.
Wrightwood Tap	1059 W Wrightwood Ave	773-549-4949	Neighborhood feel-good spot.

Map 30 • Lincoln Park

B.L.U.E.S.	2519 N Halsted St	773-528-1012	Smaller but notorious blues bar with an older African-American crowd.
Bacchus	2242 N Lincoln Ave	773-477-5238	Yup-to-be dance club.
Gamekeepers	345 W Armitage Ave	773-549-0400	Where young singles mingle.
Glascott's	2158 N Halsted St	773-281-1205	Wannabe Irish joint with frat-boy written all over it.
GoodBar	2512 N Halsted St	773-296-9700	Candles, DJ, wine bar.
Hidden Shamrock	2723 N Halsted St	773-883-0304	We played darts with Joe Walsh here one night. Righteous.
Kingston Mines	2548 N Halsted St	773-477-4646	Chicago blues bar in a neighborhood safe for tourists.
Lion Head Pub & The Apartment	2251 N Lincoln Ave	773-348-5100	DePaul nightspot.
Neo	2350 N Clark St	773-528-2622	Popular eighties retro night. Gag me with a spoon.
Park West	322 W Armitage Ave	773-929-1322	Costs extra to reserve a table.
The Second City	1616 N Wells St	312-664-4032	Drama and food in front of you.
Victory Liquors	2610 N Halsted St	773-348-5600	Hope you like Notre Dame.
Wise Fools Pub	2270 N Lincoln Ave	773-929-1300	Vibes are high for live local legends and jam sessions.

Map 31 • Old Town / Near North

boutique	809 W Evergreen Ave	312-751-2900	Hip-hop club with Asian vibe.
Burton Place	1447 N Wells St	312-664-4699	Great late night; good bar food.
McGinney's Tap	313 W North Ave	312-943-5228	Laid-back crowd.
Old Town Ale House	219 W North Ave	312-944-7020	Crusty old-timers meet performing arts crowd.
Spoon	1240 N Wells St	312-642-5522	Trendy young crowd.
Weeds	1555 N Dayton St	312-943-7815	Pinball, bras, shoes, poetry, and tequila.
Zanies Comedy Club	1548 N Wells St	312-337-4027	After a few drinks, everything is funny. Well, almost.

Map 32 • Gold Coast / Mag Mile

Backroom	1007 N Rush St	312-751-2433	Old jazz club w/ lots of baby boomers.
Butch McGuire's	20 W Division St	312-337-9080	Wet T-shirt contests anyone?
Coq d'Or	140 E Walton St	312-932-4623	A sophisticate's lodge: red leather, dark wood, torch singers and pub food. Inside the Drake Hotel.
Cru Wine Bar	25 E Delaware Pl	312-337-4001	Another little wine bar.
Dublin's	1050 N State St	312-266-6340	Gold Coast pub.
Finn McCool's	15 W Division St	312-337-4349	McNot.
The Hunt Club	1100 N State St	312-988-7887	The ultimate yuppy sports bar.
Jilly's Retro Club	1007 N Rush St	312-664-1001	Gold digger's haven. Jerry Springer's old hangout.
Le Passage	937 N Rush St	312-255-0022	Jeremy Piven tried to pick up one of our friends here one time.
Leg Room	7 W Division St	312-337-2583	Huge singles scene.
loft	15 W Division St	312-337-4349	Dance clubs with poles above Finn McCools. Cringing as we type.
Mothers	26 W Division St	312-642-7251	The mother of frat-boy shenanigans.
She-nanigans	16 W Division St	312-642-2344	Another Rush vicinity hellhole.
Signature Lounge	875 N Michigan Ave	312-787-9596	Unbelievable view from the women's room.
Underground Wonder Bar	10 E Walton St	312-266-7761	Mostly jazz.
The Whisky	1015 N Rush St	312-475-0300	Great summer place where hip and trendy folks abound.
Zebra Lounge	1220 N State St	312-642-5140	Garish, cramped piano bar—in other words, it's a hit.

Map 33 • West Rogers Park

Cary's Lounge	2251 W Devon Ave	773-743-5737	Locals' place to go for a nightcap.
McKellin's	2800 W Touhy Ave	773-973-2428	Cozy neighborhood Irish bar.
Mullen's Sports Bar and Grill	7301 N Western Ave	773-465-2113	Food until 1 am (10 pm on Sundays).

Map 34 • East Rogers Park

Duke's Bar	6920 N Glenwood Ave	773-764-2826	Start boozin' at 7 am.
Hamilton's Pub	6341 N Broadway St	773-764-8133	Watering hole popular with Loyola students.
Jackhammer	6406 N Clark St	773-743-5772	Gay bar with a welcoming neighborhood vibe.
Lamp Post	7126 N Ridge Blvd	773-465-9571	Friendly place to catch a game or toss darts.
No Exit	6970 N Glenwood Ave	773-743-3355	Standard coffee house.
Poitin Stil	1502 W Jarvis Ave	773-338-3285	What's in a name? Cozy little neighborhood Irish joint.
Red Line Tap	7006 N Glenwood Ave	773-274-5463	Brews and bands on the Red Line.
Touche	6412 N Clark St	773-465-7400	Drunken gay leather bar.

Map 35 • Arcadia Terrace / Peterson Park

Emerald Isle	2537 W Peterson Ave	773-561-6674	Ahh, the Emerald Isle!
Hidden Cove	5338 N Lincoln Ave	773-275-6711	Sports bar with trivia, darts, and karaoke.

Map 36 • Bryn Mawr / Bowmanville

Big Joe's 2 & 6 Pub	1818 W Foster Ave	773-784-8755	Corner bar endorsed by the Windy City Darters.
Claddagh Ring	2306 W Foster Ave	773-271-4794	Traditional Irish-American bar with plentiful pub fare.
Fireside Restaurant & Lounge	5739 N Ravenswood Ave	773-561-7433	Good late-night bar with above average grub.

K's Dugout	1930 W Foster Ave	773-561-2227	Drink and watch sports, drink and watch sports, drink and…
Leadway Bar & Café	5233 N Damen Ave	773-728-2663	Artsy bar with free picture-painting and pool-playing.
Mike's Ale House	5652 N Western Ave	773-784-2143	The perfect local spot for the aging hipsters who've been moving into this 'hood.

Map 37 • Edgewater / Andersonville

@tmosphere	5355 N Clark St	773-784-1100	Trendy gay bar with dance floor and DJs.
Charlie's Ale House	5308 N Clark St	773-751-0140	Family-friendly spot with reliable grub.
Edgewater Lounge	5600 N Ashland Ave	773-878-3343	Alehouse with open-mike on Tuesdays for singers.
Farraguts Tavern	5240 N Clark St	773-728-4903	Neighborhood dive, less yuppy than Simon's.
Granville Anvil	1137 Granville Ave	773-973-0006	Gay old-timers drink here.
Joie de Vine	1744 W Balmoral Ave	773-989-6846	Casual wine bar popular with local lesbians.
Kitty Moon	6237 N Clark St	773-856-6667	Shots, beer, and madly eclectic live music.
Marty's Wine and Martini Bar	1511 W Balmoral Ave	773-561-6425	Compact and classy.
Moody's Pub	5910 N Broadway St	773-275-2696	Best beer garden in the city. Long wait times.
Ole St Andrew's Inn	5938 N Broadway St	773-784-5540	Food and spirits…of the haunted sort.
Ollie's	1064 W Berwyn Ave	773-784-5712	A rare quiet neighborhood joint.
Pumping Company	6157 N Broadway St	773-465-9500	Cozy neighborhood dive with a fireplace and beergarden.
Simon's	5210 N Clark St	773-878-0894	Casual joint replete with thrift-store-attired hipsters.
Sovereign	6202 N Broadway St	773-274-0057	Cheap, laidback neighborhood joint frozen in time.
StarGaze	5419 N Clark St	773-561-7363	Lesbian bar with salsa on Friday nights.

Map 38 • Ravenswood / Albany Park

Lincoln Square Lanes	4874 N Lincoln Ave	773-561-8191	Brews and bowling above a hardware store. Cheap date.
Montrose Saloon	2933 W Montrose Ave	773-463-7663	Classic Chicago "Old Style." No cell phones, please.
Peek Inn	2825 W Irving Park Rd	773-267-5197	Cool little dive worth a peek.

Map 39 • Ravenswood / North Center

Bowman's Bar and Grill	4356 N Leavitt St	773-478-9999	Cozy, upscale bar with obligatory exposed brick.
Celtic Crown Public House	4301 N Western Ave	773-588-1110	Great specials without over-Irishing it!
Chicago Brauhaus	4732 N Lincoln Ave	773-784-4444	More German than Germany…even in Oktober.
Daily Bar & Grill	4560 N Lincoln Ave	773-561-6198	Bar food in retro ambiance.
The Globe Pub	1934 W Irving Park Rd	773-871-3757	Great music venue gone sportsbar.
Grafton Pub	4530 N Lincoln Ave	773-271-9000	Outstanding bar food and friendly atmosphere.
Huettenbar	4721 N Lincoln Ave	773-561-2507	German-town favorite with great beer selection.
Jury's Food & Drink	4337 N Lincoln Ave	773-935-2255	Local spot with bar food.
Katerina's	1920 W Irving Park Rd	773-348-7592	Live jazz, gypsy music, and local rock at this European lounge.
Laschet's Inn	2119 W Irving Park Rd	773-478-7915	Pull on the Lederhosen!
The Long Room	1612 W Irving Park Rd	773-665-4500	Yes, it's long, but not as long as you might think.
Margie's Pub	4145 N Lincoln Ave	773-477-1644	Bikers and burnouts and boozers…oh my!
O'Donovan's	2100 W Irving Park Rd	773-478-2100	It's a neighborhood bar. You can watch sports.
O'Lanagan's	2335 W Montrose Ave	773-583-2252	Not an Irishman in sight!
The Rail	4709 N Damen Ave	773-878-9400	One-time dive, the rail rocks in Ravenswood.
Resi's Bierstube	2034 W Irving Park Rd	773-472-1749	Wear your leiderhosen.
Wild Goose	4265 N Lincoln Ave	773-281-7112	Guy's bar. Cheap eats, TVs and games.

Map 40 • Uptown

Bar on Buena	910 W Buena Ave	773-619-6973	Microbrews and tasty burgers in this plush neighborhood café. All-you-can-eat pasta on Wednesdays!
Big Chicks	5024 N Sheridan Rd	773-728-5511	Friendly gay bar with fabulous art collection.
Carol's Pub	4659 N Clark St	773-334-2402	Hillbillies gone yuppie…thanks to a little press.
Crew Bar & Grill	4804 N Broadway St	773-784-CREW	Gay sports bar with 50 beers and several televisions, or vice versa.
Green Mill Pub	4802 N Broadway St	773-878-5552	Chicago legend… And birthplace of the poetry slam.
Holiday Club	4000 N Sheridan Rd	773-348-9600	The Rat Pack is back! With food.
Hopleaf	5148 N Clark St	773-334-9851	Tons of imports if you can get a seat.
Konak	5150 N Clark St	773-271-6688	Overflow option for when Hopleaf is too packed, which means always.
Max's Place	4621 N Clark St	773-784-3864	At $1.25 per draft, who wouldn't pass out?
Nick's Uptown	4015 N Sheridan Rd	773-975-1155	Open late with a great beer selection.
The Spot	4437 N Broadway St	773-728-8933	Three floors and constant special events.
T's	5025 N Clark St	773-784-6000	Popular with local gays and lesbians.
The Uptown Lounge	1136 W Lawrence Ave	773-878-1136	Former dump becomes trendy lounge in up-and-coming neighborhood.

Map 41 • Avondale / Old Irving

Angie's Bar & Grill	3700 N Kedzie Ave	773-509-9372	Neighborhood hangout.
Chief O'Neill's	3471 N Elston Ave	773-583-3066	Celtic music and top-of-the-line pub food.
Kuma's Corner	2900 W Belmont Ave	773-604-8769	Heavy metal bar with great microbrew selection and kobe beef sliders.
N	2977 N Elston Ave	773-866-9898	Argentine flair with electro grooves.

| Nelly's Saloon | 3256 N Elston Ave | 773-588-4494 | Romanian hangout with occasional live music. |
| Small Bar | 2956 N Albany Ave | 773-509-9888 | This Logan Square watering hole offers great domestic and imported booze and a chill vibe. |

Map 42 · North Center / Roscoe Village / West Lakeview

Beat Kitchen	2100 W Belmont Ave	773-281-4444	Hip music spot in a not so hip hood.
Black Rock	3614 N Damen Ave	773-348-4044	Not sure what this place is.
Cody's Public House	1658 W Barry Ave	773-528-4050	Named after the owner's dog.
Four Moon Tavern	1847 W Roscoe St	773-929-6666	Neighborhood tavern. Cozy back room. Thespian crowd.
Four Treys	1952 W Henderson St	773-549-8845	One of 5,000 drinking options in this area.
G&L Fire Escape	2157 W Grace St	773-472-1138	Attention ladies! It's a fireman's hangout!
Hungry Brain	2319 W Belmont Ave	773-935-2118	Mellow, friendly artist hangout. Experimental jazz on Sundays.
Martyrs'	3855 N Lincoln Ave	773-404-9494	Great stage for live acts.
Mulligan's Public House	2000 W Roscoe St	773-549-4225	Villagers do not go thirsty.
Riverview Tavern & Grill	1958 W Roscoe St	773-248-9523	Another Roscoe Village watering hole.
Roscoe Village Pub	2159 W Addison St	773-472-6160	Karaoke in a dive bar... doesn't get much better than that.
The Village Tap	2055 W Roscoe St	773-883-0817	Neighborhood icon with a touch of class.
Waterhouse	3407 N Paulina Ave	773-871-1200	Local lounge aiming for a classy feel.
Xippo	3759 N Damen Ave	773-529-9135	Martini lounge in unlikely 'hood.

Map 43 · Wrigleyville / East Lakeview

Bar Celona	3474 N Clark St	773-244-8000	Two bars, one in the basement, DJ spins upstairs.
Berlin	954 W Belmont Ave	773-348-4975	Tiny classic "pansexual" dance club.
Bernie's	3664 N Clark St	773-525-1898	Favored Wrigleyville spot.
Bottle Bar	950 W Wolfram St	773-665-5660	All kinds of beer from cheap malts to craft brew.
Bourbon	3244 N Lincoln Ave	773-880-9520	31 flavors to wet your whistle.
Bungalow Bar and Lounge	1622 W Belmont Ave	773-244-0400	Quirky lounge in a blue-collar neighborhood.
Cooper's	1232 W Belmont Ave	773-929-2667	Beer. Stylish/casual bar food.
Cubby Bear	1059 W Addison St	773-327-1662	Drunk cubs fans and bar bands.
Elbo Room	2871 N Lincoln Ave	773-549-5549	Didn't RATT play here?
Fizz Bar and Grill	3220 N Lincoln Ave	773-348-6000	Good specialty drinks. Tiki nights and more.
Ginger Man Tavern	3740 N Clark St	773-549-2050	Plays classical music to ward off Cubs fans.
Ginger's Ale House	3801 N Ashland Ave	773-348-2767	European Futbol. Goal!
Gunther Murphy's	1638 W Belmont Ave	773-472-5139	German-Irish = Beer.
Guthrie's Tavern	1300 W Addison St	773-477-2900	Comfortable atmosphere, good drinks, a range of board games to play with.
Higgins' Tavern	3259 N Racine Ave	773-281-7637	Yuppies and drunks.
Improv Olympic	3541 N Clark St	773-880-0199	Get laughs and drunk.
Jack's Bar & Grill	2856 N Southport Ave	773-404-8400	Classy wine bar.
Justin's	3358 N Southport Ave	773-929-4844	Great bar for Sunday football.
Lange's Lounge	3500 N Southport Ave	773-472-6030	Total dive, but not disgusting.
Lincoln Tap Room	3010 N Lincoln Ave	773-868-0060	Great mix of people, comfortable couches.
Metro	3730 N Clark St	773-549-0203	Internationally renowned venue for top local and touring rock music.
Moxie	3517 N Clark St	773-935-6694	Trendy, narrow bar with expensive fancy drinks.
Murphy's Bleachers	3655 N Sheffield Ave	773-281-5356	Outdoor Cubbie haven with drunks galore.
Newport Bar & Grill	1344 W Newport Ave	773-325-9111	For an ass-whooping in Pictionary, meet us here tomorrow night.
Raw Bar	3720 N Clark St	773-348-7291	Post-Metro rock star hangout.
Risque Cafe	3419 N Clark St	773-525-7711	Tangy BBQ and over 300 craft beers
Schuba's	3159 N Southport Ave	773-525-2508	Top live music staple with attached restaurant.
Sheffield's	3258 N Sheffield Ave	773-281-4989	Outdoor area attracts afternoon revelers. Great beer selection.
Slugger's	3540 N Clark St	773-248-0055	Batting cages—some people's heaven, others' hell.
Smart Bar	3730 N Clark St	773-549-0203	Club kids unite!
Sopo Lounge & Grill	3418 N Southport Ave	773-348-0100	Really popular with the local yuppie crowd, but great specials.
Tai's Til 4	3611 N Ashland Ave	773-348-8923	Well, they're open till 4 am, so you can probably guess what it's like. Hookup central.
Ten Cat Tavern	3931 N Ashland Ave	773-935-5377	Artsy type relaxing spot.
Toons Bar	3857 N Southport Ave	773-935-1919	Buncha characters in that joint (groan). But seriously, folks, check out the black-light mural by the bathrooms.
Uncommon Ground Café	3800 N Clark St	773-929-3680	Local acts play while sipping a latte.
Underground Lounge	952 W Newport Ave	773-327-2739	Cool music spot tucked away below the street.
Vida Lounge	1248 W. George	773-935-5700	South-American Dance Club and Lounge.
Y*k-zies-Clark	3710 N Clark St	773-525-9200	Loud post-Cubs hangout.

Map 44 · East Lakeview

Bridget McNeill's	420 W Belmont Av	773-248-6654	A fun hangout and godsend for those living along the lake.
Charlie's Chicago	3726 N Broadway St	773-871-8887	Gay country and western bar. That's right.
Circuit	3641 N Halsted St	773-325-2233	Huge Boys Town dance club—recently remodeled.
The Closet	3325 N Broadway St	773-477-8533	Boy-friendly lesbian bar, 4 am license.
Cocktail	3359 N Halsted St	773-477-1420	Small dance floor, occasional male strippers.
Duke of Perth	2913 N Clark St	773-477-1741	Shades of Edinburgh, along with requisite whiskies and haddock.
Friar Tuck	3010 N Broadway St	773-327-5101	Enter through a barrel. Yup, a barrel.

Hydrate	3458 N Halsted St	773-975-9244	Just what Boystown needs—a gay-friendly fern bar!
Kit Kat Lounge	3700 N Halsted St	773-525-1111	Live drag queen shows.
Little Jim's	3501 N Halsted St	773-871-6116	Halsted Street Gay Dive.
minibar	3341 N Halsted St	773-871-6227	Fancy cocktails in a smoke-free lounge.
Monsignor Murphy's	3019 N Broadway St	773-348-7285	Irish Pub with plenty of board games.
Roscoe's	3356 N Halsted St	773-281-3355	Cavernous mingling for the gay sweater set.
Sidetrack	3349 N Halsted St	773-477-9189	Popular showtune sing-a-longs!
Spin	800 W Belmont Ave	773-327-7711	Lots of theme days throughout the week.
Town Hall Pub	3340 N Halsted St	773-472-4405	Unassuming, mixed clientele, live music.
Wilde	3130 N Broadway St	773-244-0404	Classy bar for bookish set.

Northwest

5th Province Pub	4626 N Knox Ave	773-282-7035	Authentic pub located in the Heritage Center.
Abbey Pub	3420 W Grace St	773-478-4408	Reputable live music venue.
Babe's	4416 N Milwaukee Ave	773-477-5238	Warm, pleasant Jeff Park local option.
The Burlington	3425 W Fullerton Ave	773-384-3243	Low-key candlelit drinks
Edison Park Inn	6715 N Olmsted Ave	773-755-1404	All in one bowling, pizza parlor & sports bar.
Emerald Isle	6686 N Northwest Hwy	773-775-2848	The brothers and sisters of Kerry gather here.
Fantasy Lounge	4400 N Elston	773-685-8083	Neighborhood place with eclectic live music offerings.
Fischman Liquors	4780 N Milwaukee Ave	773-545-0123	We call beer "piwo" 'round here.
Flo's Algiers Lounge	5436 W Montrose Ave	773-736-1111	The name evokes Casablanca, the environment, Kiev.
Ham Tree	5333 N Milwaukee Ave	773-792-2072	Neigborhood place with beer garden.
Hollywood Lounge	3301 W Bryn Mawr Ave	773-588-9707	Friendly neighborhood bar with extensive beer selection.
Jimmy Mack	5581 N Northwest Hwy	773-631-1466	After 9 pm, lots of Bikers but no Bears.
Moretti's	6727 N Olmsted Ave	773-631-1223	Sports-guy type of hangout.
New Polonia Club	6101 W Belmont Ave	773-237-0571	A polish bar on the NW side? Go figure.
Original Dugan's	6051 N Milwaukee Ave	773-467-5555	The perfect neighborhood dive.
Rosa's Lounge	3420 W Armitage Ave	773-342-0452	Revered Chicago Blues staple.
Three Counties	5856 N Milwaukee Ave	773-631-3351	Popular afterwork neighborhood bar.
Vaughan's Pub	5485 N Northwest Hwy	773-631-9206	Cozy neighborhood joint with nice beer selection and Irish food.
Weegee's Lounge	3659 W Armitage Ave	773-384-0707	Swank pub with craft beers and a '50s cocktail menu.

West

Black Beetle	2532 W Chicago Ave	773-384-0701	Displaced suburbanites in the heart of Humbolt Park.
California Clipper	1002 N California Ave	773-384-2547	An art-dork and hipster haven.
Grandma Sally's	5225 W Madison	312-718-8311	Friday night stand-up comedy.
La Justicia	3901 W 26th St	773-522-0041	Live rock-en-español on Friday nights only!

Southwest

Cork & Kerry	10614 S Western Ave	773-445-2675	We think we've actually seen a Leprechaun here.
Groucho's	8355 S Pulaski Rd	773-767-4838	Mainstream and big-hair live rock venue.
Jeremy Lanigan's Irish Pub	3119 W 111th St	773-233-4004	Live celtic music from time-to-time.
Keegan's Pub	10618 S Western Ave	773-233-6829	Another Irish joint on the South Side. Go figure.
Mrs O'Leary's Dubliner	10910 S Western Ave	773-238-0784	Quaint, with locals and expats and hand-carved booths.
Patrick's	6296 S Archer Ave	773-581-4036	Sing along to old Irish jukebox tunes. A classic neighborhood spot.
Sean's Rhino Bar	10330 S Western Ave	773-238-2060	The new kid on the block (1999) offers darts, pool, drink specials and decent pub grub.

South

Jeffrey Pub	7041 S Jeffery Blvd	773-363-8555	Gay men and lesbians mingle at this southside dance club.
New Apartment Lounge	504 E 75th St	773-483-7728	Where Von Freeman jams every Tuesday night.
Red Pepper's Masquerade Lounge	428 E 87th St	773-873-5700	Sports bar and grill with live entertainment.
Reds	6926 S Stony Island Ave	773-643-5100	Popular place to mack on the opposite sex.

Evanston

1800 Club	1800 Sherman Ave	847-733-7900	Always busy, thanks to cheap drinks and trivia night.
Bill's Blues Bar	1029 Davis St	847-424-9800	Chicago transplant Bill Gilmore invades Evanston.
Keg of Evanston	810 Grove St	847-869-9987	DJ on the weekends. Dollar drafts on Wednesdays!
Prairie Moon	1502 Sherman Ave	847-864-8328	Weekly drink specials.
The Stained Glass Wine Bar	1735 Benson Ave	847-864-8600	240 varieties of wine, braised rabbit, and frog legs.
Tommy Nevin's Pub	1450 Sherman Ave	847-869-0450	Evanston's answer to live music joints.

Oak Park

Avenue Ale House	825 S Oak Park Ave	708-848-2801	Really great place to grab a beer (or frozen margarita or sangria) and watch a game. Tasty grub. Great patio.

Skokie

Champps	134 Old Orchard Ctr	847-673-4778	Sports bar chain. Just about perfect.
Don's Fishmarket Tavern and Grill	9335 Skokie Blvd	847-677-3424	Yuppy watering hole connected to Don's Fishmarket.
Principal's Pub	4249 Main St	847-675-7773	Local beer and shot option.

Mag Mile and Oak Street: Bring Your Bars of Gold

The Mag Mile has long replaced State Street as downtown Chicago's premier (and tourist-friendly) shopping strip. This stretch of prime real estate, spanning from the Chicago River to Oak Street features Chicago outposts of many destination shopping spots, including **Niketown (Map 3)**, **The Apple Store (Map 3)**, **Needless-Markup** (a.k.a. **Neiman-Marcus (Map 3)**, **American Girl Place (Map 2)**, and the high-end boutiques and department stores, (think **Tiffany (Map 3)**, **Gucci (Map 32)**, and **Hermes (Map 32)**) connected to **Water Tower Place (Map 32)** and the **900 North Michigan Mall (Map 32)**.

Around the corner on Oak Street lay tonier boutiques. While Mag Mall attracts goggle-eyed Midwestern families, who'll likely stop for lunch at the Cheesecake Factory or Bubba Gump, Oak Street appeals more to the Gold Coast and North Shore set: **Prada (Map 32)**, **Ultimo (Map 32)**, **Barney's (Maps 30, 32)** and BCBG **(Map 32)** are all located on this tiny strip.

Boutique Shopping

You don't have to go down to Oak Street to find funky designer boutiques selling everything from original fashions by local designers to housewares and hostess gifts. Lincoln Park and Wicker Park in particular are heavy on cool women's fashion boutiques. In Lincoln Park, check out Armitage, Clark, and Halsted for shops such as **Lori's Designer Shoes (Map 30)**, **Cynthia Rowley (Map 30),** and **Kaveri (Map 29)**. In Wicker Park, the highest concentration of cool little shops, like the fashion boutiques **Habit (Map 21)** and **Penelope (Map 21)**, line Division street, but if you love to shop, you'll want to work the whole Bermuda triangle of Division, Milwaukee and North Avenue.

Best of the 'Hoods

In many cases, Chicago's neighborhood shopping destinations say something unique about the character of the 'hood. Funky little punk-rock indie shops in Logan Square for example, or gay-friendly places like **GayMart (Map 44)**, **Unabridged Bookstore (Map 44)**, and **He Who Eats Mud (Map 44)** in Boystown. Lincoln Square caters to the NPR-lovin' Hupsters that call that 'hood home, and Andersonville has something for everyone: feminist books (**Women & Children First (Map 37)**), chic home furnishings, men's and women's fashions, Swedish souvenirs, and, count them, two clean, friendly and non-oogly-feeling sex-toy stores (**Early to Bed (Map 37)** and **Tulip (Maps 37, 44)**).

Ethnic enclaves also make for great shopping. Try gifts and cookware in Chinatown, gorgeous saris and Bollywood flicks on West Devon, hookahs and Moroccan teas sets on north Kedzie in Albany Park, and Irish arts and crafts in Beverly.

One Man's Trash...

Is another man's treasure. Whether you wants are driven by the desire to save the planet or you just want to save a buck, Chicago offers a plentitude of places to buy other people's old crap. Vintage wear boutiques thrive in arty 'hoods like Wicker Park, East Lakeview, and Roscoe Village. Some faves: **Disgraceland (Map 43)**, **Una Mae's Freak Boutique (Map 21)**, **Yellow Jacket (Map 43)**, **Silver Moon (Map 21)**, and the **Hollywood Mirror Map 43)**. **The Ragstock (Maps 43, 21)** used-and-off sale clothing chain has two Chicago outposts—one near Clark and Belmont, the other on Milwaukee Avenue.

For one-stop antique shopping, check out one of Chicago's many antique malls—huge enclosed spaces that lease space to small dealers. Not to be missed are the **Broadway Antique Mall (Map 37)**, the **Edgewater Antique Market (Map 37)**, and the **Lincoln Antique Mall (Map 38)**.

In terms of thrift stores, there's either a **Salvation Army (Maps 25, 29, 40, NW)**, a **Unique Thrift (Map 40)** or a **Village Discount (Maps 28, 38, 40, 42, NW, W, SW)** in nearly every neighborhood in the city. Meanwhile, the **Brown Elephant (Maps 21, 37)** thrift stores benefit Howard Brown Health Center's HIV research, whereas the **White Elephant (Map 30)** benefits the Children's Memorial Hospital.

Audiophilia

Although two huge chain record stores (Tower Records and the Virgin Superstore) have folded in the past few years, Chicago loves our independent record stores. Among our faves, **Reckless Records (Maps 21, 44)** serves the indie rock crowd. **Borderline (Maps 21, 44)** spins Euro dance hits. Gramaphone is where Chicago's DJs pick-up the hottest wax. Speaking of wax, **Dr. Wax (Map 19)** supplies Hyde Parkers with all its old-school vinyl needs, while **Dusty Groove (Map 22)**, which specializes in old R&B and soul, provides the same service to West Towners. **Laurie's Planet of Sound (Map 39)**, in Lincoln Square, offers an eclectic array of mostly-indie music without the attitude that is often associated with record store clerks.

For stereo equipment and electronics, DJ's shop at **Midwest Stereo (Map 43)**. **DeciBel (Map 21)** serves the Wicker Park and Bucktown crew. Saturday **Audio Exchange (Map 43)**, only open on Thursdays, Saturdays, and Sundays, sells high-end stereo brands for cheap, (well, relatively cheap, anyways) as well as used and refurbished woofers, tweeters, receivers, and all that other audio-geek stuff.

Get Foodie

The gourmet and specialty food trade has exploded in the past few years, as have the high-end houseware stores that are supplying upscale home cooks with their Le Creuset pans and Wustof knives. Today, if you find yourself hard-up for locally-produced caviar, lavender extract, stinky artisinal cheese, curry leaves, or whatever other weird ingredient they don't stock at the Jewel, all you have to do is follow your nose. Of Chicago's many, many gourmet or specialty food shops, there are a few that are particularly dear to our hearts. **Pastoral Artisan (Map 44)**, a specialty cheese and wine shop, is a great stop on your way to a dinner party to pick up cheese, wine, olives, or other tasty treats. **The Cheese Stands Alone (Map 39)** is a super-friendly store specializing, obviously, in the stinky stuff. We also love **Goddess and the Grocer (Maps 28, 32)**, **Provenance Food and Wine (Map 27)**, and, perhaps, the best-smelling shop in town, Old Town's **The Spice House (Map 31)**. Ethnic markets are great places to track down hard-to-find ingredients. **Middle East Bakery (Map 37)** in Andersonville sells amazing homemade hummus and falafel, as well as olive oil, pine nuts, and dried fruit at prices significantly lower than Whole Paycheck. Oh, and that local caviar? Look no further than **The Fishguy Market (Northwest)**.

Mall Rats

Normally we'd scoff, but look, it's Chicago, and it gets damn cold. So, if occasionally you want to do your shopping without having to venture too far into the great outdoors, we're not going to point any fingers.

On the Mag Mile, **Water Tower Place (Map 32)** offers pretty typical mall fare—there's a Gamer's Paradise, Godiva, and Victoria's Secret—but their food court has more in common with a Las Vegas buffet than anywhere

you'd be able to grab an Orange Julius or a Mrs. Fields cookie. A block north, the shops at **900 N Michigan (Map 32)**, offer higher-end fare, (no surprise, as it's attached to the super-luxe Four Seasons hotel). Shops here include Coach, Diesel, MaxMara, and Williams-Sonoma. In East Lakeview, the **Century Shopping Mall (Map 44)** is kept in business by its fine art house cinema and Bally's outpost, certainly not by the mundane shops contained within (Limited, Express, or Bath & Body Works, anyone?). Housed in a building where bombers were built during WWII, today the huge **Ford City Mall (Southwest)** is a popular hang-out for local kids without much else to do, but otherwise boasts nothing very exceptional – a few low-end department stores, a movie theater, and all of the shops and fast food joints you'd expect to find in a mall. Anchored by a Target and a Kohl's, **Harlem Irving Plaza (Northwest)**, like the Ford City Mall, is a popular stomping ground for high school students but offers little beyond the same old shops despite that location-specific nom de mall.

Oddities

Some of our favorite Chicago shops defy easy definition. Among them, **American Science and Surplus (Northwest)** offers one-stop shopping for professional-quality laboratory beakers, school supplies, crime-scene tape, pirate flags, and life-sized anatomy models. At **Uncle Fun (Map 43)** you can find all the coolest vintage and wind-up toys, as well as oodles of strange and playful things for under $5, making it the gag gift headquarters of Chi-town. Recent acquisitions: a bacon-scented air-freshener, a week's worth of fake moustaches, and a "Mr. T in Your Pocket" keychain. Ah, youth. Relive it again at again at **Izzy Rizzy's House of Tricks (Southwest)**, where you can stock up on plastic vomit, hand-buzzers, and stink bombs. Finally, to cast a curse or break one, stop by **Athenian Candle Company (Map 4)**, where, in addition to 12-foot, gold-detailed, church-quality candles, you can also pick up a bottle of "Law Be Gone" floor wash or "Love Come Back" air spray.

Map 1 • River North / Fulton Market District

Doolin's	511 N Halsted St	312-243-9424	Party decorations galore, closed Sundays.

Map 2 • Near North / River North

American Girl Place	111 E Chicago Ave	877-247-5223	Stepford dolls for your tween.
Jazz Record Mart	27 E Illinois St	312-222-1467	Jazz lover's emporium.
Jonathan Adler	676 N Wabash Ave	312-274-9920	Hip and happy home furnishings.
Mig and Tig Furniture	540 N Wells St	312-644-8277	Classic, well-made furniture.
Montauk	401 N Wells St	312-951-5688	The most comfortable sofas.
Paper Source	232 W Chicago Ave	312-337-0798	Great paper and invitations.

Map 3 • Streeterville / Mag Mile

Apple Store	679 N Michigan Ave	312-981-4104	All of their newest and shiniest offerings, plus classes and seminars.
Chicago Place	700 N Michigan Ave	312-266-7710	Upscale mall.

Map 3 · Streeterville / Mag Mile—*continued*

Disney Store	717 N Michigan Ave	312-654-9208	M-i-c-k-e-Why?
Garrett Popcorn Shop	670 N Michigan Ave	312-944-4730	Everything you could possibly think of related to popcorn.
Neiman-Marcus	737 N Michigan Ave	312-642-5900	Affectionately known as "Needless Mark-up" by those who can afford it anyway.
Niketown	669 N Michigan Ave	312-642-6363	Nike label sports clothing.
Ralph Lauren	750 N Michigan Ave	312-280-1655	If you love those little polo horses...
Tiffany & Co	730 N Michigan Ave	312-944-7500	Deluxe jeweler.

Map 4 · West Loop Gate / Greek Town

Athenian Candle Co	300 S Halsted St	312-332-6988	Candles, curse-breakers, Greek trinkets, and much more.
Greek Town Music	330 S Halsted St	312-263-6342	Music, T-shirts, hats—everything Greek!

Map 5 · The Loop

American Music World	111 N State St	312-781-4050	The place to go if you're looking to buy an instrument.
Carson Pirie Scott	1 S State St	312-641-7000	Department store.
Gallery 37 Store	66 E Randolph St	312-744-8925	Speciality gifts.
Kramer's Health Food Center	230 S Wabash Ave	312-922-0077	Healthy hippie haven.
Rock Records	175 W Washington St	312-346-3489	Good CD store.
Sears	2 N State St	312-373-6000	Blue-collar stalwart.

Map 6 · The Loop / Grant Park

Art & Artisans	108 S Michigan Ave	312-641-0088	Art gallery.
Museum Shop of the Art Institute	111 S Michigan Ave	800-518-4214	Art Institute gift shop.
Poster Plus	200 S Michigan Ave	800-659-1905	Vintage posters and custom framing.
Precious Possessions	28 N Michigan Ave	312-726-8118	Mineral shop.

Map 7 · South Loop / River City

Adam Joseph's Hats	544 W Roosevelt Rd	312-913-1855	Haberdashery and menswear.
Fishman's Fabrics	1101 S Des Plaines St	312-922-7250	Huge fabric wholesaler.
Lee's Foreign Car Service	727 S Jefferson St	312-663-0823	Import parts and service.
Morris & Sons	557 W Polk St	312-243-5635	Mostly men, off-price Italian designers.

Map 8 · South Loop / Printers Row / Dearborn Park

Printers Row Fine & Rare Books	715 S Dearborn St	312-583-1800	Fine and rare books.
Sandmeyer's Book Store	714 S Dearborn St	312-922-2104	Dream come true if you love books and atmosphere.

Map 9 · South Loop / South Michigan Ave

Spertus Shop	610 S Michigan Ave	312-322-1740	Unique Hanukkah gifts include yiddishwear and the Moses action figure.

Map 10 · East Pilsen / Chinatown

Chinatown Bazaar	2221 S Wentworth Ave	312-225-1088	Part clothing store, part knick-knack shop.
Pacific Imports	2200 S Wentworth Ave	312-808-0456	Mostly home furnishings.
Sun Sun Tong	2260 S Wentworth Ave	312-842-6398	Stock up on Chinese herbs and teas.
Ten Ren Tea & Ginseng Co	2247 S Wentworth Ave	312-842-1171	The only place to buy ginseng.
Woks 'n' Things	2234 S Wentworth Ave	312-842-0701	Stir-fry utensils and cookware.

Map 11 · South Loop / McCormick Place

Blue Star Auto Stores	2001 S State St	312-225-0717	All your auto needs.
Cycle Bicycle Shop	1465 S Michigan Ave	312-987-1080	Bike shop, obviously.
Waterware	1829 S State St	312-225-4549	Designer plumbing fixtures.

Map 12 · Bridgeport (West)

Best's Kosher Outlet Store	1000 W Pershing Rd	773-650-6338	Packaged deli meats and made-to-order sandwiches.
Bridgeport Antiques	2963 S Archer Ave	773-927-9070	Old stuff.

Map 13 · Bridgeport (East)

Ace Bakery	3241 S Halsted St	312-225-4973	Excellent breads and pastries.
Augustine's Spiritual Goods	3327 S Halsted St	773-843-1933	Mystical and religious knick-knacks.
Bridgeport News Travel & Tours	3252 S Halsted St	312-225-6311	Travel store.

Health King Enterprises Chinese Medicinals	238 W 31st St	312-567-9978	Natural remedies.
Henry's Sports & Bait Shop	3130 S Canal St	312-225-8538	Fishing mecca.
Let's Boogie Records & Tapes	3321 S Halsted St	773-254-0139	Music.

Map 14 · Prairie Shores / Lake Meadows

Ashley Stewart	3455 S Dr Martin L King Jr Dr	312-567-0405	Women's clothing.
Avenue	3429 S Dr Martin L King Jr Dr	312-697-1219	Modern plus-size clothes.

Map 16 · Bronzeville

Afrocentric Bookstore	4655 S King Dr	773-924-3966	The authority on Afrocentic literature.
Ibiza	233 E 47th St	773-924-5199	High-fashion hip-hop rock star gear & denim.
Issues Barber & Beauty Salon	3958 S Cottage Grove Ave	773-924-4247	Beauty salon.
Jordan's Closets	106 E 51st St	773-624-4104	Adorable resale shop for sassy little girls and fashionista mommies.
Leaders 1354	4351 S Cottage Grove Ave	773-285-1067	The place for hip-hop fit and skateboards and spray-pained murals of Harold Washington, Marley, Che, and Malcolm.
New Approach Health Foods	641 E 47th St	773-373-6900	Restaurant and store that caters to residents who don't want to clog their arteries at the local fast food joints.
Sensual Steps	4518 S Cottage Grove Ave	773-548-FEET	A sanctuary for fancy kicks, handbags, camisoles, jewelry, and shawls by black designers.
Synx Galleria	4700 S Prairie Ave	773-548-4110	Fashionable & upscale athletic shoe shop.

Map 17 · Kenwood

South Shore Decor	1328 E 47th St	773-373-3116	Wall coverings, paint, blinds, and window treatments galore.

Map 19 · Hyde Park

57th Street Books	1301 E 57th St	773-684-1300	Brainy, independent bookstore.
The Baby PhD Store	5225 S Harper Ave	773-684-8920	For the smart kid.
Borders	1539 E 53rd St	773-752-8663	Check out the outside Patio.
Dr Wax Records and Tapes	5225 S Harper Ave	773-493-8696	Old-style vinyl.
Futons N More	1370 E 53rd St	773-324-7083	Futons 'n' more.
House of Africa	1510 E 63rd St	773-324-6858	Afrocentric everything.
Hyde Park Records	1377 E 53rd St	773-288-6588	Buy/sell vintage LPs.
O'Gara & Wilson	1448 E 57th St	773-363-0993	Rare and out-of-print books.
Powell's	1501 E 57th St	773-955-7780	Famous bookstore.
Toys Et Cetera	1502 E 55th St	773-324-6039	Just for fun.
Wesley's Shoe Corral	1506 E 55th St	773-667-7463	Shoes.
Wheels and Things	5210 S Harper Ave	773-493-4326	Bike sales and repairs.

Map 20 · East Hyde Park / Jackson Park

Art's Cycle Sales & Service	1652 E 53rd St	773-363-7524	Bike sales and repairs.

Map 21 · Wicker Park / Ukrainian Village

Akira	1814 W North Ave	773-489-0818	High fashion for wanna-be Eurotrash.
American Apparel	1563 N Milwaukee Ave	773-235-6778	Sweatshop-free clothes.
An Je Nu	1747 W Division St	773-469-2212	Excellent paper store offering a bevy of local and letterpressed cards.
Asrai Garden	1935 W North Ave	773-782-0680	Flowers and garden.
Black Walut Gallery	2135 W Division St	773-772-8870	Handcrafted hardwood furniture along with modern art and accessories.
The Brown Elephant	1459 N Milwaukee Ave	773-252-8801	Resale boutique benefits Howard Brown Health Center.
Casa de Soul	1919 W Division St	773-252-2520	Asian/African-inspired global lifestyle boutique for men and women.
Cattails	1935 W Division St	773-486-1621	A unique flower market.
City Soles	2001 W North Ave	773-489-2001	Up to $600 a pop for the latest European soles.
DeciBel Audio	1429 N Milwaukee Ave	773-862-6700	New and used stereo equipment.
G-Star	1525 N Milwaukee Ave	773-342-2623	More denim than your little heart could desire.
Grow	1943 W Division St	773-489-0009	Stylish, organic wares for your tots.
Habit	1951 W Division St	773-342-0093	Indie/local designer's collective.
hejfina	1529 N Milwaukee Ave	773-772-0002	Sleek, sophisticated boutique.
Jade	1557 N Milwaukee Ave	773-342-5233	Hip women's boutique.
Language	1537 N Milwaukee Ave	773-777-2574	Hip yet sophisticated wares hang in this small women's boutique.
Lille	1923 W North Ave	773-342-0563	Great little things for the home.
Myopic Books	1564 N Milwaukee Ave	773-862-4882	A Wicker Park brainy-hipster institution.

Arts & Entertainment • **Shopping**

Map 21 • Wicker Park / Ukrainian Village—continued

Nina	1655 W Division St	773-486-8996	Yarn shop includes delicate, frayed thread from old saris.
Paper Doll	2048 W Division St	773-227-6950	Paper, cards, and great gifts.
Penelope's	1913 W Division St	773-395-2351	Casual, stylish women's clothes.
Plein Aire	2036 W Division St	773-227-3722	Cute, affordable boutique.
Porte Rouge	1911 W Division St	773-269-2800	Fancy French housewares and free tea.
Quimby's Bookstore	1854 W North Ave	773-342-0910	Books and music.
Ragstock	1433 N Milwaukee Ave	773-486-1783	Funky vintage clothes and trendy irregulars.
Reckless Records	1532 N Milwaukee Ave	773-235-3727	Mostly indie music-new and used.
Ruby Room	1743 W Division St	773-235-2323	A "spa for the spirit" of the chic.
Silver Moon	1755 W North Ave	773-235-5797	Amazing vintage.
The Silver Room	1442 N Milwaukee Ave	773-278-7130	Clothing and accessories.
Symmetry	1925 W Division St	773-645-0502	Upscale/modern furniture and décor featuring Tibetan rugs.
Tatine	1742 W Division St	773-342-1890	Fancy candle/soap store.
Una Mae's Freak Boutique	1422 N Milwaukee Ave	773-276-7002	A Wicker Park staple—vintage and new clothing.
Untitled	1941 W North Ave	773-342-0500	Uber-hipster clothing.

Map 22 • Noble Square / Goose Island

Cost Plus World Market	1623 N Sheffield Ave	312-587-8037	Like Pier One, but with food and wine.
Dusty Groove Records	1120 N Ashland Ave	773-342-5800	Vinyl and CDs. Specializes in funk, soul, rare groove, now sound, and world music.
Irv's Luggage Warehouse	820 W North Ave	312-787-4787	Carries some discounted luggage and briefcases.
Restoration Hardware	938 W North Ave	312-475-9116	Fancy housewares.
Transitions Bookplace	1000 W North Ave	312-951-7323	Books on spirituality, health, etc. Has a café.
Vintage Pine	904 W Blackhawk St	312-943-9303	Custom-made furniture from the English and French countrysides.

Map 23 • West Town / Near West Side

Alcala's	1733 W Chicago Ave	312-226-0152	Western-wear emporium sells boots, jeans and cowboy hats.
Donofrio's Double Corona Cigars	2058 W Chicago Ave	773-342-7820	Brian Donofrio sells very fine imported cigars.
Guess Hookah	1829 W Chicago Ave	312-666-8801	Head shop meets the hookah trend with a lounge to show off your purchase.
H&R Sports	1739 W Chicago Ave	312-226-8737	Soccer gear.
Modern Times	2100 W Grand Ave	773-772-8871	Vintage mid-century modern funishings.
Painted Lady Organic Eatery	2018 W Chicago Ave	773-327-6931	Proof that politically-correct pastry—organic, sustainable—tastes good.
Pistol Bazaar	1717 W Chicago Ave	312-929-2350	Funky vintage boutique.
Rotofugi	1953 W Chicago Ave	312-491-9501	Really cool toy store with urban vinyl figures.
Salvage One Architectural Elements	1840 W Hubbard St	312-733-0098	Warehouse of antique, vintage and salvaged architectural pieces for home/loft restoration.
SoKo Fashion	1925 W Chicago Ave	773-592-1089	Well-chosen women's fashion.
Sprout Home	745 N Damen Ave	312-226-5950	Plants and gardening supplies meet modernism.
Tomato Tattoo	1855 W Chicago Ave	312-226-6660	Every hip strip needs a tattoo parlor.

Map 24 • River West / West Town

Aesthetic Eye	1520 W Chicago Ave	312-243-1520	Art gallery, irregular hours.
Casati	949 W Fulton Market	312-421-9905	Mid-century Italian furniture and accessories.
Chicago Avenue Discount	1637 W Chicago Ave	312-226-0004	Shoes for $1.93!
Design Inc	1359 W Grand Ave	312-243-4333	Architecturally centered home design.
Douglas Dawson Gallery	400 N Morgan St	312-226-7975	Fancy artifacts from around the world.
duchess	1043 W Grand Ave	312-933-5317	Two young curators turn their living room into a contemporary gallery.
Jan's Antiques	225 N Racine Ave	312-563-0275	Mind-boggling antique emporium.
MK Brody	1101 W Randolph St	800-652-7639	Piñatas and balloons!
Ouest	1063 W Madison St	312-421-2799	From Philip Lim to Rozae Nichols…need we say more?
Pet Care Plus	1328 W Lake St	312-397-9077	For the pet-obsessed.
Phaiz	673 N Milwaukee Ave	312-226-9070	Handmade couture arranged with eclectic art collection.
The Realm	1430 W Chicago Ave	312-491-0999	Exotic furniture from far-away places.
Roots	1140 W Grand Ave	312-666-6466	Trendy hair salon.
RR#1 Chicago Apothecary	814 N Ashland Blvd	312-421-9079	Old-school pharmacy.
Snap	470 N Ogden Ave	312-226-5110	Hair and nail salon.
Terry's Toffee	1117 W Grand Ave	312-733-2700	Gourmet, house-made toffee, ice creams, and biscotti.
Upgrade Cycle Works	1130 W Chicago Ave	312-226-8650	Bikes, accessories and servicing.
Xyloform	1423 W Chicago Ave	312-455-7949	Furniture store.

Map 25 • Illinois Medical District

Accents Flowers and Gifts	2246 W Taylor St	312-850-4438	Flower shop conveniently located near major hospitals.
Salvation Army Thrift Store	2024 S Western Ave	773-254-1127	Good 'ol fashioned thrifting.

Map 26 • University Village / Little Italy / Pilsen

Conte Di Savoia	1438 W Taylor St	312-666-3471	European and Italian specialties.
Lush Wine and Spirits	1306 S Halsted St	312-738-1900	Wine, microbrews, and booze.
Scafuri Bakery	1337 W Taylor St	312-733-8881	The secret's in the bread.

Map 27 • Logan Square

Boulevard Bikes	2535 N Kedzie Blvd	773-235-9109	Friendly neighborhood bike shop.
Disco City	2630 N Milwaukee Ave	773-486-1495	Latin music emporium.
Fleur	3149 W Logan Blvd	773-395-2770	Not your mother's floral arrangements, plus handmade goods from locals.
Provenance Food and Wine	2528 N California Ave	773-384-0699	Reasonably priced wines and unreasonably priced groceries.
Threads, Etc	2327 N Milwaukee Ave	773-276-6411	Resale clothes and furniture.
Wolfbait & B-Girls	3131 W Logan Blvd	312-698-8685	Two young designers showcase funky wares by dozens of locals.

Map 28 • Bucktown

Beta Boutique	2016 W Concord Pl	773-276-0905	Everything you'd find at your favorite sample sale.
Bleeker Street Antiques	1946 N Leavitt St	773-862-3185	Fine selection of antiques.
G Boutique	2131 N Damen Ave	773-235-1234	Lingerie and bedroom accessories.
Goddess and the Grocer	1646 N Damen Ave	773-342-3200	Gourmet groceries and take-out.
Jean Alan	2134 N Damen Ave	773-278-2345	House and home.
Mark Shale Outlet	2593 N Elston Ave	773-772-9600	Great deals on grown-up clothes.
p.45	1643 N Damen Ave	773-862-4523	Edgy women's boutique.
Pagoda Red	1714 N Damen Ave	773-235-1188	Fine Asian antiques.
Pavilion Antiques	2055 N Damen Ave	773-645-0924	Antique furniture.
Red Balloon Company	2060 N Damen Ave	773-489-9800	A unique store for children—toys, clothes and furniture.
Robin Richman	2108 N Damen Ave	773-278-6150	Arty, indie boutique.
Scoop NYC	1702 N Milwaukee Ave	773-227-9930	On top of the trends.
T-Shirt Deli	1739 N Damen Ave	773-276-6266	Pricey—but quality—custom-made t-shirts.
Tangerine	1719 N Damen Ave	773-772-0505	Feminine women's boutique.
Veruca Salt	1937 N Damen Ave	773-276-3888	Flirty ladies fashions.
Vienna Beef Factory Store	2501 N Damen Ave	773-278-7800	Here's the beef.
Village Discount Outlet	2032 N Milwaukee Ave	866-545-3866	Tons of clothes and weekly specials.
Vive La Femme	2115 N Damen Ave	773-772-7429	Style beyond size.

Map 29 • DePaul / Wrightwood / Sheffield

Active Endeavors	853 W Armitage Ave	773-281-8100	Playing sports or heading into the great outdoors? This is your place for gear.
Dirk's Fish	2070 N Clybourn Ave	773-404-3475	Carry out fresh fish and seafood spot.
Isabella Fine Lingerie	1101 W Webster Ave	773-281-2352	Fine after-hours wear.
Jayson Home & Garden	1885 N Clybourn Ave	773-248-8180	Flowers and garden.
Kaveri	1211 W Webster Ave	773-296-2141	Boutique lines by designers like Trovata and Ulla Johnson.
Left Bank	1155 W Webster Ave	773-929-7422	Jewelry and home décor.
Lush Cosmetics	859 W Armitage Ave	773-281-5874	Handmade soaps and natural cosmetics—too bad they aren't edible!
Mint	2150 N Seminary Ave	773-322-2944	Boutique featuring Midwestern artists.
Sam's Wine and Liquor Warehouse	1720 N Marcey St	312-664-4394	Great selection, accessories, classes, and free samples.
Tabula Tua	1015 W Armitage Ave	773-525-3500	Housewares.
Uncle Dan's	2440 N Lincoln Ave	773-477-1918	One-stop shopping for survivalists.
Vosges Haut Chocolat	951 W Armitage Ave	773-296-9866	Delicious exotic gourmet chocolates flavored with Indian spices, whiskey, etc.
Wine Discount Center	1826 N Elston Ave	773-489-3454	Wine warehouse—free tastings every Saturday.

Map 30 • Lincoln Park

A New Leaf	1818 N Wells St	312-642-8553	Perhaps the most elegantly designed flower shop in Chicago.
Art & Science	1971 N Halsted St	312-787-4247	Beauty salon.
Barneys New York Co-Op	2209 N Halsted St	773-248-0426	Barney's "affordable" sister.
Buy Popular Demand	2629 N Halsted St	773-868-0404	Consignment shop offering affordable fashions.
Cynthia Rowley	808 W Armitage Ave	773-528-6160	Apparel and accessories.

Map 30 • Lincoln Park—*continued*

Dave's Records	2604 N Clark St	773-929-6325	All LPs, from Janacek to Jay-Z.
Ethan Allen	1700 N Halsted St	312-573-2500	Furniture store.
GNC	2740 N Clark St	773-883-3008	General nutrition center.
Lori's Designer Shoes	824 W Armitage Ave	773-281-5655	Designer shoes.
Lululemon	2104 N Halsted St	773-883-8860	Canadian-based yoga wear brand brings soft-as-cashmere soy clothes and sleek attire.
Nau	2118 N Halsted St	773-281-1363	Eco-friendly attire for the athetic set.
Old Town Triangle	1763 N North Park Ave	312-337-1938	Don't miss their openings.
Sally Beauty Supply	2727 N Clark St	773-477-6222	Wholesale for stylists, but open to the public.
White Elephant	2300 Childrens Plz	773-880-4031	Resale shop at the Children's Memorial Hospital.

Map 31 • Old Town / Near North

Crate & Barrel Outlet Store	1864 N Clybourn Ave	312-787-4775	Housewares.
Etre	1361 N Wells St	312-266-8101	Upscale boutique.
Fleet Feet Sports	210 W North Ave	312-587-3338	The staff watches you run to make sure the shoes fit.
Fudge Pot	1532 N Wells St	312-943-1777	A chocolate institution.
Jumbalia	1429 N Wells St	312-335-9082	Great gift store.
Nicole Miller	1419 N Wells St	312-664-3532	The high-end designer sells her wares—from lingerie to bridal and formal attire—to the ladies who can afford to look this good.
Old Town Gardens	1555 N Wells St.	312-266-6300	Beautiful plants and flowers.
The Spice House	1512 N Wells St	312-274-0378	Spice up your cooking.
Up Down Tobacco	1550 N Wells St	312-337-8025	Great selection of cigars, cigarettes, and accessories.
Village Cycle	1337 N Wells St	312-751-2488	Good urban cycling store.

Map 32 • Gold Coast / Mag Mile

900 North Michigan Shops	900 N Michigan Ave		Hi-end mall stores.
Anthropologie	1120 N State St	312-255-1848	Hip clothing and knick-knacks.
Barney's New York	25 E Oak St	312-587-1700	Upscale boutique, clothing and accessories.
BCBG	55 E Oak St	312-787-7395	Apparel and accessories.
Bloomingdale's	900 N Michigan Ave	312-440-4460	Upscale department store.
Bravco Beauty Center	43 E Oak St	312-943-4305	For those who like to be pampered.
Chanel at the Drake Hotel	935 N Michigan Ave	312-787-5000	Classic, expensive clothing, accessories, and fragrances.
Club Monaco	900 N Michigan Ave	312-787-8757	Fashion-forward clothing that doesn't try too hard.
Diesel	923 N Rush St	312-255-0157	Edgy styles keep on coming.
Elements	102 E Oak St	312-642-6574	Cool house-y stuff.
Europa Books	832 N State St	312-335-9677	International magazines.
Flight 001	1133 N State St	312-944-1001	Modern retro-style travel gear.
Frette	41 E Oak St	312-649-3744	European furniture and accessories.
G'bani	949 N State St	312-440-1718	Shoes.
Gucci	900 N Michigan Ave	312-664-5504	Tom Ford's alluring and provocative clothes and accessories.
H&M	840 N Michigan Ave	312-640-0060	European department store taking Chicago by storm.
Hermes	110 E Oak St	312-787-8175	Fancy scarves and more.
Hershey's Chicago	822 N Michigan Ave	312-337-7711	Dumb and fun chocoholic tourist trap.
Intermix	40 E Delaware Pl	312-640-2922	The NYC shoppers' mecca.
Jake	939 N Rush St	312-664-5553	Fashionista favorite for men and women.
Lush Cosmetics	835 N Michigan Ave	312-573-1805	Handmade soaps and natural cosmetics—too bad they aren't edible!
MAC	40 E Oak St	312-951-7310	Fabulous make-up.
Paul Stuart X/S	875 N Michigan Ave	312-640-2650	Located on the second floor, one of only two Paul Stuart outlets in the world. So far.
Prada	30 E Oak St	312-951-1113	Expensive, but delightful, clothing and accessories.
Pratesi	67 E Oak St	312-943-8422	Linens.
Tod's	121 E Oak St	312-943-0070	Clothing.
Ultimate Bride	106 E Oak St	312-337-6300	Bridal gear.
Ultimo	114 E Oak St	312-787-1171	Apparel and accessories.
Urban Outfitters	935 N Rush St	312-640-1919	Retro clothing, nifty gifts, and cool accessories.
Water Tower	835 N Michigan Ave	312-440-3166	Marshall Fields, er, Macy's.

Map 33 • West Rogers Park

Al Mansoor	2600 W Devon Ave	773-764-7576	All-in-one Bollywood music and DVD.
Argo Georgian Bakery	2812 W Devon Ave	773-764-6322	Some Russian baked goods for your trouble?
AutoZone	2555 W Touhy Ave	773-764-5277	Stuff for your car.

Cheesecakes by JR	2841 W Howard St	773-465-6733	Over 20 flavors of cheesecakes.
Chicago Harley Davidson	6868 N Western Ave	773-338-6868	Hogs, gear, etc.
Levinson's Bakery	2856 W Devon Ave	773-761-3174	Always fresh!
Office Mart	2801 W Touhy Ave	773-262-3924	Combination office supply store and and Internet coffee shop.
Raj Jewels	2652 W Devon Ave	773-465-5755	For all your Indian wedding needs.
Resham's	2540 W Devon Ave	773-764-9692	Saris and fabric fill the store.
Taj Sari Palace	2553 W Devon Ave	773-338-0177	Beautiful Indian clothing and accessories.
Tel-Aviv Kosher Bakery	2944 W Devon Ave	773-764-8877	Under the supervision of Rabbi Chaim Goldzweig!
Three Sisters Deli	2854 W Devon Ave	773-973-1919	Russian deli with fresh herring, smoked meats, and caviar.

Map 34 • East Rogers Park

Mar-Jen Discount Furniture	1536 W Devon Ave	773-338-6636	Cheap futons, dorm furniture.
New Leaf Natural Grocery	1261 W Loyola Ave	773-743-0400	Adorable, horribly expensive organic grocery, as per usual.

Map 35 • Arcadia Terrace / Peterson Park

Grazer's Gourmet	5333 N Lincoln Ave	773-561-5500	Homemade granola minus the macramé.

Map 36 • Bryn Mawr / Bowmanville

Target	2112 W Peterson Ave	773-761-3001	All you need, under one roof.

Map 37 • Edgewater / Andersonville

Alamo Shoes	5321 N Clark St	773-334-6100	Large selection for the soles from local retailer.
Blue Hydrangea	1113 W Berwyn Ave	773-293-1113	Friendly flower shop.
Bon Bon	5410 N Clark St	773-784-9882	Sweet handmade chocolate boutique.
Broadway Antique Market	6130 N Broadway St	773-743-5444	BAM! Calling all mallrats and antique freaks—one of America's most reviewed antique stores.
The Brown Elephant	5404 N Clark St	773-271-9382	Resale shop benefits local HIV clinic.
Cassona	5241 N Clark St	773-506-7882	Gorgeous home furnishings.
Early to Bed	5232 N Sheridan Rd	773-271-1219	Woman-oriented grown-up toys. Boy friendly.
Edgewater Antique Mall	6314 N Broadway St	773-262-2525	20th century antiques and vintage.
Elda de la Rosa	5555 N Sheridan Rd	773-769-3128	Custom gowns and dresses.
Erickson Jewelers	5304 N Clark St	773-275-2010	Large selection of jewelry.
Gethsemane Garden Center	5739 N Clark St	773-878-5915	Like mini-trip to a botanical garden; but you can take it home.
Hip Fit	1513 W Foster Ave	773-878-4447	Funky jeans shop.
Johnny Sprocket's	1052 W Bryn Mawr Ave	773-293-1695	Caters to all your bicycle needs.
Kate the Great Bookstore	5550 N Broadway	773-561-1932	Friendly staff actually knows something about books.
Middle East Bakery	1512 W Foster Ave	773-561-2224	So good, so cheap.
Paper Trail	5309 N Clark St	773-275-2191	Paper boutique and cards galore.
Presence	5216 N Clark St	773-989-4420	Cool boutique for young women.
Scout	5221 N Clark St	773-275-5700	Beautiful urban antiques.
Soothe Your Senses Day Spa	6260 N Broadway St	773-262-4246	Bringing Southern charm to Chicago.
Surrender	5225 N Clark St	773-784-4455	Health and beauty.
Toys Etcetera	5311 N Clark St	773-769-5311	Educational toys and quality books for kids.
True Nature Foods Community Market	6034 N Broadway St	773-465-6400	Pick up your weekly CSA box of fruits and veggies from your local farmers.
Tulip Toy Gallery	1480 W Berwyn Ave	773-275-6110	Woman-owned, inviting sex paraphenalia shop.
White Attic	5408 N Clark St	773-907-9800	Clean home furnishings and art work.
Wickstrom's Swedish Deli	5247 N Clark St	773-275-6100	The Swedish epicenter of Andersonville.
Women & Children First	5233 N Clark St	773-769-9299	World's biggest feminist book and music store.

Map 38 • Ravenswood / Albany Park

Lincoln Antique Mall	3115 W Irving Park Rd	773-604-4700	Mid-sized antique mall.
The Music Store	3121 W Irving Park Rd	773-478-7400	Guitars and other musical instruments.
Odin Tatu	3313 W Irving Park Rd	773-442-8288	Get inked.
Rave Sports	3346 W Lawrence Ave	773-588-7176	Athletic shoes and clothing.
Sassy Boutique	3210 W Lawrence Ave	773-539-1738	Cute partywear for 20-somethings. (Sign on store inexplicably reads "Tomato.")
Scents & Sensibility	4654 N Rockwell St	773-267-3838	Cards. And things to put your cards and candles and flowers into.
Village Discount Outlet	3301 W Lawrence Ave	866-545-3866	Tons of clothes and weekly specials.
Village Discount Outlet	4027 N Kedzie Ave	866-545-3866	Tons of clothes and weekly specials.

Map 39 • Ravenswood / North Center

Architectural Artifacts	4325 N Ravenswood Ave	773-348-0622	Renovator's dream.
Book Cellar	4736 N Lincoln Ave	773-293-2665	Book store/coffee shop/wine bar. Also has sandwiches.

Map 39 • Ravenswood / North Center—*continued*

The Cheese Stands Alone	4547 N Western Ave	773-293-3870	Artisinal cheeses from Europe and America in this delightfully stinky shop.
The Chopping Block	4747 N Lincoln Ave	773-472-6700	Gourmet cooking utensils and cooking classes.
Different Strummer	4544 N Lincoln Ave	773-728-6000	Guitars and such.
East Meets West	2118 W Lawrence Ave	773-275-1976	Handpicked fair-trade global wares; totally boring.
European Import Center	4752 N Lincoln Ave	773-561-8281	Beer steins and other gifts from Bavaria.
Gallimaufry Gallery	4712 N Lincoln Ave	773-728-3600	Artisan crafts including instruments, incense, stone fountains.
Glass Art & Decorative Studio	4507 N Lincoln Ave	773-561-9008	Stained glass and gifts.
Griffins & Gargoyles Antiques	2140 W Lawrence Ave	773-769-1255	Pine furniture from Europe.
Hazel	1902 W Montrose Ave	773-769-2227	Stylish gifts and jewelry, plus an extensive stationery section.
Laurie's Planet of Sound	4639 N Lincoln Ave	773-271-3569	Funky CD shop with unpretentious service.
Margie's Candies	1813 W Montrose Ave	773-348-0400	Second generation of a Chicago classic.
Merz Apothecary	4716 N Lincoln Ave	773-989-0900	German and other imported toiletries, herbal supplements, etc. The original.
Patina	4907 N Damen Ave	773-334-0400	Vintage designer furniture.
Quake Collectables	4628 N Lincoln Ave	773-878-4288	Vintage toys and fun!
Timeless Toys	4749 N Lincoln Ave	773-334-4445	Old-fashioned toys.

Map 40 • Uptown

Angel Food Bakery	1636 W Montrose Ave	773-728-1512	Whimsical bakery with interesting sandwiches to go.
Eagle Leathers	5005 N Clark St	773-728-7228	Come to daddy.
Foursided	5061 N Clark St	773-506-8300	Framing and more at this funky shop.
Play It Again Sports	3939 N Ashland Ave	773-463-9900	Sporting goods.
Salvation Army Thrift Store	4315 N Broadway St	773-348-1401	Good 'ol fashioned thrifting.
Shake Rattle and Read Book Box	4812 N Broadway St	773-334-5311	Funky used bookstore, great finds, but cluttered.
Tai Nam Market Center	4925 N Broadway St	773-275-5666	Vietnamese. Very good.
Tattoo Factory	4441 N Broadway St	773-989-4077	High-profile place to get inked.
Unique so Chique	4600 N Magnolia Ave	773-561-0324	A small but quirky collection of gifties.
Unique Thrift Store	4445 N Sheridan Rd	773-275-8623	Half-price Mondays.
Uptown Bikes	4653 N Broadway St	773-728-5212	Cool, grungy bike shop.
Village Discount Outlet	4898 N Clark St	866-545-3866	Tons of clothes and weekly specials.
Wilson Broadway Mall	1114 W Wilson Ave	773-561-0300	Socks, shoes, ethnic shopping, music, luggage—it's all here.
Wooden Spoon	5047 N. Clark	773-293-3190	Heaven for foodies.

Map 42 • North Center / Roscoe Village / West Lakeview

Antique Resources	1741 W Belmont Ave	773-871-4242	Large inventory of antique furniture.
Caravan Beads	3361 N Lincoln Ave	773-248-9555	Loads of beads for all your beady needs.
Father Time Antiques	2108 W Belmont Ave	773-880-5599	Antiques store.
Glam to Go	2002 W Roscoe St	773-525-7004	Girly-girls get pampered.
Good Old Days Antiques	2138 W Belmont Ave	773-472-8837	Antiques and treasures.
Lynn's Hallmark	3353 N Lincoln Ave	773-281-8108	Cards, stationery, and gift wrap.
My Closet	3350 N Paulina St	773-388-9851	Marked-down designer wear from Bloomingdale's and Macy's.
The Pleasure Chest	3436 N Lincoln Ave	773-525-7151	Sextastic adult store.
Sacred Art	2040 W Roscoe St	773-404-8790	Featuring up and coming local designers.
Village Discount Outlet	2043 W Roscoe St	866-545-3866	Tons of clothes and weekly specials.

Map 43 • Wrigleyville / East Lakeview

The Alley	3228 N Clark St	773-883-1800	Skulls, tattoos, big boots.
Bookworks	3444 N Clark St	773-871-5318	Friendly, well-organized used books.
Disgraceland	3338 N Clark St	773-281-5875	Two floors of decent resale clothing.
Fashion Tomato	937 W Belmont Ave	773-281-2921	Cheap, trendy clothes for girls who go to clubs and like to "party."
Hollywood Mirror	812 W Belmont Ave	773-404-2044	Vintage clothes and kitschy doo-dads.
Izzy	3406 N Ashland Ave	773-880-0994	For metrosexuals only.
J. Toguri Mercantile Co	851 W Belmont Av	773-929-3500	Find Japanese books, paper, and foodstuffs here.
Krista K	3458 N Southport Ave	773-248-1967	Snobby clothes for snobby women but good selection of jeans.
Leahy & LaDue Consignment	3753 N Southport Ave	773-929-4865	Classy resale shop, mostly expensive, but good buys on the sale rack.
Midwest Stereo	1613 W Belmont Ave	773-975-4250	DJ equipment, fog machines, strobe lights.
Namaskar Boutique	3950 N Southport Ave	773-472-0930	Yoga accessories.
Never Mind	953 W Belmont Ave	773-472-4922	Trendy accessories and clothes for trixie girls.
Ragstock	812 W Belmont Ave	773-868-9263	Vintage resale and trendy off-price clothes.
Saturday Audio Exchange	1021 W Belmont Ave	773-935-4434	Great bargains on name brand audio.

Strange Cargo	3448 N Clark St	773-327-8090	Hip affordable threads for the 20-somethings.
Thousand Waves Spa	1212 W Belmont Ave	773-549-0700	Get away from it all at this female-only spa.
Trousseau	3543 N Southport Ave	773-472-2727	Beautiful and unique lingerie—tres chic.
Uncle Fun	1338 W Belmont Ave	773-477-8223	Cramped and crazy retro toys and novelties.
Yellow Jacket	2959 N Lincoln Ave	773-248-1996	Funky vintage shop with great window displays.

Map 44 • East Lakeview

Borderline	3333 N Broadway St	773-975-9533	Dance music store named after Madonna song.
Century Mall	2828 N Clark St	773-929-8100	Most notable occupants include the cinema and Bally's Fitness.
Clothes Optional	2918 N Clark St	773-296-6630	Funky thrift store.
Cupcakes	613 W Briar Pl	866-525-0817	Just fancy cupcakes.
Equinox	3401 N Broadway St	773-281-9151	Gifts and glassware—great Xmas ornament selection.
GayMart	3459 N Halsted St	773-929-4272	Gay Barbie and other homo kitsch and gifts.
Gramaphone	2843 N Clark St	773-472-3683	DJ's shop here for the latest wax.
He Who Eats Mud	3247 N Broadway St	773-525-0616	Cards, cards, and more cards.
P&L	2956 N Clark St	773-248-3758	The latest from Bangkok designers.
Pastoral Artisan Cheese, Bread & Wine	2945 N Broadway St	773-472-4781	One of Chicago's favorite cheese shops. Start your picnic here.
Reckless Records	3161 N Broadway St	773-404-5080	Oldies and new releases on vinyl.
skinstinct	3343 N Broadway St	773-857-6900	Tiny boutique featuring bamboo and organic clothing.
Spare Parts	2947 N Broadway St	773-525-4242	Cool bags, purses, and man purses.
Tulip Toy Gallery	3448 N Halsted St	773-975-1515	Woman-owned, inviting sex paraphenalia shop.
Unabridged Books	3251 N Broadway St	773-883-9119	Helpful bookstore with great travel, kids and gay sections.
Windy City Sweets	3308 N Broadway St	773-477-6100	Old-fashioned candy shop with homemade fudge.

Northwest

Albany Office Supply	3419 W Lawrence Ave	773-267-6000	A substantial portion of the store is devoted to Hello Kitty. Some other stuff too, but who cares about that?
American Science & Surplus	5316 N Milwaukee Ave	773-763-0313	Your one-stop obscure gizmo shop.
Fishguy	4423 N Elston Ave	773-283-7400	Get your local caviar here.
Harlem Irving Plaza	Irving Park Rd & Forest Preserve Ave	773-625-3036	Every tacky, low-end, wholesale-to-public you could ever want.
NY Shoes Imports	3546 W Lawrence Ave	773-509-9903	Has slightly fetishistic edge; interesting lingerie in back.
Perfumes R' Us	3608 W Lawrence Ave	773-463-9575	Well-known name brand perfumes including Nina Ricci, Chanel, DNKY, etc., discounted and wholesale.
Rolling Stone Records	7300 W Irving Park Rd	708-456-0861	The place to rock, with lots of big-haired in-store appearances.
Salvation Army Thrift Store	3837 W Fullerton Ave	773-276-1955	Good 'ol fashioned thrifting.
Srpska Tradicija	3615 W Lawrence Ave	773-588-7372	Music, books, religious icons, and gifts from Serbia and Montenegro.
Sweden Shop	3304 W Foster Ave	773-478-0327	Gifts from Scandinavia.
Village Discount Outlet	4635 N Elston Ave	866-545-3866	Tons of clothes and weekly specials.

West

Buyer's Flea Market	4545 W Division St	773-227-1889	A weekend bargain hunter's dream.
Family Dollar	5410 W Chicago Ave	773-287-7050	All your convenient(ce) store needs for under a dollar.
Moo & Oink	4848 W Madison St	773-473-4800	A barbeque enthusiast's Mecca.
Village Discount Outlet	4020 W 26th St	866-545-3866	Tons of clothes and weekly specials.
Village Discount Outlet	2514 W 26th St	866-545-3866	Tons of clothes and weekly specials.

Southwest

African American Images Bookstore	1909 W 95th St	800-552-1991	Books, art, and jewelry with an African-American theme.
Beverly & Novelty Costume Shop	11626 S Western Ave	773-779-0068	Lifeline of trick-or-treaters and masquerade ballers on Far Southwest Side.
The Beverly Cigar Company	10513 S Western Ave	773-239-3264	More than 65 types of stogies, including a Honduras-rolled house brand.
Beverly Records	11612 S Western Ave	773-779-0066	Flip through actual vinyl here. Remember that stuff?
Bobak's	5275 S Archer Ave	773-735-5334	A melange of Polish buffet and supermarket, Chicago style.
Borders Book, Music, Movies & Café	2210 W 95th St	773-445-5471	The hub of Beverly's literary universe.

Southwest—*continued*

Calabria Imports	1905 W 103rd St	773-396-5800	Italian deli foodstuffs.
County Fair	10800 S Western Ave	773-238-5576	Classic family-owned market with produce, organics, butcher, and deli!
Ford City Shopping Center	7601 S Cicero Ave	773-767-6400	One-stop shopping for everyone on the Southwest Side and Suburbs. Multiplex cinema shows blockbusters.
Grich Antiques	10857 S Western Ave	773-233-8734	Furniture, housewares, and vintage electronics.
Izzy Rizzy's House of Tricks	6356 S Pulaski Rd	773-735-7370	Where to get your whoopy cushions, hand-buzzers, and fake puke.
Mr Peabody Records	11832 S Western Ave	773-881-9299	One of two black-owned, thriving retailers of rare vinyl in the world.
Ms Priss	9915 S Walden Pkwy	773-233-7747	Clubby young woman's fashion haven.
My Sisters' Knits	9907 S Walden Pkwy	773-238-4555	Beverly stitch and bitch knitter's paradise.
Optimo Hat	10215 S Western Ave	773-238-2999	Custom-made men's hats.
Village Discount Outlet	6419 S Kedzie Ave	866-545-3866	Tons of clothes and weekly specials.
Village Discount Outlet	7443 S Racine Ave	866-545-3866	Tons of clothes and weekly specials.
World Folk Music	1808 W 103rd St	773-779-7059	Weird instruments and lessons for kids and adults.

South

African Hedonist	8501 S Cottage Grove Ave	773-651-8511	Disc store features African and Caribbean tunage.
Halsted Indoor Mall	11444 S Halsted St	773-995-0265	Lots of bargains under one roof in historically black Morgan Park, on site of former golf course.
Underground Afrocentric Bookstore	1727 E 87th St	773-768-8869	New and used books of African-American interest.

Evanston

Active Endeavors	901 Church St	847-869-7070	New Evanston location for casual chic clothing.
Art & Science Hair Salon	811 Church St	847-864-4247	Beakers bring you back to science class. Student discounts available.
Asinamali Women's Boutique	1722 Sherman Ave	847-866-6219	Great clothes in a reasonable price range.
Bookman's Alley	1712 Sherman Ave	847-869-6999	Great selection of used books in good condition.
Campus Gear	1717 Sherman Ave	847-869-7033	Cheaper than the campus bookstore for Northwestern apparel. If that's your thing.
Uncle Dan's Great Outdoors	700 Church St	847-475-7100	Camping gear with a granola, Grateful Dead kind of feel.
William's Shoes	710 Church St	847-328-0527	Great boot and sneaker selection.

Oak Park

Antiques, Etc	125 N Marion St	708-386-9194	30+ dealers in one spot. Beautiful furniture, art, jewelry, rugs, and more.
Fly Bird	719 Lake St	708-383-3330	Warmly off-beat housewares and treats, 5-armed plush monsters to lemon-lychee candles.
Magic Tree Bookstore	141 N Oak Park Ave	708-848-0770	Welcoming children's bookstore that also has music, puzzles, and gifts.
Pumpkin Moon	1028 North Blvd	708-524-8144	The place for nostalgic collectables. Includes toys, T-shirts, and candy. Super fun.

Chicago's status as a city of neighborhoods extends to its arts scene, which can be grouped into several notable gallery districts:

River North (**Map 2**)—a scary industrial district in the 1970s—has grown into a glitzy nightlife district that's home to scores of Chicago's most established art dealers. **Jean Albano, Mary Bell, Catherine Edelman, Byron Roche, the Vale Craft Gallery, Zg,** and **Zolla/Lieberman** are just a few places where you can count on finding splendid original— and costly—works from recognized artists. The area hosts a variety of gallery walks and art fairs, such as a gala fall opening night and the annual River North Rendezvous and Feast of the Senses festivals, which pair art spaces with local chefs.

In search of larger, cheaper, and more contemporary spaces, many River North dealers have removed to the burgeoning West Loop (**Map 24**), turning it into a nexus of cutting-edge galleries. **Carrie Secrist** and **Kavi Gupta** are good starting points, while a gaggle of smaller spaces, such as **Bucket Rider, Packer Schopf, Peter Miller, ThreeWalls,** and **Tony Wight Bodybuilder & Sportsman,** to name a few standouts, also showcase quality art.

Wicker Park/Bucktown has been a focal point of progressive and experimental work for nearly 20 years, centering on the historic Flatiron Arts Building at the intersection of North, Damen, and Milwaukee avenues, although to find the art you may have to climb stairs—most of the gallery space is in lower-rent digs above street level. Look for promising artists at such galleries as **AllRise (Map 21), Around the Coyote (Map 21), Heaven (Map 21),** and **Johnsonese (Map 28)**.

The district teems with art events, most notably the semi-annual Around the Coyote festivals.

Pilsen (**Map 26**) became the next haven for young artists priced out of the gentrifying Bucktown/Wicker Park, as well as a focal point of Latino art. Collectives like the **Chicago Arts District** and **Polvo Art (Map 26)** and galleries such as **Metzli (Map 10)** and **Vespine (Map 26)** showcase a broad array of emerging artists. The area hosts several annual open-studios events as well as coordinated Second Friday openings.

Fine art can be found in many parts of the city, and it's worth seeking out more isolated showcases as well as **Gallery Guichard (Map 11),** which exhibits artists from the African diaspora; **Woman Made (Map 24),** whose focus is obvious; **R.H. Love (Map 2),** which deals in museum-quality American masterpieces; and the studios and galleries in the historic **Fine Arts Building (Map 6)**. Finally, for the most adventurous, be sure to try some of the many alternative gallery spaces in the city. Chicago's reputation as an incubator for start-ups is well-deserved—there are more unorthodox galleries than ever before. Though they are a little dicier as far as exhibition schedules and locations, they often pay off with some of the most unusual and thought-provoking work Chicago has to offer: **Deadtech (Map 27)** and **Dogmatic (Map 24)** are examples.

Check www.chicagoart.net or www.chicagogallerynews.com for more info on galleries in the city, as well as details on openings. The opening celebrations of new exhibits usually take place on Friday evenings. A great web resource for working artists is www.chicagoartistsresource.org.

Map 1 • River North / Fulton Market District

Northeastern Illinois University Fine Arts Center Gallery	5500 N St Louis Ave	773-442-4944
Stuart-Rodgers Gallery	375 W Erie St	312-787-8696

Map 2 • Near North / River North

Alan Koppel Gallery	210 W Chicago Ave	312-640-0730
Aldo Castillo Gallery	675 N Frankin St	312-337-2536
Andrew Bae Gallery	300 W Superior St	312-335-8601
Ann Nathan Gallery	212 W Superior St	312-664-6622
Belloc Lowndes Fine Art	226 W Superior St	312-266-2222
Byron Roche Gallery	750 N Franklin St, Ste 105	312-654-0144
Carl Hammer Gallery	740 N Wells St	312-266-8512
Catherine Edelman Gallery	300 W Superior St	312-266-2350
Gwenda Jay/Addington Gallery	704 N Wells St	312-664-3406
Habatat Galleries	222 W Superior St	312-440-0288
Hildt Galleries	617 N State St	312-255-0005
I Space	230 W Superior St	312-587-9976
Jean Albano Gallery	215 W Superior St	312-440-0770
Judy A Saslow Gallery	300 W Superior St	312-943-0530
Kass Meridian Gallery	325 W Huron St	312-266-5999
Lydon Fine Art	309 W Superior St	312-943-1133
Marx-Saunders Gallery	230 W Superior St	312-573-1400
Mary Bell Gallery	740 N Franklin St	312-642-0202
Maya Polsky Gallery	215 W Superior St	312-440-0055
Melanee Cooper Gallery	740 N Franklin St	312-202-9305
Mongerson Gallery	704 N Wells St	312-943-2354
Nicole Gallery	230 W Huron St	312-787-7716
Oskar Friedl Gallery	1029 W 35th St	312-493-4330
Perimeter Gallery	210 W Superior St	312-266-9473
Peter Bartlow Gallery	226 W Superior St	312-337-1782
Portals	742 N Wells St	312-642-1066
Printworks	311 W Superior St	312-664-9407
RH Love Galleries	645 N Michigan Ave	800-437-7568
Richard Norton Gallery	612 Merchandise Mart Plz	312-644-8855
Rita Bucheit Fine Art & Antiques	449 N Wells St	312-527-4080
Robert Henry Adams Fine Art	715 N Franklin St	312-642-8700
Rosenthal Fine Art	3 E Huron St	312-475-0700
Roy Boyd Gallery	739 N Wells St	312-642-1606
Russell Bowman Art Advisory	311 W Superior St, Ste 115	312-751-9500
Schneider Gallery	230 W Superior St	312-988-4033
Spencer Weisz Galleries	46 E Superior St	312-527-9420
Stephen Daiter Gallery	311 W Superior St	312-787-3350
Trowbridge Gallery	703 N Wells St	312-587-9575
Vale Craft Gallery	230 W Superior St	312-337-3525
Zg Gallery	300 W Superior St	312-654-9900
Zg Gallery	300 W Superior St	312-654-9900

Arts & Entertainment • **Art Galleries**

Map 2 • Near North / River North—*continued*

Zolla/Lieberman Gallery	325 W Huron St	312-944-1990
Zygman Voss Gallery	222 W Superior St	312-787-3300

Map 3 • Streeterville / Mag Mile

The Arts Club of Chicago	201 E Ontario St	312-787-3997
City Gallery	806 N Michigan Ave	312-742-0808
Inspire Fine Art	435 E Illinois St, Ste 131	312-595-9475
Joel Oppenheimer Gallery	410 N Michigan Ave	312-642-5300
Lora D Art Gallery	435 E Illinois St	312-245-9005
Ogilvie/Pertl Gallery	435 E Illinois St, Ste 151	312-321-0750
RS Johnson Fine Art	645 N Michigan Ave, Ste 234	312-943-1661
Worthington Gallery	645 N Michigan Ave	312-266-2424

Map 4 • West Loop Gate / Greek Town

Gallery 2	847 W Jackson Blvd	312-563-5162
Primitive Art Works	130 N Jefferson St	312-575-9600
Thomas McCormick Gallery	835 W Washington Blvd	312-226-6800

Map 5 • The Loop

Donald Young Gallery	933 W Washington Blvd	312-455-0100
Illinois State Museum Chicago Gallery	100 W Randolph St, 2nd Fl	312-814-5322

Map 6 • The Loop / Grant Park

Beacon Street Gallery	410 S Michigan Ave	312-212-1323
Cliff Dwellers Gallery	200 S Michigan Ave	312-922-8080
Hilligoss Gallery	520 N Michigan Ave	312-755-0300

Map 10 • East Pilsen / Chinatown

Metzli Gallery & Cultural Organization	556 W 18th St	312-738-0860
Meztli Gallery	556 W 18th St	312-738-0860
Rogeramsay Gallery	711 N Milwaukee Ave	312-491-1400

Map 11 • South Loop / McCormick Place

Framing Mode	1526 S Wabash Ave	312-566-0027
Gallery Guichard	3521 S Dr Martin Luther King Jr Dr	773-373-8000

Map 13 • Bridgeport (East)

MN Gallery	3524 S Halsted St	773-847-0573

Map 16 • Bronzeville

Nicole Gallery II	4653 S King Dr	312-787-7716

Map 19 • Hyde Park

Artisans 21	5225 S Harper Ave	773-288-7450

Map 20 • East Hyde Park / Jackson Park

Hyde Park Art Center	5020 S Cornell Ave	773-324-5520

Map 21 • Wicker Park / Ukrainian Village

AllRise Gallery	1542 N Milwaukee Ave, Third Floor	773-292-9255
Around the Coyote Gallery	1935 1/2 W North Ave	773-342-6777
Carlos E Jimenez Gallery	2301 W North Ave	773-235-5328
David Leonardis Gallery	1346 N Paulina St	773-278-3058
Gallery 203	1579 N Milwaukee Ave	773-252-1952
Heaven Gallery	1550 N Milwaukee Ave, 2nd Fl	773-342-4597
JoJo's Closet	1579 N Milwaukee Ave Ste 206	773-862-5656

Map 22 • Noble Square / Goose Island

1112 Gallery	1112 N Milwaukee Ave	773-486-9612
Madron LLC	1000 W North Ave, 3rd Fl	312-640-1302

Map 23 • West Town / Near West Side

Open-End Art Gallery	2000 W Fulton St	312-738-2140

Map 24 • River West / West Town

ARC Gallery	832 W Superior St	312-733-2787
Bucket Rider Gallery	835 W Washington Blvd	312-421-6993
Carrie Secrist Gallery	835 W Washington Blvd	312-491-0917
Dogmatic	1319 W Lake St	312-375-7757
Douglas Dawson Gallery	400 N Morgan St	312-226-7975
Flatfile Galleries	217 N Carpenter St	312-491-1190
Frederick Baker Gallery	1230 W Jackson Blvd	312-243-2980
Function + Art	1046 W Fulton Market	312-243-2780
Gallery 400	400 S Peoria St	312-996-6114
Gallery 40000	119 N Peoria St	312-738-0179
Gescheidle	1039 W Lake St	312-226-3500
Giola Gallery	118 N Peoria St	312-850-4487
GR N'Namdi Gallery International Center For Documentary Arts	110 N Peoria St 1303 W Chicago Ave	312-563-9240 312-226-5902
Kasia Kay Art Projects Gallery	1044 W Fulton Market	312-492-8828
Kavi Gupta Gallery	835 W Washington Blvd	312-432-0708
Linda Warren Gallery	1052 W Fulton Market	312-432-9500
Lisa Boyle Gallery	1821 W Hubbard St	773-655-5475
Monique Meloche Gallery	118 N Peoria St	312-455-0299
NavtaSchulz Gallery	1039 W Lake St	312-421-5506
Packer Schopf Gallery	942 W Lake St	312-226-8984
Peter Miller Gallery	118 N Peoria St	312-951-1700
Rhona Hoffman Gallery	118 N Peoria St	312-455-1990
Rowland Contemporary	1118 W Fulton Market	312-421-6275
Rowley Kennerk Gallery	119 N Peoria St	773-983-0077
Shane Campbell Gallery	1431 W Chicago Ave	312-226-2223
Skestos Gabriele Gallery	212 N Peoria St	312-243-1112
ThreeWalls	119 N Peoria St	312-432-3972

Tony Wight Bodybuilder & Sportsman Gallery	119 N Peoria St, #2C	312-492-7261
Walsh Gallery	118 N Peoria St, 2nd Fl	312-829-3312
Western Exhibitions	1821 West Hubbard St	312-307-4685
Woman Made Gallery	685 N Milwaukee Ave	312-738-0400

Map 26 • University Village / Little Italy / Pilsen

Polvo Art Studio	1458 W 18th St	773-344-1940
Vespine Gallery & Studios	1907 S Halsted St	312-962-5850

Map 27 • Logan Square

Deadtech	3321 W Fullerton Ave	n/a

Map 28 • Bucktown

Johnsonese Gallery	2149 W Armitage Ave	773-252-8750
Morlen Sinoway-Atelier	1052 W Fulton Market	312-432-0100

Map 29 • DePaul / Wrightwood / Sheffield

Chicago Art Source/ 2nd Floor Gallery	1871 N Clybourn Ave	773-248-3100
Chicago Center for the Print	1509 W Fullerton Ave	773-477-1585
DePaul University Art Museum	2350 N Kenmore Ave	773-325-7506
Havana Gallery	1139 W Webster Ave	773-549-2492
La Llorona Gallery	1474 W Webster Ave	773-281-8460

Map 30 • Lincoln Park

Contemporary Art Workshop	542 W Grant Pl	773-472-4004
Triangle Gallery of Old Town	1763 N North Park Ave	312-337-1938

Map 31 • Old Town / Near North

Thomas Masters Gallery	245 W North Ave	312-440-2322

Map 32 • Gold Coast / Mag Mile

Armstrong Fine Arts	200 E Walton St	312-664-9312
Colletti Gallery	67 E Oak St	312-664-6767
FL Braswell Fine Art	73 E Elm St	312-636-4399
Galleries Maurice Sternberg	875 N Michigan Ave	312-642-1700
Richard Gray Gallery	875 N Michigan Ave, Ste 2503	312-642-8877
Valerie Carberry Gallery	875 N Michigan Ave, Ste 2510	312-397-9990

Map 37 • Edgewater / Andersonville

Las Manos Gallery	5220 N Clark St	773-728-8910

Map 39 • Ravenswood / North Center

Peter Jones Gallery	1806 W Cuyler Ave	773-472-6725

Map 42 • North Center / Roscoe Village / West Lakeview

August House Studio	2113 W Roscoe St	773-327-5644
Chicago Photography Center	3301 N Lincoln Ave	773-549-1631

Map 43 • Wrigleyville/ East Lakeview

Bell Studio	3428 N Southport Ave	773-281-2172
Fourth World Artisans	3727 N Southport Ave	773-404-5200

Map 44 • East Lakeview

Billy Hork Galleries	3033 N Clark St	773-528-9090
Leigh Gallery	3306 N Halsted St	773-472-1865

LOWER LEVEL

Price Auditorium
To Teacher Resource Center
16 19
18
17
15
Family Shop
24
Architecture Study Room
Architecture
Morton Auditorium
1 Photography
10
Kraft Education Center
14
Thorne Miniature Rooms
2
3 Photography Study Room
4
11
Touch Gallery

European Decorative Arts 1900-Present
50 McKinlock Court
Garden Restaurant
Cafe
59 55
58 Textiles Study Room
60
63 61 69 57
European Decorative Arts 1600-1900
64 71 68
65 66 67
Textiles
Paperweight Collection

MAP 6

FIRST LEVEL

Print Study Room
123
126
124
127
125
Fullerton Hall
African & Ancient American
Arms & Armor
141
101 130 Gunsaulus Hall 140
101A 131A 142
107 102 103 131B
104 105 European Decorative Arts
106 132
133
Museum Shop
Ryerson & Burnham Libraries
109 108 134
135
Chinese, Japanese, & Korean
136
Contemporary
137
138
139
American to 1900

Indian & Southeast Asian
Arthur Rubloff Auditorium
151 152 153t
143 150 McKinlock Court
154 Chicago Stock Exchange Trading Room
155
Chagall Windows
159 158 157 156
179
163 161 178 American 1901-Present
164 Sculpture 177
165 Court 176
166 161 175
170
167 174
173
168 171
169 172
Ancient Egyptian Greek, Etruscan, & Roman
The School of the Art Institute
Betty Rymer Gallery (School)

SECOND LEVEL

European 1600s-1700s
218 219 220 221 222
European Prints & Drawings
217
216
215
Architecture
European
214
213
212
211
200 201
227
209 208 207 206
European 1400s
223
225 224
226
230 240
231
202 232
204 203
205 233
234B 234A
235
236
237B 237A
237C 237E
237D 237F
238B 238A
239
European 1800s
Modern
241 244 248
242 243 245 246 247 249
Impressionism & Postimpressionism
Modern

Arthur Rubloff Auditorium
Millennium Park Room

262 261 273
263 272
264
265 266 271
267 Museum Shop

Regenstein Hall Special Exhibitions

General Information

NFT Map:	6
Address:	111 S Michigan Ave
	Chicago, IL 60603
Phone:	312–443–3600
Website:	www.artic.edu
Hours:	Mon–Wed & Fri: 10:30 am–5 pm;
	Thurs: 10:30 am–8 pm;
	Sat & Sun: 10 am–5 pm; Thanksgiving,
	Christmas, & New Year's Days: closed
	Summer hours: Memorial Day through
	Labor Day open till 9pm on Thursdays
	and Fridays (free from 5–9 pm)
Admission:	$12 for adults, $7 for students/children/
	seniors, free for kids under twelve, free
	for all on Thursday evenings 5– 8pm

Overview

Built in 1892 as the only permanent structure of the 1893 Columbian Exposition, the Classical Revival-style Allerton Wing of the Art Institute of Chicago began life as the "Palace of Culture" for the World's Fair. (The lions were added two years later.) Today the Art Institute is one of the preeminent art museums in the country, housing the largest collection of 19th–Century French art outside of Paris (and its modern art collection isn't anything to sneeze at, either). Walking up the grand staircase in the main entrance, visitors are presented with an eclectic collection of architectural fragments wrenched from Chicago buildings that were standing in the way of, well, you know: "progress." There are also impressive exhibitions such as the Japanese wood block prints, the Touch Gallery designed specifically for the visually impaired, as well as really, really old vases and things, but who are we kidding? Everyone comes here for an up–close and personal look at such celebrated paintings as Caillebotte's *Paris Street; Rainy Day,* Seurat's *Grand Jatte,* Grant Wood's *American Gothic,* and Hopper's *Nighthawks,* along with their impressive collection of Monets, Manets, Van Goghs, and Picassos.

After delays that seem trifling compared to those of neighboring Millenium Park, the Art Institute intends to unveil its $200 million Renzo Piano-designed modern art wing in 2009. If you cant wait, plans for the wing are available at the museum in the Galley 50 exhibit, *"Zero Gravity."*

Restaurants and Services

The Café, on the lower–level of the Rubloff Building, offers self–service dining with burgers, pizza, and deli sandwiches at reasonable prices 11 am–4 pm daily (11 am–7 pm on Thursdays). For a more elegant lunch, dine next door at the Garden Restaurant. Now open year–round from 11:30 am to 3 pm daily, the restaurant features patio dining with seasonal cuisine and a full bar. The museum also offers free jazz concerts for Garden diners with their Jazz in the Garden program on Thursday evenings from July to September.

While postcards, books, and magnets may be purchased at kiosks throughout the museum, the Museum Shop, just off the main lobby, offers an extensive collection of art–oriented gifts and souvenirs (and you don't have to pay admission to shop there!). The lower–level Woman's Board Family Shop, adjacent to the Kraft Education Center and the Touch Gallery, hawks kid–oriented goodies.

School of the Art Institute of Chicago

Boasting such illustrious alumni as Georgia O'Keefe, Claes Oldenburg, Laurie Anderson, and David Sedaris, the School of the Art Institute of Chicago (SAIC) offers a fine art higher education for tomorrow's budding Renoirs.

Gene Siskel Film Center

160 N State St, 312–846–2600;
www.siskelfilmcenter.org

The film branch of the Art Institute offers art house, foreign films, and revivals, with frequent lectures by academics and industry professionals. Highlights include an Annual European Union Film Festival, and Oscar Night America, Chicago's only Academy-sanctioned party.

How to Get There

By Car: The Art Institute is located on Michigan Avenue between Monroe and Jackson. From I–90/94 N (the Dan Ryan), exit to Congress East (Loop exit). From I–90/94 S (Kennedy Expressway), exit Monroe Steet East. Affordable parking is located underground at Millennium Park garages (enter at Columbus and Monroe) and Grant Park garages (enter on Michigan, either between Madison and Randolph or between Van Buren and Adams).

By Metra: Nearest stops are the Randolph and Van Buren stations served by the Metra Electric and South Shore Lines. For other Metra lines, transfer to the 151 Sheridan Avenue bus at Union Station.

By Bus: Numerous lines serve this strip of Michigan Avenue. Important buses include (from the south) the 3 King Drive, the 4 Collage Grove, and the 6 Jackson Park Express, (from the west) the 126 Jackson and 20 Madison, and (from the north) the 151 Sheridan, the 145 Wilson–Michigan Express, and the 146 Inner Drive/ Michigan Express.

By L: From the Red and Blue lines, exit at Monroe. Brown, Orange, Purple and Green exit at Adams and Wabash.

Is the "city of big shoulders" also the city of big readers? Oprah and Da Mare would have you think so, what with their "One Book, One City" and "Oprah's Book Club" campaigns. To be sure, there's no lack of bookshops in the city, and Chicago's multitude of quirky, independent stores stand defiantly side–by–side with the bookselling super chains that continue to pop up every day.

Independent Bookstores

For general, all–purpose bookshops, **Barbara's (Map 3, Map 5)** is a Chicago Institution, as is 26–year–old **Unabridged Books (Map 44)** with its specialties in literary fiction, kids' books, travel, cookbooks, and gay and lesbian titles. Down by the University of Chicago campus, **57th Street Books (Map 19)** and **Seminary Co-op Bookstore (Map 19)** both appeal to the brainiac set, whereas **Beck's Book Store (Map 2, Map 5, Map 34, Map 40)** specializes in textbooks for Chicago's community colleges.

Specialty Bookstores

Specialty stores abound in the city. We think **Women & Children First (Map 37)** may have the largest selection of feminist and woman–focused books in the country, and their children's section is also top-notch. **Afrocentric Bookstore (Map 16)** specializes in black literature and culture. Heal thyself at **Transitions Bookplace (Map 22, Map 36)**—a peaceful, feng shui enclave in the chaotic Clybourn Corridor shopping district. The **Occult Bookstore (Map 21)** on Milwaukee Avenue offers everything a budding witch or warlock could desire. And you can overthrow your repressed bookshelf with works by Marx and Mao from **Revolution Books (Map 22)** on Ashland.

Quimby's (Map 21) in Wicker Park specializes in esoteric small–press books and 'zines with a marked counter–culture feel. You'll find your John Fante, Kathy Acker, and Georges Bataille here. **Printer's Row Fine & Rare Books (Map 8)** has a focus on architecture titles.

Used Bookstores

Shuffle through the used stacks at **Bookworks (Map 43)** on North Clark, **Kate the Great's (Map 37)** in Edgewater, or **Myopic (Map 21)** in Wicker Park. **Selected Works (Map 44)** on Broadway sells used books and sheet music. **Powell's (Map 8, Map 19, Map 43)** has made a name for itself for its great selection of remaindered and off–price lit.

Chain Bookstores

If you must chain it, the **Barnes & Noble (Map 29)** near the Webster Place cinema has a convenient parking lot. **Borders (Map 32)** on North Michigan is accessible for Mag Mile shoppers, ditto the address at 150 **North State (Map 5)** for State Street excursions.

Chicago Books on the Web

www.literago.org is a fun, hip site that highlights readings and other literary events throughout chicago .

www.bookslut.com is a fun, snarky book review and industry gossip forum based out of Chicago .

www.womenandchildrenfirst.com is the site of the indie, feminist bookstore that hosts an active, (usually) free reading series that has featured such authors as Katha Pollitt, Margaret Atwood, Alice Walker, and many, many more.

Map 1 • River North / Fulton Market District

N Fagin Books	459 N Milwaukee Ave	312-829-5252	Social sciences.

Map 2 • Near North / River North

Abraham Lincoln Book Shop	357 W Chicago Ave	312-944-3085	History and military specialty store.
After-Words	23 E Illinois St	312-464-1110	New and used.
B Dalton	222 Merchandise Mart Plz	312-329-1881	Chain.
Beck's Book Store	50 E Chicago Ave	312-944-7685	Where there's a Beck's, there's a campus.

Map 3 • Streeterville / Mag Mile

Abbott Hall Book Center	710 N Lake Shore Dr	312-503-8486	Textbooks.
Barbara's	201 E Huron St	312-926-2665	Branch of local chain.
University of Chicago Graduate School of Business	450 N Cityfront Plz Dr	312-464-8650	Textbooks.

Map 4 • West Loop Gate / Greek Town

Waldenbooks	500 W Madison St	312-627-8334	Chain.

Map 5 • The Loop

Barbara's	111 N State St	312-781-3033	Branch of local chain.
Barbara's	233 S Wacker Dr	312-466-0223	Branch of local chain.
Barnes & Noble	1 E Jackson Blvd	312-362-8792	Chain.
Beck's Book Store	60 E Lake St	312-630-9113	Where there's a Beck's, there's a campus.
Beck's Book Store	315 S Plymouth Ct	312-913-0650	Where there's a Beck's, there's a campus.
Books-a-Million	144 S Clark St	312-857-0613	Chain.
Borders	150 N State St	312-606-0750	State Street books.
Brent Books & Cards	309 W Washington St	312-364-0126	General.
Graham Crackers Comics	77 E Madison St	312-629-1810	Comics.
Prairie Avenue Bookshop	418 S Wabash Ave	312-922-8311	Le Corbusier, you say? Architecture bookstore and more.

Map 6 • The Loop / Grant Park

Art Institute of Chicago	111 S Michigan Ave	312-443-3583	Art books and souvenirs.
Chicago Architecture Foundation	224 S Michigan Ave	312-922-3432	Lots of pretty pictures.

Map 8 • South Loop / Printers Row / Dearborn Park

Books In The City South Loop	545 S State St	312-291-1111	Textbooks.
Powell's	828 S Wabash Ave	312-341-0748	Used and remainders.
Printers Row Fine & Rare Books	715 S Dearborn St	312-583-1800	The name says it all.
Sandmeyer's Book Store	714 S Dearborn St	312-922-2104	General.

Map 9 • South Loop / South Michigan Ave

Columbia College	624 S Michigan Ave	312-427-4860	Some general books, mostly textbooks.

Map 10 • East Pilsen / Chinatown

Chinese Champion Book & Gift	2167 S China Pl	312-326-3577	Chinese books.
World Journal	2116 S Archer Ave	312-842-8005	A world of Chinese books.

Map 11 • South Loop / McCormick Place

Paragon Book Gallery	1507 S Michigan Ave	312-663-5155	Asian arts.

Map 14 • Prairie Shores / Lake Meadows

Matthews Illinois College of Optometry Bookstore	3241 S Michigan Ave	312-949-7471	Textbooks.

Map 16 • Bronzeville

Afrocentric Bookstore	4655 S King Dr	773-924-3966	Celebrates the African-American literary tradition.

Map 19 • Hyde Park

57th Street Books	1301 E 57th St	773-684-1300	Frequented by U of C brainiacs.
Borders	1539 E 53rd St	773-752-8663	General/chain.
Frontline Books & Crafts & Crystal Power	5206 S Harper Ave	773-288-7718	New age.
O'Gara & Wilson	1448 E 57th St	773-363-0993	Used books.
Powell's	1501 E 57th St	773-955-7780	Remainders and off-price books. Mostly scholarly.
Seminary Co-op Bookstore	5757 S University Ave	773-752-4381	Underground trove of scholarly books for all.
University of Chicago Bookstore	970 E 58th St	773-702-7712	Textbooks.

Map 21 • Wicker Park / Ukrainian Village

Brainstorm	1648 W North Ave	773-384-8721	Comic books.
hejfina	1529 N Milwaukee Ave	773-772-0002	Fine art and Architecture.
Myopic Books	1564 N Milwaukee Ave	773-862-4882	Rare and collectable books.
Occult Bookstore	1164 N Milwaukee Ave	773-292-0995	I put a spell on you.
Quimby's Bookstore	1854 W North Ave	773-342-0910	Edgy, counter-culture bookshop.

Map 22 • Noble Square / Goose Island

Revolution Books	1103 N Ashland Ave	773-489-0930	Radical and revolutionary books.
Transitions Bookplace	1000 W North Ave	312-951-7323	Heal thyself.

Map 23 • West Town / Near West Side

CNW Book Store	1900 W Van Buren St	312-829-6482	Get your Malcolm X College textbooks here.

Map 24 • River West / West Town

Joyce & Company	400 N Racine Ave	312-738-1933	Out of print books.

Map 25 • Illinois Medical District

Logan Medical Bookstore	600 S Paulina St	312-733-4544	Medical books.
UIC Medical Bookstore	828 S Wolcott Ave	312-413-5550	Reading material for when you're laid up.

Map 26 • University Village / Little Italy / Pilsen

Chicago Textbook	1076 W Taylor St	312-733-8398	Textbooks.
Libreria Giron	1443 W 18th St	312-226-2086	Spanish.

Map 28 • Bucktown

Libreria Nazareth De Lourves	1907 N Milwaukee Ave	773-342-8890	Spanish books.
Micro Center	2645 N Elston Ave	773-292-1700	Department store chain.

Map 29 • DePaul / Wrightwood / Sheffield

Barnes & Noble	1441 W Webster Ave	773-871-3610	Convenient for the run-in-and-grab-something shopper.
Transitions Bookplace	1000 W North Ave	312-951-7232	New Age.

Map 30 • Lincoln Park

Books in the City	2428 N Lincoln Ave	773-472-2665	Textbooks.
Graham Crackers Comics	2562 N Clark St	773-665-2010	Where good and evil meet.

Map 31 • Old Town / Near North

Borders	755 W North Ave	312-266-8060	General/chain.

Map 32 • Gold Coast / Mag Mile

Barnes & Noble	1130 N State St	312-280-8155	Chain.
Borders	830 N Michigan Ave	312-573-0564	Mag Mile books.
Europa Books	832 N State St	312-335-9677	Foreign language books.
Newberry Bookstore	60 W Walton St	312-255-3520	Connected to the cultural library.
Waldenbooks	900 N Michigan Ave	312-337-0330	Chain.

Map 33 • West Rogers Park

India Book House & Journals	2551 W Devon Ave	773-764-6567	Spiritual/cultural.
Iqra Book Center	2751 W Devon Ave	773-274-2665	Islamic books.
Russian American Book Store	2746 W Devon Ave	773-761-3233	Floor to ceiling with musty books, as it should be.

Map 34 • East Rogers Park

Armadillos Pillow	6753 N Sheridan Rd	773-761-2558	General used.
Beck's Book Store	6550 N Sheridan Rd	773-743-2281	Where there's a Beck's, there's a campus.

Map 35 • Arcadia Terrace / Peterson Park

Korean Books	5773 N Lincoln Ave	773-769-1010	Korean books.

Arts & Entertainment • Bookstores

Map 37 • Edgewater / Andersonville

Ginkgo Leaf Books	1759 W Rosehill Dr	773-989-2200	Rare and collectable books.
Heritage Books	1135 W Granville Ave	773-262-1566	Books of African-American interest.
Kate the Great Bookstore	5550 N Broadway St	773-561-1932	Used and New.
Women & Children First	5233 N Clark St	773-769-9299	Spacious feminist bookshop.

Map 39 • Ravenswood / North Center

Book Cellar	4736 N Lincoln Ave	773-293-2665	General books and café.
Darktower Comics	4835 N Western Ave	773-506-0400	Comics.
Ravenwood Used Books	4626 N Lincoln Ave	773-593-9166	General used. Classic literature.
Variety Comic Book Store	4602 N Western Ave	773-334-2550	Comic books.

Map 40 • Uptown

Beck's Book Store	4520 N Broadway St	773-784-7963	Where there's a Beck's, there's a campus.
Borders	4718 N Broadway St	773-334-7338	General/chain.
Shake Rattle and Read Book Box	4812 N Broadway St	773-334-5311	Weird little store. Mostly used, some new.
Stern's Psychology Book Store	1256 W Victoria St	773-506-0683	Psychology books.

Map 41 • Avondale / Old Irving

Devry Follett Bookstore-Chicago	3300 N Campbell Ave	773-477-2600	Textbooks, etc.

Map 42 • North Center / Roscoe Village / West Lakeview

Casa de Carina	2834 N Western Ave	773-395-2834	Spanish language self-help and personal growth.
Galaxy Comic Zone	3804 N Western Ave	773-267-1043	Comic books.

Map 43 • Wrigleyville/ East Lakeview

Beasley Books	1533 W Oakdale Ave, 2nd Fl	773-472-4528	Jazz/Blues, Labor History.
Bookworks	3444 N Clark St	773-871-5318	Used and rare books.
Chicago Comics	3244 N Clark St	773-528-1983	Fun! Not geeky, really...
Gallery Bookstore	923 W Belmont Ave	773-975-8200	Used books.
Hanley's	923 W Belmont Ave	773-975-8200	Mystery, sci-fi, and horror genre shop.
Powell's	2850 N Lincoln Ave	773-248-1444	Remainders and off-price books. Large art, architecture, photography and rare departments.

Map 44 • East Lakeview

Barnes & Noble	659 W Diversey Pkwy	773-871-9004	Chain.
Bookleggers Used Books	2907 N Broadway St	773-404-8780	Used books.
Borders	2817 N Clark St	773-935-3909	Behemoth on Clark and Broadway.
City Bookshop	3125 N Broadway	773-880-8003	Used books.
Selected Works Bookstore	3510 N Broadway St	773-975-0002	Quirky, junky used book store.
Unabridged Books	3251 N Broadway St	773-883-9119	Great literary bookshop, best gay selection in town.

The Grande Dames of Chicago's museum scene, **The Art Institute of Chicago (Map 6)**, the **Museum of Science and Industry (Map 20)**, and the Museum Campus's **Adler Planetarium (Map 11)**, **Field Museum (Map 11)**, and **Shedd Aquarium (Map 9)**, may offer a lifetime of wonder, speculation, and enrichment; but impressive as they are, these cultural epicenters are only the tip of the iceberg when it comes to our city's museum offerings.

Art Museums

Although the Art Institute's collection *is* undeniably impressive (see p385), Chicago's true art lovers know to look past the lions to some of Chicago's less-celebrated treasures.

Columbia College's **Museum of Contemporary Photography (Map 9)** is one of two accredited photography museums in the nation. Other campus–linked art museums include University of Chicago's **Smart Museum (Map 19)**, where the collection spans some 5,000 years. Catch the Lunch at **Loyola University Museum of Art (Map 34)** series for a quick bite with artists and experts on exhibits. Artwork created by and commemorating veterans (from both sides) of the Vietnam War hangs on the walls of the **National Vietnam Veterans Art Museum (Map 11)**.

One of the country's largest collections of art post–1945 is housed at the always eye-opening **Museum of Contemporary Art (Map 3)**. The first Friday of the month, hundreds of twenty–something singles converge here for cocktails, live entertainment, and friendly flirtation.

History

The **Chicago History Museum (Map 32)** (previously the Chicago Historical Society) is a tremendous archive of the city's past and present. African–American history is celebrated at the nation's oldest museum focusing on the black experience, the **DuSable Museum of African–American History (Map 18)**. The **Oriental Institute (Map 19)** specializes in artifacts from the ancient Near–East, including Persia, Mesopotamia, and Egypt. Nobel Prize–winning sociologist **Jane Addams's Hull–House (Map 26)** examines Chicago's history of immigration, ethnic relations, and social work. "Artifacts" such as a John Lennon guitar and song lyrics by Bono are highlights of the collection at **The Peace Museum (West)**. Exhibits focus on individual peacemakers and artists, human rights, women's leadership, and the horrors of war. Contemplate big thoughts behind little objects like Mother Theresa's coffee mug, Martin Luther King Jr.'s toothbrush, and Nelson Mandela's sunglasses.

Science and Technology

As if the aforementioned **Adler Planetarium (Map 11)**, **Shedd Aquarium (Map 9)**, and **Field Museum (Map 11)** (all of which get special treatment within the Parks & Places listings under "Museum Campus") and the **Museum of Science and Industry (Map 20)** (listed with "Jackson Park") weren't enough to satisfy your inner nerd, Chicago is also home to a handful of quirky, smaller science museums. The **International Museum of Surgical Science (Map 32)** offers a window to the world of questionable surgical practices of yore. The **Museum of Holography (Map 24)** examines the art and technology of making things appear 3–D. For kids, the **Children's Museum (Navy Pier)** presents a hands–on approach to learning about science and geography. Conservation and the environment are the focus of the **Peggy Notebaert Nature Museum (Map 30)**, which also features a butterfly haven, delighting the child in us all.

Architecture

The city itself is perhaps one of the best architecture museums in the world. Examine it by embarking on one of the tours offered by the **Chicago Architecture Foundation (Map 6)**. Frank Lloyd Wright's influence on Chicago architecture can be examined at the **Robie House (Map 19)** in Hyde Park and the Frank Lloyd Wright Home and Studio in Oak Park. Chicago's Prairie Avenue District offers an architectural glimpse at Chicago's Victorian Golden Age. Joint tours of the oldest house in Chicago, the **Clarke House (Map 11)** (c. 1836), and the neighboring **Glessner House (Map 11)** offer the curious an interesting inside peek.

Ethnic Museums

Immigration made Chicago into the "City of Neighborhoods." The **Swedish American Museum Center (Map 37)**, the **Chinese Historical Society of America (Map 10)**, the **Balzekas Museum of Lithuanian Culture (Map 53)**, and the **Polish Museum of America (Map 22)** all explore the impact of immigration on Chicago. The **Hellenic Museum and Cultural Center (Map 6)** is a celebration of all things Greek. The **Mexican Fine Arts Center (Map 25)** is the largest such museum in the country, and examines the Mexican experience through art and culture. The **Spertus Museum (Map 9)**, scheduled to reopen in the fall of 2007, specializes in Jewish history and heritage. Its hands–on reproduction of an archeological dig is eternally popular with kids.

Miscellaneous

Housed in the former home of the legendary, influential blues label, Chess Records, Willie Dixon's **Blues Heaven Foundation (Map 11)** offers tours of where Chuck Berry, Muddy Waters, and even the Rolling Stones once recorded. (The site is memorialized in the Stones' song "2120 South Michigan.")

For the darker side of sightseeing, the **Leather Archives and Museum (Map 34)** exhibits eight galleries of fetish, bondage, and S&M artifacts including photographs, clothing, toys, and more. The **Antiques Fabricare Museum (Map 48)** offers a seemingly "cleaner" afternoon out with the chance to view antique irons, washing machines, and decades–old washing powders.

The **Museum of Broadcast Communications (Map 2)**, one of only three broadcast museums and home to the only Radio Hall of Fame in the nation, recently moved from the Chicago Cultural Center to its own space on State Street.

Museum	Address	Phone	Map
A Philip Randolph Pullman Porter Museum	10406 S Maryland Ave	773-928-3935	South
ABA Museum of Law	321 N Clark St	312-988-6222	32
Adler Planetarium & Astronomy Museum	1300 S Lake Shore Dr	312-922-7827	11
Antiques Fabricare Museum	4213 W Irving Park Rd	773-282-6216	South
Art Institute of Chicago	111 S Michigan Ave	312-443-3600	6
Balzekas Museum of Lithuanian Culture	6500 S Pulaski Rd	773-582-6500	SW
Bronzeville Children's Museum	9600 S Western Ave	708-636-9504	SW
Charnley-Persky House	1365 N Astor St	312-915-0105	32
Chicago Architecture Foundation	224 S Michigan Ave	312-922-3432	6
Chicago Blues Museum	3636 S Iron St	773-828-8118	12
Chicago Children's Museum	700 E Grand Ave, Navy Pier	312-527-1000	p234
Chicago History Museum	1601 N Clark St	312-642-4600	32
Chicago Maritime Society	310 S Racine Ave	312-421-9096	24
Chinese Historical Society of America	238 W 23rd St	312-949-1000	10
Clarke House Museum	1827 S Indiana Ave	312-745-0040	11
Columbia College Center for Book & Paper Arts	1104 S Wabash Ave	312-344-6630	8
DePaul University Art Museum	2350 N Kenmore Ave	773-325-7506	29
DL Moody Museum	820 N La Salle Dr	312-329-4000	32
DuSable Museum of African-American History	740 E 56th Pl	773-947-0600	18
The Field Museum	1400 S Lake Shore Dr	312-922-9410	11
Frank Lloyd Wright Home and Studio	951 Chicago Ave, Oak Park	708-848-1976	p236
Glessner House Museum	1800 S Prairie Ave	312-326-1480	11
Hellenic Museum and Cultural Center	801 W Adams St	312-655-1234	6
Holocaust Memorial Foundation of Illinois	4255 Main St, Skokie	847- 677-4640	p240
Hyde Park Historical Society	5529 S Lake Park Ave	773-493-1893	19
International Museum of Surgical Science	1524 N Lake Shore Dr	312-642-6502	32
Intuit: Center for Intuitive and Outsider Art	756 N Milwaukee Ave	312-243-9088	24
Irish-American Heritage Center	4642 N Knox Ave	773-282-7035	NW
Jane Addams Hull-House Museum	800 S Halsted St	312-413-5353	26
Jazz Institute of Chicago	410 S Michigan Ave	312-427-1676	6
Leather Archives & Museum	6418 N Greenview Ave	773-761-9200	34
Loyola University Museum of Art	820 N Michigan Ave	312-915-7600	32
Mexican Fine Arts Center	1852 W 19th St	312-738-1503	25
The Museum of Broadcast Communications	400 N State St	312-245-8200	2
Museum of Contemporary Art	220 E Chicago Ave	312-280-2660	3
Museum of Contemporary Photography	600 S Michigan Ave - Columbia College	312-663-5554	9
Museum of Holography-Chicago	1134 W Washington Blvd	312-226-1007	24
Museum of Science and Industry	5700 S Lake Shore Dr	773-684-1414	20
National Vietnam Veterans Art Museum	1801 S Indiana Ave	312-326-0270	11
The Newberry Library	60 W Walton St	312-943-9090	32
Oriental Institute Museum	1155 E 58th St	773-702-9514	19
The Peace Museum	100 N Central Park Ave	773-638-6450	West
Peggy Notebaert Nature Museum	2430 N Cannon Dr	773-755-5100	30
Polish Museum of America	984 N Milwaukee Ave	773-384-3352	22
Ridge Historical Society	10621 S Seeley Ave	773-881-1675	SW
Robie House	5757 S Woodlawn Ave	773-834-1847	19
Rogers Park/West Ridge Historical Society	7344 N Western Ave	773-764-4078	33
Shedd Aquarium, John G	1200 S Lake Shore Dr	312-939-2438	9
Skokie Heritage Museum	8031 Floral Ave, Skokie	847-677-6672	p240
Smart Museum of Art	5550 S Greenwood Ave	773-702-0200	19
Smith Museum of Stained Glass	700 E Grand Ave, Navy Pier	312-595-5024	p234
Spertus Museum	610 S Michigan Ave	312-322-1700	9
Swedish American Museum	5211 N Clark St	773-728-8111	37
Ukrainian Institute of Modern Art	2320 W Chicago Ave	773-227-5522	23
Ukrainian National Museum	2249 W Superior St	312-421-8020	23
Willie Dixon's Blues Heaven Foundation	2120 S Michigan Ave	312-808-1286	11

The impeccably restored **Music Box Theatre (Map 43)**, built in 1929, features fantastic Moorish architecture, floating clouds on the ceilings, and live organ music at many weekend screenings. Specialties include the latest art house and international releases, as well as restored classics and weekend matinee double–features that follow monthly themes. Holiday season sing–alongs of White Christmas are huge hits that sell out in advance. The Music Box is also the major screening ground for International Film Festival and Gay and Lesbian Film Festival releases.

Other worthy art–house screening rooms include the **Landmark Century Centre Cinema (Map 44)** at the Century Mall and **Lowes Piper's Alley Theater (Map 31)** in Old Town. For even more refined or esoteric options, pick up schedules for the **Gene Siskel Film Center (Map 5)** of the Art Institute, **Facets Multimedia (Map 29)** in the DePaul neighborhood, **Chicago Filmmakers (Map 37)** in Andersonville and the **LaSalle Bank Cinema (Northwest)** on Irving Park Road.

The latest action features should be seen at **Loews (Map 29)** at Webster Place, **ICE Chatham (South)** off of 87th & the Dan Ryan, and Streeterville's **AMC River East (Map 3)**, which offer ample theaters and show times. Cheap seats on relatively new releases can be had at Lincoln Square's **Davis Cinema (Map 39)**, the **Village Art Theater (Map 32)** along the Gold Coast, and the **Village North Theater (Map 34)** in East Rogers Park. The legendary **University of Chicago Doc Films (Map 19)** in Hyde Park has the perfect balance of historical, contemporary and international films. This student-run film society boasts cheap shows and seduces the intellectual crowd.

One of Chicago's most notorious places to catch a flick is **The Vic's "Brew and View," (Map 43)** where the drunken frat boy audiences are almost as annoying as the movies that they show.

Movie Theaters	Address	Phone	Map	
The Alliance Francaise	810 N Dearborn St	312-337-1070	32	Sparse, almost free French films.
AMC Ford City 14	7601 S Cicero Ave	773-582-1839	SW	Mainly teeny-boppers & families coming from the mall.
AMC Loews 600	600 N Michigan Ave	312-255-9347	3	Good concession options, limited times, expensive parking.
AMC Loews Gardens 1/6	175 Old Orchard Ctr, Skokie	847-674-0072	p240	Standard Megaplex.
AMC Loews Norridge 10	4520 N Harlem Ave	708-452-6677	NW	Megaplex suburbanite hell, unless you're a suburbanite.
AMC Loews Pipers Alley 4	1608 N Wells St	312-642-6275	31	Gorgeous backdrop & great independent films.
AMC River East	322 E Illinois St	312-596-0333	3	Blockbuster flicks, billiards, bar & bowling.
Brew & View	3145 N Sheffield Ave	312-618-8439	43	For the lush who likes old movies.
Chicago Cultural Center	78 E Washington St	312-744-6630	5	Free, cultural films and docs.
Chicago Filmmakers	5243 N Clark St	773-293-1447	37	Classes and films, no mainstream mess & no pretense.
Davis Theater	4614 N Lincoln Ave	773-784-0893	39	Four screens. Old, cute, cash-only, homie.
Facets Multimedia	1517 W Fullerton Ave	773-281-4114	29	Obscure independent films anyone?
Gene Siskel Film Center	164 N State St	312-846-2800	5	Tasty smorgasbord of international films.
Henry Crown MSI Omnimax	5700 S Lake Shore Dr	773-684-1414	20	Bring kids, 3-D glasses, and loot, cuz it ain't cheap.
ICE Chatham 14	210 87th St	773-783-8711	South	Mega-theater with comfy seats and fab parking.
Kerasotes Chicago City North 14	2600 N Western Ave	312-394-1600	28	Multiple spacious theaters, diverse crowd, plenty of parking.
Kerasotes Chicago Webster	1471 W Webster Ave	773-327-1314	29	Huge crowds, common date spot, latest movies.
Landmark Century Centre Cinema	2828 N Clark St	773-248-7759	44	Get stimulated by international films, then go shopping at mall.
LaSalle Bank Cinema	4901 W Irving Park Rd	312-904-9442	NW	Cheap vintage films, great parking, cash only.
Logan Theater	2646 N Milwaukee Ave	773-252-0628	27	Charming neighborhood spot, second-run, $3 flicks.
Museum of Contemporary Art Movie Theater	220 E Chicago Ave	312-397-4010	3	Few films, more live performance art.
Music Box Theatre	3733 N Southport Ave	773-871-6604	43	Antiquated theater with character, bad seats & great films.
Navy Pier IMAX Theatre	600 E Grand Ave, Navy Pier	312-595-5629	p234	Expensive, but cute spot for families with youngens.
University of Chicago Doc Films	1212 E 59th St	773-702-8575	19	Student-run film society, kickass variety of films, dirt cheap.
Village Art Theater	1548 N Clark St	312-642-2403	32	Small and dank, but cheap price for slightly old flicks.

If you live in Chicago, you know a few things for sure: Hot dogs should have sweet relish, pickles, tomato, onion, sport peppers, and yellow mustard; the Cubs always lose; deep-dish is the best kind of pizza; and Chicago is a *theater* town. You can't swing Mrs. O'Leary's cow without hitting a tiny, struggling off-Loop storefront theater. The storefront theaters are so prevalent here that the city's Department of Cultural Affairs, in its effort to bring smaller productions to the newly revitalized "theater district" (more on that later), named its new downtown venue after them (**Storefront Theater (Map 5)**).

General Tips

The Theater section of the *Chicago Reader*, a free weekly available citywide in bookstores, cafés, bars, and in boxes on street corners (or online at www.chicagoreader.com) is the best friend of the Chicago theatergoer-in-the-know. Turn to the Short List, look for "Highly Recommended" status, or search for Critic's Choices to ferret out your best bets. Another source is the *New City's* "Top Five Shows to See Now" list. Look for free copies of *New City* in the same places as the *Reader*. Hottix (www.hottix.org), a program of the League of Chicago Theaters, offers half-price tickets to same-day shows on a first-come-first-served basis. Most small theatres, however, won't charge you more than $15 or $20 for a seat—and the larger houses tend to have day-of and student rush tickets available in person at the box office. Also, if you are new in town and want to break into the biz, drop by any theater in your 'hood and pick up a copy of *PerformInk*, the Chicago trade paper for theater and the performing arts, or check 'em out online at www.performink.com. Many auditions and theatre-related gigs are also listed at www.chicagoplays.com via the "industry" link. Also, for the budget conscious, The Saints (a volunteer usher program used by most of the large and medium-sized theaters in Chicago) offers opportunities to usher and see multiple plays for free. You have to join their ranks for an annual $55 fee, but think of how much you'll save on theater tickets. Check out www.saintschicago.org for more information.

Let's get this out of the way. If you want to see a big, traveling Broadway show, check out www.broadwayinchicago.com. There you can find the listings for **Cadillac Palace Theatre (Map 5)**, **Ford Center for the Performing Arts/Oriental Theatre (Map 5)**, the **LaSalle Bank Theatre (Map 5)**, or the beautiful and historic **Auditorium Theatre (Map 5)** (designed by Louis Sullivan). When in doubt, the city will always have *Wicked* (at least it seems that way). But Chicago, my friends, offers so much more than just second runs…

Downtown Theaters a.k.a. "The Downtown Theater District"

There are many large theaters producing quality work in downtown Chicago. One of the oldest theaters in Chicago, **The Goodman Theatre (Map 5)** is a stalwart of the downtown theater scene. Now in its new location at 170 North Dearborn, the Goodman is a professional theater featuring high-quality plays by well-known and lesser-known playwrights. One of the classic Chicago theaters,

Steppenwolf Theatre Co. (Map 30) in Old Town produces wonderful ensemble productions with notable Chicago actors. Among their famous ensemble members are John Mahoney, John Malkovich, Laurie Metcalf, Martha Plimpton, and Gary Sinise. Similarly, **Lookingglass Theatre (Map 43)** (known for ensemble member David Schwimmer of *Friends* fame) creates productions that incorporate skills and acts you might otherwise find in the circus. Their new location (in Chicago's Water Tower Water Works building, one of the few structures to survive the famous 1871 Chicago fire) is well worth a trip downtown. Known as a playwright's theater, **Victory Gardens Theater (Map 30)** produces original works by contemporary, living playwrights in a newly renovated space in the historic Biograph Theatre on Lincoln Avenue. On Navy Pier, you'll find **Chicago Shakespeare Theater (Map 3)**, which offers up classy (but pricey) stagings of the Bard. Another Chicago theatre staple is *Blue Man Group*, which has completely taken over **Briar Street Theatre (Map 44)** with paint, drums, and marshmallows. Finally, the **Storefront Theater (Map 5)**, at the Chicago Department of Cultural Affairs, remounts the best of the neighborhood theater productions in its state of the art venue at 66 E Randolph.

Medium-Sized Neighborhood Theaters

Really amazing productions can be found at medium-sized neighborhood theaters. Some of the best picks include the longest running show in Chicago today, *Too Much Light Makes the Baby Go Blind* (at **The Neo-Futurarium (Map 37)**). Proclaiming to perform thirty plays in sixty minutes, the show ends when one or the other is over. Other good bets include **Stage Left Theatre (Map 43)** (whose work has cultivated some of the best national playwrights), **Live Bait Theater (Map 43)** (first-run plays), **About Face Theatre (Map 44)** (high-quality gay/lesbian/bisexual works), **Famous Door Theatre (Map 43)** (original and "seldom-produced" works), and **Redmoon Theater (Map 24)** (highly unique large-scale puppetry productions).

Improv

Chicago is also well known for its improv scene. The original, **The Second City (Map 31)** (the famed training ground for most of *Saturday Night Live's* original cast) keeps on going with its many shows at four venues in Chicago. Check out www.secondcity.com for show times. Other improv venues include **The Playground Theater (Map 42)**, **ImprovOlympic Theater (Map 43)** (with its free Friday and Saturday midnight "Cage Match"), **Annoyance Theatre (Map 40)**, **Comedy Sportz (Map 44)**, and **WNEP Theater (Map 39)**. Most of these venues feature improv teams battling against one another for audience approval. Information about all venues can be found on www.improvchicago.com.

Fringe/Performance Art/Other

At the **Museum of Contemporary Art (Map 3)** (www.mcachicago.org), a new theatre built of concrete offers a stage for a variety of theatre, dance, performance art, and readings of all ilks.

But if you don't catch the bigger shows (read: more expensive) at the MCA, some of Chicago's best productions occur in alternative spaces. They are created by smaller companies who don't have a venue (whether by choice or by size). These are the tiny, glittering gems of the Chicago theater scene. Find these productions in the Performance Listings in the *Reader*. Don't shy away from a theater company you've never heard of producing at a rented venue. You might just find your new favorite group of artists—and it's fun to latch onto a company, watch them grow, and then say "I knew them when." We can't list them all here (for they are too numerous), but here are some of our favorites.

For girl-on-girl combat action, check out *Babes with Blades* (www.babeswithblades.com) in semi-regular productions at various venues. 500 Clown (www.500clown.com) produces loose adaptations of classic tales (*Frankenstein, Macbeth*) in original, dangerous clown theater that the authors wouldn't recognize. *Defiant Theatre* (www.defianttheatre.org) subverts the social, moral, and aesthetic expectations of the theater with edgy productions at varied venues. At Strawdog, you'll find fresh takes on everything from classics to contemporary works to radio plays presented by a cohesive ensemble (www.strawdog.org). Collaboration (known mainly for its *Sketchbook* series of ultra-short new plays) is a collective comprising cross-disciplinary artists presenting unique works in all media. Check them out at www.collaboration. org. The House Theatre of Chicago (www.thehousetheatre. org) has drawn major critical praise (and major audiences) with its smart, witty adaptations and new works that incorporate dance, music, and magic. For super-intellectual takes on classic plays, seek out the Hypocrites (www.the-hypocrites.com). Uma (www.umaproductions.org) offers interesting, thought-provoking productions in a variety of styles. At Theater Oobleck (www.theateroobleck.com), you can expect to find quirky plays written by the ensemble and rehearsed without the help of a director. Drawing from diverse sources, Goat Island Performance Ensemble (www. goatislandperformance.org) offers up heady movement-based performance created in a lengthy ensemble process. *Plasticene* (www.plasticene.com) confronts audiences with rare physical theater. In the summer, look for remounts of favorite local productions at **Theater on the Lake (Map 30)** (www.chicagoparkdistrict.com), a screened-in theater venue (and former TB sanitarium) situated near Fullerton Avenue on Chicago's lakefront. Curious Theater Branch (www.curioustheaterbranch.com) has presented original, engaging theater for the last eleven years.

Out of Town

There also are some fantastic theatrical adventures just beyond the borders of our fair city. For outstanding productions of plays that focus on writing and language, check out Writer's Theatre in Glencoe. A little bit closer to home, Evanston offers some quality productions by Next Theatre, Light Opera Works, and acclaimed theater department at Northwestern University. West of the City, Oak Park offers up gems at the Village Players and the Oak Park Festival Theatre (which offers outdoor plays and musicals during the summer months). In Wilmette, an annual musical production is presented at the Wallace Bowl, in Gillson Park, just across the street from the Bahai temple.

All told, Chicago boasts somewhere in the neighborhood of 250 theatre companies – all of which believe they have something new and different to offer to the city. Any given weekend is likely to offer scores of theatrical options—so make it your business to get out to see some of them.

Theater	Address	Phone	Map
A Red Orchid Theatre	1531 N Wells St	312-943-8722	31
About Face Theatre	1222 W Wilson Ave	773-784-8565	44
American Girl Place	111 E Chicago Ave	877-247-5223	2
American Theater Company	1909 W Byron St	773-929-1031	42
Angel Island Theater	735 W Sheridan Rd	773-871-0442	44
Annoyance Productions	4840 N Broadway St	773-561-4665	40
Apollo Theater Chicago	2540 N Lincoln Ave	773-935-6100	29
Arie Crown Theatre	2301 S Lake Shore Dr	312-791-6190	11
Athenaeum Theatre	2936 N Southport Ave	773-935-6860	43
Auditorium Theatre	50 E Congress Pkwy	312-922-2110	5
Bailiwick Repertory Theatre	1229 W Belmont Ave	773-883-1090	43
Black Ensemble Theater	4520 N Beacon St	773-769-4451	40
Briar Street Theatre	3133 N Halsted St	773-348-4000	44
Cadillac Palace Theatre	151 W Randolph St	312-977-1700	5
Casa Aztlan	1831 S Racine Ave	312-666-5508	26
Chase Park	4701 N Ashland Ave	312-742-7518	40
Chicago Center for the Performing Arts	777 N Green St	312-733-6000	1
Chicago Cultural Center	78 E Washington St	312-744-6630	5
Chicago Dramatists	1105 W Chicago Ave	312-633-0630	24
Chicago Shakespeare Theater	800 E Grand Ave	312-595-5600	3
The Chicago Theatre	175 N State St	312-462-6363	5

Theater	Address	Phone	Map
Chopin Theater	1543 W Division St	773-278-1500	22
Civic Opera House	20 N Wacker Dr	312-419-0033	5
Cornservatory	4210 N Lincoln Ave	312-409-6435	39
Court Theatre	5535 S Ellis Ave	773-753-4472	19
Dance Center of Columbia College	1306 S Michigan Ave	312-344-8300	11
Drury Lane Theatre at Water Tower Place	175 E Chestnut St	312-642-2000	32
Ford Center for the Performing Arts/Oriental Theatre	24 W Randolph St	312-782-2004	5
Free Street Theater	1419 W Blackhawk St	773-772-7248	22
Getz Theater (Columbia College)	72 E 11th St	312-344-6126	8
The Goodman Theatre	170 N Dearborn St	312-443-3800	5
Gorilla Tango Theatre	1919 N Milwaukee Ave	773-598-4549	28
Harold Washington Cultural Center	4701 S Dr Martin L King Jr Dr	773-373-1900	16
Harris Theater for Music and Dance	205 E Randolph St	312-334-7777	5
The Heartland Café Studio Theater	7016 N Glenwood Ave	773-465-8005	34
Improv Olympic	3541 N Clark St	773-880-0199	43
Kathleen Mullady Memorial Theatre	1125 W Loyola Ave	773-508-3847	34
Lakeshore Theatre	3175 N Broadway Ave	773-472-3492	44
LaSalle Bank Theatre	22 W Monroe St	312-977-1710	5
Lifeline Theatre	6912 N Glenwood Ave	773-761-4477	34
Links Hall Studio	3435 N Sheffield Ave	773-281-0824	43
Live Bait Theater	3914 N Clark St	773-871-1212	43
Lookingglass Theatre	821 N Michigan Ave	312-337-0665	43
Mercury Theater	3745 N Southport Ave	773-325-1700	43
Merle Reskin Theatre	60 E Balbo Ave	312-922-1999	8
Museum of Contemporary Art	220 E Chicago Ave	312-280-2660	3
National Pastime Theater	4139 N Broadway St	773-327-7077	40
The Neo-Futurarium	5153 N Ashland Ave	773-275-5255	37
North Shore Center for the Performing Arts	9501 Skokie Blvd, Skokie	847-673-6300	p240
O'Malley Theater-Roosevelt University	430 S Michigan Ave	312-341-3831	6
O'Rourke Center for the Performing Arts	1145 W Wilson Ave	773-878-9761	40
Piccolo Theater	600 Main St, Evanston	847-424-0089	p214
The Playground Theater	3209 N Halsted St	773-871-3793	42
Profiles Theatre	4147 N Broadway St	773-549-1815	40
Prop Theatre	3504 N Elston Ave	773-539-7838	39
Raven Theatre	6157 N Clark St	773-338-2177	33
Redmoon Theater Co	1463 W Hubbard St	312-850-8440	24
Royal George Theatre Center	1641 N Halsted St	312-988-9000	30
Ruth Page Center Theater	1016 N Dearborn St	312-337-6543	32
The Second City	1616 N Wells St	312-664-4032	30
The Second City e.t.c./Donny's Skybox	1608 N Wells St	312-337-3992	31
The Side Project	1439 W Jarvis Ave	773-973-2105	34
Stage Left Theatre	3408 N Sheffield Ave	773-883-8830	43
Steep Theatre	3902 N Sheridan Rd	312-458-0722	43
Steppenwolf Theatre	1650 N Halsted St	312-335-1650	31
Storefront Theater	66 E Randolph St	312-742-8497	5
Strawdog Theatre	3829 N Broadway St	773-528-9696	44
Theater on the Lake	2400 N Lake Shore Dr	312-742-7994	30
Theatre Building	1225 W Belmont Ave	773-327-5252	43
TimeLine Theatre Co	615 W Wellington Ave	773-281-8463	44
TinFish Theatre	4247 N Lincoln Ave	773-549-1888	39
Trap Door Productions	1655 W Cortland St	773-384-0494	28
UIC Theatre	1044 W Harrison St	312-996-2939	26
Viaduct Theater	3111 N Western Ave	773-296-6024	42
Victory Gardens	2257 N Lincoln Ave	773-871-3000	30
Vittum Theater	1012 N Noble St	773-342-4141	22

FIELD GUIDE
TO THE URBAN
ENVIRONMENT
CHICAGOREADER.COM

**FOR ADVERTISING INFORMATION
CALL 312-828-0350**

Think local. Act global.

When Volunteers return home from
making a difference in another country,
they bring back real-world skills and
experience for their own community.

800.424.8580
www.peacecorps.gov

Life is calling. How far will you go?

PEACE CORPS

GOLD STAR

BAR

1755 W. Division

Understanding Your World, So You Don't Have To

Lead anchor Brandon Armstrong and the rest of the Onion team bring you, the ignorant masses, hard-hitting news, videos, and opinions you can't find anywhere else.

FREE IN PRINT WEEKLY AND ONLINE DAILY AT ONION.COM

America's Finest News Source

Butch McGuire's - The Legendary Saloon of Division St.

Great Pub Grub
Spectacular Brunch
Daily Specials
Private Parties

Famous Holiday Decorations
a must see!

20 West Division Street
Chicago, IL 60610
312-337-9080
butchmcguires.com

Some of the townships and communities immediately adjoining Chicago proper thought it would be a fun joke to restart street numbering at their borders—or name a street exactly the same name as an entirely unrelated Chicago street. These cases are designated with an asterisk.*

Street Index

Street Index

Street Index

Street	Page	Grid
W Estes Ave		
(1300–2029)	34	B1/B2
(2030–3598)	33	B1/B2
(3800–5199)	46	B3/B4
(5824–7599)	45	B1/B2
Euclid Ave	45	B1
S Euclid Ave		
(6700–9549)	58	A3/B3/C3
(9550–9699)	60	A3
W Eugenie St	30	C1/C2
S Evans Ave		
(4300–5099)	16	B2/C2
(6100–6349)	18	C2
(6350–9399)	57	—
(13000–13499)	59	C2
E Evans Ct	2	A2
W Evelyn Ln	47	A1
W Everell Ave	45	C1/C2
S Everett Ave	20	A1/B1
W Evergreen Ave		
(200–839)	31	B1/B2
(840–1663)	22	B1/B2
(1664–2199)	21	A2/B1/B2
(2600–3249)	50	A3
(3250–3599)	49	A2
(6800–6899)	55	C1
Ewing Ave	46	A4
S Ewing Ave		
(9200–9549)	58	C3
(10600–12099)	60	B3
S Exchange Ave		
(7100–9549)	58	B3/C3
(9550–13299)	60	A3/C3
W Exchange Ave		
(788–849)	15	A1
(850–1199)	52	B4
Executive Ct	47	A1

F

Street	Page	Grid
W Fair Pl	31	B1
N Fairbanks Ct	3	A1/B1
Fairfax St	55	B2
N Fairfield Ave		
(200–1549)	50	A3/B3
(1550–2799)	27	A2/B2/C2
(2900–2999)	41	C2
(4800–4999)	38	A2
(5600–6349)	35	A2/B2
(6350–7499)	33	A1/C1
S Fairfield Ave		
(900–2199)	50	C3
(4146–5049)	52	B3/C3
(5050–8849)	54	A3/B3/C3
(8850–11500)	56	A3/B3
Fairlane Dr	55	A1
Fairview Ave		
(5500–5699)	45	C1
(12400–12699)	56	C3
S Fairview Ave	45	A1/B1/C1
Fairview Ln	46	B3
Fairway Cir	56	C3
W Fargo Ave		
(1300–2065)	34	A1/A2
(2066–3199)	33	A1/A2
(3800–5499)	46	B3/B4
(6900–7750)	45	B1/B2

Street	Page	Grid
Farnsworth Dr	45	A1
W Farragut Ave		
(1400–1749)	37	C1
(1750–2449)	36	C1/C2
(2450–2999)	35	C1/C2
(5500–5599)	46	C3
(6900–8399)	47	A1/A2
S Farragut Dr	58	B3
S Farrar Dr	50	C3
S Farrell St	12	A2
W Farwell Ave		
(1100–2024)	34	B1/B2
(2025–2999)	33	B1/B2
(4700–5299)	46	B3
(7200–7399)	45	B2
Father Burns Dr	55	B2
S Federal St		
(300–449)	5	C2
(450–1259)	8	A1/C1
(1260–2549)	10	A2/B2/C2
(2550–3987)	13	A2/B2/C2
(3988–5168)	15	A2/B2/C2
(5169–5499)	57	A1
Feldner Ct	55	C1
N Felton Ct	31	B2
W Ferdinand St		
(1600–2398)	23	A1/A2
(3630–5499)	49	B1/B2
N Fern Ct	30	C1
Fernald Ave	45	A2
Ferris Ave	45	A2
W Fey Ln	55	C2
N Field Blvd	6	A2/B2
Field Dr	45	A1
Field Plaza Dr	9	C2
S Fielding Ave	57	B1
W Fillmore St		
(1300–1599)	26	A1
(1800–2549)	25	A1/A2
(2550–3249)	50	C3
(3250–5933)	49	C1/C2
S Financial Pl		
(300–499)	5	C1
(600–999)	8	A1/B1
Fireside Dr	55	B1
W Fitch Ave		
(2400–2999)	33	B1/B2
(3800–5199)	46	B3/B4
(5900–7346)	45	B2
Fitzjames Walk		
(4000–4019)	56	A3
(4020–4099)	55	A2
S Flambeau Dr	55	C1
W Fletcher Ave		
(700–819)	44	C1
(820–999)	43	B2
W Fletcher St		
(1200–1649)	43	B1
(1650–2449)	42	C1/C2
(2450–3099)	41	B1/B2
(4100–5399)	48	B3/B4
(6000–7999)	47	B1/B2
Floral Ave	46	A3
Florence Ave	33	A2
W Florence St	56	C4

Street	Page	Grid
W Flournoy St		
(1205–1669)	26	A1
(1670–2538)	25	A1/A2
(2539–3249)	50	B3/C3
(3250–5599)	49	C1/C2
S Ford Ave	26	C2
W Ford City Dr		
(4000–4045)	54	C3
(4046–4999)	53	C2
E Foreman Dr	60	A3
Forest Ave	47	C1
S Forest Ave		
(9100–9449)	57	C1
(9450–13499)	59	A2/B2/C2
Forest Ln	55	B1
N Forest Glen Ave	46	C3
W Forest Preserve Dr		
	47	A2/B1/B2
Forest View Ave	59	C1
(2400–2699)	47	C1
W Forest View Ln	45	B2
N Forestview Ave	47	A1
Forestview Rd	46	A4
S Forrestville Ave		
(4300–5099)	16	B2/C2
(11100–13434)	59	B2/C2
W Foster	47	A1
W Foster Ave		
(800–1749)	37	C1/C2
(1750–2499)	36	C1/C2
(2500–3215)	35	C1/C2
(3216–3599)	38	A1
(3601–5720)	48	A3/A4
(5721–8799)	47	A1/A2
W Foster Dr	37	C2
W Foster Pl	47	A2
Foxfire Dr	53	C1
Foxwoods Ct	55	B2
Foxwoods Dr	55	B2
Frances Pky	45	C1
W Francis Pl	27	B2
N Francisco Ave		
(1–1199)	50	A3/B3
(1600–2749)	27	A1/B1/C1
(2750–3949)	41	A1/B1/C1
(3950–5163)	38	A1/B1/C1
(5164–6349)	35	A1/B1/C1
(6350–7599)	33	A1/B1/C1
S Francisco Ave		
(1–1199)	50	B3/C3
(2400–4699)	52	A3/B3/C3
(5100–8849)	54	A3/B3/C3
(8850–12898)	56	A3/B3/C3
Frank Pky	47	A1
Franklin Ave	55	A2
W Franklin Blvd		
(3000–3257)	50	B3
(3231–3628)	49	B2
N Franklin St		
(1–248)	5	A1/B1
(219–815)	2	A1/B1/C1
(816–1125)	31	B2/C2
S Franklin St		
(1–399)	5	B1/C1
(400–599)	7	A2
N Franks Ave	45	B2

Street	Page	Grid
N Fremont St		
(1500–1599)	22	A2
(1700–3549)	29	B2/C2
(3550–3964)	43	A2
(3965–3999)	40	C2
S Front Ave	59	B2
Frontage Rd	46	A3/B3
E Frontage Rd	46	A3
N Frontage Rd	46	B3
W Frontage Rd	46	A3
S Frontenac Ave	57	A1
N Frontier Ave		
(1500–1599)	31	A1
(3900–3999)	40	C2
W Fry St	22	C1/C2
W Fuller St	12	A1
W Fullerton Ave		
(1–823)	30	A2/B1/B2
(824–1676)	29	B1/B2
(1677–2499)	28	B1/B2
(2477–3599)	27	B1/B2
(3600–5865)	48	C3/C4
(5866–8929)	47	C1/C2
W Fulton Blvd	49	B2
W Fulton St		
(500–864)	1	C1/C2
(865–1649)	24	B1/B2
(1650–2524)	23	B1/B2
(2525–3199)	50	B3
(3800–5933)	49	B1/B2

G

Street	Page	Grid
W Gale St	48	A3
Galitz St	46	A3
Garden St	45	B1
E Garfield Blvd	18	A2/B1/B2
W Garfield Blvd		
(1–99)	18	A1/B1
(100–799)	57	A1
(801–4655)	54	A3/A4
Garfield Sq	49	B2
N Garland Ct		
(1–261)	5	A2/B2
(262–299)	2	C2
N Garvey Ct		
(200–260)	5	A2
(261–299)	2	C2
W Gaslight Square Dr		
	56	C3
N Geneva Ter	30	A1/B1
S Genoa Ave		
(8700–8999)	57	C1
(9200–9999)	56	A4
W George St		
(800–849)	44	C1
(850–1599)	43	C1/C2
(1900–2449)	42	C1/C2
(2450–3399)	41	C1/C2
(3600–5815)	48	B3/B4/C3
(5816–7799)	47	B1/B2
Georgia Ave	55	B2
Georgia Dr		
(6900–7099)	45	A2
(10700–10899)	55	B2
Georgiana Ave	45	A2

Street Index

Street Index

General

All emergencies	**911**
AIDS Hotline	800-342-AIDS
Animal Anti-Cruelty Society	312-644-8338
Chicago Dental Referral Service	312-836-7305
Chicago Department of Housing	773-285-5800
City of Chicago Board of Elections	312-269-7900
Dog License (City Clerk)	312-744-6875
Driver's Licenses	312-793-1010
Emergency Services	312-747-7247
Employment Discrimination	312-744-7584
Gas Leaks	312-240-7000
Income Tax (Illinois)	800-732-8866
Income Tax (Federal)	800-829-3676
Legal Assistance	312-332-1624
Mayor's Office	312-744-4000
Parking (City Stickers)	312-742-9200
Parking Ticket Inquiries	312-744-7275
Report Crime in Your Neighborhood	312-372-0101
Passports	312-341-6020
Police Assistance (non-emergency)	311
Social Security	773-890-2492
Streets and Sanitation	312-744-5000
Telephone Repair Service	888-611-4466
Voter Information	312-269-7900
Water Main Leaks	312-744-7038

Helplines

Alcoholics Anonymous	312-346-1475
Alcohol, Drug and Abuse Helpline	800-234-0420
Alcoholism and Substance Abuse	312-988-7900
Domestic Violence Hotline	800-799-7233
Drug Care, St. Elizabeth's	773-278-5015
Gamblers Anonymous	312-346-1588
Illinois Child Abuse Hotline	800-252-2873
Narcotics Anonymous	708-848-4884
Parental Stress Services	312-372-7368
Runaway Switchboard	800-621-4000
Sexual Assault Hotline	888-293-2080
United Way Community Information and Referral	312-876-0010
Violence – Anti-Violence Project	773-871-CARE

Complaints

Better Business Bureau of Chicago	312-832-0500
Consumer Fraud Division (Attorney General's Office)	312-814-3000
Chicago Department of Consumer Services	312-744-9400
Citizen's Utility Board	800-669-5556
Department of Housing Inspection Complaints	312-747-9000
Mayor's Office	312-744-4000
Postal Service Complaints	312-983-8400

NOT FOR TOURISTS™ Guidebooks

Not For Tourists™ Guide to CHICAGO

2009

Your ad here

or here.

We offer half- and full-page advertising options inside each of the **Not For Tourists**™ Guidebooks, including multi-city packages for national companies and organizations, as well as space on our website. Advertising in **NFT**™ means that the city dwellers who rely on our indispensable guidebooks everyday will literally have your business information right at their fingertips wherever they go. Come on. Everybody's doing it.

For a media kit and space rates, call 212 965 8650 x231 or email us at advertising@notfortourists.com

Not For Tourists™
www.notfortourists.com
Atlanta · Boston · Chicago · London · Los Angeles · New York City · Philadelphia · San Francisco · Seattle · Washington DC